HOLLYWOOD SCREENWRITING DIRECTORY

SPRING / SUMMER - VOLUME 8

BURBANK, CALIFORNIA

Printed and bound in the United States of America.

Published by F+W Media, Inc.
3510 West Magnolia Boulevard
Burbank, California 91505
www.fwcommunity.com

Disclaimer

Every reasonable effort has been made to ensure the accuracy of the information contained in the *Hollywood Screenwriting Directory*. F+W Media, Inc. cannot be held responsible for any inaccuracies, or the misrepresentation of those listed in the *Hollywood Screenwriting Directory*.

Updates/Change Listing

Please submit corrections and updates to corrections@screenwritingdirectory.com

Print ISBN 13: 978-1-4403-4735-1
Print ISBN 10: 1-4403-4735-2
EPUB ISBN 13: 978-1-44034-747-4
EPUB ISBN 10: 1-44034-747-6
PDF ISBN 13: 978-1-44034-741-2
PDF ISBN 10: 1-44034-741-7

Contents

Letter from the Editor

Dear Fellow Screenwriter,

Thank you for purchasing the *Hollywood Screenwriting Directory*. Whether this is your first volume or your eighth, you'll find that this Spring/Summer edition has the most comprehensive Industry contact information and submission guidelines you can find. That's because we thoroughly check each entry to ensure that it's always the most accurate information available. The updates you'll find include new contact info, along with updated Twitter, Facebook, and LinkedIn details, and changes to submission policies.

The *HSD* is a very specialized directory created by The Writers Store based on our extensive experience serving the screenwriting community since 1982. It contains a range of people to contact, from ambitious upstarts to established studio Execs, along with management companies who package production deals. For each listing, you'll find the kind of useable information you need: Street and email addresses, whether or not they accept unsolicited material, and how they prefer to receive submissions.

The Screenwriting Directory is also online as an active marketplace that allows you to post your project for consideration in an area accessible only to verified Industry Execs looking for new writers and fresh material. Visit screenwritingdirectory.com/c/HSD8TZ5 now for a **free Silver subscription**.

While having access to this data is crucial, just as essential is an understanding of the right way to use it. These insiders are flooded with submissions daily. Any indication of incorrect format or other amateur flubs in the first few pages will quickly send your script to the trash.

The first thing these A-listers see is your query letter. This is your one shot to impress an agent or exec enough to request a read of your script. So it's essential that this all-important doc is perfect before you send it out. We recommend using our top-rated ScriptXpert Query Critique service to ensure it's ready for the big leagues. For just $39, you receive a high-level review of your query, offering up helpful advice and pointing out reasons that an agent or buyer may stop reading your letter. We also offer detailed Screenplay Coverage and Development Notes, in which our professional readers and coaches will help you take your work to the saleable level.

We also can't emphasize enough how important it is that your submission is polished and professional before you send it out for consideration. Screenwriting software makes producing an Industry-standard screenplay simple and straightforward. Final Draft and Movie Magic Screenwriter put your words into proper format as you type, letting you focus on a well-told story rather than the chore of margins and spacing. In these pages, we've also included a guide to proper screenplay format, along with sample title and first pages to help you send out a professional script.

Besides a properly packaged submission, it's also wise to know your audience before you send out any materials. If your script is an action thriller with a strong female lead, don't send it to Paul Giamatti's production company. Actors establish their own companies so that they're not reliant on studios for roles. Pad an actor's vanity (and his pipeline) by submitting materials catered specifically to him.

You may find that a good number of companies do not want unsolicited submissions. It's not that they're not open to new ideas; they're not open to liability. A script is property, and with it, come ramifications if not handled properly. If you choose to disregard "no unsolicited submissions," sending your script with a submission release form gives it a better chance of getting read. Consult with an entertainment attorney to draft an appropriate form, or consult a guide like *Clearance and Copyright* by Michael C. Donaldson, which has submission release form templates. It's also prudent to protect your work. We recommend registering your script with the WGA (Writers Guild of America, West) or the ProtectRite registration service.

While Hollywood is a creative town it is, above all, professional. Do a service to yourself and the potential buyer by being courteous. If you choose to follow up by phone, don't be demanding and frustrated. These people are overworked and do not owe you anything. It's okay to follow up, but be sure to do so with respect. And if you pique a buyer's interest and she asks for a treatment, you must be ready to send off this vital selling tool at once! That's why we've also included a handy guide to writing treatments in this volume.

While it may oftentimes feel like the opposite, the Entertainment Industry *is* looking for new writers and fresh material. BUT (and this is important) they're also looking for those aspiring scribes to take the time to workshop their scripts with an experienced professional and get them to a marketable level. The Writers Store can help you get ready for the big leagues through our slate of screenwriting courses, personalized coaching and more, which works in a format that mirrors the same process occurring in the studio ranks.

Hollywood is the pinnacle of competition and ambition. But that's not to say that dreams can't happen—they can, and they do. By keeping to these professional guidelines and working on your craft daily, you can find the kind of screenwriting success you seek.

Speaking of success, we'd love to hear all about your achievements. Be sure to contact us at 800.272.8927 or via our website to tell us about your Hollywood experiences.

Wishing you the best of luck,

Jesse Douma
Editor

What is a Screenplay?

In the most basic terms, a screenplay is a 90-120 page document written in Courier 12pt font on 8.5" x 11" bright white three-hole punched paper. Wondering why Courier font is used? It's a timing issue. One formatted script page in Courier font equals roughly one minute of screen time. That's why the average page count of a screenplay should come in between 90 and 120 pages. Comedies tend to be on the shorter side (90 pages, or 1 ½ hours) while Dramas run longer (120 pages, or 2 hours).

A screenplay can be an original piece, or based on a true story or previously written piece, like a novel, stage play or newspaper article. At its heart, a screenplay is a blueprint for the film it will one day become. Professionals on the set including the producer, director, set designer and actors all translate the screenwriter's vision using their individual talents. Since the creation of a film is ultimately a collaborative art, the screenwriter must be aware of each person's role and as such, the script should reflect the writer's knowledge.

For example, it's crucial to remember that film is primarily a visual medium. As a screenwriter, you must show what's happening in a story, rather than tell. A 2-page inner monologue may work well for a novel, but is the kiss of death in a script. The very nature of screenwriting is based on how to show a story on a screen, and pivotal moments can be conveyed through something as simple as a look on an actor's face. Let's take a look at what a screenplay's structure looks like.

The First Page of a Screenplay

Screenwriting software makes producing an Industry-standard script simple and straightforward. While screenplay formatting software such as Final Draft, Movie Magic Screenwriter, Movie Outline and Montage frees you from having to learn the nitty-gritty of margins and indents, it's good to have a grasp of the general spacing standards.

The top, bottom and right margins of a screenplay are 1". The left margin is 1.5". The extra half-inch of white space to the left of a script page allows for binding with brads, yet still imparts a feeling of vertical balance of the text on the page. The entire document should be single-spaced.

Find software, books, courses and more on WritersStore.com

Screenplay Elements

Following is a list of items that make up the screenplay format, along with indenting information. Again, screenplay software will automatically format all these elements, but a screenwriter must have a working knowledge of the definitions to know when to use each one.

Ⓐ Fade In

The very first item on the first page should be the words FADE IN:.

Ⓑ Page Numbers

The first page is never numbered. Subsequent page numbers appear in the upper right hand corner, 0.5" from the top of the page, flush right to the margin.

Ⓒ Mores and Continueds

Use mores and continueds between pages to indicate the same character is still speaking.

Ⓓ Scene Heading

Left Indent: 0"   Right Indent: 0"   Width: 6"

A scene heading is a one-line description of the location and time of day of a scene, also known as a "slugline." It should always be in CAPS. Example: EXT. WRITERS STORE – DAY reveals that the action takes place outside The Writers Store during the daytime.

Ⓔ Subheader

Left Indent: 0"   Right Indent: 0"   Width: 6"

When a new scene heading is not necessary, but some distinction needs to be made in the action, you can use a subheader. But be sure to use these sparingly, as a script full of subheaders is generally frowned upon. A good example is when there are a series of quick cuts between two locations, you would use the term INTERCUT and the scene locations.

Ⓕ Action

Left Indent: 0"   Right Indent: 0"   Width: 6"

The narrative description of the events of a scene, written in the present tense. Also less commonly known as direction, visual exposition, blackstuff, description or scene direction. Remember—only things that can be seen and heard should be included in the action.

Sample Screenplay Page

A FADE IN:

D EXT. WRITERS STORE - DAY

F In the heart of West Los Angeles, a boutique shop's large
OPEN sign glows like a beacon.

 M DISSOLVE TO:

INT. WRITERS STORE - SALES FLOOR - DAY

Writers browse the many scripts in the screenplay section.

G ANTHONY, Canadian-Italian Story Specialist extraordinaire,
30s and not getting any younger, ambles over.

 H ANTHONY
I Hey, how's everyone doin' here?

A WRITING ENTHUSIAST, 45, reads the first page of "The
Aviator" by John Logan.

                    ENTHUSIAST
          Can John Logan write a killer first
          page or what?

                    ANTHONY
          You, sir, are a gentleman of
          refined taste. John Logan is my
          non-Canadian idol.

The phone RINGS. Anthony goes to--

E THE SALES COUNTER

And answers the phone.

                    ANTHONY (CONT'D)
          Writers Store, Anthony speaking.

                    VOICE
          J (over phone)
          Do you have Chinatown in stock?

I/E LUXURIOUS MALIBU MANSION - DAY

A FIGURE roams his estate, cell phone pressed to his ear.

                    ANTHONY (O.S.)
          'Course we have Chinatown!
          Robert Towne's masterpeice is
          arguably the Great American
          Screenplay...
                    (MORE) **C**

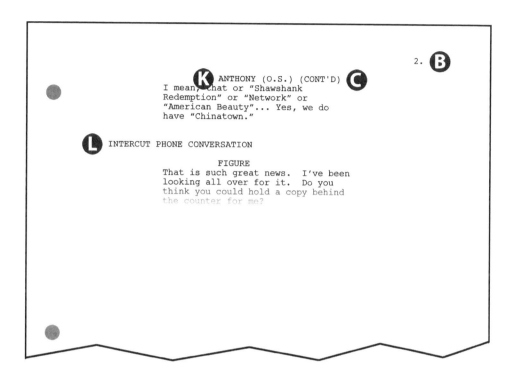

Character

Left Indent: 2" Right Indent: 0" Width: 4"

G When a character is introduced, his name should be capitalized within the action. For example: The door opens and in walks LIAM, a thirty-something hipster with attitude to spare.

H A character's name is CAPPED and always listed above his lines of dialogue. Minor characters may be listed without names, for example TAXI DRIVER or CUSTOMER.

I Dialogue

Left Indent: 1" Right Indent: 1.5" Width: 3.5"

Lines of speech for each character. Dialogue format is used anytime a character is heard speaking, even for off-screen and voice-overs.

J Parenthetical

Left Indent: 1.5" Right Indent: 2" Width: 2.5"

A parenthetical is direction for the character, that is either attitude or action-oriented. Parentheticals are used very rarely, and only if absolutely necessary. Why? First, if you need to use a parenthetical to convey what's going on with your dialogue, then it probably needs a good re-write. Second, it's the director's job to instruct an actor, and everyone knows not to encroach on the director's turf!

(K) Extension

Placed after the character's name, in parentheses

An abbreviated technical note placed after the character's name to indicate how the voice will be heard onscreen, for example, if the character is speaking as a voice-over, it would appear as LIAM (V.O.).

(L) Intercut

Intercuts are instructions for a series of quick cuts between two scene locations.

(M) Transition

Left Indent: 4"   Right Indent: 0"   Width: 2"

Transitions are film editing instructions, and generally only appear in a shooting script. Transition verbiage includes:

```
CUT TO:
DISSOLVE TO:
SMASH CUT:
QUICK CUT:
FADE TO:
```

As a spec script writer, you should avoid using a transition unless there is no other way to indicate a story element. For example, you might need to use DISSOLVE TO: to indicate that a large amount of time has passed.

Shot

Left Indent: 0"   Right Indent: 0"   Width: 6"

A shot tells the reader the focal point within a scene has changed. Like a transition, there's rarely a time when a spec screenwriter should insert shot directions. Examples of Shots:

```
ANGLE ON --
EXTREME CLOSE UP --
LIAM'S POV --
```

Spec Script vs. Shooting Script

A "spec script" literally means that you are writing a screenplay on speculation. That is, no one is paying you to write the script. You are penning it in hopes of selling the script to a buyer. Spec scripts should stick stringently to established screenwriting rules. Once a script is purchased, it becomes a shooting script, also called a production script. This is a version of the screenplay created for film production. It will include technical instructions, like film editing notes, shots, cuts and the like. All the scenes are numbered, and revisions are marked with a color-coded system. This is done so that the production assistants and director can then arrange the order in which the scenes will be shot for the most efficient use of stage, cast, and location resources.

A spec script should never contain the elements of shooting script. The biggest mistake any new screenwriter can make is to submit a script full of production language, including camera angles and editing transitions.

It can be very difficult to resist putting this type of language in your script. After all, it's your story and you see it in a very specific way. However, facts are facts. If you want to direct your script, then try to go the independent filmmaker route. But if you want to sell your script, then stick to the accepted spec screenplay format.

Script Presentaction and Binding

Just like the format of a script, there are very specific rules for binding and presenting your script. The first page is the title page, which should also be written in Courier 12pt font. No graphics, no fancy pictures, only the title of your script, with "written by" and your name in the center of the page. In the lower left-hand or right-hand corner, enter your contact information.

In the lower left-hand or right-hand corner you can put Registered, WGA or a copyright notification, though this is generally not a requirement.

Sample Screenplay Title Page

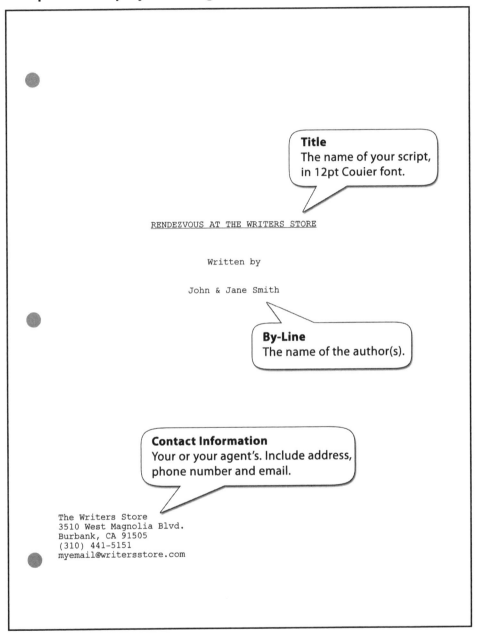

Title
The name of your script, in 12pt Couier font.

RENDEZVOUS AT THE WRITERS STORE

Written by

John & Jane Smith

By-Line
The name of the author(s).

Contact Information
Your or your agent's. Include address, phone number and email.

The Writers Store
3510 West Magnolia Blvd.
Burbank, CA 91505
(310) 441-5151
myemail@writersstore.com

Find software, books, courses and more on WritersStore.com

Query Letters

A query is a one-page, single-spaced letter that quickly tells who you are, what the work is, and why the work is appropriate for the market in question. Just as queries are used as the first means of contact for pitching magazine articles and novels, they work just the same for scripts.

A well-written query is broken down into three parts.

Part I: Your Reason for Contacting/Script Details

Before even looking at the few sentences describing your story, a producer wants to see two other things:

1. **What is it?** State the title, genre, and whether it's a full-length script or a shorter one.
2. **Why are you contacting this market/person in particular?** There are thousands of individuals who receive scripts. Why have you chosen this person to review the material? Is it because you met them in person and they requested to see your work? Have they represented writers similar to yourself? Did you read that they were actively looking for zombie comedies? Spelling out your reason upfront shows that you've done your research, and that you're a professional.

Part II: The Elevator Pitch

If you wrote the first paragraph correctly, you've got their attention, so pitch away. Explain what your story is in about 3-6 sentences. The point here is to intrigue and pique only. Don't get into nitty-gritty details of any kind. Hesitate using a whole lot of character names or backstory. Don't say how it ends or who dies during the climax or that the hero's father betrays him in Act II. Introduce us to the main character and his situation, then get to the key part of the pitch: the conflict.

Try to include tidbits here and there that make your story unique. If it's about a cop nearing retirement, that's nothing new. But if the story is about a retiring cop considering a sex change operation in his bid to completely start over, while the police union is threatening to take away his pension should he do this, then you've got something different that readers may want to see.

Sample Query Letter

John. Q. Writer
123 Main St.
Writerville, USA
(212) 555-1234
johnqwriter@email.com

Agent
JQA & Associates
678 Hollywood St.
Hollywood, CA 90210

B Dear Mr./Ms (Last Name):

C My name is John Q. Writer and we crossed paths at the Screenwriters World Conference in Los Angeles in October 2012. After hearing the pitch for my feature-length thriller, October Surprise, you requested that I submit a query, synopsis and the first 10 pages of the script. All requested materials are enclosed. This is an exclusive submission, as you requested.

D U.S. Senator Michael Hargrove is breaking ranks with his own political party to endorse another candidate for President of the United States. At the National Convention, he's treated like a rock star V.I.P. -- that is, until, he's abducted by a fringe political group and given a grim ultimatum: Use your speech on live TV to sabotage and derail the presidential campaign you're now supporting, or your family back home will not live though the night.

E The script was co-written with my scriptwriting partner, Joe Aloysius. I am a produced playwright and award-winning journalist. Thank you for considering October Surprise. I will be happy to sign any release forms that you request. May I send the rest of the screenplay?

Best,
John Q. Writer

Part III: The Wrap Up

Your pitch is complete. The last paragraph is where you get to talk about yourself and your accomplishments. If the script has won any awards or been a finalist in a prominent competition, this is the place to say so. Mention your writing credentials and experience. Obviously, any paid screenwriting experience is most valuable, but feel free to include other tidbits such as if you're a magazine freelancer or a published novelist.

Sometimes, there won't be much to say at the end of a query letter because the writer has no credits, no contacts and nothing to brag about. As your mother would tell you: If you don't have anything nice to say, don't say anything at all. Keep the last section brief if you must, rather than going on and on about being an "active blogger" or having one poem published in your college literary magazine.

Following some information about yourself, it's time to wrap up the query and propose sending more material. A simple way to do this is by saying "The script is complete. May I send you the treatment and full screenplay?"

Here are the elements of a query letter in the example on the facing page:

(A) Include all of your contact information—including phone and e-mail—as centered information at the top.

(B) Use proper greetings and last names.

(C) Include a reason for contacting the reader.

(D) Try and keep the pitch to one paragraph.

(E) Regarding your credentials, be concise and honest.

Treatments and Log Lines

Introduction to the Treatment

Nobody reads a full script in Hollywood anymore. Execs don't want to put in the time to read a 90-page comedy script, much less a 180-page epic. They want to know if the goods are there before they invest their precious time, and this is where the treatment comes in. Think of it as reading the back cover of a book before you invest in buying it. You'd never just pay for a book without knowing what type of story to expect. So it is with the movie industry. The treatment is the essential selling tool that can make or break your script.

What is a Treatment

A treatment is a short document written in prose form and in the present tense that emphasizes, with vivid description, the major elements of a screenplay.

That's a very broad definition, to be sure. And while the main purpose of a treatment is as a selling tool, there are variations of the definition to consider.

1. A treatment could be your first attempt toward selling your screenplay to a producer, your first try at getting someone to pay you to write the script.
2. A treatment could be a sales tool for a script that you've already written—a shorter, prose version of the screenplay's story for producers to read, to pique their interest in your project and entice them to read your screenplay.
3. A treatment could describe how you intend to attack a rewrite, either of your own script or of another writer's script. Often when a producer hires a writer to do a rewrite, they'll ask for a treatment first.
4. A treatment could be the first step toward writing your screenplay—it could be one of the first steps toward getting your story down on paper. Maybe you don't have time to write the screenplay yet—a treatment can help cement the story in your mind (and on paper) so that you can work on it later.

Why Write a Treatment?

Ultimately, the best reason to write a treatment is that the process of writing your treatment can help you write a better script. It can be easier to find and solve structural challenges, plot incongruities, lapses in logic, etc. in the prose treatment format than it is to find and solve those challenges in the screenplay format.

Find software, books, courses and more on WritersStore.com

Writing a screenplay is a step-by-step process, and some steps are more involved than others. Writing a treatment is a very achievable step in the screenwriting process, and taking that step from beginning to end can be a rewarding boost for your writing ego.

Writing a treatment helps give tangible shape to your story, and makes sharing your story with others simpler and more precise. If you can share your story with others, you can get feedback, which may open up more channels in your brain and help your story to grow. The treatment format is much easier to read and comprehend for people who aren't familiar with the screenplay format.

You might not be ready to write your complete screenplay yet—you might not have time, you might not be fully committed to the idea. Writing a treatment is a good stopgap measure, so that an idea doesn't just exist as an idea—it may exist as something you can sell, share with a collaborator, or simply file away for a rainy day.

When is a Treatment Used

A treatment is usually used when you begin the process of selling your script. When you pitch your script to a producer and he shows interest in your script, he will most likely ask you to send over the treatment. This way, he can review the story and see if he is interested in reading the full script.

Think of the treatment as your business card—the thing you leave behind after you've pitched your story.

You may have heard of writers who sell a script based only a treatment. Yes, this happens, but this happens only for established writers with a track record of produced scripts. They have proven to Hollywood that they can write a blockbuster script, so buyers know that if they like the treatment, they will most likely love the script.

The treatment can also be used as an outline for the writer before he begins his script. It's smart to either outline or summarize a script before you begin writing. If you can complete the story in a smaller form, you know that you'll be able to sustain it in the longer script format. Architects don't erect a building without first designing a blueprint and then creating a model of the structure. The outline is your blueprint and the treatment is your model.

Treatment vs. Synopsis, Coverage, Beat Sheet and Outline

The term treatment is thrown around loosely in Hollywood, and you can be sure that you'll hear a different definition each time you ask. Some buyers will request a treatment when they really want a synopsis, an outline or a beat sheet. So what are the definitions of the other items?

Synopsis

A Synopsis is a brief description of a story's plot or a straightforward presentation of the scenes and events in a story. It is not a selling tool, but rather a summation of the story, and is typically no more than 2 pages long. It's generally used by professional script readers when writing coverage on a script.

Coverage

Coverage is the name of the document generated by the buyer's in house script readers. The main purpose of this document is to assess the commercial viability of the script. The reader supplies the buyer with the basic identifying information of the script, a synopsis, their comments on the script and a rating chart on all of the elements of the script, including characters, dialogue, action, setting, and commercial appeal. The reader then rates the script "pass" (no, thanks. Don't call us, cause we're certainly not gonna call you) "consider" (maybe someone we know can rewrite this puppy into something marketable) or "recommend" (this is the script that will move me from script reader hell to producing heaven!).

Beat Sheet

A Beat Sheet lists the sequence of major events that takes place in a script. It shows what will happen to the main character, and the order in which the events will occur. It can be anywhere from a short paragraph to three pages. Each beat is described in only 1-2 sentences.

Here is an extremely short example from "Die Hard."

1. New York Detective John McClane flies to Los Angeles to reconcile with his wife Holly at her company Christmas party.
2. When he arrives at Holly's high-rise office building, they argue and Holly leaves McClane alone in her executive bathroom.
3. From the bathroom, McClane hears terrorists, lead by Hans Gruber, break in and take over the building.
4. McClane witnesses the murder of Takagi, the CEO of the company, by Gruber and decides to take action.
5. McClane kills the brother of the lead henchman, Karl, and many other terrorists. He greatly angers Hans and Karl in the process.
6. McClane battles the terrorists with the help of a lone police officer.
7. The other police are against McClane and he feels alone in his fight. The police approach fails, so McClane is totally alone.
8. McClane fights Karl, kills him and prepares to go save Holly from Gruber.
9. Seemingly outnumbered, McClane appears to give up.
10. Using his New York wits, McClane kills Gruber and saves Holly.

Outline

An outline is a list of the scenes that make up a screenplay, from FADE IN to FADE OUT. Every writer has a different method of outlining—some are very detailed, while some list only a sentence or even just a word for each scene.

A good way to start a screenplay is to write a beat sheet, an outline and then a treatment. If you work out the story problems with these three tools, you will find that writing the actual script is a breeze.

Why Do I Need a Treatment

Besides being an important selling tool, a treatment allows you to see if your idea can sustain a feature-length film. Many writers take an idea straight to screenplay form, and then find 30 pages in that there is not enough story to continue the script. In this short summary form, you will also be able to identify any weaknesses in your plot, theme and characters.

It is much easier to find and solve these challenges in the prose treatment form than it is to locate them in the screenplay format.

How Long Should It Be?

Sadly, there is no cut and dry length for a treatment. Generally, treatments vary in length from 1-25 pages.

A general rule—the more power the executive holds, the shorter the treatment you should send them. It is recommended to have a few different versions of your treatment. Besides a lengthy summary of the story, have a quick one pager on hand.

What Is the Format?

Your treatment should be written in prose form, and in 12 point Courier font. In essence, the treatment looks like a short story. There should be one line of space between each paragraph, and no indenting.

DON'T insert dialogue, slug lines, or anything else in screenplay format.

DO use standard punctuation for dialogue.

However, be careful not to rely on much dialogue in your treatment in order to effectively tell the story in 10 pages or less. A few carefully chosen thematic lines will suffice. For instance, the treatment for "Forrest Gump" would likely use the line, "Life is like a box of chocolates. You never know what you're gonna get," because it is used throughout the script as a thematic tag line.

What Should I Aspire to Do with the Treatment?

The treatment should not look, sound or read like an outline, a beat sheet or a screenplay. The essence of the story and the characters should be evoked through exhilarating language and imagery. It should sound like an excited moviegoer recanting the details of a film he just saw that was thought provoking, exhilarating and made him feel like he just had to share all the details with his friends. The prose you use in a treatment should be different than the narrative lines of a screenplay.

The beginning of the treatment has to grab the reader and not let go until the very end. Your reader should be able to see the script play out on the silver screen in front of his or her very eyes. After reading the treatment, the reader should be on fire to get this script to her boss, pronto!

The Log Line

A Log Line is a one sentence description of your film. It's really that simple. You've seen log lines, even if you're not aware of it. In essence, TV Guide descriptions of films are log lines. A log line may describe the following elements:

- Genre—comedy, drama, thriller, love story, etc.
- Setting—time and place, locale, other pertinent information
- Plot—the main narrative thrust of the story
- Character—the lead character or group of characters
- Theme—the main subject of the movie

A log line need not contain the following elements:

- Character names (unless the characters are historical figures)
- Back story
- Qualitative judgments—"A hilarious story..." "A fascinating tale..."
- Comparisons to other films—"It's 'Jaws' meets 'Mary Poppins'..."

Here are a few examples of log lines for well-known films. See if you can guess the film being described (the answers are right below, so don't cheat!):

1. A throwback to the serial adventure films of the 1930s, this film is the story of a heroic archeologist who races against the Nazis to find a powerful artifact that can change the course of history.
2. Set at a small American college in the early 1960s, this broad comedy follows a fraternity full of misfits through a year of parties, mishaps and food fights.
3. An illiterate boy looks to become a contestant on the Hindi version of "Who Wants to be A Millionaire" in order to re-establish contact with the girl he loves, who is an ardent fan of the show.

4. A man decides to change his life by saying 'yes' to everything that comes his way. On his journey, he wins $45,000, meets a hypnotic dog, obtains a nursing degree, travels the globe, and finds romance.

5. A behind-the-scenes view of the 2000 presidential election and the scandal that ensued in the weeks following.

Get the idea? The log line is designed to describe and to tease, like a line of advertising copy for your film. It has to be accurate, it can't be misleading. It's the first sentence a producer or executive is going to read, and you've got to make sure it isn't the last. Make it count.

By the way, the log lines above are for:

1. "Raiders of the Lost Ark"
2. "Animal House"
3. "Slumdog Millionaire"
4. "Yes Man"
5. "Recount"

Why Is the Log Line Important in a Treatment?

The log line is the first sentence an executive will ever read from your hand. It's also the shorthand that executives will use to discuss your project with each other. If a junior executive reads your treatment and likes it, she'll need to tell her boss about the project in order to move it to the next step (probably a meeting between you and the boss).

The boss will ask the junior executive "What's it about?" The junior executive will respond with your log line, if you've written it well and accurately. You are helping to provide the junior executive with the tools she needs to help move your project forward. If you don't provide a log line at the beginning of your treatment, you rely on the junior executive's ability to digest your treatment and come up with a good log line of her own. Even in a collaborative art form like filmmaking, it's never a good idea to leave a job undone for someone else to do if you are more capable of doing it yourself. And who knows your story better than you do? Write a great log line for your treatment, and you'll know that your treatment is being discussed in your own words.

Who Is the Log Line For

The log line is for the buyer: the executive, the producer, the agent. By writing a log line for your treatment, you are helping them to process your material more efficiently. Getting a movie made is a sales process, a constant, revolving door sales process. You sell your work to an agent, who then sells your work to a producer, who then sells it to a director, who then sells it to actors and key crew members.

Once the movie is made, the sales process starts all over again, as the producer has to sell the movie to distributors and marketing executives, who have to sell the film to theater owners who have to sell the film to audiences. A good log line can ride the film all the way from start to finish, helping to sell it at each step.

Should the Log Line Refer to Other Movies?

No. It used to be popular to write log lines that were entirely film references. This practice became so prevalent that it became a cliché, and should be avoided if at all possible. Nothing says "schlock" as quickly as a "Die Hard" reference—the classic action movie reference that every movie strived for in the early 1990s. "Speed" was called "Die Hard" on a bus. "Passenger 57" was called "Die Hard" on a plane. Descriptive as these log lines may be, they read as lazy writing, and if your writing isn't even original in the log line, who will be interested in reading your treatment or your script? Avoid hucksterism, overselling and hype. It's a turnoff.

How Long Should the Log Line Be

Your log line should be one sentence long. Pare it down to its essence, and don't let your sentence become a run-on. Try it out loud, see if it works. You don't have to follow every twist and turn of the plot in your log line, you only have to convey the flavor of the script. One sentence will do it.

What Is the Difference Between the Log Line and the Theme?

Your log line is a sales tool that is a teaser and an invitation to read your script. The theme may be contained in the log line, but not necessarily. Theme is the real answer to "What is your script about?" and Theme need not be confined to a one sentence answer. Theme is often related to the discovery that your main character makes during the course of the film. For instance, in "Raiders of the Lost Ark," Indiana Jones discovers that people are actually more important to him than historical artifacts. In "Animal House," the Deltas discover that the camaraderie that they've discovered in their fraternity is the real lasting value of their college experience, not their class work or their social status on campus.

In Closing

You've spent months or years (or even decades) on your script, and so it may be frustrating to jump through the hoops of the submission process—but it's important. Don't give readers an excuse to ignore your work. You must craft a killer query, treatment and log line before the script gets its big shot. Compose them well, and you're on your way to selling that screenplay.

Legal 411 for Screenwriters

By Dinah Perez, Esq.

As a practicing entertainment attorney for nearly two decades, I have represented many writers. I have counseled them on the legal issues related to their writing endeavors, negotiated their agreements with agents and managers, helped them sell their screenplays, and settled their disputes with other writers and producers.

You need to be diligent when it comes to dealing with the legal issues that may arise while you are writing and selling your screenplay, including hiring an agent and manager. Otherwise, you may end up jointly owning your screenplay with another writer, though it was not your intention; may be sued for copyright infringement for incorporating copyright protected material into your screenplay that you thought was in the public domain; could waste your time writing a derivative work based on an original whose rights you cannot acquire; may not be paid all the compensation and may not secure rights you're entitled to when you sell your screenplay; may not be able to shop or sell your screenplay; and may find it impossible to replace your current agent or manager. Overall, consulting with an entertainment attorney up front is much more cost efficient that attempting to fix mistakes and settle disputes that could have been avoided. Whenever I say "attorney" herein, I mean "entertainment attorney."

This chapter endeavors to inform you of the legal issues that exist as you navigate through the process of writing, shopping, selling your screenplay, and hiring an agent, manager, and attorney. This is not a full exploration of the law, nor is it intended to make you an expert in the field. Rather, it is meant to help you spot the issues that may require legal counsel and the important deal terms of the agreements into which you may enter into as a screenwriter. There is a primer on the basics of copyright law up front. Thereafter, I have organized the information in a sequential manner that guides you on your journey, start to finish.

Copyright

A "copyright" is a form of protection for the authors of original content which, with few exceptions, bestows upon authors of intellectual property, such as a book, play, magazine article, news story, video game, screenplay, motion pictures, etc., the exclusive right to reproduce, distribute, perform, prepare and sell their creations.[1] Copyright protection does not extend to ideas—only to their expression. The current term of copyright is the life of the author plus 70 years.[2] Copyright is automatic the moment the work is fixed in a tangible medium, like a printed page, a hard drive, a flash drive, digital recording, film, etc.[2] Copyright law may impact your use of any of the source material you incorporate into your screenplay, and the ownership of your screenplay if you collaborate with another writer.

Copyright protection means that you own the object of your creation and that anyone who wants to use it needs to acquire the right to do so from you. In fact, absent an exception, anyone who uses your copyright protected work without your assent is infringing on your copyright. Likewise, you cannot use another's work without permission unless said work is in the public domain (the work does not have a valid copyright), or you are claiming your use is a "Fair Use." This latter exception to the Copyright Act allows you to utilize another's work without permission for the purpose of "criticism, comment, news reporting, teaching (including multiple copies for classroom use), scholarship, or research" without infringing copyright.[3] I advise that you proceed with caution and consult with an attorney if you are claiming a Fair Use exception to the Copyright Act because the exception is far narrower than most people realize.

Though copyright protection is automatic, I strongly urge you to pay the U.S. Copyright Office the $35 it costs to formally register a copyright for your completed treatment and screenplay. You can register a copyright at any time, but I recommend you do so before you start shopping and submitting your treatment and/or screenplay. The benefits that you gain from the registration far outweigh the cost and time it takes to complete the registration form online. Copyright registration within five years of first publication provides proof of ownership and affords you the opportunity to litigate against infringers, since registration is a prerequisite to filing a legal claim. Registration within three month of first publication and prior to an infringement allows a court to award you statutory damages of up to $150,0000 (or actual damages and profits, if they are more than the statutory damages) as well as attorneys' fees. You may only be awarded actual damages and profits if you do not register within the first three months of publication or prior to an infringement.[4]

Registration of your copyright with the U.S. Copyright Office is the only registration that affords the benefits in the preceding paragraph. The "poor man's copyright," which entails you mailing your screenplay (or other creation) to yourself and you saving the unopened package, provides no more protection than the unregistered copyright. The Writers Guild of America ("WGA") script registration service, which allows you to register ideas, treatments, screenplays, and teleplays, may serve to potentially provide proof as to the day of existence of your registered material, but does not convey the benefits of copyright registration. I recommend registering with WGA when a production company requests it, or when what you have created is not entitled to copyright protection. WGA registration costs $20 for non-members and $10 for members.

Note that in order for anyone to infringe on your screenplay's copyright they actually have to copy it. There is no infringement unless the party you are accusing had access to your screenplay and there is substantial similarity of the copyright protected elements in your screenplay and the screenplay or picture you are claiming is infringing on yours. You have no copyright infringement claim if someone independently creates a screenplay that is similar to yours.

Ready, Set ... Pause

You have come up with an idea for a screenplay which you want to begin writing. I suggest that you stop and ponder what you intend to write and the potential legal issues that may exist at this juncture. Pausing long enough to consider what may be required legally of you at the start of every writing endeavor will help you avoid legal errors and costly mistakes that may undermine your goals.

Ask yourself the questions that follow in order to determine if you need to consult with and/ or hire an attorney. Are you writing by yourself or with a writing partner? Is the story you want to tell completely fictional and original to you? Is your screenplay based on, or inspired by, outside source material, like a book, play, news article, magazine article, or trial transcript? Are you writing about a living person? It is important that you ask yourself these questions at the outset so that you do not waste time writing something you cannot sell.

Resist the temptation to use a boilerplate agreement not specifically drafted for you by an attorney. Chances are you do not know enough about the law, or crafting an agreement, to revise the agreement without creating a litigation worthy mistake, or one that forces you to shelve your screenplay. The time that you are investing writing warrants the cost of hiring an attorney to do things right.

Writing the Screenplay

Collaborations

A "collaboration" occurs when you write with another writer. You have to consider the long term implications of any writing partnership because the term of copyright, in the proceeds of your collaboration, is your life plus 70 years. As such, it is important that your writing partner and you share a similar vision for the screenplay you intend to write, that you agree on the deal terms of your writing partnership, and that you assess the relationship and its long term viability. Note that your writing partner and you will equally co-own the screenplay you write together the moment you fix it in a tangible medium because copyright automatically attaches regardless of oral agreements or intention to the contrary.

I strongly urge that you retain an attorney, if you do not already have one, and that you enter into a "Collaboration Agreement," a three to four page agreement that addresses all of the pertinent terms of your writing partnership, e.g., split of copyright and revenues, who gets the first position credit, who gets to make the final decision if you disagree on a creative or business issue, who will be responsible for shopping the screenplay, who approves the sale, etc.

Your attorney will help you compromise when your writing partner and you cannot seem to agree on a deal term so that you both feel fairly treated. When a client and collaborator cannot agree on the credit, I suggest that one take the first position credit on screen and the other in ads. When both want final approval, I suggest that one have it on business decisions and the other on creative ones. You can start writing once you have executed the Collaboration Agreement. If you cannot agree, despite the attorney's efforts, then you both just walk away, only having expended the legal fees. This is a small price to pay to avoid a time-intensive and potentially costly dispute down the line.

What happens if you started writing without a Collaboration Agreement and now realize that you do not want to complete the screenplay with your writing partner? You may not have to shelve what you have written thus far if your writing partner is willing to assign it to you. To "assign" means to transfer an asset. You want the other writer to transfer his/her interest in the screenplay to you. This is done via an "Assignment," since copyright law requires that a transfer of a copyright interest be affected by a written document signed by the party assigning rights.[3] I suggest that you execute an Assignment, even if what you have written does not qualify for copyright protection. In addition to drafting the Assignment, an attorney can motivate a recalcitrant collaborator by negotiating terms whereby he/she is paid a portion of the screenplay's sale price. Unfortunately, you may have to chalk this experience up to a lesson learned if your collaborator and you are at an impasse. The alternative, in such a circumstance, is that you assign the results and proceeds of your collaboration to the other writer.

Original Fictional Screenplays

You can proceed to write without regard to any legal issues if you are writing a completely original screenplay either on your own or with a writing partner, as long as you have entered into a Collaboration Agreement. For the purposes of this chapter, "completely original to you" means that you are writing a work of fiction that is not based on outside material, be it a book, play, magazine article, life story, video game, etc. If you are doing research, then it is best that you determine if any of the other sections of this chapter apply to your use of the source materials you may be incorporating into your screenplay.

Screenplays Based on Public Domain Material

You may write a screenplay that is an adaptation of, or based upon, a work that is in the public domain without infringing its copyright. A work is in "Public Domain" when no one owns that work's copyright or if the work never qualified for copyright protection. A work is in the public domain because it was not registered for copyright at a time when an actual registration was mandatory, did not comply with the formalities of the Copyright Act, or the copyright term has expired. You can use a work that is in public domain without securing permission to do so from the author. Works in the public domain include the following:

Works published between 1923 and 1977 that were never registered for copyright; works published prior to 1923; works published between 1923 and 1963 that were registered for copyright but published without a copyright notice; works published between 1978 and March 1, 1989 without a copyright notice and without a subsequent registration (within 5 years); unpublished works from authors who died prior to 1944; unpublished anonymous or pseudonymous works created prior to 1894; unpublished works created prior to 1894 when the author's date of death is unknown; and, foreign works that are in the public domain in their country of origin.[5]

Facts, numbers, events, government works (written by government employees), and ideas do not qualify for copyright protection and are, therefore, also in the public domain. Keep in mind that though the aforementioned are in the public domain, their expression and any theories that are original to the author may be protected by copyright. Be extremely careful when using material in historical biographies. Do extensive research in order to separate the historical facts from the author's theories and expression thereof.

Keep your notes and research and annotate your screenplay if you are including any public domain works or information in your screenplay; this may seem burdensome, but you will be grateful you did it if you are ever accused of copyright infringement, since you may have to provide it to prove your innocence. Furthermore, whoever produces your screenplay is going to purchase Errors and Omissions Insurance which, among other things, insures producers against copyright infringement law suits. The insurance carrier may require an opinion letter from an attorney, who may request the annotated script from you. It is far easier to annotate a script as you write than to try to piece it together after the fact.

You are not required to credit the source of your public domain materials. Notwithstanding, I recommend that you credit the author and work if your screenplay is an adaptation of it, or if your screenplay is based upon the work. You do not need to credit your research sources for facts, numbers and such.

Derivative Works

You need to secure the author's or publisher's ("author/publisher") permission if you want to adapt or write a screenplay based upon or inspired by another literary work, such as a book, play, magazine article, essay, etc. Do not take the risk of writing first and attempting to acquire rights afterwards. You are not only infringing copyright when you do this—you are also potentially wasting your time because the author/publisher of the literary work may refuse to let you acquire the rights you need to proceed. They do not always want to have their literary works adapted to the big screen and, even if they do, may prefer to do business with a studio, which is more likely to pay them hefty option fees and purchase prices. If that is the case, it is best that you discover it up front before you invest your time.

Copyright protection applies to that portion of a derivative work created by you, but not to the original work itself. If you adapt a book, your adaptation is protected by copyright, but you acquire no rights in the original materials from the underlying book. In other words, the characters, locations, dialogue, storyline and other elements from the book belong to its author/publisher. The same goes any for public domain facts you incorporate into your screenplay; they remain in the public domain while your expression of those facts is subject to copyright protection.

You acquire the rights to a literary work by entering into an "Option/Purchase Agreement" whereby you have the exclusive option to buy said literary work for a determined period of time. The Option/Purchase Agreement has two components: the Option Agreement ("Option") itself states how much time you have to buy the literary work, and the purchase agreement includes the sale price and rights to be granted. You purchase the literary work by exercising the Option and paying the purchase price prior to the Option's expiration date. You do not actually purchase the literary work until the commencement of principal photography—when you know that the picture is being produced.

Options usually run in one year increments ("option period(s)") and can have one or more extensions. I recommend a one year initial option period with a minimum of two one year extension periods. You pay an "option fee" at the commencement of each option period. Option fees are considered advances and, therefore, may be applicable against the purchase price. If you have paid $20,000 in applicable option fees, when you exercise the Option, you pay $80,000 of the total $100,000 purchase price. If you do not make the option fees applicable, then you pay the full purchase price irrespective of the option fees paid. The Option expires if you let it lapse due to non-payment of the applicable option fee, so be sure to extend the Option one month prior to its expiration; to avoid any mishaps mail the option fee and notice of extension via registered mail return receipt requested.

My clients have paid option fees as low as $1 and as high as $25,000 per option period. Expect to deplete your bank account if you are entering into an Option/Purchase Agreement on behalf of a best-selling book or play, or a magazine article or news story from a well known publication. Authors/publishers in the know expect an option fee equal to 10% of the purchase price. Some may consider this an industry standard—I do not because this is a point of negotiation versus a hard and fast rule. If you cannot afford to pay an option fee equal to 10% of the purchase price, then offer what you can pay, keeping in mind that you do not want to insult the author/publisher. Among other things, I may offer to make one or more of the option fees non-applicable if they are on the low end and it seems like they may be keeping the author/publisher from agreeing to the Option/Purchase Agreement. A "free" Option may be possible if you are acquiring a self-published or obscure book or play, or an article published in a relatively unknown publication. Notwithstanding that the Option is free, you should pay at least one dollar per option period so that the Option/Purchase Agreement does not fail for lack of consideration of some kind. "Consideration" is necessary for the formation of a binding contract—each party to the transaction needs to get a benefit.

The Option/Purchase Agreement for the literary work upon which you are basing your screenplay will determine whether you can sell your creation upon its completion. You will not be able to sell your screenplay if you go about it incorrectly or offer too high a purchase price. I advise that you hire an attorney to help you negotiate and draft an Option/Purchase Agreement that provides you with all the rights you need to deliver to your screenplay's buyer.

Remakes and Sequels Based on Pre-Existing Pictures

Do not write a screenplay based on a previously released motion picture or television show. This is not only copyright infringement—it is a monumental waste of your time! Under no uncertain terms will the motion picture studio or television network ("studio/network") which produced the original ever give you permission to write a sequel or remake based on their original motion picture or television show; they do not let third parties acquire an interest in their library. When the studio/network is ready, it will develop the remake or sequel in-house, with writers of their own choosing. Delete the screenplay if you have already written it, since you cannot use it as a writing sample or share it with anyone due to copyright infringement. Do not waste your money hiring an attorney to attempt to make a submission for you since the studio/network always responds with a resounding, "no." They do not want to read your screenplay because they do not want to risk you filing a copyright infringement, unjust enrichment, and/or breach of implied contract law suit against them, when they produce a remake or sequel that contains elements that were in your submitted screenplay. This happened to MGM and Sylvester Stallone when a writer submitted his version of "Rocky IV" to them. MGM and Sylvester Stallone prevailed over the writer because the "Rocky" characters were entitled to copyright protection.

Life Stories

"Private Persons"

Every living person has the "right of privacy"—the right to be left alone and the right to keep private facts from the public. As a consequence thereof, you need to enter into a Life Story Agreement if the subject of your screenplay is a "private person" whose story has not been in the national news and, hence, is not known by the general public. Do not commence writing until you have entered into a Life Story Agreement. The only exception here is if you are writing about a deceased person, since the right of privacy terminates upon death.

A Life Story Agreement is an agreement whereby the person whose life story you are writing (the "subject" of your screenplay) gives you permission to base your screenplay on his/her life story. It also allows your screenplay's buyer to produce and distribute the picture based on your screenplay. The Life Story Agreement is an Option/Purchase Agreement which takes into account the personal nature of the rights being acquired. The option fee and purchase price for a private person's Life Story Agreement are generally on the low end, because the life story is arguably not in big demand. Both tend to be far lower than the subject usually expects. It is more likely that the purchase price will be in the $80,000 range than the $1 million—the sum a subject asked of a client of mine a couple of years ago. You will not be able to find a buyer for your screenplay if you overpay for the rights, so that is something to always keep in mind.

The Life Story Agreement will give you access to the subject's life story via any news clippings, journals, and interviews. Do not be surprised if the subject wants "final approval" of the screenplay. You can grant the subject the right to comment on a draft of your screenplay, but never final approval. The former is just feedback, the latter means that the subject can stop you from producing any version of the screenplay he/she does not like. Needless-to-say, you never give a subject final approval of the screenplay.

The Life Story Agreement conveys upon you the right to write the screenplay, but it does not give you permission to defame or portray the subject of your screenplay in a false light without legal repercussions. You can take certain dramatic license with the story, but cannot depict the subject in an untrue and in an inaccurate manner—especially one that would be offensive or damaging to him/her. Let the subject comment on the screenplay so that you know where you have potential issues. It is much easier and cost efficient to fix the issues during the writing process than to address them in a court of law. Note that defamation and false light are not the same thing: the former is making false statements that harm a person's reputation and the latter is making untrue statements that depict a person in a false light and are offensive or cause the person embarrassment.

"Public Persons"

Celebrities, politicians, and other persons in whom the general public has great interest are all considered "public persons" because they have disclosed their private facts and live so much of their lives out in the public. As a consequence, public persons have a more limited right of privacy than the private person, and have a lesser expectation of it.

You have a lot of leeway to write about a politician because of the First Amendment and the public's right and need to know about any individual running for, or in, political office.[6] You may disclose truthful facts about politicians, e.g., that a politician is taking bribes, is an alcoholic or drug addict, has cancer, etc. Limit disclosure to facts that impact the politician's ability to do his/her job or how he/she carries out the responsibilities of office. You do not have the same berth where a living celebrity is concerned. If you want to avoid a costly judgment in favor of a celebrity, use facts that are already in the public consciousness, garnered from the likes of a trial transcript, news story, magazine article, biography, autobiography, television interviews, etc.

In the category of public persons are criminals whose crimes have catapulted them to celebrity status. Casey Anthony, Amy Fisher, Ted Bundy, and David Berkowitz aka the Son of Sam are what I call "celebrity criminals." The aforementioned have all had pictures produced about them, but not all entered into Life Story Agreements with the television networks that produced movies about them. In fact, two of the three networks that produced pictures about Amy Fisher, the "Long Island Lolita," did so without a Life Story Agreement. You can write about a celebrity criminal as long as you stick to the facts disclosed in court during a trial and/ or are in the public domain.

Notwithstanding, since the public person has a right to privacy, limited though it may be, I always recommend that you consult with an attorney and that you enter into a Life Story Agreement rather than proceed without one. In order to sell your screenplay, you are going to have to warrant and represent that you have not invaded anyone's right of privacy, and will be required to agree to indemnify and hold harmless the producer if you breach that warranty and representation. This means that you have to reimburse the producer for any damages the producer suffers due to your breach of the right of privacy via your screenplay. The Life Story Agreement greatly eliminates the risk of litigation and a costly judgment, as long as you do not defame or portray your subject in a false light (there has to be an element of maliciousness where celebrities are concerned). The producer and distributor may want the assurances and rights granted via the Life Story Agreement and may make it a condition of financing and distribution. Also, you may want the public person's cooperation either because you may want to interview him/her to gain access to information that was not previously disclosed and/or need his/her help in securing any releases from other individuals integral to the life story.

The Right of Publicity

Every person, be they private or public, also has the "right of publicity," which gives everyone the right to control the commercial exploitation of their name, likeness, voice, and any other identifying aspect of their persona. In other words, your screenplay's producer cannot advertise and distribute a picture based on your screenplay unless you acquired the subject's right of publicity. This is best done via a Life Story Agreement, which grants the buyer the right to use the subject's, name, voice and likeness to produce, advertise, and distribute the picture.

Also, though the right of privacy terminates at death, the right of publicity does not always because state law determines whether the right dies or survives. For example, in New York, the right of publicity is extinguished at death for persons domiciled there[7] and, as per California statute, the right of publicity is a descendible property right that currently survives death by 70 years (for persons who died there prior to 1985).[8] You need to know where the subject of your screenplay died in order to ascertain whether the right of publicity ended with, or outlived, your subject's life.

Representation: Signing with an Agent or Manager

You are going to need representation via an agent or manager once you are done writing your screenplay. The California Talent Agency Act ("TAA") says that only licensed "agents" may procure, offer, promise, or attempt to procure employment or engagements for you. Agents must limit their commissions to 10% of what you earn, post a $50,000 surety bond with the Labor Commissioner, submit their artist agreement for approval by the Labor Commissioner, and segregate client monies from agency monies in a client trust fund.[9] In addition, agents are not supposed to have a conflict of interest with their clients, which means that they do not attach themselves to produce their clients' screenplays.

Managers are not licensed agents and, therefore, are not supposed to engage in agent type activities, such as pitching, shopping screenplays, and attempting to secure writing assignments. Because of the TAA, managers are limited to advising their clients on matters related to their careers, helping their clients secure agency representation, and assisting in the development of their clients' screenplays. They cannot procure, promise to procure or attempt to procure work. Since managers are not agents, they are not required to post a surety bond or maintain a client trust account, and have no limit on their commissions—though the industry standard is 10%. Notwithstanding the TAA, most literary managers do engage in agent type activities on behalf of their clients when their clients lack agency representation. Managers risk rescission of the management agreement with you, and forfeiture of past and future commissions from you, if you file a complaint against them with the California Labor Commissioner alleging that the manager engaged in activities in violation of the TAA, and the California Labor Commissioner determines that your allegations are true.

I am grateful for every reputable manager who works to create and improve the career of any writer—more so when the writer is not represented by an agent. I believe managers should be paid for the value of services they render regardless of the TAA. They should get to collect commissions if their services contributed to your success and earnings. The only problem I have with managers is that their interests are very often in conflict with those of their clients. This occurs when managers attempt to attach themselves to produce their clients' screenplays. A manager friend tells me that she should be credited and paid as a producer because the development work that she does with her clients is actually a producer's job. I disagree.

My biggest concern with managers attaching themselves to produce is that it might deter a producer from going forward—especially if the manager has not produced before. It's best to have an agreement with the manager whereby the manager does not insist on being attached, or will step aside if his/her attachment negatively impacts the negotiation. If necessary, I would offer the manager a higher commission (up to 20% total) to compensate him/her for development services.

Notwithstanding the possible drawbacks, there are a couple of advantages when a manager produces: you have someone advocating on your behalf and you pay a lower commission because the manager's producing fee is credited against the commission you owe. (A commission of $100,000 gets reduced to $20,000 if the manager's producing fee is $80,000.) Whether you want a manager/producer representing you is something that you need to consider prior to entering into the management agreement. Very often, managers will decline representation if they cannot produce the material they develop.

Standard agency and management agreements include a variety of clauses related to your relationship with the agent and/or manager, their duties, compensation, the term of the agreement, how you may be able to terminate the agreement do to non-performance, etc. The agreement you sign most likely will not contain a "sunset clause" unless your attorney makes it a requirement.

A "sunset clause" reduces and eventually terminates continuing commissions owed to the agent and/or manager once the agreement terminates. The need for a sunset clause most often arises when your agent and/or manager secures you a position as a staff writer on a television series, sells your screenplay and it spins off into a series, or your screenplay becomes a studio franchise. The agent or manager wants to receive his/her commission on any monies earned by you, in perpetuity, from agreements you entered into during the term of their representation—even after their agreement with you terminates. The problem with this is that whoever represents you next is going to want to commission *all* your earnings as payment for the services they are rendering in the present. Since agents individually or jointly cannot charge you in excess of 10%, you are in the position of not being able to hire any agent that wants to commission the pre-existing deal, which is likely most of them. You could end up paying a double commission to your managers, since there is no restriction as to how much they can charge.

The alternative is the sunset clause whereby the commission to the previous agent and/or manager is reduced by 33 ⅓% per year until it zeroes out—you pay the new agent or manager that commission on an escalating basis until he/she is receiving 100% of the commission on those earnings. You will only reap the benefit of the sunset clause if it is negotiated into your agreement up front, since the agent will not incorporate it after the fact because it impacts them negatively.

Whether you need both an agent and manager depends on where you are in your career. As I said above, the agent's job is to sell you while the manager's job is to develop you. You are more likely to need a manager earlier in your career, when you do not have an agent, need help getting your career off the ground, and need help developing your talent. You always need an agent. It is highly unlikely that you are going to be able to secure an agent or manager with the top five companies early in your career—unless you are introduced by someone whose opinion they value or you have been extremely successful in another medium, e.g., you have a best-selling novel, graphic novel or video game. Sign with the most reputable agent and/or manager you can at this time. You can upgrade later if the opportunity presents itself.

Your relationship with your agent or manager, how much money you get to keep, what expenses you are reimbursing the manager for, how much help you get from both, and how long you are tied to them is going to be dictated by the agreement you sign. You will regret not having hired an attorney to advise you where this agreement is concerned when you realize that you could have made a better deal and/or that the deal you made has drawbacks.

As far as your attorney goes, be sure to keep him/her in the loop at all times. My clients always end up with a better deal when their representatives and I work together. I always improve the financial terms, credit, make sure that my client reaps the benefits of a box office success, and/or include clauses that protect my client and maintain my client's involvement if the picture or series has a life beyond the original production.

Shopping and Submissions

Shopping

Your agent (or manager if you do not have an agent) will shop and submit your screenplay once you have completed it. "Shopping" is defined in the industry to mean marketing your screenplay in an effort to entering into an Option/Purchase Agreement. A "pitch" is a three to four minute oral summary of your screenplay. The producer and your agent will negotiate the terms of the Option/Purchase Agreement if the producer wants to develop and potentially produce a picture based on your screenplay. Again, I strongly recommend that you insist that your agent work jointly with your attorney to get you the best option fee, purchase price, and overall terms. Whatever additional monies you have to pay your attorney will be justified by the end result.

You can shop your screenplay directly to producers if you do not have an agent or manager. This directory includes within it the information you need to contact producers. When dealing with a producer that has a development department, contact a development executive, unless you have a pre-existing relationship with the producer. You will pitch your screenplay on that first call if you make contact, so be sure to have a prepared pitch and logline. A "logline" is a sentence summary of your script.

Protecting Your Ideas

You have to be careful not to "blurt out" the idea for your screenplay, since ideas are not protected by copyright law. A "blurt out" most often occurs when a writer meets a producer by chance, like at a party, restaurant, or in an elevator, and takes advantage of the moment by sharing the idea without asking for permission to do so. Producers do not want to be liable for hearing an unsolicited idea, nor should they be. Since it is not entitled to copyright protection, your idea is in the public domain and is up for grabs once you blurt it out. For the reasons stated below, I prefer that you pitch in a formal setting even if the producer grants you permission to pitch during the chance encounter.

Pitching your idea and/or screenplay in a business meeting goes a long way in protecting it because contract law fills the void that exists in copyright law. You can protect your idea by setting up an oral agreement or an implied-in-fact contract. Both require that you work smart and be patient enough to pitch in formal settings only.

An oral agreement is a spoken versus written contract. You protect your idea by creating an oral agreement with the producer for that purpose. You create the oral agreement during your pitch meeting by making disclosure of the idea contingent on the producer's agreement to your terms. Prior to pitching say, "As you know, I'm here to pitch my screenplay (or the idea for a screenplay), but before I do, I just want to make sure you are willing to credit me and purchase my screenplay for no less than WGA minimum if you use it. Can we agree to that?" Oral agreements are difficult to prove so be sure to create a paper trail to substantiate its existence. You do this by sending an email to confirm the scheduled meeting and its purpose beforehand. Afterwards, send the producer an email thanking him/her for the meeting, the purpose of the meeting, and reiterate the agreed upon oral agreement.

You can also protect an idea via an implied-in-fact contract, which is formed when you pitch in a formal setting and it is clear from the conduct that you met with the producer for the purpose of selling your idea and, hence expect payment for its use. The idea can even be based on material that is in the public domain, like a Shakespearean play, as was the case with *Blaustein v. Burton*.

Julian Blaustein, came up with the idea to produce "The Taming of the Shrew", starring Elizabeth Taylor and Richard Burton. He pitched the idea to Richard Burton's agent. Blaustein conditioned the disclosure on the agent being interested in his idea and Burton and Taylor being available to star in it. The agent confirmed both. Blaustein went ahead with the pitch. The agent responded positively and confirmed that it was something Burton and Taylor had not previously considered. Burton and Taylor went ahead and produced the picture without Blaustein's involvement. Blaustein sued for breach of an implied-in-fact contract and prevailed even though the idea was for material in the public domain.[10]

You see here why the conduct and circumstances under which the idea is pitched are so important. Blaustein would not have prevailed if the agent had informed him that Burton and Taylor were already developing the idea, had previously considered it, if they had produced the picture based on a screenplay they had received from an independent source, or if Blaustein had blurted out the idea in an informal setting. As with the oral agreement, I recommend that you create a paper trail as evidence of your meeting and your intentions. Send an email confirming the meeting and its purpose. Send another afterward to evidence the fact that the meeting took place, what you pitched, and why.

Notwithstanding, the above, be aware that idea theft is rather rampant and difficult to prove. The trend is for courts tend to side with the studios/networks and producers versus the writers. The conundrum is that you risk theft when you pitch, but that you can never sell anything unless you do. In light of that, do everything you can to protect your idea. Never pitch without permission to do so, only do so in a formal setting, and create a paper trail. Do not pitch the idea for your completed screenplay until you have registered it with the U.S. Copyright Office since, among other things, it is prima facie evidence as to the date of your screenplay's existence. If you are pitching an idea for a screenplay that you have yet to write, at least write up a summary and register it with the WGA; this does not provide copyright protection, but you at least have proof as to the date of your idea's existence.

Submission Releases

If you are not represented by an agent or manager, it is likely that you will be required to sign a "Submission Release" when you ask to submit your screenplay to a producer or studio/network. A "Submission Release" is a written agreement whereby you relieve the recipient of your screenplay from liability should he/she use any of the content in your screenplay that is not protected by copyright, such as your idea or the public domain material incorporated therein. It also relieves the producer and studio/network of the obligation to pay you if it independently creates material similar to yours, or comes by it from an independent source. Furthermore, the Submission Release also states that the recipient will pay you fair market value if they use of your screenplay, or any portion thereof that is protected by copyright. The Submission Release is going to override any oral agreement you have made to the contrary with the producer once you sign it.

As onerous as Submission Releases are, I understand that producers and studios/networks require them as a form of protection against lawsuits that may or may not be warranted. You can pay an attorney to explain the Submission Release to you, but it is unlikely that the attorney will be able to convince the producer to revise it. You might be tempted to throw caution to the wind and sign the Submission Release if you are unrepresented by an agent or manager. I recommend that you ask the producer if he/she will accept an attorney submission instead. Your lawyer can make the submission for you if the producer agrees to accept it. If not, then I suggest that you continue pounding doors until you do find an agent or manager willing to represent you. I know that it is difficult to walk away from what you may think is your only opportunity, but you have to be patient unless you are willing to risk your screenplay.

Note that agents will also require that you sign a Submission Release as a condition to reading your screenplay. You cannot submit otherwise. Be aware that agents can share your screenplay with other agents and the agency's clients with impunity once you sign the Submission Release. You might try having your manager make the submission, or asking if the agent will accept an attorney submission. Otherwise, you will have to take the risk if you want to the agent to consider representing you.

Sample Submission Release

_____ (Name of Production Company)

_____ (Title of Screenplay)

Dear _____:

I am submitting to you herewith the above referenced screenplay (hereinafter referred to as the "material") pursuant to the following terms and conditions.

1. I am interested in having you evaluate my material. I know that because of your stature in the industry that you receive many screenplays, treatments, ideas, stories, formats, and suggestions for screenplays. As a consequence thereof, I understand that you cannot read, accept, and evaluate the material unless I sign and return this Submission Release.

[The production company wants to protect itself from copyright infringement and breach of implied or oral contract claims on behalf of your submitted screenplay. This Submission Release, which is a binding agreement, will release the production company from liability for the aforementioned types of legal claims initiated by the person submitting the material.]

2. I represent and warrant that I am the material's author; that I am sole owner of the right, title and interest in and to the material; that I have the authority to make this submission and to grant the rights being conveyed to you hereunder; that the material does not infringe upon a third party's copyright; that the material does not violate anyone's right of privacy nor is it defamatory. I agree to indemnify you and hold you harmless from any claims, losses, judgments, and expenses (including reasonable legal fees and costs) that are incurred by you due to my breach of the aforementioned warranties and this Submission Release.

[You own the screenplay because you either wrote it or commissioned it as a work-for-hire. The production company wants you to warrant that you have the legal right and authority to submit the screenplay and to contract on its behalf. The production company wants an assurance that the screenplay is not going to result in a third party copyright infringement, right of privacy, or defamation claim against it should they to produce your screenplay. Via this clause, you agree to pay all of the losses and costs incurred by the production company if a legal claim is brought against the production company due to you breach of the warranties in this clause and the overall Submission Release.]

3. I understand that you create screenplays in-house and, as such, that you may be developing a screenplay that is similar to the material that I am submitting to you. Furthermore, I am also aware that a third party may submit a screenplay to you that is comparable to mine, which you may decide to acquire and produce. You may produce said screenplay, without any obligation

Find software, books, courses and more on WritersStore.com

to me of any kind, a screenplay that though similar to the material was independently created by a third party or you.

[The production company is disclosing the scenarios under which it may produce a screenplay that may resemble yours but which it asserts is independently created by the production company or a third party. You are agreeing that the production company does not have to pay or credit you under these circumstances.]

4. I agree that any portion of the material that may be freely used by the public, because it is not protected under copyright law or is in the public domain, may be utilized by you. The material which you are free to use without any obligation to me shall be referred to as "unprotected material" henceforth. If all or any part of said material is not unprotected material because it is protected under copyright law, then it shall be referred to herein as "protected material."

[Ideas, theories, names, titles, formats, and content in the public domain are not protected by copyright law. The production company wants the right to use this unprotected material without having to credit or pay you. For example, if you adapt, update and give an urban spin to a Jane Austen book, the production company can do the same without paying you because Austen's works are in the public domain. The production company cannot use your exact word for word adaptation, but it take utilize your idea without payment to you if you sign this Submission Release.]

5. If you use or cause to be used any of the protected material, you will pay me industry standard compensation or the fair market value of said material, whichever is greater.

[I have seen many different clauses regarding use of protected material and compensation therefor. Some companies will wait to reach an agreement with you prior to using the protected material—others want free reign to use it at will. Some will agree to pay you fair market value while others agree to industry standards, or what they say they typically pay for similar material. Regardless of the formula, you usually give up your ability to negotiate the purchase price of your protected material via the agreement.]

6. I acknowledge that no fiduciary or confidential relationship now exists or will ever exist between us by reason of this agreement or submission of the material to you. No express or implied agreements will be exist between us as a consequence of this unsolicited submission or conversations in reference thereto.

[This eliminates the possibility that you may be paid for use of the unprotected material in your screenplay. If you will remember, I discuss in the chapter how contract law protects elements of your screenplay that are not protected by copyright law—this clause eliminates that possibility.]

7. This agreement shall be governed by the laws of the state of California applicable to agreements executed and to be fully performed therein.

[This means that California state law will apply to this agreement regardless of where you reside.]

8. In the event of any dispute concerning the material or concerning any claim of any kind or nature whatsoever, arising in connection with the material or arising in connection with this agreement, such dispute will be submitted to arbitration. We hereby waive any and all rights and benefits, which we may otherwise have or be entitled to under the laws of California to litigate any such dispute in court, it being the intention of the parties to arbitrate, according to the provisions hereof, all such disputes. Either party may commence arbitration proceedings by giving the other party written notice thereof by registered mail and proceeding thereafter in accordance with the rules and procedures of the American Arbitration Association. The arbitration shall be conducted in the County of Los Angeles, State of California and shall be governed by and subject to the laws of the State of California and the then prevailing rules of the American Arbitration Association. The arbitrators' award shall be final and binding and a judgment upon the award may be enforced by any court of competent jurisdiction.

[An arbitration is a proceeding that takes place outside of a court room. There is no judge or jury—just an arbitrator. Furthermore, the prevailing party usually recuperates reasonable legal fees and expenses associated with the arbitration proceeding. Arbitration clauses are touted by the production entities as more financially efficient and less time consuming than litigation. After discussing the issue of arbitration clauses with various transactional and litigation attorneys and witnessing my own clients' arbitrations, I have come to the conclusion that I prefer for my clients to litigate than arbitrate: arbitration is not necessarily less costly than litigation, it is most definitely not less time consuming, can result in an unprecedented decisions, and may result in an outcome that is biased in favor of a motion picture studio or television network. I make an effort to negotiate out of the arbitration clause whenever possible.]

9. I hereby state that I have read and understand this agreement and that no oral representations of any kind have been made to me and that this agreement states our entire understanding with reference to the subject matter hereof. Any modification or waiver of any of the provisions of this agreement must be in writing and signed by both of us.

[This clause eliminates the possibility of an oral agreement that contradicts the terms of the Submission Release. Modifications after-the-fact need to be agreed to in writing by the production company and you.]

Sincerely,

_____   Date: _____
(Writer's Signature)

[The Submission Release is a contract of adhesion, which means that the agreement is presented to you on a take or leave it basis. They will not modify the Submission Release if you object to any of

its content, and they will not accept your material without it if you lack an agent or manager and the production company does not accept attorney submissions.

I have presented the most basic of Submission Releases. Every company has their own basic form. It is a good idea to have an attorney explain a Submission Release to you at least once, so that you may know up front how signing it may negatively impact you.

You may download a PDF edition of this Sample Submission Release form here: http://www.scriptmag.com/features/submission-releases]

Selling Your Screenplay: The Option/Purchase Agreement

The Option

Any producer who is serious about producing a picture based on your screenplay will offer to Option it. The "Option/Purchase Agreement," in this instance, is a written agreement whereby a producer acquires the exclusive right to develop, produce and distribute a picture based on your screenplay. The Option automatically expires at the end of each option term unless the producer renews it (if it has any remaining terms), or the producer exercises it and purchases the screenplay. The producer will not buy your screenplay until the commencement of principal photography.

Typically, producers want a minimum one year option term with a one year extension. This is not excessive considering that it takes an average of seven years to get a picture produced. You need to give the producer a realistic amount of time to develop the screenplay with you, to attach talent and a director, and to shop it for financing. In fact, do not be surprised if the producer wants an extension at the end of the second option term. I advise my clients to extend if the producer is paying a decent option fee, or has made good use of the time, e.g., talent or a director capable of attracting funding are attached.

The option fee that the producer offers to pay you is influenced by a number of factors: your track record, the producer's track record, the heat generated by your screenplay (if any), the subject's notoriety if the screenplay is based on a true life story, whether you are a WGA member, the screenplay's purchase price, the option term, and whether the producer is a studio or independent producer. Due to the foregoing, I disagree with the notion that the industry standard option fee is 10% of the purchase price. I always try to negotiate the highest option fee possible; in my experience, they generally tend to be under 10% for unproduced writers unless the purchase price is less than WGA low budget minimum. They are in the 10% range for writers with a successful track record.

Whether a writer is a WGA member will influence the option fee because the WGA requires that its members be paid an option fee equal to no less than 10% of the applicable WGA minimum purchase price (for a term not to exceed 18 months). From May 2016 through May 2017, the WGA minimums for a low budget and high budget completed screenplay are $48,695 and $98,455 respectively. The option fee required for a purchase price of $250,000 is only $9,845. The producer can offer a higher option fee, but he/she is not required to do so by the WGA. If the producer does so, it will likely be because the writer's track record warrants it or the screenplay has generated a bidding war.

When considering option fees, you have to take into account the fact that most independent producers lack development funds. As such, be flexible and consider the entirety of the circumstances, e.g., the producer's track record, connections, and ability to raise financing. I do recommend that you consider an earnest and reasonable offer. I consider a reasonable offer to be one that takes into consideration the benefit the producer gets by having your screenplay available to develop and produce and the legal fees you will incur to enter into the Option/ Purchase Agreement. I appreciate the time, effort and money that the producer is going to invest in getting your screenplay made; I also believe you should not be out-of-pocket on the legal fees.

Options fees are technically advances against the purchase price, but whether they are applied against the purchase price is up to negotiation. Most often, the end result is that the first option fee is applicable against the purchase price and the subsequent ones are not.

I advise you against entering into "free" Options. Free Options usually result in a waste of time, money and opportunity, since you are out-of-pocket on legal fees, cannot shop the screenplay while it is under Option, and producers tend to be less productive when they have no money at stake. An alternative to the free Option is a "Shopping Agreement" wherein you allow the producer to shop the screenplay without acquiring the right to purchase it from you. This arrangement usually works well when you are dealing with a proven producer, who has studio or production company connections, and who could potentially enter into an Option/ Purchase Agreement directly with you and pay you an option fee. Shopping Agreements are usually in the 60-90 day range and get extended if you are in the midst of negotiations with a studio/network or production company interested in entering into an Option/Purchase Agreement with you. The producer does not negotiate the terms of the Option/Purchase Agreement on your behalf. He/she only gets the ball rolling so that your agent and attorney can step in and negotiate for you. Keep in mind that if the producer is not successful, that you will not be able to shop your screenplay where he/she shopped it for at least a year—or until there are new executives working there. Other producers may not be interested in paying you for an Option if the previous producer has limited his/her opportunities for success, so this is something to keep in mind.

Purchase Price

There is no such thing as a "standard" purchase price for a screenplay. WGA members cannot accept less than the sum prescribed in the WGA Schedule of Minimums, but can exceed the minimum, and non-WGA members can sell their screenplays for any price they are able to negotiate. Sale prices typically range between 1% and 3% of the cash production budget of the picture. How much you are offered for your screenplay depends on who you are and what you bring to the table. Producers consider your track record; whether there is a bidding war for your screenplay; whether the screenplay is based on a best-selling novel; whether it is about a salacious, interesting or well publicized person or event; the screenplay's genre; and, if known ahead of time, the picture's potential production budget. If the production budget is not known going into the negotiations, I suggest a purchase price based on a sliding scale, e.g., "for a picture not to exceed $15,000,000 dollars, the purchase price shall be 2 ½% of the cash budget of the picture, but in no event less than WGA low budget minimum and no more than $250,000. The purchase price will be increased by $10,000 for every $1 million increase in the picture's production above $15,000,000 not to exceed a total purchase price equal to $500,000." The attorney attempts to secure the highest ceiling possible while the producer tries to limit it.

Additional Compensation

If the purchase price is on the lower end due to limited financing, I ask for additional compensation in the form of a deferment. "Deferred compensation" is a sum of money that is paid at a future date, from first revenues on a pari passu basis with the other parties being paid on a deferred basis. "Pari passu" means dollar for dollar. For example, if you and four cast members are entitled to deferred monies, where you are due $100,000 and each cast member $25,000, and the production company receives $100,000 in revenues, then you each receive $20,000 from the $100,000. Monies received by the production company will be distributed this way until each deferral is satisfied. Deferred compensation is usually paid prior to investor recoupment, since it is considered part of the screenplay's purchase price and is a production cost.

Whenever possible, I negotiate for my clients to receive a "Box Office Bonus," which is not guaranteed and only gets paid when, and if, the picture reaches a specific and pre-determined sales goal. Box Office Bonus compensation may be expressed as follows: "Writer shall be entitled to a Box Office Bonus of $50,000 when, and if, the picture's domestic and international gross box office, as reported in Variety, exceeds three times the picture's production budget." The bonus is only paid if you are a credited writer. I also negotiate for Nomination/Award Bonus that is paid for award nominations and wins, e.g., Golden Globes and Academy Awards.

Sequels, Remakes…

It is standard for a producer to pay the writer of an original screenplay additional monies if he/she produces a sequel, remake, or television series based on the writer's original screenplay. These additional monies are passive payments, which means that the writer does not have to render additional writing services in order receive them. As per industry standard, if a sequel based on your original screenplay is produced, you are paid 50% of the original screenplay's purchase price and 50% of the profit participation allocated to you for the original screenplay. The passive payment drops from 50% to 33 ⅓% on behalf of remakes based on your original screenplay. As such, if you were paid a $100,000 purchase price and 5% of picture's net profits for your original screenplay, you will be paid $50,000 plus 2 ½% of picture's net profits for any sequels and $33,333 plus 1 ⅔% of picture's net profits for any remakes produced. For any television series based on your screenplay, you will receive passive payments based on the running time of each episode, on its first airing and a portion thereof up to the sixth rerun. I usually refer to the WGA schedule of minimums to calculate the television payments even if my client is not a WGA member.

I always negotiate for my clients to have the Right of First Refusal to write any subsequent versions of their original screenplay, be it a sequel, remake, prequel, television series, or television motion picture. How much you are paid to write any of the aforementioned may depend on whether you are a WGA member, the success of your original screenplay, whether you were credited on your original screenplay (sometimes requires sole credit), and whether you are a working writer at the time of the subsequent version's negotiation. The terms for these writing services will not be negotiated until your services are required, and whether you are engaged to write is contingent upon the producer and you coming to an agreement for your services, since this is just a "Right of First Refusal." Passive payments are generally offered in lieu of writing fees.

Separated Rights

The WGA may determine that you are entitled to "Separated Rights" if you are a WGA member: these are a bundle of rights that the WGA has determined belong to writers of original screenplays. Dramatic stage and publication rights are both included in Separated Rights, as is the mandatory first rewrite of your original screenplay for WGA minimum; the right to meet with a senior production executive if the producer wants to replace you with another writer; the right to reacquire the screenplay if it has not been produced within five years; and, WGA minimum payment for sequel theatrical motion pictures, television movies, and television series.

As far as the dramatic stage rights are concerned, you will be entitled to a royalty free license to produce the screenplay as a dramatic stage play after the producer's holdback period of two years from the picture's general release or five years from the purchase agreement. A "holdback period" is a period of time during which the producer has exclusivity to exploit the right. If the producer exploits the dramatic stage rights prior to expiration of the holdback period, then you shall be paid 50% of the minimum sum paid to authors under the Minimum Basic Contract of the Dramatist Guild of the Author's League of America, Inc. Regarding publishing, you will be able to publish the script or novelization of the script subject to a holdback period equal to six months from the picture's general release or three years from date of the purchase agreement. The producer has to give you the opportunity to negotiate directly with the publisher to write a novel based on your screenplay, if the producer publishes it during the holdback period. The producer has to pay you WGA minimum if you do not write the novel and it is published.

Remember, the compensation and the rights guaranteed via the WGA Basic Agreement are the bare minimum to which you are entitled as a WGA member. Sometimes industry standards are higher, as is the case for passive payments for sequels and remakes. Your attorney can always negotiate for more rights and compensation than that required by the WGA.

Profit Participation

"Net Profits," an additional form of remuneration, are paid when, and if, the Picture based on your screenplay reaches a profit position. Net profits are usually calculated by subtracting all of the costs incurred in the making, marketing and distributing the Picture; this calculation includes the production budget, all financing costs, legal fees, bank interest, production company overhead, collection costs, prints, ads, distribution fees, residuals paid to any union, etc. I negotiate for my clients to have net profits allocated, knowing that it is unlikely that they will ever receive them due to the industry's accounting practices and distribution expenses. In other words, it would be nice if you received net profits—just do not count on it.

It is standard to allocate writers 5% of the picture's net profits, though independent producers tend to offer 5% of producer's net profits instead. It is important for you to understand the difference between the two calculations: "Picture's net profits" refers to 100% of the net profits of the picture whereas "producer's net profits" accounts for only 50% of the net profits. Independent producers prefer the latter formula because they generally only retain 50% of the picture's net profits themselves. Rather than push for 5% of Picture's Net Profits, my clients prefer for me to negotiate a Box Office Bonus instead.

Credit

You are entitled to a "Written by" credit if the screenplay was completely original to you, or "Screenplay by" credit if the screenplay is derived from another work, e.g., a book or play. Your credit should appear in the main credits of the picture, on a single card, in a size and type equal to the size and type of the director's credit. The credit should also appear on screen, in the position prior to the director's credit, and in paid ads whenever the director or producers are credited (excepting paid ads which are award/congratulatory type ads). If you are not the only credited writer, as happens so often, then you will have to share the writing credit on the same card with the other credited writer(s).

The WGA has a credit determination process[11] whereby it decides who gets credited (and how) when there are multiple writers on any one screenplay. The WGA compares the written drafts against the produced draft and then determines who gets the credit and in what order, and who does not. The basic credit determination rule is this: Any writer whose work equals 33% of a non-original screenplay, e.g., an adaptation, or 50% an original screenplay will be credited. Credits are limited to two writers unless the credit determination rules otherwise.

Non-members of the WGA do not get the benefit of the WGA's credit determination process. Notwithstanding, I always negotiate into my client's agreements that the producer will apply the WGA rules to determine my client's credit if he/she is not the only writer who worked on the screenplay. This way the subsequent writer only receives a credit if his/her contribution to the screenplay is substantial. I avoid credit provisions whereby the producer is given sole discretion over all aspects of your credit.

If the writer is not a member of the WGA and is entering into an Option/Purchase Agreement with a producer, who is not a WGA signatory, it is a good idea to include language in the credits clause that states that the writer will be "upgraded" (and become a WGA member) if the production company becomes a WGA signatory, or finances the Picture through a WGA signatory company, such as a studio/network. I suggest this additional terminology because a writer, who is not WGA member, will not get the benefit of a WGA credit determination or the credit he/she agreed to in the Option/Purchase Agreement, if the screenplay is rewritten by a WGA member.

Rewrites

You always want the opportunity to do the first paid rewrite of your screenplays, since whether you are credited or share credit hinges on how much of your writing ends up in the final screenplay. I attempt to secure this right for my client regardless of their WGA membership status. I always ask for the rewrite fee to be no less than WGA minimum—more if the writer has a track record. Sometimes producers attempt to credit the rewrite fee against the purchase price—whether it is will depend on your bargaining power. Either way, the goal is to not only do the first rewrite but all of them. The better you rewrite and collaborate with the producer, the more likely it is that you will be the only credited writer. I had a client who Optioned her screenplay to a major studio, refused to do the rewrite that the development executive wanted, breached her contract with the studio, and gave up the career she could have had. You may not believe in the rewrite the producer wants of you, but you have to do it if you want to stay on board and get that credit.

Occasionally, an independent producer without development funding may ask you to do a free rewrite if you are not a WGA member. Whether or not you should do it is contingent on the circumstances. I would not advise you to undertake writing for free for a producer without a good track record, since you will likely be wasting your time. If you are unproduced or need to get a screenplay produced, and a producer asks you to rewrite for free, then I might advise you to do it if the producer lacks development funding, has a very good track record, has the ability to help you develop a production worthy screenplay, and has the connections and capacity to get your screenplay produced. The caveat here is that you have to own the rewrite.

Warranties & Representations

The Option/Purchase Agreement will include a paragraph whereby you will have to make certain representations and warranties in order to sell the screenplay. You will have to warrant and represent the following: that your screenplay is original; that if any material in the screenplay is not original, that said material came from the public domain; that if any material in the screenplay is not original or in the public domain, that it is included with the permission of the original material's author; that your screenplay does not defame anyone; that it does not infringe on another person's right to privacy, and that you are the screenplay's sole and exclusive proprietor and, hence, have the authority to enter into the Option/Purchase Agreement. You cannot enter into the Option/Purchase Agreement knowing that you will be in breach of this clause the moment you sign it because the repercussions are great: you are going to be liable for whatever damages are caused to the producer via an indemnification and hold harmless clause whereby you have to reimburse the producer for any and all damages and legal fees. You need for there to be a reciprocal indemnity and hold harmless clause from the producer to you for damages incurred by you as a consequence of the production and distribution of the picture.

Rights Sold

The Option/Purchase Agreement will, at the very least, require that you sell exclusively and forever all motion picture rights, all television motion picture, all television series and all television spin-off rights and all allied and ancillary rights for the term of the copyright and all renewals and extensions thereof. The allied and ancillary rights include the right to create and sell the picture's soundtrack, merchandise, video games, etc.

In the end, what rights you get to reserve for yourself will depend on your bargaining position and the buyer. For example, studios/networks want to acquire any and all rights in and to your screenplay, whether now in existence or yet to be invented, because in addition to creating filmed entertainment, they may want the right to sell books, create theme parks or theme park rides, stage plays, etc. I try to reserve dramatic, publishing and radio rights. It is next to impossible to reserve them if you are an unproduced writer entering into an Option/ Purchase Agreement with a studio/network and more likely with an independent producer. Notwithstanding, you may be entitled to Separated Rights as a WGA member.

Option Reversion

The Option on your screenplay expires if the producer does not renew or exercise the Option prior to its termination date. All rights in and to the screenplay automatically revert to you when the Option expires. You retain any and all option and writing fees paid to you by the producer without the obligation of repayment.

Turnaround Right

You will have a "turnaround right" that provides you with the opportunity to buy back your screenplay if the producer purchased the screenplay, but did not produce it within the time specified in the Option/Purchase Agreement—usually five years. You will have an 18 to 24 month window to reacquire the screenplay. You, or whoever is buying your screenplay, will have to reimburse the producer's direct out-of-pocket cost to purchase and develop the screenplay.

Works-For-Hire: Getting Paid to Write

Most working writers in the film industry work on a for hire basis. A "work-for-hire", as it is known, means that the writer is specifically hired and paid to write on behalf of someone who employs his/her services. In the film industry, this usually occurs when a producer hires you to write a treatment, outline, or screenplay either based on the producer's idea, your screenplay pitch, or assigned material, such as a book, news story, or life story. I strongly recommend that you engage an attorney to negotiate and review the producer's draft of the Work-for-Hire Agreement.

Copyright in the Work-For-Hire

Although copyright normally vests in the author of an original work, copyright to your work vests in the producer if the producer and you entered into a written Work-for-Hire Agreement prior to the commencement of services. The Work-for-Hire Agreement will, among other things, clearly state that you are working on a for-hire basis and, therefore, that all results and proceeds of your labor and the copyright to your work are the property of the producer. It is imperative that the producer and you enter into the Work-for-Hire Agreement beforehand so that the copyright vests in the producer versus you. Otherwise, you will have to assign the results and proceeds of your labor and the copyright to the producer.

Compensation

Any producer who asks you to write for "free" is not treating you with respect and, is likely, a producer without the power and ability to get the screenplay he/she expects you to write produced. You have to value yourself and your talent if you expect anyone else to do the same. Whether I advise my client to write depends on the reasonableness of the compensation and terms offered by the producer.

Work-for-Hire Agreements are done on a "flat deal" or "step deal" basis. "Flat deal" means that the producer is going to pay you a lump sum to write the treatment, outline, first draft, second draft, final draft, polish, etc. It is important that the flat deal be well defined in the agreement, so that you know exactly how many steps you need to write for that flat deal payment. Otherwise, you could end up writing an infinite number of steps until the producer is satisfied, if ever. Payments pursuant to the Work-for-Hire Agreement occur at commencement and delivery of each step, e.g., treatment/outline, first draft, second draft, and final draft. A "step deal" means that the producer is hiring you on a step-by-step basis, so that he/she has the discretion to order the next step in the writing process, or not, and only paying for the steps ordered.

The compensation the producer offers you will take into account your track record, whether you are a member of the WGA, and whether the producer has a development deal or financing. "Development deal" refers to an arrangement between a studio/network and producer whereby the studio/network funds the producer's overhead and development expenses. It is unlikely that the producer will offer you WGA minimum compensation if you are not a WGA member, and not much beyond it if you are, but do not have track record that warrants more.

Additional Compensation

I ask the producer for deferred compensation if you are being offered a less than competitive flat deal or step deal. In addition, I negotiate for a Set Up Bonus, Box Office Bonus and a Nomination/Award Bonus. A "Set Up Bonus" gets paid when, and if, the producer sets up the screenplay at a studio/network.

Profit Participation

The producer should agree to allocate you a portion of net profits as part of your overall compensation, which as per industry standard is five percent (5%) of the net profits of the picture or producer's net profits. If I have to choose between net profits and actual money, I always chose the latter. Whether you are paid net profits, even assuming the picture is profitable, is going to depend on whether you are a credited writer (more on credits below). Your five percent (5%) will get cut in half if you share the credit. Uncredited writers get zero net profits unless the Work-for-Hire Agreement specifically states otherwise.

Credit

Your credit is not eliminated because the copyright is vesting in the producer. You are the screenplay's writer irrespective of copyright law because you wrote it. How, when, and if you are credited is more a function of the WGA or the Work-for-Hire Agreement. There is nothing you can do about your credit if the producer is a WGA signatory, you are WGA member, and you are not the screenplay's only writer due to the WGA's credit determination process. Your credit is completely up to the terms of the Work-For-Hire Agreement if you are not a WGA writer and the producer is not a WGA signatory. Notwithstanding, I try to make the producer follow the WGA's rules for credit determination, so that you are treated fairly should another writer be engaged after you.

Sequels, Remakes...

You may be entitled to passive payments if you are not a WGA member and your attorney was successful in negotiating for them. Whether you need to be the sole writer in order to get paid passive payments will be a function of the Work-for-Hire Agreement. The WGA will determine whether you are entitled to Separated Rights if you are WGA member; this is possible even though you worked on assigned material if your screenplay is substantially different from what was assigned to you, or the assigned material was not available to you, i.e., you adapt a book without referring to it.

Right of First Refusal

You may have the ability to write subsequent versions of the screenplay, e.g., sequel, remakes, television series, if you are granted the Right of First Refusal in your Work-for-Hire Agreement and are a credited writer. I find that it is always worth asking for this right, since you should benefit if your work resulted in a screenplay with a life beyond the original. As I previously mentioned, how much you are paid to write any of the aforementioned will depend on whether you are a WGA member, the success of the screenplay, and whether you are a working writer. Whether you get to write the subsequent version will depend on whether the producer and you are able to reach an agreement for your engagement to do so.

Warranties and Representations

As with the Option/Purchase Agreement, you will have to warrant and represent that whatever you write is original to you with the exception of any material assigned to you. You will have to indemnify and hold harmless the producer should you breach this warranty and representation. You need for there to be a reciprocal indemnity and hold harmless clause for any of the assigned materials provided by the producer and producer's production and distribution of the picture, since you do not want to be legally and financially liable for the producer's actions.

Becoming a WGA Member

Joining the WGA requires that you earn 24 units in the three years preceding the application and payment of a $2,500 initiation fee. You accumulate units by writing for, selling, or by entering into an Option/Purchase Agreement on behalf your screenplay with a WGA signatory producer. Below is the WGA Schedule of Units that applies to screenplays:

- 8 units for a short subject theatrical screenplay.
- 12 units for story for a feature-length theatrical screenplay.
- 24 units for a feature-length theatrical screenplay.

A rewrite will earn you half of the units applicable to the category, e.g., you get four units for rewriting a short subject theatrical screenplay.

A polish will earn you one-quarter of the units applicable to the category, e.g., you get two units for polishing a short subject theatrical screenplay.

An Option will earn one-half of the units you would be entitled to on the purchase up to a maximum of eight units per year, e.g., you are allocated four units if you Option a short subject theatrical screenplay. You are only entitled to units for the initial option period. You receive no units for extensions and renewals.

You can refer to WGA's website for the Schedule of Units available for television, radio, and New Media.[12]

Hiring an Attorney

I have discussed above the reasons why and when you may need to retain an attorney. Now the issue is, how do you find the attorney that is right for you? I suggest you do a little research: ask friends and colleagues for referrals, read legal articles and books written by attorneys, and refer to the posts by attorneys you have read and liked on Linkedin.com or another social forum. Narrow your list down to five attorneys and then interview them. Most attorneys offer a free half hour initial consultation, which is for both your benefit and the attorney's. Take advantage of it. I use the consultation to get to know the potential client, his/her needs and expectations, the likelihood that I can be of service, and to determine if our personalities are compatible. My advice to you is that you retain an attorney that you feel comfortable asking questions, who respects you, who tells you the truth—even if you do not want to hear it—and who you feel is going to be a good advocate for you. If you want an attorney for the long term, which I recommend, steer clear of attorneys that intimidate you or are arrogant. Use the free consultation to shop for an attorney—not for the purpose of picking the attorney's brain when you have no intention of retaining legal counsel.

Attorneys most often get paid an hourly fee, a flat fee, or a percent of the gross monies earned by you. Hourly rates run the gamut. How much you pay by the hour is going to depend on the attorney's experience and whether the attorney is with a large law firm. The average hourly rate is in the $300-$500 range. When billing on an hourly basis, the attorney charges for all the time spent on your behalf: negotiating, drafting, redlining (revising agreements presented to you), phone calls on your behalf or with you, copies, messenger, etc. You might be able to convince an attorney to represent you on a flat fee basis if your financial resources are limited. A flat fee entails the attorney quoting you a price that is inclusive of all the phone calls and work to be done by the attorney on your behalf. The attorney gets no more than the flat fee quoted regardless of how long it takes to conclude the task. Flat fees are on a task by task basis. Either way, you are going to have to provide an up-front deposit based on the attorney's guesstimate or flat fee quote. Whether an attorney will represent you on a percentage basis will depend on whether you are currently making money writing, are represented by a reputable agency or manager, have a track record, or have an offer on the table that will result in a payment to you large enough to compensate the attorney. It is unlikely that an attorney will represent you on a percentage basis otherwise. The average percent is 5%, but it can be as high as 10% if the attorney is representing you on a very low paying matter. Sometimes an attorney will structure a hybrid billing arrangement so that you are paying a portion of your fee up front and the other portion as a percent of the monies earned by you. Attorneys do this sometimes to accommodate a client's limited financial resources.

You will have to sign an engagement agreement with the attorney, which explains the basis of the representation, the fees, deposits (if any), and contains any necessary disclosures. The California State Bar requires one whenever the matter is going to result in payment to the attorney exceeding $1,000 and in contingent fee arrangements. The deposit that you give the attorney will go into an Attorney/Client Trust Account until it is earned by the attorney. Any monies remaining at the end of representation, if any, are returned to you. If you do not understand the engagement agreement have the attorney explain it to you, or consult with another attorney about it.

Is the cost of hiring an attorney worth it if you have an agent or manager? Absolutely, yes! The attorney is an important part of your team who is responsible for not only improving the deal terms but, also, making sure you are protected. I have yet to work on a negotiation with an agent or manager where I did not substantially improve the overall deal. Among other things, I have secured deferrals and bonuses for my clients that were not offered up front and improved my client's credit and the likelihood that he/she would retain it. I always say, "When you think you cannot afford attorney is exactly when you cannot afford to go without one."

Conclusion

As I hope you have realized by reading this chapter, writing is not just about sitting down and creating, it is also about working smart to avoid the types of situations that might detour your writing career. When in doubt, consult with an attorney. Do not rely on advice from "friends," or attorneys who are not familiar with entertainment and intellectual property law. Do not use boilerplates or attempt to draft your own agreements. It is better that you consult and determine that you are in the clear, than discover that you have made a very costly mistake.

This chapter is not a complete review of the subject matter. You should consult with an attorney if you have questions, need additional information, or require legal representation.

About the Author

Dinah Perez graduated from Loyola Law School and has been in the practice of entertainment law since 1996. She practices film, television, theater, music, new media, publishing, copyright, and trademark law. She enjoys her practice because she has great respect for the arts and those who create, and relishes helping her clients attain their professional goals.

Ms. Perez has been published in *Story Board Magazine*, *Release Print*, and *Script Magazine*, *The Screenwriter's Guide to Agents and Managers*, and the *Hollywood Screenwriting Directory*. The *Hollywood Producing Directory* authored by Ms. Perez is due to be published in April 2016. She has been quoted in *Entertainment Weekly*, *Wired Magazine*, *Wired.Com*, and *Alone in a Room*.

Ms. Perez has participated in panels and/or spoken at the Black Hollywood Film Festival, the Latin Heat Film Festival, Women in Film, Cinewomen, Independent Feature Project West, American Film Market, the Inktip Pitch Summit, The Writers Store, the Showbiz Store and Cafe, the Screenwriters World Conference, the Beverly Hills Bar Association, New York Film Academy, and California Institute for the Arts.

She is a member of the Beverly Hills Bar Association (Entertainment Law Section, Executive Committee) and the California State Bar. She was a founding board member of Cinewomen in Los Angeles, CA.

Ms. Perez is available for consultation. She may be reached by phone at (323) 935-7955, via her website at www.dinahperezlaw.com, or email at dinahperezlaw@gmail.com.

[1] 17 U.S.C. §302.

[2] 17 U.S.C. §102

[3] 17 U.S.C. §107.

[4] U.S. Copyright Office, *Copyright Basics Circular 1*, Library of Congress, May 2012.

[5] http://www.unc.edu/~unclng/public-d.htm

[6] Michael C. Donaldson, *Clearance & Copyright* (Silman James Press 2008), 332-335.

[7] N.Y. CVR. LAW § 50 and 51.

[8] CAL. CIV. CODE §3344.1

[9] Cal. Labor Code §1700.4.

[10] *Blaustein v. Burton* (1970) 9 Cal.App.3d 161, 88 Cal.Rptr. 319.

[11] http://www.wga.org/subpage_Writersresources.aspx?id=170

[12] http://www.wga.org/

The Directory

100% ENTERTAINMENT
Production company

203 N Irving Blvd
Los Angeles, CA 90004
323-630-0632 (phone)
323-871-8203 (fax)

sisaacs100@mac.com
100percentent.com
imdb.com/company/co0077804

Does not accept any unsolicited material. Project types include feature films. Genres include science fiction, horror, and drama. Established in 1998.

Stanley Isaacs
President
323-461-6360
sisaacs100@mac.com
imdb.com/name/nm0410570
linkedin.com/pub/stanley-isaacs/4/50b/5bb
twitter.com/Stanley100

meet dhillon
CEO
meetasingh108@gmail.com

100M FILMS
Production company

6 1F
Honshiocho
Shinjuku, Tokyo 160 0003
Japan
03 3358 3411

info@100meterfilms.com
imdb.com/company/co0061420

Does not accept any unsolicited material. Project types include feature films and short films. Genres include drama.

John Williams
Producer
imdb.com/name/nm0930942

100% TERRYCLOTH
Production company

421 Waterview St
Playa Del Rey, CA 90293
917-737-2368

contact@terencemichael.com
terencemichael.com
imdb.com/company/co0194989
facebook.com/pages/100-Percent-Terry-Cloth-Inc/147268518656038

Accepts query letters from unproduced, unrepresented writers via email. Project types include feature films and TV. Genres include comedy and reality. Established in 2008.

Terence Michael
Producer
310-823-3432
tm@terencemichael.com
imdb.com/name/nm0006709

Erik Adams
Development
linkedin.com/in/erikmichaeladams
twitter.com/ErikMAdams

1019 ENTERTAINMENT
Production company

1680 N Vine St, Suite 600
Hollywood, CA 90028
323-645-6840 (phone)
323-645-6841 (fax)

info@1019ent.com
1019ent.com
imdb.com/company/co0263748
twitter.com/1019Ent

Does not accept any unsolicited material. Project types include TV. Genres include comedy, non-fiction, and drama.

Ralph Winter
Partner
imdb.com/name/nm0003515
linkedin.com/pub/ralph-winter/7/1a8/8a9

Terry Botwick
Partner
imdb.com/company/co0263748

101 DISTRIBUTION
Distributor

2375 E Camelback Rd
6 Fl
Phoenix, AZ 85016
602-357-3288 (phone)
602-387-5001 (fax)

info@101d.com
101distribution.com
imdb.com/company/co0386624
facebook.com/arenadotcom
twitter.com/arenadotcom

Does not accept any unsolicited material. Genres include horror and action.

108 MEDIA
Production company, distributor, and sales agent

225 Commissioners St
Ste 204
Toronto, ON M4M 0A1
Canada
647-837-3312

info@108mediacorp.com
108mediacorp.com
imdb.com/company/co0370213
linkedin.com/company/108-media-corp-
facebook.com/108mediacorp
twitter.com/108MediaCorp

Does not accept any unsolicited material. Genres include drama.

Julien Sexsmith
Producer
imdb.com/name/nm6592381

10TH HOLE PRODUCTIONS
Production company and financing company

1071 Post Rd East
Westport, CT 06880
203-222-0707

info@10thholeproductions.com
10thholeproductions.com
imdb.com/company/co0278302

Accepts query letters from unproduced, unrepresented writers via email. Project types include TV. Genres include comedy and drama.

Andy Sawyer
Producer
imdb.com/name/nm1238818

120DB FILMS, INC.
Financing company

75 Mill River Rd. South Salem, NY 10590
914-533-5241 (phone)
914-533-5242 (fax)

hays@120dbfilms.com
120dbfilms.com

Does not accept any unsolicited material. Genres include reality, science fiction, thriller, comedy, detective, horror, family, non-fiction, romance, sociocultural, drama, crime, animation, action, documentary, fantasy, myth, and period.

12 FORWARD ENTERTAINMENT
Production company

500 Church St, Ste 600.
Nashville, TN 37219

4228 N. Central Expwy
Suite 200
Dallas, TX 75206
214-855-0500 (phone)
214-855-0500 (fax)

2601 Gaston Ave
Dallas, Texas 75226

melanie@12forward.com
12forward.com
imdb.com/company/co0175822

Does not accept any unsolicited material. Project types include short films and TV. Genres include drama and comedy.

16X9 PRODUCTIONS
Production company

7312 COVERED BRIDGE DR
Austin, TX 78736
818-749-6608

imdb.com/company/co0156846

Does not accept any unsolicited material. Project types include TV. Genres include comedy and documentary.

1821 MEDIA
Production company

205 S Beverly Dr, Suite 206, Beverly Hills, CA, United States, 90212
310-860-1121 (phone)
310-860-1123 (fax)

asst@1821media.com
1821pictures.com
imdb.com/company/co0237137

Does not accept any unsolicited material. Project types include TV. Genres include family, drama, animation, thriller, and romance.

1821 PICTURES
Production company

205 S. Beverly Dr.
Suite 206
Beverly Hills, CA 90212
310-860-1121 (phone)
310-860-1123 (fax)

asst@1821pictures.com
1821pictures.com
imdb.com/company/co0237259
facebook.com/1821Pictures

Accepts query letters from unproduced, unrepresented writers via email. Project types include TV. Genres include animation, non-fiction, comedy, and drama. Established in 2005.

Billy Piché
Director of Development
310-860-1121
imdb.com/name/nm5046038
linkedin.com/pub/billy-pich%C3%A9/16/7b9/9b4

Paris Latsis
310-860-1121
imdb.com/company/co0237259

Terry Douglas
Principal
310-860-1121
imdb.com/name/nm0234806
facebook.com/td007

19 ENTERTAINMENT
Production company

8560 W Sunset Blvd, 9th Floor
West Hollywood, CA 90069
310-777-1940 (phone)
310-777-1949 (fax)

1071 Ave of the Americas,
New York, NY 10018
212-784-7770

inquiries@19entertainment.com
coremediagroup.com/19.html
imdb.com/company/co0085773
linkedin.com/company/19-entertainment
facebook.com/19EntertainmentLtd
twitter.com/COREMediaGrp

Does not accept any unsolicited material. Project types include TV. Genres include animation, comedy, and drama.

Peter Hurwitz
President
310-777-1940
linkedin.com/pub/peter-hurwitz/b/a6b/7b7

1ST MIRACLE PICTURES
Distributor and sales agent

3439 W Chauenga Blvd. Hollywood, CA 90068
323-874-6000 (phone)
323-874-4252 (fax)

sales@1stmiracleproductions.com
imdb.com/company/co0063241

Does not accept any unsolicited material. Genres include crime, science fiction, thriller, action, documentary, reality, detective, myth, comedy, fantasy, drama, non-fiction, horror, family, animation, period, romance, and sociocultural.

20TH CENTURY FOX
Production company and distributor

6F, 3-16-33 Roppongi
Minato-ku
Tokyo 106-0032
Japan

info@foxjapan.com
foxjapan.com
imdb.com/company/co0051477
facebook.com/20thfox.video
twitter.com/20foxvideo

Does not accept any unsolicited material. Project types
include feature films and short films. Genres include
action.

John Flanagan
VP Marketing (Executive)
imdb.com/name/nm2675851

21 LAPS/ADELSTEIN
Production company

10201 W. Pico Blvd.
Building 41, Suite 500B
Los Angeles, CA 90064
310-369-7402

imdb.com/company/co0372539

Does not accept any unsolicited material.

Marty Adelstein
Producer
310-270-4570
imdb.com/name/nm1374351

21 LAPS ENTERTAINMENT
Production company

c/o Twentieth Century Fox
10201 W Pico Blvd
Building 41, Suite 400
Los Angeles, CA 90064
310-369-7170 (phone)
310-969-0443 (fax)

imdb.com/company/co0158853
facebook.com/pages/21-Laps-Entertainment/
    185829081580687

Does not accept any unsolicited material. Project types
include TV and feature films. Genres include action,
comedy, and drama.

Dan Levine
President of Production
imdb.com/name/nm0505782

Shawn Levy
Principal
310-369-4466
imdb.com/name/nm0506613

Billy Rosenberg
Senior Vice President Development
310-369-7170
imdb.com/name/nm1192785

Will Rack
Director of Development
310-369-7170
imdb.com/name/nm5211280

25/7 PRODUCTIONS
Production company

4119 Burbank Blvd.
Burbank, CA 91505
818-432-2800 (phone)
818-432-2810 (fax)

info@257productions.com
257productions.com
imdb.com/company/co0200336

Accepts query letters from unproduced, unrepresented
writers. Project types include TV. Genres include non-
fiction, drama, comedy, and animation. Established in
2003.

David Broome
President
818-432-2800
imdb.com/company/co0200336

26 FILMS
Production company and distributor

8748 Holloway Dr
Los Angeles, CA, 90069
310-205-9922 (phone)
310-206-9926 (fax)

asst@26films.com
imdb.com/company/co0107215

Accepts query letters from unproduced, unrepresented writers via email. Project types include feature films and short films. Genres include comedy, myth, non-fiction, and action.

Nathalie Marciano
Principal
310-205-9922
asst@26films.com
imdb.com/name/nm0545695

Elena Brooks
Director of Development
310-205-9922
asst@26films.com
imdb.com/name/nm4542983
linkedin.com/pub/elena-brooks/7/229/4b5

289 FILMS DISTRIBUTING INC.
Distributor

5707 Lakemoore Dr., Ste. G
Austin, TX 78731
512-689-5867 (phone)
512-382-4327 (fax)

sales@289filmsdistributing.com
imdb.com/company/co0157978

Does not accept any unsolicited material. Project types include short films and feature films. Genres include documentary and comedy. Established in 2003.

2929 INTERNATIONAL
Distributor and sales agent

9100 Wilshire Blvd., Ste. 500W Beverly Hills, CA 90212
310-309-5200 (phone)
310-309-5200 (fax)

kkelly@2929entertainment.com
2929entertainment.com/Home.aspx
imdb.com/company/co0139479

Does not accept any unsolicited material. Genres include drama, science fiction, action, comedy, period, detective, myth, fantasy, reality, romance, sociocultural, thriller, animation, crime, documentary, family, horror, and non-fiction.

2929 PRODUCTIONS
Production company and distributor

1437 Seventh St, Suite 250
Santa Monica, CA 90401
310-309-5200 (phone)
310-309-5716 (fax)

2929entertainment.com
imdb.com/company/co0005596

Accepts query letters from unproduced, unrepresented writers. Genres include action, drama, and non-fiction.

Todd Wagner
Principal
310-309-5200
todd@2929entertainment.com
imdb.com/company/co0005596
linkedin.com/pub/todd-wagner/52/977/ba4

Shay Weiner
Director of Development
310-309-5200
sweiner@2929ent.com
imdb.com/name/nm1674317

2ND FIDDLE ENTERTAINMENT
Production company

2601 Long Ln
Flower Mound, TX 75022
972-965-7391

imdb.com/company/co0271697
facebook.com/MaggiesPassage

Does not accept any unsolicited material. Project types include feature films. Genres include fantasy, action, and drama. Established in 2009.

2ND LIFE FILM PRODUCTION
Production company, distributor, and sales agent

10741 NW 45th St
Ste 12
Coral Springs, FL 33065
954-401-4220

2movie@gmail.com
imdb.com/company/co0209728

Does not accept any unsolicited material. Genres include drama, horror, and crime.

2S FILMS

Production company

10390 Santa Monica Blvd
Suite 210
Los Angeles, CA 90025
310-789-5450 (phone)
310-789-3060 (fax)

info@2sfilms.com
2sfilms.whoiskenjackson.com
imdb.com/company/co0238996

Does not accept any unsolicited material. Project types include feature films. Genres include comedy and romance. Established in 2007.

Allison Rayne
Vice President of Development
310-789-5450
info@2sfilms.com
imdb.com/name/nm2588349
linkedin.com/pub/allison-rayne/5/56/9a8

Jon Schumacher
Development Executive
imdb.com/name/nm2749499

Molly Smith
Principal
310-789-5450
info@2sfilms.com
imdb.com/company/co0238996

2THESKY ENTERTAINMENT

Production company and distributor

1606 Willowview St.
Longview, TX 75604
903-736-8311

jena@2theskyentertainment.com
2theskyentertainment.com
imdb.com/company/co0480013
facebook.com/pages/Emmas-Song/
    1460496420871726
twitter.com/2theSky2

Does not accept any unsolicited material. Project types include short films. Genres include drama.

2WAYTRAFFIC - A SONY PICTURES ENTERTAINMENT COMPANY

Production company

Middenweg 1
PO Box 297
Hilversum 1217 HS
The Netherlands
+31(0)357508000 (phone)
+31(0)357508020 (fax)

info@2waytraffic.com
2waytraffic.com
imdb.com/company/co0211160
linkedin.com/company/2waytraffic

Does not accept any unsolicited material. Project types include feature films and TV. Established in 2004.

3311 PRODUCTIONS

Production company

3522 Hayden Ave
Culver City, CA 90232
323-319-5060 (phone)
323-306-5534 (fax)

info@3311productions.com
3311productions.com
imdb.com/company/co0312478
linkedin.com/company/3311-productions-inc

Accepts query letters from produced or represented writers. Project types include feature films. Genres include drama and comedy.

Mark Roberts
Executive
imdb.com/name/nm4224736

Ross Jacobson
CEO
imdb.com/name/nm2278951
linkedin.com/pub/ross-jacobson/6/6bb/60a

Eddie Vaisman
imdb.com/name/nm4224744

34TH STREET FILMS

Production company

8200 Wilshire Blvd, Suite 300
Beverly Hills, CA 90211

323-315-7963 (phone)
323-315-7117 (fax)

imdb.com/company/co0248547
facebook.com/34thstreetfilms

Does not accept any unsolicited material. Project types include feature films. Genres include romance, action, comedy, and family.

Matt Moore
Executive Vice President
323-315-7963
imdb.com/name/nm0601597

Amber Rasberry
Director of Development
323-315-7963
imdb.com/name/nm2248393
linkedin.com/in/amberrasberry
twitter.com/arazz

Poppy Hanks
Senior Vice President (Production & Development)
323-315-7963
imdb.com/name/nm1585325
linkedin.com/pub/poppy-hanks/6/9b8/4a0

369 PRODUCTIONS
Production company

+44 7540 653 783

harriet@369productions.co.uk
imdb.com/company/co0367023

Does not accept any unsolicited material. Project types include feature films. Genres include animation and romance.

Victor Glynn
Producer
imdb.com/name/nm0323376

3 ALLIANCE ENTERPRISES, INC
Distributor

703 Pier Ave., Ste 627 Hermosa Beach, CA 90254
323-756-0940 (phone)
323-756-2435 (fax)

submissions@3alliance.com
alliance.com

imdb.com/company/co0140135
linkedin.com/company/3-alliance-enterprises-inc.
facebook.com/3Alliance

Does not accept any unsolicited material. Genres include family and documentary.

3 ARTS ENTERTAINMENT
Production company

9460 Wilshire Blvd 7th Floor
Beverly Hills, CA 90212
310-888-3200 (phone)
310-888-3210 (fax)

16 W 22nd St
Suite 201
New York, NY 10010

3arts.com
imdb.com/company/co0070636
linkedin.com/company/3-arts-entertainment

Accepts query letters from unproduced, unrepresented writers. Project types include feature films and TV. Genres include comedy and drama. Established in 1992.

Howard Klein
Partner
310-888-3200
hklein@3arts.com
imdb.com/name/nm2232433

Erwin Stoff
Partner (Chairman)
310-888-3200
estoff@3arts.com
imdb.com/name/nm0831098
linkedin.com/pub/erwin-stoff/41/70a/a1b

3 BALL ENTERTAINMENT
Production company and distributor

3650 Redondo Beach Ave
Redondo Beach, CA 90278
424-236-7500 (phone)
424-236-7501 (fax)

reception@3ballentertainment.com
3ballentertainment.com
imdb.com/company/co0100000
linkedin.com/company/3-ball-productions

facebook.com/3BallEntertainment

Does not accept any unsolicited material. Project types include TV. Genres include drama.

Brant Pinvidic
Chief Creative Officer
424-236-7500
imdb.com/name/nm1803480

J.D. Roth
Co-Founder and Non-Executive Board Member
424-236-7500
imdb.com/name/nm0744870

3GZ PRODUCTIONS
Production company and distributor

2000 N. Bayshore Dr, #314
Miami, FL 33137
305-917-5257

franceasca@3gzproductions.com
3gzproductions.com
imdb.com/company/co0181238
facebook.com/3gzproductions

Does not accept any unsolicited material. Project types include short films and feature films. Genres include documentary and drama. Established in 2006.

408 FILMS
Production company and financing company

20111 Stevens Creek Blvd., Suite 160, Cupertino, CA, United States, 95014
408-516-9676

5/F Two Exchange Square 8 Connaught Place
Central Hong Kong
011-852-30172046

info@408films.com
408films.com
imdb.com/company/co0236057

Does not accept any unsolicited material. Project types include TV. Genres include drama, thriller, and family.

40 ACRES & A MULE FILMWORKS, INC.
Production company

75 S Elliot Place
Brooklyn, NY 11217
718-624-3703 (phone)
718-624-2008 (fax)

40acres.com
imdb.com/company/co0029134
facebook.com/40AcresAndAMuleFilmworks

Does not accept any unsolicited material. Project types include TV. Genres include drama, non-fiction, comedy, and action.

Spike Lee
Chairman
718-624-3703
imdb.com/name/nm0000490
facebook.com/SpikeLee
twitter.com/SpikeLee

44 BLUE PRODUCTIONS, INC.
Production company

4040 Vineland Ave, Suite 105
Studio City, CA 11217
818-760-4442 (phone)
818-760-1509 (fax)

reception@44blue.com
44blue.com
imdb.com/company/co0012712
linkedin.com/company/44-blue-productions
facebook.com/44blueproductions
twitter.com/44blue

Does not accept any unsolicited material. Project types include TV. Genres include action, drama, non-fiction, comedy, reality, and documentary.

Rasha Drachkovitch
President
818-760-4442
reception@44blue.com
imdb.com/name/nm0236624
linkedin.com/pub/rasha-drachkovitch/8/735/598
facebook.com/rasha.drachkovitch

Stephanie Drachkovitch
Executive Vice-President
818-760-4442
reception@44blue.com
imdb.com/name/nm1729517
linkedin.com/pub/stephanie-drachkovitch/47/218/113

48 HOUR FILM FESTIVAL
Distributor

PO Box 40008
Washington, DC 20016

info@48hourfilm.com
imdb.com/company/co0167544
facebook.com/48hourfilmproject
twitter.com/48HourFilmProj

Does not accept any unsolicited material. Project types include short films. Genres include comedy.

495 PRODUCTIONS
Production company

4222 Burbank Blvd, 2nd Floor
Burbank, CA 91505
818-840-2750 (phone)
818-840-7083 (fax)

info@495productions.com
495productions.com
imdb.com/company/co0192481
facebook.com/495Productions
twitter.com/495Prods

Does not accept any unsolicited material. Project types include TV. Genres include comedy, drama, non-fiction, and reality.

SallyAnn Salsano
President
818-840-2750
info@495productions.com
imdb.com/name/nm1133163
linkedin.com/pub/sallyann-salsano/38/2a2/3b5
twitter.com/sallyannsalsano

James Bianco
Head (Production)
imdb.com/name/nm1291179

4KIDS ENTERTAINMENT
Distributor

1414 Ave Of The AmeriCAs New York, NY 10019
212-758-7666

JNarvaez@4KidsEnt.com
kidsentertainment.com
imdb.com/company/co0052177

Does not accept any unsolicited material. Genres include family.

4TH ROW FILMS
Production company and distributor

27 W 20th St, Suite 1006
New York, NY 10011
212-974-0082 (phone)
212-627-3090 (fax)

info@4throwfilms.com
4throwfilms.com
imdb.com/company/co0117932
linkedin.com/company/4th-row-films
facebook.com/4thRowFilmsNYC
twitter.com/4thRowFilms

Does not accept any unsolicited material. Project types include TV. Genres include non-fiction, comedy, and drama.

Susan Bedusa
Senior Vice President, Production & Development
imdb.com/name/nm1513256
linkedin.com/pub/susan-bedusa/5/578/aa0

Douglas Tirola
President
imdb.com/name/nm0864263
linkedin.com/pub/douglas-tirola/4/427/856
facebook.com/douglas.tirola

4 VISIONS
Production company

5403 Galahad Ln
Richardson, TX 75082
214-563-1506

moody@4visions.com
imdb.com/company/co0221847

Does not accept any unsolicited material. Genres include romance and comedy.

501 POST
Production company

501 N. I-35
Austin, TX 78702

501studios.com

imdb.com/company/co0147102
linkedin.com/company/501-post

Does not accept any unsolicited material. Genres include action, thriller, horror, and crime.

51 MINDS ENTERTAINMENT
Production company

5200 Lankershim Blvd. Ste. 200
North Hollywood CA 91601
818-643-8200 (phone)
323-466-9202 (fax)

info@51minds.com
51minds.com
imdb.com/company/co0166565
linkedin.com/company/51-minds-entertainment
facebook.com/51Minds
twitter.com/51Minds

Accepts query letters from unproduced, unrepresented writers via email. Project types include TV. Genres include reality, drama, and comedy. Established in 2003.

Mark Cronin
Co-President
323-466-9200
info@51minds.com
imdb.com/name/nm0188782

David Caplan
Vice President (Development)
323-466-9200
info@51minds.com
imdb.com/name/nm4933376

Cris Abrego
Co-President
323-466-9200
info@51minds.com
imdb.com/name/nm0009312

59TH STREET FILMS
Production company

101 Destiny Dr
Lafayette, LA 70506
337-280-9370

59thstreetfilms@gmail.com

59thstreetfilms.com
imdb.com/company/co0285087
linkedin.com/company/59th-street-films
facebook.com/59thStreetFilms
twitter.com/59thstreetfilms

Accepts scripts from unproduced, unrepresented writers. Project types include TV. Genres include comedy and drama.

Alfred Rubin Thompson
Producer
imdb.com/name/nm0867022

Nicholas Scott
imdb.com/name/nm4641966

Jennifer Jarrett
Producer
imdb.com/name/nm1838264

Steve Sirkis
imdb.com/name/nm2401659
linkedin.com/pub/dir/nicholas/scott

Sarah Agor
Producer
imdb.com/name/nm2706070
linkedin.com/pub/sarah-agor/7/36/216

5IVE SMOOTH STONES PRODUCTIONS
Production company

8500 Wilshire Blvd, Suite #527
Beverly Hills, CA 90211

imdb.com/company/co0332052

Accepts query letters from unproduced, unrepresented writers via email. Project types include feature films. Genres include comedy and family.

Terry Crews
Actor/CEO
imdb.com/name/nm0187719
facebook.com/realterrycrews
twitter.com/terrycrews

5 NEN D GUMI
Production company

1-6-1-1F
Shoto

Shibuya, Tokyo 150-0046
Japan
03-5790-5577 (phone)
03-5790-5595 (fax)

info@5-d.co.jp
5-d.co.jp
imdb.com/company/co0321455

Does not accept any unsolicited material. Project types include TV. Genres include drama.

Shûichi Nakayama
Producer
imdb.com/name/nm3357390

5TH QUARTER PRODUCTIONS
Production company and distributor

70 Perimeter Ctr E
Atlanta, GA 30346
404-789-7634

directorapar@gmail.com
directorapar.com
imdb.com/company/co0449332

Does not accept any unsolicited material. Project types include short films. Genres include crime and drama.

6 DEGREE MEDIA
Production company

37 Berwick St
London W1F 8RS
UK
+44 0207-734-6194

info@6degreemedia.co.uk
imdb.com/company/co0282374

Does not accept any unsolicited material. Project types include feature films and TV. Genres include drama, thriller, and comedy.

Alan Greenspan
Producer
imdb.com/name/nm0339171

70/30 PRODUCTIONS
Production company

81 Wakefield Dr NE
Atlanta, GA 30309
404-352-4724

imdb.com/company/co0025188

Does not accept any unsolicited material. Project types include short films and TV. Genres include comedy.

72ND STREET PRODUCTIONS
Production company

1041 N Formosa Ave
Formosa Building, Suite 3
West Hollywood, CA 90046
323-850-3139 (phone)
323-850-3179 (fax)

contact@72ndstreetproductions.com
imdb.com/company/co0180596

Accepts query letters from unproduced, unrepresented writers via email. Project types include feature films, TV, and commercials. Genres include drama.

Tim Harms
Principal
323-850-3139
tharms@72ndstreetproductions.com
imdb.com/name/nm0363608

Lee Toland Krieger
Principal
323-850-3139
lkrieger@72ndstreetproductions.com
imdb.com/name/nm1767218

Steven Krieger
Principal
323-850-3139
skrieger@72ndstreetproductions.com
imdb.com/name/nm2544844

72 PRODUCTIONS
Production company

39 Mesa St #207
San Francisco, CA 94129
415-292-7100 (phone)
310-278-1224 (fax)

72productions.com
imdb.com/company/co0196483

Accepts query letters from unproduced, unrepresented writers. Project types include feature films. Genres include science fiction and thriller.

Jennifer Chaiken
Principal
310-278-1221
imdb.com/name/nm0149671
linkedin.com/pub/jen-chaiken/37/779/945

Sebastian Dungan
Principal
310-278-1221
imdb.com/name/nm0242253
facebook.com/sebastian.dungan

7&7 PRODUCERS'S SALES
Production company and sales agent

122 Walton St
London SW3 2JJ
UK
+44 020 7584 6402

info@7and7.co.uk
7and7.co.uk
imdb.com/company/co0330284

Does not accept any unsolicited material. Project types include commercials. Genres include comedy, drama, and horror.

Maura Hoy
Producer
imdb.com/name/nm1084040

7ATE9 ENTERTAINMENT
Production company

740 N. La Brea Ave
Los Angeles, CA 90038
323-936-6789 (phone)
323-937-6713 (fax)

andrea@7ate9.com
7ate9.com
imdb.com/company/co0171281
linkedin.com/company/7ate9-entertainment
facebook.com/
    7ATE9-Entertainment-201426896556397

Does not accept any unsolicited material. Project types include TV.

Artur Spigel
Creative Director
imdb.com/name/nm1742493
linkedin.com/pub/artur-spigel/25/982/926
facebook.com/art.spigel

8:38 PRODUCTIONS
Production company

10390 Santa Monica Blvd.
Suite 200
Los Angeles, CA 90064
310-789-3056 (phone)
310-789-3077 (fax)

imdb.com/company/co0252672

Does not accept any unsolicited material. Genres include romance and family.

Kira Davis
Principal
310-789-3056
imdb.com/name/nm0204987

8790 PICTURES, INC.
Production company

11400 W Olympic Blvd, Suite 590
Los Angeles, CA 90064
310-471-9983 (phone)
310-471-6366 (fax)

8790pictures@gmail.com
imdb.com/company/co0159892
facebook.com/pages/8790-Pictures-Inc/
    109963982365708

Accepts query letters from unproduced, unrepresented writers via email. Project types include feature films and TV. Genres include animation, drama, action, comedy, and romance.

Ralph Singleton
310-471-9983
8790pictures@gmail.com
imdb.com/name/nm0802326

Joan Singleton

310-471-9983
8790pictures@gmail.com
imdb.com/name/nm0802306
linkedin.com/pub/joan-singleton/4/336/62b

8TH WONDER LIVE EVENTS

4147 1/2 N. Brand Blvd.
Glendale, CA 91203
818-571-9073

info@8thwonderent.com
8thwonderliveevents.com
imdb.com/company/co0226729
facebook.com/pages/8th-wonder-entertainment

Accepts query letters from unproduced, unrepresented writers via email.

David Luong

Director of Development
info@8thwonderent.com

Michael McQuarn

mcq@8thwonderent.com
linkedin.com/pub/michael-mcquarn/33/953/793
facebook.com/Iammcq
twitter.com/IamMcQ

900 FILMS

Production company

1611A South Melrose Dr
Vista, CA 92081
760-477-2470 (phone)
760-477-2478 (fax)

asst@900films.com
900films.com
imdb.com/company/co0086829
facebook.com/900films

Accepts query letters from unproduced, unrepresented writers via email. Project types include feature films, TV, and commercials. Genres include action, non-fiction, and reality. Established in 1999.

Angela Rhodehamel

Production Manager/ Producer
linkedin.com/pub/angela-rhodehamel/86/520/979

Tony Hawk

Skateboarder/Principal
imdb.com/name/nm0005000

9.14 PICTURES

Production company

1804 Chestnut St, Suite 2
Philadelphia, PA 19103
215-238-0707 (phone)
215-238-0663 (fax)

info@914pictures.com
914pictures.com
imdb.com/company/co0145535
facebook.com/pages/914-Pictures/117299371642553

Accepts query letters from unproduced, unrepresented writers via email. Established in 2002.

Sheena Joyce

Owner
215-238-0707 ext. 11#
info@914pictures.com
imdb.com/name/nm1852224
linkedin.com/pub/sheena-joyce/6/230/852
twitter.com/sheenamjoyce

Don Argott

Owner
215-238-0707 ext. 12#
info@914pictures.com
imdb.com/name/nm0034531
linkedin.com/pub/don-argott/6/7a5/634
twitter.com/dargott

9 STORY MEDIA GROUP

Production company and distributor

23 Fraser Ave
Toronto, ON M6K 1Y7
Canada
416-530-9900

info@9story.com
9story.com
imdb.com/company/co0124707
linkedin.com/company/140126
facebook.com/9StoryMediaGroup
twitter.com/9StoryMG

Does not accept any unsolicited material. Genres include comedy and family.

Vince Commisso
Producer
imdb.com/name/nm0173886

A51FILMS
Production company and distributor

188 Steelmanville Rd.
Egg Harbor Township, NJ 08234

HDFilmMaker2112@gmail.com
imdb.com/company/co0203534

Does not accept any unsolicited material. Project types include TV. Genres include comedy, thriller, and drama.

A71 PRODUCTIONS
Production company and distributor

25 Atlantic Ave
Toronto, ON M6K 3E7
Canada
416-778-5571

miller@agency71.com
a71productions.com
imdb.com/company/co0336760
linkedin.com/company/a71-productions
facebook.com/A71productionsinc
twitter.com/a71productions

Does not accept any unsolicited material. Project types include short films. Genres include comedy.

David Miller
Producer
imdb.com/name/nm2418763

A AND S ANIMATION
Production company

8137 Lake Crowell Circle
Orlando, FL 32836
407-370-2673 (phone)
407-370-2602 (fax)

mark@funnytoons.tv
funnytoons.tv
imdb.com/company/co0186525

Does not accept any unsolicited material. Project types include short films. Genres include animation.

AARDMAN ANIMATIONS
Production company

Gas Ferry Rd
Bristol BS1 6UN
United Kingdom
+44117-984-8485 (phone)
+44117-984-8486 (fax)

1410 Aztec West
Bristol
BS32 4RT
014-548-59000

mail@aardman.com
aardman.com
imdb.com/company/co0103531
twitter.com/aardman

Does not accept any unsolicited material. Genres include animation.

Alicia Gold
Head (Feature Development)
+44117-984-8485
mail@aardman.com
imdb.com/name/nm1664759imdb.com/name/
    nm4211100
linkedin.com/pub/alicia-gold/50/1a6/575

AARDWOLF ENTERTAINMENT
Production company, distributor, and sales agent

3200 N Lakeshore
709
Chicago, IL 60657
312-656-9926

mvadik13@gmail.com
imdb.com/company/co0371400

Does not accept any unsolicited material. Project types include TV. Genres include drama and crime.

Mark Vadik
Producer
imdb.com/name/nm1067375

AARON KOGAN PRODUCTIONS
Production company

10474 S. Santa Monica Blvd., Ste. 301
Los Angeles, CA 90025
310-474-4000 (phone)
310-474-4431 (fax)

linkedin.com/in/aaron-kogan-a83b1650

Does not accept any unsolicited material. Project types include feature films. Genres include crime and drama.

Aaron Kogan
Producer/Manager
imdb.com/name/nm1179939

ABACAB PRODUCTIONS INC.
Production company

11156 Cashmere St.
Los Angeles, CA 90049
310-476-1278 (phone)
310-471-0879 (fax)

judith@abacabproductions.com
abacabproductions.com

Does not accept any unsolicited material. Genres include comedy, documentary, thriller, horror, science fiction, animation, reality, period, crime, fantasy, sociocultural, romance, myth, detective, drama, family, action, and non-fiction.

ABANDON INTERACTIVE ENTERTAINMENT
Production company

711 Route 302
Pine Bush, NY 12566
845-361-9317 (phone)
845-361-9150 (fax)

info@abandoninteractive.com
imdb.com/company/co0025591
linkedin.com/company/abandon-interactive-
    entertainment

Does not accept any unsolicited material.

Karen Lauder
COO
845-361-9317
info@abandoninteractive.com
imdb.com/name/nm0490746

ABANDON PICTURES
Production company

711 Route 302
Pine Bush, NJ 12566
845-361-9317 (phone)
212-397-8361 (fax)

imdb.com/company/co0025591

Does not accept any unsolicited material. Project types include feature films. Genres include thriller.

Karen Lauder
Producer
imdb.com/name/nm0490746

Deborah Marcus
imdb.com/name/nm3359316

Lizzie Friedman
Producer
imdb.com/name/nm0295288

ABBOLITA PRODUCTIONS
Production company

New York, NY

abbolita.com
imdb.com/company/co0419092
twitter.com/abbolita13

Accepts scripts from unproduced, unrepresented writers via email. Project types include feature films. Established in 2014.

Tim Nye
Principal
imdb.com/name/nm5470167

ABBY LOU ENTERTAINMENT
Production company

1411 Edgehill Pl.
Pasadena, CA 91103
626-795-7334 (phone)
626-795-4013 (fax)

ale@full-moon.com
abbylouent.com
imdb.com/company/co0094888
facebook.com/abbylouent
twitter.com/AbbyLouEnt

Does not accept any unsolicited material. Project types include feature films.

George Le Fave
President
imdb.com/name/nm2247957

Cheryl Pestor
imdb.com/name/nm2453743

ABC SIGNATURE
Production company

500 S Buena Vista St
Burbank, CA 91521

imdb.com/company/co0492993

Does not accept any unsolicited material. Project types include TV. Genres include comedy and drama.

Tracy Underwood
Head
imdb.com/name/nm0881046

ABC STUDIOS
Production company

500 S Buena Vista St
Burbank, CA 91505
818-460-7777

imdb.com/company/co0209226
facebook.com/ABCNetwork
twitter.com/ABCNetwork

Does not accept any unsolicited material. Project types include TV and commercials. Genres include drama and comedy.

Brenda Kyle
Vice President (Television Production)
imdb.com/name/nm0477368
linkedin.com/pub/brenda-kyle/1/a09/9b1

Gary French
Senior Vice President (Production)
imdb.com/name/nm2380686

Patrick Moran
Executive Vice President (Creative & Production)
imdb.com/name/nm3988896
facebook.com/patrick.moran.18400

ABERRATION FILMS
Production company

1425 N Crescent Heights Blvd, #203
West Hollywood, CA 90046
323-656-1830

info@aberrationfilms.com
imdb.com/company/co0164476
linkedin.com/company/aberration-films

Accepts query letters from unproduced, unrepresented writers. Project types include feature films. Genres include drama.

Susan Dynner
323-656-1830
aberrationfilms@yahoo.com
imdb.com/name/nm1309839
linkedin.com/pub/susan-dynner/8/739/83

A BIGGER BOAT
Production company

275 S. Beverly Dr, Suite 210
Beverly Hills, CA 90212
310-860-1113

imdb.com/company/co0247116

Does not accept any unsolicited material. Project types include feature films.

Peter Block
Producer
imdb.com/name/nm0088756

Amanda Essick
imdb.com/name/nm2302699

A BIRD'S EYE PRODUCTIONS
Production company, distributor, and sales agent

9663 Santa Monica Blvd
Ste 441
Beverly Hills, CA 90210
424-204-2094 (phone)
310-388-0956 (fax)

info@birdseyeproductions.com
abirdseyeproductions.com
imdb.com/company/co0343658

Does not accept any unsolicited material. Genres include crime, drama, and action.

ABOMINABLE PICTURES
Production company

3400 Cahuenga Blvd. West Building, 2nd Floor
Los Angeles, CA 90068

info@abominablepictures.com
abominablepictures.com
imdb.com/company/co0295946
facebook.com/pages/Abominable-Pictures/
337127229732998
twitter.com/AbominablePix

Does not accept any unsolicited material. Project types include TV. Genres include comedy.

Jonathan Stern
Producer
imdb.com/name/nm0827746

ABRAMORAMA
Distributor and sales agent

23 Washington Ave
Pleasantville, NY 10570
914-741-1818

info@abramorama.com
abramorama.com
imdb.com/company/co0096337
linkedin.com/company/abramorama
facebook.com/AbramoramaInc
twitter.com/abramorama

Does not accept any unsolicited material. Project types include feature films. Genres include documentary and comedy.

ABSOLUTE PRODUCTIONS
Production company and distributor

545 SW 15th Ave
Fort Lauderdale, FL 33312
954-763-7939

Rob@531themovie.com
531themovie.com
imdb.com/company/co0202367

Does not accept any unsolicited material. Project types include short films. Genres include romance and comedy. Established in 2007.

ABSURDA FILMS
Production company

16782 Redhill Ave., Suite B
Irvine, CA 92606
949-250-8090

facebook.com/filmabsurda

Does not accept any unsolicited material. Project types include feature films. Genres include horror and drama.

Norm Hill
Producer
imdb.com/name/nm2147362

David Lynch
Producer/Director/Writer
imdb.com/name/nm0000186

ACADEMY ENTERTAINMENT, INC.
Production company and distributor

59 Westminster Ave.
Bergenfield, NJ 07621
201-394-1849 (phone)
201-357-8482 (fax)

alanmacacademy@aol.com
imdb.com/company/co0043995

Does not accept any unsolicited material. Genres include drama, romance, and crime.

ACAPPELLA PICTURES
Production company

8271 Melrose Ave, Suite 101
Los Angeles, CA 90046
323-782-8200 (phone)
323-782-8210 (fax)

charmaine@acappellapictures.com
acappellapictures.com
imdb.com/company/co0055414
linkedin.com/company/acappella-pictures

Accepts query letters from unproduced, unrepresented writers via email.

Charles Evans
President
323-782-8200
charmaine@acappellapictures.com
imdb.com/name/nm0262509
linkedin.com/pub/dir/Charlie/Evans

Charmaine Parcero
Development Executive
323-782-8200
charmaine@acappellapictures.com
imdb.com/name/nm0661019
linkedin.com/pub/charmaine-parcero/7/200/520

ACCELERATED ENTERTAINMENT LLC
Production company

10201 W Pico Blvd, Building 6
Los Angeles, CA 90064

cleestorm@acceleratedent.com
imdb.com/company/co0208920

Does not accept any unsolicited material. Project types include feature films. Genres include non-fiction and drama.

Christina Lee Storm
cleestorm@acceleratedent.com
imdb.com/name/nm0497028
linkedin.com/pub/dir/christina/storm

Jason Perr
jperr@acceleratedent.com
imdb.com/name/nm1280790
linkedin.com/pub/dir/%20/Perr

ACCESS
Production company

Tokyo,
Japan
03-5259-3511

ir_o@access.co.jp
access-company.com
imdb.com/company/co0198697

Does not accept any unsolicited material. Project types include TV. Genres include comedy and animation.

Toru Arakawa
CEO
imdb.com/name/nm2525771

ACCESS INDUSTRIES
Financing company

730 Fifth Ave
New York City NY 10019

10 Uspensky Pereulok
Moscow Russia 127006

85 Tottenham Court Rd
London United Kingdom W1T 4TQ
011-440-2072683639

post@ai-film.com
accessindustries.com
imdb.com/company/co0316046

Does not accept any unsolicited material. Project types include TV and feature films. Genres include action, drama, and thriller.

ACE CREW ENTERTAINMENT
Distributor

2-20-1-701
Tomigaya
Shibuya, Tokyo 151-0063
Japan
03-5452-3531

info@acecrew.co.jp
acecrew.co.jp
imdb.com/company/co0311522

Does not accept any unsolicited material. Genres include drama and comedy.

ACIEM STUDIOS
Production company

7 N Mountain Ave
Montclair, NJ 07042
973-707-7987

brian@aciemstudios.com
aciemstudios.com
imdb.com/company/co0457339

Does not accept any unsolicited material. Project types include TV. Genres include documentary.

A.C. LYLES PRODUCTIONS, INC.
Production company

5555 Melrose Ave, Hart Building 409
Hollywood, CA 90038-3197
323-956-5819

imdb.com/company/co0074718

Accepts query letters from unproduced, unrepresented writers via email. Project types include feature films. Genres include action.

ACME PRODUCTIONS
Production company

4000 Warner Blvd, Building 19, Room 221-B
Burbank, CA 91522
818-954-7779

imdb.com/company/co0066048

Does not accept any unsolicited material. Project types include TV. Genres include comedy and family.

Michael Hanel
Partner/Producer
imdb.com/name/nm0995625

Mindy Schultheis
Partner/Producer
imdb.com/name/nm0995547
linkedin.com/pub/mindy-mindy-schultheis/43/967/
507

ACORT INTERNATIONAL
Distributor and sales agent

6929 N Hayden Rd
Ste C4-246
Scottsdale, AZ 85250
480-966-4070 (phone)
480-966-4570 (fax)

contact@acortinternational.com
acortinternational.com
imdb.com/company/co0309963

Does not accept any unsolicited material. Project types include TV and feature films. Genres include crime, drama, and horror.

ACT 4 ENTERTAINMENT
Production company

1323 Ocean Ave, Santa Monica, CA, United States, 90401
310-458-4390 (phone)
310-458-4399 (fax)

info@act4ent.com
act4entertainment.com
imdb.com/company/co0198377

Does not accept any unsolicited material. Project types include TV and short films. Genres include drama, comedy, and family.

Jesse Singer
Vice President (Development & Production)
310-458-4396
imdb.com/name/nm3112930

ACT III PRODUCTIONS
Production company and distributor

100 N Crescent Dr, Suite 250
Beverly Hills, CA 90210
310-385-4111 (phone)
310-385-4148 (fax)

normanlear.com/act_iii.html
imdb.com/company/co0030401

Accepts query letters from unproduced, unrepresented writers. Project types include short films, TV, and feature films. Genres include comedy, animation, family, action, non-fiction, drama, and crime. Established in 2006.

Lara Bergthold
Director of Development
310-385-4111
imdb.com/name/nm2401887

Norman Lear
310-385-4111
normanl@actiii.com
normanlear.com
imdb.com/name/nm0005131

ACTION
Production company

10-2-403
Udagawa-Cho
Shibuya-Ku, Tokyo 150-0042
Japan
813-3770-3936 (phone)
813-3770-3938 (fax)

actioninfo@action-inc.co.jp
action-inc.co.jp
imdb.com/company/co0071113

Does not accept any unsolicited material. Project types include TV, feature films, and short films. Genres include drama and action.

ACTION!!! ENTERTAINMENT
Production company

12165 Viewcrest Rd
Studio City, CA 91604
818-980-0889

info@aaandaction.com
aaandaction.com
imdb.com/company/co0358723
facebook.com/pages/ActionVisuals/142054852531756
twitter.com/actionvisuals

Does not accept any unsolicited material. Project types include feature films. Genres include drama.

Chris Darling
Producer
imdb.com/name/nm3827939

Susan Feiles
Producer
imdb.com/name/nm4716424
facebook.com/fourthrt

ACTIVE CINE CLUB (ACC) K.K.
Production company and distributor

43-7F
Tansucho
Shinjuku, Tokyo
Japan
03-3268-8606 (phone)
03-3268-7725 (fax)

acc@actcine.com
actcine.com/iid
imdb.com/company/co0154908

Does not accept any unsolicited material. Project types include TV. Genres include drama.

Mikiyo Miyata
Executive
imdb.com/name/nm2206215

ACTIVE ENTERTAINMENT
Sales agent

170 Camino Viejo
Santa Barbara, CA 93108
805-969-2151 (phone)
310-388-0496 (fax)

1000 Celtic Dr
Baton Rouge, LA 70809
225-906-5440 (phone)
225-906-5445 (fax)

activeentertainment.com
imdb.com/company/co0098277
facebook.com/activentertainment
twitter.com/ActiveEntertain

Does not accept any unsolicited material. Project types include TV. Genres include fantasy and horror.

Daniel Lewis
COO
imdb.com/name/nm2786983
linkedin.com/pub/daniel-lewis/22/bbb/846

Kenneth M. Badish
President/Producer
imdb.com/name/nm0046168
linkedin.com/pub/ken-badish/a/126/9a1
facebook.com/kenneth.badish
twitter.com/kbadish

Griff Furst
Creative Director/Producer
imdb.com/name/nm0975225
linkedin.com/pub/griff-furst/47/246/b49
facebook.com/griff.furst
twitter.com/GEFURST

ACTUAL REALITY PICTURES
Production company

310-202-1272 (phone)
310-202-1502 (fax)

questions@arp.tv
imdb.com/company/co0004087
linkedin.com/company/actual-reality-pictures

Does not accept any unsolicited material. Project types include TV. Genres include reality.

R.J. Cutler
President
310-202-1272
imdb.com/name/nm0191712

ADAM FIELDS PRODUCTIONS
Production company

1601 Cloverfield Suite 2000 North
Santa Monica, CA 90404
310-745-5454 (phone)
310-859-4795 (fax)

imdb.com/company/co0064962

Accepts query letters from unproduced, unrepresented writers. Project types include feature films and TV. Genres include science fiction and thriller.

Adam Fields
President
310-859-9300
imdb.com/name/nm0276178
linkedin.com/pub/adam-fields/3/685/907

ADAPTIVE STUDIOS
Studio

3623 Hayden Ave
Culver City, CA 90232

info@adaptivestudios.com
adaptivestudios.com
imdb.com/company/co0394662
linkedin.com/company/adaptive-studios
facebook.com/adaptivestudios
twitter.com/adaptivestudios

Does not accept any unsolicited material. Project types include TV.

Perrin Chiles
Founder/CEO
imdb.com/name/nm1406232
linkedin.com/pub/perrin-chiles/2/b18/351
facebook.com/perrin.chiles
twitter.com/perrinchiles

Marc Joubert
Founder/Head of Business Development
linkedin.com/pub/marc-joubert/2b/82a/571

ADDICTIVE PICTURES
Production company

Los Angeles, CA

imdb.com/company/co0124727

Does not accept any unsolicited material. Project types include feature films. Genres include science fiction. Established in 2014.

John Schoenfelder
imdb.com/name/nm4964008

Russell Ackerman
imdb.com/name/nm1652438

ADES FILMS, MIKE
Production company

1028 12th St, Suite 8
Santa Monica, CA 90403
310-699-0242

imdb.com/name/nm1400460
linkedin.com/in/michael-ades-ba15819

Does not accept any unsolicited material. Project types include feature films.

Mike Ades
Producer
imdb.com/name/nm1400460

AD HOMINEM ENTERPRISES
Production company

506 Santa Monica Blvd
Suite 400
Santa Monica, CA 90401
310-394-1444 (phone)
310-394-5401 (fax)

imdb.com/company/co0171502
facebook.com/pages/Ad-Hominem-Enterprises/
    165041236847752

Does not accept any unsolicited material. Project types
include feature films.

Jim Burke
Partner
310-394-1444
jwb@adhominem.us
imdb.com/name/nm0121724
Assistant: Adam Wagner

Alexander Payne
Partner
310-394-1444
imdb.com/name/nm0668247

Adam Wagner
Director of Development
310-394-1444
twitter.com/linkedin.compubadam-wagner15326b07

ADIRONDACK PICTURES
Production company and distributor

267 W 17th St, 2nd Floor, New York City , NY,
United States, 10011
212-343-2405

info@adirondackpics.com
adirondackpics.com
imdb.com/company/co0175996

Does not accept any unsolicited material. Project types
include feature films and TV. Genres include action,
family, drama, and thriller.

ADITI PICTURES
Production company

244 5th Ave, Suite 2658
New York, NY 10001
646-861-8777

borozco@aditipictures.com
aditipictures.com
imdb.com/company/co0416283
facebook.com/pages/Aditi-Pictures-Incorporated/
    167187393297937

Accepts query letters from unproduced, unrepresented
writers via email. Project types include TV and feature
films. Genres include comedy and family.

Beverly Orozco
President/CEO
imdb.com/name/nm3869619
linkedin.com/pub/beverly-orozco/4/7a/750
twitter.com/beverlyorozco

ADJACENT PRODUCTIONS
Production company

10351 Santa Monica Blvd., Suite 250
Los Angeles, CA 90025
310-228-1001

imdb.com/company/co0490085

Does not accept any unsolicited material. Project types
include TV. Genres include drama.

ADVENTURES IN FILM
Production company

Burbank, CA 91505
310-880-0222 (phone)
310-867-2004 (fax)

jeff@adventuresinfilm.com
adventuresinfilm.com
imdb.com/company/co0348285
facebook.com/AdventuresInFilm

Does not accept any unsolicited material. Project types
include feature films. Genres include drama.

Ira Besserman
Producer
imdb.com/name/nm0078810
linkedin.com/pub/ira-besserman/12/1a9/b55
facebook.com/ira.besserman

ADV FILMS
Production company and distributor

10114 W Sam Houston Pkwy South, Suite 200,
Houston , TX, United States, 77099
713-341-7100

info@advfilms.com
advfilms.com
imdb.com/company/co0037660

Does not accept any unsolicited material. Project types include TV and feature films. Genres include family, drama, comedy, thriller, animation, and action.

ADVOCATE PICTURES
Production company

PO Box 118014
Carrollton, TX 75011
972-394-7334

Info@AdvocatePictures.com
imdb.com/company/co0295552
linkedin.com/company/advocate-pictures-llc

Does not accept any unsolicited material. Project types include feature films. Genres include drama, action, family, and thriller. Established in 2013.

AEC STUDIOS
Production company

2828 N Speer Ave
Suite 140
Denver, CO 80211
303-446-8170 (phone)
303-446-8173 (fax)

info@aecstudios.com
aecstudios.com
imdb.com/company/co0177777

Does not accept any unsolicited material. Genres include thriller and science fiction.

Brian McCulley
Owner / Project and Talent Development (Executive)
imdb.com/name/nm0567115

A+E FILMS
Production company and distributor

235 E 45th St, Fourth Floor, New York City, NY, United States, 10017
212-210-1400 (phone)
212-210-9755 (fax)

aetv.com/shows/ae-indiefilms
imdb.com/company/co0056790

Does not accept any unsolicited material. Project types include TV. Genres include family, drama, and thriller.

AEGIS FILM GROUP
Production company

7510 Sunset Blvd
Ste 275
Los Angeles, CA 90046
818-588-3545 (phone)
323-650-9954 (fax)

aegisfilmgroup@ca.rr.com
aegisfilmgroup.com
imdb.com/name/nm1985255
linkedin.com/company/aegis-film-group-inc-

Does not accept any unsolicited material. Project types include TV and feature films. Genres include documentary. Established in 2003.

Steven Shultz
President (Production)
323-848-7977
imdb.com/name/nm0795789

Arianna Eisenberg
CEO
323-848-7977
imdb.com/name/nm1985255
linkedin.com/pub/arianna-eisenberg/22/818/b21

AEI - ATCHITY ENTERTAINMENT INTERNATIONAL, INC.
Production company

9601 Wilshire Blvd, #1202
Beverly Hills, CA 90210
323-932-0407 (phone)
323-932-0321 (fax)

kja@aeionline.com
aeionline.com
imdb.com/company/co0010944
twitter.com/kennja

Does not accept any unsolicited material. Project types include TV. Genres include family.

Ken Atchity
Writer
kja@aeionline.com
imdb.com/name/nm0040338

A&E NETWORK
Production company and distributor

235 E 45th St
New York, NY 10017
212-210-1400 (phone)
212-210-9755 (fax)

2049 Century Park East Tenth Floor
Los Angeles, CA 90067
310-556-7500

feedback@aetv.com
aetv.com
imdb.com/company/co0056790
facebook.com/AETV
twitter.com/intentuser

Does not accept any unsolicited material. Project types include TV. Genres include drama and documentary.

Thomas Moody
Senior Vice President
212-210-1400
feedback@aetv.com
imdb.com/name/nm1664759

AESOP ENTERTAINMENT
Production company

12-13 Greek St
Soho W1D 4DL London

269 S Beverly Dr, Suite 950
Beverly Hills, CA 90212

la@AesopEntertainment.com
aesopentertainment.com
imdb.com/name/nm5764189
linkedin.com/company/aesop-entertainment-limited

Does not accept any unsolicited material. Project types include feature films. Genres include comedy.

Michael Kasher
Head
imdb.com/name/nm1183606

A&E STUDIOS
Studio

2049 Century Park East Tenth Floor
Los Angeles, CA 90067
310-556-7500

aetv.com
linkedin.com/company/a-e-networks

facebook.com/AETV
twitter.com/AETV

Does not accept any unsolicited material. Project types include feature films. Established in 2014.

Robert DeBitetto
President
imdb.com/name/nm2248039

Barry Jossen
Vice President
imdb.com/name/nm0430904

AFFIRMATIVE ENTERTAINMENT

425 N Robertson Blvd.
West Hollywood, CA 90048
310-858-3200 (phone)
310-858-8999 (fax)

imdb.com/company/co0244988

Does not accept any unsolicited material. Project types include feature films and TV. Genres include comedy, thriller, and drama.

Nicholas Bogner
Producer/Manager
imdb.com/name/nm0091851
linkedin.com/pub/nicholas-bogner/2b/312/912
facebook.com/nicholas.bogner.75

Melanie Greene
Producer/Manager
linkedin.com/pub/melanie-greene/3a/782/912

AFFIRM FILMS
Production company and distributor

10202 W. Washington Blvd., Stage 6/513
Culver City, CA 90232
310-244-4000

AF-Questions@spe.sony.com
sonypictures.com/homevideo/affirmfilms
imdb.com/company/co0248867
facebook.com/sonyaffirm
twitter.com/AFFIRMFilms

Does not accept any unsolicited material. Project types include feature films. Genres include family and drama.

Rich Peluso
VP
imdb.com/name/nm3553062
linkedin.com/in/richpeluso

AFTER DARK FILMS
Production company

844 Seward St
Los Angeles, CA 90038
310-270-4260 (phone)
310-270-4262 (fax)

info@afterdarkfilms.com
afterdarkfilms.com
imdb.com/company/co0166161
linkedin.com/company/after-dark-films
facebook.com/afterdarkfilms
twitter.com/afterdarkfilms

Does not accept any unsolicited material. Genres include horror. Established in 2006.

Richard Cardona
Creative Executive
linkedin.com/pub/richard-cardona/3/b63/591

AGAMEMNON FILMS
Production company

650 N Bronson Ave, Suite B225
Los Angeles, CA 90004
323-960-4066

mmmgmt42@gmail.com
agamemnon.com
imdb.com/company/co0004137

Accepts query letters from unproduced, unrepresented writers via email. Project types include TV. Genres include reality, action, family, thriller, non-fiction, and drama. Established in 1981.

Fraser Heston
President
imdb.com/name/nm0381699
linkedin.com/pub/fraser-heston/34/419/936
Assistant: Heather Thomas

Alex Butler
Senior Partner
imdb.com/name/nm0124808

AGENCY FOR THE PERFORMING ARTS (APA)
Studio

405 S Beverly Dr, Beverly Hills , CA, United States, 90212
310-888-4200 (phone)
310-888-4242 (fax)

135 W 50th St, 17th Floor
New York NY 10020
212-205-4320 (phone)
212-245-5062 (fax)

3010 Poston Ave
Nashville TN 37203
615-297-0100 (phone)
615-297-5434 (fax)

apa-agency.com
imdb.com/company/co0078069

Does not accept any unsolicited material. Project types include TV. Genres include family and drama.

AGGREGATE FILMS
Production company

100 Universal City Plaza
Bungalow 4144
Universal City, CA 91608
818-777-8180

imdb.com/company/co0369082
facebook.com/pages/Aggregate-Films/
    1421345828081841

Does not accept any unsolicited material. Project types include feature films and TV. Genres include drama, comedy, and crime. Established in 2013.

Jason Bateman
Founder
imdb.com/name/nm0000867

Jim Garavente
President
imdb.com/name/nm4814574

AGILITY STUDIOS
Production company

11928 Ventura Blvd
Studio City, CA 91604
310-314-1440 (phone)
310-496-3292 (fax)

creators@agilitystudios.com
imdb.com/company/co0293230
linkedin.com/company/agility-studios-llc

Accepts query letters from unproduced, unrepresented writers via email. Established in 2008.

Scott Ehrlich
Principal
310-314-1440
info@agilitystudios.com
imdb.com/name/nm3796990
linkedin.com/in/scottehrlich

AGRON PRODUCTIONS, CHARLES
Production company

PO Box 7302
Beverly Hills, CA
310-203-1450

info@charlesagronproductions.com
imdb.com/company/co0361904
facebook.com/pages/Charles-Agron-Productions/
   284039284962368

Does not accept any unsolicited material. Project types include feature films. Genres include horror.

Charles Agron
Producer
imdb.com/name/nm4469602
facebook.com/charles.agron.7
twitter.com/CAgronProducer

AGUA FILMS
Production company, distributor, and sales agent

5482 Wilshire Blvd., Suite 193
Los Angeles, CA 90036
323-571-2723 (phone)
323-571-0210 (fax)

information@aguafilms.com
imdb.com/company/co0175993

Does not accept any unsolicited material. Project types include feature films and TV. Genres include comedy, drama, science fiction, and fantasy.

Leyani Diaz
Creative Executive
imdb.com/name/nm2250587
facebook.com/leyanid
twitter.com/LEYANIWRITER

Lourdes Diaz
Producer
imdb.com/name/nm0969006
linkedin.com/in/lourdesdiaz

AGUNG
Production company and distributor

10-1-3-3F
Hachobori
Chuo, Tokyo 104-0032
Japan

mail@agunginc.com
agunginc.com
imdb.com/company/co0194094
facebook.com/agunginc.cinema

Does not accept any unsolicited material. Project types include TV. Genres include fantasy.

Mikiko Anzai
Producer
imdb.com/name/nm2023162

AHIMSA FILMS
Production company

6671 Sunset Blvd, Suite 1593
Los Angeles, CA 90028
323-464-8500 (phone)
323-464-8535 (fax)

imdb.com/company/co0202538

Accepts query letters from unproduced, unrepresented writers.

Rebecca Yeldham
President
imdb.com/name/nm0947344
Assistant: Alex Killian

AHIMSA MEDIA
Production company and studio

8060 Colonial Dr, Suite 204
Richmond, BC V7C 4V1
Canada
604-785-3602

info@ahimsamedia.com
ahimsamedia.com
imdb.com/company/co0222513
linkedin.com/company/ahimsa-media
facebook.com/ahimsamedia
twitter.com/ahimsamedia

Accepts query letters from unproduced, unrepresented writers via email. Project types include commercials. Genres include comedy and drama.

Erica Hargreave
President/Head of Creative and Interactive
604-785-3602
info@ahimsamedia.com
imdb.com/name/nm2988128
twitter.com/EricaHargreave

AI-FILM
Production company and sales agent

4th Floor, 8 – 12 Broadwick St
London, W1F 8HW
44 (0) 20 7439 9547

post@ai-film.com
ai-film.com
imdb.com/company/co0465607

Does not accept any unsolicited material. Project types include TV, feature films, and short films. Genres include thriller, crime, and drama.

Len Blavatnik
Producer
imdb.com/name/nm4131373

AIMIMAGE PRODUCTIONS
Production company and distributor

22 & 24 St Pancras Way
London NW1 0NT
UK

+44 20 7391 2650 (phone)
+44 20 7391 2669 (fax)

atif@aimimage.com
aimimage.com
imdb.com/company/co0103789
facebook.com/aimimagecameras
twitter.com/AimimageGroup

Does not accept any unsolicited material. Project types include feature films and TV. Genres include horror, thriller, action, and crime.

AIRCRAFT PICTURES
Production company

147 Liberty St
Toronto, ON M6K 3G3
Canada
416-536-9179 (phone)
416-536-9178 (fax)

info@aircraftpictures.com
aircraftpictures.com
imdb.com/company/co0005198
twitter.com/aircraftpix

Does not accept any unsolicited material. Project types include TV and feature films. Genres include comedy, non-fiction, animation, fantasy, and family.

Anthony Leo
Producer
imdb.com/name/nm1479800

AIRMONT PICTURES
Production company

1115 Berkeley St
Santa Monica, CA 90403

imdb.com/company/co0176167

Accepts query letters from unproduced, unrepresented writers.

Matthew Gannon
Producer
imdb.com/name/nm0304478
linkedin.com/pub/matt-gannon/5/b28/385

AJ PRODUCTIONS
Production company

8313 Hillsborough Ave
Suite #250
Tampa, FL 33615

imdb.com/company/co0305117
facebook.com/ajproductions.tv

Does not accept any unsolicited material. Genres include comedy and action.

AKIL PRODUCTIONS
Production company

Los Angeles, CA
212-608-2000

info@akilproductions.com
akilproductions.com
imdb.com/company/co0372929
facebook.com/akilproductionstv
twitter.com/AKILPRODUCTIONS

Does not accept any unsolicited material. Project types include TV. Genres include drama. Established in 2000.

Salim Akil
Founder
imdb.com/name/nm0015328

Mara Brock Akil
Founder
imdb.com/name/nm0015327
linkedin.com/pub/mara-akil/74/50/3b7

AKSHAR MEDIA
Production company

30 Hillside Ave
Suite 201
Springfield, New Jersey 07081
973-912-8392 (phone)
973-912-9256 (fax)

info@aksharmedia.com
imdb.com/company/co0129928

Does not accept any unsolicited material. Project types include TV. Genres include crime, drama, and thriller.

AK WATERS PRODUCTIONS
Production company and distributor

San Diego, CA
310-801-6507

mikalvega@me.com
akwatersproductions.com/home.html
imdb.com/company/co0483715
linkedin.com/in/a-k-waters-2aab1b49
facebook.com/AK-Waters-Productions-
    LLC-311968815525286

Does not accept any unsolicited material. Project types include feature films. Genres include thriller, horror, and action. Established in 2013.

ALAMO DRAFTHOUSE FILMS
Studio

info@drafthousefilms.com
drafthousefilms.com
imdb.com/company/co0313579
facebook.com/drafthousefilms
twitter.com/DrafthouseFilms

Does not accept any unsolicited material. Project types include feature films. Genres include action, thriller, drama, documentary, and comedy. Established in 1997.

Evan Husney
Creative Director
imdb.com/name/nm3432889
linkedin.com/pub/evan-husney/9/3b0/5aa
facebook.com/evanhusney
twitter.com/evanhusney

Tim League
CEO
imdb.com/name/nm1382506
linkedin.com/in/timleague
facebook.com/timleague
twitter.com/timalamo

James Emanuel Shapiro
COO
imdb.com/name/nm4874938

ALAN BARNETTE PRODUCTIONS
Production company

8899 Beverly Blvd # 800
Los Angeles, CA 90048
310-922-2688

dabarnette@aol.com
imdb.com/company/co0056462

Does not accept any unsolicited material.

Alan Barnette
Executive Producer
imdb.com/name/nm0056002
linkedin.com/pub/alan-barnette/6/122/752

Nancy Mosher Hall
Development Executive
imdb.com/name/nm0355945

ALAN DAVID MANAGEMENT
Production company and distributor

8840 Wilshire Blvd,
Suite 200
Beverly Hills, CA 90211
310-358-3155 (phone)
310-358-3256 (fax)

ad@adgmp.com
imdb.com/company/co0097077
facebook.com/pages/Alan-David-Management/
109890892393822

Does not accept any unsolicited material. Project types include feature films and TV. Genres include comedy, thriller, action, detective, drama, family, non-fiction, and science fiction.

Alan David
President
310-358-3155
ad@adgmp.com
imdb.com/name/nm2220960

ALAN GASMER & FRIENDS
Studio

10877 Wilshire Blvd., Suite 1404
Los Angeles, CA 90024
310-208-7338

imdb.com/company/co0283191

Does not accept any unsolicited material. Project types include feature films. Genres include comedy.

Alan Gasmer
Producer/Manager
imdb.com/name/nm2231517

ALAN SACKS PRODUCTIONS
Production company

11684 Ventura Blvd, Suite 809
Studio City, CA 91604
323-957-1952

asacks@pacbell.net
imdb.com/company/co0013945

Does not accept any unsolicited material.

Alan Sacks
Executive Producer
imdb.com/name/nm0755286

ALCHEMY BROS.
Production company and distributor

1-7-5-2F
Kanda Izumicho
Chiyoda, Tokyo 101-0024
Japan
+81 03-5823-4536 (phone)
+81 03-5823-4558 (fax)

info@alchemybros.com
alchemybros.com
imdb.com/company/co0433968

Does not accept any unsolicited material. Project types include TV. Genres include drama.

ALCHEMY ENTERTAINMENT
Production company

7024 Melrose Ave, Suite 420
Los Angeles, CA 90038
323-937-6100 (phone)
323-937-6102 (fax)

ouralchemy.com
imdb.com/company/co0094892
linkedin.com/company/millennium-entertainment

Does not accept any unsolicited material.

Jason Barrett
Principal (Manager)
323-937-6100
imdb.com/name/nm2249074

ALCIDE BAVA PICTURES
Production company

Los Angeles, CA

imdb.com/company/co0482803

Does not accept any unsolicited material. Project types include feature films. Genres include horror and comedy. Established in 2014.

ALCINA PICTURES
Production company and distributor

1 Atlantic Ave
Ste 100
Toronto, ON M6K3E7
Canada
416-364-3777 (phone)
416-364-7123 (fax)

info@alcinapictures.com
alcinapictures.com
imdb.com/company/co0138023
linkedin.com/company/alcina-pictures
facebook.com/alcinapictures

Does not accept any unsolicited material. Genres include drama.

Paul Barkin
Producer
imdb.com/name/nm0055050

ALCINE TERRAN

2F Tokiwa Bldg.
4-5-6 Shibuya
Shibuya-Ku, Tokyo 150-0002
Japan
+81 3 5467 3730 (phone)
+81 3 5467 3731 (fax)

alcine@epcott.co.jp
imdb.com/company/co0022964

Does not accept any unsolicited material. Project types include TV. Genres include comedy and drama.

Minori Ikeda
Acquisition (Executive)
imdb.com/name/nm3096784

ALCON ENTERTAINMENT, LLC
Production company

10390 Santa Monica Blvd, Suite 250
Los Angeles, CA 90025
310-789-3040 (phone)
310-789-3060 (fax)

info@alconent.com
alconent.com
imdb.com/company/co0054452
facebook.com/AlconEntertainment

Does not accept any unsolicited material. Project types include feature films.

Broderick Johnson
Co-CEO/Co-Founder
310-789-3040
info@alconent.com
imdb.com/name/nm0424663

Steven Wegner
Executive Vice President of Production
310-789-3040
info@alconent.com
imdb.com/name/nm1176853

ALCOVE ENTERTAINMENT
Production company

+44 20 7642 2703

info@alcoveentertainment.com
alcoveentertainment.com
imdb.com/company/co0282748

Does not accept any unsolicited material. Genres include drama, comedy, and thriller.

Robin C. Fox
Producer
imdb.com/name/nm1929951

ALDAMISA INTERNATIONAL
Distributor and sales agent

15760 Ventura Blvd # 1450, Encino, CA, United States, 91436
818-783-4084 (phone)
818-753-2310 (fax)

sales@aldamisa.com
aldamisa.com
imdb.com/company/co0337582

Does not accept any unsolicited material. Project types include TV. Genres include comedy, drama, family, and romance.

ALEBRIJE ENTERTAINMENT
Distributor

1421 SW 107 Ave
#261
Miami, FL 33174
954-442-6777 (phone)
954-442-2411 (fax)

info@alebrije.tv
alebrije.tv
imdb.com/company/co0389821

Does not accept any unsolicited material. Genres include thriller.

ALEXANDER CONTENT
Production company

8033 Sunset Blvd. Suite 507
Los Angeles, CA 90046

info@alexandercontent.com
imdb.com/company/co0240231
twitter.com/Alexanderrcc

Does not accept any unsolicited material. Project types include feature films. Genres include science fiction, action, thriller, and comedy.

Rick Alexander
President/Producer
imdb.com/name/nm1006153

ALEXANDER/MITCHELL PRODUCTIONS
Production company

201 Wilshire Blvd Third Floor
Santa Monica, CA 90401

310-458-3003 (phone)
310-393-7238 (fax)

imdb.com/company/co0241249
facebook.com/pages/AlexanderMitchell-Productions/
    109975532363448

Accepts query letters from unproduced, unrepresented writers via email. Project types include feature films and TV. Genres include drama.

Jonathan Mitchell
imdb.com/name/nm2927057

Les Alexander
imdb.com/name/nm0018573

ALEXIUS DISTRIBUTION
Distributor and sales agent

PO Box 504
Roy, UT 84067
801-644-0980

imdb.com/company/co0252226

Does not accept any unsolicited material. Genres include horror and comedy.

ALEX ROSE PRODUCTIONS
Production company

8291 Presson Place
Los Angeles, CA 90069
323-654-8662 (phone)
323-654-0196 (fax)

imdb.com/company/co0177705

Accepts query letters from unproduced, unrepresented writers.

Alexandra Rose
President
imdb.com/name/nm0741228

ALIANZA FILMS INTERNATIONAL
Production company

11941 Weddington St, Suite #106
Studio City, CA 91607
310-933-6250 (phone)
310-388-0874 (fax)

shari@alianzafilms.com
alianzafilms.com
imdb.com/company/co0022267

Accepts query letters from unproduced, unrepresented writers. Established in 1984.

Shari Hamrick
Executive
shari@alianzafilms.com
imdb.com/name/nm0359089

ALIBABA
Production company

US Office 3945 Freedom Circle Suite 600
Santa Clara CA 95054
408-748-1200 (phone)
408-748-1218 (fax)

6/F, Meridien House 42-43 Upper Berkeley St
London England United Kingdom W1H 5QL
011-442-072585111 (phone)
011-442-072585112 (fax)

Corporate Headquarters, 699 Wang Shang Rd,
Binjiang District, Hangzhou, 33, China, 310052
011-865-7185022088 (phone)
011-865-7189815505 (fax)

news.alibaba.com/newsHome.htm
imdb.com/company/co0482193

Does not accept any unsolicited material. Project types include TV, feature films, short films, and commercials. Genres include action and thriller.

ALIGNED ENTERTAINMENT
Production company

201 Wilshire Blvd., 2nd Floor
Santa Monica, CA 90401
424-208-3773

aligned-ent.com
imdb.com/company/co0275686

Does not accept any unsolicited material. Project types include feature films. Genres include comedy.

Brett Carducci
Producer/Manager
imdb.com/name/nm2248023
linkedin.com/pub/brett-carducci/1a/4b8/71a
facebook.com/brett.carducci.7
twitter.com/BrettCarducci

A-LINE PICTURES
Production company

info@a-linepictures.com
a-linepictures.com
imdb.com/company/co0156447

Does not accept any unsolicited material. Established in 2005.

Caroline Baron
Producer
212-496-9496
info@a-linepictures.com
imdb.com/name/nm0056205

A-LIST FEATURE FILMS
Production company

8313 Hillsborough Ave
#250
Tampa, FL 33760
727-595-7135

PacAtlanticPR@mail.com
imdb.com/company/co0256443

Does not accept any unsolicited material. Genres include action and comedy.

ALIVE ENTERTAINMENT
Production company and distributor

7955 W. 3rd St, Unit C
Los Angeles, CA 90048
323-939-3130 (phone)
323-939-3132 (fax)

info@aliveentertainment.com
aliveentertainment.com
imdb.com/company/co0008174
linkedin.com/company/alive-entertainment

Does not accept any unsolicited material. Genres include drama.

Isabell von Alvensleben
Partner/Producer
imdb.com/name/nm0901879
facebook.com/isabell.vonalvensleben

Philip von Alvensleben
Partner/Producer
imdb.com/name/nm0901880

AL JAZEERA AMERICA
Production company and distributor

Via Maroncelli 9
Milan Italy 20154

305 W 34th St, New York, NY, United States, 10001
646-273-8700

42 Tuscaloosa Ave
Atherton CA 94027

San Francisco CA
415-995-8200 (phone)
415-995-8201 (fax)

america@aljazeera.net
america.aljazeera.com
imdb.com/company/co0442998

Does not accept any unsolicited material. Project types include TV. Genres include reality, non-fiction, and family.

ALL3MEDIA
Production company and distributor

Berkshire House
168-173 High Holborn
London WC1V 7AA
UK
+44 (0)20 7845 4377

info@all3media.com
all3media.com
imdb.com/company/co0136768
facebook.com/All3Media
twitter.com/all3media

Does not accept any unsolicited material. Project types include feature films, TV, and short films. Genres include drama, crime, and action.

Maartje Horchner
Producer
imdb.com/name/nm2626944

ALL CHANNEL FILMS DISTRIBUTION
Distributor and sales agent

2662 Carmar Dr
Los Angeles, CA 90046
323-654-5800 (phone)
323-654-5828 (fax)

info@allchannelfilms.net
allchannelfilms.net
imdb.com/company/co0068672

Does not accept any unsolicited material. Project types include feature films. Genres include thriller, horror, and comedy.

ALLEGIANCE THEATER, THE
Production company

Los Angeles , CA
424-260-3340

info@theallegiance.com
theallegiancetheater.com
imdb.com/company/co0370262
facebook.com/TheAllegianceTheater/timeline

Does not accept any unsolicited material. Project types include feature films. Genres include drama, thriller, and comedy.

Carly Norris
Head of Development
imdb.com/name/nm1771200

Lara Alameddine
Partner/Producer
imdb.com/name/nm1240783
facebook.com/lara.alameddine

Torus Tammer
Partner (Australia)
imdb.com/name/nm0848709
linkedin.com/pub/torus-tammer/7/208/b27
facebook.com/pages/Torus-Tammer/
   139179796109857

Timothy Crane
Partner/Producer
linkedin.com/pub/tim-crane/a/605/29b

Daniel Dubiecki
Partner/Producer
imdb.com/name/nm0239277
linkedin.com/pub/daniel-dubiecki/a/256/10a
facebook.com/daniel.dubiecki
twitter.com/danieldubiecki

ALLEN ENTERTAINMENT
Production company and distributor

5015 Louetta # 1037
Spring, TX 77379
281-251-6348

Allen_Entertainment@Yahoo.Com
allenentertainment.net
imdb.com/company/co0172599

Does not accept any unsolicited material. Project types include short films. Genres include comedy.

ALLEN MORRIS PRODUCTIONS
Production company

#4 Forest Shores
Kingwood, TX 77339
713-304-2750

allen@belaymedia.com
belaymedia.com
imdb.com/company/co0265158

Does not accept any unsolicited material. Project types include short films. Genres include documentary.

ALLENTOWN PRODUCTIONS
Production company

100 Universal City Plaza
Building 2372B, Suite 114
Universal City, CA 91608
818-733-1002 (phone)
818-866-4181 (fax)

writetous@allentownproductions.com
allentownproductions.com
imdb.com/company/co0122945
facebook.com/AllentownProductions

twitter.com/JamesMoll

Does not accept any unsolicited material. Genres include non-fiction. Established in 1994.

James Moll
Principal
imdb.com/name/nm0002224

Chris W. King
Director of Development
imdb.com/name/nm1648242

ALL GIRL PRODUCTIONS
Production company

2625 Piedmont Rd NE
Ste 56-30
Atlanta, GA 30324
404-949-9955

imdb.com/company/co0023403

Does not accept any unsolicited material. Project types include TV. Genres include drama and comedy.

ALLIANCE ATLANTIS COMMUNICATIONS
Production company and distributor

121 Bloor St. E
Ste 1500
Toronto, ON M4W 3M5
Canada
416-967-1174

imdb.com/company/co0054762

Does not accept any unsolicited material. Project types include TV. Genres include thriller and action.

Andrew Callum
Executive
imdb.com/name/nm2451439

ALLIANCE CINEMA ENTERTAINMENT
Production company and distributor

MMC Studios Am Coloneum 1 Geb. B
Cologne Germany 50829
011-490-2212501195

468 N Camden Dr, Suite 200, Beverly Hills, CA, United States, 90210
310-601-3113

info@alliancecinema.com
alliancecinema.com
imdb.com/company/co0168721

Does not accept any unsolicited material. Project types include TV. Genres include family, thriller, reality, comedy, and drama.

ALLIANCE FILMS
Production company

22 Harbor Park Dr
Port Washington, NY 11050

9465 Wilshire Blvd.
Suite 500
Beverly Hills, CA 90212

145 Kings St East
Suite 300
Toronto, ON, Canada, M5C2Y7
416-309-4200 (phone)
416-309-4290 (fax)

info@alliancefilms.com
alliancefilms.com
imdb.com/company/co0224509
linkedin.com/company/alliance-films-inc

Does not accept any unsolicited material. Project types include feature films. Genres include science fiction, thriller, horror, drama, romance, fantasy, action, crime, and comedy.

Xavier Marchand
President
imdb.com/name/nm0545421

ALLIED ARTISTS
Production company and distributor

15810 E Gale Ave, Suite 133
Hacienda Heights, CA 91745
626-330-0600 (phone)
626-961-0411 (fax)

info@alliedartists.net
us.alliedartists.com/default.php
imdb.com/company/co0119902

Does not accept any unsolicited material. Project types include feature films. Genres include horror.

ALL NIPPON ENTERTAINMENT WORKS
Production company

5225 Wilshire Blvd., Suite 700
Los Angeles, CA 90036
323-904-3787 (phone)
323-904-3788 (fax)

an-ew.com
imdb.com/company/co0349144

Does not accept any unsolicited material. Project types include feature films and TV. Genres include thriller, science fiction, and action.

Sandy Climan
CEO
imdb.com/name/nm0166787

Annmarie Sairrino Bailey
VP of Creative Affairs
imdb.com/name/nm2913118

ALLOY ENTERTAINMENT
Production company

4000 Warner Blvd.
Building 146, Room 203
Burbank, CA 91522
818-954-3074 (phone)
818-954-3508 (fax)

151 W. 26th St
11th Floor
New York, NY 10001
212-329-8448

laassistant@alloyentertainment.com
alloyentertainment.com
imdb.com/company/co0142434
facebook.com/alloyent
twitter.com/alloyent

Accepts query letters from unproduced, unrepresented writers via email.

Josh Bank
Executive Vice President
212-329-8448
imdb.com/name/nm2987370

ALOE ENTERTAINMENT

Production company

433 N Camden Dr.
Suite 600
Beverly Hills, CA 90210
310-288-1886 (phone)
310-288-1801 (fax)

info@aloeentertainment.com
aloeentertainment.com
imdb.com/company/co0261920
facebook.com/theofficialaloeentertainment

Does not accept any unsolicited material. Established in 1999.

Mary Aloe
imdb.com/name/nm0022053

ALONESTAR FILMS

Production company

5200 Canella Dr.
Austin, TX 78744

eric@alonestar.com
alonestar.com
imdb.com/company/co0316773

Does not accept any unsolicited material. Genres include thriller and action.

ALORIS ENTERTAINMENT

Production company

275 W Natick Rd
Warwick, RI 02886
401-374-0249

alorisentertainment.com
imdb.com/company/co0301850
facebook.com/Alorisentertainment
twitter.com/AlorisEnt

Does not accept any unsolicited material. Project types include feature films. Genres include thriller, horror, and crime.

John Santilli
Producer
imdb.com/name/nm2530923
linkedin.com/pub/john-santilli/6/480/82b

ALOUPIS PRODUCTIONS

Production company

PO Box 103
Brielle, NJ 08730

info@aloupisproductions.com
aloupisproductions.com
imdb.com/company/co0377210
facebook.com/AloupisProductions

Does not accept any unsolicited material. Project types include TV. Genres include drama.

ALP ENTERTAINMENT

Sales agent

3333 Piedmont Rd
Atlanta, GA 30305
Usa
678-288-6212

Accounting@alpentertainment.com
alpentertainment.com
imdb.com/company/co0381132

Does not accept any unsolicited material. Project types include TV. Genres include fantasy and family.

Alander 'Big Aj' Pulliam
Producer
imdb.com/name/nm4021285

AL ROKER PRODUCTIONS

Production company

250 W 57th St
Suite 1525
New York, NY 10019
212-757-8500 (phone)
212-757-8513 (fax)

info@alroker.com
alrokerproductions.com
imdb.com/company/co0095131
facebook.com/AlRokerEntertainment
twitter.com/AlRoker_Entmnt

Does not accept any unsolicited material. Project types include feature films. Established in 1994.

Al Roker
CEO
imdb.com/name/nm0737963
twitter.com/alroker

Tracie Brennan
imdb.com/name/nm2200420
linkedin.com/in/traciebrennan

ALTA LOMA ENTERTAINMENT
Production company

9346 Civic Center Dr.
Beverly Hills, CA 90210
310-424-1800

imdb.com/company/co0008514
linkedin.com/company/alta-loma-entertainment-inc

Does not accept any unsolicited material.

J.W. Starrett
Director of Development
323-276-4211
imdb.com/name/nm2852786

ALTERNATIVE FUEL
Production company

25 Highland Park Village
Suite 100-528
Dallas, TX 75205
214-521-4962

altfueltv.com
imdb.com/company/co0258716
twitter.com/altfueltv

Does not accept any unsolicited material. Project types include TV. Genres include science fiction and thriller.

ALTERNATIVE STUDIO
Production company and distributor

100 Universal City Plaza
Universal City, CA 91608
818-777-1000

nbcuni.com
imdb.com/company/co0096447
linkedin.com/company/universal-pictures
facebook.com/UniversalTV

twitter.com/UniversalTV

Does not accept any unsolicited material. Project types include TV. Genres include drama, action, and comedy.

Paul Telegdy
President, Alter.Prgrmming/Late Night
imdb.com/name/nm2350150

ALTITUDE FILM ENTERTAINMENT
Production company, distributor, and sales agent

34 Fouberts Place
London W1F 7PX
England
44207-478-7612

info@altitudefilment.com
altitudefilment.com
imdb.com/company/co0398856
facebook.com/altitudefilmdistribution
twitter.com/AltitudeFilmUK

Does not accept any unsolicited material. Project types include TV, feature films, and short films. Genres include action and horror.

Will Clarke
Producer
imdb.com/name/nm1676089

ALTITUDE FILM SALES
Production company and distributor

34 Fouberts Place
London W1F 7PX
England
+44 (020)-478-7612

info@altitudefilment.com
altitudefilment.com
imdb.com/company/co0397603
facebook.com/altitudefilmdistribution
twitter.com/AltitudeFilmUK

Does not accept any unsolicited material. Project types include TV. Genres include drama.

Mike Runagall
Managing Director, International Sales (Executive)
imdb.com/name/nm2553445

ALTURAS FILMS
Production company

2403 Main St
Santa Monica, CA 90405
310-230-6100 (phone)
310-314-2135 (fax)

reception@alturasfilms.com
alturasfilms.com
imdb.com/company/co0169508

Does not accept any unsolicited material. Established in 2004.

Marshall Rawlings
CEO (Producer)
310-401-6200
reception@alturasfilms.com
imdb.com/name/nm1987844
linkedin.com/pub/marshall-rawlings/0/a63/489

AMADEUS PICTURES
Production company

578 Washington Blvd., Suite 578
Marina Del Rey, CA 90292
310-923-4356

info@amadeuspictures.com
imdb.com/company/co0224596
facebook.com/amadeuspictures

Does not accept any unsolicited material. Genres include drama.

Damian Chapa
Writer/Producer/Director/Actor
imdb.com/name/nm0152082
facebook.com/pages/Damian-Chapa/
    108140612539942

A-MARK ENTERTAINMENT
Production company

233 Wilshire Blvd, Suite 200
Santa Monica, CA 90401
310-255-0900

info@amarkentertainment.com
amarkentertainment.com
imdb.com/company/co0135086
linkedin.com/company/a-mark-entertainment

Does not accept any unsolicited material. Established in 2004.

Bruce McNall
Co-Chairman
310-255-0900
info@amarkentertainment.com
imdb.com/name/nm1557652

AMARO FILMS
Production company

18 Broadwick St
London, UK W1F 8HS
England

info@amarofilms.com
imdb.com/company/co0524825

Does not accept any unsolicited material. Project types include feature films. Genres include drama, family, and romance.

Cora Palfrey
Producer
imdb.com/name/nm4367953

AMASIA ENTERTAINMENT
Production company

12300 Wilshire Blvd, Suite 420, Los Angeles, CA, United States, 90025
310-820-0757

info@amasiaent.com
amasiaentertainment.com
imdb.com/company/co0415896

Does not accept any unsolicited material. Project types include feature films and TV. Genres include thriller, family, and drama.

AMAZON
Distributor

440 Terry Ave North, Seattle, WA, United States, 98109
206-266-1000

amazon.com
imdb.com/company/co0515031

Does not accept any unsolicited material. Project types include TV and feature films. Genres include fantasy, drama, family, and action.

AMBASSADOR ENTERTAINMENT, INC.
Production company

310-862-5200 (phone)
310-496-3140 (fax)

aspeval@ambassadortv.com
ambassadortv.com
imdb.com/company/co0175998
linkedin.com/company/ambassador-entertainment-group
facebook.com/ambassadorentertainment

Does not accept any unsolicited material. Established in 1999.

Albert Spevak
President
aspeval@ambassadortv.com
imdb.com/name/nm0818411
linkedin.com/in/albertspevak

AMBER ENTERTAINMENT
Production company

21 Ganton St, 4th Floor
London
United Kingdom
W1F 98N
+44207-292-7170

info@amberentertainment.com
amberentertainment.com
imdb.com/company/co0266476
linkedin.com/company/amber-entertainment
twitter.com/amber_ent

Does not accept any unsolicited material. Project types include feature films. Genres include crime, horror, thriller, fantasy, and drama. Established in 2010.

Lawrence Elman
Executive Producer
imdb.com/name/nm3793846

Ileen Maisel
Executive
+44207-292-7170
info@amberentertainment.com
imdb.com/name/nm0537884

AMBI DISTRIBUTION
Distributor

9454 Wilshire Blvd
Suite 208
Beverly Hills, CA 90212
310-274-2000

office@ambidistribution.com
ambidistribution.com
wwwimdb.com/company/co0478960

Does not accept any unsolicited material. Genres include science fiction, thriller, and animation.

AMBLIN ENTERTAINMENT
Production company

100 Universal Plaza
Bldg 5121
Universal City, CA 91608
818-733-7000

imdb.com/company/co0009119

Does not accept any unsolicited material. Project types include feature films. Genres include fantasy, science fiction, drama, comedy, and action.

Steven Spielberg
Chairman
imdb.com/name/nm0000229
facebook.com/pages/Steven-spielberg

AMBUSH ENTERTAINMENT
Production company

360 N. La Cienega Blvd. Third Floor
Los Angeles, CA 90048
323-951-9197 (phone)
323-951-9998 (fax)

info@ambushentertainment.com
imdb.com/company/co0091524
linkedin.com/company/ambush-entertainment

Accepts scripts from produced or represented writers. Established in 2000.

Miranda Bailey
Partner (CEO)
323-951-9197
323-951-9998
imdb.com/name/nm0047419

Amanda Marshall
Head (Production)
imdb.com/name/nm1622973

AMC NETWORKS
Distributor

11 Penn Plaza, New York City , NY, United States, 10001
212-324-8500

amcnetworks.com
imdb.com/company/co0332012

Does not accept any unsolicited material. Project types include TV. Genres include thriller, drama, and family.

AMERICAN CHAINSAWS
Production company

10950 Washington Blvd., Suite 300
Culver City, CA 90232
213-241-9500

americanchainsaws.com
imdb.com/company/co0361572

Does not accept any unsolicited material. Project types include TV.

Colt Straub
Producer
imdb.com/name/nm2324836
linkedin.com/pub/colt-straub/48/a74/886
facebook.com/colt.straub.92
twitter.com/cougarcolt

Royal Malloy
Producer
imdb.com/name/nm3735876
linkedin.com/pub/royal-malloy/31/950/749
facebook.com/royal.malloy
twitter.com/royalmalloy

Duke Straub
Producer
imdb.com/name/nm0833702
linkedin.com/pub/duke-straub/12/b63/437

AMERICAN CINEMA INTERNATIONAL
Production company

15363 Ventura Blvd.
Sherman Oaks, CA 91406
818-907-8700

aci-americancinema.com
imdb.com/company/co0004425
facebook.com/pages/American-Cinema-International/
   166267290065693

Does not accept any unsolicited material. Project types include feature films. Genres include action, drama, and romance.

George Shamieh
CEO
imdb.com/name/nm0787864

Chevonne O'Shaughnessy
President
imdb.com/name/nm1367679
linkedin.com/pub/chevonne-o-shaughnessy/11/8a2/
   5b8
facebook.com/chevonne.oshaughnessy.5

AMERICAN GENRE FILM ARCHIVE
Production company

612A E 6th St
Austin, TX 78701
512-861-7009

sebastian@americangenrefilm.org
americangenrefilm.com
imdb.com/company/co0396277

Does not accept any unsolicited material. Genres include documentary and thriller.

AMERICAN LIFE TELEVISION NETWORK
Distributor

650 Massachusetts Ave., NW
Washington, DC 20001

202-289-6633 (phone)
202-289-6632 (fax)

goodtv.com
imdb.com/company/co0151317
facebook.com/goodtvcom

Does not accept any unsolicited material. Genres include drama.

AMERICAN PUBLIC TELEVISION
Production company, distributor, and sales agent

55 Summer St.
Boston, MA 02110
617-338-4455 (phone)
617-338-5369 (fax)

info@aptonline.org
aptonline.org
imdb.com/company/co0120663

Does not accept any unsolicited material. Project types include TV. Genres include documentary.

AMERICAN SOCIETY OF CINEMATOGRAPHERS
Production company

1313 Vine St, Hollywood , CA, United States, 90028
323-969-4333

office@theasc.com
theasc.com/site
imdb.com/company/co0065738

Does not accept any unsolicited material. Project types include feature films. Genres include science fiction and animation.

AMERICAN TELEVISION DISTRIBUTION
Distributor

4008 E Side Ave
Dallas, TX 75226
214-720-1300

tommy@americantvd.com
americantvd.com
imdb.com/company/co0143524

Does not accept any unsolicited material. Project types include TV.

AMERICAN UNITED ENTERTAINMENT
Production company

7119 W. Sunset Blvd., Suite 403
Hollywood, CA 90046
424-235-0030

info@americanunitedent.com
americanunitedent.com
imdb.com/company/co0223507
linkedin.com/in/robert88
facebook.com/pages/Beverly-Hills-CA/American-United-Entertainment/210968482563

Does not accept any unsolicited material. Project types include TV and feature films. Genres include drama, family, action, and comedy.

Art Camacho
VP of Entertainment
imdb.com/name/nm0131064

Kevin Hicks
President
imdb.com/name/nm1649077

Todd Chamberlain
President of Production
imdb.com/name/nm1956927

Robert Rodriguez
CEO/Producer
imdb.com/name/nm0001675

AMERICAN WORK INC.
Production company

7030 Delongpre
Los Angeles, CA 90028
323-668-1100

imdb.com/company/co0167015

Accepts query letters from unproduced, unrepresented writers. Project types include feature films and TV. Genres include comedy and drama. Established in 2009.

Ravi Nandan
imdb.com/name/nm2249298

Scot Armstrong
Partner
imdb.com/name/nm0035905

AMERICAN WORLD PICTURES
Production company

8255 Sunset Blvd.
West Hollywood, CA 90046
323-848-7700 (phone)
323-848-7744 (fax)

info@americanworldpictures.com
americanworldpictures.com
imdb.com/company/co0054536
linkedin.com/company/american-world-pictures

Accepts scripts from unproduced, unrepresented writers. Project types include feature films. Genres include drama, family, thriller, romance, comedy, horror, and action.

Mark Lester
818-340-9004
mark@americanworldpictures.com
imdb.com/name/nm0504495
linkedin.com/pub/mark-l-lester/44/503/a57

Dana Dubovsky
818-340-9004
dana@americanworldpictures.com
imdb.com/name/nm0239541
linkedin.com/pub/dana-dubovsky/40/868/268

AMERICAN ZOETROPE
Studio

916 Kearny St Sentinel Building
San Francisco, CA 94133
415-788-7500 (phone)
415-989-7910 (fax)

1641 N Ivar Ave
Los Angeles, CA 90028

contests@zoetrope.com
zoetrope.com
imdb.com/company/co0020958

Accepts scripts from unproduced, unrepresented writers. Genres include thriller, action, crime, and non-fiction. Established in 1972.

Francis Coppola
Emeritus
415-788-7500
imdb.com/name/nm0000338

Michael Zakin
Vice President (Production & Acquisitions)
323-460-4420
imdb.com/name/nm2943902

AMG ENTERTAINMENT
Distributor

Seishin Ebisu Bldg. 5F
1-5-2, Ebisu Minami
Tokyo 150-0022
Japan
+81 3 5720 2461 (phone)
+81 3 5720 2462 (fax)

info@amg-e.co.jp
amg-e.co.jp
imdb.com/company/co0166527

Does not accept any unsolicited material. Project types include TV. Genres include drama, romance, and comedy.

Naotaka Yoshida
Chairman (Producer)
imdb.com/name/nm0948912

AMPLIFY
Distributor

333 Park Ave S, Suite 5B, New York, NY, United States, 10010
212-537-6769

info@amplifyreleasing.com
amplifyreleasing.com
imdb.com/company/co0464994

Does not accept any unsolicited material. Project types include TV. Genres include family and drama.

Dylan Marchetti
Chief Creative Officer (Theatrical Distribution & Marketing)
212-537-6769
imdb.com/name/nm2543241

AM PRODUCTIONS & MANAGEMENT
Production company

8899 Beverly Blvd. Suite 713
Los Angeles , CA 90048
310-275-9081 (phone)
310-275-9082 (fax)

imdb.com/company/co0094894

Does not accept any unsolicited material.

Alan Marguilies
Producer/Manager
imdb.com/name/nm0546865

AMS PICTURES
Production company and distributor

16986 Dallas Pkwy.
Dallas, TX 75248
972-818-7400 (phone)
866-691-3660 (fax)

4407 Bee Caves Rd
Suite 612
Austin, TX 78746
512-330-9434 (phone)
866-691-3660 (fax)

creative@amspictures.com
amspictures.com
imdb.com/company/co0279324
linkedin.com/company/ams-pictures
facebook.com/ams.pictures
twitter.com/AMSPicturesOP

Does not accept any unsolicited material. Project types include TV and feature films. Genres include reality, documentary, family, and crime. Established in 1982.

ANCHOR BAY
Distributor

70 The Esplanade
Ste 300
Toronto, ON M5E 1R2
Canada
416-862-1700

info.canada@anchorbayent.com
anchorbayentertainment.com
imdb.com/company/co0223306

facebook.com/AnchorBay
twitter.com/Anchor_Bay

Does not accept any unsolicited material. Genres include drama and horror.

ANCHOR BAY ENTERTAINMENT
Production company and distributor

1699 Stutz Dr, Troy, MI, United States, 48084
248-816-0909 (phone)
248-816-3335 (fax)

anchorbayentertainment.com/Entertainment.aspx
imdb.com/company/co0067793

Does not accept any unsolicited material. Project types include feature films and TV. Genres include romance, drama, family, and thriller.

ANCHOR BAY FILMS
Production company and distributor

9242 Beverly Blvd Suite 201
Beverly Hills, CA 90210
424-204-4166

1699 Stutz Dr.
Troy, MI 48084
248-816-0909

anchorbayent.com
imdb.com/company/co0249289
linkedin.com/company/anchor-bay-entertainment-inc
facebook.com/AnchorBay
twitter.com/Anchor_Bay

Does not accept any unsolicited material. Project types include feature films. Genres include drama, action, horror, thriller, crime, science fiction, comedy, and romance. Established in 1997.

Bill Clark
President
424-204-4166
imdb.com/name/nm0163694

ANDARES PRODUCTIONS
Production company

1100 Business Parkway# 140
Richardson, TX 75081
682-222-6042

aksmith@andaresproductions.com
imdb.com/company/co0480021
facebook.com/andaresproductions

Does not accept any unsolicited material. Project types include feature films and short films. Genres include thriller, drama, and action. Established in 2015.

ANDELL ENTERTAINMENT
Production company

10877 Wilshire Blvd. Suite 2200
Los Angeles , CA 90024
310-954-4890 (phone)
310-954-4881 (fax)

imdb.com/company/co0064187

Does not accept any unsolicited material. Project types include feature films. Genres include drama.

ANDELL ENTERTAINMENT
Production company

10877 Wilshire Blvd. Suite 2200
Los Angeles , CA 90024
310-954-4890 (phone)
310-954-4881 (fax)

imdb.com/company/co0064187

Does not accept any unsolicited material. Project types include feature films. Genres include drama.

Eric Hayes
President
imdb.com/name/nm2498510
linkedin.com/pub/eric-hayes/5/b77/540

Andrew Hauptman
Producer
imdb.com/name/nm0369448
facebook.com/pages/Andrew-Hauptman/
143071572375642
twitter.com/andrew_hauptman

Lisbeth Vitallo-Hook
Development
imdb.com/name/nm1025460

ANDERSON PRODUCTIONS, CRAIG
Production company

444 N. Larchmont Blvd., Suite 109
Los Angeles, CA 90004
323-463-2000 (phone)
323-463-2022 (fax)

info@cappix.com
cappix.com
imdb.com/company/co0062854
linkedin.com/company/craig-anderson-productions

Accepts query letters from produced or represented writers. Project types include TV. Genres include drama.

Craig Anderson
Producer
imdb.com/name/nm0026544
linkedin.com/pub/craig-anderson/5/839/14

Nathan Santell
Development
imdb.com/name/nm2731214

David Markus
VP of Development
imdb.com/name/nm0549007

ANDREA SIMON ENTERTAINMENT
Production company

4230 Woodman Ave.
Sherman Oaks, CA 91423
818-380-1901 (phone)
818-380-1932 (fax)

asimon@andreasimonent.com
imdb.com/company/co0102747
linkedin.com/company/andrea-simon-entertainment
facebook.com/pages/Andrea-Simon-Entertainment/
109513095743968

Accepts query letters from unproduced, unrepresented writers. Project types include TV and feature films. Genres include drama and comedy.

Andrea Simon
Principal
asimon@andreasimonent.com
imdb.com/name/nm2231084
linkedin.com/pub/andrea-simon/18/AB/885

ANDREW LAUREN PRODUCTIONS
Production company

36 E 23rd St, Suite 6F
New York, NY 10010
212-475-1600 (phone)
212-529-1095 (fax)

asst@andrewlaurenproductions.com
andrewlaurenproductions.com
imdb.com/company/co0032488
linkedin.com/company/andrew-lauren-productions

Accepts scripts from unproduced, unrepresented writers. Project types include feature films and TV. Genres include drama.

Andrew Lauren
Principal
212-475-1600
asst@andrewlaurenproductions.com
imdb.com/name/nm0491054

Dave Platt
Creative Executive
212-475-1600
asst@andrewlaurenproductions.com
imdb.com/name/nm5255879

ANGEL ARK PRODUCTIONS
Production company

5042 Wilshire Blvd,. Suite 592
Los Angeles, CA 90036
818-981-8833

imdb.com/company/co0030722

Does not accept any unsolicited material. Project types include TV. Genres include comedy and crime.

Michael A. Jackman
Partner
imdb.com/name/nm0413182
linkedin.com/pub/michael-a-jackman/1/74/a63
twitter.com/jackmantwo

Jenny Birchfield-Eick
Partner
imdb.com/name/nm0083316
linkedin.com/pub/jenny-birchfield-eick/27/b7/50b
facebook.com/jenny.birchfieldeick

Jason Alexander
Partner
imdb.com/name/nm0004517
facebook.com/pages/Jason-Alexander/
    108011235885841
twitter.com/IJasonAlexander

ANGELWORLD ENTERTAINMENT LTD.
Production company

New Bridge House
30-34 New Bridge St
London
EC4 V6BJ

6 Triq Ta Fuq Il Widien
Mellieha
Malta

asst@angelworldentertainment.com
angelworldentertainment.com
imdb.com/company/co0295879

Accepts query letters from unproduced, unrepresented writers via email. Project types include feature films. Established in 2007.

Darby Angel
CEO/Producer
chris@angelworldentertainment.com
imdb.com/name/nm3786007
linkedin.com/pub/darby-angel/0/963/b50
Assistant: Christopher Tisa

ANGOSTURA FILM COMPANY
Production company

4380 NW 128th St
Miami, FL 33054
646-209-2274

angostura@angosturafilms.com
angosturafilms.com
imdb.com/company/co0223248
facebook.com/pages/Angostura-Media/
    676778792381652
twitter.com/angostura_media

Does not accept any unsolicited material. Genres include drama and documentary.

ANGRY FILMS

Production company

1416 N. La Brea Ave
Los Angeles, CA
323-802-1715 (phone)
323-802-1720 (fax)

donmurphy.net
imdb.com/company/co0000612

Does not accept any unsolicited material. Project types include feature films. Genres include action, drama, and thriller.

Susan Montford
Producer
imdb.com/name/nm1848205
facebook.com/pages/Susan-Montford/
    141299689229919

Don Murphy
Producer
donmurphy.net
imdb.com/name/nm0006613
facebook.com/pages/Don-Murphy/100330733356089

ANGRY OTTER PRODUCTIONS

Production company

1810 Flowerdale St
San Antonio, TX 78232
210-277-7237

info@angryotter.com
angryotter.com
imdb.com/company/co0346211

Does not accept any unsolicited material. Project types include TV. Genres include horror.

ANGST PRODUCTIONS LTD.

Production company

1st Fl, Kenilworth House
79-80 Margaret S
London, England W1W 8TA
UK

info@angstproductions.tv
mocktheweek.tv
imdb.com/company/co0149700

Does not accept any unsolicited material. Project types include TV. Genres include comedy.

Mark Leveson
Producer
imdb.com/name/nm0505386

ANIMAL KINGDOM

Production company and financing company

242 W 30th St Suite 602
New York, NY 10001
212-206-1801

info@animalkingdomfilms.com
animalkingdomfilms.com
facebook.com/pages/Animal-Kingdom-Films/
    472303949497226
twitter.com/AnimalFilms

Does not accept any unsolicited material. Project types include feature films. Genres include drama. Established in 2014.

Frederick Green
Principal
imdb.com/name/nm2677259

Joshua Astrachan
Principal
imdb.com/name/nm0040120
linkedin.com/pub/joshua-astrachan/16/602/2a5
facebook.com/joshua.astrachan

ANIMAL LOGIC ENTERTAINMENT

Production company

4000 Warner Blvd Building 95, Suite 120
Burbank CA 91522
818-333-4777

38 Drr Ave, Moore Park, Building 54, FSA 19, Sydney
, Australia, NSW 2021
011-612-93834800 (phone)
011-612-93834801 (fax)

info@al.com.au
animallogic.com
imdb.com/company/co0456655

Does not accept any unsolicited material. Project types include TV. Genres include family, reality, and drama.

ANIMALS ARE PEOPLE TOO
Production company and sales agent

2780 S Jones Blvd
Ste 3373
Las Vegas, NV 89146
702-290-3135

sales@animalsarepeopletoo.com
animalsarepeopletoo.com
imdb.com/company/co0183771
facebook.com/LeoGrilloActor

Does not accept any unsolicited material. Project types include TV. Genres include documentary.

ANIMA SOLA PRODUCTIONS
Production company

1041 N. Formosa Ave Writers Building, Suite 6
West Hollywood, CA 90046
323-850-3530

info@animasolaproductions.com
animasolaproductions.com
imdb.com/company/co0050662
linkedin.com/company/anima-sola-productions
facebook.com/animasolaproductions
twitter.com/animasolaprods

Does not accept any unsolicited material. Project types include TV. Genres include drama and comedy.

Lisa Bellomo
SVP of Production & Development
imdb.com/name/nm0069185
linkedin.com/pub/lisa-bellomo/6/403/98b
facebook.com/lisa.bellomo.71
twitter.com/lisagbellomo

Will Scheffer
Writer/Producer
imdb.com/name/nm0770504
linkedin.com/in/willscheffer
facebook.com/pages/Will-Scheffer/110837282298444

Mark V. Olsen
Writer/Producer
imdb.com/name/nm0647739

ANIME INTERNATIONAL COMPANY (AIC)
Production company

3-19-9
Nakamura Kita
Nerima, Tokyo 176-0023
Japan

business@aicanime.com
imdb.com/company/co0097219

Does not accept any unsolicited material. Project types include TV. Genres include animation and family.

Tôru Miura
President (Producer)
imdb.com/name/nm0594258

ANIMUS FILMS
Production company

914 Hauser Blvd
Los Angeles, CA 90036
323-988-5557 (phone)
323-571-3361 (fax)

info@animusfilms.com
animusfilms.com
imdb.com/company/co0092860
facebook.com/AnimusFIlms

Accepts query letters from unproduced, unrepresented writers. Genres include thriller and non-fiction. Established in 2003.

Jim Young
Principal
323-988-5557
info@animusfilms.com
imdb.com/name/nm1209063
linkedin.com/pub/jim-young/8/176/28

ANNAPURNA PICTURES
Production company

310-724-5678

annapurnapics.com
imdb.com/company/co0323215
facebook.com/annapurnapics
twitter.com/annapurnapics

Does not accept any unsolicited material. Project types include TV and feature films. Genres include crime, non-fiction, drama, comedy, action, and thriller.

Megan Ellison
Principal
imdb.com/name/nm2691892

David Distenfeld
Development Executive
imdb.com/name/nm3367048

ANNIE PLANET
Distributor

2-12-14-6F
Tsukiji
Chuoku, Tokyo 104-0045
Japan
03-3549-1266 (phone)
03-3541-1326 (fax)

info@annieplanet.co.jp
annieplanet.co.jp
imdb.com/company/co0135315

Does not accept any unsolicited material. Genres include drama and comedy.

Junko Satô
President (Executive)
imdb.com/name/nm2846581

ANOINTED PICTURES
Distributor

1516 K St S.E
Suite 303
Washington, DC 20602
202-547-1591 (phone)
202-547-0013 (fax)

info@anointedpictures.com
anointedpictures.com
imdb.com/company/co0442446

Does not accept any unsolicited material. Genres include drama.

AN OLIVE BRANCH PRODUCTIONS, INC.
Production company

9100 Wilshire Blvd, Suite 616
East Tower
Beverly Hills, CA 90212

310-860-6088 (phone)
310-362-8922 (fax)

38 Highbridge Place
Toronto, ON M1V4R9

info@anolivebranchmedia.com
anolivebranchmedia.com
imdb.com/company/co0308344
linkedin.com/company/an-olive-branch-productions-
   inc-
facebook.com/AnOliveBranchMedia

Accepts scripts from produced or represented writers. Project types include feature films. Genres include drama.

Cybill Lui
310-860-6088
info@anolivbranchmedia.com
imdb.com/name/nm3359236

George Zakk
310-860-6088
info@anolivbranchmedia.com
imdb.com/name/nm0952327
linkedin.com/pub/george-zakk/b/863/2a6

ANONYMOUS CONTENT
Production company

3532 Hayden Ave
Culver City, CA 90232
310-558-3667 (phone)
310-558-2724 (fax)

588 Broadway Suite 308
New York, NY 10012
212-925-0055 (phone)
212-925-5030 (fax)

litmanagement@anonymouscontent.com (script submissions)
filmtv@anonymouscontent.com (general)
anonymouscontent.com
imdb.com/company/co0017525
linkedin.com/company/23201

Does not accept any unsolicited material. Project types include feature films, TV, and commercials. Genres include drama, family, thriller, non-fiction, crime, comedy, and action. Established in 1999.

Emmeline Yang
Executive (Features)
310-558-3667
imdb.com/name/nm2534779
linkedin.com/pub/emmeline-yang/5/b2a/65a

Steve Golin
CEO
imdb.com/name/nm0326512

Matt DeRoss
Vice President (Features)
310-558-3667
mattd@anonymouscontent.com
imdb.com/name/nm2249185
linkedin.com/pub/matt-derossi/18/582/229

ANOVA PICTURES
Production company

12400 Wilshire Blvd., Suite 1275
Los Angeles, CA 90025
310-985-7335 (phone)
310-362-8922 (fax)

info@anovapictures.com
anovapictures.com
imdb.com/company/co0442499

Accepts query letters from produced or represented writers. Project types include feature films.

Cybill Lui
Producer
imdb.com/name/nm3359236
linkedin.com/profile/view
facebook.com/cyb.lui
twitter.com/TheCybills

ANSUR PICTURES
Distributor

3-19-8-105
Okamoto
Setagaya, Tokyo 157-0076
Japan
03-3417-6709 (phone)
03-3417-6709 (fax)

info@ansurpictures.com
ansurpictures.com
imdb.com/company/co0196488

Does not accept any unsolicited material. Project types include feature films. Genres include family.

ANTAGONIST PICTURES
Production company

20 Island Ave Suite 205
Miami Beach, FL 33139-1303
786-380-9870

info@antagonistpictures.com
antagonistpictures.ch
imdb.com/company/co0527454
facebook.com/antagonistpict

Does not accept any unsolicited material. Genres include horror and thriller.

ANTENA LATINA FILMS
Distributor

3545 NE 166st
Apt 802
North Miami Beach, FL 33160

alfonsorodriguez@antenalatina7.com
imdb.com/company/co0322727

Does not accept any unsolicited material. Genres include crime, action, and thriller.

ANTHEM PICTURES
Production company

5137 Clareton Dr, Suite 120
Agoura Hills, CA 91301
818-597-2344 (phone)
818-706-8553 (fax)

info@anthemdvd.com
anthempictures.tv
imdb.com/company/co0106574
facebook.com/Anthem-Pictures-135089656504352

Does not accept any unsolicited material. Project types include feature films and TV.

Charles Adelman
President
imdb.com/name/nm0011828
linkedin.com/in/charlesadelman
facebook.com/chuck.adelman
twitter.com/charles_adelman

Keith Walley
Vice President
imdb.com/name/nm0909120
linkedin.com/pub/keith-walley/37/185/96b

ANTIDOTE FILMS
Production company

PO Box 150566
Brooklyn, NY 11215-0566
646-486-4344

info@antidotefilms.com
antidotefilms.com
imdb.com/company/co0011355

Does not accept any unsolicited material. Project types include feature films. Genres include documentary. Established in 2000.

Gerry Kim
imdb.com/name/nm2332388
linkedin.com/pub/dir/gerald/kim

James Debbs
646-486-4344 x305
imdb.com/name/nm0999455
linkedin.com/pub/james-debbs/9/9b/1a5

Jeffrey Kusama-Hinte
President
646-486-4344 x301
jeff@antidotefilms.com
imdb.com/name/nm0506664

Takeo Hori
646-486-4344 x300
imdb.com/name/nm0394659
linkedin.com/in/takeohori

AOI PROMOTION
Production company and distributor

1-6-1
Ohsaki
Shinagawa, Tokyo 141-8580
Japan
03-3779-8000 (phone)
03-3779-8029 (fax)

webmaster@aoi-pro.co.jp
aoi-pro.com

imdb.com/company/co0172041

Project types include TV. Genres include drama.

Yoshio Sasanuki
Executive
imdb.com/name/nm7436205

AOL
Production company and distributor

22000 AOL Way
Dulles VA 20166
703-265-1000

770 Broadway, New York, NY, United States, 10003
212-206-4400

aol.com
imdb.com/company/co0328940

Does not accept any unsolicited material. Project types include TV and feature films. Genres include reality, non-fiction, family, and drama.

A ONE ENTERTAINMENT
Distributor

611 Cedar Ln
Teaneck, NJ 07666
201-394-1849 (phone)
201-357-8482 (fax)

a-one-entertainment.com
imdb.com/company/co0390652

Does not accept any unsolicited material. Genres include horror.

APACHE CO.
Production company

37-14-301
Udagawacho
Shibuya, Tokyo 150-0042
Japan
03-6407-4700 (phone)
03-6407-4701 (fax)

info@apache2001.co.jp
apache2001.co.jp
imdb.com/company/co0314444

Does not accept any unsolicited material. Project types include feature films, short films, and TV. Genres include drama.

APARTMENT 3B
Production company

3000 W Olympic Blvd., Suite 2363
Santa Monica, CA 90404
310-264-4264

imdb.com/company/co0117528

Does not accept any unsolicited material. Project types include TV and feature films. Genres include horror, comedy, drama, and thriller.

Jennifer Klein
Producer/President
imdb.com/name/nm0458813

APATOW PRODUCTIONS
Production company

11788 W Pico Blvd
Suite 141
Los Angeles, CA 90064
310-943-4400 (phone)
310-479-0750 (fax)

apatowproductions.tumblr.com
imdb.com/company/co0073081

Does not accept any unsolicited material. Project types include feature films and TV. Genres include drama, comedy, action, documentary, and romance. Established in 2000.

Judd Apatow
imdb.com/name/nm0031976
twitter.com/JuddApatow
Assistant: Amanda Glaze, Rob Turbovsky, Michael Lewen

APERTURE ENTERTAINMENT
Production company

7620 Lexington Ave
West Hollywood, CA 90046
323-848-4069

agasst@aperture-ent.com
aperture-ent.com

imdb.com/company/co0265611
facebook.com/pages/Aperture-Entertainment
twitter.com/aperturee

Accepts scripts from unproduced, unrepresented writers. Project types include feature films and TV. Genres include action, fantasy, thriller, science fiction, and horror. Established in 2009.

Adam Goldworm
Principal
323-848-4069
adam@aperture-ent.com
imdb.com/name/nm0326411
linkedin.com/in/adamgoldworm
twitter.com/goldworm

APEX ENTERTAINMENT
Production company

15760 Ventura Blvd, Suite 1020, Encino, CA, United States, 91436
818-479-7040

info@apexentertainment.com
apexentertainment.com
imdb.com/company/co0132135

Does not accept any unsolicited material. Project types include feature films and TV. Genres include thriller, family, and drama.

APIS FILMS
Production company

London
England
+44 (0)20 7978 8586

info@apisfilms.co.uk
apisfilms.co.uk
imdb.com/company/co0279256

Does not accept any unsolicited material. Project types include feature films. Genres include horror, drama, romance, and comedy.

Ben Hughes
Producer
imdb.com/name/nm0400467

APOLLO CINEMA
Production company and distributor

P.O. Box 35036, Los Angeles , CA, United States, 90035

info@apollocinema.com
imdb.com/company/co0112126

Does not accept any unsolicited material. Project types include TV, short films, and feature films. Genres include animation, family, action, drama, and thriller.

APOLLO CINEMA SHORT FILM DISTRIBUTION

Distributor

519 Hillcrest Rd.
Los Angeles, CA 90210
323-939-1122 (phone)
323-939-1133 (fax)

info@apollocinema.com
imdb.com/company/co0158394

Does not accept any unsolicited material. Project types include short films. Genres include drama and comedy.

APOSTLE

Production company

9696 Culver Blvd Suite 108
Culver City, CA 90232
310-945-2991

568 Broadway, Suite 301
New York, NY 10012
212-541-4323 (phone)
212-541-4330 (fax)

apostlenyc.com
imdb.com/company/co0072799
twitter.com/ApostleTvFilm

Does not accept any unsolicited material. Project types include TV and feature films.

Jim Serpico

President/Producer
jimserpico.com
imdb.com/name/nm0785351
linkedin.com/pub/jim-serpico/10/b67/2a8
facebook.com/pages/Jim-Serpico/140494332642978
twitter.com/jimserpico

Denis Leary

Producer/Director/Actor
denisleary.com
imdb.com/name/nm0001459
facebook.com/denisleary
twitter.com/denisleary

Molly Irwin

Assistant
imdb.com/name/nm2630329
linkedin.com/pub/molly-irwin/6/664/9bb

Tom Sellitti

SVP of Production/Producer
imdb.com/name/nm0783418
linkedin.com/pub/tom-sellitti/25/9b7/195
facebook.com/tom.sellitti.3

APPARATUS PRODUCTIONS

Production company

8633 Washington Blvd.
Culver City, CA 90232
310-424-1300

apparatusproductions.com
imdb.com/company/co0073189

Does not accept any unsolicited material. Project types include feature films. Genres include drama.

Marc Forster

Director, Producer
imdb.com/name/nm0286975
facebook.com/pages/Marc-Forster/112920088719735
twitter.com/MarcForster

Jessica Kumai Scott

Creative Executive
imdb.com/name/nm1869626
linkedin.com/pub/jessica-kumai-scott/a/64/a96
facebook.com/jkumai
twitter.com/jkumai

Brad Simpson

Producer
imdb.com/name/nm0800922
linkedin.com/pub/brad-simpson/99/987/459

APPIAN WAY

Production company

9255 Sunset Blvd., Suite 615
West Hollywood, CA 90069
310-300-1390 (phone)
310-300-1388 (fax)

imdb.com/company/co0088354
facebook.com/LeonardoDiCaprio
twitter.com/LeoDiCaprio

Does not accept any unsolicited material. Project types include TV and feature films. Genres include horror, crime, science fiction, drama, and thriller.

Leonardo DiCaprio

CEO, Actor, Producer
leonardodicaprio.com
imdb.com/name/nm0000138
facebook.com/LeonardoDiCaprio
twitter.com/LeoDiCaprio

Jennifer Davisson Killoran

President/Producer
imdb.com/name/nm2248832

Michael Hampton

Co-VP
imdb.com/name/nm6280536

Nathaniel Posey

Co-VP
imdb.com/name/nm2929952

Aaron Criswell

Creative Executive
imdb.com/name/nm2082839
linkedin.com/pub/aaron-criswell/52/b89/a58

APPLE CART PRODUCTIONS

Production company

11684 Ventura Blvd. #544
Studio City, CA 91604
818-274-9609 (phone)
818-763-5319 (fax)

info@applecartproductions.com
imdb.com/company/co0221107

Does not accept any unsolicited material. Project types include feature films. Genres include romance and drama.

Benjamin Oberman

President / Producer
boberman@applecartproductions.com
imdb.com/name/nm2589353
linkedin.com/pub/benjamin-oberman/0/649/b1
facebook.com/BenjaminOberman
twitter.com/TheFilmChampion

Jordana Oberman

VP of Development/Producer
joberman@applecartproductions.com
resumes.actorsaccess.com/JordanaOberman
imdb.com/name/nm3037696
linkedin.com/pub/jordana-oberman/8/330/831
facebook.com/jordana.oberman
twitter.com/jordanaoberman

APPLE COMPUTER, INC.

Production company, distributor, and financing company

1 Infinite Loop, Cupertino , CA, United States, 95014
408-996-1010

8560 Sunset Blvd Suite 100
West Hollywood CA 90069

apple.com

Does not accept any unsolicited material. Project types include TV and feature films. Genres include family and drama.

APPLE CORE HOLDINGS

Production company

1450 Broadway, 40th Floor, New York City , NY, United States, 10018
212-209-2300 (phone)
212-209-2301 (fax)

info@applecoreholdings.com
applecoreholdings.com
imdb.com/company/co0280324

Does not accept any unsolicited material. Genres include family, drama, and thriller.

APPLECREEK PRODUCTIONS

Production company

55 Mill St
Bldg 5, Ste 510
Toronto, ON M5A 3C4
Canada
905-893-1725 (phone)
905-552-0459 (fax)

andy@applecreekfilms.com
applecreekfilms.com
imdb.com/company/co0032540

Does not accept any unsolicited material. Genres include drama and romance.

Andy Emilio
Producer
imdb.com/name/nm0256410

APPLESEED ENTERTAINMENT
Production company

7715 W Sunset Blvd
Hollywood, CA 90046
818-718-6000 (phone)
818-556-5610 (fax)

films@appleseedent.com
appleseedent.com
imdb.com/company/co0176039

Does not accept any unsolicited material. Project types include feature films. Genres include drama, comedy, and family.

Ben Moses
Founder
ben@appleseedent.com
imdb.com/name/nm0608558

Lynne Moses
Founder
lynne@appleseedent.com
imdb.com/name/nm1030988
facebook.com/lynne.moses
twitter.com/lynne_moses

APPLOFF ENTERTAINMENT
Production company

5900 Wilshire Blvd, Suite 2250
Los Angeles, CA 90036
310-975-9707

imdb.com/company/co0213781
facebook.com/pages/Apploff-Entertainment/
  137269886288644

Does not accept any unsolicited material. Project types include TV.

Jeff Apploff
Executive Producer
imdb.com/name/nm2201741
linkedin.com/pub/jeff-apploff/0/439/b55
facebook.com/japploff
twitter.com/japploff

APRIL FILMS
Production company

17644 Rancho St
Encino, CA 91316
818-757-7680 (phone)
818-757-7437 (fax)

info@aprilfilms.com
aprilfilms.com
imdb.com/company/co0089035

Does not accept any unsolicited material. Project types include feature films.

Adam Dunlap
Producer
imdb.com/name/nm318441

Rudy Cohen
Producer
imdb.com/company/co0080027
linkedin.com/pub/rudy-cohen/7/764/450

APT WORLDWIDE
Distributor and sales agent

55 Summer St
Boston, MA 02110
617-338-5369

aptww.org
imdb.com/company/co0212599

Does not accept any unsolicited material. Project types include TV. Genres include drama, comedy, and documentary.

AQUA FOXX PRODUCTIONS
Production company

7880 San Felipe
Suite 110
Houston, TX 77063
323-931-2027

lauriefoxx.com/Site/
    Aqua%20Foxx%20Productions,%20LLC.html
imdb.com/company/co0228592
linkedin.com/in/laurie-foxx-258ab412

Does not accept any unsolicited material. Project types
include short films. Genres include drama, comedy,
and action.

AQUAMOTION FILM AND TV
Production company

PO Box 403042 Miami Beach, FL 33140

sea@aquamotion.tv
aquamotion.tv
imdb.com/company/co0116176

Does not accept any unsolicited material. Project types
include TV. Genres include documentary.

AQUARIUM STUDIOS
Production company

122 Wardour St
Soho
London W1F 0TX
UK
+44 (0)20 7734 1611

pam@aquariumstudios.co.uk
aquariumstudios.co.uk
imdb.com/company/co0245996
facebook.com/aquariumstudios
twitter.com/AquariumStudios

Does not accept any unsolicited material. Genres
include animation and comedy.

Ben Baird
Producer
imdb.com/name/nm1496435

AQUOS ENTERTAINMENT GROUP
Distributor

20533 Biscayne Blvd.
Suite 153
Aventura, FL 33180
305-389-5859

probles@aquosentertainment.com
aquosentertainment.com
imdb.com/company/co0304249
facebook.com/AquosEntertainment
twitter.com/aquosgroup

Does not accept any unsolicited material. Genres
include comedy and romance.

ARAD PRODUCTIONS, AVI
Production company

10203 Santa Monica Blvd., Suite 301
Los Angeles, CA 90067
310-772-2723

imdb.com/company/co0180492

Does not accept any unsolicited material. Project types
include feature films. Genres include action.

Emmy Yu
Development
linkedin.com/pub/emmy-yu/35/226/454

Avi Arad
Producer
imdb.com/name/nm0032696
facebook.com/pages/Avi-Arad/110917875627509
twitter.com/AviArad

Alexandra Bland
Executive
imdb.com/name/nm6348549

ARCANE PICTURES
Production company and sales agent

25 Floral St
London WC2E 9DS
UK
+44 20 7189 5525 (phone)
+44 20 7031 8101 (fax)

info@arcanepictures.com
imdb.com/company/co0104093

Does not accept any unsolicited material. Project types
include TV. Genres include documentary and drama.

Meg Thomson
Producer
imdb.com/name/nm0861052

ARC ENTERTAINMENT
Distributor

3212 Nebraska Ave, Santa Monica, CA, United States, 90404
310-857-5200 (phone)
310-857-5201 (fax)

info@arc-ent.com
arc-ent.com
imdb.com/company/co0435023

Does not accept any unsolicited material. Project types include TV. Genres include drama, family, and thriller.

ARC FILMS
Distributor

2-17-55-109
Akasaka
Minato, Tokyo 107-0052
Japan
090-3439-4608 (phone)
03-3551-6004 (fax)

info@arc-films.co.jp
arc-films.co.jp
imdb.com/company/co0363547

Does not accept any unsolicited material. Project types include TV, feature films, and short films. Genres include action.

Hiroyuki Ueno
Executive
imdb.com/name/nm7090019

ARCHER GRAY PRODUCTIONS
Production company

142 Greene St, 4th Floor
New York, NY 10012
212-203-4955

info@archergray.com
archergrayproductions.com
imdb.com/company/co0423953

linkedin.com/company/archer-gray-productions
facebook.com/ArcherGrayProductions
twitter.com/Archer_Gray

Does not accept any unsolicited material. Project types include feature films and TV. Genres include drama and romance.

Anne Carey
President of Production
imdb.com/name/nm0136904
linkedin.com/pub/anne-carey/28/237/661
facebook.com/pages/Anne-Carey/112360425443946

Amy Nauiokas
Founder/CEO
amynauiokas.com
imdb.com/name/nm2602846
linkedin.com/in/amynauiokas
facebook.com/amy.nauiokas
twitter.com/AmyNauiokas

Shani Geva
Creative Executive
imdb.com/name/nm2802616
linkedin.com/pub/shani-geva/54/165/752
facebook.com/shani.geva.7
twitter.com/shanigeva

ARCHER'S MARK
Production company

First Floor
120-124 Curtain Rd
London EC2A 3SQ
UK
+44 20 7426 5160

info@archersmark.co.uk
archersmark.co.uk
imdb.com/company/co0439202

Does not accept any unsolicited material. Project types include TV. Genres include drama and documentary.

ARCHERY PICTURES
Production company and distributor

3 Archery Close
London W2 2BE
UK
44207-224-1221

hello@archerypictures.com
archerypictures.com
imdb.com/company/co0501538

Does not accept any unsolicited material. Project types include TV. Genres include family and drama.

Liza Marshall
Producer
imdb.com/name/nm0551017

ARCHETYPE PRODUCTIONS

1608 Argyle Ave
Los Angeles, CA 90028
323-468-3600 (phone)
323-784-7842 (fax)

info@archetypela.com
archetypela.com
imdb.com/company/co0156755
linkedin.com/company/archetype
facebook.com/ArchetypeLA
twitter.com/ArchetypeLA

Does not accept any unsolicited material. Project types include feature films. Genres include action.

David Server
Producer
imdb.com/name/nm2159992
facebook.com/david.server.3

Ray Miller
Producer/Manager
ray.miller@archetypela.com
linkedin.com/pub/ray-miller/1/b31/63b
facebook.com/raymillerla
twitter.com/LARayRay

ARCHSTONE DISTRIBUTION

Distributor and sales agent

1201 W Fifth St
Ste T-420, 4th Fl
Los Angeles, CA 90017
310-622-8773 (phone)
310-492-5369 (fax)

info@archstonedistribution.com
archstonedistribution.com
imdb.com/company/co0291889

facebook.com/pages/Archstone-Distribution/
 144349352276960
twitter.com/ArchstoneDistb

Does not accept any unsolicited material. Project types include feature films. Genres include action, drama, and thriller.

ARCIMBOLDO Y.K.

Production company and distributor

3-11-12-701
Shinjuku
Shinjuku, Tokyo 160-0022
Japan
03-5361-3121 (phone)
03-5361-3122 (fax)

arcimboldo@jmpd.jp
imdb.com/company/co0155099

Does not accept any unsolicited material. Project types include feature films. Genres include comedy and horror.

ARCLIGHT FILMS

Production company

9107 Wilshire Blvd, Suite 600
Beverly Hills, CA 90210
310-777-8855 (phone)
310-777-8882 (fax)

90/330 Wattle St
Ultimo NSW 2007, Australia
06028-353-2440

info@arclightfilms.com
arclightfilms.com
imdb.com/company/co0003093
facebook.com/ArclightFilms

Accepts query letters from unproduced, unrepresented writers via email. Project types include feature films.

Gary Hamilton
Co-Chairman
310-528-5888
gary@arclightfilms.com
imdb.com/name/nm0357861
linkedin.com/pub/hamilton-gary/32/ba/a12

Mike Gabrawy
CCO
310-475-2330
info@arclightfilms.com
imdb.com/name/nm0300166
linkedin.com/pub/mike-gabrawy/1/667/729

ARCLIGHT FILMS PTY LTD.
Production company and distributor

90/330 Wattle St
Ultimo NSW Australia 2007
011-612-83532440

9107 Wilshire Blvd, Suite 600, Beverly Hills, CA,
United States, 90210
310-777-8855

info@arclightfilms.com
arclightfilms.com

Does not accept any unsolicited material. Project types
include TV and feature films. Genres include thriller,
family, action, and drama.

Mike Gabrawy
Chief Creative Officer
310-475-2330
imdb.com/name/nm0300166

ARC PRODUCTIONS
Production company and distributor

230 Richmond St East
Toronto, ON M5A 1P4
Canada
416-682-5200 (phone)
416-682-5209 (fax)

info@arcproductions.com
arcproductions.com
imdb.com/company/co0328433
linkedin.com/company/arc-productions
facebook.com/pages/Arc-Productions-Animation-
    Visual-Effects%20/219230164759377
twitter.com/arcproductions

Does not accept any unsolicited material. Genres
include animation.

Rob Silvestri
Director
imdb.com/name/nm3241556

ARCTIC PICTURES LIMITED
Production company

75 Oxford Gardens
London W10 5UL
UK

info@arctic-pictures.com
arctic-pictures.com
imdb.com/company/co0506369

Does not accept any unsolicited material. Project types
include feature films. Genres include thriller.

Tobias Queisser
Producer
imdb.com/name/nm5422565

ARDABAN
Production company

1741 Ivar Ave
Los Angeles, CA 90028
323-790-8000

chachi@ardaban.com
ardaban.com
imdb.com/company/co0396320
linkedin.com/company/shine-group
facebook.com/ShineGroup.tv
twitter.com/ShineGroupTV

Does not accept any unsolicited material. Project types
include TV. Genres include reality.

Chachi Senior
CEO
imdb.com/name/nm1551847
linkedin.com/pub/chachi-senior/5/544/a5
facebook.com/chachi.senior
twitter.com/ChachiSenior

AREA 51 ENTERTAINMENT
Production company

188 Steelmanville Rd
Egg Harbor Township, NJ 08234

HDFilmMaker2112@gmail.com
imdb.com/company/co0321460

Does not accept any unsolicited material. Project types include TV. Genres include comedy and thriller.

AREMCO PRODUCTIONS

Production company

6-17-7-201
Akasaka
Minato, Tokyo 107-0052
Japan
03-6426-5866 (phone)
03-6426-5865 (fax)

info@aremco-bobby.com
aremco-bobby.com
imdb.com/company/co0428518

Does not accept any unsolicited material. Project types include feature films. Genres include comedy.

ARENAS ENTERTAINMENT

Production company

3375 Barham Blvd
Los Angeles, CA 90068
323-785-5555 (phone)
323-785-5560 (fax)

2121 N. Bayshore Dr.
Miami, FL 33137

general@arenasgroup.com
arenasgroup.com
imdb.com/company/co0051527
facebook.com/ArenasEntertainment
twitter.com/ArenasEnt

Does not accept any unsolicited material. Project types include feature films. Established in 1988.

Santiago Pozo
CEO
imdb.com/name/nm0694815

ARGONAUT PICTURES

Production company

310-359-8481

info@argonaughtpictures.co.uk

argonautpictures.co.uk
imdb.com/company/co0015041
twitter.com/ArgonautPicture

Does not accept any unsolicited material. Project types include feature films. Genres include drama.

Paul Marashlian
paul@argonautpictures.com
imdb.com/name/nm2281671

Giovanni Agnelli
Owner
imdb.com/name/nm1278301
facebook.com/public/Giovanni-Agnelli

Karim Mashouf
Owner
imdb.com/name/nm3196690

Scott Bloom
Owner
imdb.com/name/nm0089231
linkedin.com/in/scottbloomedit1

Manny Mashouf
Owner
imdb.com/name/nm3196705

Carter Hall
carter@argonautpictures.com
imdb.com/name/nm3050292

ARGO PICTURES

Production company and distributor

4-10-21-4F
Akasaka
Minato, Tokyo 107-0052
Japan
03-3584-6237 (phone)
03-3584-6238 (fax)

mail@argopictures.jp
argopictures.jp
imdb.com/company/co0046532

Does not accept any unsolicited material. Project types include TV. Genres include drama, fantasy, and comedy.

Yutaka Okada
Producer
imdb.com/name/nm0645448

ARIESCOPE PICTURES
Production company

10750 Cumpston St
North Hollywood, CA 91601

info@ariescope.com
ariescope.com
imdb.com/company/co0132426

Does not accept any unsolicited material. Project types include TV and feature films. Genres include horror, romance, fantasy, thriller, crime, drama, and comedy. Established in 1998.

Cory Neal
Principal
imdb.com/name/nm1425628

Will Barratt
Principal
imdb.com/name/nm1701139
facebook.com/pages/Will-Barratt-Productions

Adam Green
Principal
imdb.com/name/nm1697112
facebook.com/AdamFnGreen

ARISTAR ENTERTAINMENT
Production company and sales agent

19320 Stone Oak pkwy STE: 308
San Antonio, TX 78260
210-687-8755

derekonthetv@hotmail.com
aristarfilms.com
imdb.com/company/co0252754
facebook.com/Aristar-Entertainment-
    Group-174783065907694/timeline
twitter.com/dereknixon

Does not accept any unsolicited material. Project types include feature films. Genres include horror, family, drama, thriller, and fantasy. Established in 2006.

ARJAY ENTERTAINMENT
Production company

441 Maple Ave
Phillipsburg, NJ 08865

908-387-0114 (phone)
908-387-0144 (fax)

rj@arjayent.com
arjayent.com
imdb.com/company/co0096657

Does not accept any unsolicited material. Project types include short films. Genres include comedy.

ARLOOK GROUP
Production company

205 S Beverly Dr, Suite 209
Beverly Hills, CA 90212
310-550-5714 (phone)
310-550-8714 (fax)

arlookgroup.com
imdb.com/company/co0242042
facebook.com/pages/The-Arlook-Group/
    366944246680789

Does not accept any unsolicited material. Project types include feature films. Genres include drama.

Richard Arlook
Producer/Manager
imdb.com/name/nm0035207
facebook.com/pages/Richard-Arlook/
    143404012338857
twitter.com/richardarlook

ARMANDO MONTELONGO PRODUCTIONS
Production company

2935 Thousand Oaks Dr
#6-285
San Antonio, TX 78247
210-501-0077

armandomontelongoproductions.com
imdb.com/company/co0488307
facebook.com/armandomontelongoproductions
twitter.com/AMPSATX

Does not accept any unsolicited material. Project types include feature films. Genres include drama. Established in 2014.

ARMORY FILMS
Production company

6671 W. Sunset Blvd., Suite 1585
Los Angeles, CA 90028
323-461-1613

armoryfilms.com
imdb.com/company/co0368217
facebook.com/pages/Armory-Films/
 221193544620551

Does not accept any unsolicited material. Project types include feature films. Genres include action, thriller, horror, and comedy.

Christopher Lemole
CCO
imdb.com/name/nm4043287
linkedin.com/pub/chris-lemole/76/805/927
twitter.com/clemole

Tim Zajaros
Partner/Producer
imdb.com/name/nm2591283
linkedin.com/pub/tim-zajaros/4/9a6/434
facebook.com/TimZajaros
twitter.com/TimZajaros

ARRIVAL PICTURES
Production company and distributor

PO Box 219
Austin, TX 78767

ArrivalPictures@gmail.com
imdb.com/company/co0119406

Does not accept any unsolicited material. Genres include crime, romance, and comedy.

ARROYO PICTURES
Production company

3000 Olympic Blvd., Suite 1100
Santa Monica, CA 90404

imdb.com/company/co0067151

Does not accept any unsolicited material. Project types include feature films and TV. Genres include crime, drama, and thriller.

Scott Frank
President/Writer/Producer
imdb.com/name/nm0291082

ARSENAL PICTURES
Production company, distributor, sales agent, and financing company

433 N. Camden Dr
6th floor
Los Angeles, CA 90210
310-279-5270

info@arsenal-pictures.com
arsenal-pictures.com
imdb.com/company/co0176772
facebook.com/ArsenalPictures
twitter.com/ArsenalPictures

Does not accept any unsolicited material. Project types include feature films. Genres include action, thriller, drama, and comedy. Established in 2006.

Yarek Danielak
Founder/Producer
imdb.com/name/nm1345948
linkedin.com/pub/yarek-danielak/1/4ba/560
facebook.com/yarek.danielak

ARS NOVA
Production company and distributor

511 W 54th St
New York, NY 10019
212-586-4200 (phone)
212-489-1908 (fax)

info@arsnovaent.com
arsnovaent.com
imdb.com/company/co0176042
twitter.com/arsnova

Accepts scripts from unproduced, unrepresented writers. Genres include myth, science fiction, fantasy, comedy, and action.

Jon Steingart
Producer
212-586-4200
japfelbaum@arsnovaent.com
imdb.com/name/nm0826050

Jillian Apfelbaum
Producer
212-586-4200
japfelbaum@arsnovaent.com
imdb.com/name/nm2249752
linkedin.com/pub/jillian-apfelbaum/5/294/51b

ART4NOISE
Production company

16, Ingestre Place
Soho
London W1F 0JJ
UK
+44(0207-287-7873 (phone)
+44(0207-099-8381 (fax)

info@art4noise.com
art4noise.com
imdb.com/company/co0106536
facebook.com/Art4noise-163348943679114
twitter.com/art4noise

Does not accept any unsolicited material. Project types include feature films and TV. Genres include thriller, action, and drama.

Peter Baldock
Actor
imdb.com/name/nm0049792

ARTEMIS FILMS
Production company

Suite 3, Berkeley Square House
Berkeley Square
London W1J 6BY
UK
+44203-675-0499

info@artemisfilms.org
artemisfilms.org
imdb.com/company/co0103851

Does not accept any unsolicited material. Project types include feature films. Genres include drama and thriller.

Iain Sinclair
Producer
imdb.com/name/nm7323960

ARTHAUS PICTURES
Production company

Granville Towers, 1424 N. Crescent Heights, Suite 57
West Hollywood, CA 90046
323-848-8257 (phone)
323-848-8267 (fax)

imdb.com/company/co0211409

Does not accept any unsolicited material. Genres include drama.

Chuck Rock
Producer
imdb.com/name/nm3066606

ARTHOUSE FILMS
Production company, distributor, and sales agent

601 W 26th St, 11th Floor, New York City , NY, United States, 10001
212-320-3600 (phone)
212-320-3609 (fax)

arthousefilmsdk@gmail.com
arthousefilmsonline.com
imdb.com/company/co0008561

Does not accept any unsolicited material. Project types include feature films and TV. Genres include thriller, family, action, and drama.

David Koh
Head (Acquisitions & Production)
imdb.com/name/nm1646295

ARTICLE 19 FILMS
Production company and distributor

247 Centre St, Suite 7W
New York, NY 10013
212-777-1987

info@article19films.com
imdb.com/company/co0164965
facebook.com/Article-19-Films-410967495625491

Accepts query letters from unproduced, unrepresented writers. Project types include feature films. Genres include drama, documentary, and non-fiction. Established in 2006.

Filippo Bozotti
Executive
imdb.com/name/nm1828075

ARTICULUS ENTERTAINMENT
Production company

9440 Santa Monica Blvd., Suite 708
Beverly Hills, CA 90210
310-691-1401 (phone)
877-724-8651 (fax)

articulusentertainment.com
imdb.com/company/co0097887

Does not accept any unsolicited material. Project types include feature films. Genres include drama and action.

Steven Sawalich
Founder, Producer
imdb.com/name/nm1367960
linkedin.com/in/stevesawalich
facebook.com/steven.sawalich
twitter.com/stevensawalich

Jennifer Perchalla
Director of Development
imdb.com/name/nm1339702
linkedin.com/pub/jen-perchalla/23/54a/1b

ARTIFICIAL EYE
Production company and distributor

+44207-240-5353 (phone)
+44207-240-5242 (fax)

info@artificial-eye.com
artificial-eye.com
imdb.com/company/co0053637

Does not accept any unsolicited material. Genres include romance and drama.

Philip Knatchbull
Producer
imdb.com/name/nm0460552

ARTINA FILMS
Production company

1416 N La Brea Ave
Los Angeles, CA 90028
323-802-1500

info@artinafilms.com
artinafilms.com
imdb.com/company/co0193161

Does not accept any unsolicited material. Project types include feature films. Genres include thriller, drama, and comedy.

Robert Salerno
Producer/Director
imdb.com/name/nm0007011
facebook.com/pages/Robert-Salerno/
    133011346736225

Naomi Despres
Producer
imdb.com/name/nm0221638
linkedin.com/pub/naomi-despres/16/baa/117

ARTISTS-PRODUCERS ASSOCIATES INC.
Production company and distributor

745 Fifth Ave
New York, NY 10151

imdb.com/company/co0022036

Does not accept any unsolicited material. Genres include drama.

ARTISTS PRODUCTION GROUP
Production company

9348 Civic Center Dr.
2nd Fl.
Beverly Hills, CA 90210
310-300-2400 (phone)
310-300-2424 (fax)

imdb.com/company/co0024601

Does not accept any unsolicited material. Project types include feature films. Genres include comedy, drama, romance, science fiction, action, horror, and crime. Established in 1998.

Chris George
Development
imdb.com/name/nm0313383

ARTISTS PUBLIC DOMAIN
Production company

225 W 13th St
New York, NY 10011

info@artistspublicdomain.com
artistspublicdomain.com
imdb.com/company/co0203133
facebook.com/artistspublicdomain
twitter.com/apdfilms

Accepts query letters from unproduced, unrepresented
writers. Project types include feature films. Genres
include thriller, drama, sociocultural, romance, family,
non-fiction, and comedy.

Alex Orlovsky
Producer
imdb.com/name/nm0650164

Andrew Adair
imdb.com/name/nm4253715

Hunter Gray
Producer
imdb.com/name/nm0336683

ARTISTS STUDIO
Production company

London, England
UK
+44 (0208-222-4343

info@artists-studio.tv
artists-studio.tv
imdb.com/company/co0262794

Does not accept any unsolicited material. Project types
include TV. Genres include drama, thriller, and crime.

Gub Neal
Producer
imdb.com/name/nm0623614

ARTIST VIEW ENTERTAINMENT
Production company

4425 Irvine Ave
Studio City, CA 91602
818-752-2480 (phone)
818-752-9339 (fax)

info@artistviewent.com
artistviewent.com
imdb.com/company/co0054865
linkedin.com/company/artist-view-entertainment
facebook.com/artistviewent

Does not accept any unsolicited material. Project types
include feature films. Genres include action, romance,
comedy, and drama.

Jay E. Joyce
Vice President
imdb.com/name/nm0431543
linkedin.com/in/jayjoyce1

Scott J. Jones
President
imdb.com/name/nm0429222
linkedin.com/pub/scott-j-jones/89/508/272
facebook.com/profile.php

ART PORT
Distributor

1-2-23
Higashi
Shibuya, Tokyo 150-0011
Japan
03-5469-8766 (phone)
03-3407-9980 (fax)

info@artport.co.jp
artport.co.jp
imdb.com/company/co0038312

Does not accept any unsolicited material. Project types
include TV. Genres include thriller and science fiction.

Jun'ichi Matsushita
International Acq. & Sales (Producer)
imdb.com/name/nm0559657

ARTS+LABOR
Production company

7010 Easy Wind Dr
Suite 210

Austin, TX 78752
512-374-0000

info@artsandlabor.co
arts-and-labor.com
imdb.com/company/co0472567
linkedin.com/company/arts---labor
facebook.com/artsandlabor
twitter.com/artsandlabor

Does not accept any unsolicited material. Project types include feature films. Genres include comedy, documentary, drama, and thriller. Established in 2001.

ARTSPLOITATION

Production company, distributor, and sales agent

234 Market St, Fifth Floor, Philadelphia, PA, United States, 19106
215-733-0608 (phone)
215-733-0637 (fax)

info@artsploitation.com
artsploitationfilms.com
imdb.com/company/co0380129

Does not accept any unsolicited material. Project types include TV, short films, and feature films. Genres include family, action, drama, and thriller.

ASCENDANT PICTURES

Production company and distributor

406 Wilshire Blvd.
Santa Monica CA 90401
310-288-4600 (phone)
310-288-4601 (fax)

info@ascendantpictures.com
ascendantpictures.com
imdb.com/company/co0094902
facebook.com/pages/Ascendant-Pictures/
    154899421215569

Does not accept any unsolicited material. Project types include feature films. Genres include thriller, comedy, drama, and crime.

Christopher Roberts
CEO/Founder
imdb.com/name/nm0730932
linkedin.com/pub/chris-roberts/39/132/351
facebook.com/pages/Chris-Roberts-game-developer/
    427661267297625
twitter.com/croberts68

ASCENT MEDIA MANAGEMENT EAST

Distributor

235 Pegasus Ave.
Northvale, NJ 07647
201-767-3800 (phone)
201-767-4568 (fax)

ascentmedia.com
imdb.com/company/co0190166

Does not accept any unsolicited material. Project types include TV. Genres include fantasy, drama, and comedy.

ASF

Distributor and sales agent

121 Bloor St. East #1500
Toronto, ONTARIO M4W 3M5
Canada
416-967-1174 (phone)
416-967-0044 (fax)

corporate.inquiries@shawmedia.ca
allianceatlantis.com
imdb.com/company/co0212412

Does not accept any unsolicited material. Genres include comedy.

ASH & D CO.

Production company

2-1-1411
Udagawacho
Shibuya, Tokyo 150-0042
Japan
03-5456-8130 (phone)
03-5456-8132 (fax)

ash-d@aioros.ocn.ne.jp
ash-d.info
imdb.com/company/co0315569

Does not accept any unsolicited material. Project types include feature films. Genres include drama.

Ryôta Ohtake
Manager
imdb.com/name/nm7408550

ASHRAK MEDIA

ashrak@yahoo.com
ashrak.com

Does not accept any unsolicited material. Project types include feature films and theater.

ASH QFH
Actor
ashrakbd@outlook.com

ASIA PRESS INTERNATIONAL
Production company and sales agent

No. 301 Otsuki Bd., 40-4, Kamiyama
Shibuya-ku
Tokyo 150-0047
Japan
+81 3 5465 6605 (phone)
+81 3 5465 6606 (fax)

info@riporipo.com
imdb.com/company/co0285279

Does not accept any unsolicited material. Project types include TV. Genres include documentary.

Takeharu Watai
Director
imdb.com/name/nm3747219

AS IS PRODUCTIONS
Production company

11661 San Vicente Blvd # 9
Los Angeles, CA 90049

imdb.com/company/co0420272

Does not accept any unsolicited material. Project types include TV and feature films. Genres include drama. Established in 1998.

Jeff Bridges
President/Actor
jeffbridges.com
imdb.com/name/nm0000313
facebook.com/JeffBridgesOfficial
twitter.com/TheJeffBridges

A. SMITH & COMPANY PRODUCTIONS
Production company

9911 W Pico Blvd
Suite 250
Los Angeles, CA 90035
310-432-4800 (phone)
310-551-3085 (fax)

4130 Cahuenga Blvd. Suite 108
Toluca Lake, CA 91602
818-432-2900 (phone)
818-432-2940 (fax)

info@asmithco.com
asmithco.com
imdb.com/company/co0095150
linkedin.com/company/a--smith-&-company
facebook.com/ASmithCoProductions

Accepts query letters from unproduced, unrepresented writers via email.

Arthur Smith
CEO
imdb.com/name/nm0807368
linkedin.com/pub/arthur-smith/B/A76/91B

Christmas Rini
Senior Vice President (Development)
imdb.com/name/nm2859471

A SQUARED ENTERTAINMENT (A2)
Production company

9401 Wilshire Blvd. #608
Beverly Hills, CA 90212
310-273-4442 (phone)
310-273-4202 (fax)

info@a2entertain.com
imdb.com/company/co0375311

Does not accept any unsolicited material. Genres include animation and family.

ASSYU JAPAN CO.
Production company

2-6-1-39F
Nishi Shinjuku
Shinjuku, Tokyo 163-0239
Japan
03-5339-5013 (phone)
03-5339-5014 (fax)

mail@assyu.co.jp
imdb.com/company/co0324723

Does not accept any unsolicited material. Project types include TV. Genres include drama.

ASTAIRE
Distributor

42-3-4F
Udagawacho
Shibuya, Tokyo 150-0042
Japan
03-5459-1173 (phone)
03-5459-1174 (fax)

info@astaire.co.jp
imdb.com/company/co0225375

Does not accept any unsolicited material. Project types include feature films and TV. Genres include fantasy, action, and comedy.

Hiroyasu Hirano
President (Executive)
imdb.com/name/nm2868060

A SUPERIOR BREED OF WANNABEES
Production company

6118 Knollview Dr
Spring, TX 77389
832-533-6366

laragwinn@hotmail.com
heathersilvio.com
imdb.com/company/co0210103
facebook.com/silvio.heather
twitter.com/HeatherSilvio

Does not accept any unsolicited material. Project types include short films.

ASYLUM ENTERTAINMENT
Production company

15503 Ventura Blvd.
Suite 240
Encino, CA 91436
310-696-4600

info@asylument.com
asylument.com
imdb.com/company/co0017595
facebook.com/AsylumEnt
twitter.com/AsylumEnt

Accepts scripts from unproduced, unrepresented writers. Project types include TV. Genres include non-fiction, horror, fantasy, crime, action, drama, science fiction, and thriller.

A-TEAM
Production company

3-6-9-B1
Moto Azabu
Minato, Tokyo 106-0046
Japan
03-3404-3370 (phone)
03-3404-3460 (fax)

info@ateam-japan.com
ateam-japan.com
imdb.com/company/co0313438

Does not accept any unsolicited material. Project types include short films, feature films, and TV. Genres include action.

Yû Kojima
Manager
imdb.com/name/nm6172325

AT ENTERTAINMENT
Distributor

Takeda, # 2, Bldg.2-3-3
Ebisunishi Shibuya-ku
Tokyo 150-0021
Japan
+81 3 3476 2550 (phone)
+81 3 3476 2551 (fax)

info@at-e.co.jp
at-e.co.jp

imdb.com/company/co0074908

Does not accept any unsolicited material. Project types include TV. Genres include drama.

Yoshiyasu Ikezaki
Executive Vice President - COO (Executive)
imdb.com/name/nm1963049

ATHÉNÉÉ FRANÇAIS CULTURE CENTRE
Distributor

2-11-4F
Kanda Surugadai
Chiyoda, Tokyo 101-0062
Japan
03-3291-4339

infor@athenee.net
athenee.net
imdb.com/company/co0336150
twitter.com/afcc1970

Does not accept any unsolicited material. Project types include feature films. Genres include documentary.

A THING OR TWO PRODUCTIONS
Production company

Los Angeles, CA

imdb.com/company/co0476877
facebook.com/pages/A-Thing-or-Two-Productions/
    563880260365062

Does not accept any unsolicited material. Project types include feature films. Genres include drama. Established in 2014.

Benjamin McKenzie
imdb.com/name/nm1360270

Logan Marshall-Green
imdb.com/name/nm1334869

ATLANTIC SWISS PRODUCTIONS
Production company

52-54 High Holborn
Holborn
London WC1V 6RB
UK

+44 0 8706 260 250 (phone)
+44 0 8706 260 255 (fax)

mailroom@atlanticswiss.com
atlanticswiss.com
imdb.com/company/co0304644

Does not accept any unsolicited material. Genres include thriller, drama, and action.

James Gallimore
Producer
imdb.com/name/nm3919063

ATLANTIC VIDEO
Production company and distributor

650 Massachusetts Ave
Washington, DC 20001
202-408-0900

salesdc@atlanticvideo.com
theatlantic.com/video
imdb.com/company/co0160741

Does not accept any unsolicited material. Genres include science fiction and comedy.

ATLAS 2 PRODUCTIONS
Production company

56 N. Haddon Ave
3rd Floor
Haddonfield, NJ 08033
310-826-5000

info@atlasshruggedmovie.com
imdb.com/company/co0431646

Does not accept any unsolicited material. Project types include TV and feature films. Genres include science fiction.

ATLAS DISTRIBUTION COMPANY
Distributor

56 N Haddon Ave
3rd Fl
Haddonfield, NJ 08033
856-359-4258

HKaslow@atlasdistribution.com
atlasdistribution.com

imdb.com/company/co0390285
twitter.com/atlasmovies

Does not accept any unsolicited material. Genres include comedy, science fiction, and drama.

ATLAS ENTERTAINMENT (PRODUCTION BRANCH OF MOSAIC)
Production company

9200 W Sunset Blvd, 10th Floor
Los Angeles, CA 90069
310-786-4900

imdb.com/company/co0028338

Does not accept any unsolicited material. Project types include feature films and TV.

Andy Horwitz
Producer
imdb.com/name/nm2191045

Alex Gartner
Producer
imdb.com/name/nm0308672
linkedin.com/pub/alex-gartner/1a/695/69a

Jake Kurily
Vice-President
imdb.com/name/nm2464228
linkedin.com/pub/jake-kurily/1/785/26b

ATLAS MEDIA CORPORATION
Production company

242 W 36th St
New York, NY, 10018
212-714-0222 (phone)
212-714-0240 (fax)

info@atlasmediacorp.com
atlasmedia.tv
imdb.com/company/co0280783
facebook.com/atlasinteractiveagency
twitter.com/atlasinteract

Does not accept any unsolicited material. Genres include non-fiction.

Glen Freyer
Senior Vice President (Development)
imdb.com/name/nm0294662
linkedin.com/pub/glen-freyer/4/18b/62b

Andrew Jacobs
Director of Development
linkedin.com/in/andrewejacobs
facebook.com/manofstats

ATL-NYC PRODUCTIONS
Production company and distributor

1801 Peachtree St NE
Suite 155
Atlanta, GA 30309
800-401-1533

info@atl-nyc.com
imdb.com/company/co0347202

Does not accept any unsolicited material.

ATMOSPHERE ENTERTAINMENT MM, LLC
Production company

844 Seward St.
Los Angeles, CA 90038
310-270-4262

imdb.com/company/co0014103

Accepts scripts from produced or represented writers. Genres include fantasy, thriller, and horror. Established in 2003.

David Hopwood
Senior Vice President (Production & Development)
imdb.com/name/nm2055027

ATOMIC ENTERTAINMENT

Los Angeles, CA
323-739-3999

Mississippi
800-859-0450

info@atomicent.com
atomicent.com

Does not accept any unsolicited material. Project types include feature films. Genres include drama. Established in 2014.

Adam Rosenfelt
Principal
imdb.com/name/nm0742580

Maureen Meulen
Principal
imdb.com/name/nm1371473

ATO PICTURES
Production company

44 Wall St, 23rd Floor
New York, NY 10005
646-292-7500 (phone)
646-292-7550 (fax)

jd@atopictures.com
atopictures.com
imdb.com/company/co0075964
linkedin.com/company/ato-pictures-llc

Does not accept any unsolicited material. Project types include feature films. Genres include comedy.

A TRUE STORY PRODUCTION
Production company

P. O. Box 1899
Winter Park, FL 32790
310-739-1406

sheri@saytruefilms.com
saytruefilms.com
imdb.com/company/co0339353
facebook.com/ATrueStoryProduction
twitter.com/SayTrueFilms

Does not accept any unsolicited material. Genres include documentary.

ATTABOY FILMS
Production company

8335 Sunset Blvd., Suite 102
Los Angeles, CA 90069
323-337-9037

info@attaboyfilms.com
imdb.com/company/co0186937

Does not accept any unsolicited material. Project types include TV and feature films. Genres include drama and comedy.

AT THE HELM PRODUCTIONS
Production company and distributor

15 Iceboat Terrace
Toronto, ON M5V4A5
Canada

lisa.munsterhjelm@utoronto.ca
atthehelmproductions.com
imdb.com/company/co0373520

Does not accept any unsolicited material. Project types include feature films. Genres include science fiction, drama, and documentary.

ATTICUS ENTERTAINMENT
Production company

7025 Santa Monica Blvd.
Hollywood, CA 90038
310-550-2720

imdb.com/company/co0368174

Does not accept any unsolicited material. Project types include feature films and TV.

AUDAX FILMS

100 Wilshire Blvd, Suite 650
Santa Monica, CA 90401
310-870-3771

info@audaxfilms.com
audaxfilms.com
facebook.com/AudaxFilms
twitter.com/audaxfilms

Does not accept any unsolicited material. Project types include feature films. Genres include drama.

AU FILMS
Production company

2319 Fargo St
Los Angeles, CA 90039
213-926-9098

david@aufilms.com

aufilms.com

Does not accept any unsolicited material. Project types include feature films. Genres include drama. Established in 2014.

David Au
Producer
david@aufilms.com
imdb.com/name/nm1614404

AUSTIN FILM SOCIETY
Production company

1901 E 51st St
Austin, TX 78723
512-322-0145

afs@austinfilm.org
austinfilm.org
www/.imdb.com/company/co0139303
facebook.com/austinfilm
twitter.com/afs1985

Does not accept any unsolicited material. Genres include action, thriller, comedy, and science fiction.

AUTOMATIC PICTURES
Production company

5225 Wilshire Blvd
Suite 525
Los Angeles, CA 90036
323-935-1800 (phone)
323-935-8040 (fax)

automaticstudio@mail.com
imdb.com/company/co0227149
linkedin.com/company/automatic-pictures

Accepts query letters from unproduced, unrepresented writers via email. Project types include video games. Genres include fantasy.

Frank Beddor
imdb.com/name/nm0065980
linkedin.com/pub/frank-beddor/6/191/4ba
facebook.com/goaskalyss
Assistant: Bo Liebman

Nate Barlow
nate@automaticpictures.net
imdb.com/name/nm0055269
linkedin.com/in/natebarlow
facebook.com/natebarlowfans

Liz Cavalier
Creative Executive
imdb.com/name/nm2248983
linkedin.com/pub/liz-cavalier/59/b66/b27

AUTONOMOUS FILMS
Production company

10203 Santa Monica Blvd. Suite 300A
Los Angeles, CA 90067
310-270-4260

afterdarkfilms.com
imdb.com/company/co0217659
facebook.com/afterdarkfilms
twitter.com/afterdarkfilms

Does not accept any unsolicited material. Project types include feature films. Genres include comedy and action.

AV1 PRODUCTIONS
Production company

2300 Central Parkway
Suite H
Houston, TX 77092
713-680-0554

amirv@av1productions.com
av1productions.com
imdb.com/company/co0175512

Does not accept any unsolicited material. Genres include thriller, drama, horror, and science fiction.

AVALON PICTURES
Production company

imdb.com/company/co0036419

Does not accept any unsolicited material. Project types include feature films. Genres include drama. Established in 2009.

AVALON TELEVISION

Production company and distributor

9171 Wilshire Blvd, Suite 320
Beverly Hills, CA 90210
310-424-1700

31 W 26th St, 6th Floor
New York, NY 10010
212-400-4822

info@avalonuk.com
avalontelevision.com
imdb.com/company/co0175958

Does not accept any unsolicited material. Project types include feature films and TV. Genres include documentary and comedy. Established in 2005.

AVENUE PICTURES PRODUCTIONS

Production company and distributor

1112 Montana Ave.
Suite 710
Santa Monica, CA 90403
310-292-7400

imdb.com/company/co0091390

Does not accept any unsolicited material. Project types include feature films. Genres include drama, comedy, and crime.

AVER MEDIA

Financing company

55 Bloor St W
2nd Fl
Toronto, ON M4W 3N5
Canada
416-643-4224

imdb.com/company/co0243211

Does not accept any unsolicited material. Project types include commercials. Genres include thriller, action, and drama.

AVERSANO FILMS

Production company

2011 Benedict Canyon
Beverly Hills , CA 90210
310-246-2392

info@aversanofilms.com
aversanofilms.com
imdb.com/company/co0258142

Does not accept any unsolicited material. Project types include TV and feature films. Genres include science fiction, action, drama, and comedy.

AVEX MANAGEMENT

Production company

3-1-30-7F
Minami Aoyama
Minato, Tokyo 107-0062
Japan
03-5772-4302 (phone)
03-5413-8792 (fax)

sports_casting@ax.avex.co.jp
avex-management.jp
imdb.com/company/co0281161

Does not accept any unsolicited material. Project types include TV. Genres include drama.

Ryuhei Chiba
Co-CEO (Executive)
imdb.com/name/nm2273845

AVIATION CINEMAS INC.

Production company

231 W Jefferson Blvd.
Oak Cliff, TX 75208
214-948-1546

info@aviationcinemas.com
aviationcinemas.com
imdb.com/company/co0412596
linkedin.com/company/aviation-cinemas-inc-
facebook.com/TexTheatre
twitter.com/texastheatre

Does not accept any unsolicited material. Project types include feature films and short films. Genres include documentary and thriller. Established in 2010.

AVISPA FILMS

Production company

1601 Miriam Ave
Suite 218
Austin, TX 78702

imdb.com/company/co0476447

Does not accept any unsolicited material. Genres include drama, crime, and comedy.

AV PICTURES
Sales agent

+44207-317-0140 (phone)
+44207-224-5149 (fax)

info@avpictures.co.uk
avpictures.co.uk
imdb.com/company/co0158518

Does not accept any unsolicited material. Project types include feature films and TV. Genres include horror.

Angad Paul
Producer
imdb.com/name/nm0666756

AWAAZ PRODUCTIONS
Production company

1850 Houret Court
Mipitas, CA 95035
408-823-4811 (phone)
408-461-7944 (fax)

awaazproduction.com
imdb.com/company/co0441851
facebook.com/Awaaz-Productions-168677646658077
twitter.com/AwaazProduction

Does not accept any unsolicited material. Project types include feature films. Genres include horror. Established in 2010.

AWARE FILMS
Production company

PO Box 246
Grapevine, TX 76051

courtney@awarefilms.com
awarefilms.com
imdb.com/company/co0358273
facebook.com/awarefilms

twitter.com/_awarefilms

Does not accept any unsolicited material. Project types include short films. Genres include drama.

AWESOMENESSTV
Production company

11821 Mississippi Ave, Los Angeles, CA, United States, 90025
310-601-1960 (phone)
310-601-1961 (fax)

info@awesomenesstv.com
dashboard.awesomenesstv.com
imdb.com/company/co0553901

Does not accept any unsolicited material. Project types include TV and feature films. Genres include family and drama.

AWESOMETOWN ENTERTAINMENT
Production company

157 Princess St. 3rd Flr
Toronto, ON M5A 4M4
Canada
416-603-2000

info@awesometownent.ca
awesometownent.ca
imdb.com/company/co0474561
linkedin.com/company/awesometown-entertainment
facebook.com/awesometownent
twitter.com/awesometownTO

Does not accept any unsolicited material. Genres include animation.

AWOUNDEDKNEE
Production company

48 W 25th St, 9th Floor
New York, NY 10010
212-255-4440 (phone)
212-255-4494 (fax)

info@awkfilms.com
awkfilms.com

Does not accept any unsolicited material. Genres include crime.

AXIOM FILMS
Production company

87 Notting Hill Gate
London W11 3JZ
UK
+44 20 7243 3111 (phone)
+44 20 7243 3152 (fax)

mail@axiomfilms.co.uk
axiomfilms.co.uk
imdb.com/company/co0086527
twitter.com/axiomfilmsindie

Does not accept any unsolicited material. Project types include feature films. Genres include drama.

Douglas Cummins
Producer
imdb.com/name/nm0191995

AXN
Production company and distributor

1-11-1 Kaigan, Takeshiba Nosutawa Nyupia
Minato-Ku
Tokyo 105-0022
Japan
03-5402-1760

contact@axn.co.jp
axn.co.jp
imdb.com/company/co0186281
facebook.com/axnjapan
twitter.com/AXNJapan

Does not accept any unsolicited material. Project types include feature films and TV. Genres include crime and drama.

AXON ENTERTAINMENT
Production company

2-22-4-407
Minami-Aoyama, Minato-Ku
Tokyo 107-0062
Japan
81-3-3479-0616 (phone)
81-3-3479-0617 (fax)

info@axonentertainment.co.jp
imdb.com/company/co0256410

Does not accept any unsolicited material. Project types include TV. Genres include drama.

Keisuke Asada
President (Manager)
imdb.com/name/nm2048893

AYA PRO
Production company and distributor

#4-5F, 5-17-12 Tsurumake Setagaya-Ku
Tokyo 154 0016
Japan
+81 3 3428 7874 (phone)
+81 3 3428 7874 (fax)

ayapro@pluto.dti.ne.up
imdb.com/company/co0173740

Does not accept any unsolicited material. Project types include feature films, TV, and short films. Genres include horror.

Yoko Kawahara
Director (Executive)
imdb.com/name/nm2588564

AZRO MEDIA
Production company

5510 W. LaSalle
Tampa, FL 33607
650-701-0220

steve@anderson.org
imdb.com/company/co0523406

Does not accept any unsolicited material. Genres include drama.

BABY COW PRODUCTIONS
Production company and distributor

5-6 Portland Mews,
London W1F 8JG
020-369-65200

info@babycow.co.uk
babycow.co.uk
imdb.com/company/co0104255
facebook.com/BabyCowProductions
twitter.com/BabyCowLtd

Does not accept any unsolicited material. Project types include feature films. Genres include drama and comedy.

BACH ENTERPRISES
Production company

10235 W. Sample Rd
Suite 205
Coral Springs, FL 33065
954-806-4077

andrewbachelor1@gmail.com
imdb.com/company/co0384646
facebook.com/KingBach
twitter.com/KingBach

Does not accept any unsolicited material. Project types include short films and TV. Genres include comedy.

BACK LOT PICTURES
Production company

1351 N. Genesee Ave.
Los Angeles, CA 90046
323-876-1057

imdb.com/company/co0143583

Does not accept any unsolicited material. Project types include feature films. Genres include drama, horror, and comedy.

Glenn Williamson
Owner/Producer
imdb.com/name/nm0932037

Brian Schornak
VP of Production
imdb.com/name/nm1935985

BACK ROADS ENTERTAINMENT
Production company

7 Penn Plaza, Suite 1105
New York, NY 10001

contact@backroadsentertainment.com
backroadsentertainment.com
imdb.com/company/co0464900
linkedin.com/company/back-roads-entertainment
twitter.com/backroadsent

Does not accept any unsolicited material. Project types include TV. Genres include comedy.

Zach Messner
Development Associate
imdb.com/name/nm4130410

Charles Taylor Goubeaud
Producer
imdb.com/name/nm3982977

Colby Gaines
Founder
imdb.com/name/nm1454469

BAD BOY WORLDWIDE ENTERTAINMENT
Production company

1440 Broadway, 30th Floor
New York, NY 10036
212-381-1540 (phone)
212-381-1599 (fax)

badboyonline.com
imdb.com/company/co0125541
linkedin.com/company/bad-boy-entertainment
facebook.com/bbweg

Does not accept any unsolicited material. Project types include feature films. Genres include thriller, action, comedy, and crime.

Anthony Maddox
VP
imdb.com/name/nm1474016

Sean Combs
Chairman/Producer/Actor
imdb.com/name/nm0004835

BAD HAT HARRY PRODUCTIONS
Production company

10201 W Pico Blvd
Building 50
Los Angeles, CA 90064
310-369-2260

imdb.com/company/co0057712

Accepts scripts from produced or represented writers. Project types include TV. Genres include fantasy, drama, thriller, science fiction, myth, and action.

Bryan Singer
CEO
imdb.com/name/nm0001741
twitter.com/BryanSinger

Mark Berliner
Vice President (Development)
imdb.com/name/nm2249392

BAD ROBOT
Production company

1221 Olympic Blvd
Santa Monica, CA 90404
310-664-3456 (phone)
310-664-3457 (fax)

badrobot.com
imdb.com/company/co0021593
facebook.com/Bad-Robot-
    Productions-214632218556454
twitter.com/bad_robot

Does not accept any unsolicited material. Project types include feature films and TV. Genres include fantasy, drama, science fiction, and action. Established in 2001.

Kevin Jarzynski
Executive (Film)
imdb.com/name/nm1704653
Assistant: Veronica Baker

Bryan Burk
Partner (Vice President)
imdb.com/name/nm1333357
Assistant: Max Taylor

David Baronoff
Executive (New Media, Film, & Television)
imdb.com/name/nm2343623

Kathy Lingg
Head (Television)
imdb.com/name/nm2489727
Assistant: Matthew Owens

Lindsey Paulson Weber
Head (Film)
imdb.com/name/nm1439829
Assistant: Corrine Aquino

Athena Wickham
Executive (Television)
imdb.com/name/nm2204043
Assistant: Casey Haver

J.J. Abrams
CEO
imdb.com/name/nm0009190

BAGDASARIAN PRODUCTIONS
Production company

1192 C. Mountain Dr
Montecito, CA 93108
805-969-3349 (phone)
805-969-7466 (fax)

info@chipmunks.com
chipmunks.com
imdb.com/company/co0026227
facebook.com/AlvinAndTheChipmunks
twitter.com/officialalvinnn

Does not accept any unsolicited material. Project types include feature films. Genres include comedy and family.

Ross Bagdasarian Jr.
Producer
imdb.com/name/nm0046559

Janice Karman
Producer
imdb.com/name/nm0439739

BAIN FILMS, BARNET
Production company

4250 Wilshire Blvd.
Los Angeles, CA 90010
323-656-8829

imdb.com/company/co0123754
facebook.com/pages/Barnet-Bain-Films/
    548666401854501

Does not accept any unsolicited material. Project types include feature films. Genres include drama and fantasy.

Barnet Bain
Producer
barnetbain.com
imdb.com/name/nm0047685
linkedin.com/pub/barnet-bain/1/112/441
facebook.com/barnet.bain
twitter.com/BarnetBain

BAKER ENTERTAINMENT INC, DAVID E.
Production company

146 N San Fernando Blvd. Suite 206
Burbank, CA 91502
818-843-8700

info@davidebaker.com
davidebaker.com
imdb.com/company/co0129945
linkedin.com/company/david-e-baker-entertainment-inc-

Accepts query letters from unproduced, unrepresented writers via email. Project types include TV and feature films. Genres include myth, animation, comedy, reality, family, action, non-fiction, crime, detective, documentary, drama, fantasy, horror, period, sociocultural, romance, science fiction, and thriller.

David E. Baker
Executive Producer
imdb.com/name/nm0048380

BALAGAN PRODUCTIONS
Production company

Suite 124
100 Hatton Garden
London EC1N 8NX
UK
+44203-590-0155

info@balagan.biz
balagan.biz
imdb.com/company/co0104704
facebook.com/BalaganFilmProductions
twitter.com/Balagan_Films

Does not accept any unsolicited material. Project types include feature films. Genres include action and thriller.

Jonathan Weissler
Producer
imdb.com/name/nm0919277

BALDWIN ENTERTAINMENT GROUP, LTD.
Production company

3000 W Olympic Blvd
Suite 2510
Santa Monica, CA
310-243-6634

225 Parkway North
Waterford, CT 06385
806-326-2870

info@baldwinent.com
imdb.com/company/co0145519

Does not accept any unsolicited material. Project types include feature films. Genres include drama, non-fiction, comedy, action, and romance. Established in 2009.

Howard Baldwin
President
310-243-6634
imdb.com/name/nm0049920

Karen Baldwin
Executive Vice President
310-243-6634
imdb.com/name/nm0049945

BALLISTIC DISTRIBUTION
Distributor

100 Wilshire Blvd
Ste 950
Santa Monica, CA 90401
213-207-6871

imdb.com/company/co0349114

Does not accept any unsolicited material. Genres include action, science fiction, crime, and horror.

BALLPARK FILM DISTRIBUTORS

Distributor

24 Hanover Square
London W1S 1JD
UK
077-707-76245

contact@ballparkfilmdistributors.com (script
submissions)
ballparkgb@aol.com (general)
ballparkfilmdistributors.com
imdb.com/company/co0350668
facebook.com/ballparkfilms

Does not accept any unsolicited material. Project types
include TV. Genres include comedy and drama.

Mark Thomas
Producer
imdb.com/name/nm1623493

BALLYHOO, INC.

Production company and studio

6738 Wedgewood Place
Los Angeles, CA 90068
323-874-3396

imdb.com/company/co0094858

Accepts scripts from unproduced, unrepresented
writers. Project types include feature films. Genres
include comedy and action.

Michael Besman
Producer
323-874-3396
imdb.com/name/nm0078698
linkedin.com/pub/michael-besman/4/b9/455

BALTIMORE PICTURES

Production company

8306 Wilshire Blvd
PMB 1012
Beverly Hills, CA 90211
310-234-8988

levinson.com/index_bsc.htm
imdb.com/company/co0038108

Does not accept any unsolicited material. Project types
include feature films. Genres include romance, thriller,
crime, comedy, drama, and science fiction.

Barry Levinson
Principal
imdb.com/name/nm0001469
facebook.com/pages/Barry-Levinson/50880796633

Jason Sosnoff
Director of Development
imdb.com/name/nm0815369

BAMBOO FOREST GROUP LLC

csavan@hotmail.com
imdb.com/name/nm6554230

Does not accept any unsolicited material. Project types
include feature films.

Cheryl Savan
Producer
csavan@hotmail.com

BAM ENTERTAINMENT

Distributor

Suite 608 The Chandlery
50 Westminister Bridge Rd
London SE1 7QY
UK
+44843-289-2785 (phone)
+44844-357-2155 (fax)

info@bamentertainment.co.uk
bamentertainment.co.uk
imdb.com/company/co0434762

Does not accept any unsolicited material. Project types
include video games. Genres include crime, family,
and animation.

Sam Brown
Producer
imdb.com/name/nm5757282

BANDAI ENTERTAINMENT

Production company

5551 Katella Ave
Cypress , CA 90630
1-877-77-ANIME

bandai-ent.com
imdb.com/company/co0040281

Does not accept any unsolicited material.

BANDITO BROTHERS
Production company and studio

3249 S. La Cienega Blvd,
Los Angeles, CA 90016
310-559-5404 (phone)
310-559-5230 (fax)

Hangar 102
14850 NW 44th Court
Miami, FL 33054

jay@banditobrothers.com
imdb.com/company/co0195602
linkedin.com/company/bandito-brothers
facebook.com/BanditoBrothers
twitter.com/BanditoBrothers

Does not accept any unsolicited material. Project types
include feature films. Genres include science fiction,
fantasy, drama, comedy, action, and thriller.

Max Leitman
COO
imdb.com/name/nm2649648

Suzanne Hargrove
Managing Director
imdb.com/name/nm2597628

Jacob Rosenberg
CTO
imdb.com/name/nm0742230

Mike McCoy
CEO
imdb.com/name/nm0566788

Scott Waugh
Founder
imdb.com/name/nm0915304

BARBARA LIEBERMAN PRODUCTIONS
Production company

10510 Culver Blvd.
Culver City, CA 90232
310-204-0404

imdb.com/company/co0021842
linkedin.com/in/barbara-lieberman-478b7a37

Does not accept any unsolicited material. Project types
include TV. Genres include comedy and drama.

Barbara Lieberman
Executive Producer
imdb.com/name/nm0509365

Devlin McCluskey
Development
imdb.com/name/nm3052185

BARBARIAN FILM FUND
Production company

1801 Century Park East, 25th Floor
Los Angeles, CA 90067
310-553-2300 (phone)
310-553-2345 (fax)

imdb.com/company/co0228488

Does not accept any unsolicited material. Project types
include feature films. Genres include comedy and
thriller.

Ron Hartenbaum
Producer
imdb.com/name/nm2735439

Aaron Kaufman
Principal, Producer
imdb.com/name/nm2721926

Doug Kuber
Principal, Producer
imdb.com/name/nm2739787

BARBARIAN FILMS, LLC
Production company

110 Greene St, Suite 402, New York City , NY,
United States, 10012
212-561-5294 (phone)
646-224-8270 (fax)

info@wearebarbarians.com
wearebarbarians.com

imdb.com/company/co0228488

Does not accept any unsolicited material. Project types include feature films. Genres include family, thriller, and action.

BARNSTORM FILMS
Production company

73 Market St
Venice, CA 90291
310-396-5937 (phone)
310-450-4988 (fax)

tbtb@comcast.net
barnstormfilms.com
imdb.com/company/co0044065

Accepts query letters from unproduced, unrepresented writers.

Tony Bill
Producer
tbtb@comcast.net
imdb.com/name/nm0082300

BARNYARDGROUP ENTERTAINMENT
Production company

175 Atlantic St - 3rd Floor
Stamford, CT 06901
646-532-1512

15 Central Park West, Suite G104
New York, NY 10023

thebarnyardgroup.com
linkedin.com/company/thebarnyardgroup
facebook.com/TheBarnYardGroup
twitter.com/BarnyardGroup

Does not accept any unsolicited material.

Elaine Rogers
Co-Founder/Co-CEO/Producer
imdb.com/name/nm1199976

BARRY FILMS
Production company

4081 Redwood Ave
Los Angeles, CA 90066
310-871-3392

mail@barryfilms.com
barryfilms.com
imdb.com/company/co0075789

Does not accept any unsolicited material. Project types include feature films. Genres include detective, horror, drama, animation, romance, fantasy, and action.

Benito Mueller
Principal
benito@barryfilms.com
imdb.com/name/nm1762339

BARRY MENDEL PRODUCTIONS
Production company

11788 W. Pico Blvd. 3rd Floor
Los Angeles, CA 90064
310-943-4473

barrycmendel@gmail.com.
barrymendel.com/Home.html
imdb.com/company/co0018092

Does not accept any unsolicited material. Project types include feature films. Genres include drama, comedy, and horror.

Barry Mendel
Producer
imdb.com/name/nm0578814

BARWOOD FILMS
Production company

5670 Wilshire Blvd., Suite 2400
Los Angeles, CA 90036
323-653-1555 (phone)
323-653-1593 (fax)

imdb.com/company/co0073376
linkedin.com/company/barwood-films
facebook.com/barbrastreisand

Does not accept any unsolicited material. Project types include feature films. Genres include drama.

Jason Gould
President
imdb.com/name/nm0332410

Cis Corman
Chairman/Producer
imdb.com/name/nm0180015

Barbra Streisand
Actor/Director/Producer
imdb.com/name/nm0000659
facebook.com/barbrastreisand
twitter.com/BarbraStreisand

BASE PRODUCTIONS
Production company

4540 W Valerio St
Burbank, CA 91505
818-333-5700

info@baseproductions.com
baseproductions.com
imdb.com/company/co0010298
linkedin.com/company/base-productions
facebook.com/pages/BASE-Productions/
    109436385749283

Does not accept any unsolicited material. Project types
include TV.

Mickey Stern
Co-CEO (Washington, DC)
imdb.com/name/nm0827790

John Brenkus
Co-CEO
imdb.com/name/nm0107228

BASRA ENTERTAINMENT
Production company

68-444 Perez Rd, Suite O
Cathedral City, CA 92234
760-324-9855 (phone)
760-324-9035 (fax)

daniela@basraentertainment.com (script submissions)
info@basraentertainment.com (general)
basraentertainment.com
imdb.com/company/co0092056

Accepts query letters from unproduced, unrepresented
writers via email. Established in 2002.

Daniela Ryan
Producer
daniela@basraentertainment.com
imdb.com/name/nm0752491
linkedin.com/pub/daniela-ryan/10/7b9/815

Tony Shawkat
President
tony@basraentertainment.com
imdb.com/name/nm0790059
linkedin.com/pub/abdul-tony-shawkat/27/7a/a2b

Dina Burke
Producer
dina@basraentertainment.com
imdb.com/name/nm1318482

BASS FILMS, EDWARD
Production company

511 Stonewood Dr
Beverly Hills, CA 90210

358 Broadway, 3A
New York, NY 10013
212-937-5999 (phone)
310-601-7628 (fax)

info@edwardbassfilms.com
edwardbassfilms.com
facebook.com/pages/Edward-Bass-Films/
    163000960933
twitter.com/EdwardBassFilm

Does not accept any unsolicited material. Project types
include feature films. Genres include romance and
comedy.

Edward Bass
Producer/Writer/Financier
linkedin.com/in/edwardbass1

BAT BRIDGE ENTERTAINMENT
Production company

504 W 7th St
Austin, TX 78701
512-400-0570

imdb.com/company/co0462903
facebook.com/BatBridge

Does not accept any unsolicited material. Genres include documentary.

BATTLE GROUND
Production company

1948 N Van Ness Ave
Los Angeles, CA 90068
323-962-9913 (phone)
323-962-9903 (fax)

imdb.com/company/co0295113

Does not accept any unsolicited material. Project types include feature films. Genres include drama, romance, and comedy. Established in 2007.

David Mackay
Producer/Director
imdb.com/name/nm0533145

Mark Witsken
Producer
imdb.com/name/nm0936837

BATTLEPLAN PRODUCTIONS
Production company

1041 N. Formosa Ave.
Santa Monica West Bldg. #222
West Hollywood, CA 90046
323-850-2940

imdb.com/company/co0089304

Does not accept any unsolicited material. Project types include feature films and TV. Genres include action, drama, crime, horror, and thriller. Established in 1999.

Marc Frydman
Partner/Producer
imdb.com/name/nm0296827

Rod Lurie
Partner/Writer/Director
imdb.com/name/nm0527109

BAUER MARTINEZ STUDIOS
Production company

601 Cleveland St, Suite 501
Clearwater, FL 33755

727-210-1408 (phone)
727-210-1470 (fax)

sales@bauermartinez.com
bauermartinez.com
imdb.com/company/co0025891
linkedin.com/company/bauer-martinez-studios

Accepts query letters from unproduced, unrepresented writers.

Philippe Martinez
CEO
imdb.com/name/nm0553662
linkedin.com/pub/philippe-martinez/2b/71a/b11

BAUMANT ENTERTAINMENT
Production company

14 Greenway Plaza 4L
Houston, TX 77046

imdb.com/company/co0326941

Does not accept any unsolicited material. Genres include drama and horror.

BAUMGARTEN MANAGEMENT AND PRODUCTIONS
Production company

9595 Wilshire Blvd., Suite 1000
Beverly Hills, CA 90212
310-445-1601

craigbaumgarten@yahoo.com
imdb.com/company/co0191075

Does not accept any unsolicited material. Project types include short films and feature films. Genres include documentary, action, drama, thriller, science fiction, crime, and horror. Established in 2000.

Craig Baumgarten
Producer/Manager
imdb.com/name/nm0062332

BAY FILMS
Production company

631 Colorado Ave
Santa Monica, CA 90401

310-319-6565 (phone)
310-319-6570 (fax)

imdb.com/company/co0049752

Does not accept any unsolicited material. Project types include feature films. Genres include science fiction, drama, thriller, fantasy, comedy, and action.

Matthew Cohan
Vice President
imdb.com/name/nm0169134
linkedin.com/in/matthewcohan

Michael Bay
CEO
michaelbay.com
imdb.com/name/nm0000881
linkedin.com/company/bay-films
facebook.com/MichaelBayMovies
Assistant: Talley Singer

BAYONNE ENTERTAINMENT
Production company

8560 W Sunset Blvd
9th Floor
West Hollywood, CA 90069
310-777-1940

assistant@bayonne-ent.com
imdb.com/company/co0070871
facebook.com/pages/Bayonne-Entertainment/
   179679728756461

Accepts query letters from produced or represented writers. Project types include TV. Genres include comedy, science fiction, drama, and fantasy.

Rob Lee
President
imdb.com/name/nm0498098
linkedin.com/pub/rob-lee/14/46B/295

BAZELEVS PRODUCTIONS
Production company

9229 Sunset Bvld.
Suite 820
West Hollywood, CA 90069
424-288-4822

Pudovkina St
6/1
Moscow, Russia, 119285
Moscow 119285
Russia
+7 495-223-04-00

film@bazelevs.ru
bazelevs.ru
imdb.com/company/co0042742
linkedin.com/company/bazelevs-group

Does not accept any unsolicited material. Project types include feature films.

Alan Khamoui
Development Executive
imdb.com/name/nm3081242
linkedin.com/pub/alan-khamoui/44/12/641

Timur Bekmambetov
Founder
+7 495-223-04-00
film@bazelevs.ru
imdb.com/name/nm0067457
linkedin.com/pub/timur-bekmambetov/4/9b1/863

BBC FILMS
Production company

Zone A, 7th Floor BBC Broadcasting House Portland Place
London, United Kingdom, W1A 1AA
011-440-2036144445

bbc.co.uk/bbcfilms
imdb.com/company/co0103694
twitter.com/BBCFilms

Accepts scripts from unproduced, unrepresented writers. Project types include feature films and TV. Genres include action, thriller, science fiction, romance, myth, non-fiction, horror, fantasy, drama, detective, crime, and comedy.

Nichola Martin
Development Executive
imdb.com/name/nm1660581

Beth Pattinson
Development Executive
imdb.com/name/nm3179273

BBCG FILMS

Production company

466 W. Montgomery Ave
Haverford, PA 19041

tamtiehel@aol.com
imdb.com/company/co0396231

Does not accept any unsolicited material. Project types include feature films. Genres include romance and comedy. Established in 2011.

Tammy Tiehel-Stedman
Producer
imdb.com/name/nm0862843

BBC WORLDWIDE

Production company and distributor

1120 Ave of the Americas, Fifth Floor, New York, NY, United States, 10036
212-705-9300 (phone)
212-888-0576 (fax)

Dubai Media City Building Sheikh Zayed Rd Number 10 Office #309
Dubai United Arab Emirates
011-009-7143678090 (phone)
011-009-7143678077 (fax)

255 Alhambra Circle 10th Floor
Coral Gables FL 33134
305-461-6999

10351 Santa Monica Blvd. Suite 250
Los Angeles CA 90025
310-228-1001

Media Centre London 201 Wood Ln
London United Kingdom W12 7TQ
011-442-084332000 (phone)
011-442-087490538 (fax)

bbcworldwide.com
imdb.com/company/co0168805

Does not accept any unsolicited material. Project types include TV. Genres include comedy, reality, documentary, non-fiction, family, and sociocultural.

BCDF PICTURES

Production company

7 Old Pilgrims Way
Kerhonkson, NY 12446
845-834-4300 (phone)
917-591-7589 (fax)

submissions@bcdfpictures.com (script submissions)
info@bcdfpictures.com (general)
bcdfpictures.com
imdb.com/company/co0303915
linkedin.com/company/bcdf-pictures

Accepts query letters from unproduced, unrepresented writers via email. Project types include feature films. Genres include romance, drama, comedy, thriller, crime, and family.

Brice Dal Farra
Principal
imdb.com/name/nm3894454
facebook.com/brice.dalfarra

Paul Prokop
COO (Executive Producer)
imdb.com/name/nm2373782

Claude Dal Farra
Principal
imdb.com/name/nm3894387

Lauren Munsch
Producer
imdb.com/name/nm3907323

BCII

Production company

16135 Roscoe Blvd.
North Hills, CA 91343
818-333-3680 (phone)
818-487-2713 (fax)

dennis@bciitv.com
bciitv.com
imdb.com/company/co0398777
facebook.com/BCIItv

Does not accept any unsolicited material. Project types include short films and TV. Genres include reality and documentary. Established in 1997.

Bud Brutsman
CEO/Producer
imdb.com/name/nm0116782

Cynthia Whorton
Director of Operations
cynthia@bciitv.com
imdb.com/name/nm1469778

Ashley Yoder
Producer
imdb.com/name/nm1825095

Greg Glass
President
greg@bciitv.com
imdb.com/name/nm2374944

BCUT PRODUCTIONS
Production company and distributor

276 Morris Ave
Springfield, NJ 07081-1214

bcut15.prod@gmail.com
imdb.com/company/co0196890

Does not accept any unsolicited material. Project types include TV and feature films. Genres include action, comedy, drama, and thriller.

BDE ENTERTAINMENT
Production company and distributor

9903 Santa Monica Blvd, Suite 230
Beverly Hills, CA 90212
310-606-0092

imdb.com/company/co0186277

Does not accept any unsolicited material. Project types include feature films and TV. Genres include crime, reality, drama, action, and comedy. Established in 2006.

Bob Debrino
Producer
imdb.com/name/nm1754593

BEACHSIDE FILMS
Production company

625 Mildred Ave.
Venice, CA 90291
310-230-3999

info@beachsidefilms.com

beachsidefilms.com
imdb.com/company/co0421107
facebook.com/beachsidefilms
twitter.com/Beachsidefilms

Does not accept any unsolicited material. Project types include feature films and TV. Genres include romance, drama, comedy, and documentary. Established in 2013.

Alex Turtletaub
Partner/Producer
imdb.com/name/nm2801211

Michael B. Clark
Partner/Producer
imdb.com/name/nm0164290

BEACON PICTURES
Production company

2900 Olympic Blvd
2nd Floor
Santa Monica, CA 90404
Santa Monica, CA 90404
310-260-7000 (phone)
310-260-7096 (fax)

info@beaconpictures.com
beaconpictures.com
imdb.com/company/co0097246

Does not accept any unsolicited material. Project types include feature films and TV. Genres include drama, fantasy, family, action, romance, science fiction, thriller, crime, comedy, and detective. Established in 1990.

Jeffrey Crooks
Director (Special Projects)
imdb.com/name/nm3715349
linkedin.com/pub/dir/jeff/crooks

Armyan Berstein
Chairman
imdb.com/name/nm0077000

Suzann Ellis
President
sellis@beaconpictures.com
imdb.com/name/nm0255104

Joeanna Sayler
Executive (Television)
imdb.com/media/rm2798096896/nm1376366

Glenn Klekowski
Vice President (Internet Content)
imdb.com/name/nm0459192
linkedin.com/pub/glenn-klekowski/17/3b3/8b3

BEDFORD FALLS COMPANY
Production company and studio

409 Santa Monica Blvd
Penthouse Suite
Santa Monica, CA 90401
310-394-5022 (phone)
310-394-5825 (fax)

imdb.com/company/co0110946
linkedin.com/company/bedford-falls-productions
facebook.com/pages/Bedford-Falls-Productions/
    143292225689760

Does not accept any unsolicited material. Project types
include feature films. Genres include action and
drama. Established in 1985.

Troy Putney
Creative Executive
imdb.com/name/nm1586726

BEDLAM PRODUCTIONS
Production company

London
UK
+ 44 20 7287 6317

info@bedlamproductions.co.uk
bedlamproductions.co.uk
imdb.com/company/co0095111
facebook.com/Bedlam-
    Productions-127172314069095
twitter.com/Bedlam_Prods

Does not accept any unsolicited material. Project types
include feature films and TV. Genres include horror.

Gareth Unwin
Producer
imdb.com/name/nm1060902

BEDROCK STUDIOS
Production company

2115 Colorado Ave
Santa Monica, CA 90404
310-264-6480

imdb.com/company/co0299258

Does not accept any unsolicited material. Project types
include TV and feature films. Genres include drama,
science fiction, fantasy, action, family, and animation.
Established in 2011.

Spike Seldin
Head of Television
imdb.com/name/nm1749292

Cary Granat
Co-Founder/Producer
imdb.com/name/nm0334665

BEECH HILL FILMS
Production company

330 W 38th St, Suite 1004
New York, NY 10018
212-594-8095 (phone)
212-594-8118 (fax)

imdb.com/company/co0064667

Does not accept any unsolicited material. Project types
include feature films and short films. Genres include
family, comedy, drama, thriller, documentary, and
romance. Established in 1999.

Joseph Infantolino
Producer
imdb.com/name/nm0408642

Alexa Fogel
Producer
imdb.com/name/nm0283881

BEE FREE PRODUCTIONS

24139 Twin Tides Dr
Valencia, CA 91355
310-441-5151

jesse.douma+42115@gmail.com
imdb.com/company/co0274443
linkedin.com/in/jessedouma

Does not accept any unsolicited material. Project types include short films, theater, feature films, video games, TV, and commercials. Genres include myth, action, science fiction, animation, period, family, drama, reality, romance, non-fiction, horror, fantasy, comedy, documentary, crime, detective, thriller, and sociocultural. Established in 2015.

Jesse Exec Account
Development Executive
jesse.douma+42115@gmail.com

BEE HOLDER PRODUCTIONS
Production company

310-860-1005 (phone)
310-860-1007 (fax)

asst@beeholder.com
beeholder.com
imdb.com/company/co0136434

Accepts query letters from unproduced, unrepresented writers. Project types include feature films. Genres include documentary, detective, crime, comedy, thriller, and drama.

Dan Fugardi
Vice President (New Media)
dan@beeholder.com
imdb.com/name/nm2809882
linkedin.com/in/danfugardi

Steven L. Jones
Principal
imdb.com/name/nm2831867
linkedin.com/pub/steve-jones/9/1A4/ABB

John Hill
imdb.com/name/nm4787026

Michelle Jones
Executive
imdb.com/name/nm4786947

BEFORE THE DOOR PICTURES
Production company

323-644-5525

staff@beforethedoor.com
beforethedoor.com
imdb.com/company/co0271126

facebook.com/beforethedoor

Does not accept any unsolicited material. Project types include TV, feature films, and commercials. Genres include drama, thriller, action, crime, comedy, and science fiction.

Neal Dodson
Partner
imdb.com/name/nm0230306

Corey Moosa
Partner
imdb.com/name/nm0602161
facebook.com/corey.moosa

Zachary Quinto
Partner
zacharyquinto.com/before-the-door.html
imdb.com/name/nm0704270
facebook.com/zacharyquintoofficial

Sean Akers
Development Executive
imdb.com/name/nm3577109

BE GOOD PRODUCTIONS
Production company

1327 Ocean Ave., Suite L
Santa Monica, CA 90491
310-458-1600 (phone)
310-458-1665 (fax)

info@begoodinc.com
imdb.com/company/co0202350

Does not accept any unsolicited material. Project types include feature films.

BEHOLD MOTION PICTURES
Production company

Oklahoma City, OK
213-260-1670

info@beholdmotionpictures.com
beholdmotionpictures.com

Does not accept any unsolicited material. Project types include feature films. Genres include documentary and drama. Established in 2014.

BELIEVE ENTERTAINMENT
Production company and distributor

638 Carmel Dr
Lafayette, LA 70501
337-235-4383

info@believe-entertainment.com
believe-entertainment.com
imdb.com/company/co0158325
linkedin.com/company/believe-entertainment
facebook.com/pages/Believe-Entertainment/
    149232458511959

Accepts query letters from unproduced, unrepresented writers via email. Project types include TV and feature films. Genres include drama, documentary, and action. Established in 2007.

Cary Solomon
Producer
imdb.com/name/nm0813301

Chuck Konzelman
Producer
imdb.com/name/nm0465484

BELISARIUS PRODUCTIONS
Production company

1901 Ave of the Stars
Second Floor
Los Angeles, CA 90067
310-461-1361 (phone)
310-461-1362 (fax)

imdb.com/company/co0114905

Does not accept any unsolicited material. Project types include TV. Genres include thriller, crime, detective, and drama.

Chas Floyd Johnson
imdb.com/name/nm0424759

Mark Horowitz
imdb.com/name/nm0395317

Shane Brennan
Producer
imdb.com/name/nm0107402

Donald Bellisario
Executive Producer
imdb.com/name/nm0069074
linkedin.com/pub/donald-bellisario/15/99/355

John C. Kelley
imdb.com/name/nm0445931

David Bellisario
Producer
imdb.com/name/nm0069072

BELLADONNA PRODUCTIONS

164 W 25th St 9th Floor
New York, NY 10001
212-807-0108 (phone)
212-807-6263 (fax)

mail@belladonna.bz
belladonna.bz
imdb.com/company/co0003224
facebook.com/belladonnaproductions
twitter.com/belladonnaprods

Accepts scripts from unproduced, unrepresented writers via email. Project types include feature films and commercials. Genres include comedy, thriller, and non-fiction. Established in 1994.

René Bastian
Owner/Producer
212-807-0108
mail@belladonna.bz
imdb.com/name/nm0060459
linkedin.com/company/belladonna-productions
facebook.com/rene.bastian.167
twitter.com/renebastian

BELLE FILMS
Production company

17 Perrers Rd
London W6 0EY
UK
447-935-815727

alexandra@bellefilms.co.uk
bellefilms.co.uk
imdb.com/company/co0499376

Does not accept any unsolicited material. Project types include short films. Genres include romance and drama.

Alexandra Billington Billington
Producer
imdb.com/name/nm1345646

BELLTOWER PRODUCTIONS
Production company and distributor

PO Box 360161
Cleveland, OH 44136
216-251-5600

belltowerpro@gmail.com
imdb.com/company/co0024842
facebook.com/BELLTOWER-
    Productions-57893946430

Does not accept any unsolicited material. Project types include TV and feature films. Genres include science fiction, action, romance, documentary, thriller, family, and drama. Established in 1995.

BELLUM ENTERTAINMENT
Production company and distributor

2901 W. Alameda Ave Suite 500
Burbank, CA 91505
818-480-4600

bellument.com
imdb.com/company/co0361925
linkedin.com/company/bellum-entertainment
facebook.com/BellumEntertainment
twitter.com/BellumEnt

Does not accept any unsolicited material. Project types include TV. Genres include documentary, reality, period, family, and comedy. Established in 2011.

BELLWETHER PICTURES
Production company

73 Moody Rd
Tunbridge, VT 05077
802-889-3474 (phone)
802-889-3412 (fax)

john@bellwetherfilms.com
bellwetherfilms.com

imdb.com/company/co0359041
twitter.com/BellwetherPics

Accepts query letters from unproduced, unrepresented writers via email. Project types include feature films and commercials. Genres include drama, science fiction, comedy, and action. Established in 2011.

Joss Whedon
Principal
imdb.com/name/nm0923736

Kai Cole
Principal
imdb.com/name/nm4740874

BELVEDERE FILM
Production company and distributor

Colorado Springs, CO
719-310-8233

belvederefilm@yahoo.com
belvederefilm.com
imdb.com/company/co0004808

Does not accept any unsolicited material. Project types include feature films. Genres include drama, documentary, and romance.

BENAROYA PICTURES
Production company, distributor, and sales agent

8383 Wilshire Blvd, Suite 310, Beverly Hills, CA, United States, 90211
323-883-0056 (phone)
866-220-5520 (fax)

general@benaroyapics.com
imdb.com/company/co0232586

Does not accept any unsolicited material. Project types include TV and feature films. Genres include family, action, thriller, and drama.

BENAROYA PICTURES
Production company and sales agent

8383 Wilshire Blvd
Suite 310
Beverly Hills, CA 90211
323-883-0056 (phone)
866-220-5520 (fax)

general@benaroyapics.com
benaroyapictures.com
imdb.com/company/co0232586
facebook.com/Benaroya-Pictures-271526159554814
twitter.com/BenaroyaPics

Accepts query letters from unproduced, unrepresented writers via email. Project types include feature films. Genres include science fiction, drama, comedy, crime, period, horror, action, thriller, and romance. Established in 2006.

Michael Benaroya
CEO
323-883-0056
imdb.com/name/nm2918260

Joe Jenckes
Head (Production)
323-883-0056
joel@benaroyapics.com
imdb.com/name/nm3765270
linkedin.com/pub/joe-jenckes/7/bb7/5a8

Clayton Young
323-883-0056
clay@benaroyapics.com
imdb.com/name/nm4464240
facebook.com/clayton.young.5851

BENDERSPINK
Production company

8447 Wilshire Blvd.
Suite 250
Los Angeles, CA 90211
323-904-1800 (phone)
323-297-2442 (fax)

info@benderspink.com
benderspink.com
imdb.com/company/co0044439
facebook.com/pages/Benderspink/177855663106

Does not accept any unsolicited material. Project types include TV. Genres include drama, thriller, science fiction, romance, myth, non-fiction, horror, fantasy, detective, crime, comedy, and action.

J.C. Spink
Founder
imdb.com/name/nm0818940

Chris Bender
Founder
imdb.com/name/nm0818940
linkedin.com/pub/chris-bender/10/B22/569

BENGE, WENDY
Production company

15 Brooks Ave
Venice, CA 90291

wb@wbesquire.com
wbesquire.com
imdb.com/name/nm3076187

Does not accept any unsolicited material. Project types include feature films. Genres include comedy, crime, thriller, and drama.

Wendy Benge
Producer/Attorney
imdb.com/name/nm3076187
linkedin.com/in/wendybenge
facebook.com/wendy.benge.9

BENNETT ROBBINS PRODUCTIONS
Production company

116 Thompson St. #2A
New York, NY 10012
212-586-0500 (phone)
212-918-9138 (fax)

info@bennettrobbins.com
imdb.com/company/co0233377

Does not accept any unsolicited material. Project types include short films and feature films. Genres include thriller, drama, comedy, romance, crime, documentary, and horror. Established in 2009.

Lawrence Robbins
imdb.com/name/nm2797178

BENTO BOX ENTERTAINMENT
Production company

2600 W Magnolia Blvd.
Burbank, CA 91505
818-333-7700

info@bentoboxent.com

bentoboxent.com
imdb.com/company/co0239674
linkedin.com/company/bento-box-entertainment-llc
facebook.com/bentoboxent
twitter.com/BentoBoxEnt

Does not accept any unsolicited material. Project types include short films. Genres include family and comedy.

Mark McJimsey
Principal/Producer
imdb.com/name/nm0570877

Joel Kuwahara
Principal/Producer
imdb.com/name/nm0476669

Scott Greenberg
Principal/Producer
imdb.com/name/nm2092115

BERKELEY FILMS
Production company

25 Withrow Ave
Toronto, ON M4K 1C8
Canada
416-518-3785

jonathan@berkeleyfilms.com
berkeleyfilms.com
imdb.com/company/co0110459
facebook.com/BerkeleyFilms
twitter.com/Berkeley_Films

Does not accept any unsolicited material. Project types include TV and short films. Genres include documentary and comedy.

Jonathan Hayes
Director
imdb.com/name/nm1419056

BERK/LANE ENTERTAINMENT
Production company

9595 Wilshire Blvd, Suitee 900
Beverly Hills, CA 90212
310-300-8410

info@berklane.com
berklane.com

imdb.com/company/co0183891

Does not accept any unsolicited material. Genres include crime, comedy, and action.

Jason Berk
imdb.com/name/nm1357809

Matt Lane
imdb.com/name/nm2325262

BERLANTI TELEVISION
Production company

4000 Warner Blvd.
Burbank, CA 91522
818-954-4319 (phone)
818-977-9728 (fax)

imdb.com/company/co0192672

Accepts query letters from unproduced, unrepresented writers. Project types include TV. Genres include drama.

Ryan Lindenberg
Director of Development
imdb.com/name/nm1742204

Greg Berlanti
Principal
imdb.com/name/nm0075528

BERNERO PRODUCTIONS
Production company

500 S. Buena Vista St, Suite 2D-4
Burbank, CA 91521
818-560-1442

info@berneroproductions.com
berneroproductions.com
imdb.com/company/co0281008

Accepts query letters from unproduced, unrepresented writers via email.

Bob Kim
Producer
imdb.com/name/nm2344755

BETH GROSSBARD PRODUCTIONS
Production company

5168 Otis Ave
Tarzana, CA 91356
818-758-2500 (phone)
818-705-7366 (fax)

bgpix@sbcglobal.net
imdb.com/company/co0037144

Accepts query letters from produced or represented writers. Project types include TV. Genres include comedy and drama.

Beth Grossbard
Executive Producer
bgpix@sbcglobal.net
imdb.com/name/nm0343526
linkedin.com/pub/beth-grossbard/12/989/996

BET NETWORKS
Distributor

BET Atria West
10635 Santa Monica Blvd.
Second Floor
Los Angeles, CA 90025
310-481-3700

1443 Park Ave.
New York, NY 10029
212-975-4048

One BET Plaza
1235 W St NE
Washington, DC 20018-1211
202-608-2000 (phone)
206-608-2631 (fax)

bet.com
imdb.com/company/co0176390
facebook.com/BET
twitter.com/BET

Does not accept any unsolicited material. Project types include feature films and TV. Genres include drama, documentary, and comedy.

Austyn Biggers
Director of Development
310-481-3741
austyn.biggers@bet.net
imdb.com/name/nm2056137
linkedin.com/in/austynb

BETRON PRODUCTIONS
Production company

2400 Augusta Dr
Ste 355
Houston, TX 77057

betronproductions.com
imdb.com/company/co0178286

Does not accept any unsolicited material. Genres include comedy and drama.

BEYOND DREAMS PRODUCTIONS
Production company

247 SW 8th St. #895
#895
Miami, FL 33130

contact@beyondreams.com
beyondreams.com
imdb.com/company/co0188512
facebook.com/BeyondDreamsEntertainmentPvtLtd

Does not accept any unsolicited material. Genres include drama and documentary.

B GOOD PICTURE COMPANY
Production company

London
UK

info@bgoodpicturecompany.com
bgoodpicturecompany.com
imdb.com/company/co0285978

Does not accept any unsolicited material. Project types include feature films and TV. Genres include drama and comedy.

Joe Stephenson
Producer
imdb.com/name/nm3087240

BICKFORD PRODUCTIONS, LAURA
Production company

10153 1/2 Riverside Dr, Suite 683
Toluca Lake, CA 91602
323-850-8191

imdb.com/company/co0214437

facebook.com/pages/Laura-Bickford-Productions/
  507372106020086

Does not accept any unsolicited material. Project types include feature films. Genres include romance, drama, and comedy.

Laura Bickford
Producer
imdb.com/name/nm0081046
facebook.com/laura.bickford.526

Patrick Reese
Assistant
imdb.com/name/nm3101321

BIERLEIN ENTERTAINMENT
Production company

2000 Bay City Rd, Midland, MI, United States, 48642
989-921-9510

info@bierleinentertainment.com
imdb.com/company/co0235422

Does not accept any unsolicited material. Project types include short films. Genres include crime and thriller.

BIFROST PICTURES
Production company and financing company

8730 Wilshire Blvd, Suite 350, Beverly Hills, CA, United States, 90211
424-204-9330

info@bifrostpictures.com
imdb.com/company/co0420227

Does not accept any unsolicited material.

Daniel Wagner
Producer
424-204-9330
imdb.com/name/nm1016628

BIG BEACH
Production company

625 Mildred Ave
Venice CA 90291
310-230-3999

648 Broadway, 7th Floor, New York City, NY, United States, 10012
212-473-5800 (phone)
212-473-5805 (fax)

info@bigbeachfilms.com
bigbeach.com
imdb.com/company/co0148020

Does not accept any unsolicited material. Project types include feature films and TV. Genres include thriller, drama, and family.

BIG BELLI
Production company

411 Commercial Ave
Cliffside Park, NJ 07010
888-318-4075

info@bigbelli.com
bigbelli.com
imdb.com/company/co0488500
facebook.com/pages/40-Weeks-Movie/
  544802182248138
twitter.com/FortyWeeksMovie

Does not accept any unsolicited material. Project types include TV. Genres include documentary.

BIGEL ENTERTAINMENT, LLC
Production company

1450 Broadway, 41st Floor
New York, NY 10018
212-475-4333

info@bigelentertainment.com
imdb.com/company/co0163248
linkedin.com/company/bigel-entertainment

Accepts query letters from produced or represented writers. Project types include feature films and TV. Genres include comedy and drama.

Daniel Bigel
Producer
imdb.com/name/nm0081730

BIG FISH ENTERTAINMENT
Studio

609 Greenwich St, 7th Floor
New York, NY 10014
646-797-4102

info@bigfishusa.com
bigfishusa.com
imdb.com/company/co0203789
facebook.com/pages/Big-Fish-Entertainment/
    199241686772035
twitter.com/BigFishUSA

Does not accept any unsolicited material. Project types
include TV.

Doug DePriest
Co-Owner/Producer
imdb.com/name/nm2685128

Dan Cesareo
Co-Owner/Producer
imdb.com/name/nm2389863

BIG FOOT ENTERTAINMENT, LTD.
Production company

Bigfoot Entertainment Inc.
246 W Broadway
New York NY 10013
212-666-9000

help@bigfoot.com
bigfoot.com
imdb.com/company/co0261687

Accepts query letters from unproduced, unrepresented
writers via email. Project types include feature films
and TV. Genres include myth, action, fantasy, science
fiction, thriller, animation, and drama. Established in
2004.

Ashley Jordan
CEO
ashley@bigfootcorp.com
imdb.com/name/nm1248442
linkedin.com/pub/dir/ashley/jordan

BIG GREEN MACHINE
Production company

2213 S 1st St
Suite #B3

Austin, TX 78704
512-910-3330

7119 W Sunset Blvd, #702
Los Angeles, California 90046
213-444-6240

gearheads@big-green-machine.com
big-green-machine.com
imdb.com/company/co0534182
linkedin.com/company/big-green-machine
facebook.com/gobiggreenmachine
twitter.com/bigmachinegreen

Does not accept any unsolicited material. Project types
include short films. Genres include documentary.
Established in 2014.

BIG INDIE PICTURES
Production company

55 Main St, 2nd Floor
Yonkers, NY 10701
914-420-1447

declanbaldwin@gmail.com
bigindiepictures.com
imdb.com/company/co0203259

Does not accept any unsolicited material. Project types
include feature films. Genres include drama.

Corey Deckler
Producer
corey@bigindiepictures.com
imdb.com/name/nm4224057

Declan Baldwin
Producer
declanbaldwin@gmail.com
imdb.com/name/nm0049888

BIG JOURNEY PRODUCTIONS

9100 Wilshire Blvd., Suite 400W
Beverly Hills, CA 90212
310-595-0100

facebook.com

Project types include TV. Genres include drama.

Steve Shill
Writer/Producer/Director
imdb.com/name/nm0793455

BIG KID PICTURES
Production company

9000 Sunset Blvd., Suite 1010
West Hollywood, CA 90069

bigkidpictures.com
imdb.com/company/co0246151
facebook.com/pages/David-Dobkin/
    107565629266878

Does not accept any unsolicited material. Project types include feature films. Genres include comedy and action.

David Dobkin
Writer/Producer
imdb.com/name/nm0229694

BIG KIDS PRODUCTIONS
Production company and distributor

2120 Oxford Ave.
Austin, TX 78704
512-441-0737 (phone)
512-441-0339 (fax)

bigkidsvideo.com
imdb.com/company/co0152721
facebook.com/Big-Kids-
    Productions-101439903277555

Does not accept any unsolicited material. Project types include short films. Genres include family.

BIG LIGHT PRODUCTIONS
Production company

500 S. Buena Vista St, Animation Bldg.
Burbank, CA 91521
818-560-4782

biglightquestions@gmail.com
biglight.com
imdb.com/company/co0172688
facebook.com/biglightprod
twitter.com/FrankSpotnitz

Does not accept any unsolicited material. Project types include TV and feature films. Genres include thriller, drama, crime, and science fiction.

BIG PITA, LIL' PITA
Production company

231 Park Place, Suite 31
Brooklyn, NY 11238
646-395-3371

imdb.com/company/co0184052

Does not accept any unsolicited material. Project types include TV and feature films. Genres include family and fantasy.

Alicia Keys
Partner/Producer
imdb.com/name/nm1006024

BIG SCREEN ENTERTAINMENT GROUP
Production company

5555 Melrose Ave, Wallis Bldg. Suite 221
Hollywood, CA 90038
323-956-4321 (phone)
323-862-1172 (fax)

5440 W. Sahara Ave, Suite 202
Las Vegas, Nevada 89146

info@bigscreenent.com
bigscreenentertainmentgroup.com
imdb.com/company/co0145769
linkedin.com/company/big-screen-entertainment-
    group
facebook.com/BigScreenEntertainmentGroup
twitter.com/bigscreenbuzz

Does not accept any unsolicited material. Project types include feature films. Genres include romance, drama, and thriller.

BIG STAR PICTURES
Production company

1041 Formosa Ave
Writer's Building #309
West Hollywood, CA 90046
424-245-0015

info@bigstarpictures.com
bigstarpictures.com
imdb.com/company/co0504046
facebook.com/bigstarpix
twitter.com/BigStarPictures

Does not accept any unsolicited material. Project types include TV and feature films. Genres include drama and documentary. Established in 2013.

Christopher Quinn

Principal
imdb.com/name/nm1077724
linkedin.com/pub/christopher-quinn/b/2b2/855
facebook.com/christopher.quinn.940
twitter.com/BigStarPictures

BIG TALK PRODUCTIONS

Studio

26 Nassau St
London
W1W 7AQ
+44 (0) 20-7255-1131 (phone)
+44 (0) 20-7255-1132 (fax)

info@bigtalkproductions.com
bigtalkproductions.com
linkedin.com/company/big-talk-productions
facebook.com/bigtalk
twitter.com/bigtalk

Does not accept any unsolicited material. Project types include TV. Genres include drama, comedy, crime, science fiction, and action.

Rachael Prior

Head (Development/Film)
imdb.com/name/nm0975099

BILL AND BEN PRODUCTIONS

Production company

20 Great Chapel St
Soho
London W1F 8FW
UK
+44207-734-4933

enquiries@billandben.net
billandben.net
imdb.com/company/co0115595

Does not accept any unsolicited material. Project types include short films, TV, and feature films. Genres include animation, science fiction, comedy, and drama.

Bill Jones

Producer
imdb.com/name/nm0427580

BILL KENWRIGHT FILMS

Production company

1 Venice Walk
London W2 1RR
+44207-446-6200

info@kenwright.com
kenwright.com
imdb.com/company/co0103798
facebook.com/BKLProductions
twitter.com/bkl_productions

Does not accept any unsolicited material. Project types include TV and feature films. Genres include drama, comedy, and romance.

Daniel-Konrad Cooper

Producer
imdb.com/name/nm2257360

BILL & MELINDA GATES FOUNDATION

Production company and distributor

P.O. Box 23350, Seattle , WA, United States, 98102
206-709-3140

info@gatesfoundation.org
gatesfoundation.org
imdb.com/company/co0150454

Does not accept any unsolicited material. Project types include TV. Genres include reality, documentary, family, non-fiction, and fantasy.

BILL'S MARKET & TELEVISION PRODUCTIONS

Production company

17328 Ventura Blvd., Suite 191
Encino, CA 91316

bmtvp.com

imdb.com/company/co0410317

Does not accept any unsolicited material. Project types include TV. Genres include comedy.

David Hurwitz
Co-Founder/Partner
imdb.com/name/nm0975188

BILL THOMPSON PRODUCTIONS

149 N Cambridge St
Orange, CA 92866
714-450-9000

imdb.com/name/nm4719971

Does not accept any unsolicited material. Project types include TV. Genres include drama. Established in 2014.

Bill Thompson
Principal
imdb.com/name/nm0859892
linkedin.com/pub/bill-thompson/8/A54/8B8

BIO-TIDE FILMS (I)
Production company and distributor

3-13-10-3F
Chuo
Nakano, Tokyo 164-0011
Japan
03-3369-8221 (phone)
03-3369-8228 (fax)

info@biotide-films.com
imdb.com/company/co0134171

Does not accept any unsolicited material. Genres include comedy.

BIRCH TREE ENTERTAINMENT
Production company

10620 Southern Highlands Parkway
Suite 103
Las Vegas, NV 89141
Las Vegas, NV 89141
702-858-2782 (phone)
702-583-7928 (fax)

sales@birchtreefilms.com

birchtreeentertainment.com
imdb.com/company/co0114722
facebook.com/pages/Las-Vegas-NV/Birch-Tree-Entertainment/178085089631
twitter.com/BIRCHTREEFILMS

Accepts scripts from produced or represented writers. Project types include feature films. Genres include action.

Art Birzneck
CEO
sales@birchtreefilms.com
imdb.com/name/nm1010723
linkedin.com/pub/art-birzneck/36/ab8/5a7
linkedin.com/pub/art-birzneck/36/ab8/5a7

BISCAYNE PICTURES
Production company

Los Angeles, CA

info@biscaynepictures.com
biscaynepictures.com
imdb.com/company/co0152645

Does not accept any unsolicited material. Project types include feature films. Genres include thriller, horror, action, crime, and drama. Established in 2005.

Jeffrey Silver
Principal
310-777-2007
info@biscaynepictures.com
imdb.com/name/nm0798711
linkedin.com/pub/jeffrey-silver/16/833/503

BISCHOFF-HERVEY ENTERTAINMENT
Production company

1033 N Hollywood Way, Suite F
Burbank, CA 91505

bhe.tv
imdb.com/company/co0165662
linkedin.com/company/bischoff-hervey-entertainment-television-llc
facebook.com/bischoffhervey
twitter.com/bhetv

Does not accept any unsolicited material. Project types include TV.

Eric Bischoff
Partner/Producer
imdb.com/name/nm0083888

Jason Hervey
Partner/Producer
imdb.com/name/nm0381155

BITTERS END
Distributor

13-3 Nampeidaicho
3F
Shibuya-ku, Tokyo 150-0036
Japan
+81 3 34 62 03 45 (phone)
+81 3 34 62 06 21 (fax)

info@bitters.co.jp
bitters.co.jp
imdb.com/company/co0061630

Does not accept any unsolicited material. Project types include TV. Genres include drama and romance.

Yuji Sadai
President (Executive)
imdb.com/name/nm0755406

BIX PIX ENTERTAINMENT
Production company

11630 Tuxford St.
Sun Valley, CA 91352
818-252-7474 (phone)
818-252-7410 (fax)

jodidowns@bixpix.com
bixpix.com
imdb.com/company/co0187260
facebook.com/Bix-Pix-Entertainment-
    Inc-185406288160456
twitter.com/bix_pix

Accepts query letters from unproduced, unrepresented writers. Project types include feature films and short films. Genres include fantasy and animation. Established in 1998.

Kelli Bixler
Founder
imdb.com/name/nm1064778
linkedin.com/pub/kelli-bixler/4/577/426

BKGTH PRODUCTIONS
Production company

PO Box 800646
Dallas, TX 75380
212-712-7336

info@badkidsgotohell.com
badkidsgotohell.com
imdb.com/company/co0370228
facebook.com/BadKidsGoToHell
twitter.com/BadKidsGoToHell

Does not accept any unsolicited material. Genres include thriller and comedy.

BLACK BEAR PICTURES
Production company and financing company

1739 Berkeley St
Santa Monica, CA 90404
424-291-6000

515 Greenwich St
Suite 202
New York, NY 10013
212-931-5714

info@blackbearpictures.com
blackbearpictures.com
imdb.com/company/co0319513
linkedin.com/company/black-bear-pictures-llc
facebook.com/pages/Black-Bear-Pictures/
    166891590022937
twitter.com/blackbearpics

Does not accept any unsolicited material. Project types include feature films. Genres include romance, thriller, crime, drama, comedy, and horror. Established in 2011.

Ben Stillman
Creative Executive
imdb.com/name/nm4212466
linkedin.com/pub/ben-stillman/2b/11b/433

Amanda Greenblatt
imdb.com/name/nm1716375
linkedin.com/pub/amanda-greenblatt/0/8b/829

Teddy Schwarzman
imdb.com/name/nm3267061
linkedin.com/pub/teddy-schwarzman/11/50a/27a

BLACK & BLUE FILMS
Production company

Portland House
12-13 Greek St
London W1D4DL
UK

info@blackandbluefilms.com
imdb.com/company/co0206513

Does not accept any unsolicited material. Project types include feature films. Genres include horror, thriller, and action.

BLACK BULL MEDIA
Production company

1101 The Plaza
Tenafly, NJ 07670

blackbull.com
facebook.com/pages/Black-Bull-Media/
 178772705557048
twitter.com/blackbullnews

Does not accept any unsolicited material. Genres include drama and action.

Gareb Shamus
Principal/Producer
imdb.com/name/nm1347437
linkedin.com/in/garebshamus

BLACK CASTLE PRODUCTIONS
Production company

1041 N Formosa Ave., Formosa Bldg. Suite 195
West Hollywod, CA 90046
323-426-9208

blackcastleproductions@ymail.com
blackcastleprod.com
imdb.com/company/co0311113

linkedin.com/company/black-castle-productions
facebook.com/BlackCastleProductions
twitter.com/BlackCastleProd

Does not accept any unsolicited material. Project types include feature films. Genres include drama, horror, and thriller.

Sabrina Cooper
Producer
imdb.com/name/nm3735458

BLACK CLOUD MOTION PICTURES
Production company

602 Gembler Rd
San Antonio, TX 78219
775-230-1933

blackcloudproduction@yahoo.com
imdb.com/company/co0504639

Does not accept any unsolicited material. Project types include short films. Genres include comedy and drama.

BLACK FAMILY CHANNEL PRODUCTIONS
Production company and distributor

800 Forrest St. NW
Atlanta, GA 30318
404-350-2509 (phone)
404-350-0356 (fax)

imdb.com/company/co0147354

Does not accept any unsolicited material. Project types include TV. Genres include comedy,

BLACKFIN
Production company

25 Broadway, 9th Floor
New York, NY 10004

info@blackfin.tv
blackfin.tv
imdb.com/company/co0466165
facebook.com/pages/Blackfin/589135057798131
twitter.com/GENO_TV

Does not accept any unsolicited material. Project types include TV. Genres include reality.

Joanne Inglott
Partner/Producer
imdb.com/name/nm1531940

Geno McDermott
Partner/CEO/Producer
imdb.com/name/nm6183414

BLACK FOREST FILM GROUP
Production company

8383 Wilshire Blvd. Suite 355
Beverly Hills, CA 90210
310-990-8680

info@blackforestfg.com
imdb.com/company/co0369400
twitter.com/BlackForestFG

Does not accept any unsolicited material. Project types include feature films. Genres include thriller.

Mark Morgan
Partner
imdb.com/name/nm0604878

Brett Hudson
Partner
imdb.com/name/nm0399791

Eric Thompson
Partner
imdb.com/name/nm0860095

Kami Garcia
Partner
imdb.com/name/nm3721581

BLACK INDEPENDENT MEDIA CHANNEL
Distributor

PO BOX 23274
Houston, TX 77228-3274

imdb.com/company/co0387042

Does not accept any unsolicited material. Genres include comedy.

BLACKLIGHT
9560 Wilshire Blvd
4th Floor
Beverly Hills, CA 90212
310-285-9000

pr@blacklighttransmedia.com
blacklighttransmedia.com
imdb.com/company/co0333337
facebook.com/BlacklightTransmedia
twitter.com/BlacklightMedia

Accepts scripts from produced or represented writers. Project types include feature films, TV, and video games. Genres include fantasy, non-fiction, action, animation, drama, and crime.

Zak Kadison
CEO
imdb.com/name/nm1780162
linkedin.com/in/zakkadison

Justin Catron
Director of Development
imdb.com/name/nm2031037

BLACKMALED PRODUCTIONS
Production company

5700 Arlington Ave
Bronx, NY 10471
718-601-5353

malcolmdlee.com
imdb.com/company/co0425503
linkedin.com/company/blackmaled-productions
facebook.com/pages/Malcolm-D-Lee-Blackmaled-
    Productions/408778477872

Does not accept any unsolicited material. Project types include feature films. Genres include comedy and drama.

Malcolm D. Lee
Writer/Director/Producer
imdb.com/name/nm0002700
twitter.com/malcolmdlee

BLAIRWOOD ENTERTAINMENT
Production company, distributor, and sales agent

2505 Anthem VIllage Dr
Ste E-493
Henderson, NV 91608
323-319-3978 (phone)
323-686-5379 (fax)

blairwoodentertainment.com
imdb.com/company/co0332352

Does not accept any unsolicited material. Project types
include feature films and TV. Genres include drama
and thriller.

Ana Clavell
Producer
imdb.com/name/nm0165410

Ana Clavell
Producer
imdb.com/name/nm0165410

BLANK PAIGE PRODUCTIONS
Production company

611 N. Bronson Ave, Suite 2
Los Angeles, CA 90004
323-461-2300 (phone)
323-461-1320 (fax)

info@blankpaige.com
blankpaige.com
imdb.com/company/co0324748
facebook.com/BlankPaigeProductions
twitter.com/blankpaigetv

Does not accept any unsolicited material. Project types
include TV.

Liane Su
Executive Producer
imdb.com/name/nm1015692

Edward Paige
Executive Producer
imdb.com/name/nm2302761
linkedin.com/pub/edward-paige/1b/ba9/4a8

BLAST! FILMS
Production company and distributor

blast@blastfilms.co.uk
imdb.com/company/co0104495

Does not accept any unsolicited material. Project types
include TV and feature films. Genres include drama,
comedy, action, and thriller.

BLEECKER STREET
Distributor

381 Park Ave South, 14th floor, New York, NY,
United States, 10016

imdb.com/company/co0494731

Does not accept any unsolicited material. Project types
include feature films and TV. Genres include thriller,
action, drama, comedy, and family.

BLEIBERG ENTERTAINMENT
Production company and studio

225 S Clark Dr
Beverly Hills, CA 90211
310-273-1034 (phone)
310-273-0007 (fax)

sales@bleibergent.com
bleibergent.com
imdb.com/company/co0165151
facebook.com/Bleiberg-
    Entertainment-167059083344929

Accepts query letters from unproduced, unrepresented
writers via email. Project types include feature films
and TV. Genres include drama, comedy, action, and
romance.

Ehud Bleiberg
Chairman
ehud@bleibergent.com
imdb.com/name/nm0088173
linkedin.com/pub/ehud-bleiberg/11/679/595

Nicholas Donnermeyer
Vice President of Acquisitions & Development
nick@bleibergent.com
imdb.com/name/nm2223730

BLINDING EDGE PICTURES
Production company

1055 Westlakes Dr
Berwyn, PA 19312

610-251-9200 (phone)
610-260-9879 (fax)

imdb.com/company/co0054054

Does not accept any unsolicited material. Project types include feature films. Genres include horror, drama, and thriller.

Ashwin Rajan
Head of Production/Producer
imdb.com/name/nm2248864

M. Night Shyamalan
Writer/Director/Producer
mnightshyamalan.com
imdb.com/name/nm0796117
facebook.com/pages/M-Night-Shyamalan/
    116097218498409
twitter.com/MNightShyamalan

BLIND WINK PRODUCTIONS
Production company

8 Mills Place 2nd Floor
Pasadena, CA 91105
626-600-4100

info@blindwink.com
imdb.com/company/co0230970

Does not accept any unsolicited material. Project types include feature films. Genres include science fiction, thriller, family, comedy, fantasy, action, drama, and crime. Established in 2011.

Nils Peyron
Executive Vice President
imdb.com/name/nm3741163

Gore Verbinski
Principal
imdb.com/name/nm0893659

Jonathan Krauss
Head of Film Production & Development
imdb.com/name/nm0470310

BLKNEON
Production company

244 5th Ave, Ste 2077
New York, New York
917-370-5396

info@blkneon.com
blkneon.com
imdb.com/company/co0474121
facebook.com/blkneonproductions
twitter.com/blkneon

Accepts scripts from unproduced, unrepresented writers. Project types include short films. Genres include action, drama, romance, thriller, comedy, reality, and horror. Established in 2015.

zaher saleh
President
zmsnyc@gmail.com

BLONDIE GIRL PRODUCTIONS
Production company

Relativity Television
1040 N. Las Palmas Ave.
Building 40
Hollywood, CA 90038
323-860-8610 (phone)
323-860-8601 (fax)

jessica@blondiegirlprod.com
blondiegirlproductions.com
imdb.com/company/co0261290
facebook.com/BlondieGirlProductions
twitter.com/blondiegirlprod

Does not accept any unsolicited material. Project types include TV. Genres include comedy.

Ashley Tisdale
Owner
misstisdale.net/jessica-rhoades-of-blondie-girl-prod-
    interview
imdb.com/name/nm0864308

Jennifer Rhoades
VP Development and Production
imdb.com/name/nm1056279

BLOOD MOON PRODUCTIONS
Production company

75 Saint Marks Place
Staten Island, NY 10301
718-556-9410 (phone)
718-816-4092 (fax)

danforthprince@gmail.com
bloodmoonproductions.com
imdb.com/company/co0511521
facebook.com/pages/Blood-Moon-Productions-Ltd/
    258733018503
twitter.com/BloodyandLunar

Does not accept any unsolicited material. Project types
include feature films. Genres include drama.

Danforth Prince
Publisher/Executive Producer
imdb.com/name/nm3362710

BLOODY EARTH FILMS
Distributor

PO Box 132
Butler, NJ 07405
973-838-3030 (phone)
973-492-8988 (fax)

info@popcinema.com
alternativecinema.com
imdb.com/company/co0216429

Does not accept any unsolicited material. Genres
include horror.

BLOOMFIELDS WELCH MANAGEMENT
Production company

Garden Studios
71-75 Shelton St
London WC2H 9JQ
UK
+44 (0)20 7659 2001 (phone)
+44 (0)20 7659 2101 (fax)

info@bloomfieldswelch.com
bloomfieldsmanagement.com
imdb.com/company/co0134824
twitter.com/bwmgt

Does not accept any unsolicited material. Project types
include feature films, short films, and TV. Genres
include thriller, reality, family, drama, and action.

BLUE BAY PRODUCTIONS
Production company

1119 Colorado Ave., Ste. 105C
Santa Monica, CA 90404
310-440-9904

imdb.com/company/co0176188
facebook.com/bluebayprod

Does not accept any unsolicited material. Established
in 1999.

Rodney Liber
Producer
imdb.com/name/nm0508764

BLUE COLLAR PRODUCTIONS
Production company

1041 N. Formosa Ave.
West Hollywood, CA 90046
323-850-2530

info@bluecollarproductions.com
bluecollarproductions.com
imdb.com/company/co0121663
linkedin.com/company/blue-collar-productions-inc.
facebook.com/pages/Blue-Collar-Productions-Inc/
    152776894868030
twitter.com/BlueCollarLA

Does not accept any unsolicited material. Project types
include TV, feature films, and short films. Genres
include drama, thriller, period, comedy, crime, action,
and romance. Established in 2001.

Mark Rowen
Producer
imdb.com/name/nm0746651

Jeffrey Lerner
Partner
imdb.com/company/co0121663

BLUE PRINT PICTURES
Production company

43-45 Charlotte St
London W1T 1RS
United Kingdom
+44 0207-580-6915

enquiries@blueprintpictures.com
blueprintpictures.com
imdb.com/company/co0010002

Does not accept any unsolicited material. Project types include feature films. Genres include family, drama, comedy, action, and non-fiction. Established in 2004.

Graham Broadbent
Principal
asst@blueprintpictures.com
imdb.com/name/nm0110357

BLUE RIDER PICTURES
Production company and distributor

2801 Ocean Park Blvd., Suite 193
Santa Monica, CA 90405
310-314-8405 (phone)
310-314-8402 (fax)

info@blueriderpictures.com
blueriderpictures.com
imdb.com/company/co0042650
linkedin.com/company/blue-rider-pictures

Does not accept any unsolicited material. Project types include TV and feature films. Genres include comedy, drama, and crime.

Walter Josten
CEO/Executive Producer
imdb.com/name/nm0430943

Jeff Geoffray
CFO/Executive Producer
imdb.com/name/nm0313258

BLUE SHIRT PRODUCTIONS
Production company

506 Santa Monica Blvd., Suite. 200
Santa Monica, CA 90401
310-917-5000

imdb.com/company/co0255230

Does not accept any unsolicited material. Project types include feature films. Genres include family. Established in 2015.

Karey Kirkpatrick
Writer/Director
imdb.com/name/nm0456732

BLUE SKY CINEMA
Distributor

52 Brunswick Woods Dr
East Brunswick, NJ 08816
732-613-1194 (phone)
866-465-5470 (fax)

movie@blueskycinemas.com
blueskycinemas.com
imdb.com/company/co0274633

Does not accept any unsolicited material. Project types include TV. Genres include romance and comedy.

BLUE SKY STUDIOS
Production company and distributor

One American Ln
Greenwich, CT 06831
203-992-6000 (phone)
203-992-6001 (fax)

info@blueskystudios.com
blueskystudios.com
imdb.com/company/co0047265
facebook.com/BlueSkyStudios
twitter.com/blueskystudios

Does not accept any unsolicited material. Project types include feature films. Genres include non-fiction, animation, comedy, family, and fantasy. Established in 1997.

Chris Wedge
Vice-President (Creative Director)
imdb.com/name/nm0917188
linkedin.com/in/chrispinkuswesselman

Lisa Fragner
Head (Feature Development)
imdb.com/name/nm0289591
linkedin.com/in/lisafragner

BLUE THREE PRODUCTIONS
Production company

Los Angeles, CA

kyle@blue3llc.com
blue3llc.com
imdb.com/company/co0357214
linkedin.com/company/blue-three-productions-llc
twitter.com/kylehs

Accepts scripts from unproduced, unrepresented writers via email. Project types include TV, commercials, short films, and feature films. Genres include crime, documentary, detective, sociocultural, thriller, drama, science fiction, action, and romance. Established in 2010.

Kyle Hausmann-Stokes
Owner
kylehs@gmail.com
kylehausmannstokes.com
imdb.com/name/nm3492571
linkedin.com/in/kylehs
twitter.com/kylehs

BLUE TULIP PRODUCTIONS
Production company

1708 Berkeley St.
Santa Monica, CA 90404
310-582-1587

imdb.com/company/co0007610

Does not accept any unsolicited material. Project types include feature films. Genres include romance, action, science fiction, drama, and comedy. Established in 1997.

Jan De Bont
Director/Producer
imdb.com/name/nm0000957
linkedin.com/pub/jan-de-bont/36/b24/25a

Chris Stanley
Vice President
imdb.com/name/nm0000957

BLUEWATER RANCH ENTERTAINMENT
Production company

1433 Sixth St
Santa Monica, CA 90401
310-395-1882 (phone)
310-395-8939 (fax)

rancher@bluewaterranch.com
imdb.com/company/co0201577
linkedin.com/company/bluewater-ranch-entertainment
twitter.com/BluewaterRanch

Does not accept any unsolicited material. Project types include feature films. Genres include thriller, drama, and comedy. Established in 1991.

Mindy Marin
Producer
imdb.com/name/nm0547484

BLUMHOUSE PRODUCTIONS
Production company

2401 Beverly Blvd.
Los Angeles, CA 90057
213-835-1000

blumhouseproductionsinfo@gmail.com
blumhouse.com
imdb.com/company/co0098315
facebook.com/Blumhouse
twitter.com/blumhouse

Accepts query letters from unproduced, unrepresented writers. Project types include feature films and TV. Genres include horror, action, and thriller. Established in 2000.

Jason Blum
President
imdb.com/name/nm0089658

Jessica Hall
Director of Development
imdb.com/name/nm4148859
linkedin.com/pub/jessica-hall/1/703/a07

BLUR STUDIO INC.
Production company

589 Venice Blvd.
Venice, CA 90291
310-581-8848 (phone)
310-851-8850 (fax)

jobs@blur.com
blur.com
imdb.com/company/co0064973
linkedin.com/company/blur-studio

facebook.com/therealblurstudio
twitter.com/TheBlurStudio

Does not accept any unsolicited material. Project types include feature films. Genres include action, science fiction, and fantasy.

Chris Kubsch
Executive Producer
imdb.com/name/nm5477852

Tim Miller
Writer, Director
imdb.com/name/nm1783265

BLUR STUDIO INC.
Production company

589 Venice Blvd.
Venice, CA 90291
310-581-8848 (phone)
310-851-8850 (fax)

blur.com
imdb.com/company/co0064973

Does not accept any unsolicited material. Project types include feature films. Genres include animation, action, and science fiction.

B MOVIES
Production company and distributor

1000 Universal Studios Plaza
Orlando, FL 32819
321-445-1568

info@bmoviesllc.com
imdb.com/company/co0051848

Does not accept any unsolicited material. Genres include thriller.

BMP LATIN
Production company and distributor

6007 Sepulveda Blvd.
Van Nuys, CA 91411
818-756-5100 (phone)
818-756-5140 (fax)

contactus@bunim-murray.com
bunim-murray.com/bmp-latin

imdb.com/company/co0031439
linkedin.com/company/bunim-murray-productions
facebook.com/BunimMurrayProductions
twitter.com/BunimMurray

Does not accept any unsolicited material. Project types include short films, TV, and feature films. Genres include reality, documentary, and comedy. Established in 1987.

Gabriela Cocco-Sanchez
Co-Head
imdb.com/name/nm6419869

BMW FILMS
Production company and distributor

PO Box 1227
Westwood, NJ 07675-1227

imdb.com/company/co0004108

Does not accept any unsolicited material. Project types include TV. Genres include action and comedy.

BN FILMS
Production company

1531 14th St
Santa Monica, CA 90404
310-881-6334

info@bnfilms.tv
bnfilms.tv
imdb.com/company/co0403621
facebook.com/bnfilmsLA
twitter.com/BNFilmsLA

Does not accept any unsolicited material. Project types include feature films. Genres include thriller and drama.

Alex Garcia
Producer
imdb.com/name/nm4111213

Jonathan Gray
Executive (NY)
imdb.com/name/nm1807745

Lucas Akoskin
Producer
imdb.com/name/nm1993666

Katrina Wolfe
President of Production/Producer
imdb.com/name/nm2302501

BOAT ANGEL / CAR ANGEL
Production company, distributor, and sales agent

1641 E University Dr Suite 104
Mesa, AZ 85203
602-903-1844 (phone)
480-668-4855 (fax)

boatangel@gmail.com
boatangel.com
imdb.com/company/co0241196

Does not accept any unsolicited material. Project types
include TV. Genres include drama.

BOAT ANGEL DONATION CENTER
Financing company

1641 E University Dr Suite 104
Mesa, AZ 85203
602-903-1844

bstewart@boatangel.org
boatangel.org
imdb.com/company/co0444447

Does not accept any unsolicited material. Project types
include commercials. Genres include drama.

Brian Stewart
Producer
imdb.com/name/nm2772668

BOBBCAT FILMS
Production company

800 Forest Rd
Atlanta, GA 30318
404-351-5353 (phone)
404-351-5327 (fax)

info@bobbcatfilms.com
bobbcatfilms.com
imdb.com/company/co0351552
linkedin.com/company/bobbcat-films
facebook.com/pages/bobbcatfilms/224619900913110
twitter.com/BobbcatFilms

Does not accept any unsolicited material. Project types
include feature films and TV. Genres include drama,
comedy, family, reality, and romance. Established in
2011.

Roger Bobb
CEO/Producer/Director
imdb.com/name/nm0090292

BOBKER/KRUGAR FILMS
Production company and distributor

1416 N La Brea Ave
Hollywood, CA 90028
323-469-1440 (phone)
323-802-1597 (fax)

imdb.com/company/co0163148
facebook.com/pages/BobkerKruger-Films/
114336545247226

Accepts query letters from unproduced, unrepresented
writers.

Daniel Bobker
Producer
imdb.com/name/nm0090394
linkedin.com/pub/daniel-bobker/62/1b9/59b

Ehren Kruger
imdb.com/name/nm0472567

BOB STICKS WORLDWIDE
Production company

219 S Barrington Ave
Apt 116
Los Angeles, CA 90049

nikki@bobsticks.com
bobsticks.com
imdb.com/company/co0486412
facebook.com/pages/Bob-Sticks-Worldwide/
781362418604280

Does not accept any unsolicited material. Project types
include feature films and TV. Genres include thriller,
comedy, and action. Established in 2014.

Nikki Stanghetti
Producer
nikki@bobsticks.com
imdb.com/name/nm2325595

BOGNER ENTERTAINMENT INC.
Production company

269 S Beverly Dr, Suite 8
Beverly Hills, CA 90212
310-569-7525

Relativity / Bogner Entertainment
1040 N. Las Palmas Ave., Bldg 40
Hollywood, CA 90028
323-860-8670

info.beitv@gmail.com
bognerentertainment.com
imdb.com/company/co0068550
facebook.com/beitv
twitter.com/share

Accepts scripts from unproduced, unrepresented writers. Genres include thriller, horror, comedy, family, and action. Established in 2000.

Oliver Bogner
oliverbogner@gmail.com
imdb.com/name/nm3331124
linkedin.com/in/oliverbogner
facebook.com/oliverbogner
twitter.com/oliver_bogner

Jonathan Bogner
President
jsbogner@aol.com
imdb.com/name/nm0091845
linkedin.com/pub/jonathan-bogner/1/37b/91a

BOIES/SCHILLER FILM GROUP
Production company

2200 Corporate Blvd NW
Ste 400
Boca Raton, FL 33431
310-752-2460 (phone)
561-866-6006 (fax)

info@bsfgllp.com
bsfgllp.com
imdb.com/company/co0377076

Does not accept any unsolicited material. Project types include TV and feature films. Genres include crime, thriller, romance, drama, action, and comedy. Established in 2013.

BOIES/SCHILLER FILM GROUP, LLC
Production company

401 Wilshire Blvd, Suite 850, Santa Monica, CA, United States, 90401
310-597-4984

info@bsfgllp.com
imdb.com/company/co0377076

Does not accept any unsolicited material.

David Boies
Actor
imdb.com/name/nm7635641

BOKU FILMS
Production company

45 E Coast Rd
Singapore 428765

katgoh@bokufilms.com
bokufilms.com
imdb.com/company/co0047458

Does not accept any unsolicited material. Project types include TV. Genres include thriller and drama.

Alan Poul
Principal
imdb.com/name/nm0693561

BOLD FILMS
Production company and distributor

6464 Sunset Blvd,
Suite 800
Los Angeles, CA 90028
323-769-8900 (phone)
323-769-8954 (fax)

17-19 Maddox St , 5th Floor
London W1S 2QH

info@boldfilms.com
boldfilms.com
imdb.com/company/co0135575

Does not accept any unsolicited material. Project types include feature films and TV. Genres include action, fantasy, thriller, and horror.

Stephanie Wilcox
Director of Development
imdb.com/name/nm3432545

Garrick Dion
Senior Vice President (Development)
imdb.com/name/nm1887182

BONA FIDE PRODUCTIONS
Production company

8899 Beverly Blvd
Suite 804
Los Angeles, CA 90048
310-273-6782 (phone)
310-273-7821 (fax)

imdb.com/company/co0063938
facebook.com/pages/Bonafide-Production-LLC/
    202153449861231

Accepts query letters from unproduced, unrepresented writers. Project types include feature films. Genres include comedy and animation. Established in 1993.

Albert Berger
Partner
imdb.com/name/nm0074100
linkedin.com/pub/albert-berger/6/b49/493

BONANZA PRODUCTIONS
Production company

3727 Magnolia Blvd
Ste 255
Burbank, CA 91505
818-841-0561 (fax)

1175 Chattahoochee Ave NW
Atlanta, GA 30318
404-351-3004 (fax)

imdb.com/company/co0265986

Does not accept any unsolicited material. Project types include TV. Genres include science fiction, comedy, and action.

BONTRAGER TWINS PRODUCTIONS
Production company

1440 Dutch Valley Place
Suite 620
Atlanta, GA 30324
404-664-9907

mail@twiinmedia.com
twiinmedia.com
imdb.com/company/co0390558

Does not accept any unsolicited material. Project types include short films. Genres include family, drama, and comedy.

BORDERLINE FILMS
Production company and sales agent

310 Bowery, 2nd Floor
New York, NY 10012
212-254-2272

9336 Civic Center Dr
Beverly Hills, CA 90210
301-273-6700

contact@blfilm.com
blfilm.com
imdb.com/company/co0155943

Does not accept any unsolicited material. Project types include feature films and short films. Genres include detective, crime, thriller, and drama. Established in 2003.

Sean Durkin
Principal
imdb.com/name/nm1699934

Josh Mond
Principal
imdb.com/name/nm1317614
linkedin.com/pub/dir/Josh/Mond/us-70-Greater-New-
    York-City-Area

Antonio Campos
Principal
imdb.com/name/nm1290515

BORG
Production company

700 W. 6th St
Austin, TX 78701

844-THE-BORG (phone)
844-THE-BORG (fax)

hello@borg.agency
imdb.com/company/co0499593

Does not accept any unsolicited material. Project types include feature films and TV. Genres include drama, documentary, and fantasy.

BOSS MEDIA

9440 Santa Monica Blvd.
Suite 200
Beverly Hills, CA 90210
310-205-9900 (phone)
310-205-9909 (fax)

boss-media.com
imdb.com/company/co0341936
linkedin.com/company/boss-media-ab
twitter.com/bossmediacomm

Does not accept any unsolicited material. Genres include science fiction, thriller, and comedy.

Frank Mancuso
President
310-205-9900
imdb.com/name/nm0541548

Jennifer Nieves Gordon
Vice President (Development)
310-205-9900
imdb.com/name/nm2707034

BOULDER CREEK INTERNATIONAL

Production company, distributor, and sales agent

45 Great Guildford St
London
UK
442-076-420810

info@bouldercreekinternational.com
bouldercreekinternational.com
imdb.com/company/co0250719
facebook.com/bouldercreekinternational
twitter.com/bouldercreekint

Does not accept any unsolicited material. Genres include documentary and drama.

BOUNDLESS PICTURES
Production company

500 W Putnam Ave
Ste 400
Greenwich, CT 06830
203-295-0350

233 Wilshire Blvd
4th Floor
Santa Monica, CA 90401
310-957-2041

contact@boundlesspictures.com
boundlesspictures.com
imdb.com/company/co0302100
facebook.com/BoundlessPictures

Project types include feature films. Genres include action, drama, thriller, horror, and fantasy. Established in 2008.

BOW & ARROW ENTERTAINMENT
Production company

Los Angeles, CA

bowandarrow.la
imdb.com/company/co0488623
linkedin.com/company/bow-and-arrow-entertainment

Does not accept any unsolicited material. Project types include feature films. Genres include drama and documentary. Established in 2014.

Michael Sherman
Principal
imdb.com/name/nm5554634

Matthew Perniciaro
Principal
imdb.com/name/nm0674362
linkedin.com/pub/matthew-perniciaro/47/976/73b

BOWJAPAN
Distributor

TOKYO,
Japan
03-3545-3411

info@bowjapan.com
imdb.com/company/co0092272

Does not accept any unsolicited material. Project types include feature films. Genres include fantasy and drama.

BOX INC.
Production company

4440 El Camino Real
Los Altos, CA 94022
877-729-4269

twitter.com/boxHQ

Does not accept any unsolicited material. Project types include TV. Genres include drama.

Aaron Levie
CEO
imdb.com/name/nm3085736

BOXING CAT PRODUCTIONS
Production company and distributor

11500 Hart St
North Hollywood, CA 91605
818-765-4870 (phone)
818-765-4975 (fax)

bradb@boxingcats.ca
imdb.com/company/co0080834

Does not accept any unsolicited material. Project types include feature films and TV. Genres include comedy and family.

Tim Allen
timallen.com/misc/bcf.php?xpt=1
imdb.com/name/nm0000741

BOY WONDER PRODUCTIONS
Production company

347-632-2961 (phone)
347-332-6953 (fax)

info@boywonderproductions.net
boywonderproductions.net
imdb.com/company/co0255525
facebook.com/pages/Boy-Wonder-Productions/
    239113204508

Accepts query letters from unproduced, unrepresented writers via email. Project types include TV. Genres

include non-fiction, comedy, and drama. Established in 2006.

BOZ PRODUCTIONS
Production company

323-697-5340

bozenga@sbcglobal.net
bozproductions.com
imdb.com/company/co0068487

Accepts query letters from unproduced, unrepresented writers. Project types include feature films.

Bo Zenga
bozenga@sbcglobal.net
imdb.com/name/nm0954848

BRAD LACHMAN PRODUCTIONS
Production company

4450 Lakeside Dr, Suite 280
Burbank, CA 91505
818-954-0473

reception@bradlachmanprods.com
bradlachmanprods.com
imdb.com/company/co0091962
linkedin.com/company/brad-lachman-productions

Does not accept any unsolicited material. Project types include TV.

Brad Lachman
Producer
imdb.com/name/nm0480044

BRADS MOVIES
Production company

P.O. Box 16256
North Hollywood, CA 91615
818-298-2750

bradsmovies@gmail.com
bradsmovies.com
imdb.com/company/co0108268

Does not accept any unsolicited material. Genres include drama.

BRAIN DAMAGE FILMS

Production company, distributor, and sales agent

6929 N Hayden Rd
Ste C4-246
Scottsdale, AZ 85250
480-966-4070 (phone)
480-966-4570 (fax)

contact@braindamagefilms.com
braindamagefilms.com
imdb.com/company/co0000908
facebook.com/BrainDamageFilms
twitter.com/BrainDamageFilm

Does not accept any unsolicited material. Project types include TV. Genres include horror.

Darrin Ramage
Producer
imdb.com/name/nm0198582

BRAINSTORM MEDIA

Production company, distributor, and sales agent

280 S Beverly Dr, Suite 208, Beverly Hills , CA,
United States, 90212
310-285-0812 (phone)
310-285-0772 (fax)

info@brainmedia.com
brainmedia.net
imdb.com/company/co0091979

Does not accept any unsolicited material. Project types include TV. Genres include drama, comedy, family, and romance.

BRAINWAVE FILM GROUP

Production company

827 Hollywood Way, Suite 539
Burbank, CA 91505
818-429-4238

info@brainwavefilms.net
facebook.com/brainwavefilms01
twitter.com/BrainwaveFilms

Does not accept any unsolicited material. Project types include feature films. Genres include drama.

Emily Pearson
Producer
imdb.com/name/nm0962588

Duane Andersen
Producer
imdb.com/name/nm1104565

BRANDED FILMS

Production company

4000 Warner Blvd
Building 139, Suite 107
Burbank, CA 91522
818-954-7969

info@branded-films.com
imdb.com/company/co0347637

Does not accept any unsolicited material. Project types include feature films and TV. Genres include comedy. Established in 2011.

Nik Linnen
Producer
imdb.com/name/nm3800556

Russell Brand
Principal
imdb.com/name/nm1258970
Assistant: Lee Sacks

BRANDI BROTHERS PRODUCTIONS

Production company, distributor, and sales agent

PO Box 3373
Park City, UT 84060

info@brandibrothers.com
brandibrothers.com
imdb.com/company/co0285865

Does not accept any unsolicited material. Project types include feature films and TV. Genres include drama.

Jamison Brandi
Producer
imdb.com/name/nm2720731

BRASSCO PAGE PRODUCTIONS

Production company

8373 Genova Way
Lake Worth, FL 33467
561-632-5977

brasscopage@hotmail.com
imdb.com/company/co0236344

Does not accept any unsolicited material. Genres include comedy, romance, and drama.

BRAT ENTERTAINMENT
Distributor

PO Box 591850
San Antonio, TX 78259

BratEntertainment@yahoo.com
imdb.com/company/co0082581

Does not accept any unsolicited material. Project types include feature films. Genres include romance, drama, and comedy. Established in 2002.

BRAUN ENTERTAINMENT GROUP
Production company

3685 Motor Ave, Suite 150
Los Angeles, CA 90034
310-204-6000 (phone)
310-204-6005 (fax)

braunent@aol.com
braunentertainmentgroup.com
imdb.com/company/co0150508
linkedin.com/company/braun-entertainment-group

Accepts query letters from unproduced, unrepresented writers via email. Project types include feature films and TV. Genres include drama.

Zev Braun
CEO/President
imdb.com/name/nm0105881

Philip M. Krupp
EVP
imdb.com/name/nm0472803

Michael Swidler
Development
imdb.com/name/nm4522103

BRAUNSTEIN FILMS
Production company

12301 Wilshire Blvd., Suite 110
Los Angeles, CA 90025
310-207-6600 (phone)
310-207-6069 (fax)

imdb.com/company/co0462935

Does not accept any unsolicited material. Project types include TV. Genres include comedy, drama, and crime.

Howard Braunstein
Producer
imdb.com/name/nm0105946

BRAVEN FILMS
Production company

33 W 19th St, New York, NY, United States, 10011
646-619-1247 (phone)
212-400-7201 (fax)

info@bravenfilms.com
bravenfilms.com
imdb.com/company/co0313103

Does not accept any unsolicited material. Project types include TV. Genres include drama and family.

Ross Saxon
Executive (Creative Development)
imdb.com/name/nm3136259

BRAVERMAN PRODUCTIONS
Production company

3000 Olympic Blvd.
Santa Monica, CA 90404
310-264-4184 (phone)
310-388-5885 (fax)

chuck@bravermanproductions.com
bravermanproductions.com
imdb.com/company/co0093100
facebook.com/pages/Braverman-Productions-Inc/
    411951145571125

Does not accept any unsolicited material. Project types include feature films.

Chuck Braverman
Producer/Director
imdb.com/name/nm0106015
facebook.com/chuck.braverman

BRAY ENTERTAINMENT
Production company

80 River St
5D
Hoboken, NJ 07030
212-993-7222

info@brayentertainment.com
brayentertainment.com
imdb.com/company/co0371080
facebook.com/pages/Bray-Entertainment/
    111633412259172
twitter.com/bray_ent

Does not accept any unsolicited material.

BREAKFAST ANYTIME PRODUCTIONS
Production company

13701 Riverside Dr, Suite 400
Sherman Oaks, CA 91423

imdb.com/company/co0333901

Does not accept any unsolicited material. Project types include TV.

Ari Shofet
Producer
imdb.com/name/nm1597896

Rick Hurvitz
President/Producer
imdb.com/name/nm1539523

BREAKING GLASS PICTURES
Production company and distributor

133 N 4th St, Philadelphia, PA, United States, 19106
267-324-3934 (phone)
267-687-7533 (fax)

bgpics.com

Does not accept any unsolicited material. Project types include TV. Genres include drama and family.

BREAKOUT WORLDWIDE ENTERTAINMENT
Production company

1438 N. Gower St, Bldg. 70, Suite 226 Box 70
Hollywood, CA 90028
323-860-7100 (phone)
323-468-4665 (fax)

imdb.com/company/co0198150

Does not accept any unsolicited material. Project types include feature films. Genres include horror.

Christina Rosenberg
VP of Development
imdb.com/name/nm0479447

Sherri Strain
President
imdb.com/name/nm0833173

BREAKTHROUGH DISTRIBUTION
Distributor

2910 Main St
Second Floor
Santa Monica, CA 90405
310-399-9453

breakthroughentertainment.com
imdb.com/company/co0204051
linkedin.com/company/breakthrough-distribution

Does not accept any unsolicited material.

BREAKTHROUGH ENTERTAINMENT
Production company, distributor, and sales agent

35 Britain St
Toronto, ON M5A 1R7
Canada
416-766-6588 (phone)
416-769-1436 (fax)

breakthroughentertainment.com
imdb.com/company/co0008941

Does not accept any unsolicited material. Project types include TV. Genres include family and comedy.

BREAKTHROUGH FILMS AND TELEVISION
Production company

122 Sherbourne St
Toronto, ON M5A 2R4
Canada
416-766-6588 (phone)
416-366-7796 (fax)

breakthroughentertainment.com
imdb.com/company/co0187905
twitter.com/breakthru_ent

Does not accept any unsolicited material. Project types include TV. Genres include comedy and drama.

Alethea Robinson
Executive
imdb.com/name/nm2657611

BREATH
Production company and distributor

3-7-10-203
Ebisu Minami
Shibuya, Tokyo 150-0022
Japan
+81 3 5724 6401 (phone)
+81 3 5722 6615 (fax)

info@breathinc.com
breathinc.com
imdb.com/company/co0217854

Does not accept any unsolicited material. Project types include TV. Genres include drama.

BREGMAN PRODUCTIONS, MARTIN
Production company

34-12 36th St, Suite 2/201
Astotia, NY 11106
718-706-4700

imdb.com/company/co0056556
facebook.com/pages/Martin-Bregman-Productions/
    146196798738142

Does not accept any unsolicited material. Project types include feature films. Genres include thriller.

Martin Bregman
Producer
imdb.com/name/nm0106840

Michael Bregman
Director/Writer
imdb.com/name/nm0106841

BRICK TOP PRODUCTION
Production company

433 Plaza Real
Ste 275
Boca Raton, FL 33432
561-962-4175

imdb.com/company/co0354871
linkedin.com/company/brick-top-productions-inc-
facebook.com/BrickTopProductions

Does not accept any unsolicited material.

BRIDGE FILMS
Production company

149 S Barrington Ave #762
Los Angeles, CA 90049
310-472-0780 (phone)
310-472-4781 (fax)

mriklin@bridgefilms.com
imdb.com/company/co0013928

Does not accept any unsolicited material. Project types include feature films. Genres include thriller.

Matthew Riklin
President/Producer
imdb.com/name/nm1930450

BRIDGEHEAD
Production company

3-5-6-3F
Kita Aoyama
Minato, Tokyo 107-0061
Japan
080-4209-1984

ogawa@bridgehead-jp.com
imdb.com/company/co0389200

Does not accept any unsolicited material. Project types include feature films and TV. Genres include thriller and horror.

Shinji Ogawa
President (Producer)
imdb.com/name/nm1654405

BRIDGEMAN ROCK
Production company

3006 Cole Ave.
Dallas, TX 75204
214-744-4242 (phone)
214-748-7625 (fax)

info@languageofabrokenheart.com
languageofabrokenheart.com
imdb.com/company/co0298227

Does not accept any unsolicited material. Genres include romance and comedy.

BRIDGET JOHNSON FILMS
Production company

1416 N. La Brea Ave
Los Angeles, CA 90028
323-802-1749

imdb.com/company/co0095018

Does not accept any unsolicited material. Project types include TV and feature films. Genres include drama, thriller, and comedy.

Bridget Johnson
Producer
imdb.com/name/nm0424660

BRIGHTLIGHT PICTURES
Production company and distributor

The Bridge Studios
2400 Boundary Rd
Burnaby, BC V5M 3Z3
Canada
604-628-3000 (phone)
604-628-3001 (fax)

info@brightlightpictures.com
brightlightpictures.com
imdb.com/company/co0065717

Does not accept any unsolicited material. Project types include feature films and TV. Genres include drama and comedy. Established in 2001.

Shawn Williamson
Chairman
imdb.com/name/nm0932144
linkedin.com/pub/shawn-williamson/13/442/124

BRILLIANT DIGITAL ENTERTAINMENT
Production company

14011 Ventura Blvd, Suite 501
Sherman Oaks, CA 91423
818-386-2179

brilliantdigital.com
imdb.com/company/co0004768
linkedin.com/company/brilliant-digital-entertainment

Does not accept any unsolicited material. Project types include TV.

BRISTOW GLOBAL MEDIA
Production company

Berkeley Castle
208-2 Berkeley St
Toronto ON M5A 4J5
CANADA
416-306-6455

info@bristowglobalmedia.com
bristowglobalmedia.com
imdb.com/company/co0473988
twitter.com/jbristowBGM

Does not accept any unsolicited material. Genres include documentary.

Claire Adams
Producer
imdb.com/name/nm3346038

BRITISH FILM INSTITUTE (BFI)
Production company and distributor

information@bfi.org.uk
bfi.org.uk
imdb.com/company/co0061324
facebook.com/BritishFilmInstitute
twitter.com/bfi

Does not accept any unsolicited material. Project types include feature films. Genres include comedy.

Tanya Seghatchian
Producer
imdb.com/name/nm0782036

BRITISH LION FILM CORPORATION
Production company, distributor, and sales agent

Pinewood Studios
Pinewood Rd.
Iver Heath, Buckinghamshire SL0 0NH
UK
+44 17 5365 1700 (phone)
+44 17 5365 6844 (fax)

petersnell@britishlionfilms.com
britishlionfilms.com
imdb.com/company/co0103038

Does not accept any unsolicited material. Project types include short films and feature films. Genres include documentary, science fiction, and animation.

Peter Snell
Producer
imdb.com/name/nm0811056

BRITS IN LA DISTRIB
Distributor

6424 Ivarene Ave
Los Angeles, CA 90068
310-666-9905

craigyoung26@aol.com
imdb.com/company/co0340255

Does not accept any unsolicited material.

BROAD GREEN PICTURES
Production company and distributor

6555 W Barton Ave, Los Angeles, CA, United States, 90038
323-688-1800

info@broadgreen.com
broadgreen.com
imdb.com/company/co0471578

Does not accept any unsolicited material. Project types include TV and feature films. Genres include thriller, family, action, and drama.

Victor Moyers
President (Production)
imdb.com/name/nm2098196

BROKEN CAMERA PRODUCTIONS

San Antonio, TX
210-446-8103

info@brokencameraproductions.com
brokencameraproductions.com
imdb.com/company/co0224909
facebook.com/brokencameraproductions

Accepts query letters from unproduced, unrepresented writers via email. Project types include feature films. Genres include comedy, drama, and thriller.

Matthew Garth
Producer
210-454-8103
matthew@brokencameraproductions.com
imdb.com/name/nm2123288

Lynette C. Aleman
Producer
210-317-4647
lynette@brokencameraproductions.com
imdb.com/name/nm4074593

Sommer Bostick
Editor
830-998-5017
sommer@brokencameraproductions.com
imdb.com/name/nm5223266

David Y. Duncan
Producer
210-884-5234
dave@brokencameraproductions.com
imdb.com/name/nm2839229

BROKEN SILENCE
Production company and distributor

scripts@broken-silence.co.uk
broken-silence.co.uk
imdb.com/company/co0537707

facebook.com/brokensilencedistro
twitter.com/brokensilence

Accepts query letters from unproduced, unrepresented writers. Project types include feature films and short films. Genres include action, thriller, crime, drama, and detective. Established in 2005.

Zaid Alkayat
Director
scripts@broken-silence.co.uk

BROKEN WINGS FILMS
Production company

1221 20th Ave NE
Naples, FL 34120
239-580-7406

jimdavis30@hotmail.com
emptychairmovie.wix.com/brokenwings
imdb.com/company/co0476496

Does not accept any unsolicited material. Genres include horror and drama.

BRON MEDIA CORP.
Production company and studio

5542 Short St, Burnaby, BC, Canada, V5J 1L9
604-628-5568 (phone)
604-435-4384 (fax)

contact@bronstudios.com
bronstudios.com

Does not accept any unsolicited material. Project types include TV. Genres include family and drama.

BROOKLYN FILMS
Production company

3815 Hughes Ave.
Culver City, CA 90232
310-838-2500 (phone)
310-204-3464 (fax)

inquiries@brooklynfilms.com
brooklynfilms.com
imdb.com/company/co0088618
facebook.com/pages/New-York-NY/Brooklyn-Films/
    12482289393

Accepts query letters from unproduced, unrepresented writers. Project types include TV and feature films. Genres include crime and drama.

Marsha Oglesby
Executive Producer
imdb.com/name/nm0644749

Robin Adams
Co-Founder
robin.adams@brooklynfilms.com
linkedin.com/in/robincadams

Michael Helman
michael.helman@brooklynfilms.com

Jon Avnet
Principal
imdb.com/name/nm0000816

BROOKSFILMS
Production company

9336 W. Washington Blvd.
Culver City , CA 90232
310-202-3292 (phone)
310-202-3225 (fax)

imdb.com/company/co0000858
facebook.com/pages/Mel-Brooks/109496505734925

Does not accept any unsolicited material. Project types include feature films. Genres include drama and comedy.

Mel Brooks
President/Director/Writer
imdb.com/name/nm0000316

BROOKSIDE ARTIST MANAGEMENT
Production company

250 W. 57th St
New York, NY 10019
212-489-4929 (phone)
212-489-9056 (fax)

imdb.com/company/co0084962
linkedin.com/company/brookside-artist-management
facebook.com/pages/Brookside-Artist-Management/
    170654672948747

Does not accept any unsolicited material. Project types include feature films. Genres include comedy.

Emily Gerson Saines
President/Producer/Manager
imdb.com/name/nm0756593

BROTHERS DOWDLE PRODUCTIONS
Production company

13323 W Washington Blvd.
Los Angeles, CA 90066

imdb.com/company/co0114058

Does not accept any unsolicited material. Project types include feature films. Genres include thriller and drama.

John Dowdle
Director/Writer
imdb.com/name/nm0235719

Drew Dowdle
Producer/Writer
imdb.com/name/nm1803105

BROWN EYED BOY
Production company

The Shepherds Bldg 5th Floor
Charecroft Way, London
W14 0EE
44 (0870-333-1700

richard.tan@browneyedboy.com
browneyedboy.com
imdb.com/company/co0186906
facebook.com/BrownEyedBoyTV
twitter.com/BrownEyedBoyTV

Does not accept any unsolicited material. Project types include TV. Genres include drama and thriller.

Gary Reich
Producer
imdb.com/name/nm0716933

BROWNIE
Distributor

6-7-1-212
Shinjuku

Shinjuku, Tokyo 160-0022
Japan
03-3354-6274

info@brownie-project.com
brownie-project.com
imdb.com/company/co0297899

Does not accept any unsolicited material. Project types include feature films and TV. Genres include comedy and horror.

Taishi Suzuki
imdb.com/name/nm4666237

BROWNSTONE PRODUCTIONS
Production company

100 Universal Plaza
Universal City, CA 91608

imdb.com/company/co0019749

Does not accept any unsolicited material. Project types include feature films and TV. Genres include comedy, fantasy, and drama.

Max Handelman
Producer
imdb.com/name/nm2583641

Elizabeth Banks
Actor/Producer
imdb.com/name/nm0006969

BRUCE COHEN PRODUCTIONS
Production company

8292 Hollywood Blvd
Los Angeles, CA 90069
323-650-4567 (phone)
323-843-9534 (fax)

imdb.com/company/co0297426
twitter.com/brucecohen83

Does not accept any unsolicited material. Project types include TV. Genres include drama.

Bruce Cohen
Principal
imdb.com/name/nm0169260
facebook.com/bruce.cohen.908

Jessica Leventhal
Director of Development
imdb.com/name/nm4202199
linkedin.com/pub/jessica-leventhal/25/453/196

BRUCKS ENTERTAINMENT
Production company

6363 Wilshire Blvd., Suite 416
Los Angeles, CA 90046
323-556-6419

imdb.com/company/co0284585
twitter.com/bryanbrucks

Does not accept any unsolicited material. Project types include feature films. Genres include action.

Bryan Brucks
Producer/Manager
imdb.com/name/nm1834398

BRUSH FIRE FILMS
Production company

2727 Inwood Rd
Dallas, TX 75235
214-350-2676 (phone)
214-352-1427 (fax)

martins@brushfirefilms.com
imdb.com/company/co0224019
linkedin.com/company/brush-fire-films

Does not accept any unsolicited material. Project types include TV. Genres include documentary.

BRYAN HICKOX PRODUCTIONS
Production company

1120 Hideaway Dr. N
Jacksonville, FL 32259
904-509-4790 (phone)
904-230-4162 (fax)

b.hickox@comcast.net
bryanhickox.com/BryanHickox.com/
    Welcome_Page.html
imdb.com/company/co0032875
linkedin.com/company/bryan-hickox-productions

Does not accept any unsolicited material. Project types include TV and feature films. Genres include drama, documentary, and thriller. Established in 1996.

BS PRODUCTIONS
Production company

9229 Sunset Blvd., Suite 608
Los Angeles, CA 90069
310-717-5187

barrett_stuart@bsproductions.org
bsproductions.org
imdb.com/company/co0191476

Does not accept any unsolicited material. Genres include drama.

Barrett Stuart
Producer
imdb.com/name/nm2302967

BUCK 50 PRODUCTIONS
Production company and distributor

123 Town Square Place
Jersey City, NJ 07310
646-619-9977

buck50productions.com
imdb.com/company/co0144923
facebook.com/buck50productions

Does not accept any unsolicited material. Genres include comedy.

BUENA ONDA PICTURES
Production company

PO BOX 403137
Miami Beach, FL 33140
305-600-2785

info@silviosardi.com
imdb.com/company/co0130531

Does not accept any unsolicited material. Genres include documentary.

BUFFALO JUMP PRODUCTIONS
Production company

6100 Primrose St, Suite 12
Los Angeles, CA 90068
323-461-3422

info@buffalojumpproductions.com
buffalojumpproductions.com
imdb.com/company/co0061609

Does not accept any unsolicited material.

Bill Kalmenson
Actor/Writer/Director
imdb.com/name/nm0436105

BUNGALOW MEDIA + ENTERTAINMENT
Production company

7 Penn Plaza, Suite 1105
New York, NY 10001
646-753-5037

1888 Century Park East, 7th Floor
Los Angeles, CA 90067
310-734-0451

ahoffman@bungalowentertainment.com
bungalowentertainment.com
imdb.com/company/co0533703
linkedin.com/company/bungalow-media-
    entertainment

Does not accept any unsolicited material. Project types include feature films and TV. Genres include drama and comedy.

Robert Friedman
CEO/Producer
imdb.com/name/nm2473259

BUNIM-MURRAY PRODUCTIONS
Production company

6007 Sepulveda Blvd
Van Nuys, CA 91411
818-756-5100 (phone)
818-756-5140 (fax)

bmp@bunim-murray.com
bunim-murray.com
linkedin.com/company/bunim-murray-productions
facebook.com/BunimMurrayProductions
twitter.com/bunimmurray

Does not accept any unsolicited material. Project types include TV. Genres include documentary and reality.

Scott Freeman
Executive Vice President (Current Programming and Development)
imdb.com/name/nm1321720
linkedin.com/pub/dir/Scott/Freeman

John Greco
Vice President (Production)
linkedin.com/pub/erin-cristall/9/545/549

Gil Goldschein
President
imdb.com/name/nm2251455
linkedin.com/pub/gil-goldschein/0/a33/17

Jonathan Murray
Chairman
imdb.com/name/nm0615086

Erin Cristall
Vice President (Development)
imdb.com/name/nm0188058
linkedin.com/pub/dir/erin/cristall

Jeff Jenkins
Executive Vice President
imdb.com/name/nm0420870
linkedin.com/pub/jeff-jenkins/9/B09/79B

Cara Goldberg
Production Executive
linkedin.com/in/caraleigh

BUREAU OF MOVING PICTURES
Production company

1548 Hedgepath Ave
Hacienda Heights, CA 91745
626-961-3465

imdb.com/company/co0211360

Does not accept any unsolicited material. Project types include feature films. Genres include drama.

Andrew Meieran
Producer/Financier
imdb.com/name/nm2677942

Matthew Tabak
Producer
imdb.com/name/nm0845860

BUREAU, THE
Production company

42 Glasshouse St
2nd Fl
London W1B 5DW
UK
+44 20 7439 8257

mail@thebureau.co.uk
thebureau.co.uk
imdb.com/company/co0104435

Does not accept any unsolicited material. Project types include feature films. Genres include thriller, drama, and horror.

Tristan Goligher
Producer
imdb.com/name/nm2571063

BURLEIGH FILMWORKS
Production company

22287 Mulholland Highway, Suite 129
Calabasas, CA 91302
818-224-4686 (phone)
818-223-9089 (fax)

imdb.com/company/co0176271

Accepts query letters from unproduced, unrepresented writers. Project types include TV.

Steve Burleigh
Principal
steve.burleigh@burleighfilmworks.com
imdb.com/name/nm0122114
linkedin.com/pub/steve-burleigh/8/a35/813
facebook.com/steve.burleigh

BURNING IMAGE
Production company

41 S. Haddon Ave Haddonfield, NJ 08033
856-428-9330

imdb.com/company/co0124499

Does not accept any unsolicited material. Project types include TV. Genres include documentary, comedy, and crime.

BURNSIDE ENTERTAINMENT, INC.
Production company

265 W 19th St
New York, NY 10011
323-902-7384

mail@burnsideentertainment.com
imdb.com/company/co0180518

Accepts query letters from unproduced, unrepresented writers.

Seth William Meier
Partner
323-902-7384
sethwilliammeier@burnsideentertainment.com
imdb.com/name/nm0576720

Glen Trotiner
Owner
212-727-7665
gtrotiner@burnsideentertainment.com
imdb.com/name/nm0873641

BUSBOY PRODUCTIONS
Production company

375 Greenwich St, Fifth Floor
New York, NY 10013
212-965-4700

imdb.com/company/co0176273
facebook.com/pages/Busboy-Productions/
    112760302071089

Does not accept any unsolicited material. Project types include TV and feature films. Genres include comedy.

Chris McShane
Co-Head of Production and Development
imdb.com/name/nm1457370

Jon Stewart
Principal
imdb.com/name/nm0829537

BUSHIROAD
Production company

1-38-1-2F
Chuo
Nakano, Tokyo 164-0011
Japan
03-5348-0852 (phone)
03-5348-0854 (fax)

support@bushiroad.com
bushiroad.com/en
imdb.com/company/co0337428

Does not accept any unsolicited material. Project types include TV. Genres include drama and animation.

Takaaki Kidani
President (Executive)
imdb.com/name/nm2154825

BY HAND MEDIA
Production company

926 Bergen Ave Ste. 167
Jersey City, NJ 07306
201-417-3852

web@byhandmedia.com
byhandmedia.com
imdb.com/company/co0351309

Does not accept any unsolicited material. Genres include documentary.

C2 ENTERTAINMENT
Production company

2917 W Olive Ave
Burbank, CA 91505
818-450-3425

Info@c2creates.com
c2creates.com
facebook.com/pages/C2-Entertainment/
    106245599449496
twitter.com/c2creates

Does not accept any unsolicited material. Project types include feature films. Genres include action.

CABIN CREEK FILMS
Production company

270 Lafayette St, Suite 710
New York, NY 10012

212-343-2545 (phone)
212-343-2585 (fax)

info@cabincreekfilms.com
cabincreekfilms.com
imdb.com/company/co0050052
linkedin.com/company/cabin-creek-films
facebook.com/pages/Cabin-Creek-Films/
    196118677070312
twitter.com/cabincreekfilms

Does not accept any unsolicited material. Project types include feature films and TV. Genres include drama.

Barbara Kopple
Producer/Director
imdb.com/name/nm0465932

CAIRO/SIMPSON ENTERTAINMENT
Production company

10764 Rochester Ave.
Los Angeles, CA 90024
310-470-9309

imdb.com/company/co0039501

Does not accept any unsolicited material. Project types include feature films. Genres include romance and horror.

Judy Cairo
Producer
imdb.com/name/nm0003437

Michael A. Simpson
Producer/Director/Writer
imdb.com/name/nm0801121

C A KAPLAN ENTERTAINMENT
Production company

917-804-8229

charles@cakaplanent.com
cakaplanent.com

Does not accept any unsolicited material. Project types include feature films and TV. Genres include drama, detective, action, thriller, crime, science fiction, sociocultural, non-fiction, horror, and animation. Established in 2001.

Charles Kaplan
Literary Manager\Owner
charles@cakaplanent.com

CALAMITY FILMS
Production company

Unit 2 Waldo Works
Waldo Rd
London NW10 6AW
UK
+44208-964-1315

info@calamityfilms.com
calamityfilms.co.uk
imdb.com/company/co0400365

Does not accept any unsolicited material. Genres include drama, family, and comedy.

David Livingstone
Producer
imdb.com/name/nm5928339

CALIBER MEDIA COMPANY
Production company

5670 Wilshire Blvd.
Ste 1600
Los Angeles, CA 90036
310-786-9210

calibermediaco.com
imdb.com/company/co0228420
facebook.com/CALIBERMEDIACO
twitter.com/calibermediaco

Accepts query letters from unproduced, unrepresented writers. Project types include feature films. Genres include sociocultural, action, crime, horror, drama, family, and thriller. Established in 2008.

Dallas Sonnier
Partner
imdb.com/name/nm2447772

Jack Heller
Partner
imdb.com/name/nm2597331
linkedin.com/pub/jack-heller/12/60/967

CALLAHAN FILMWORKS
Studio

4000 Warner Blvd.
Building 138, Room 209
Burbank, CA 91522
323-878-0645 (phone)
323-878-0649 (fax)

imdb.com/company/co0113274

Does not accept any unsolicited material. Project types include TV and feature films. Genres include fantasy, romance, action, crime, comedy, family, and drama.

Michael Ewing
Partner
imdb.com/name/nm0263989
linkedin.com/pub/michael-ewing/56/545/728

Peter Segal
Partner
imdb.com/name/nm0781842
linkedin.com/pub/pete-segal/11/996/a90

Chris Osbrink
Creative Executive
imdb.com/name/nm1644713
linkedin.com/pub/chris-osbrink/6/b33/a1a

CALLA PRODUCTIONS
Production company

3019 Effie St
Los Angeles, CA 90026
310-392-3775 (phone)
310-399-5594 (fax)

debcalla@callaproductions.com
callaproductions.com
imdb.com/company/co0131004
linkedin.com/company/calla-productions
facebook.com/pages/Calla-Productions/
    166894293323398

Does not accept any unsolicited material. Project types include TV and feature films. Genres include drama.

Deborah Calla
Producer
imdb.com/name/nm0130111

CALUV FILMS

Production company

1825 Ponce De Leon Blvd.
#465
Coral Gables, FL 33134

imdb.com/company/co0386562

Does not accept any unsolicited material. Genres include action, horror, and science fiction.

CAMELOT DISTRIBUTION GROUP

Distributor and sales agent

300 Spectrum Center Dr
Suite 400
Irvine, CA 92618
949-754-3030

info@camelotfilms.com
camelotfilms.com
imdb.com/company/co0176716
twitter.com/camelotent

Does not accept any unsolicited material. Genres include action, horror, and comedy.

CAMELOT ENTERTAINMENT

Distributor

300 Spectrum Center Dr
Suite 400
Irvine, CA 92618
949-754-3030

submissions@camelotfilms.com (script submissions)
info@camelotfilms.com (general)
camelotent.com
imdb.com/company/co0006731

Accepts scripts from unproduced, unrepresented writers. Project types include feature films and TV. Genres include animation, drama, romance, science fiction, thriller, comedy, action, non-fiction, family, and horror.

Steven Istock
Partner
imdb.com/name/nm1916408

Robert Atwell
Chairman
imdb.com/name/nm0041164

CAMERA SPEEDS

Production company

Denver, CO 80516
303-408-7715

admin@cameraspeeds.com
cameraspeeds.com
imdb.com/company/co0472526

Does not accept any unsolicited material. Project types include short films. Genres include drama and documentary.

Kyle Woodiel
Lead Producer of Production Development (Producer)
imdb.com/name/nm2946459

CAMPBELL GROBMAN FILMS

Production company

9461 Charleville Blvd, Suite 301
Beverly Hills, CA 90212
310-422-8444

imdb.com/company/co0360646
facebook.com/pages/Campbell-Grobman-Films/
336999609674457

Does not accept any unsolicited material. Project types include feature films. Genres include horror, comedy, and drama.

Christa Campbell
Partner/Actor/Producer
imdb.com/name/nm0132300

Lati Grobman
Partner/Producer
imdb.com/name/nm0342788

CAMPFIRE PRODUCTIONS

Production company and distributor

16890 County Rd 558
Farmersville, TX 75442

imdb.com/company/co0400459

Does not accept any unsolicited material.

CAMP GREY PRODUCTIONS

Production company

9229 W Sunset Blvd.
West Hollywood, CA 90069
424-283-3900

imdb.com/company/co0477188

Does not accept any unsolicited material. Project types include feature films. Genres include thriller and drama.

CAMP MOTION PICTURES

Production company and distributor

PO Box 132
Butler, NJ 07405
973-838-3030

CampPictures@aol.com
imdb.com/company/co0052772

Does not accept any unsolicited material. Project types include TV. Genres include comedy and horror.

CANADA FILM CAPITAL

Production company

130 Bloor St W
Ste 500
Toronto, ON M5S 1N5
Canada
416-927-2228 (phone)
416-920-9134 (fax)

scardinale@canadafilmcapital.com
canadafilmcapital.com
imdb.com/company/co0311606

Does not accept any unsolicited material. Project types include TV. Genres include fantasy and family.

Sante Cardinale
Executive
imdb.com/name/nm2776692

CANADIAN BROADCASTING COMPANY (CBC)

Studio

181 Queen St
Ottawa, ON, Canada, K1P 1K9
613-288-6000

liaison@cbc.ca

cbc.ca
imdb.com/company/co0045850
linkedin.com/company/cbc

Does not accept any unsolicited material. Project types include feature films and TV. Genres include comedy, documentary, non-fiction, action, animation, period, family, crime, and drama. Established in 2007.

Kim Wilson
linkedin.com/pub/dir/Kimberly/Wilson

Trevor Walton
imdb.com/name/nm4280633

Hubert Lacroix
President
imdb.com/name/nm4522750

Suzanne Colvin-Goulding
imdb.com/name/nm0003681
linkedin.com/pub/suzanne-colvin-goulding/17/704/10B

CANDESCENT FILMS

Production company and financing company

New York, NY, United States

info@candescentfilms.com
candescentfilms.com
imdb.com/company/co0320035

Does not accept any unsolicited material. Project types include feature films and TV. Genres include action, thriller, drama, and family.

CANNELL STUDIOS

Production company

7083 Hollywood Blvd., Ste. 600
Hollywood , CA 90028
323-465-5800 (phone)
323-856-7390 (fax)

questions@cannell.com
cannell.com
imdb.com/company/co0369010
linkedin.com/company/cannell-studios
facebook.com/StephenCannell

Does not accept any unsolicited material. Genres include drama, horror, and action.

Theresa Peoples
Development
imdb.com/name/nm1323919

CANNY LADS PRODUCTIONS
Production company

500 S. Buena Vista St, Animation 3B-10
Burbank, CA 91521
818-560-1314

cannyladsproductions.com

Does not accept any unsolicited material. Project types include TV. Genres include comedy and drama.

Julie Anne Robinson
Director/Producer
imdb.com/name/nm1455688

CANTON THEATRICAL
Production company

PO Box 852
Edison, NJ 08818
732-586-3493

anthony@cantontheatrical.com
cantontheatrical.com
imdb.com/company/co0447064

Does not accept any unsolicited material. Project types include short films. Genres include comedy and drama.

CAPACITY PICTURES
Production company

310-247-8534

capacitypictures@gmail.com
imdb.com/company/co0192878

Does not accept any unsolicited material. Project types include feature films. Genres include crime, drama, thriller, horror, and comedy. Established in 2008.

Wayne Rice
Principal
imdb.com/name/nm0723573

Richard Heller
Principal
imdb.com/name/nm0375378
linkedin.com/pub/richard-heller/10/8B5/95A
twitter.com/richardheller

CAPITAL ARTS ENTERTAINMENT

23315 Clift on Plaza
Valencia, CA 91354
818-343-8950 (phone)
818-343-8962 (fax)

info@capitalarts.com
sandmancommunications.com
imdb.com/company/co0009722
facebook.com/capitalartsentertainmentinc

Accepts query letters from unproduced, unrepresented writers via email. Genres include thriller, comedy, horror, and action. Established in 1995.

Joe Genier
Partner
imdb.com/name/nm0312856
linkedin.com/pub/joe-genier/11/a67/851

Rob Kerchner
Partner
imdb.com/name/nm0449246

Mike Elliot
imdb.com/name/nm0254291
linkedin.com/pub/mike-elliott/8/443/509

CAPITAL ENTERTAINMENT
Production company and distributor

217 Seaton Place NE
Washington, DC 20002
202-506-5051

billcarpenter@capitalentertainment.com
capitalentertainment.com
imdb.com/company/co0139813
facebook.com/capital64chicago

Does not accept any unsolicited material. Genres include drama and comedy.

CAPITAL FILMS
Production company

London
UK
+44 (0) 20 8318 6227

info@capital-films.com
capital-films.com
imdb.com/company/co0364206
facebook.com/Capital-Films-
    Limited-164020987035183
twitter.com/CapitalFilms

Does not accept any unsolicited material. Project types
include TV and feature films. Genres include thriller,
science fiction, comedy, and drama.

Claire Daly
Producer
imdb.com/name/nm5011217

CAPITOL PICTURES
Production company

PO Box 2057
Palm Beach, FL 33480

featurefilms@capitol-pictures.com
capitol-pictures.com
imdb.com/company/co0096343

Does not accept any unsolicited material. Project types
include feature films and short films. Genres include
drama and comedy. Established in 2002.

CAPRI FILMS
Production company

123 -B Davenport Rd
Toronto, ON M5R1H8
Canada
416-960-3003 (phone)
416-535-3414 (fax)

info@caprifilms.com
caprifilms.com
imdb.com/company/co0304922

Does not accept any unsolicited material. Genres
include fantasy and drama.

CAPTIVATE ENTERTAINMENT
Studio

3111 Camino Del Rio North, Suite 400
San Diego, CA 92108
323-658-7760 (phone)
818-733-4303 (fax)

paul@captive-entertainment.com
captive-entertainment.com
imdb.com/company/co0263292

Does not accept any unsolicited material. Project types
include TV and feature films. Genres include fantasy,
thriller, comedy, myth, drama, science fiction,
romance, and action.

Jeffrey Weiner
Chairman (CEO)
imdb.com/name/nm1788648

Ben Smith
President
imdb.com/name/nm3328356
linkedin.com/in/bensmithonline

Tony Shaw
Creative Executive
tony.shaw@univfilms.com
imdb.com/name/nm4130192
linkedin.com/pub/tony-shaw/9/958/86a
facebook.com/public/Tony-Shaw

CAPTURE
Production company

36c Junction Rd
London N19 5RD
UK
+44(0)20 7739 3319

all@wearecapture.com
wearecapture.com
imdb.com/company/co0309862
twitter.com/Capture_tweets

Does not accept any unsolicited material. Project types
include feature films. Genres include drama.

M.J. McMahon
Production Manager |
imdb.com/name/nm1702155

CAPTURED LIGHT WORKS
Production company

1699 S Trenton St Suite #82
Denver, CO 80231
303-941-0886

Stephen@capturedlightworks.com
imdb.com/company/co0232123

Does not accept any unsolicited material. Genres
include science fiction.

Stephen McKissen
Owner (Executive)
imdb.com/name/nm1744656

CAREER ARTIST MANAGEMENT
Production company

1100 Glendon Ave, Suite 1100
Los Angeles, CA 90024
310-776-7640 (phone)
310-776-7659 (fax)

camanagement.com
imdb.com/company/co0175522
linkedin.com/company/career-artist-management
facebook.com/pages/Career-Artist-Management-
    CAM/1571532839756068

Does not accept any unsolicited material. Project types
include TV. Genres include drama and comedy.

Jordan Feldstein
Producer
imdb.com/name/nm3206443

CARGO ENTERTAINMENT
Production company, distributor, and sales agent

135 W 29th St
Ste 300
New York, NY 10001
US
646-354-7160 (phone)
212-674-0081 (fax)

info@cargoentertainment.com
cargoentertainment.com
www/www.imdb.com/company/co0370684

Does not accept any unsolicited material. Project types
include TV and feature films. Genres include thriller.

Marina Grasic
Producer
imdb.com/name/nm1628464

CARMEN BEDFORD

carmenbedford2@gmail.com
facebook.com/Ms.CeeBee

Does not accept any unsolicited material. Project types
include feature films and TV. Genres include
documentary, detective, crime, comedy, animation,
action, sociocultural, period, family, drama, non-
fiction, fantasy, horror, myth, reality, romance, science
fiction, and thriller.

Carmen Bedford
CEO
carmenbedford2@gmail.com

CARNABY FILMS
Distributor

8th Fl
55 New Oxford St
London WC1A 1BS
UK
+44 0800 022 33 45 (phone)
+44 0800-234-6146 (fax)

thelounge@carnabyentertainment.com
carnabyfilms.com
imdb.com/company/co0197493

Does not accept any unsolicited material. Project types
include TV and feature films. Genres include thriller.

Michael Loveday
Producer
imdb.com/name/nm2548860

CARNABY FILM SALES &
DISTRIBUTION
Distributor and sales agent

57-61 Mortimer St
Ste 412
London W1W 8HS
UK
+44207-434-0185

ashley@carnabyinternational.com

carnabysales.com
imdb.com/company/co0444365
twitter.com/CarnabyFilms

Does not accept any unsolicited material. Project types include feature films. Genres include action and drama.

CARNABY INTERNATIONAL
Production company, distributor, and sales agent

55 New Oxford St
8th Fl
London WC1A 1BS
UK
+44 0 800 022 33 45 (phone)
+44 0800-234-6146 (fax)

info@carnabyinternational.com
carnabyinternational.com
imdb.com/company/co0104601
facebook.com/carnabyinternational
twitter.com/carnabyfilms

Does not accept any unsolicited material. Project types include TV. Genres include drama.

CARNIVAL FILM & TELEVISION
Production company and distributor

100 Universal City Plaza
Universal City, CA 91608

info@carnivalfilms.co.uk
carnivalfilms.co.uk
imdb.com/company/co0106806
linkedin.com/company/carnival-film-&-television-
    limited
facebook.com/carnivalfilm
twitter.com/Carnival_Films

Does not accept any unsolicited material. Project types include feature films, short films, and TV. Genres include documentary, drama, science fiction, thriller, action, crime, and romance. Established in 1978.

Kimberly Hikaka
Production Executive
imdb.com/name/nm2529465
linkedin.com/pub/kimberley-hikaka/5/10/aa4

Sam Symons
Development Executive
imdb.com/name/nm1599585
linkedin.com/pub/symons-sam/23/647/2

CAROL BAUM PRODUCTIONS
Production company

8899 Beverly Blvd., Suite 721
Los Angeles, CA 90048
310-550-4575

imdb.com/company/co0058685
linkedin.com/company/carol-baum-productions

Does not accept any unsolicited material. Project types include feature films. Genres include drama, comedy, crime, and romance. Established in 2001.

Carol Baum
Producer
imdb.com/name/nm0062071

CAROUSEL TELEVISION
Production company

12925 Riverside Dr, 4th Floor
Sherman Oaks, CA 90068
818-849-3900

imdb.com/company/co0303652
facebook.com/pages/Carousel-Television/
    109347619094709

Does not accept any unsolicited material. Project types include TV. Genres include comedy.

Steve Carell
Actor/Owner/President
imdb.com/name/nm0136797

Campbell Smith
Co-Head of TV
imdb.com/name/nm0962607

CARRIE PRODUCTIONS
Production company

2625 Alcatraz Ave, Suite 243
Berkeley, CA 94705
510-450-2500

imdb.com/company/co0059331

facebook.com/pages/Carrie-Productions-Inc/
   113680898643029

Does not accept any unsolicited material. Project types include TV and feature films. Genres include drama.

Karen Bolt
Development Executive
imdb.com/name/nm1163463

Danny Glover
Producer/Actor
imdb.com/name/nm0000418

CARSON SIGNATURE FILMS
Production company

10 Universal City Plaza, 20th Floor
Universal City, CA 91608
818-753-2333 (phone)
818-753-2310 (fax)

imdb.com/company/co0176330

Does not accept any unsolicited material. Project types include feature films. Genres include thriller.

Darby Connor
Sr. Vice President/ Writer
imdb.com/name/nm1915279

Beaux Carson
President/Producer
imdb.com/name/nm0141185

CARTOON NETWORK
Production company and studio

300 N 3rd St.
6th Floor
Burbank, CA 91502
818-729-4000 (phone)
818-729-4220 (fax)

10 Columbus Circle
New York, NY 10019
212-275-7800

1065 Techwood Dr. NW
Atlanta, GA 30318
404-885-2263 (phone)
404-885-4312 (fax)

adultswim.com

imdb.com/company/co0153115
twitter.com/cartoonnetwork

Accepts query letters from unproduced, unrepresented writers. Project types include video games.

Mike Lazzo
Executive Vice President (Creative Director, Adult Swim)
imdb.com/name/nm0494020

Katie Krentz
Development Executive (Comedy Animation)
imdb.com/name/nm1872617
twitter.com/katiekrentz

CARYN MANDABACH PRODUCTIONS
Production company

135 Bay St, Unit 7
Santa Monica, CA 90405
310-399-6700

info@mandabachtv.com
mandabachtv.com
imdb.com/company/co0275656

Does not accept any unsolicited material. Project types include TV. Genres include crime, comedy, and drama.

Michael Besman
Executive
imdb.com/name/nm0078698

Caryn Mandabach
Producer
imdb.com/name/nm0541591

CASEY SILVER PRODUCTIONS
Production company

1411 5th St
Santa Monica, CA 90401
310-566-3750 (phone)
310-566-3751 (fax)

imdb.com/company/co0058884

Does not accept any unsolicited material. Project types include feature films. Genres include family, drama, comedy, thriller, and action.

Casey Silver
Owner
casey@caseysilver.com
imdb.com/name/nm0798661
facebook.com/pages/Casey-Silver-Productions

Matthew Reynolds
Creative Executive
matthew@caseysilver.com
imdb.com/name/nm2303863
linkedin.com/pub/matthew-reynolds/66/345/258

CASPIAN PICTURES
Production company

839 E. Orange Grove Ave
Burbank, CA 91501
818-567-1565 (phone)
818-567-1560 (fax)

info@caspianpictures.net
caspianpictures.net
imdb.com/company/co0246517
facebook.com/pages/Caspian-Pictures/
    221682464537498

Does not accept any unsolicited material. Project types include feature films. Genres include drama.

Will Raee
Producer, Director
imdb.com/name/nm0706091

Brian Bullock
Producer
imdb.com/name/nm3068149

CASSADAGA FILM PRODUCTION
Production company

324 E. Par St
Suite 202
Orlando, FL 32804
407-529-6989

scottbpoiley@gmail.com
cassadaga-movie.com
imdb.com/company/co0317069
facebook.com/cassadagafilm
twitter.com/CassadagaFilm

Does not accept any unsolicited material. Project types include feature films. Genres include thriller and horror. Established in 2011.

CASTLE MOUNTAIN PRODUCTIONS
Production company

476 Ossington Ave
Toronto, ON M6G 3T2
Canada
416-666-3516

colin@rogerspassmovie.com
imdb.com/company/co0305918

Does not accept any unsolicited material. Genres include drama and comedy.

CASTLE ROCK ENTERTAINMENT
Production company

9169 W. Sunset Blvd.
Los Angeles, CA 90069
310-285-2300 (phone)
310-285-2345 (fax)

imdb.com/company/co0040620

Accepts scripts from produced or represented writers.

Andrew Scheinman
andres.scheinman@castle-rock.com
imdb.com/name/nm0770650

Rob Reiner
rob.reiner@castle-rock.com
imdb.com/name/nm0001661

CATALYST MEDIA
Production company

85 Linden Ave
Verona NJ

imdb.com/company/co0057146

Does not accept any unsolicited material. Project types include TV. Genres include comedy and drama.

CATAPULT FILM FUND
Production company and financing company

39 Mesa St, Suite 209
San Francisco, CA 94129
415-738-8337

info@catapultfilmfund.org
catapultfilmfund.org
facebook.com/pages/Catapult-Film-Fund/
    199055386793333
twitter.com/CatapultFilmFnd

Accepts scripts from unproduced, unrepresented writers. Genres include documentary. Established in 2014.

Lisa Kleiner Chanoff
Founder
imdb.com/name/nm5137916

Bonni Cohen
Founder
imdb.com/name/nm1010896

CATAPULT FILMS INC.
Production company

832 Third St, Suite 303
Santa Monica, CA 90403-1155
310-395-1470 (phone)
310-401-0122 (fax)

info@catapult.ee
catapult.ee
imdb.com/company/co0100754

Accepts scripts from produced or represented writers.

Lawrence Levy
Executive
imdb.com/name/nm0506504

Lisa Josefsberg
Producer
imdb.com/name/nm2248853

CATCHPHRASE ENTERTAINMENT
Production company

3575 Cahuenga Blvd West, Suite 360
Los Angeles, CA 90068
310-622-4273 (phone)
310-826-6886 (fax)

info@catchphraseentertainment.com

catchphraseentertainment.com
imdb.com/company/co0205963
linkedin.com/company/catchphrase-entertainment
facebook.com/pages/Catchphrase-Entertainment/
    159079530776013

Does not accept any unsolicited material. Project types include feature films and TV.

Shahrook Oomer
Producer
imdb.com/name/nm1551082

Dean Shull
CEO
imdb.com/name/nm1306561

CATEGORY 5 ENTERTAINMENT
Production company

9229 Sunset Blvd., Suite 601
Los Angeles, CA 90069
310-273-9400 (phone)
310-273-9494 (fax)

imdb.com/company/co0231993
linkedin.com/company/category-5-entertainment

Does not accept any unsolicited material.

Brian Sher
Producer/Manager
imdb.com/name/nm0792033

CATFISH STUDIOS
Production company and distributor

17 Oxford Terrace
West Orange, NJ 07052

contact@catfishstudios.com
catfishstudios.com
imdb.com/company/co0140244

Does not accept any unsolicited material. Project types include TV. Genres include horror.

CAT HOLLOW FILMS
Production company

334 Pavonia Ave #3
Jersey City, NJ 07302
646-688-3499

info@windfallmovie.com
imdb.com/company/co0315997

Does not accept any unsolicited material. Project types include TV. Genres include drama and documentary.

CAVE PAINTING PICTURES
Production company

401 Logan Ave
Ste 20A
Toronto, ON M4M2P2
Canada

info@cavepaintingpics.com
cavepaintingpics.com
imdb.com/company/co0201838
facebook.com/cavepaintingpics

Does not accept any unsolicited material. Genres include horror, science fiction, and comedy.

Casey Walker
Producer
imdb.com/name/nm1043587

CAVIAR FILMS
Production company

6320 W Sunset Blvd, Los Angeles, CA, United States, 90028
310-396-3400 (phone)
310-396-3410 (fax)

info.losangeles@caviarcontent.com
imdb.com/company/co0169332

Does not accept any unsolicited material. Project types include feature films. Genres include action and drama.

Bert Hamelinck
Producer
imdb.com/name/nm0353012

CBS FILMS
Production company and distributor

11800 Wilshire Blvd
Los Angeles, CA 90025
310-575-7700

cbsfilms.com

imdb.com/company/co0047306
facebook.com/pages/CBS-Films/86622447300
twitter.com/CBSFilms

Does not accept any unsolicited material. Project types include feature films. Genres include science fiction, drama, romance, action, and fantasy.

Terry Press
imdb.com/name/nm1437110

Mark Ross
imdb.com/name/nm0743653

Maria Faillace
imdb.com/name/nm1299267

CBS TELEVISION DISTRIBUTION
Production company, distributor, and sales agent

2450 Colorado Ave., Suite 500E
Santa Monica, CA 90404
310-264-3300

825 Eighth Ave
30th Fl
New York, NY 10019
212-315-4000

dtvlegal@cbsparamount.com
cbstvd.com
imdb.com/company/co0213710

Does not accept any unsolicited material. Project types include feature films. Genres include action, comedy, and crime.

CCI ENTERTAINMENT
Production company and distributor

18 Dupont St
Toronto, ON M5R 1V2
Canada
416-964-8750

info@ccientertainment.com
ccientertainment.com
imdb.com/company/co0087343
linkedin.com/company/cci-entertainment

Does not accept any unsolicited material. Genres include drama and comedy.

Arnie Zipursky
Producer
imdb.com/name/nm0957160

CECCHI GORI PRODUCTIONS
Production company

5555 Melrose Ave
Bob Hope 203
Los Angeles, CA 90038
323-956-5954 (phone)
323-862-2254 (fax)

info@cgglobalmedia.com
imdb.com/company/co0078943

Does not accept any unsolicited material. Project types include feature films. Genres include horror, romance, thriller, drama, and family.

Niels Juul
CEO
imdb.com/name/nm3887220

Alex Shub
VP of Business and Legal Affairs
linkedin.com/pub/alex-shub/24/467/971
facebook.com/alex.shub.1

Andy Scott
Art Director
imdb.com/name/nm4866101

Jennifer Parker
Development Executive
imdb.com/name/nm4487725

Dana Galinsky
imdb.com/name/nm1919300

C.E.D. ENTERTAINMENT DISTRIBUTION
Distributor and sales agent

10635 Santa Monica Blvd.
Ste. 140
Los Angeles, CA 90025
310-475-2111

imdb.com/company/co0048523

Does not accept any unsolicited material. Genres include comedy and fantasy.

CELADOR ENTERTAINMENT
Production company

39 Long Acre
London, WC2E 9LG
United Kingdom
+44 20-7845-6800 (phone)
+44 20-7845-6801 (fax)

vrogers@celador.co.uk
celador.co.uk
imdb.com/company/co0152921

Accepts scripts from produced or represented writers. Established in 1989.

Paul Smith
psmith@celador.co.uk
imdb.com/name/nm0809531

Michelle Davies
44 020 7845 6800
mdavies@celador.co.uk

CELEBRITY VIDEO DISTRIBUTION
Distributor

6380 Wilshire Blvd
Ste 1115
Los Angeles, CA 90048
323-655-0303

myrna@celebrityhe.com
imdb.com/company/co0251533
facebook.com/pages/Celebrity-Home-Entertainment/
164884793578835
twitter.com/CelebrityHE

Does not accept any unsolicited material. Genres include drama and horror.

CELLULOID DISTRIBUTION
Distributor

974 Estes Ct.
Schaumburg, IL 60193

imdb.com/company/co0172961

Does not accept any unsolicited material.

CENTER FOR ASIAN AMERICAN MEDIA (CAAM)
Production company, distributor, and sales agent

145 Ninth St, Suite 350, San Francisco, CA, United States, 94103
415-863-0814 (phone)
415-863-7428 (fax)

info@asianamericanmedia.org
asianamericanmedia.org
imdb.com/company/co0200316

Does not accept any unsolicited material. Project types include feature films. Genres include comedy, thriller, drama, family, action, and romance.

CENTROPOLIS ENTERTAINMENT
Production company

1445 N Stanley
3rd Floor
Los Angeles, CA 90046
Los Angeles, CA 90046
323-850-1212 (phone)
323-850-1201 (fax)

info@centropolis.com
centropolis.com
imdb.com/company/co0050111
twitter.com/rolandemmerich

Accepts scripts from produced or represented writers. Genres include action, fantasy, romance, myth, and non-fiction. Established in 1985.

Roland Emmerich
imdb.com/name/nm0000386

Ute Emmerich
imdb.com/name/nm0256498

CENTSLESS PICTURES
Production company and distributor

176 E 77th St
New York, NY 10075
917-297-1829

info@centslesspictures.com
centslessblog.wordpress.com
imdb.com/company/co0326610
facebook.com/CentslessPictures

twitter.com/centslesspix

Does not accept any unsolicited material. Project types include short films and TV. Genres include comedy and non-fiction. Established in 2009.

Stephen Cavaliero
Principal
imdb.com/name/nm3308912
facebook.com/stephen.cavaliero
twitter.com/centslesspix

CESS SILVERA MUVEES
Production company

555 Washington Ave
Suite 240
Miami Beach, FL 33139
305-673-3530

hmadison@madison-si.com
imdb.com/company/co0450141

Does not accept any unsolicited material. Genres include action.

CHAIKEN FILMS
Studio

802 Potrero Ave
San Francisco, CA 94110
415-826-7880 (phone)
415-826-7882 (fax)

info@chaikenfilms.com
chaikenfilms.com
imdb.com/company/co0064208

Accepts query letters from unproduced, unrepresented writers. Project types include feature films and commercials. Genres include non-fiction. Established in 1998.

Jennifer Chaiken
Producer
jen@chaikenfilms.com
imdb.com/name/nm0149671

CHAKO FILM COMPANY
Production company

MBE713 Yebisu Garden Place Tower 1F
4-20-3 Ebisu

Shibuya-ku, Tokyo 150-6001
Japan
+81 3 34 47 77 97 (phone)
+81 3 34 47 77 97 (fax)

ixfilmgroup@gmail.com
ixfilmgroup.com
imdb.com/company/co0038754

Does not accept any unsolicited material. Project types include TV. Genres include comedy.

Chako van Leeuwen
Producer
imdb.com/name/nm0498799

CHAMBER SIX PRODUCTIONS
Production company

6815 Willoughby St, Los Angeles , CA, United States, 90038
323-960-0777

info@chambersix.com
imdb.com/company/co0163234

Does not accept any unsolicited material. Project types include feature films. Genres include thriller.

CHAMELEON FILMWORKS
Production company and distributor

14375 Myer Lake Circle
Clearwater, FL 33760
727-230-1033

info@hallowspoint.com
imdb.com/company/co0204933
facebook.com/chameleon.filmworks

Does not accept any unsolicited material. Genres include horror.

CHAMPION ENTERTAINMENT
Production company

2620 Fountain View, Suite 220
Houston, TX 77057
713-522-4701 (phone)
713-522-0426 (fax)

info@championentertainment.com
championentertainment.com

imdb.com/company/co0036127
facebook.com/CEI-Information
twitter.com/filmsbychampion

Does not accept any unsolicited material. Project types include TV and feature films. Genres include drama, horror, and family.

Bob Willems
Owner/Producer
imdb.com/name/nm0929721

CHANCHO PANZA MEDIA
Production company and distributor

3705 Surrey Ln
Colorado Springs, CO 80918
719-640-2835

ffeliu@chanchopanza.com
imdb.com/company/co0319628

Does not accept any unsolicited material. Genres include documentary.

CHANGEWORX
Production company

522 Stephanie Dr
North Caldwell, NJ 07006
212-380-8213

info@changeworx.com
changeworx.com
imdb.com/company/co0326154
facebook.com/changeworxconsulting
twitter.com/changeworxfilms

Does not accept any unsolicited material. Genres include documentary.

CHAPPELL ENTERTAINMENT
Production company and distributor

214 N Griffin Dr.
Casselberry, FL 32707
407-831-0942 (phone)
407-831-8196 (fax)

cec@chappellentertainment.com
chappellentertainment.com
imdb.com/company/co0084988
facebook.com/Chappell.Entertainment

Does not accept any unsolicited material. Genres include family and animation.

CHARLOTTE STREET FILMS

Production company

1901 Ave of the Stars, Suite 200
Los Angeles, CA 90067
310-499-4949

imdb.com/company/co0157676

Does not accept any unsolicited material. Project types include feature films and TV.

CHARTOFF PRODUCTIONS

Production company

1250 Sixth St, Suite 101
Santa Monica, CA 90401
310-319-1960 (phone)
310-319-3469 (fax)

hendeechartoff@cs.com
imdb.com/company/co0094865

Accepts scripts from produced or represented writers. Established in 1986.

Robert Chartoff
imdb.com/name/nm0153590

CHASE FILM CO.

Production company and distributor

3-38-3-2F
Jingumae
Shibuya, Tokyo 150-0001
Japan
03-5775-3692 (phone)
03-5770-3210 (fax)

information@chasefilm.com
imdb.com/company/co0223332

Does not accept any unsolicited material. Project types include TV. Genres include action.

Yasuhiro Kawakami
Producer
imdb.com/name/nm1921934

CHATTERBOX PRODUCTIONS INC.

Production company

2311 S Bayshore Dr Miami, FL 33133-4728
305-285-1058

meleposky@aol.com
ampersandcom.com/chatterbox
imdb.com/company/co0086854

Does not accept any unsolicited material. Project types include short films. Genres include action.

CHEERLAND FILM GROUP.

Production company

302-2-B No.55 Da Shi Qiao Hutong
Xicheng District, Beijing
China
86-10-84044597 (phone)
86-10-84044597-806 (fax)

chenxiaonansy@gmail.com
qixinran.com
imdb.com/name/nm2279694

Accepts query letters from unproduced, unrepresented writers. Project types include feature films. Genres include drama, animation, and family. Established in 1992.

Suey chen
Head of Production & Development
86138-111-97845
chenxiaonansy@gmail.com

CHERNIN ENTERTAINMENT

Production company

1733 Ocean Ave, Suite 300
Santa Monica, CA 90401
310-899-1205

imdb.com/company/co0286257

Accepts scripts from produced or represented writers. Project types include TV and feature films. Genres include comedy, drama, and action. Established in 2009.

Pavun Shetty
ps@cherninent.com
imdb.com/name/nm0792904

Jenno Topping
jt@cherninent.com
imdb.com/name/nm0867768

Peter Chernin
Principal
imdb.com/name/nm1858656

Katherine Pope
kp@cherninent.com
imdb.com/name/nm0691142

Ivana Schechter-Garcia
Creative Executive
imdb.com/name/nm1190974

Dylan Dark
dc@cherninent.com
imdb.com/name/nm1249995

CHERRY SKY FILMS
Production company and studio

2100 Sawtelle Blvd.,
Suite 101
Los Angeles, CA 90025
310-479-8001 (phone)
310-479-8815 (fax)

contact@cherryskyfilms.com
cherryskyfilms.com
imdb.com/company/co0032062
facebook.com/pages/Cherry-Sky-Films/
    172702119443857
twitter.com/cherryskyfilms

Does not accept any unsolicited material. Project types include feature films. Genres include comedy, drama, romance, and family. Established in 2001.

Joan Huang
Producer
imdb.com/name/nm0399009

Jeffrey Gou
Producer
imdb.com/name/nm2370188

CHESTNUT RIDGE PRODUCTIONS
Production company

8899 Beverly Blvd, Suite 800
Los Angeles, CA
310-285-7011

imdb.com/company/co0273538
linkedin.com/in/paula-wagner-53432847

Does not accept any unsolicited material. Established in 2009.

Paula Wagner
imdb.com/name/nm0906048

CHEYENNE ENTERPRISES LLC
Production company

406 Wilshire Blvd
Santa Monica, CA 90401
310-455-5000 (phone)
310-688-8000 (fax)

imdb.com/company/co0041195

Accepts scripts from produced or represented writers. Established in 2000.

Joshua Rowley
Director of Development
imdb.com/name/nm2282373

Arnold Rifkin
imdb.com/name/nm0726476

CHIAROSCURO PRODUCTIONS
Production company and distributor

400 Interstate North Parkway
Suite 1210
Atlanta, GA 30338
404-895-8368 (phone)
404-303-1598 (fax)

CDickert@PlasticShark.com
imdb.com/company/co0049191
linkedin.com/company/chiaroscuro-productions-ltd.

Does not accept any unsolicited material. Genres include drama and horror.

CHICAGOFILMS
Production company

253 W 72nd St
Suite 1108
New York, NY 10023
212-721-7700 (phone)
212-721-7701 (fax)

Editor@chicagofilm.com
chicagofilm.com
imdb.com/company/co0012485

Accepts scripts from produced or represented writers.

Bob Balaban
imdb.com/name/nm0000837

CHICKEN IN THE GATE PRODUCTIONS
Production company

1978 Hill Top Circle
Weatherford, TX
817-599-8273

imdb.com/company/co0433521

Does not accept any unsolicited material. Genres include drama and family.

CHICKFLICKS
Studio

8861 St Ives Dr
Los Angeles, CA 90069
310-854-7210

info@chickflicksinc.com
chickflicksinc.com
imdb.com/company/co0156986

Accepts scripts from produced or represented writers. Genres include non-fiction, fantasy, comedy, myth, and romance.

Stephanie Austin
310-854-7210
stephanie@chickflicksinc.com
imdb.com/name/nm0042520

Sara Risher
310-854-7210
sara@chickflicksinc.com
imdb.com/name/nm0728260

CHINA LION FILM DISTRIBUTION
Distributor

10100 Santa Monica Blvd, Suite 600,
Los Angeles, California 90067
310-461-3066

info@chinalionentertainment.com
chinalionentertainment.com
imdb.com/company/co0316267
facebook.com/chinalionfilm
twitter.com/chinalionfilm

Does not accept any unsolicited material. Project types include feature films. Genres include drama, action, comedy, and romance.

CHIPSHOT FILMS
Production company

1140 Highland Ave. #123
Manhattan Beach, CA 90266
310-772-8126

tbennett@chipshotfilms.com
chipshotfilms.com

Does not accept any unsolicited material. Project types include feature films. Genres include thriller.

Tracy Bennett
Producer
imdb.com/name/nm0072100

Lee Ross
Producer
imdb.com/name/nm0743605

CHOCKSTONE PICTURES
Production company

22355 Carbon Mesa Rd
Malibu, CA 90265
310-456-2945

steves@chockstonepictures.com
chockstonepictures.com
imdb.com/company/co0192912
facebook.com/chockstonepictures

Accepts query letters from unproduced, unrepresented writers via email. Project types include feature films. Established in 2004.

Paula Mae Schwartz
CEO
paulamae@chockstonepictures.com
imdb.com/name/nm2445382

Roger Schwartz
Development Executive
310-600-6840
rogers@chockstonepictures.com
imdb.com/name/nm0970118
linkedin.com/pub/roger-schwartz/1a/2a5/2b6

Steve Schwartz
President
steves@chockstonepictures.com
imdb.com/name/nm0777455
linkedin.com/pub/steve-schwartz/1b/8/329

CHOCOLATE SUPERSTAR PRODUCTIONS
Production company

PO Box 91145
Atlanta, GA 30364

chris@chocolatesuperstar.com
imdb.com/company/co0376954

Does not accept any unsolicited material. Project types include TV. Genres include drama.

CHOICE ONE TV
Distributor

6131 Pettiford Rd
Jacksonville, FL 32209

choiceonetv.tv
imdb.com/company/co0511287
facebook.com/ChoiceOneTV
twitter.com/ChoiceOneTV

Does not accept any unsolicited material. Genres include drama.

CHOTZEN/JENNER PRODUCTIONS
Production company

4178 Dixie Canyon Ave.
Sherman Oaks, CA 91423
323-465-9877 (phone)
323-460-6451 (fax)

imdb.com/company/co0176334

Accepts scripts from produced or represented writers. Project types include TV. Genres include drama and comedy. Established in 1990.

Yvonne Chotzen
Movie Producer
imdb.com/name/nm0159278

William Jenner
imdb.com/name/nm0421076

CHRIS/ROSE PRODUCTIONS
Production company

3131 Torreyson Place
Los Angeles, CA 90046
323-851-8772 (phone)
323-851-0662 (fax)

imdb.com/company/co0040069

Accepts scripts from produced or represented writers. Project types include TV. Genres include non-fiction, drama, and comedy.

Robert Christiansen
Executive Producer
310-781-0833
imdb.com/name/nm0160222

CHRISTIANO FILM GROUP
Production company and distributor

7512 Dr. Phillips Blvd
#50-124
Orlando, FL 32819
828-215-1860

4117 Hillsboro Pike, #103-149
Nashville TN 37215
321-961-7774

contact@christianfilms.com
christianfilms.com
imdb.com/company/co0032279
facebook.com/pages/Five-Two-Pictures/
    126882045205
twitter.com/intentfollow

Does not accept any unsolicited material. Genres include fantasy, family, and drama.

CHUBBCO FILM CO.
Studio

1550 E. Valley Rd.
Santa Barbara, CA 93108

751 N. Fairfax Ave.
#10
Los Angeles, CA 90046
310-729-5858 (phone)
310-933-1704 (fax)

chubbco@gmail.com
imdb.com/company/co0026094
facebook.com/pages/ChubbCo-Film-Co/
    114221475257012

Does not accept any unsolicited material. Genres include non-fiction, crime, and action.

Caldecot Chubb
Producer
chubbco@gmail.com
imdb.com/name/nm0160941

CHUCK FRIES PRODUCTIONS, INC.
Production company and distributor

1880 Century Park East
Suite 213
Los Angeles, CA 90067
310-203-9520 (phone)
310-203-9519 (fax)

imdb.com/company/co0040068

Does not accept any unsolicited material. Project types include TV. Genres include science fiction, crime, and detective.

Charles Fries
imdb.com/name/nm0295594

CHUCK LORRE PRODUCTIONS
Production company

4000 Warner Blvd, Bldg. 160
Burbank, CA 91522

imdb.com/company/co0004981

Does not accept any unsolicited material. Project types include TV and feature films. Genres include comedy and drama.

Robert Broder
Executive
imdb.com/name/nm2516638

Chuck Lorre
Producer/Writer
imdb.com/name/nm0521143

CINDY COWAN ENTERTAINMENT
Production company

8265 W Sunset Blvd
Suite 205
Los Angeles, CA 90046
323-822-1082 (phone)
323-822-1086 (fax)

info@cowanent.com
cowanent.com
imdb.com/company/co0094925

Does not accept any unsolicited material. Project types include feature films. Genres include drama and thriller.

Cindy Cowan
President
imdb.com/name/nm0184546

CINE BAZAR
Production company

Toho Studio
1-4-1 Seijo, Setagaya-ku
Tokyo 157-8561
Japan
+81 3 5727 2120 (phone)
+81 3 5727 2121 (fax)

hee-koo@jd5.so-net.ne.jp
imdb.com/company/co0051902

Does not accept any unsolicited material. Project types include feature films and TV. Genres include crime, drama, and action.

CINECO DISTRIBUTION
Distributor

1901 Ave Of The Stars Suite 200
Los Angeles, CA 93740

310-461-1313 (phone)
310-461-1304 (fax)

imdb.com/company/co0176060

Does not accept any unsolicited material. Genres include romance, action, and drama.

CINEDIGM
Production company and distributor

1901 Ave of the Stars 12th Floor
Los Angeles CA 90067

5550 Topanga Canyon Blvd Suite 300
Woodland Hills CA 91367
818-961-0801 (phone)
818-587-4890 (fax)

902 Broadway Ninth Floor
New York NY 07960
212-206-8600 (phone)
212-206-9001 (fax)

2049 Century Park East, Suite 1900, Los Angeles, CA, United States, 90067
424-281-5400

info@cinedigm.com
cinedigm.com
imdb.com/company/co0268731

Does not accept any unsolicited material. Project types include feature films and TV. Genres include family, thriller, drama, and action.

CINEFIL IMAGICA
Production company and distributor

5-4-14 Kitashinagawa
Shinagawa ku
Tokyo 141
Japan
+81 0 3 3280 1179 (phone)
+81 0 3 3280 7598 (fax)

info@cinefil.imagica.co.jp
cinefilimagica.com
imdb.com/company/co0180507

Does not accept any unsolicited material. Project types include TV. Genres include drama.

CINEMA EPHOCH
Production company and distributor

2600 W. Olive Ave.
5th Floor
Burbank, CA 91505
818-753-2345

info@cinemaepoch.com
cinemaepoch.com
imdb.com/company/co0028810

Does not accept any unsolicited material. Genres include action, horror, non-fiction, thriller, crime, myth, comedy, and detective.

Gregory Hatanaka
imdb.com/name/nm0368693

CINEMAGIC DISTRIBUTIONS
Production company and distributor

1507 7th St.
Suite 201
Santa Monica, CA 90401-2605

imdb.com/company/co0347352

Does not accept any unsolicited material.

CINEMAGIC ENTERTAINMENT
Studio

9229 Sunset Blvd, Suite 610
West Hollywood, CA 90069
310-385-9322 (phone)
310-385-9347 (fax)

cinemagicent.com
imdb.com/company/co0183883
facebook.com/cinemagicentertainmentproduction

Accepts query letters from unproduced, unrepresented writers. Genres include fantasy, horror, myth, action, detective, thriller, crime, and science fiction.

Lee Cohn
imdb.com/name/nm2325144

CINEMA GUILD, INC.
Production company and distributor

115 W 30th St, Suite 800, New York City , NY,
United States, 10001
212-685-6242 (phone)
212-685-4717 (fax)

info@cinemaguild.com
cinemaguild.com
imdb.com/company/co0014382

Does not accept any unsolicited material. Project types
include feature films and TV. Genres include drama,
thriller, family, and action.

CINEMA INVESTMENT
Production company

Tokyo,
Japan

info@cinv.biz
cinv.biz
imdb.com/company/co0209549

Does not accept any unsolicited material. Project types
include TV. Genres include drama and science fiction.

CINEMA LIBRE STUDIO
Studio

120 S. Victory Blvd, First Floor
Burbank, CA 91502
818-588-3033 (phone)
818-349-9922 (fax)

project@cinemalibrestudio.com
cinemalibrestudio.com
imdb.com/company/co0132224
linkedin.com/company/cinema-libre-studio
facebook.com/cinemalibrestudio
twitter.com/cinemalibre

Accepts query letters from unproduced, unrepresented
writers. Established in 2003.

Philippe Diaz
imdb.com/name/nm0225034

CINEMA MANAGEMENT GROUP LLC
Production company and distributor

8383 Wilshire Blvd, Suite 320, Beverly Hills, CA,
United States, 90211

310-300-9959 (phone)
310-300-9960 (fax)

info@cinemamanagementgroup.com
cinemamanagementgroup.com
imdb.com/company/co0179243

Does not accept any unsolicited material. Project types
include TV and theater. Genres include drama, family,
reality, and thriller.

CINEMANX
Production company and distributor

3rd Fl
12 Great Portland St
London W1W 8QN
UK
+44207-637-2612

films@cinemanx.com
imdb.com/company/co0229198

Does not accept any unsolicited material. Project types
include short films. Genres include crime, drama,
romance, thriller, comedy, and action.

Steve Christian
Producer
imdb.com/name/nm0160091

CINEMA PARISIEN
Production company and distributor

202 Hikida Bldg.
1-14-2 Nishi-Azabu
Minato, Tokyo
Japan
81 3 5786 1590 (phone)
81 3 5786 1591 (fax)

info@wisepolicy.com
imdb.com/company/co0040807

Does not accept any unsolicited material. Project types
include feature films. Genres include drama.

CINEMA ROSA
Distributor

1-37-12
Nishi Ikebukuro
Ikeukuro, Tokyo 171-0021

Japan
03-3986-3713 (phone)
03-3986-3714 (fax)

info@cinemarosa.net
cinemarosa.net
imdb.com/company/co0301167

Does not accept any unsolicited material. Project types include feature films. Genres include comedy and drama.

CINEMA TEX
Production company

6802 Rocky Top Cr
Dallas, TX 75252
972-523-2136

fred@cinematexinc.com
cinematexinc.com
imdb.com/company/co0008665
linkedin.com/company/cinema-tex-partners

Does not accept any unsolicited material. Project types include short films. Genres include drama and thriller.

CINEMAVAULT
Distributor and sales agent

1240 Bay St
Ste 307
Toronto, ON M5R 2A7
Canada
416-363-6060 (phone)
416-363-2305 (fax)

cinemavault.com
imdb.com/company/co0002267
linkedin.com/company/255517
facebook.com/people/Line-Up-Cinemavault/
    100000982967052
twitter.com/Cinemavault

Does not accept any unsolicited material. Project types include TV. Genres include romance, drama, and comedy.

Michael da Silva
Executive
imdb.com/name/nm6220092

CINE MOSAIC
Production company

130 W 25th St, 12th Floor
New York, NY 10001
212-625-3797 (phone)
212-625-3571 (fax)

info@cinemosaic.net
cinemosaic.net
imdb.com/company/co0124029
linkedin.com/company/cine-mosaic
facebook.com/cinemosaic
twitter.com/queendean

Accepts scripts from produced or represented writers. Project types include TV. Genres include drama, non-fiction, and action. Established in 2002.

Lydia Pilcher
imdb.com/name/nm0212990

CINEREACH
Production company and financing company

126 Fifth Ave, Fifth Floor, New York, NY, United States, 10011
212-727-3224

info@cinereach.org
cinereach.org
imdb.com/company/co0200307

Does not accept any unsolicited material. Project types include TV and feature films. Genres include thriller, family, action, and drama.

CINERGI
Production company

406 Wilshire Blvd.
Santa Monica, CA 90401
310-315-6000 (phone)
310-315-6015 (fax)

imdb.com/company/co0009350

Does not accept any unsolicited material. Project types include feature films. Genres include drama, romance, and action.

Andrew Vajna
CEO
imdb.com/name/nm0883351

CINESAVVY
Production company and sales agent

20 Butterick Rd
Toronto, ON M8W 3Z8
Canada
416-598-2525 (phone)
416-599-2223 (fax)

brad@cinesavvyinc.com
cinesavvyinc.com
imdb.com/company/co0236034

Does not accept any unsolicited material. Genres include drama.

Hassain Zaidi
Producer
imdb.com/name/nm2817574

CINÉ-SHOP
Production company

10217 Plano Rd.
Dallas, TX 75238-1702
214-348-0025 (phone)
214-348-7173 (fax)

photocineshop.com/en
imdb.com/company/co0017743
facebook.com/cineshop254

Does not accept any unsolicited material. Project types include short films. Genres include drama.

CINESON ENTERTAINMENT
Production company

4519 Varna Ave.
Sherman Oaks, CA 91423
818-501-8246 (phone)
818-501-3647 (fax)

imdb.com/company/co0127539

Does not accept any unsolicited material. Project types include feature films and TV. Genres include crime, comedy, period, non-fiction, thriller, drama, and romance.

Andy Garcia
imdb.com/name/nm0000412

CINETELFILMS
Sales agent

8255 Sunset Blvd
Los Angeles, CA 90046
323-654-4000 (phone)
323-650-6400 (fax)

info@cinetelfilms.com
cinetelfilms.com
imdb.com/company/co0017447
facebook.com/pages/CineTel-Films/
628876050561279

Does not accept any unsolicited material. Project types include TV. Genres include horror, drama, crime, and thriller. Established in 1985.

Paul Hertzberg
imdb.com/name/nm0078473

CINETEL FILMS
Production company, distributor, and sales agent

8255 Sunset Blvd, Los Angeles , CA, United States, 90046
323-654-4000 (phone)
323-650-6400 (fax)

info@cinetelfilms.com
cinetelfilms.com
imdb.com/company/co0017447

Does not accept any unsolicited material. Project types include feature films and TV. Genres include romance, thriller, drama, action, and family.

Bill Berry
Vice President (Production)
imdb.com/name/nm2694429

CINETIC MEDIA
Sales agent and financing company

555 W 25th St
4th Floor
New York, NY 10001
212-204-7979 (phone)
212-204-7980 (fax)

info@cineticmedia.com
cineticmedia.com
imdb.com/company/co0120476

Does not accept any unsolicited material. Project types include TV and feature films. Genres include drama, crime, and action.

John Sloss
Producer
imdb.com/name/nm0806189

CINEVILLE
Production company and distributor

3400 Airport Ave
Santa Monica, CA 90405
310-397-7150 (phone)
310-397-7155 (fax)

info@cineville.com
cineville.com
imdb.com/company/co0063993
facebook.com/cinevilleUSA

Does not accept any unsolicited material. Genres include romance, comedy, and non-fiction.

Carl Colpaert
President
imdb.com/name/nm0173207

CINEVOYAGE
Production company

848 N Rainbow Blvd, Suite 2054, Las Vegas, NV, United States, 89017
702-490-0783

cinevoyage2001@gmail.com
imdb.com/company/co0425487

Does not accept any unsolicited material.

Michael Harpster
Producer
imdb.com/name/nm0364021

CIPHER FILMS
Production company

58-60 Stamford St
Waterloo
London , England SE1 9LX
UK

info@cipher-films.com

imdb.com/company/co0138244

Does not accept any unsolicited material. Project types include feature films. Genres include crime, drama, and thriller.

CIRCA FILM
Production company and distributor

329 Bernard Ave
Sarasota, FL 34243
941-544-8888

circafilm@aol.com
cinando.com/DefaultController.aspx?PageID
imdb.com/company/co0447034
linkedin.com/company/cinando
facebook.com/pages/Cinando/149338658420294
twitter.com/Cinando_Films

Does not accept any unsolicited material. Genres include documentary and drama.

CIRCLE OF CONFUSION

8931 Ellis Ave
Los Angeles, CA 90034
310-691-7000 (phone)
310-691-7099 (fax)

queries@circleofconfusion.com
circleofconfusion.com
imdb.com/company/co0090153
facebook.com/pages/Circle-of-Confusion/258459361785
twitter.com/ofconfusion

Accepts query letters from unproduced, unrepresented writers via email. Project types include TV. Genres include horror, non-fiction, myth, drama, science fiction, action, comedy, crime, detective, fantasy, thriller, and romance.

Stephen Emery
Executive Vice-President Production and Development
stephen@circleofconfusion.com
imdb.com/name/nm1765323

CIRCUS ROAD FILMS
Distributor and sales agent

Studio City, CA
310-862-4006 (phone)
310-494-0808 (fax)

Austin, TX
512-815-3901

josh@circusroadfilms.com (script submissions)
glen@circusroadfilms.com (general)
circusroadfilms.com
imdb.com/company/co0198009
facebook.com/Circus-Road-Films-373259509459592
twitter.com/CircusRoadFilms

Accepts query letters from unproduced, unrepresented writers via email. Project types include TV and feature films. Genres include drama, family, and comedy.

CITY ENTERTAINMENT
Production company and distributor

266 1/2 S Rexford Dr
Beverly Hills, CA 90212
310-273-3101 (phone)
310-273-3676 (fax)

imdb.com/company/co0093881

Does not accept any unsolicited material. Project types include TV. Genres include thriller, documentary, and drama.

Joshua Maurer
imdb.com/name/nm0561027

CLARENDON ENTERTAINMENT
Production company and distributor

C/O CEI Media Partners LLC
One Bridge Plaza North, Suite 275
Fort Lee, NJ 07024
201-790-2872

info@clarendon-entertainment.com
clarendon-entertainment.com
imdb.com/company/co0009658

Does not accept any unsolicited material. Project types include short films. Genres include drama.

CLARITY PICTURES, LLC
Production company

1107 Fair Oaks Ave
Ste 155
South Pasadena, CA 91030
310-388-5846 (phone)
310-226-7046 (fax)

info@claritypictures.net
imdb.com/company/co0151012

Does not accept any unsolicited material. Project types include feature films and TV. Genres include documentary, horror, and comedy.

Loren Basulto
imdb.com/name/nm1457923

David Basulto
imdb.com/name/nm0060617

CLARIUS CAPITAL GROUP, LLC
Production company, distributor, and sales agent

9100 Wilshire Blvd, Suite 520E, Beverly Hills, CA, United States, 90211
310-360-7000

info@clarius.com
clarius.com/capital.html
imdb.com/company/co0241200

Does not accept any unsolicited material. Project types include TV. Genres include drama and family.

CLASS 5 FILMS
Production company

200 Park Ave South, 8th Floor
New York, NY 10003
917-414-9404

imdb.com/company/co0113781

Does not accept any unsolicited material. Project types include TV. Genres include documentary, comedy, drama, and romance.

Edward Norton
imdb.com/name/nm0001570

CLEAN CUTS
Production company

4455 Connecticut Ave NW
Suite A 500
Washington, DC 20008
202-237-8884

tetiana@cleancuts.com
cleancuts.com
www/www.imdb.com/company/co0308201
facebook.com/cleancutsbarbershops

Does not accept any unsolicited material. Genres
include family.

CLEANUP KITTY PRODUCTIONS
Production company

155 Holmes St, Barnesville, GA, United States, 30204
770-358-9383

roger@cleanupkitty.com
imdb.com/company/co0186322

Does not accept any unsolicited material. Project types
include feature films. Genres include drama.

Roger McLeod
Director
imdb.com/name/nm1177150

CLEAR PICTURES ENTERTAINMENT
Production company

12400 Ventura Blvd, Suite 306
Studio City, CA 91604
818-980-5460 (phone)
818-980-4716 (fax)

clearpicturesinc@aol.com
imdb.com/company/co0171732
linkedin.com/.../clear-pictures-entertainment
facebook.com/Clear-Pictures-
    Entertainment-212760035420860

Accepts query letters from unproduced, unrepresented
writers via email. Project types include TV and feature
films. Genres include non-fiction and drama.
Established in 2009.

Elizabeth Fowler
Principal
imdb.com/name/nm2085583

CLEARPOINT ENTERTAINMENT
Production company

18807 Ave Biarritz
Suite 101
Tampa, FL 33558
813-675-5120 (phone)
813-385-0772 (fax)

info@clearpointentertainment.com
imdb.com/company/co0199391

Does not accept any unsolicited material.

CLEAR SCOPE MEDIA
Production company

513 W Jefferson St #200,
Grand Prairie, TX 75051, USA
214-997-3677

contact@clearscopemedia.com
clearscopemedia.com
imdb.com/company/co0422788
facebook.com/ClearScopeMedia
twitter.com/ClearScopeMedia

Does not accept any unsolicited material. Project types
include short films. Genres include drama.

CLEAR SLATE FILMS
Production company

10197 SE 144th Place
Summerfield, FL 34491
352-288-3999 (phone)
352-288-5538 (fax)

nickgmiller@aol.com
imdb.com/company/co0219115

Does not accept any unsolicited material. Genres
include romance.

CLEARVIEW PRODUCTIONS
Production company

1180 S Beverly Dr, Suite 700
Los Angeles, CA 90035
310-271-7698 (phone)
310-278-9978 (fax)

clearviewproductionsllc.com

imdb.com/company/co0464904
facebook.com/Clearview-
    Productions-739447106134701

Does not accept any unsolicited material.

Albert Ruddy
Producer
imdb.com/name/nm0748665

CLICK PRODUCTIONS
Production company

6399 Wilshire Blvd, Suite 1007
Los Angeles, CA 90048
323-655-6845

Alain Sirtzky Productions
23 Rue Raynouard
Paris 75016, France

asproductions@usa.net
imdb.com/company/co0011751
facebook.com/CLICKproductions

Does not accept any unsolicited material. Project types include feature films and TV. Genres include comedy and drama.

Alain Sirtzky
President
imdb.com/name/nm0802852

CLIFFORD WERBER PRODUCTIONS INC.
Production company

232 S Beverly Dr, Suite 224
Beverly Hills, CA 90212
310-288-0900 (phone)
310-288-0600 (fax)

imdb.com/company/co0097249

Accepts query letters from produced or represented writers.

Clifford Werber
Producer
imdb.com/name/nm0921222

CLINICA ESTETICO
Production company

308 Mott St
New York, NY 10012
212-219-2800

imdb.com/company/co0093046
facebook.com/pages/Clinica-Estetico/
    137878189593335

Does not accept any unsolicited material. Project types include feature films. Genres include drama and science fiction.

Jonathan Demme
Producer/Director/Writer
imdb.com/name/nm0001129

CLOSED ON MONDAYS ENTERTAINMENT
Production company

3800 Barham Blvd Suite 100
Los Angeles, CA 90068
818-526-6707

imdb.com/company/co0186526
facebook.com/pages/Closed-on-Mondays-
    Entertainment/107861705911770

Does not accept any unsolicited material. Established in 2003.

Joe Nozemack
imdb.com/name/nm1060496

CLOUD EIGHT FILMS
Production company

39 Long Acre
London WC2E 9LG
United Kingdom
+44 20-7845-6877

imdb.com/company/co0265704

Accepts scripts from produced or represented writers. Established in 2009.

Christian Colson
+44 20 7845 6988
imdb.com/name/nm1384503

CLOUDY SKY FILMS
Production company, distributor, and sales agent

4 Shelbourne Ave
Trenton, NJ 08618

cloudyskyfilms@gmail.com
cloudyskyfilms.com
imdb.com/company/co0334762
facebook.com/CloudySkyFilms

Does not accept any unsolicited material. Genres
include drama.

CMI ENTERTAINMENT

Production company

9712 Riverside Circle
Ellicott City, MD 21042
410-203-9990 (phone)
410-203-5999 (fax)

headsup21@aol.com
cmientertainment.com
imdb.com/company/co0395321

Does not accept any unsolicited material. Genres
include animation and comedy.

CMT FILMS

Production company

2600 Colorado Blvd.
Santa Monica, CA 90404
310-752-8000

cmt.com
imdb.com/company/co0155665
facebook.com/cmt

Does not accept any unsolicited material. Project types
include feature films. Genres include drama.

COACH HOUSE STUDIOS

Production company

Twickenham Studios
Twickenham
London TW12AW
UK
020-874-08000

enquiries@coachhousestudios.co.uk
coachhousestudios.co.uk
imdb.com/company/co0238091
twitter.com/CoachHouseTW1

Does not accept any unsolicited material. Project types
include TV. Genres include drama.

COALITION FILMS

Production company

33-41 Newark St
Ste 3C
Hoboken, NJ 07030
201-683-7547 (phone)
201-683-7546 (fax)

info@coalition-films.com
coalitionfilms.com
imdb.com/company/co0157918
facebook.com/pages/Coalition-Films/
    150225605173407

Does not accept any unsolicited material. Genres
include crime and drama.

COALITION GROUP

Production company

11222 Weddington St
North Hollywood, CA 91601
818-755-7941

contact@thecoalition-group.com
thecoalition-group.com
imdb.com/company/co0425053
facebook.com/coalitiongroup
twitter.com/coalitiongroup

Does not accept any unsolicited material. Project types
include feature films. Genres include fantasy and
action.

COBAIN STUDIOS

Production company and distributor

3928 Burns PL SE
Washington, DC 20019
202-391-6557

imdb.com/company/co0486861

Does not accept any unsolicited material. Genres
include comedy.

COCOON

Production company

3-10-14-3F
Kita Aoyama
Minato, Tokyo 107-0061
Japan
03-5468-5705 (phone)
03-5468-5707 (fax)

info@cocoon-jp.com
cocoon-jp.com
imdb.com/company/co0159869

Does not accept any unsolicited material. Project types include short films and TV. Genres include comedy.

CODE 3 FILMS
Production company

642 8th St
Absecon, NJ 08201
609-432-5980

dmart@code3films.net
code3films.net
imdb.com/company/co0297632
facebook.com/Code-3-Films-189914581046389

Does not accept any unsolicited material. Genres include comedy and horror.

CODEBLACK ENTERTAINMENT
Production company and distributor

111 Universal Hollywood Dr, Suite 2260
Universal City, CA 91608
818-286-8600 (phone)
818-286-8649 (fax)

info@codeblackentertainment.com
codeblack.com
imdb.com/company/co0172361
facebook.com/Codeblacklife
twitter.com/codeblacklife

Does not accept any unsolicited material. Project types include commercials. Established in 2005.

Jeff Clanagan
CEO
imdb.com/name/nm0163335

CODE ENTERTAINMENT
Production company

9229 Sunset Blvd, Suite 615
Los Angeles, CA 90069
310-772-0008 (phone)
310-772-0006 (fax)

contact@codeentertainment.com
codeentertainment.com
imdb.com/company/co0143069

Accepts scripts from produced or represented writers. Established in 2005.

Bart Rosenblatt
Producer
310-772-0008 ext. 3
imdb.com/name/nm0742386

CODEX DIGITAL
Production company

60 Poland St
London W1F 7NT
UK
+44 (0)20 7292 6919 (phone)
+44 (0)20 7990 9906 (fax)

info@codexdigital.com
codexdigital.com
imdb.com/company/co0294826

Does not accept any unsolicited material. Project types include TV and feature films. Genres include science fiction, action, and comedy.

Rainer Hercher
Producer
imdb.com/name/nm5292747

COGITO WORKS
Production company

1-14-18-2F
Setagaya
Setagaya, Tokyo 154-0017
Japan
03-6413-6664 (phone)
03-6413-6667 (fax)

contactcogito@cogitoworks.com
cogitoworks.com
imdb.com/company/co0400151

Does not accept any unsolicited material. Project types include TV. Genres include comedy.

Takaharu Inagaki
Founder (Producer)
imdb.com/name/nm5376686

COHEN PICTURES
Production company

15332 Antioch St, Suite 215
Pacific Palisades, CA 90272
310-462-2040

imdb.com/company/co0206264

Does not accept any unsolicited material. Project types include feature films. Genres include comedy and drama.

COIN FILM
Production company

Heinrich-Roller-Str. 15
Berlin-Prenzlauer Berg 10405
Germany
+49 30 3935 836

info@coin-film.de
coin-film.de
imdb.com/company/co0066704

Does not accept any unsolicited material. Project types include feature films, TV, and short films. Genres include fantasy, drama, and comedy.

COLD IRON PICTURES
Production company

360 N La Cienega Blvd, 3rd Floor, Los Angeles, CA, United States, 90048
323-951-9197 (phone)
323-951-9998 (fax)

info@coldironpictures.com
coldironpictures.com
imdb.com/company/co0184318

Does not accept any unsolicited material. Project types include TV, feature films, and short films. Genres include comedy, action, thriller, drama, and family.

Amanda Marshall
Head (Production)
imdb.com/name/nm1622973

COLLEEN CAMP PRODUCTIONS
Production company

6464 Sunset Blvd, Suite 800
Los Angeles, CA 90028
323-463-1434 (phone)
323-463-4379 (fax)

asst@ccprods.com
imdb.com/company/co0092983

Accepts query letters from unproduced, unrepresented writers.

Colleen Camp
Producer
imdb.com/name/nm0131974

COLLETON COMPANY
Production company

20 Fifth Ave, Suite 13F
New York, NY 10011
212-673-0916 (phone)
212-673-1172 (fax)

imdb.com/company/co0176685

Accepts scripts from produced or represented writers. Project types include feature films and TV. Genres include thriller, drama, crime, detective, and non-fiction.

Sara Colleton
imdb.com/name/nm0171780

COLOR BIRD INC.
Production company

1-23-14-307
Aobadai
Meguro, TOKYO 153-0042
Japan
03-6451-2885 (phone)
03-6451-2885 (fax)

info@colorbird.co.jp
colorbird.co.jp

imdb.com/company/co0530306

Does not accept any unsolicited material. Project types include feature films. Genres include drama.

Yasushi Miyamae
CMO (Producer)
imdb.com/name/nm5243006

COLOR FORCE
Production company

2 rue Saint Jospeh
38000 Grenoble
FRANCE
9 50 53 33 52 (phone)
9 55 53 33 52 (fax)

thecolorforce.com
imdb.com/company/co0212151

Accepts query letters from unproduced, unrepresented writers. Project types include short films and TV. Genres include family, action, animation, and comedy. Established in 2007.

Nina Jacobson
Producer
nina.jacobson@colorforce.com
imdb.com/name/nm1749221

COLOR OF LOVE PRODUCTION
Production company and distributor

421 New York Ave
Suite#2R
Jersey City, NJ 07307
347-423-1722

Colorofloveproduction@gmail.com
colorofloveproduction.wordpress.com
imdb.com/company/co0475368

Does not accept any unsolicited material. Project types include short films. Genres include drama.

COLOSSAL ENTERTAINMENT
Production company

: 10A Apapa Ln Dolphin Estate, Ikoyi, Lagos, Nigeria
234 -1-4537895

info@colossal-entertainment.net

colossal-entertainment.net
imdb.com/company/co0176684

Accepts query letters from unproduced, unrepresented writers. Project types include feature films. Genres include action and thriller.

Kelly Rowan
Producer
imdb.com/name/nm0746414

Graham Ludlow
imdb.com/name/nm0524905

COLOURS TV NETWORK
Production company and distributor

200 Quebec St
Building 600, Suite 209
Denver, CO 80230
303-326-0088 (phone)
303-326-0087 (fax)

info@colourstv.org
imdb.com/company/co0176498

Does not accept any unsolicited material. Genres include animation and action.

COLUMBIA PICTURES
Production company

10202 W Washington Blvd Thalberg Building
Culver City, CA 90232
310-244-4000 (phone)
310-244-2626 (fax)

sonypictures.com
imdb.com/company/co0071509
linkedin.com/company/sony-pictures-entertainment
facebook.com/SonyPictures
twitter.com/sonypictures

Does not accept any unsolicited material. Project types include feature films. Genres include comedy, horror, period, crime, science fiction, non-fiction, romance, thriller, animation, action, drama, family, and fantasy. Established in 1939.

Hannah Minghella
imdb.com/name/nm1098742
Assistant: Mahsa Moayeri
mahsa_moayeri@spe.sony.com

Amy Pascal
Chairman
imdb.com/name/nm1166871

Andy Given
imdb.com/name/nm0321429

Samuel C. Dickerman
Executive Vice President of Production
imdb.com/name/nm0225385

Pete Corral
imdb.com/name/nm0180707

Elizabeth Cantillon
Executive Vice President of Production
imdb.com/name/nm0134578
Assistant: Katherine Spada
katherine_spada@spe.sony.com

Doug Belgrad
President
imdb.com/name/nm1000411

DeVon Franklin
imdb.com/name/nm2035952

Eric Fineman
Creative Executive
imdb.com/name/nm2349857

Andrea Giannetti
Executive Vice President of Production
imdb.com/name/nm1602150

Foster Driver
Creative Executive
imdb.com/name/nm5372839

Adam Moos
imdb.com/name/nm0602149

Jonathan Kadin
imdb.com/name/nm2142367
Assistant: Ashley Johnson
ashley_johnson@spe.sony.com

Debra Bergman
imdb.com/name/nm2984630

Rachel O'Connor
imdb.com/name/nm1471418

Lauren Abrahams
imdb.com/name/nm1036268

COMEDY ARTS STUDIOS
Production company

2500 Broadway
Santa Monica, CA 90404
310-382-3677 (phone)
310-382-3170 (fax)

imdb.com/company/co0220109
facebook.com/pages/Comedy-Arts-Studios/
465841403443774

Accepts query letters from unproduced, unrepresented writers. Project types include short films and TV. Genres include comedy and drama.

Stu Smiley
imdb.com/name/nm0806979

COMEDY CENTRAL
Production company and distributor

1633 Pennsylvania Ave
Santa Monica CA 90404
310-907-2568

17-29 Hawley Crescent
London United Kingdom NW1 8TT
440-203-5803211

345 Hudson St Eighth Floor
New York NY 10014
212-767-8600 (phone)
212-767-8592 (fax)

2600 Colorado Ave, Fourth Floor, Santa Monica , CA, United States, 90404
310-752-8000

cc.com
imdb.com/company/co0362091

Does not accept any unsolicited material. Project types include TV. Genres include comedy, drama, and family.

Lu Chekowsky
Senior Vice President (Brand Creative)
310-752-8000
imdb.com/name/nm5636782

COMERICA ENTERTAINMENT GROUP
Financing company

2000 Ave of the Stars, Suite 210, Los Angeles , CA,
United States, 90067
310-712-6700

comerica_entertainment_group_mail@comerica.com
comerica.com
imdb.com/company/co0109905

Does not accept any unsolicited material. Project types
include short films and feature films. Genres include
action, horror, and thriller.

COMMON GROUND PRODUCTIONS
Production company and distributor

1601 Connecticut Ave. NW
#200
Washington, DC 20009
202-265-4300

cgp@sfcg.org
sfcg.org/programmes/cgp/programmes_cgp.html
imdb.com/company/co0098072
facebook.com/pages/Search-for-Common-Ground/
    72700460615
twitter.com/sfcg_

Does not accept any unsolicited material. Project types
include short films. Genres include documentary.

COMPANY 3
Production company

1661 Lincoln Blvd., Suite 400
Santa Monica, CA 90404
310-255-6600

company3.com
imdb.com/company/co0028470
linkedin.com/company/company-3
facebook.com/Company3
twitter.com/Company3

Does not accept any unsolicited material. Project types
include feature films. Genres include horror.

COMPANY FILMS
Production company and distributor

2629 Main St, Suite 167, Santa Monica , CA, United
States, 90405

310-399-2500 (phone)
310-399-2583 (fax)

info@companyfilms.com
companyfilms.com
imdb.com/company/co0097671

Does not accept any unsolicited material. Project types
include TV and feature films. Genres include family,
thriller, drama, and action.

COMPANY PICTURES
Production company

3-7 RAY STREET, FARRINGDON
LONDON, EC1R 3DR
+44 20 7380 3900 (phone)
+44 20 7831 5601 (fax)

enquiries@companypictures.co.uk
companypictures.co.uk
imdb.com/company/co0103820
facebook.com/companypicturestv
twitter.com/CoPicsTV

Does not accept any unsolicited material. Project types
include short films, TV, and feature films. Genres
include thriller.

Claire Ingham
Producer
imdb.com/name/nm2516204

COMPASS ENTERTAINMENT
Production company

New York, NY, United States

compass@compass-entertainment.com
imdb.com/company/co0295747

Does not accept any unsolicited material. Project types
include TV. Genres include family and drama.

COMPASS FILMS
Production company

1-3-6-436
Shimo Ochiai
Shinjuku, Tokyo
Japan
03-5389-0809 (phone)
03-5389-0809 (fax)

compass_films@mac.com
imdb.com/company/co0022671

Does not accept any unsolicited material. Project types include feature films and short films. Genres include documentary.

Toshi Fujiwara
CEO (Executive)
imdb.com/name/nm1350393

COMPLETION FILMS

60 E 42nd St, Suite 4600
New York, NY 10165
718-693-2057 (phone)
888-693-4133 (fax)

info@completionfilms.com
completionfilms.com
imdb.com/company/co0175660
linkedin.com/company/completion-films
facebook.com/pages/Completion-Films/
    109502505745410

Accepts query letters from unproduced, unrepresented writers. Genres include non-fiction.

Kisha Imani Cameron
President
imdb.com/name/nm0131650

CONCEPT ENTERTAINMENT

Production company

334 1/2 N Sierra Bonita Ave
Los Angeles, CA 90036
323-937-5700 (phone)
323-937-5720 (fax)

enquiries@conceptentertainment.biz
conceptentertainment.biz
imdb.com/company/co0096670

Accepts query letters from unproduced, unrepresented writers. Project types include TV. Genres include crime, detective, fantasy, horror, non-fiction, romance, science fiction, comedy, thriller, action, drama, and myth.

David Faigenblum
imdb.com/name/nm1584960

CONCORD FILMS

Production company and distributor

10238 W State Rd 84,
Davie, FL 33324
954-816-0100 (phone)
954-241-5134 (fax)

concordfilms.com
imdb.com/company/co0350442

Does not accept any unsolicited material. Genres include thriller and drama.

CONCRETE ENTERTAINMENT

Production company

468 N Camden Dr, Suite 200
Beverly Hills, CA 90210
310-860-5611

imdb.com/company/co0182126
linkedin.com/company/concrete-entertainment

Does not accept any unsolicited material. Project types include feature films and TV. Genres include comedy.

Carolyn Kessler
Manager/Producer
imdb.com/name/nm0450315

Alicia Silverstone
Producer/Actress
imdb.com/name/nm0000224

CONDE NAST PUBLICATIONS, INC.

Production company and distributor

6300 Wilshire Blvd
Los Angeles CA
323-965-2880

1 World Trade Center, Floor 20-44, New York, NY, United States, 10006
212-286-2860

creativity.condenast.com

Does not accept any unsolicited material. Project types include TV. Genres include drama and family.

CONGLOMERATE MEDIA

Production company

3175 SW 8 St
Miami, FL 33135
407-749-0272

info@conglomerate.com
conglomerate.com
imdb.com/company/co0446151
facebook.com/waltbeforemickey
twitter.com/armandogutierez

Does not accept any unsolicited material. Genres
include drama, comedy, and fantasy.

CONQUISTADOR ENTERTAINMENT INC
Production company, distributor, and sales agent

9595 Wilshire Blvd, #900 PMB 216, Beverly Hills ,
CA, United States, 90212
310-684-3979 (phone)
310-684-3979 (fax)

info@conquistador-ent.com
conquistador-ent.com
imdb.com/company/co0033479

Does not accept any unsolicited material. Project types
include feature films, short films, and TV. Genres
include drama, thriller, comedy, romance, family, and
action.

CONSTANTIN FILM
Production company and distributor

Feilitzschstr. 6
Munich, Bavaria D-80802
Germany
+49-89-44-44-60-0 (phone)
+49-89-44-44-60-666 (fax)

9200 W Sunset Blvd, Suite 800
West Hollywood, CA 90069
310-247-0300 (phone)
310-247-0305 (fax)

zentrale@constantin-film.de
constantin-film.de
imdb.com/company/co0002257
facebook.com/constantinfilm
twitter.com/ConstantinFilm

Accepts query letters from produced or represented
writers. Project types include TV and feature films.

Genres include action, crime, and thriller. Established
in 1950.

Robert Kultzer
Executive
310-247-0300 ext. 3
robert.kultzer@constantin-film.de
imdb.com/name/nm0474709

CONTENTFILM INTERNATIONAL
Sales agent

19 Heddon St
London W1B 4BG
UK
+44207-851-6500 (phone)
+44207-851-6506 (fax)

london@contentmediacorp.com
contentmediacorp.com
imdb.com/company/co0143763

Does not accept any unsolicited material. Project types
include TV and feature films. Genres include horror,
drama, and thriller.

CONTENT HOUSE
Production company

3500 Overland Ave. Suite 110-16
Los Angeles, CA 90034
310-277-7701 (phone)
310-277-7708 (fax)

info@contenthousela.com
imdb.com/company/co0119743
facebook.com/contenthousela/timeline

Does not accept any unsolicited material. Project types
include feature films. Genres include science fiction,
drama, horror, and action.

Mark Saffian
Partner/Producer/Manager
imdb.com/name/nm2948427

CONTENT MEDIA CORPORATION PLC
Production company

19 Heddon St
London,
W1B 4BG

UK
+44 20 7851 6500 (phone)
+44 20 7851 6506 (fax)

225 Arizona Ave, Suite #250
Santa Monica, CA 90401
310-576-1059 (phone)
310-576-1859 (fax)

80 Richmond St West
Toronto
Ontario M5H 2A4 CANADA
416-360-6103 (phone)
416-360-6065 (fax)

la@contentmediacorp.com
contentmediacorp.com
imdb.com/company/co0366223

Accepts query letters from unproduced, unrepresented writers. Project types include TV. Genres include crime, drama, and detective.

Jamie Carmichael
jamie.carmichael@contentmediacorp.com
imdb.com/name/nm0138430

CONTINENTAL ENTERTAINMENT GROUP
Production company and financing company

9701 Wilshire Blvd, Tenth Floor, Beverly Hills , CA, United States, 90212
310-203-3371 (phone)
310-203-9010 (fax)

info@continental-ent.com
continental-ent.com
imdb.com/company/co0206971

Does not accept any unsolicited material. Project types include TV, short films, and feature films. Genres include family, thriller, and drama.

CONTRADICTION FILMS
Production company

3103 Neilson Way
Santa Monica, CA 90405
310-396-8558

info@contradictionfilms.com
contradictionfilms.com

imdb.com/company/co0306436

Does not accept any unsolicited material. Project types include feature films. Genres include horror and thriller.

Tomas Harlan
Producer
imdb.com/name/nm3938576

Tim Carter
Writer/Producer
imdb.com/name/nm3939975

CONTRAFILM
Production company

1531 N Cahuenga Blvd
Los Angeles, CA 90028
323-467-8787 (phone)
323-467-7730 (fax)

imdb.com/company/co0128546

Accepts query letters from unproduced, unrepresented writers. Project types include feature films. Genres include horror, drama, and thriller.

Tripp Vinson
Producer
imdb.com/name/nm1246087
Assistant: Tara Farney

Tucker Williams
Creative Executive
imdb.com/name/nm2606099

Alexandra Church
Creative Executive
imdb.com/name/nm0161344

CONUNDRUM ENTERTAINMENT
Production company

325 Wilshire Blvd, Suite 201
Santa Monica, CA 90401
310-319-2800 (phone)
310-319-2808 (fax)

imdb.com/company/co0030016

Accepts scripts from produced or represented writers. Genres include comedy.

Peter Farrelly
Executive
imdb.com/name/nm0268380

Bobby Farrelly
Executive
imdb.com/name/nm0268370

CONVERGENT MEDIA
Production company and sales agent

3rd Floor Kirkman House
12 - 14 Whitfield St
London W1T2RF
UK

info@convergent.media
convergent.media
imdb.com/company/co0534732

Does not accept any unsolicited material. Project types include feature films. Genres include documentary.

Zak Kilberg
Producer
imdb.com/name/nm1815953

COOPER'S TOWN PRODUCTIONS

302A West 12th St, Suite 214
New York, NY 10014
212-255-7566 (phone)
212-255-0211 (fax)

info@cooperstownproductions.com
cooperstownproductions.com/index2.html
imdb.com/company/co0132168

Accepts query letters from unproduced, unrepresented writers. Project types include feature films. Genres include non-fiction.

Sara Murphy
imdb.com/name/nm2072976

Phillip Hoffman
Partner
imdb.com/name/nm0000450

COPIAPOA FILM
Distributor

2-6-11-2F
Shibuya
Shibuya, Tokyo 150-0002
Japan

info@copiapoafilm.com
copiapoafilm.com
imdb.com/company/co0432313

Does not accept any unsolicited material. Project types include TV. Genres include drama.

Shigeki Itô
President (Executive)
imdb.com/name/nm5995218

COPPERHEART ENTERTAINMENT
Production company

121 John St
Ste 1
Toronto, ON M5V 2E2
Canada
416-516-4950 (phone)
416-516-1712 (fax)

info@copperheart.ca
copperheart.ca
imdb.com/company/co0028055

Does not accept any unsolicited material. Genres include fantasy and action.

Steven Hoban
Producer
imdb.com/name/nm0387541

COQUETTE PRODUCTIONS
Production company and distributor

8105 W Third St
Los Angeles, CA 90048
323-801-1000 (phone)
323-801-1001 (fax)

imdb.com/company/co0142408

Does not accept any unsolicited material. Project types include TV. Genres include romance, comedy, crime, and drama.

Thea Mann
Head of Development
imdb.com/name/nm0542996

David Arquette
imdb.com/name/nm0000274

Courtney Cox
imdb.com/name/nm0001073

Jeff Bowland
Executive
imdb.com/name/nm0101188

CORNER BAR PICTURES
Production company

36 Beekman Terrace
Summit, NJ 07901
908-608-9099 (phone)
908-608-9099 (fax)

info@cornerbarpictures.com
imdb.com/company/co0462246

Does not accept any unsolicited material. Project types include short films and TV. Genres include drama.

CORNER STORE ENTERTAINMENT
Production company

9615 Brighton Way
Ste 201
Beverly Hills, CA 90210
310-276-6400 (phone)
310-276-6410 (fax)

cornerstoreentertainment.com
imdb.com/company/co0223726

Does not accept any unsolicited material. Project types include feature films. Genres include drama, comedy, and romance.

Matthew Weaver
imdb.com/name/nm2822461

Scott Prisand
imdb.com/name/nm1964055

CORNICE ENTERTAINMENT
Production company

421 S Beverly Dr, 8th Floor
Beverly Hills, CA 90212
310-279-4080

imdb.com/company/co0094922

Does not accept any unsolicited material. Project types include TV and feature films.

CORNICHE PICTURES
Production company

25 Brooks Mews
London W1K 4DZ
UK
+44207-290-8220 (phone)
+44207-290-8221 (fax)

info@corniche-group.com
corniche-group.com
imdb.com/company/co0279263

Does not accept any unsolicited material. Project types include TV. Genres include drama.

Hani Farsi
Producer
imdb.com/name/nm2354776

CORNUCOPIA PRODUCTIONS
Production company

510 Shotgun Rd
Suite 520
Sunrise, FL 33326
954-475-9311 (phone)
954-475-8392 (fax)

imdb.com/company/co0094923
linkedin.com/company/cornucopia-productions-inc
facebook.com/CornucopiaProductions

Does not accept any unsolicited material. Genres include drama.

CORONET FILMS
Production company

736 Seward St
Los Angeles, CA 90038
323-957-3213 (phone)
323-957-5405 (fax)

coronetentertainment@gmail.com
coronetfilms.net
imdb.com/company/co0273550

Does not accept any unsolicited material. Project types include feature films. Genres include drama.

Deborah Del Prete
Producer
imdb.com/name/nm0215769

CORPORATION FOR PUBLIC BROADCASTING
Production company and distributor

401 Ninth St, NW, Washington , DC, United States, 20004
202-879-9600

cpb.org
imdb.com/company/co0024370

Does not accept any unsolicited material. Project types include TV and feature films. Genres include animation, comedy, action, thriller, family, and drama.

CORUS ENTERTAINMENT
Production company, distributor, and sales agent

25 Dockside Dr
Toronto, ON M5A 0B5
Canada
416-479-7000 (phone)
416-479-7006 (fax)

corusent.com
imdb.com/company/co0080912

Does not accept any unsolicited material. Project types include TV. Genres include comedy.

CORWOOD INDUSTRIES
Distributor

Post Office Box 15375
Houston, TX 77220
713-926-4044

corwood@corwoodindustries.com
corwoodindustries.com
imdb.com/company/co0189954
twitter.com/TheRealJandek

Does not accept any unsolicited material. Project types include feature films. Established in 2008.

COURT FIVE
Production company

6030 Wilshire Blvd., Suite 300
Los Angeles, CA 90036
310-242-6445

information@courtfive.com
courtfive.com
imdb.com/company/co0242577
linkedin.com/company/court-five
facebook.com/courtfive
twitter.com/court_five

Does not accept any unsolicited material. Project types include feature films. Genres include fantasy and family.

Mark Ordesky
Producer
imdb.com/name/nm0649507

Jane Fleming
Producer
imdb.com/name/nm3794057

COURYGRAPH PRODUCTIONS
Production company, distributor, and sales agent

5802 W Palmaire Ave
Glendale, AZ 85301
623-435-1522

couryhouse@aol.com
imdb.com/company/co0275683

Does not accept any unsolicited material. Project types include short films. Genres include documentary.

COVENANT ROAD ENTERTAINMENT
Production company

334 4th Ave
Venice, CA 90291
310-598-3317

imdb.com/company/co0355555

Does not accept any unsolicited material. Project types include TV.

COVERT MEDIA
Production company

11601 Wilshire Blvd, Suite 1900, Los Angeles, CA,
United States, 90025
213-618-3750 (phone)
213-618-3760 (fax)

imdb.com/company/co0551691

Does not accept any unsolicited material. Project types
include TV. Genres include non-fiction, family,
drama, and reality.

Elissa Friedman
Vice President (Production and Development)
imdb.com/name/nm2438504

COWBOY FILMS
Production company

48 Russell Square London WC1B 4JP UK
44 (0)20 3434 4415

info@cowboyfilms.co.uk
cowboyfilms.co.uk
imdb.com/company/co0104135
facebook.com/Cowboy-Films-134957019905704
twitter.com/Cowboy_Films

Does not accept any unsolicited material. Project types
include feature films. Genres include drama.

Charles Steel
Producer
imdb.com/name/nm0824395

CPG
Production company

2800 Speer Blvd
Denver, CO 80211
303-455-5200

info@cpgtv.com
imdb.com/company/co0216752

Does not accept any unsolicited material. Genres
include documentary.

CRACKLE
Production company and distributor

9336 W Washington Blvd, Culver City, CA, United
States, 90232
310-244-4000

crackle_sales@spe.sony.com
crackle.com
imdb.com/company/co0242397

Does not accept any unsolicited material. Project types
include TV. Genres include family and drama.

Jake Munsey
Vice President (Creative)
imdb.com/name/nm2132830

CRAFTSMAN FILMS
Production company

4108 Riverside Dr, Suite 2
Burbank, CA 91505
818-567-0700

craftsmanfilms.com/main.html?src=%2F
imdb.com/company/co0176721
linkedin.com/company/craftsman-films

Does not accept any unsolicited material. Project types
include TV.

Kerry McCluggage
Producer
imdb.com/name/nm1394315

CRAVE FILMS

3312 Sunset Blvd
Los Angeles, CA 90026
323-669-9000 (phone)
323-669-9002 (fax)

cravefilms.com
imdb.com/company/co0146364

Does not accept any unsolicited material. Project types
include feature films. Genres include drama.

David Ayer
david@cravefilms.com
imdb.com/name/nm0043742

Alex Ott
alex@cravefilms.com
imdb.com/name/nm1944773

CRAVEN CORNER ENTERPRISES
Production company and financing company

Bluegrass Division
1234 Man O War Place #8
Lexington, KY 40504
859-948-3444 (phone)
859-948-3444 (fax)

ccetalent@yahoo.com
imdb.com/company/co0205609

Does not accept any unsolicited material. Project types
include feature films and TV. Genres include horror
and action.

CRAZY LEGS PRODUCTIONS
Production company

1781 Peachtree St. NE
Atlanta, GA 30309
404-891-0199 (phone)
866-753-8666 (fax)

info@crazylegsproductions.com
crazylegsproductions.com
imdb.com/company/co0234132
linkedin.com/company/crazy-legs-productions
facebook.com/clpstorytellers
twitter.com/crazylegsprods

Does not accept any unsolicited material. Genres
include documentary.

CRE8TIVE WORKS
Production company

1000 Fifth St
Suite 200-B3
Miami Beach, FL 33139
786-924-6579 (phone)
305-436-3714 (fax)

info@Cre8tiveWorks.net
cre8tiveworks.net
imdb.com/company/co0475188
facebook.com/Cre8tiveWorksInc
twitter.com/Cre8tive_Works

Does not accept any unsolicited material. Project types
include short films. Genres include drama.

CREAM PRODUCTIONS
Production company and distributor

380 Adelaide St West
3rd Fl
Toronto, ON M5V 1R7
Canada
416-979-8458 (phone)
416-979-3654 (fax)

info@creamproductions.ca
creamproductions.ca
imdb.com/company/co0136362
facebook.com/CREAMPRODUCTIONS
twitter.com/CREAMprductions

Does not accept any unsolicited material. Project types
include TV. Genres include drama.

Jenn Kuzmyk Ruch
Producer
imdb.com/name/nm5369685

CREANSPEAK PRODUCTIONS, LLC
Production company

120 S El Camino Dr
Beverly Hills, CA 90212
310-273-8217

info@creanspeak.com
imdb.com/company/co0097231
linkedin.com/pub/creanspeak-productions/3/a16/8ab

Accepts query letters from unproduced, unrepresented
writers via email. Project types include feature films,
commercials, and TV. Genres include family, comedy,
reality, drama, non-fiction, and action.

Jon Freis
310-273-8217
info@creanspeak.com
imdb.com/name/nm2045371

Kelly Crean
310-273-8217
info@creanspeak.com
imdb.com/name/nm1047631

CREATED BY
Production company

9415 Culver Blvd.
Culver City, CA 90232
424-298-2500

imdb.com/company/co0471110

Does not accept any unsolicited material. Genres include science fiction, drama, and thriller.

Vincent Gerardis
Manager
imdb.com/name/nm1136210

Ralph M. Vicinanza
President
imdb.com/name/nm2088223

CREATION FILM AND TELEVISION
Production company and distributor

Creation Film And Television
Fintex House
19 Golden Square, London W1F 9HD
UK
+44207-127-0021 (phone)
+44870-133-5818 (fax)

info@creationfilm.com
creationfilm.com
imdb.com/company/co0168955

Does not accept any unsolicited material. Project types include feature films. Genres include comedy, thriller, action, and drama.

Jake Seal
Producer
imdb.com/name/nm0780655

CREATIVE ADVANCEMENT ENTERTAINMENT
Production company

3000 Custer Rd, Suite 270-180
Plano, TX 75075

admin@dallasreuniondvd.com
imdb.com/company/co0299871

Does not accept any unsolicited material. Project types include feature films. Genres include documentary. Established in 2010.

CREATIVE ARTISTS
Production company and distributor

822-11 Ave S.W. Suite 204
Calgary AB Canada T2R 0E5
403-206-3120 (phone)
403-775-4338 (fax)

2000 Ave of the Stars, Los Angeles, CA, United States, 90067
424-288-2000 (phone)
424-288-2900 (fax)

Bryggavägen 133
Ekerö Sweden 178 31
011-454-686674110

222 S Central Ave Suite 1008
St. Louis MO 63105
314-862-5560 (phone)
314-862-4754 (fax)

caa.com
imdb.com/company/co0002521

Does not accept any unsolicited material. Project types include commercials and TV. Genres include drama, family, and comedy.

Chris Lawson
Executive (Creative Group)
424-288-2000
imdb.com/name/nm0493180

CREATIVE ASSOCIATES LIMITED (CAL)
Production company

8-14-14-5F
Ginza
Chuo, Tokyo 104-0061
Japan
03-3545-2911 (phone)
03-3545-3475 (fax)

cal.info@cal-pro.jp
imdb.com/company/co0259926

Does not accept any unsolicited material. Project types include TV. Genres include drama.

Tôichirô Shiraishi
Producer
imdb.com/name/nm3160100

CREATIVE CONTROL ENTERTAINMENT
Production company

3427 Overland Ave
Los Angeles, CA 90034
310-273-5311 (fax)

info@creativecontrolent.com
creativecontrolent.com
imdb.com/company/co0372971
facebook.com/pages/Creative-Control/
    173142216084589
twitter.com/cre8ve_ctrl

Does not accept any unsolicited material. Project types include TV. Genres include drama.

Joel C. High
President/Producer
imdb.com/name/nm0383573

CREATIVE PROJECTS GROUP
Production company

900 Third Ave, 20th Floor
New York, NY 10022
212-751-3001 (phone)
212-751-3113 (fax)

14011 Ventura Blvd. Suite 206 East
Sherman Oaks, CA 91423
818-763-0374

wnix@creativeprojectsgroup.com
creativeprojectsgroup.com
imdb.com/name/nm2773807
linkedin.com/profile/view
facebook.com/pages/Creative-Projects-Group/
    139727129373379

Does not accept any unsolicited material. Project types include feature films. Genres include drama.

CREATIVE REBELLION
Production company

18 Yorkville Ave
Toronto, ON M4W 3Y8
Canada
416-551-0370

info@creativerebellion.com

creativerebellion.com
imdb.com/company/co0382000

Does not accept any unsolicited material. Project types include feature films and TV. Genres include documentary.

CREATIVITY MEDIA
Production company

International House
1 St Katharine's Way
London E1W 1UN
UK
+44 20 3411 365 (phone)
+44 20 3411 365 (fax)

hello@creativitymedia.co.uk
creativitymedia.co.uk
imdb.com/company/co0315755

Does not accept any unsolicited material. Project types include TV. Genres include thriller and drama.

Patrick Fischer
Producer
imdb.com/name/nm1936918

CREATURE PRODUCTIONS
Production company and distributor

1545 Highland Ave South
P.O. Box 261
Clearwater, FL 33756

imdb.com/company/co0185006

Does not accept any unsolicited material. Project types include feature films. Genres include horror and science fiction. Established in 2005.

CRESCENDO PRODUCTIONS
Production company

252 N Larchmont Blvd, Suite 200
Los Angeles, CA 90004
323-465-2222 (phone)
323-464-3750 (fax)

crescendo-productions.com
imdb.com/company/co0025116

Accepts query letters from unproduced, unrepresented writers. Project types include TV and feature films. Genres include non-fiction and reality.

Don Cheadle
323-465-2222
imdb.com/name/nm0000332

CREST ANIMATION PRODUCTIONS, INC.
Production company

333 N Glenoaks Blvd, Suite 300
Burbank, CA 91502
818-846-0166 (phone)
818-846-6074 (fax)

info@crestcgi.com
imdb.com/company/co0218880

Accepts query letters from unproduced, unrepresented writers via email. Project types include feature films. Genres include animation.

Richard Rich
818-846-0166
info@crestcgi.com
imdb.com/name/nm0723704

Gregory Kasunich
818-846-0166
gkasunich@crestcgi.com
imdb.com/name/nm3215310

CRIME SCENE PICTURES
Production company

3450 Cahuenga Blvd W, Suite 701
Los Angeles, CA 90068
323-963-5136 (phone)
323-963-5137 (fax)

info@crimescenepictures.net
imdb.com/company/co0326645

Does not accept any unsolicited material. Project types include feature films. Established in 2010.

Adam Ripp
imdb.com/name/nm0728063

Jennifer Marmor
Creative Executive
imdb.com/name/nm4420063

Brett Hedblom
Director of Development
imdb.com/name/nm3916261

CRIMSON FOREST ENTERTAINMENT GROUP
Production company

8335 Sunset Blvd. Suite #238
West Hollywood CA 90069

U9 NO. 241 Caochangdi, Cuiezhuang District,
Beijing , China, 100015
011-861-051273279 (phone)
011-861-051273280 (fax)

info@cff.tv
cff.tv
imdb.com/company/co0483509

Does not accept any unsolicited material. Project types include TV and feature films. Genres include thriller, family, and drama.

CROGAN FILMWORKS
Production company, distributor, and sales agent

110 E. Crogan St.
Lawrenceville, GA 30046

submissions@croganfilmworks.com
imdb.com/company/co0427451

Accepts query letters from unproduced, unrepresented writers via email. Project types include feature films and TV. Genres include action, comedy, and crime.

Stanislav Shkilnyi
Producer
imdb.com/name/nm3390315

CROSS CREEK PICTURES

9220 W Sunset Blvd, Suite 100
West Hollywood, CA 90069
310-248-4061 (phone)
310-248-4068 (fax)

info@crosscreekpictures.com

crosscreekpictures.com
imdb.com/company/co0285648
facebook.com/crosscreekpictures

Does not accept any unsolicited material. Project types include TV and feature films. Genres include drama.

John Shepherd
Creative Executive
310-248-4061
info@crosscreekpicture.com
imdb.com/name/nm3005173
linkedin.com/pub/john-hilary-shepherd/5a/560/456

Brian Oliver
President
brian@crosscreekpicture.com
imdb.com/name/nm1003922
linkedin.com/pub/brian-oliver/3a/806/3a8

Stephanie Hall
stephanie@crosscreekpicture.com
imdb.com/name/nm24206

CROSSDAY PRODUCTIONS LTD.
Production company

14 Rathbone Place
London W1T 1HT
UK
+44 0 20 7637 0182

info@crossdayproductions.com
crossdayproductions.com
imdb.com/company/co0139826

Does not accept any unsolicited material. Project types include TV. Genres include drama.

Pippa Cross
Producer
imdb.com/name/nm0189248

CROSSROADS FILMS
Production company

1722 Whitley Ave
Los Angeles, CA 90028
310-659-6220 (phone)
310-659-3105 (fax)

imdb.com/company/co0061179
linkedin.com/company/crossroads-films_2

twitter.com/crossroadsfilms

Accepts query letters from unproduced, unrepresented writers. Project types include commercials, feature films, and TV. Genres include drama, thriller, comedy, crime, and romance.

Camille Taylor
310-659-6220
imdb.com/name/nm0852088

CRUCIAL PICTURES
Production company

629 Eastern Ave, Toronto
Ontario, Canada, M4M 1E3
310-865-8249 (phone)
310-865-7068 (fax)

crucialfilms.asst@gmail.com
crucialpictures.com
imdb.com/company/co0049027
linkedin.com/company/crucial-pictures
facebook.com/CrucialPictures
twitter.com/crucialpictures

Does not accept any unsolicited material. Project types include feature films and TV. Genres include thriller, drama, action, fantasy, horror, romance, crime, and comedy.

Daniel Schnider
310-865-8249
crucialfilms.asst@gmail.com
imdb.com/name/nm3045845

CRYBABY MEDIA
Production company, distributor, and sales agent

130 W 25th St, Suite 5C
New York, NY 10001

info@crybaby-media.com
crybaby-media.squarespace.com
linkedin.com/company/936927
facebook.com/pages/Crybaby-Media/
    142392552443351
twitter.com/crybabymedia

Does not accept any unsolicited material. Project types include TV. Genres include drama and reality. Established in 2014.

Alyssa Lomuscio
Editor
imdb.com/name/nm5143588
linkedin.com/pub/alyssa-lomuscio/56/589/17
facebook.com/alyssa.lomuscio

Salil Gandhi
Legal Counsel
linkedin.com/pub/salil-gandhi/3/937/7b0

Dan Passman
Founder
imdb.com/name/nm0664908
linkedin.com/pub/danny-passman/3/779/708
facebook.com/passmand

CRYSTAL LAKE ENTERTAINMENT, INC.
Production company

4420 Hayvenhurst Ave
Encino, CA 91436
818-995-1585 (phone)
818-995-1677 (fax)

contact@crystallakeentertainment.com
crystallakeentertainment.com
imdb.com/company/co0067362
facebook.com/crystallakeent
twitter.com/clecampdirector

Accepts query letters from unproduced, unrepresented writers via email. Project types include feature films and TV. Genres include horror, thriller, and science fiction.

Geoff Garrett
818-995-1585
sscfilms@earthlink.net
imdb.com/name/nm0308117

Sean Cunningham
818-995-1585
sscfilms@earthlink.net
imdb.com/name/nm0192446

CRYSTAL SKY ENTERTAINMENT
Production company and distributor

10203 Santa Monica Blvd, 5th Floor, Los Angeles , CA, United States, 90067

310-843-0223 (phone)
310-553-9895 (fax)

reception@crystalsky.com
crystalsky.com
imdb.com/company/co0004724

Does not accept any unsolicited material. Project types include TV and feature films. Genres include action, family, drama, and thriller.

CRYSTAL SKY PICTURES, LLC
Production company, distributor, sales agent, and financing company

10203 Santa Monica Blvd.
5th Floor
Los Angeles, CA 90067
310-843-0223 (phone)
310-553-9895 (fax)

info@crystalsky.com
crystalsky.com
imdb.com/company/co0004724
linkedin.com/company/crystal-sky-pictures
facebook.com/Crystal-Sky-
    Pictures-222110757996636

Accepts query letters from unproduced, unrepresented writers via email. Project types include feature films. Genres include drama, horror, comedy, action, thriller, family, fantasy, crime, and science fiction.

Eric Breiman
310-843-0223
info@crystalsky.com

Steven Paul
310-843-0223
info@crystalsky.com
imdb.com/name/nm0666999

Florent Gaglio
Executive
310-843-0223
info@crystalsky.com
imdb.com/name/nm2904382

C-STATION
Production company

185-0021
Kokubunji, Tokyo 3-7-12
Japan
042-359-4280 (phone)
042-359-4281 (fax)

info@cstation.jp
cstation.jp
imdb.com/company/co0302465

Does not accept any unsolicited material. Project types include TV. Genres include drama, animation, and family.

Ryoji Maru
Representative
imdb.com/name/nm2426267

CUBEVISION
Production company

9000 W Sunset Blvd
West Hollywood, CA 90069
310-461-3490 (phone)
310-461-3491 (fax)

icecube.com
imdb.com/company/co0044714
facebook.com/IceCube
twitter.com/icecube

Accepts query letters from unproduced, unrepresented writers. Project types include feature films and TV. Genres include non-fiction, thriller, animation, romance, family, crime, drama, action, comedy, and reality.

Ice Cube
310-461-3495
imdb.com/name/nm0001084
Assistant: Nancy Leiviska

Matt Alvarez
Partner
310-461-3490
imdb.com/name/nm0023297
Assistant: Lawtisha Fletcher

CUFFLINK PRODUCTIONS
Production company

239 Herbert Ave
Closter, NJ 07624
201-497-3686

info@cufflinkproductions.com
cufflinkproductions.com
imdb.com/company/co0211191

Does not accept any unsolicited material. Genres include action, thriller, and crime.

CURB ENTERTAINMENT
Production company

3907 W Alameda Ave
Burbank, CA 91505
818-843-8580 (phone)
818-566-1719 (fax)

info@curbentertainment.com
curbentertainment.com
imdb.com/company/co0089886
linkedin.com/company/curb-entertainment-intl
facebook.com/Curb-
    Entertainment-131235890244194/timeline

Accepts query letters from unproduced, unrepresented writers via email. Project types include TV and feature films. Genres include romance, comedy, family, animation, science fiction, thriller, crime, horror, and drama. Established in 1984.

Mona Kirton
818-843-8580
mkirton@curb.com
imdb.com/name/nm1310398

Carole Nemoy
818-843-8580
ccurb@curb.com
imdb.com/name/nm0626002

Christy Peterson
818-843-8580
cpeterson@curb.com

CURB ENTERTAINMENT INTERNATIONAL CORPORATION
Production company and distributor

3907 W Alameda Ave, Burbank , CA, United States, 91505

818-843-8580 (phone)
818-566-1719 (fax)

info@curbentertainment.com
curbentertainment.com/home

Does not accept any unsolicited material. Project types include TV. Genres include reality and thriller.

CURIOUSCOPE
Distributor

1-27-6-2F
Higashi, Shibuya
Tokyo 150-0011
Japan
+81 0-5466-8500 (phone)
+81 0-5466-8505 (fax)

info@curiouscope.jp
curiouscope.jp
imdb.com/company/co0321240
facebook.com/CURIOUSCOPE
twitter.com/CURIOUSCOPE

Does not accept any unsolicited material. Project types include feature films. Genres include horror and comedy.

CUTLER PRODUCTIONS
Production company

Los Angeles, CA, United States
310-202-1272 (phone)
310-202-1502 (fax)

questions@arp.tv
actualreality.tv
imdb.com/company/co0193868

Does not accept any unsolicited material. Project types include TV and feature films. Genres include thriller, drama, family, and action.

CUTTING CHAI PRODUCTIONS
Production company

1481 E Old Settlers Blvd
301
Round Rock, TX 78664
512-524-9342

imdb.com/company/co0325637

facebook.com/cuttingchaiproductions

Does not accept any unsolicited material. Project types include short films. Genres include drama.

CUTTING EDGE FIM AND TV
Production company

Unit 1, Beeby Rd, London, E16 1QJ
44 0207-511-2207

enquiries@cuttingedge.uk.net
cuttingedgefilmandtv.com
imdb.com/name/nm0071003

Does not accept any unsolicited material. Established in 1991.

Angus Benfield
Producer
angusbenfield@gmail.com

C WORD PRODUCTIONS
Production company and distributor

2450 Hively St
Sarasota, FL 34231
941-726-1986

ritterfan@hotmail.com
imdb.com/company/co0227086
facebook.com/CWordProductions

Does not accept any unsolicited material. Project types include feature films. Genres include horror and drama. Established in 2006.

CYAN PICTURES
Production company and distributor

410 Park Ave, 15th Floor
New York, NY 10022
212-274-1085

info@cyanpictures.com
imdb.com/company/co0080910
linkedin.com/company/cyan-pictures

Accepts query letters from unproduced, unrepresented writers via email. Project types include feature films and TV. Genres include comedy, romance, science fiction, thriller, non-fiction, crime, horror, drama, and reality.

Wes Schrader
212-274-1085
schrader@cyanpictures.com

Alexander Burns
CFO
212-274-1085
info@cyanpictures.com

Joshua Newman
CEO
212-274-1085
newman@cyanpictures.com
imdb.com/name/nm1243333

CYFUNO VENTURES
Production company and sales agent

P.O. Box 807
Pickerington, OH 43147
614-483-2728

info@cyfuno.com
cyfuno.com
imdb.com/company/co0483139
facebook.com/TLAReleasingFans
twitter.com/intentfollow

Accepts scripts from unproduced, unrepresented writers. Project types include TV. Genres include documentary and comedy.

CYPRESS FILMS, INC.
Production company

630 Ninth Ave, Suite 415
New York, NY 10036
212-262-3900

kmoarefi@cypressfilms.com (script submissions)
joseph@cypressfilms.com (general)
cypressfilms.com
imdb.com/company/co0044830
linkedin.com/company/cypress-films-inc

Accepts query letters from unproduced, unrepresented writers via email. Project types include feature films and TV. Genres include family, drama, romance, comedy, science fiction, thriller, and period. Established in 1998.

Jon Glascoe
212-262-3900
imdb.com/name/nm0321797

Joseph Pierson
212-262-3900
imdb.com/name/nm0682777

CYPRESS POINT PRODUCTIONS
Production company

3000 Olympic Blvd
Santa Monica, CA 90404
310-315-4787 (phone)
310-315-4785 (fax)

cppfilms@earthlink.net
imdb.com/company/co0038030

Accepts query letters from unproduced, unrepresented writers via email. Project types include feature films and TV. Genres include action, comedy, romance, family, drama, crime, science fiction, thriller, and non-fiction.

Michael Waldron
310-315-4787
cppfilms@earthlink.net
imdb.com/name/nm1707236

Gerald Abrams
Chairman
310-315-4787
cppfilms@earthlink.net
imdb.com/name/nm0009181

DACIAN WOLF PRODUCTIONS
Production company

520 Speedwell Ave
Suite 215
Morris Plains, NJ 07950

dacianwolfproductions.com
imdb.com/company/co0427992
facebook.com/DacianWolfProd

Does not accept any unsolicited material. Project types include short films. Genres include drama and comedy.

DAHLIA STREET FILMS

Production company

199 Monitor St
Brooklyn, NY 11222
347-535-4746

info@dahliastreetfilms.com
imdb.com/company/co0022350
linkedin.com/company/dahlia-street-films

Does not accept any unsolicited material. Project types include feature films. Genres include science fiction and comedy.

Molly Mayeux
Owner/Producer
imdb.com/name/nm0562617

DAKOTA PICTURES

Production company

4633 Lankershim Blvd
North Hollywood, CA 91602
818-760-0099 (phone)
818-760-1070 (fax)

info@dakotafilms.com
dakotafilms.com
imdb.com/company/co0009221
facebook.com/pages/Dakota-Pictures/
    154008627979358
twitter.com/dakotafilms

Does not accept any unsolicited material. Project types include feature films and TV. Genres include comedy, action, reality, crime, drama, fantasy, non-fiction, thriller, animation, and family.

Matt Magielnicki
818-760-0099
info@dakotafilms.com
imdb.com/name/nm2616148

A.J. DiAntonio
818-760-0099
info@dakotafilms.com
imdb.com/name/nm1472504

Troy Miller
818-760-0099
info@dakotafilms.com
imdb.com/name/nm0003474

DALIAN WANDA GROUP

Production company and distributor

Floor 28, Wanda Mansion, No. 9 Jiefang St, Dalian, 21, China, 116001
011-864-1182822888111 (phone)
011-864-1182820888 (fax)

Floor 25, Tower B Wanda Plaza, No. 93 Jianguo Rd
Chaoyang District
Beijing China 100022
011-861-085853888 (phone)
011-861-085853222 (fax)

wanda-group.com
imdb.com/company/co0358410

Does not accept any unsolicited material. Project types include TV and feature films. Genres include thriller, drama, family, comedy, and action.

DANCING ORANGE PRODUCTIONS

708 17th St
Santa Monica, CA 90402

facebook.com

Does not accept any unsolicited material. Project types include feature films. Genres include drama.

Jason Benesh
Producer
imdb.com/name/nm1200394

Lisa Todd
Producer
imdb.com/name/nm0865217

DAN FILMS

Production company

249 Grays Inn Rd
London, England WC1X 8QZ
UK
+44 (0)20 7916 4771 (phone)
+44 (0)20 7713 6016 (fax)

enquiries@danfilms.com
danfilms.com
imdb.com/company/co0014641
facebook.com/Dan-Films-243980392230
twitter.com/dan_films

Does not accept any unsolicited material. Project types include short films. Genres include thriller.

Julie Baines
Producer
imdb.com/name/nm0047787

DAN GORDON PRODUCTIONS
Production company

2060-D Ave. Suite #250
Thousand Oaks , CA 91362
805-496-2566

imdb.com/company/co0094966

Does not accept any unsolicited material. Project types include feature films and TV.

Dan Gordon
Writer/Producer
imdb.com/name/nm0330108

DANIEL L. PAULSON PRODUCTIONS
Production company

9056 Santa Monica Blvd, Suite 203A
West Hollywood, CA 90069
310-278-9747

dlpprods@sbcglobal.net
imdb.com/company/co0034720

Does not accept any unsolicited material. Project types include TV and feature films. Genres include reality, action, non-fiction, comedy, detective, crime, romance, drama, thriller, and family.

Daniel Paulson
310-278-9747
dlpprods@sbcglobal.net
imdb.com/name/nm0667340

Steve Kennedy
310-278-9747
dlpprods@sbcglobal.net
imdb.com/name/nm0448346

DANIEL OSTROFF PRODUCTIONS
Production company

2046 N Hillhurst Ave. #120
Los Angeles, CA 90027
323-238-8824

oteamthe@gmail.com
imdb.com/company/co0138101

Does not accept any unsolicited material. Project types include TV and feature films. Genres include non-fiction, reality, detective, and comedy.

Daniel Ostroff
Producer
323-284-8824
oteamthe@gmail.com
imdb.com/name/nm0652491
linkedin.com/pub/daniel-ostroff/6/856/28a

DANIEL PETRIE JR. & COMPANY
Production company

18034 Ventura Blvd, Suite 445
Encino, CA 91316
818-708-1602 (phone)
818-774-0345 (fax)

imdb.com/company/co0120842
linkedin.com/in/daniel-petrie-jr-136a2022

Accepts query letters from unproduced, unrepresented writers. Project types include feature films and TV. Genres include detective, horror, science fiction, drama, thriller, comedy, action, romance, and crime.

Rick Dugdale
818-708-1602
imdb.com/name/nm1067987

Daniel Petrie,
818-708-1602
imdb.com/name/nm0677943

DANIEL SLADEK ENTERTAINMENT CORPORATION

8306 Wilshire Blvd, Suite 510
Beverly Hills, CA 90211
323-934-9268 (phone)
323-934-7362 (fax)

danielsladek@mac.com
danielsladek.com

Does not accept any unsolicited material. Project types include TV and feature films. Genres include thriller, drama, science fiction, romance, action, reality, comedy, non-fiction, crime, fantasy, and horror.

Daniel Sladek
Talent Manager
323-934-9268
danielsladek@mac.com
imdb.com/name/nm0805202

DANJAQ PRODUCTIONS
Production company

2400 Broadway
Ste 310
Santa Monica, CA 90404
310-449-3185

imdb.com/company/co0024134
linkedin.com/company/eon-productions-ltd

Does not accept any unsolicited material. Project types include feature films. Genres include action.

David Pope
CEO
310-449-3185
imdb.com/name/nm0691102

Barbara Broccoli
imdb.com/name/nm0110483

Michael Wilson
President
310-449-3185
imdb.com/name/nm0933865

DAN LUPOVITZ PRODUCTIONS
Production company

936 Alandele Ave
Los Angeles, CA 90036
323-930-0769 (phone)
310-385-0196 (fax)

dlupovitz@aol.com
imdb.com/company/co0027986

Accepts query letters from unproduced, unrepresented writers via email. Project types include TV and feature films. Genres include comedy, romance, and drama.

Dan Lupovitz
323-930-0769
dlupovitz@aol.com
imdb.com/name/nm0526991

DAN WINGUTOW PRODUCTIONS
Production company

534 Laguardia Pl., Suite 3
New York, NY 10012
212-477-1328 (phone)
212-254-6902 (fax)

imdb.com/company/co0018565
linkedin.com/in/dan-wigutow-3039abb

Accepts query letters from unproduced, unrepresented writers. Project types include TV and feature films. Genres include horror, crime, drama, romance, fantasy, thriller, science fiction, and comedy.

Caroline Moore
212-477-1328
imdb.com/name/nm0601006

Dan Wigutow
Executive Producer
212-477-1328
imdb.com/name/nm0927887

DARIUS FILMS INCORPORATED
Production company

9255 Sunset Blvd
Suite 1100
Los Angeles, CA 90069
310-728-1342 (phone)
310-494-0575 (fax)

349 Carlaw Ave
Suite 204
Toronto, ON M4M 2T1
416-922-0007 (phone)
416-406-0034 (fax)

info@dariusfilms.com
dariusfilms.com
imdb.com/company/co0133523
facebook.com/Darius-Films-136427143096685
twitter.com/dariusfilms

Accepts query letters from produced or represented writers. Project types include feature films and TV. Genres include drama, detective, crime, comedy, romance, fantasy, thriller, non-fiction, and science fiction.

Nicholas Tabarrok
310-728-1342
info@dariusfilms.com
imdb.com/name/nm0002431

Daniel Baruela
310-728-1342
info@dariusfilms.com
imdb.com/name/nm3758990

DARK ARTS
Studio

65 Eckford St, Suite 4
Brooklyn, NY 11222

info@darkartsfilm.com
darkartsfilm.com
imdb.com/company/co0422626

Does not accept any unsolicited material. Project types include feature films. Genres include comedy.

Alicia Van Couvering
Producer
imdb.com/name/nm0885900

Andrea Roa
Producer
imdb.com/name/nm1978398

DARK CASTLE ENTERTAINMENT
Production company and distributor

1601 Main St
Venice, CA 90291
310-566-6100 (phone)
310-566-6188 (fax)

imdb.com/company/co0050870

Accepts query letters from produced or represented writers. Project types include feature films. Genres include crime, action, horror, thriller, and drama. Established in 1999.

Joel Silver
Partner
imdb.com/name/nm0005428

Steve Richards
imdb.com/name/nm0724345

Andrew Rona
imdb.com/name/nm0739868
Assistant: Dash Boam

DARK CLOUD STUDIOS
Production company

1395 Brickell Ave Suite 800
Miami, FL 33131
305-967-6340

Christian@DarkCloudStudios.com
darkcloudstudios.com
imdb.com/company/co0427019
facebook.com/darkcloudstudios
twitter.com/filmsbydark

Does not accept any unsolicited material. Genres include action and horror.

DARK FIBER PRODUCTIONS
Production company

5324 Gaston Ave #204
Dallas, TX 75214
682-551-1249

joethevisualist@gmail.com
imdb.com/company/co0478106
facebook.com/darkfiberproductions

Does not accept any unsolicited material. Project types include feature films. Genres include science fiction and action. Established in 2014.

DARK HORSE ENTERTAINMENT
Production company and distributor

12711 Ventura Blvd.
Suite 270
Studio City, CA 91604
323-655-3600 (phone)
323-655-2430 (fax)

dhentertainment.com

imdb.com/company/co0020061
facebook.com/darkhorsecomics
twitter.com/darkhorsecomics

Does not accept any unsolicited material. Project types include feature films. Genres include fantasy, thriller, non-fiction, romance, crime, comedy, action, family, science fiction, horror, animation, and drama.

Mike Richardson
323-655-3600
miker@darkhorse.com
imdb.com/name/nm0724700
Assistant: Pete Cacioppo

Keith Goldberg
323-655-3600
keithg@darkhorse.com
imdb.com/name/nm1378991

DARK LIGHTNING FILMS
Distributor

6406 Garden Trail Court
Housotn, TX 77072
832-289-1670

info@darklightningfilms.com
darklightningfilms.com
imdb.com/company/co0481721

Does not accept any unsolicited material. Genres include horror.

DARKMANIA DISTRIBUTION
Distributor

5300 Bee Cave Rd
Austin, TX 78746
512-689-3640

jmcadams@rdarkpro.com
rdarkpro.com
imdb.com/company/co0404872

Does not accept any unsolicited material. Project types include TV. Genres include documentary.

DARKO ENTERTAINMENT
Production company

7164 Melrose Ave.
2nd Floor

Los Angeles, CA 90046
323-592-3460 (phone)
323-850-2481 (fax)

info@darko.com
darko.com
imdb.com/company/co0118694
facebook.com/pages/Darko-Entertainment/
    184834071562799
twitter.com/darko_ent

Does not accept any unsolicited material. Project types include feature films and TV. Genres include thriller, horror, and fantasy.

Jeff Cullota
imdb.com/name/nm2261214

DARK SKY FILMS
Production company

16101 S 108th Ave
Orland Park, IL 60467
800-323-0442

info@darkskyfilms.com
darkskyfilms.com
imdb.com/company/co0152321
facebook.com/DarkSkyFilms
twitter.com/darkskyfilms

Does not accept any unsolicited material. Project types include feature films. Genres include horror and thriller.

Greg Newman
Executive
imdb.com/name/nm0628103

Malik Ali
Executive
imdb.com/name/nm0019446

Todd Wieneke
Producer
imdb.com/name/nm2663562

DARK TOY ENTERTAINMENT
Production company

3800 Barham Blvd. Suite 207
Los Angeles, CA 90068

imdb.com/company/co0317488

Does not accept any unsolicited material. Project types include TV. Genres include drama and comedy.

Todd Holland
Producer
imdb.com/name/nm0390844

DARKWOODS PRODUCTIONS
Production company and distributor

301 E Colorado Blvd, Suite 705
Pasadena, CA 91101
323-454-4580 (phone)
323-454-4581 (fax)

imdb.com/company/co0029398
facebook.com/Darkwoods-
    Productions-111244805606181
twitter.com/AMC_TV

Does not accept any unsolicited material. Project types include feature films. Genres include romance, non-fiction, horror, comedy, fantasy, crime, thriller, science fiction, and drama.

Frank Darobont
323-454-4582
imdb.com/name/nm0001104
Assistant: Alex Whit

DARLOW SMITHSON PRODUCTIONS
Production company and distributor

420 W 45th St
New York NY 10036
212-774-4513

Shepherds Building Central, Charecroft Way, London, United Kingdom, W14 0EE
011-442-074827027 (phone)
011-442-074827039 (fax)

1 Scotts Rd 21-01/03 Shaw Centre
Singapore 228208
011-656-5059300

mail@darlowsmithson.com
dsp.tv
imdb.com/company/co0000130

Does not accept any unsolicited material. Project types include TV. Genres include family, drama, thriller, and comedy.

DARREN STAR PRODUCTIONS
Production company

9200 Sunset Blvd, Suite 430
Los Angeles, CA 90069
310-274-2145 (phone)
310-274-1455 (fax)

d.star.prodco@gmail.com
imdb.com/company/co0020963

Accepts query letters from unproduced, unrepresented writers. Project types include feature films and TV. Genres include comedy, drama, romance, crime, and non-fiction.

Charles Pugliese
310-274-2145
imdb.com/name/nm1551399

Darren Star
310-274-2145
imdb.com/name/nm0823015

DARYL PRINCE PRODUCTIONS
Production company

C/O Archerfield Partners LLP
4 Pickering Place St James's St
London SW1A 1EA
UK
44 (0)7538 832 492

info@firstmarch.co.uk
imdb.com/company/co0399489

Does not accept any unsolicited material. Project types include feature films. Genres include drama and thriller.

DAS IMPERIUM
Production company

Torstrasse 129
Berlin 10119
Germany
+49.30.28879520

georg@dasimperium.com

dasimperium.com
imdb.com/company/co0092515
twitter.com/DasImperium

Does not accept any unsolicited material. Project types include feature films. Genres include drama.

DAVE BELL ASSOCIATES
Production company

3211 Cahuenga Blvd West
Los Angeles, CA 90068
323-851-7801 (phone)
323-851-9349 (fax)

dbamovies@aol.com
imdb.com/company/co0033679
facebook.com/pages/Dave-Bell-Associates-Inc/
   136800853043146

Accepts query letters from unproduced, unrepresented writers via email. Project types include TV and feature films. Genres include drama, reality, family, science fiction, romance, non-fiction, and horror.

Dave Bell
President
323-851-7801
dbamovies@aol.com
imdb.com/name/nm1037012

Ted Weiant
323-851-7801
dbamovies@aol.com
imdb.com/name/nm1059707

Fred Putman
323-851-7801
imdb.com/name/nm1729656

DAVID EICK PRODUCTIONS
Production company

100 Universal City Plaza
Universal City, CA 91608
818-501-0146 (phone)
818-733-2522 (fax)

imdb.com/company/co0176813

Accepts query letters from unproduced, unrepresented writers. Project types include TV. Genres include thriller, drama, action, and science fiction.

Stephanie Stanley
Writer's Assistant
linkedin.com/pub/stephanie-stanley/40/491/b01

David Eick
President
818-501-0146
imdb.com/name/nm0251594

DAVID E. KELLEY PRODUCTIONS
Production company

1600 Rosecrans Ave., Bldg. 4B
Manhattan Beach , CA 90266
310-727-2200

imdb.com/company/co0050201
linkedin.com/company/david-e.-kelley-productions

Does not accept any unsolicited material. Project types include feature films and TV. Genres include drama.

Robert Breeech
President of Development
imdb.com/name/nm010666

David E. Kelley
CEO/Writer/Producer
imdb.com/name/nm0005082

DAVIS DISTRIBUTING DIVISION
Distributor

9147 Venice Blvd.
Los Angeles, CA 90034

imdb.com/company/co0129584

Does not accept any unsolicited material. Project types include theater. Genres include action, science fiction, and drama.

DAVIS ENTERTAINMENT
Production company

150 S. Barrington Place
Los Angeles, CA 90049

10201 W Pico Blvd
31-301
Los Angeles, CA 90064
310-556-3550 (phone)
310-556-3688 (fax)

davis-e.com
imdb.com/company/co0022730

Accepts scripts from produced or represented writers. Project types include TV. Genres include detective, crime, comedy, drama, family, and action.

John Davis
imdb.com/name/nm0204862

John Fox
imdb.com/name/nm2470810

DAYBREAK PICTURES
Production company

Elsinore House
77 Fulham Palace Rd
London W6 8JA
UK
+44 20 7258 6722

info@daybreakpictures.com
daybreakpictures.com
imdb.com/company/co0199178
facebook.com/DaybreakPictures

Does not accept any unsolicited material. Project types include TV. Genres include drama.

David Aukin
Producer
imdb.com/name/nm0042010

DAYBREAK PRODUCTIONS
Production company

3000 W. Olympic Blvd. Bldge 5
Santa Monica, CA 90404
310-264-4202 (phone)
310-264-4222 (fax)

imdb.com/company/co0030602
linkedin.com/company/daybreak-productions
facebook.com/DaybreakTVProductions

Does not accept any unsolicited material. Project types include feature films and TV.

James Abraham
Development
imdb.com/name/nm1673506

Charles Gordon
Producer
imdb.com/name/nm0330077

DBM FILMS
Production company, distributor, and sales agent

606 Baltimore Ave.
Suite 200
Towson, MD 21204
410-825-7400 (phone)
443-269-0213 (fax)

info@dbmcommunications.com
dbmfilm.com
imdb.com/company/co0376314

Does not accept any unsolicited material. Project types include TV. Genres include action and drama.

DC DOGS
Production company

3509 Connecticut Ave NW
Suite 1450
Washington, DC 20008
202-237-7759

dcdogs.com
imdb.com/company/co0307879

Does not accept any unsolicited material. Genres include action.

DCI-LOS ANGELES
Production company

2001 Wilshire Blvd., Suite 600
Santa Monica, CA 90403
310-586-5600 (phone)
310-586-5898 (fax)

info@dentsuentertainment.com
dentsuentertainment.com
imdb.com/company/co0293867

Does not accept any unsolicited material. Project types include TV. Genres include science fiction.

DCM PRODUCTIONS
Production company

Schoenhauser Allee 8
Berlin 10119
Germany
+49 30 885 974 0 (phone)
+49 30 885 974 15 (fax)

what@dcmteam.com
dcmworld.com
imdb.com/company/co0248827

Does not accept any unsolicited material. Project types include feature films. Genres include crime, thriller, romance, and drama.

DEACON STREET PRODUCTIONS
Production company

133 E. Palmer Ave.
Collingswood, NJ 08108
856-297-4852 (phone)
818-332-4939 (fax)

imdb.com/company/co0084176

Does not accept any unsolicited material. Project types include TV. Genres include thriller and comedy.

DEAD RABBIT FILMS
Production company and distributor

215 Zelley Ave.
Moorestown, NJ 08057
856-234-5671 (phone)
856-234-5672 (fax)

thechack@aol.com
deadrabbitfilms.com
imdb.com/company/co0324017

Does not accept any unsolicited material. Genres include horror and thriller.

DEATH OF A GOOD MAN
Production company

117 78th St #3
North Bergen, NJ 07047
917-331-7393

enrique@enriq.org
imdb.com/company/co0526953

Does not accept any unsolicited material. Project types include TV. Genres include drama.

DEED FILMS
Production company

419-685-4842

sdonley@deedfilms.com
deedfilms.com
imdb.com/company/co0323092

Does not accept any unsolicited material. Project types include feature films. Genres include comedy, crime, and thriller.

Scott Donley
President
imdb.com/name/nm4238094

DEEDLE-DEE PRODUCTIONS
Production company

1875 Century Park East
Los Angeles, CA 90025

imdb.com/company/co0093771

Does not accept any unsolicited material. Project types include TV. Genres include comedy.

Greg Daniels
Writer/Producer
imdb.com/name/nm0199939

D&E ENTERTAINMENT
Production company and studio

6525 Sunset Blvd, Penthouse, Los Angeles , CA, United States, 90028
323-464-2403 (phone)
323-464-2426 (fax)

info@DandEentertainment.com
dandeentertainment.com
imdb.com/company/co0279492

Does not accept any unsolicited material. Project types include theater. Genres include family, thriller, romance, and drama.

DEEPA MEHTA FILMS
Production company

460 College St
Ste 301
Toronto, ON
Canada
416-516-0899

dmfilms@hamiltonmehta.com
imdb.com/company/co0071617

Does not accept any unsolicited material. Project types include feature films. Genres include romance and drama.

Deepa Mehta
Director
imdb.com/name/nm0576548

DEERJEN FILMS
Production company

401 E 80th St Suite 29b
New York, NY 10075

deerjen.com
imdb.com/company/co0190929

Does not accept any unsolicited material. Project types include feature films. Genres include comedy, drama, period, romance, and thriller. Established in 2007.

Jen Gatien
Producer
jen@deerjen.com
imdb.com/name/nm0309684

DEFIANCE ENTERTAINMENT
Production company

6605 Hollywood Blvd, Suite 100
Los Angeles, CA 91401
323-393-0132

info@defiance-ent.com
imdb.com/company/co0236811

Does not accept any unsolicited material. Project types include feature films, commercials, and TV. Genres include thriller, drama, comedy, fantasy, action, crime, myth, science fiction, and horror.

Brian Keathley
brian@defiance-ent.com
imdb.com/name/nm0444080

Clare Kramer
COO
clare@defiance-ent.com
imdb.com/name/nm0004456

DEFIANT PICTURES
Production company

4940 Melrose Hill St
Los Angeles, CA 90029
323-440-1267 (phone)
323-924-1882 (fax)

defiant@defiantfilmhaus.com
imdb.com/company/co0311341
twitter.com/titanpicturesme

Does not accept any unsolicited material. Project types include feature films. Genres include comedy, action, romance, horror, crime, thriller, and drama. Established in 2011.

Aaron Jackson
Producer
imdb.com/name/nm2980930
linkedin.com/pub/aaron-jackson/13/99b/611
facebook.com/aaronthejack

DE FINA PRODUCTIONS
Production company

443 Greenwich St, 5th Floor
New York, NY 10013
212-219-1525 (phone)
212-219-1859 (fax)

imdb.com/company/co0276457

Does not accept any unsolicited material. Project types include feature films. Genres include thriller.

Barbara De Fina
Principal, Producer
imdb.com/name/nm0208381

Sarah Feinberg
Head
imdb.com/name/nm5963270

DE LAURENTIIS COMPANY
Production company

100 Universal City Plaza, Bungalow 5195, Universal City , CA, United States, 91608
818-777-2111 (phone)
818-866-5566 (fax)

delaurentiisco.com
imdb.com/company/co0014380

Does not accept any unsolicited material. Project types include feature films and TV. Genres include action, drama, thriller, and family.

DE LINE PICTURES
Production company

4000 Warner Blvd Building 66, Room 147
Burbank, CA 91522
818-954-5200 (phone)
818-954-5430 (fax)

imdb.com/company/co0033149
linkedin.com/company/de-line-pictures

Does not accept any unsolicited material. Project types include feature films. Genres include fantasy, family, science fiction, drama, crime, animation, period, action, comedy, romance, and thriller. Established in 2001.

Jacob Robinson
imdb.com/name/nm1563784

Donald De Line
President
imdb.com/name/nm0209773
Assistant: Matt Gamboa matt@delinepictures.com

DEL TORO PRODUCTIONS
Production company

1000 Flower St
Glendale, CA 91201
818-695-6363

imdb.com/company/co0247699

Does not accept any unsolicited material. Project types include TV and feature films. Genres include thriller, crime, horror, and drama.

Guillermo del Toro
Producer/Director
imdb.com/name/nm0868219

DELVE FILMS

20727 High Desert Ct
Suite 4+5
Bend, OR 97701
541-728-3558

hello@delve.media
delve.media
imdb.com/company/co0315636

Accepts query letters from produced or represented writers. Project types include feature films. Genres include documentary, romance, thriller, comedy, fantasy, and drama.

Nate Salciccioli
541-788-6139
nate@delvefilms.com
imdb.com/name/nm4244606

Isaac Testerman
President
isaac@delvefilms.com
imdb.com/name/nm4107099

DEMAREST FILMS
Production company and financing company

11925 Wilshire Blvd, Suite 310
Los Angeles, CA 90025
424-789-8310

asst@demarestfilms.com
demarestfilms.com
imdb.com/company/co0317576

Does not accept any unsolicited material. Project types include TV and feature films. Genres include fantasy, drama, comedy, crime, and thriller.

Sam Englebardt
imdb.com/name/nm1583132
Assistant: Linda Goetz

William D. Johnso
imdb.com/name/nm4207924

Michael Lambert
imdb.com/name/nm2236003

DENNIS O'NEILL PRODUCTIONS
Production company and distributor

P.O. BOX 33003
Fort Worth, TX 76162
817-601-5129 (phone)
817-294-5464 (fax)

info@bailouttv.com
bailouttv.com
imdb.com/company/co0377634

Does not accept any unsolicited material. Project types include TV. Genres include drama and comedy.

DENTON DISTRIBUTION
Distributor

2033 Gateway Place
San Jose, CA 93110

ariana@dentondvd.com
imdb.com/company/co0351812

Does not accept any unsolicited material. Genres include comedy and drama.

DENTSU
Production company and distributor

1-8-1, Higashi-shimbashi
Minato-ku, Tokyo 105-7001
Japan
+81 3 62 17 15 60 (phone)
+81 3 62 17 15 01 (fax)

tohashi@dentsu.co.jp
dentsu.com
imdb.com/company/co0169264

Does not accept any unsolicited material. Project types include feature films. Genres include action, thriller, and crime.

Anna Teo
Executive
imdb.com/name/nm3196328

DENTSU MUSIC AND ENTERTAINMENT
Production company and distributor

2-10-1
17F Shin Nikko Bldg. East
Toranomon, Minato-ku, Tokyo 105-0001
Japan

03-5575-5713 (phone)
03-5575-5718 (fax)

info@dentsumusic.co.jp
dentsumusic.co.jp
imdb.com/company/co0064941

Does not accept any unsolicited material. Project types include TV. Genres include animation and fantasy.

Keiko Enomoto
Manager
imdb.com/name/nm3250974

DEON TAYLOR ENTERPRISES
Production company

320 N 10th St, Suite E
Sacramento, CA 95811
916-448-2388

info@deontaylorenterprises.com
imdb.com/company/co0203749
linkedin.com/company/deon-taylor-enterprises

Does not accept any unsolicited material. Project types include feature films. Genres include horror.

DE PASSE ENTERTAINMENT
Production company

9200 Sunset Blvd., Suite 510
West Hollywood, CA 90069
310-858-3734

imdb.com/company/co0063390

Does not accept any unsolicited material. Project types include TV and feature films. Genres include drama.

Suzanne de Passe
Producer
imdb.com/name/nm0210867

Rose Caraet
Creative Affairs
imdb.com/name/nm1122044

DEPTH OF FIELD

1724 Whitley Ave
Los Angeles, CA 90028

323-466-6500 (phone)
323-466-6501 (fax)

mir.com.my/rb/photography/fototech/htmls/
 depth.html
imdb.com/company/co0113177

Accepts scripts from produced or represented writers.
Project types include feature films.

Andrew Miano
Executive Producer
imdb.com/name/nm0583948

Chris Weitz
imdb.com/name/nm0919363

DERBY STREET FILMS
Production company

45 Pall Mall
London SW1Y 5JG
UK

info@derbystreetfilms.co.uk
derbystreetfilms.co.uk
imdb.com/company/co0371803

Does not accept any unsolicited material. Project types
include feature films. Genres include drama, action,
romance, comedy, and science fiction.

Nicola Horlick
Producer
imdb.com/name/nm2955308

DESERT WIND STUDIO
Production company

13603 Marina Pointe Dr
Ste D529
Marina Del Rey, CA 90292
310-437-0740 (phone)
310-499-5254 (fax)

info@desertwindstudios.com
desertwindstudios.com/Desert_Wind_Studios/
 HOME.html
imdb.com/company/co0298614
facebook.com/pages/Desert-Wind-Films/
 489420855503
twitter.com/DesertWindStud

Accepts query letters from unproduced, unrepresented
writers. Project types include feature films and TV.
Genres include drama.

Josh Mills
imdb.com/name/nm1836231

Steven Camp
CFO
imdb.com/name/nm3823972

Danny Amato
imdb.com/name/nm3824734

Jeffrey James Ward
imdb.com/name/nm3823932

T.J. Amato
President
imdb.com/name/nm2125600

DESTINY PICTURES
Production company

1423 Second St
Ste 411
Santa Monica, CA 90401
310-656-1034

destiny@destinypictures.biz
destinypictures.biz
imdb.com/company/co0176808
facebook.com/pages/Destiny-Pictures/
 185479521464859

Accepts query letters from unproduced, unrepresented
writers via email. Genres include non-fiction, drama,
and thriller.

Christine Redlin
Executive Producer
linkedin.com/pub/christine-redlin/1/24b/502
twitter.com/ChristineRedlin

Mark Castaldo
Founder
imdb.com/name/nm0144431
linkedin.com/pub/mark-castaldo/6/966/90b
facebook.com/markcastaldoproducer

DETOUR FILMPRODUCTION
Production company

PO Box 13351
Austin, TX 78711
512-322-0031 (phone)
512-322-0726 (fax)

kirsten@detourfilm.com
detourfilm.com
imdb.com/company/co0123642

Does not accept any unsolicited material. Project types include feature films. Genres include crime, drama, science fiction, animation, action, thriller, and fantasy. Established in 1988.

DEUCE THREE PRODUCTIONS
Production company

1041 N Formosa Ave., Santa Monica Building
Los Angeles, CA 90046

imdb.com/company/co0086846

Does not accept any unsolicited material. Project types include feature films. Genres include drama.

Carol Fenelon
Partner/Producer
imdb.com/name/nm0271770

Curtis Hanson
Partner/Producer/Director
imdb.com/name/nm0000436

DEVAN CLAN PRODUCTIONS
Production company

26893 Bouquet Canyon Rd
Ste C-201
Santa Clarita, CA 91350
818-732-9902

devanclan5@gmail.com
devanclan.com
imdb.com/company/co0475409
facebook.com/devanclanproductions
twitter.com/DeVanClan

Does not accept any unsolicited material. Project types include feature films. Genres include thriller and horror. Established in 2014.

Heather DeVan
CEO
imdb.com/name/nm2860951

Jason DeVan
CEO
imdb.com/name/nm1755962

DEVIANT FILM
Production company

6715 Hollywood Blvd., Suite 103
Hollywood, CA 90028
323-839-1345

info@deviantfilm.com
imdb.com/company/co0139919

Does not accept any unsolicited material. Project types include feature films. Genres include comedy and drama.

David Hillary
Producer
imdb.com/name/nm0975187

DEVOLVER DIGITAL FILMS
Production company and distributor

3267 Bee Caves Rd.
#107 -- Box 63
Austin, TX 78746
415-505-1350

films@devolverdigital.com
devolverdigital.com
imdb.com/company/co0443171
facebook.com/DevolverDigitalFilms
twitter.com/DevolverFlix

Does not accept any unsolicited material. Project types include TV and feature films. Genres include fantasy, science fiction, crime, documentary, myth, drama, and non-fiction. Established in 2012.

DEX ENTERTAINMENT
Production company and distributor

2-14-1-3F
Kamiuma
Setagaya, Tokyo 154-0011
Japan
03-5433-3070 (phone)
03-5486-8106 (fax)

info@dex-et.jp

dex-et.jp
imdb.com/company/co0203834

Does not accept any unsolicited material. Project types include TV and feature films. Genres include horror and thriller.

Fumio Kurokawa

President (Executive)
imdb.com/name/nm0475866

D FILMS

Production company and distributor

2 St. Clair Ave E
Ste 903
Toronto, ON M4T 2T5
Canada
416-778-5600

info@dfilmscorp.ca
dfilmscorp.ca
imdb.com/company/co0282370
facebook.com/dfilms
twitter.com/dfilms

Does not accept any unsolicited material. Genres include thriller and action.

DFTBA RECORDS

Distributor and sales agent

2291 W Broadway
Suite #6
Missoula, MT 59808

hello@dftba.com
store.dftba.com
imdb.com/company/co0514841
facebook.com/DFTBArecords
twitter.com/DFTBArecords

Does not accept any unsolicited material. Project types include TV. Genres include comedy and drama.

DFZ PRODUCTIONS

Production company

9465 Wilshire Blvd., Suite 920
Beverly Hills, CA 90212
310-274-5735

imdb.com/company/co0013073

Does not accept any unsolicited material. Project types include feature films.

Dean Zanuck

Producer
imdb.com/name/nm0953124

DGW FILMS

Production company and distributor

P.O. Box 35
Green Village, NJ 07935

dgwfilm@gmail.com
imdb.com/company/co0292918

Does not accept any unsolicited material. Genres include drama and thriller.

DIAMONDZ N DA RUFF

Production company

75 N 17th St
Prospect Park, NJ 07508
973-703-0990

artis2@optonline.net
imdb.com/company/co0184473

Does not accept any unsolicited material. Project types include TV. Genres include drama and crime.

DI BONAVENTURA PICTURES

Production company and distributor

5555 Melrose Ave
DeMille Building, 2nd Floor
Los Angeles, CA 90038
323-956-5454 (phone)
323-862-2288 (fax)

imdb.com/company/co0117723

Does not accept any unsolicited material. Project types include feature films. Genres include science fiction, thriller, action, and fantasy.

Lorenzo di Bonaventura

President
imdb.com/name/nm0225146

Erik Howsam
Senior Vice-President Production
imdb.com/name/nm1857184

Edward Fee
Director of Development
imdb.com/name/nm1825537

Mark Vahradian
President of Production
(Executive)http://www.imdb.com/name/nm1680607/
imdb.com/name/nm1680607

David Ready
VP (Executive)
imdb.com/name/nm2819401

DI BONAVENTURA PICTURES TELEVISION
Production company

500 S Buena Vista St Animation Building, Suite 3F-3
Burbank, CA 91521

imdb.com/company/co0341152

Does not accept any unsolicited material. Project types
include TV. Genres include science fiction, thriller,
and drama. Established in 2011.

Dan McDermott
Partner
imdb.com/name/nm1908145

Lorenzo di Bonaventura
Partner
imdb.com/name/nm0225146
Assistant: Elizabeth Kiernan

DIC ENTERTAINMENT
Production company

4100 W. Alamdea Ave, 4th Floor
Burbank, CA 91502
818-955-5400 (phone)
818-955-5696 (fax)

info@dicentertainment.com
dicentertainment.com
imdb.com/company/co0112669

Does not accept any unsolicited material.

DIFFERENCE CO.
Distributor

4-28-4-1F
Yotsuya
Shinjuku, Tokyo 160-0004
Japan

info-difference@rams.jp
imdb.com/company/co0390911

Does not accept any unsolicited material. Project types
include TV. Genres include science fiction and action.

DIFFERENT DUCK FILMS
Production company

18 Wardell Ave.,
Rumson, NJ 07760

differentduckfilms@hotmail.com
imdb.com/company/co0215662
facebook.com/Different-Duck-Films-
    LLC-386636801509072
twitter.com/different_duck

Does not accept any unsolicited material. Project types
include feature films. Genres include comedy, drama,
family, thriller, and fantasy.

Rob Margolies
imdb.com/name/nm1827689

DIGI DISTRIBUTION
Production company and distributor

718 I St
Reedley, CA 93654
559-530-2072

support@digidistribution.com
digidistribution.com
imdb.com/company/co0373400
linkedin.com/company/digi-distribution

Accepts query letters from unproduced, unrepresented
writers. Genres include drama, comedy, and romance.

DIGITAL DOMAIN FILMS
Studio

300 Rose Ave
Venica, CA 90291

310-314-2800 (phone)
310-664-2701 (fax)

digitaldomain.com

Does not accept any unsolicited material. Project types include feature films.

Mark Miller
President & CEO
imdb.com/name/nm0588903

DIGITAL DOMAIN MEDIA GROUP

Production company and distributor

10250 SW Village Parkway
Port Saint Lucie, FL 34987
772-345-8000

imdb.com/company/co0346278

Does not accept any unsolicited material. Project types include short films.

DIGITAL FLAMINGO

Production company

2010 SW 100 Ave
Miramar, FL 33025
954-381-4102

info@digitalflamingo.com
digitalflamingo.com
imdb.com/company/co0453329

Does not accept any unsolicited material. Project types include short films. Genres include comedy and thriller.

DIGITAL MEME

Distributor

3-27-11-12F
Shibuya
Shibuya, TOKYO 150-0002
Japan
+81-3-5467-4729 (phone)
+81-3-5467-4722 (fax)

info@digital-meme.com
digital-meme.com/jp
imdb.com/company/co0218202

Does not accept any unsolicited material. Project types include TV. Genres include drama.

Larry Greenberg
CEO
imdb.com/name/nm2464817

DIGITAL RIGHTS GROUP

Distributor

62-65 Chandos Place, London, United Kingdom, WC2N 4HG
310-285-9000

info@dgr.tv
imdb.com/company/co0194799

Does not accept any unsolicited material.

DIGNITY FILM FINANCE

Financing company

22647 Ventura Blvd, Suite 1004
Woodland Hills, CA 91364
818-436-2410

info@dignity-distribution.com
dignity-distribution.com
imdb.com/company/co0381376

Does not accept any unsolicited material. Project types include feature films.

Maggie Monteith
President/CEO
imdb.com/name/nm1803406

Chris Heltzel
Creative Executive
imdb.com/name/nm3810728

DIMENSION BLUE

Production company

3-16-24-3F
Nishi Azabu
Minatoku, Tokyo 106-0031
Japan
03-3470-7561 (phone)
03-3470-9666 (fax)

d-blue@joy.hi-ho.ne.jp
imdb.com/company/co0234681

Does not accept any unsolicited material. Project types include TV. Genres include drama.

Takahiro Koizumi
President (Manager)
imdb.com/name/nm2968426

DIMENSION FILMS
Production company and distributor

99 Hudson St
4th Floor
New York, NY 10013
212-845-8600

9100 Wilshire Blvd.
Suite 700W
Beverly Hills, CA 90212
424-204-4800

weinsteinco.com
imdb.com/company/co0019626
linkedin.com/company/the-weinstein-company
facebook.com/weinsteinco
twitter.com/WeinsteinFilms

Does not accept any unsolicited material. Project types include feature films. Genres include thriller, action, comedy, horror, and science fiction.

Matthew Signer
imdb.com/name/nm1529449

Jeff Maynard
imdb.com/name/nm0963230

Bob Weinstein
imdb.com/name/nm0918424

DINO DE LAURENTIIS COMPANY
Production company

100 Universal City Plaza Bungalow 5195
Universal City, CA 91608
818-777-2111 (phone)
818-886-5566 (fax)

ddlcoffice@ddlc.net
ddlc.net
imdb.com/company/co0014380
facebook.com/DeLaurentiisCo
twitter.com/DeLaurentiisCo

Does not accept any unsolicited material. Project types include feature films and TV. Genres include detective, horror, science fiction, action, romance, thriller, crime, and drama.

Meryl Pestano
imdb.com/name/nm2535378

Bobby Gonzales
imdb.com/name/nm5260285

Lorenzo De Maio
imdb.com/name/nm1298951

Martha De Laurentiis
President
imdb.com/name/nm0776646

Stuart Boros
imdb.com/name/nm0097214

DINOVI PICTURES
Production company

720 Wilshire Blvd, Suite 300
Santa Monica, CA 90401
310-458-7200 (phone)
310-458-7211 (fax)

imdb.com/company/co0062957

Accepts scripts from produced or represented writers. Project types include feature films. Genres include drama and romance. Established in 1993.

Denise Di Novi
Producer
imdb.com/name/nm0224145
Assistant: Maureen Poon Fear

Alison Greenspan
President
imdb.com/name/nm1327019
Assistant: Rebecca Rajkowski

DI NOVI PICTURES
Production company

720 Wilshire Blvd., Suite 300
Santa Monica , CA 90401
310-458-7200 (phone)
310-458-7211 (fax)

imdb.com/company/co0062957

Does not accept any unsolicited material. Project types include feature films and TV. Genres include romance, action, sociocultural, fantasy, and drama.

Denise Di Novi
Producer
imdb.com/name/nm0224145

Alison Greenspan
President/Producer
imdb.com/name/nm1327019

DIRECTIONS INC.
Production company

5-3-3F
Kamiyamacho
Shibuya, Tokyo 150-0047
Japan
03-5790-5111 (phone)
03-5790-5112 (fax)

web@directions.jp
directions.jp
imdb.com/company/co0283329

Does not accept any unsolicited material. Project types include TV. Genres include drama and animation.

DIRECTORS SYSTEM CO.
Production company

4-19-8-203
Jingumae
Shibuya, Tokyo 150-0001
Japan
+81 3 3746 0395 (phone)
+81 3 3746 0397 (fax)

info-ds@dsystem.jp
dsystem.jp
imdb.com/company/co0076665

Does not accept any unsolicited material. Project types include TV. Genres include documentary.

Minoru Matsui
Director
imdb.com/name/nm0997462

DIRECTORZ
Production company

1512 Edison St
#104
Dallas, TX 75207
214-747-1951

imdb.com/company/co0288570
linkedin.com/company/directorz
facebook.com/directorz911

Does not accept any unsolicited material. Project types include short films.

DIRECTV
Production company and distributor

2260 E Imperial Highway, El Segundo, CA, United States, 90245
310-964-5000

1 Rockefeller Plaza Sixth Floor
New York NY 10020

directv.com
imdb.com/company/co0096347

Does not accept any unsolicited material. Project types include feature films and TV. Genres include drama, thriller, action, romance, comedy, and family.

DIRTY MARTINI PRODUCTIONS
Production company

5131 Gramont Ave
Orlando, FL 32812
407-310-3905

dirtymartiniprod@mac.com
imdb.com/company/co0093520

Does not accept any unsolicited material. Genres include action and thriller.

DISCOTEK MEDIA
Distributor

P.O Box 160301
Altamonte Springs, FL 32716

discotekmedia.com
imdb.com/company/co0158242
facebook.com/Discotek-Media-147168055312297

Does not accept any unsolicited material. Genres include animation.

DISCOVERY STUDIOS
Studio

962 N. La Cienega Blvd.
Los Angeles, CA 90069
310-734-3400

1 Discovery Place
Silver Spring, MD 20910
240-662-2000 (phone)
301-272-1529 (fax)

discoverystudios.com
imdb.com/company/co0225759
facebook.com/DiscoveryStudios

Does not accept any unsolicited material. Project types include TV.

DISNEY CHANNEL
Production company and distributor

Tokyo,
Japan
+81 (0)3 5908 3377

info@disney.co.jp
disneychannel.jp
imdb.com/company/co0220567
facebook.com/DisneyJapan
twitter.com/disneyjp

Project types include video games, TV, and short films. Genres include animation.

DISTANT HORIZON
Production company

519 Bainum Dr
Los Angeles, CA 90290
310-455-0759 (phone)
323-848-4144 (fax)

28 Vernon Dr
Stanmore
Middlesex
Hat 7 2bt
United Kingdom
44 0 20 8861 5500 (phone)
44208-861-4411 (fax)

la@distant-horizon.com
distant-horizon.com

imdb.com/company/co0037852

Does not accept any unsolicited material. Project types include feature films and TV. Genres include action, thriller, and drama.

Brian Cox
Producer
imdb.com/name/nm0004051

Anant Singh
Producer
imdb.com/name/nm0802081

DISTANT HORIZON CORPORATION
Production company and distributor

1519 Bainum Dr, Los Angeles, CA, United States, 90290
310-455-0759

28 Vernon Dr Stanmore
Middlesex United Kingdom HAT7 2BT
011-442-088615500 (phone)
011-442-088614411 (fax)

london@distant-horizon.com
distant-horizon.com
imdb.com/company/co0037852

Does not accept any unsolicited material. Project types include feature films and TV. Genres include reality, family, sociocultural, drama, romance, action, and thriller.

DISTINCTIVE ENTERTAINMENT
Production company

1 Apolo Place
Toronto, ON M3J0H2
Canada
416-758-3701

imdb.com/company/co0446032

Does not accept any unsolicited material. Project types include feature films and TV. Genres include drama and horror.

DISTRACTION FORMATS
Production company and distributor

550 Sherbrooke St. West
Suite 1680, West Tower
Montreal, QC H3A 1B9
Canada
514-844-5800 (phone)
514-844-8210 (fax)

distraction@distraction.com
imdb.com/company/co0092657

Does not accept any unsolicited material. Project types include TV. Genres include romance and comedy.

DISTRIB FILMS
Distributor

241 Centre St, 4th Floor Left
10013 New York NY

fsk@distribfilms.com
distribfilmsus.com
imdb.com/company/co0428322
facebook.com/distribfilmsus
twitter.com/distribfilms

Does not accept any unsolicited material. Genres include crime, comedy, and drama.

DIVIDE PICTURES
Production company

11601 W Pico Blvd
Los Angeles, CA 90064
310-473-1213

info@dividepictures.com
dividepictures.com
imdb.com/company/co0178545

Does not accept any unsolicited material. Project types include feature films and TV. Genres include comedy and drama.

Milo Ventimiglia
Actor/Executive Producer
imdb.com/name/nm0893257

Russ Cundiff
Executive Producer
imdb.com/name/nm0192096

DIVIDING LINE ENTERTAINMENT
Studio

340 S. Lemon Ave. #1186
Los Angeles, CA 91789
310-567-2031

Alvaro Obregon 121, Piso 11
Colonia Roma Norte
Mexico City D.F. 06700
Mexico
+52 55 3438 5516

hello@dividinglineentertainment.com
dividinglineentertainment.com
linkedin.com/in/chrishuntphoto

Accepts query letters from unproduced, unrepresented writers via email. Project types include feature films. Genres include science fiction, comedy, romance, horror, action, and thriller. Established in 2015.

Christian Hunt
Head of Development
310-567-2031
hello@dividinglineentertainment.com
chrishunt.com
linkedin.com/in/chrishuntphoto
facebook.com/chrishuntphoto

DJ2 ENTERTAINMENT
Production company

612 Santa Monica Blvd.
Santa Monica, CA 90401
424-777-6603

contact@dj2.co
dj2.co
imdb.com/company/co0339509

Does not accept any unsolicited material. Project types include feature films. Genres include science fiction and action.

DLT ENTERTAINMENT
Production company

UK Headquarters
10 Bedford Square
London England WC1B 3RA
44 020 7631-1184 (phone)
44 020 7636-4571 (fax)

124 E 55th St
New York, NY 10022

212-245-4680 (phone)
212-315-1132 (fax)

dltentertainment.com
imdb.com/company/co0111885

Does not accept any unsolicited material. Project types include TV. Genres include drama and comedy.

Don Taffner Jr.
Head
imdb.com/name/nm0846397

D-MENTED ENTERTAINMENT
Production company

1635 N Cahuenga Blvd.
Los Angeles, CA 90028
323-860-1572 (phone)
323-860-1574 (fax)

imdb.com/company/co0141739

Does not accept any unsolicited material. Project types include feature films. Genres include horror.

Carter Reese
Partner
imdb.com/name/nm4490803

Dave Phillips
Partner
imdb.com/name/nm1707109

DMG
Production company and distributor

Yinli DMG, Level 25, Tower A, Chaowai Men 26, Chaoyangmenwai St, Beijing , China, 100020
011-862-185653333 (phone)
011-862-185653555 (fax)

info@dmgmedia.com
dmg-entertainment.com
imdb.com/company/co0338904

Does not accept any unsolicited material. Project types include TV and feature films. Genres include action, drama, thriller, and family.

DMG ENTERTAINMENT
Production company, studio, and distributor

25th Fl, Tower A
26 Chao Yang Men Wai St.
Beijing 100020
0086-010-85653333 (phone)
0086-010-85653555 (fax)

3431 Wesley St
Ste E
Culver City, CA 90232
310-275-3750 (phone)
310-275-3770 (fax)

info@dmg-entertainment.com
dmg-entertainment.com
imdb.com/company/co0338904
linkedin.com/company/dmg
facebook.com/dmgentertainment
twitter.com/DMG_LA

Does not accept any unsolicited material. Project types include feature films and TV. Genres include action, comedy, drama, horror, romance, science fiction, and thriller. Established in 1993.

Chris Cowles
Producer
imdb.com/name/nm1038319
facebook.com/chris.cowles.397

DM PRODUCTIONS
Production company and distributor

10201 W. Pico Blvd., Bldg. 12
Los Angeles, CA 90035
310-455-5526

imdb.com/company/co0325060

Does not accept any unsolicited material. Project types include feature films and TV. Genres include drama, romance, and thriller.

David Matalon
Producer
imdb.com/name/nm0558061

DNA FILMS
Production company

10 Amwell St
London EC1R 1UQ
+44 020-7843-4410 (phone)
+44 020-7843-4411 (fax)

info@dnafilms.com
dnafilms.com
imdb.com/company/co0103974

Does not accept any unsolicited material. Project types include feature films. Genres include thriller, comedy, drama, crime, romance, and horror. Established in 1999.

Andrew Macdonald
Partner
+44 020 7843 4410
imdb.com/name/nm0531602

Allon Reich
Partner
+44 020 7843 4410
imdb.com/name/nm0716924

DNA PRODUCTIONS
Production company

2201 W Royal Ln
Ste 275
Irving, TX 75063
214-352-4694

some_info@dnahelix.com
dnahelix.com
imdb.com/company/co0073465
linkedin.com/company/dna-productions
facebook.com/pages/DNA-Productions/
    104057599629728

Does not accept any unsolicited material. Project types include feature films, TV, and short films. Genres include family, animation, and comedy. Established in 1987.

DOBRE FILMS
Production company

Los Angeles, CA
310-926-6439

dobrefilms@dobrefilms.com
dobrefilms.com
imdb.com/company/co0251623
twitter.com/DobreFilms

Accepts scripts from unproduced, unrepresented writers. Project types include feature films and TV.

Genres include horror, action, detective, drama, crime, fantasy, comedy, myth, romance, and science fiction.

Michael Klein
Producer
323-510-0818
mklein@dobrefilms.com
imdb.com/name/nm3180840

Christopher D'Elia
Producer
310-926-6439
cdelia@dobrefilms.com
imdb.com/name/nm3179988

DOCUMENTARY EDUCATIONAL RESOURCES (DER)
Distributor and sales agent

101 Morse St.
Watertown, MA 02472
617-926-0491 (phone)
617-926-9519 (fax)

docucd@der.org
der.org
imdb.com/company/co0017395

Does not accept any unsolicited material. Project types include TV. Genres include documentary.

Brittany Gravely
Director
imdb.com/name/nm2471950

DOCUTAINMENT FILMS
Production company

11924 W Forest Hill Blvd
Suite 10A-406
Wellington, FL 33414
561-228-8885

info@docutainmentfilms.com
docutainmentfilms.com
imdb.com/company/co0409033
facebook.com/DocutainmentFilms

Does not accept any unsolicited material. Genres include family, documentary, and drama.

DOGAKOBO

Production company

Towa Bldg 2F
5-41-21 Higashiooizumi, Nerima-Ku
Tokyo
Japan
+81 3 39 78 63 93

doko@dogakobo.com
dogakobo.com
imdb.com/company/co0159059

Does not accept any unsolicited material. Project types
include TV. Genres include family and animation.

DOGWOOF PICTURES

Distributor and sales agent

Unit 102, Hatton Square Business Centre
16-16a Baldwins Gardens
London EC1N 7RJ
UK
+44 20 7831 7252 (phone)
+44 20 7691 7682 (fax)

info@dogwoof.com
dogwoof.com
imdb.com/company/co0132923
facebook.com/dogwoof
twitter.com/dogwoof

Does not accept any unsolicited material. Project types
include feature films. Genres include documentary.

Oli Harbottle
Producer
imdb.com/name/nm2079825

DOLGER FILMS

Production company

2325 Lake Talmadge Dr
DeLand, FL 32724

dolgerfilms.com
imdb.com/company/co0208833

Does not accept any unsolicited material. Genres
include drama.

DOLPHIN ENTERTAINMENT

Production company

804 S Douglas Rd, Suite 365
Miami, FL 33134
305-774-0407

dolphinentertainment.com
imdb.com/company/co0061061
facebook.com/pages/Dolphin-Entertainment/
170951312915443
twitter.com/dolphinent

Does not accept any unsolicited material. Project types
include feature films and TV. Genres include action
and science fiction.

Bill O'Dowd
President/Producer
imdb.com/name/nm1199803

Sarah Soboleski
SVP
imdb.com/name/nm1274279

DOLPHIN ENTERTAINMENT GROUP

Production company

2151 Lejeune Rd, Suite 150-Mezzanine, Coral Gables,
FL, United States, 33134
305-774-0407 (phone)
305-774-0405 (fax)

info@dolphinentertainment.com
dolphinentertainment.com
imdb.com/company/co0061061

Does not accept any unsolicited material. Project types
include TV. Genres include family, drama, and
comedy.

DOMAIN PICTURES

Production company and distributor

9415 N Edison Ave
Tampa, FL 33612
813-446-1814

domainpictures37@gmail.com
imdb.com/company/co0216073

Does not accept any unsolicited material. Genres
include drama and science fiction.

DOMINANT PICTURES

5750 Wilshire Blvd., 5th Floor
Los Angeles, CA 90036
323-850-1340

imdb.com/company/co0204612

Does not accept any unsolicited material. Project types
include TV and feature films. Genres include comedy.

Betty Thomas
Director/Producer
imdb.com/name/nm0858525

DON ARONOW DOCUMENTARY PRODUCTION

Production company

1225 Alton Rd
Miami Beach, FL 33139
305-534-9123 (phone)
305-534-9125 (fax)

info@silviosardi.com
imdb.com/company/co0202197

Does not accept any unsolicited material.

DON CARMODY PRODUCTIONS

Production company

30 Booth Ave
Ste 100
Toronto, ON M4M 2M2
Canada
416-778-0049

sitemail@doncarmody.com
doncarmody.com
imdb.com/company/co0229296
linkedin.com/in/don-carmody-0047295

Does not accept any unsolicited material. Genres
include science fiction, horror, and action.

Don Carmody
Producer
imdb.com/name/nm0138502

DON CARMODY TELEVISION

Production company

30 Booth Ave
Ste 100
Toronto, ON M4M 2M2
Canada

imdb.com/company/co0417902

Does not accept any unsolicited material. Project types
include feature films and TV. Genres include fantasy,
drama, and action.

DON KING PRODUCTIONS

Production company

501 Fairway Dr
Deerfield Beach, FL 33441

imdb.com/company/co0302116

Does not accept any unsolicited material. Project types
include TV. Genres include documentary.

DONNERS' COMPANY

Production company

9465 Wilshire Blvd
Ste 430
Beverly Hills, CA 90212
310-777-4600 (phone)
310-777-4610 (fax)

imdb.com/company/co0001946
facebook.com/pages/The-Donners-Company/
    111099955582478

Does not accept any unsolicited material. Project types
include feature films. Genres include science fiction,
fantasy, and action.

Richard Donner
Principal
imdb.com/name/nm0001149

DOODLE FILMS

Production company

9255 Sunset Blvd., Suite 600
West Hollywood, CA 90069

imdb.com/title/tt0225544

Does not accept any unsolicited material. Project types
include short films and feature films. Genres include
drama and animation.

DOOR 24 ENTERTAINMENT

Production company

115 W 29th St, Suite 1102
New York, NY 10001
212-868-5233

info@door24ent.com
door24ent.com
facebook.com/pages/Door-24-Entertainment/
9377016762

Does not accept any unsolicited material. Project types
include feature films.

Jill McGrath
Producer/Manager
imdb.com/name/nm0569814

Rebecca Atwood
Producer/Manager
imdb.com/name/nm2344105

DOOZER PRODUCTIONS

Production company

9336 W Washington Blvd., Bldg. K
Culver City, CA 90232
310-202-3566

imdb.com/company/co0007700
twitter.com/doozerprods

Does not accept any unsolicited material. Project types
include TV. Genres include comedy.

Bill Lawrence
Producer
imdb.com/name/nm0492639

Jeff Ingold
President/Executive Producer
imdb.com/name/nm1264835

DORADO MEDIA AND CAPITAL

Distributor and sales agent

161 Bay St, Suite 3930
Toronto, ON M5J 2S1
Canada
888-938-7968 (phone)
888-938-7968 (fax)

imdb.com/company/co0345181

Does not accept any unsolicited material. Project types
include TV. Genres include drama and comedy.

DOS TONTOS

Production company

10201 W. Pico Blvd.
Los Angeles, CA 90035
310-369-8701

imdb.com/company/co0265100

Does not accept any unsolicited material. Project types
include feature films. Genres include comedy.

DOUBLE 4 STUDIOS

Production company

8361 SW 91st. Ter.
Miami, FL 33156
305-216-8341 (phone)
305-964-7864 (fax)

office@double4studios.com
double4studios.com
imdb.com/company/co0356586
facebook.com/Double4Studio

Does not accept any unsolicited material. Genres
include family, romance, and drama.

DOUBLE DUTCH PRODUCTIONS

Production company

8033 W. Sunset Blvd., Suite 852
Los Angeles, CA 90046
323-457-4161

doubledutchproductions.biz
imdb.com/company/co0147245

Does not accept any unsolicited material. Project types
include feature films. Genres include horror and
drama.

David LaCour Simien
Development/Producer
imdb.com/name/nm1427504

Jim Evering
Writer/Producer
imdb.com/name/nm026342

DOUBLE EDGE ENTERTAINMENT

Production company

15233 Ventura Blvd # 9, Sherman Oaks, California,
United States.
310-882-5502 (phone)
310-606-2088 (fax)

inquiry@deegroup.com
imdb.com/company/co0090191
linkedin.com/company/double-edge-entertainment-inc

Does not accept any unsolicited material. Project types
include feature films. Genres include horror.

DOUBLE EDGE FILMS

Production company

Denver, CO

Info1@DoubleEdgeFilms.com
double-edge-films.myshopify.com
imdb.com/company/co0160720

Does not accept any unsolicited material. Genres
include fantasy and action.

Jamin Winans
President (Executive)
imdb.com/name/nm1985821

DOUBLE ENTENTE FILMS

Production company

1041 N Formosa Ave, Pickford Bldg. #204
Los Angeles, CA 90046
323-782-1363

40 rue des Blancs Manteaux
75004 Paris
336-09-94-06-59

info@doubleententefilms.com
doubleententefilms.com/features
imdb.com/company/co0200552
linkedin.com/company/double-entente
twitter.com/ententedouble

Does not accept any unsolicited material. Project types
include TV and feature films. Genres include comedy,
drama, and thriller.

Bailey Kobe
Writer/Director
imdb.com/name/nm1054636

Frederic Imbert
Producer
imdb.com/name/nm0408124

DOUBLE FEATURE FILMS

Production company

8425 W 3rd St.
Suite 201
Los Angeles, CA 90048
310-887-1100

dffproducerdesk@gmail.com
imdb.com/company/co0118437
facebook.com/pages/Double-Feature/18081094353
twitter.com/_ericx13

Does not accept any unsolicited material. Project types
include feature films. Genres include action, fantasy,
myth, drama, comedy, and thriller. Established in
2005.

Michael Shamberg
imdb.com/name/nm0787834

Ameet Shukla
Creative Executive
imdb.com/name/nm2627415

Taylor Latham
imdb.com/name/nm2281897

Stacey Sher
imdb.com/name/nm0792049

DOUBLE NICKEL ENTERTAINMENT

Production company

234 W 138th St
New York, NY 10030
646-435-4390 (phone)
212-694-6205 (fax)

311 N. Robertson Blvd.
Suite 385
Beverly Hills, CA 90211

admin@doublenickelentertainment.com
doublenickelentertainment.com

imdb.com/company/co0112616
facebook.com/Double-Nickel-
Entertainment-213918705318410

Accepts query letters from unproduced, unrepresented writers via email. Project types include feature films. Genres include drama.

Jenette Kahn
imdb.com/name/nm1986495

Adam Richman
imdb.com/name/nm0725013

Adam Callan
Creative Executive
imdb.com/name/nm2565555

DOWN BY THE RIVER PRODUCTIONS
Production company

812 N. Virginia St., # 202
El Paso, TX 79902
915-313-9414

imdb.com/company/co0172600

Does not accept any unsolicited material. Project types include short films. Genres include drama. Established in 2007.

DRAFTHOUSE FILMS
Production company and distributor

320 E 6th St
Austin, TX 78701
512-476-1320

info@drafthousefilms.com
drafthousefilms.com
imdb.com/company/co0313579
facebook.com/DrafthouseFilms
twitter.com/DrafthouseFilms

Does not accept any unsolicited material. Genres include romance, thriller, horror, and science fiction.

DRAGON RIDER PRODUCTIONS
Production company

391 Howe Ave
Ste 26A

Passaic, NJ 07055
973-272-3860

info@dragonriderproductions.com
dragonriderproductions.com
imdb.com/company/co0210652

Does not accept any unsolicited material. Project types include TV and short films. Genres include drama.

DRAMA REPUBLIC
Production company

8 Flitcroft St
2nd Fl
London WC2H 8DL
UK
+44 20 7557 7990 (phone)
+44 20 7557 7991 (fax)

info@dramarepublic.com
dramarepublic.com
imdb.com/company/co0415381
twitter.com/dramarepublic

Does not accept any unsolicited material. Project types include TV. Genres include thriller and drama.

Greg Brenman
Producer
imdb.com/name/nm0107231

DRAPER STREET FILMS
Production company and distributor

6 Draper St
Toronto, ON M5V 2M4
Canada
416-624-2266

shaywood2@me.com
imdb.com/company/co0500207

Does not accept any unsolicited material. Project types include feature films. Genres include drama and comedy.

DRC PRODUCTIONS
Production company and distributor

1217 Pecan Blvd
McAllen, Texas 78502
800-618-0914

contact@reelchristian.com
drcproductions.ca
imdb.com/company/co0120679
facebook.com/ReelChristian

Does not accept any unsolicited material. Genres include horror, drama, and fantasy.

DREAM BALLOON PRODUCTIONS
Production company

Dream Balloon Animation Studio
5750 Major Blvd.; Ste. 510
Orlando, FL 32819
407-704-7914 (phone)
407-704-7916 (fax)

1000 Universal Studios Plaza Backlot Building # 22A
Orlando, FL 32819
407-224-6809 (phone)
407-224-5171 (fax)

mattardi@dbastudios.com
dreamballoon.wordpress.com
linkedin.com/company/dream-balloon-enterprises

Does not accept any unsolicited material. Project types include feature films. Genres include comedy, animation, and family.

Michael Attardi
Director/Producer
imdb.com/name/nm2558815

DREAMBRIDGE FILMS
Production company

207 W 25th St
6th Floor
New York, NY 10001
323-927-1907 (phone)
323-927-1907 (fax)

todd27@mac.com
dreambridgefilms.com
imdb.com/company/co0248660

Accepts query letters from unproduced, unrepresented writers. Project types include feature films. Genres include drama, family, and comedy.

Todd J. Labarowski
CEO/Founder
todd27@mac.com
imdb.com/name/nm1132640

DREAM ENTERTAINMENT
Production company, distributor, and sales agent

PO Box 10445, Beverly Hills , CA, United States, 90213
310-855-3371

dreamenter@aol.com
dreamentertainment.net
imdb.com/company/co0073769

Does not accept any unsolicited material. Project types include TV. Genres include drama, family, and thriller.

DREAMFLY PRODUCTIONS
Production company

3107 Cole Ave
Dallas, TX 75204
214-999-0222 (phone)
214-999-0223 (fax)

lisa@dreamflyproductions.com
dreamflyproductions.com
imdb.com/company/co0228991
facebook.com/dreamflyproductions
twitter.com/dreamflyprod

Does not accept any unsolicited material. Genres include thriller and comedy.

DREAMGRIFTER PRODUCTIONS
Production company

PO Box 3056
West End, NJ 07740
203-512-2681

dreamgrifter@yahoo.com
imdb.com/company/co0246200

Does not accept any unsolicited material. Project types include feature films and TV. Genres include drama, thriller, and comedy.

DREAM MERCHANT 21 ENTERTAINMENT

1416 N. La Brea Ave.
Hollywood, CA 90028
323-802-1874

imdb.com/company/co0203107

Does not accept any unsolicited material. Project types include TV.

Randy Jackson
Producer
imdb.com/name/nm1193098

DREAMQUEST ENTERTAINMENT
Production company

2-24 34th St
Fair Lawn, NJ 07410
848-459-4973

dkinglives@yahoo.com
dreamquestentertainment.com
imdb.com/company/co0271814

Does not accept any unsolicited material. Project types include TV. Genres include drama.

DREAMREAL PICTURES
Production company and distributor

1712 E. Riverside Dr.
#395
Austin, TX 78741

DreamRealPictures@gmail.com
dreamrealpictures.com
imdb.com/company/co0344133
facebook.com/DreamReal-Pictures-and-
    Animation-101128243336917
twitter.com/DreamRealMovies

Does not accept any unsolicited material. Project types include TV, feature films, and short films. Genres include animation, documentary, drama, action, family, and thriller. Established in 2009.

DREAM RIVER FILMS
Production company, distributor, and sales agent

9021 Dry Creek Dr
Fort Worth, TX 76244

dreamriverfilms.com
imdb.com/company/co0351155
linkedin.com/company/dream-river-films-llc

Does not accept any unsolicited material. Project types include short films. Genres include comedy and action.

DREAMRUNNER PICTURES
Production company

Alpenstr. 112
5020 Salzburg
Austria

office@dreamrunnerpictures.com
dreamrunnerpictures.com
imdb.com/company/co0406794
facebook.com/pages/Dreamrunner-Pictures/
    1473881766217985
twitter.com/dreamrunnerpic

Does not accept any unsolicited material. Project types include feature films and TV. Genres include crime, fantasy, and drama.

Jennifer Skarpil
Assistant Producer
jennifer@dreamrunnerpictures.com

DREAMWORKS ANIMATION
Production company

1000 Flower St
Glendale, CA 91201
818-695-5000 (phone)
818-695-3510 (fax)

dreamworksanimation.com
imdb.com/company/co0129164
facebook.com/DreamWorksAnimation

Does not accept any unsolicited material. Project types include short films, TV, video games, and feature films. Genres include animation, comedy, family, action, horror, science fiction, documentary, and fantasy. Established in 2004.

Bill Damaschke
Chief Creative Officer
imdb.com/name/nm0198632

Kyle Arthur Jefferson
Director
imdb.com/name/nm2200868

Ben Cawood
Creative Executive
imdb.com/name/nm1374730

Karen Foster
Development Executive
imdb.com/name/nm2259946

Jeffrey Katzenberg
imdb.com/name/nm0005076

Chris Kuser
Senior Executive (Development)
imdb.com/name/nm1936914
Assistant: Beth Cannon

Damon Ross
Senior Executive (Development)
imdb.com/name/nm1842613

Nancy Bernsein
imdb.com/name/nm0077110

Tom McGrath
imdb.com/name/nm0569891

Jeffrey Wike
imdb.com/name/nm5204969

Amie Karp
Creative Executive (Development)
imdb.com/name/nm2047897

Suzanne Buirgy
Production Executive
imdb.com/name/nm1330174

DREAMWORKS DISTRIBUTION
Production company and distributor

100 Universal City Plaza
Bldg. 477
Universal City, CA 91608
818-733-7000

imdb.com/company/co0067641

Does not accept any unsolicited material. Genres include romance, drama, and action.

DREAMWORKS STUDIOS
Production company

100 Universal City Plaza
Building 5121
Universal City, CA 91608
818-733-7000

info@dreamworksstudios.com
dreamworksstudios.com
imdb.com/company/co0252576
facebook.com/DreamWorksStudios

Does not accept any unsolicited material. Project types include feature films and TV. Genres include romance, fantasy, comedy, crime, action, drama, thriller, science fiction, and period.

Mia Maniscalco
Creative Executive
mia_maniscalco@dreamworksstudios.com
imdb.com/name/nm4103271
linkedin.com/pub/mia-maniscalco/6/28a/652

Holly Bario
President
info@wif.org
imdb.com/name/nm2302370

Steven Spielberg
Chairman
imdb.com/name/nm0000229

DREYFUSS/JAMES PRODUCTIONS

2420 Laurel Pass
Los Angeles, CA 90046
323-822-0140 (phone)
323-822-0440 (fax)

djprods.com
imdb.com/company/co0021491

Does not accept any unsolicited material. Project types include feature films. Genres include documentary, comedy, drama, detective, animation, family, science fiction, crime, sociocultural, thriller, romance, fantasy, period, reality, horror, non-fiction, myth, and action.

Judith James
Principal
imdb.com/name/nm0416648

Richard Dreyfuss
Principal
imdb.com/name/nm0000377

DRIVING WITH OUR EYES SHUT
Production company and distributor

9085 E. Mississippi Ave.
Suite M207
Denver, CO 80247
720-570-5190

info@drivingeyes.com
drivingeyes.com
imdb.com/company/co0263135

Does not accept any unsolicited material. Project types include feature films. Genres include comedy and action.

Glenn Berggoetz
Berggoetz
imdb.com/name/nm3324251

D STREET PICTURES
Production company

Oranienburger Strasse 27
Berlin, 10117 Germany

1133 Broadway, Suite 708
New York, NY 10010

info@www.dstreetmediagroup.com
dstreetmediagroup.com
imdb.com/company/co0154465

Does not accept any unsolicited material. Project types include feature films. Genres include drama.

Javier Krause
VP
imdb.com/name/nm4040018

Dexter Davis
CEO
imdb.com/name/nm2089464

DUALSTAR ENTERTAINMENT
Production company

1801 Century Park East, 12th Floor
Los Angeles, CA 90067

310-553-9000 (phone)
310-945-3750 (fax)

imdb.com/company/co0050228

Does not accept any unsolicited material. Project types include TV. Genres include family and comedy.

Ashley Olsen
Actor/Producer
imdb.com/name/nm0001580

Mary Kate Olsen
Actor/Producer
imdb.com/name/nm0001581

DUCK SOUP STUDIOS
Production company

2205 Stoner Ave.
Los Angeles , CA 90064
310-478-0771 (phone)
310-478-0773 (fax)

info@duckstudios.com
imdb.com/company/co0172556
linkedin.com/company/duck-studios
facebook.com/DuckStudios
twitter.com/duckstudios

Does not accept any unsolicited material. Project types include TV and short films. Genres include animation.

DULY NOTED
Production company

5225 Wilshire Blvd., Suite 418
Los Angeles, CA 90036
323-525-1855

info@dulynotedinc.com
dulynotedinc.com
imdb.com/company/co0142547
linkedin.com/in/effie-brown-81443826
facebook.com/effie.t.brown
twitter.com/dulynotedinc

Does not accept any unsolicited material. Project types include feature films. Genres include thriller, horror, and drama.

DUNE ENTERTAINMENT
Production company

623 Fifth Ave.
New York, NY 10022
212-301-8400

2121 Ave of the Stars
Suite 2570
Los Angeles, CA 90067
310-432-2288

imdb.com/company/co0174373

Does not accept any unsolicited material. Project types include feature films. Genres include fantasy, drama, science fiction, action, thriller, horror, romance, and comedy.

Wendy Weller
imdb.com/name/nm2956152

Greg Coote
imdb.com/name/nm0178505

Larry Bernstein
imdb.com/name/nm2955628

DUNLOP ENTERTAINMENT
Production company

30346 Esperanza, Suite B
Rancho Santa Margarita, CA 92688
949-709-7727 (phone)
949-709-7737 (fax)

sdunlop@dunlop-group.com
dunlopgrp.com
imdb.com/company/co0171053

Does not accept any unsolicited material. Project types include TV.

Scott Dunlop
Producer
imdb.com/name/nm0242472

DUNSDON ENTERTAINMENT
Production company

PO Box 635
Montvale, NJ 07645
201-307-9720 (phone)
201-426-2366 (fax)

info@dunsdonentertainment.com
imdb.com/company/co0175089

linkedin.com/company/dunsdon-entertainment-llc

Does not accept any unsolicited material. Genres include drama and thriller.

DUPLASS BROTHERS PRODUCTIONS
Production company and distributor

902 E Fifth St
Austin, TX 78702

info@duplassbrothers.com
duplassbrothers.com
imdb.com/company/co0117723
twitter.com/jayduplass

Accepts query letters from unproduced, unrepresented writers via email. Project types include feature films. Genres include horror, thriller, drama, and comedy.

Stephanie Langhoff
Producer
imdb.com/name/nm1293297

Jay Duplass
Producer
imdb.com/name/nm0243231
twitter.com/jayduplass

Mark Duplass
Producer
imdb.com/name/nm0243233
twitter.com/markduplass

DUTCHMEN FILMS
Production company

500 N Rossmore Ave Suite 201
Los Angeles, CA 90004
310-772-8210

franklin@dutchmenfilms.com
dutchmenfilms.com
imdb.com/company/co0246561
linkedin.com/company/dutchmen-films

Does not accept any unsolicited material. Project types include feature films. Genres include drama.

Franklin Martin
Director/Writer/Producer/Actor
imdb.com/name/nm0552294

DVD DELUXE DISTRIBUTORS
Distributor

8306 Wilshire Blvd.
Suite 710
Beverly Hills, CA 90211
424-256-3770 (phone)
323-375-1673 (fax)

10645 N. Tatum Blvd.
Suite 200 130
Phoenix, AZ 85028
424-256-3770 (phone)
323-375-1673 (fax)

15508 W. Bell Rd.
Ste 101 109
Surprise, AZ 85374
800-416-9842

info@dvddeluxe.net
imdb.com/company/co0354122

Does not accept any unsolicited material. Project types include TV. Genres include comedy, animation, and action.

DVIDS DEFENSE VIDEO AND IMAGERY DISTRIBUTION SYSTEM
Distributor

3845 Pleasantdale Rd.
Atlanta, GA 30340
678-421-6776

sbetts@dvidshub.net
dvidshub.net
imdb.com/company/co0456570
facebook.com/dvids
twitter.com/dvidshub

Does not accept any unsolicited material. Project types include TV. Genres include reality.

DYNAMIC TELEVISION
Production company

8530 Wilshire Blvd, 5th Floor
Beverly Hills, CA 90211

dmarch@dynamictelevision.com
dynamictelevision.com
imdb.com/company/co0466320

Does not accept any unsolicited material. Project types include TV. Genres include action, drama, and fantasy.

Klaus Zimmermann
Managing Partner
imdb.com/name/nm0956842

Daniel March
Founder
imdb.com/name/nm4883495

DYNAMITE ENTERTAINMENT
Production company

155 E. 9th Ave., Ste. B
Runnemede, NJ 08078
856-312-1040 (phone)
856-312-1050 (fax)

info@dynamite.com
dynamiteentertainment.com
imdb.com/company/co0010018

Does not accept any unsolicited material. Project types include feature films. Genres include action.

Nick Barrucci
President, Producer
imdb.com/name/nm2262057

E1 ENTERTAINMENT
Production company and distributor

134 Peter St
Suite 700
Toronto
Ontario
Canada
M5V 2H2
416-646-2400

info@entonegroup.com
entertainmentonegroup.com
imdb.com/company/co0276425
linkedin.com/company/entertainment-one
facebook.com/EntertainmentOneGroup
twitter.com/entonegroup

Does not accept any unsolicited material.

Sejin Park
Executive
imdb.com/name/nm2925149

E1 ENTERTAINMENT DISTRIBUTION
Distributor

22 Harbor Park Dr
Port Washington, NY 11050
516-484-1000 (phone)
516-484-6179 (fax)

WSchmidt@e1ent.com
entertainmentone.com/home
imdb.com/company/co0280877

Does not accept any unsolicited material. Project types include theater and TV. Genres include drama, horror, crime, comedy, and thriller.

E1 FILMS CANADA
Sales agent

134 Peter St
Suite 700
Toronto
Ontario
Canada
M5V 2H2
416-646-2400 (phone)
416-646-2399 (fax)

Les Films Séville
455, rue St-Antoine Ouest, bureau 300
Montréal, Quebec
H2Z 1J1

eonefilmnews@entonegroup.com
eonefilms.com
imdb.com/company/co0254623

Does not accept any unsolicited material. Genres include comedy.

Natalie Kampelmacher
Executive
imdb.com/name/nm2470151

EAGLE MEDIA PRODUCTIONS
Production company and distributor

P.O. Box 4132
DeLand, FL 32721-4132
386-87E-AGLE

tmitchell@eaglemediaproductions.com
imdb.com/company/co0159598
facebook.com/Eagle-Media-
    Productions-648480171847155

Does not accept any unsolicited material. Project types include short films. Genres include comedy.

EALING STUDIOS
Production company and distributor

Ealing Green
W5 5EP
United Kingdom
+44-0-20-8567-6655 (phone)
+44-0-20-8758-8658 (fax)

info@ealingstudios.com
imdb.com/company/co0040024
facebook.com/ealingstudios
twitter.com/ealingstudios

Does not accept any unsolicited material. Project types include TV and feature films. Genres include documentary, family, romance, comedy, drama, and thriller.

James Spring
Producer
imdb.com/name/nm2020191

Barnaby Thompson
Producer
imdb.com/name/nm0859877

Gary Stone
Manager
gary.stone@ealingstudios.com

Sophie Meyer
Head of Development
imdb.com/name/nm1623306

EARTH STAR ENTERTAINMENT
Production company and distributor

16-17-11F
Nanpeidai
Shibuya, Tokyo 150-0036

Japan
03-5457-1471

info@earthstar.jp
earthstar.jp
imdb.com/company/co0327638

Does not accept any unsolicited material. Project types
include TV. Genres include drama.

EASTLAKE FILMS
Production company

107 Beechwood Rd
Summit, NJ 07901
908-608-0596

imdb.com/company/co0355991
facebook.com/Eastlake-Films-142324782542671

Does not accept any unsolicited material. Genres
include thriller and action.

EAST WORKS ENTERTAINMENT
Distributor

3-4-7-301
Minami Aoyama
Minatoku, Tokyo 107-0062
Japan
03-5413-7415 (phone)
03-5413-7406 (fax)

info@ewe.co.jp
ewe.co.jp
imdb.com/company/co0276488

Does not accept any unsolicited material. Project types
include TV. Genres include documentary.

Chie Ayado
Actress
imdb.com/name/nm2750770

EASYACTION GROUP
Production company

Los Angeles, CA
323-397-1050

me@ethanAction.com
easyaction.com
imdb.com/name/nm1803557

linkedin.com/in/ethanshaftel
twitter.com/eshaftel

Does not accept any unsolicited material. Project types
include theater and feature films. Genres include
drama, thriller, action, science fiction, and crime.
Established in 2007.

Ethan Shaftel
Owner
323-397-1050
submit@easyaction.com
easyaction.com
imdb.com/name/nm1803557
linkedin.com/in/ethanshaftel

EASY TIGER PRODUCTIONS
Production company

Barley Mow Centre
Barley Mow Passage
London W4 3PH
UK
+44 020 8400 7803 (phone)
+44 020 8400 7803 (fax)

mail@easytigerproductions.com
easytigerproductions.com
imdb.com/company/co0172072

Does not accept any unsolicited material. Project types
include TV. Genres include romance.

Maddy Lewis
Producer
imdb.com/name/nm1690136

EBEGINS

heartofashish@gmail.com
ebegins.com

Ashish Tank
President
heartofashish@gmail.com

EBONY EGG PRODUCTIONS
Production company

3588 Hwy 138
Suite 170
Atlanta, GA 30281

contact@ebonyegg.com
imdb.com/company/co0214721

Does not accept any unsolicited material. Genres
include comedy, family, drama, and thriller.

EBS WORLD ENTERTAINMENT
Production company

3000 W. Olympic Blvd
Santa Monica, CA 90404
310-449-4065 (phone)
310-449-4061 (fax)

imdb.com/company/co0158692
facebook.com/ebsworldentertainment

Does not accept any unsolicited material. Project types
include feature films. Genres include drama, action,
comedy, and horror.

Wayne Wong
Co-Chairman/President
imdb.com/name/nm1373710

ECG PRODUCTIONS
Production company

120 Interstate N Pkwy SE
Ste 435
Atlanta, GA 30082
678-855-5169

info@ecgprod.com
ecgprod.com
imdb.com/company/co0205476
linkedin.com/company/ecg-productions
facebook.com/ecgatlanta
twitter.com/ccg_productions

Does not accept any unsolicited material.

ECHELON STUDIOS
Production company and distributor

1440 Flower St
Glendale, CA 91201
818-500-1640

corporate@echelonstudios.us
imdb.com/company/co0192323

Does not accept any unsolicited material. Project types
include feature films. Genres include comedy, drama,
thriller, and horror.

Eric Louzil
President/CEO
imdb.com/name/nm0522218

ECHO BRIDGE ENTERTAINMENT
Production company and distributor

75 Second Ave
Suite 500
Needham, MA 02494
781-444-6767 (phone)
781-444-6472 (fax)

3089 Airport Rd
La Crosse, WI 54603
608-784-6620 (phone)
608-784-6635 (fax)

info@echobridgehe.com
echobridgeentertainment.com
imdb.com/company/co0127873
linkedin.com/company/echo-bridge-home-
    entertainment
facebook.com/echobridgehe
twitter.com/ebhomeent

Does not accept any unsolicited material. Project types
include feature films. Genres include drama, detective,
action, thriller, horror, fantasy, romance, and science
fiction.

Nathan Hart
President, Home Entertainment
nhart@echobridgehe.com

Michael Rosenblatt
CEO
mrosenblatt@ebellc.com

Tom Hammond
CFO
thammond@ebellc.com

ECHO FILMS PRODUCTIONS
Production company

407 W Bannock St Boise
Idaho 83702

208-336-0349 (phone)
209-336-0858 (fax)

echofilms.com
imdb.com/company/co0234791

Does not accept any unsolicited material. Project types include feature films. Genres include comedy, drama, and romance. Established in 2008.

ECHO LAKE ENTERTAINMENT

421 S Beverly Dr,
6th Floor
Beverly Hills, CA 90212
310-789-4790 (phone)
310-789-4791 (fax)

contact@echolakeproductions.com
echolakeentertainment.com
imdb.com/company/co0076285
linkedin.com/company/echo-lake-productions
facebook.com/pages/Echo-Lake-Productions/
    160303590658581

Does not accept any unsolicited material. Project types include TV and feature films. Genres include reality, drama, thriller, and non-fiction. Established in 1998.

Douglas Mankoff
Producer
imdb.com/name/nm0542551

Andrew Spaulding
Producer
imdb.com/name/nm1051748

Ida Diffley
Director of Development
imdb.com/name/nm3000066

Jessica Staman
Producer
imdb.com/name/nm1698445

ECHOLIGHT STUDIOS
Production company and distributor

1200 Lakeside Parkway. Bldg. 1
Flower Mound, TX 75028

echolight.com
imdb.com/company/co0391226

facebook.com/echolightstudios
twitter.com/echolightstudio

Does not accept any unsolicited material. Project types include feature films. Genres include drama and family.

ECLECTIC PICTURES
Production company

7510 W Sunset Blvd Ste. 517
Hollywood, CA 90046
323-656-7555 (phone)
323-848-7761 (fax)

info@eclecticpictures.com
eclecticpictures.com
imdb.com/company/co0147213
linkedin.com/company/2949479
facebook.com/eclecticpictures
twitter.com/eclecticpics

Accepts query letters from unproduced, unrepresented writers via email. Project types include feature films. Established in 2004.

John Yarincik
Development Executive
john@eclecticpictures.com
imdb.com/name/nm2432490

ECLECTIK VISION
Production company

9461 Charleville Blvd # 431
Beverly Hills, CA 90212
310-382-7730

Building 19 Fox Studios,
Moore Park Sydney, NSW 2021
02-9383-4590 (phone)
02-9383-4581 (fax)

eclectikvision.com.au
imdb.com/company/co0479919

Does not accept any unsolicited material. Project types include feature films. Established in 2007.

Brett Thornquest
Founder
brett@eclectikvision.com

Emma Dewhurst
Executive Assistant
evasst@eclectikvision.com

Steven Matusko
steven@eclectikvision.com

ECLIPSE
Distributor

2-8-11-801
Akasaka
Minato, TOKYO 107-0052
Japan
03-3568-4121 (fax)

info@eclipse-movie.co.jp
eclipse-movie.co.jp
imdb.com/company/co0363536
twitter.com/eclipsemoviejp

Does not accept any unsolicited material. Project types include feature films and TV. Genres include horror and drama.

Takao Arakawa
President (Executive)
imdb.com/name/nm4862355

ECOSSE FILMS
Production company

Brigade House
8 Parsons Green
London SW6 4TN
England
+44 20 7371 0290 (phone)
+44 20 7736 3436 (fax)

info@ecossefilms.com
ecossefilms.com
imdb.com/company/co0103777

Does not accept any unsolicited material. Project types include TV. Genres include drama.

ECSTASY FILM
Production company

63 Pinemeadow Blvd.
Toronto, ON M1W 1P1

Canada
905-664-8458

ecstasyfilminc@gmail.com
imdb.com/company/co0161273

Does not accept any unsolicited material. Project types include feature films. Genres include drama.

Rob Heydon
Producer
imdb.com/name/nm1406806

EDELMAN PRODUCTIONS
Production company

16170 Kennedy Rd.
Los Gatos, CA 95032
408-356-2804 (phone)
408-358-6593 (fax)

imdb.com/company/co0131274

Does not accept any unsolicited material. Project types include TV. Genres include reality.

EDEN ENTERTAINMENT
Distributor

4-8-4 #210 Matsubara
Setagaya-Ku
Tokyo 156-0043
Japan
81-3-5355-5792 (phone)
81-3-5355-5793 (fax)

eden@abelia.ocn.ne.jp
eden-entertainment.jp
imdb.com/company/co0293030

Does not accept any unsolicited material. Project types include feature films and TV. Genres include action, drama, and horror.

EDEN ROCK MEDIA, INC.

1416 N LaBrea Ave
Hollywood, CA 90028
323-802-1718 (phone)
323-802-1832 (fax)

taugsberger@edenrockmedia.com
edenrockmedia.com

imdb.com/company/co0156805

Does not accept any unsolicited material. Project types include TV, feature films, and commercials. Genres include family, non-fiction, science fiction, thriller, crime, and drama.

Thomas Ausberger
Producer
imdb.com/name/nm0041835

EDGEN FILMS
Production company and distributor

2851 Joe DiMaggio Bldg 7, Unit 13
Round Rock, TX 78665
512-522-8410

contact@edgenfilms.com
edgenfilms.com
imdb.com/company/co0191909
linkedin.com/company/edgen-films
facebook.com/pages/Edgen-Films/136229063085550
twitter.com/edgenfilms

Does not accept any unsolicited material. Project types include feature films. Genres include horror, drama, and thriller. Established in 2014.

Justin Durban
CCO
justin@edgenfilms.com
justindurban.com
imdb.com/name/nm0243943

Nicholle Walton-Durban
CEO
nicholle@edgenfilms.com
imdb.com/name/nm3546871

Leah Weinberger
Director of Development
leah@edgenfilms.com
imdb.com/name/nm3733040

EDGE OF LA PRODUCTIONS INC.

9601 Wilshire Blvd. #1138
Beverly Hills, California 90210
310-999-2714

email@edgeofla.com
edgeofla.com

Does not accept any unsolicited material. Project types include short films, TV, and feature films. Genres include period, animation, drama, documentary, comedy, fantasy, detective, family, action, non-fiction, science fiction, crime, sociocultural, myth, horror, thriller, and romance. Established in 2004.

Erik von Wodtke
Development Executive
erik@edgeofla.com

EDMONDS ENTERTAINMENT
Production company

1635 N Cahuenga Blvd, 6th Floor
Los Angeles, CA 90028
323-860-1550 (phone)
323-860-1537 (fax)

edmondsent.com/site/main.html
imdb.com/company/co0034440

Accepts scripts from produced or represented writers. Project types include TV and feature films. Genres include non-fiction, romance, family, drama, and reality.

Tracey Edmonds
CEO
imdb.com/name/nm0249525
Assistant: Amy Ficken

Sheila Ducksworth
Sr. Vice-President
imdb.com/name/nm0239923

Kenneth Edmonds
Executive Producer
imdb.com/name/nm0004892

EDUCATIONAL FILM CENTER
Production company and distributor

3314 Newark St, NW
Washington, DC 20008
202-243-1048

ruthpollak@verizon.net
efcvideo.com
imdb.com/company/co0075662
linkedin.com/company/educational-film-center

Does not accept any unsolicited material. Project types include TV. Genres include family.

EDWARDS SKERBELIS ENTERTAINMENT (ESE)
Production company

8549 Wilshire Blvd.
Suite 1052
Beverly Hills, CA 90211

info@esentertainment.net
esentertainment.net

Does not accept any unsolicited material. Project types include TV and feature films. Genres include romance, thriller, and comedy. Established in 2005.

EFISH ENTERTAINMENT, INC.
Production company, distributor, and financing company

4236 Arch St, Suite 407
Studio City, CA 91604
818-509-9377

info@efishentertainment.com
efishentertainment.com
imdb.com/company/co0272699
facebook.com/pages/eFish-Entertainment/
    105303619508702

Does not accept any unsolicited material. Project types include feature films. Genres include action, crime, science fiction, and horror. Established in 2009.

Brianna Johnson
Producer
briannaasst@efishentertainment.com
imdb.com/name/nm3776636

Eric Fischer
Producer
ericasst@efishentertainment.com
imdb.com/name/nm2737789
Assistant: Tatjana Bluchel

EFO FILMS
Production company, distributor, and financing company

Park Rotana Office Complex, Khalifa Park, Sector E-48, Office 302G,
PO Box 769324, Abu Dhabi, UAE

8200 Wilshire Blvd, Suite 300
Beverly Hills, CA 90211
323-213-4650

info@efofilms.com
efofilms.com
imdb.com/company/co0526484

Does not accept any unsolicited material. Project types include feature films and TV. Genres include horror, action, and drama.

George Furla
Partner/Producer
imdb.com/name/nm0298915

Randall Emmett
Partner/Producer
imdb.com/name/nm0256542

EGO FILM ARTS
Production company

80 Niagara St
Toronto, ON M5V 1C5
Canada
310-859-4000 (phone)
310-859-4440 (fax)

questions@egofilmarts.com
egofilmarts.com
imdb.com/company/co0093742

Does not accept any unsolicited material. Project types include TV and feature films. Genres include crime, comedy, action, romance, documentary, horror, drama, and thriller.

Atom Egoyan
Founder
imdb.com/name/nm0000382

EGOIST ENTERTAINMENT
Production company

3521 Oak Lawn
#222
Dallas, TX 75219

brian@egoistent.com

imdb.com/company/co0201863

Does not accept any unsolicited material.

EGOLI TOSSELL FILM
Production company

Wallstraße 15 A
Berlin 10179
Germany
+49 30 246565 0 (phone)
+49 30 246565 24 (fax)

contact@egolitossell.com
egolitossell.com
imdb.com/company/co0043735

Does not accept any unsolicited material. Project types include feature films. Genres include drama.

Jens Meurer
Producer
imdb.com/name/nm0582797

EIGHTH SQUARE ENTERTAINMENT
Production company

606 N Larchmont Blvd, Suite 307
Los Angeles, CA 90004
323-469-1003 (phone)
323-469-1516 (fax)

imdb.com/company/co0100233
facebook.com/pages/Eighth-Square-Entertainment/
  167378796607994

Does not accept any unsolicited material. Project types include feature films, TV, and theater. Genres include drama, comedy, thriller, and crime. Established in 1998.

Jeff Melnick
Producer
imdb.com/name/nm0578179

EISENBERG-FISHER PRODUCTIONS
Production company

5555 Melrose Ave.
Los Angeles, CA 90038

imdb.com/company/co0385521

Does not accept any unsolicited material. Project types include feature films. Genres include action and drama.

ELAINE RIDINGS
Production company

960 Larrabee St. #124
West Hollywood, CA 90069
310-387-5823

laniridings@gmail.com
linkedin.com/elaineridings

Accepts scripts from unproduced, unrepresented writers via email. Project types include feature films. Genres include comedy. Established in 2015.

Elaine Ridings
Researcher
310-387-5823
laniridings@gmail.com

ELECTRIC CITY ENTERTAINMENT
Production company

8409 Santa Monica Blvd
West Hollywood, CA 90069
323-654-7800 (phone)
323-654-7808 (fax)

imdb.com/company/co0366362
facebook.com/Electric-City-Entertainment-
  LLC-144843368963548

Accepts query letters from unproduced, unrepresented writers via email. Project types include feature films. Genres include comedy, romance, and drama. Established in 2012.

Jamie Patricof
imdb.com/name/nm1364232
Assistant: Jack Hart

Lynette Howell
imdb.com/name/nm1987578
Assistant: Jess Engel

Katie McNeill
imdb.com/name/nm3336352
linkedin.com/pub/katie-mcneill/a/758/581

Crystal Powell
imdb.com/name/nm2476235

ELECTRIC DYNAMITE
Production company

1741 Ivar Ave
Los Angeles, CA 90028
323-790-8040 (phone)
818-733-2651 (fax)

imdb.com/company/co0190357
twitter.com/el_dynamite

Accepts query letters from unproduced, unrepresented writers. Project types include feature films, TV, and commercials. Genres include science fiction, comedy, and fantasy.

Jack Black
323-790-8000
imdb.com/name/nm0085312

Priyanka Mattoo
imdb.com/name/nm3339192

ELECTRIC ENTERTAINMENT
Production company

940 N Highland Ave, Suite A
Los Angeles, CA 90038
323-817-1300 (phone)
323-467-7155 (fax)

electric-entertainment.com
imdb.com/company/co0003899

Does not accept any unsolicited material. Project types include feature films, commercials, and TV. Genres include drama, comedy, reality, animation, thriller, non-fiction, science fiction, and action.

Rachel Olschan
imdb.com/name/nm1272673

Dean Devlin
President
imdb.com/name/nm0002041
Assistant: Chase Friedman

Marc Roskin
imdb.com/name/nm0743059

ELECTRIC FARM ENTERTAINMENT
Production company and distributor

Los Angeles, CA
310-264-4199 (phone)
310-264-4196 (fax)

contact@electricfarment.com
imdb.com/company/co0217444

Does not accept any unsolicited material. Project types include TV. Genres include fantasy, science fiction, drama, and action. Established in 2007.

Stan Rogow
CEO
linkedin.com/pub/stan-rogow/11/903/335
Assistant: Allison Lurie

Brent Friedman
linkedin.com/pub/brent-friedman/4/342/72

ELECTRIC SHEPHERD PRODUCTIONS

c/o Anonymous Content
3532 Hayden Ave
Culver City, CA 90232
310-558-6538

admin@electricshepherdproductions.com
philipkdickesp.com
imdb.com/company/co0185913
linkedin.com/company/electric-shepherd-productions-llc

Accepts query letters from unproduced, unrepresented writers via email. Project types include TV, feature films, and commercials. Genres include science fiction, myth, drama, thriller, action, and fantasy.

Kalen Egan
imdb.com/name/nm2290810

Isa Dick Hackett
imdb.com/name/nm2357313

ELECTUS
Distributor

8800 W Sunset Blvd, West Hollywood, CA, United States, 90069
310-360-3422 (phone)
310-360-3408 (fax)

contact@electus.com
electus.com
imdb.com/company/co0534565

Does not accept any unsolicited material. Project types include feature films and TV. Genres include drama and family.

Montrel ` McKay
Vice President (Creative Development for Television)
imdb.com/name/nm5281557

ELEMENT PICTURES
Production company and distributor

21 Mespil Rd
Dublin 4
Ireland
353-1-618-5032 (phone)
353-1-664-3737 (fax)

14 Newburgh St
London, W1F7RT
UK
44207-287-5420 (phone)
44207-434-0146 (fax)

info@elementpictures.ie
elementpictures.ie
imdb.com/company/co0214624
facebook.com/ElementPicturesDistribution
twitter.com/ElementPictures

Does not accept any unsolicited material. Project types include TV and feature films. Genres include comedy, romance, thriller, crime, and drama. Established in 2007.

Ed Guiney
Company Director
imdb.com/name/nm0347384
linkedin.com/pub/dir/Ed/Guiney

Lee Magiday
Producer
imdb.com/name/nm3717662
linkedin.com/pub/lee-magiday/3/6a8/863

Andrew Lowe
imdb.com/name/nm1103466
linkedin.com/pub/andrew-lowe/20/1a/66

Emma Norton
Head of Development
imdb.com/name/nm4499999
linkedin.com/pub/dir/Emma/Norton

ELEPHANT EYE FILMS
Production company

89 Fifth Ave
Ste 306
New York, NY 10003
212-488-8877 (phone)
212-488-8878 (fax)

info@elephanteyefilms.com
elephanteyefilms.com
imdb.com/company/co0223262
facebook.com/pages/Elephant-Eye-Films/
    110546058997554
twitter.com/eeffilms

Does not accept any unsolicited material. Project types include feature films. Genres include drama, action, comedy, non-fiction, and fantasy.

Kim Jose
kim@elephanteyefilms.com

Dave Robinson
dave@elephanteyefilms.com

Toni Branson
toni@elephanteyefilms.com

ELEPHANT STONE PRODUCTIONS
Production company

5848 Pine Grove Run
Oviedo, FL 32765
407-233-9686

info@elephantstoneproductions.com
imdb.com/company/co0289879

Does not accept any unsolicited material. Genres include drama.

ELEVATE ENTERTAINMENT
Production company

5757 Wilshire Blvd.
Suite 460

Los Angeles, CA 90036
323-634-0748

elevateentertainment.net
imdb.com/company/co0246846

Accepts query letters from unproduced, unrepresented writers via email. Project types include feature films and TV. Genres include fantasy, drama, family, comedy, crime, animation, action, non-fiction, science fiction, and romance. Established in 2014.

Josh Moody
CCO
linkedin.com/pub/josh-moody/25/47/569
facebook.com/josh.moody.319

Dave Moody
CEO
davemoody.com/about
imdb.com/name/nm2628340
linkedin.com/in/davemoody

ELEVATION PICTURES
Production company and distributor

317 Adelaide St. W
Suite 520
Toronto, ON M5V1P9
Canada
416-583-5800

info@elevationpictures.com
elevationpictures.com
imdb.com/company/co0465489
linkedin.com/company/elevation-pictures-corp
facebook.com/ElevationPics
twitter.com/Elevation_Pics

Does not accept any unsolicited material. Genres include drama.

ELEVEN:11 FILMS
Production company

PO Box 170777
Austin, TX 78717
845-270-1816

imdb.com/company/co0310183
twitter.com/eleven11films

Does not accept any unsolicited material. Project types include short films and feature films. Genres include drama. Established in 2010.

ELEVEN ARTS JAPAN
Distributor

1-14-10, Matsuyama Bldg 4th Floor
Shinjuku
Shinjuku-Ku, Tokyo 160-0022
Japan
+81 3 3356 0662 (phone)
+81 3 6740 8441 (fax)

info@elevenarts-japan.net
elevenarts-japan.net
imdb.com/company/co0388539

Does not accept any unsolicited material. Project types include TV. Genres include drama, romance, and thriller.

ELEVEN FILM
Production company

25-26 Poland St
London W1F 8WN
UK
+44 7502 998 536

contact@elevenfilm.com
elevenfilm.com
imdb.com/company/co0197929
twitter.com/ElevenFilm

Does not accept any unsolicited material. Project types include TV. Genres include drama and crime.

ELEVENTH HOUR FILMS
Production company

2nd Floor, 104B St John St, London, EC1M 4EH
0207-251-6848

info@eleventhhourfilms.co.uk
eleventhhourfilms.co.uk
imdb.com/company/co0422985
facebook.com/eleventhhourfilms
twitter.com/eleventhhourtv

Does not accept any unsolicited material. Project types include TV. Genres include crime.

Jill Green
Producer
imdb.com/name/nm0337976

ELIXIR FILMS
Production company

8033 W Sunset Blvd, Suite 867
West Hollywood, CA 90046
323-848-9867 (phone)
323-848-5945 (fax)

info@elixirfilms.com
elixirfilms.com
imdb.com/company/co0082095
facebook.com/ELIXIRFILMSelixirfilms

Does not accept any unsolicited material. Project types include feature films. Genres include family and drama.

David Alexanian
Producer
imdb.com/name/nm1256362

Alexis Alexanian
Producer
imdb.com/name/nm0018936
Assistant: Joe Brinkman

ELIZABETH BARDSLEY AND ASSOCIATES
Production company

3727 W. Magnolia Blvd.
#450
Burbank, CA 91505
818-563-4008 (phone)
818-823-1938 (fax)

info@elizabethbardsley.com
elizabethbardsley.com
imdb.com/company/co0221527
linkedin.com/company/elizabeth-bardsley-&-
    associates-inc.

Does not accept any unsolicited material. Genres include crime and drama.

ELKINS ENTERTAINMENT
Production company

8306 Wilshire Blvd
PMB 3643
Beverly Hills, CA 90211
323-932-0400 (phone)
323-932-6400 (fax)

info@elkinsent.com
elkinsent.com
imdb.com/company/co0041590

Accepts query letters from unproduced, unrepresented writers via email. Project types include TV and feature films. Genres include romance, drama, non-fiction, reality, and comedy.

Sandi Love
imdb.com/name/nm0522418

ELLEN RAKIETEN ENTERTAINMENT
Production company

1040 N Las Palmas
Los Angeles, CA 90038
323-860-8900

imdb.com/company/co0299016
facebook.com/EllenRakietenEntertainment

Does not accept any unsolicited material. Project types include TV. Genres include reality.

ELLIOTT ANIMATION
Production company

237 Wallace Ave
Toronto, ON M6H 1V5
Canada
416-588-6364

info@elliottanimation.com
elliottanimation.com
imdb.com/company/co0248953
linkedin.com/company/1126384
facebook.com/Elliott-Animation-1448831422075345
twitter.com/Elliott_Animate

Accepts query letters from unproduced, unrepresented writers. Project types include TV. Genres include animation, comedy, and drama.

George Elliott
Producer
imdb.com/name/nm1721787

ELLIS ENTERTAINMENT
Production company and distributor

1300 Yonge St.
Suite 300
Toronto, ON M4T 1X3
Canada
416-924-2186 (phone)
416-924-6115 (fax)

info@ellisent.com
ellisent.com
imdb.com/company/co0121810

Does not accept any unsolicited material. Project types include TV and short films. Genres include documentary.

Kip Spidell
Producer
imdb.com/name/nm1827711

ELYSIAN ENTERTAINMENT

6735 Yucca St. #207
Hollywood, CA 90028
323-230-8224

submissions@elysian-entertainment.com (script submissions)
info@elysian-entertainment.com (general)
elysian-entertainment.com
imdb.com/company/co0110757
linkedin.com/company/elysian-entertainment
facebook.com/elysianentertainment

Accepts query letters from unproduced, unrepresented writers via email. Project types include feature films and TV.

Sheri Fults
Producer/Manager
imdb.com/name/nm2433977

EMBANKMENT FILMS
Distributor and sales agent

242 Acklam Rd
WE 020
London, England W10 5JJ
UK
44 (0207-183-4739

info@embankmentfilms.com
embankmentfilms.com
imdb.com/company/co0372116

Does not accept any unsolicited material. Project types include TV. Genres include drama.

Max Pirkis
Producer
imdb.com/name/nm1263986

EMBARGO FILMS
Production company

+44 (0207-494-4049 (phone)
+44 (0207-494-4056 (fax)

contact@embargofilms.com
embargofilms.com
imdb.com/company/co0295480

Does not accept any unsolicited material. Project types include feature films. Genres include action, drama, and crime.

Barnaby Southcombe
Director
imdb.com/name/nm0816090

EMBASSY ROW, LLC
Production company

6565 Sunset Blvd Suite 200
Los Angeles, CA 90028
323-417-6560 (phone)
323-469-0015 (fax)

325 Hudson St
Ste 601
New York, NY 10013
212-507-9700 (phone)
212-507-9701 (fax)

info@embassyrow.com
embassyrow.com
imdb.com/company/co0183718

Does not accept any unsolicited material. Project types include feature films, TV, and commercials. Genres include non-fiction, science fiction, drama, fantasy, comedy, action, and reality.

Tammy Johnston
imdb.com/name/nm1183748

Michael Davies
imdb.com/name/nm0203863

EMBER ENTERTAINMENT GROUP
Production company

11718 Barrington Court
Los Angeles, CA 90049

imdb.com/company/co0176815

Does not accept any unsolicited material. Genres include science fiction. Established in 1988.

Randall Frakes
President
imdb.com/name/nm0289696

Lindsay Dunlap
Producer
imdb.com/name/nm0242397

Ryan Geithman
President
linkedin.com/pub/ryan-geithman/57/242/446

Max Wagner
linkedin.com/pub/max-wagner/2/599/bba
linkedin.com/pub/max-wagner/2/599/bba
twitter.com/emeyex

EMBERWILDE PRODUCTIONS
Production company and distributor

4206 38th st. NW
Washington, DC 20016

imdb.com/company/co0184761
facebook.com/emberwildeproductions

Does not accept any unsolicited material. Genres include animation, documentary, and comedy.

EMERALD CITY PRODUCTIONS, INC.
Production company

c/o Stankevich-Gochman
9777 Wilshire Blvd, Suite 550
Beverly Hills, CA 90212
321-253-4335

ingrid@emeraldcityprod.com
imdb.com/company/co0284758

facebook.com/emeraldcityrecords

Does not accept any unsolicited material. Project types include feature films. Genres include science fiction, fantasy, and drama.

Stephen Walen
imdb.com/company/co0284758

Barrie M. Osborne
Producer
imdb.com/name/nm0651614

EMERGENCE ENTERTAINMENT
Production company

1508 E Wildflower Ln
Spokane, WA 99224
509-939-7206

mark.kratter@alumni.stanford.org
emergenceentertainment.com
imdb.com/company/co0178940

Accepts query letters from unproduced, unrepresented writers via email. Project types include TV and feature films. Genres include thriller, horror, science fiction, sociocultural, period, reality, romance, fantasy, crime, comedy, family, detective, drama, documentary, action, myth, non-fiction, and animation.

EMI CMG DISTRIBUTION
Distributor

101 Winners Circle
Brentwood, TN 37027-5017
615-371-4300

demos@motowngospel.com (script submissions)
info@motowngospel.com (general)
motowngospel.com
imdb.com/company/co0158088
web.facebook.com/MotownGospel
twitter.com/MotownGospel

Accepts query letters from unproduced, unrepresented writers via email. Genres include documentary and family.

EMINENT PRODUCTION
Production company

416-454-8421

info@eminentproduction.com
eminentproduction.com
facebook.com/Eminentvideo
twitter.com/eminent_video

Accepts scripts from unproduced, unrepresented writers via email. Project types include TV, commercials, short films, and feature films. Genres include romance, thriller, documentary, detective, horror, action, sociocultural, crime, comedy, and drama. Established in 2015.

Shiva Maharaj
Executive Producer
416-454-8421
info@eminentproduction.com
eminentproduction.com
twitter.com/Eminent_video

EMJAG PRODUCTIONS

9200 W Sunset Blvd., Suite 550
West Hollywood, CA 90069
310-786-7875

imdb.com/company/co0223721

Does not accept any unsolicited material. Project types include TV and feature films. Genres include drama, crime, and thriller.

Alexandra Milchan
Producer
imdb.com/name/nm0586968

Stephanie Dziczek
Story Editor
imdb.com/name/nm2933823

EM MEDIA
Production company

Em-Media, Inc. 2728 Sunset Blvd.
Steubenville, OH 43952
740-264-2186

info@em-media.com
em-media.com
imdb.com/company/co0091923
linkedin.com/company/em-media-inc-

Accepts query letters from unproduced, unrepresented writers. Project types include feature films. Genres

include drama, comedy, and romance. Established in 2002.

Suzanne Alizart
suzanne.alizart@em-media.org
imdb.com/name/nm2355251

Anna Seifert-Speck
Development Executive
imdb.com/name/nm3527106

Debbie Williams
CEO
0115-993-2333
debbie.williams@em-media.org.uk
imdb.com/name/nm3527737

John Tobin
imdb.com/name/nm3527690

EMMETT/FURLA FILMS

8200 Wilshire Blvd, Suite 300
Beverly Hills, CA 90211
323-213-4650

imdb.com/company/co0017712

Does not accept any unsolicited material. Project types include TV and feature films. Genres include drama and comedy.

Randall Emmett
Producer
imdb.com/name/nm0256542

George Furla
Producer
imdb.com/name/nm0298915

EMMETT/FURLA/OASIS FILMS
Production company and distributor

18th floor, Grosvenor Business Tower P.O. Box 500366
Dubai United Arab Emirates
011-971-44540300 (phone)
011-971-44540302 (fax)

8200 Wilshire Blvd, Third Floor, Beverly Hills, CA, United States, 90211
323-213-4650

efofilms.com

imdb.com/company/co0526484

Does not accept any unsolicited material. Project types include TV. Genres include drama, family, and comedy.

EMPIRE FILM DISTRIBUTORS
Production company and distributor

723 Seventh Ave.
New York, NY 10019

imdb.com/company/co0136909

Does not accept any unsolicited material. Genres include crime, romance, and drama.

EMPIRE PICTURES, INC.
Distributor

360 E First St, Suite 774
Tustin, CA 92780
323-939-2100

imdb.com/company/co0090070

Does not accept any unsolicited material. Project types include feature films and TV. Genres include comedy, drama, horror, and fantasy.

Michael Birnbaum
Producer
imdb.com/name/nm0083688

EMU FILMS
Production company

111A Wardour St
London, England W1F 0UJ
UK
+44 20 7183 0925

info@emufilms.com
emufilms.com
imdb.com/company/co0306472

Does not accept any unsolicited material. Project types include TV. Genres include drama.

Michael Elliott
Producer
imdb.com/name/nm0254560

END CUE
Production company

100 Wilshire Blvd, Suite 650, Santa Monica, CA, United States, 90401
310-870-3771

info@endcue.com
endcue.com
imdb.com/company/co0541701

Does not accept any unsolicited material. Project types include TV and feature films. Genres include action, family, romance, and drama.

ENDEMOL ENTERTAINMENT
Production company

1000 Brickell Ave.
Suite 1015
Miami, Florida 33131
305-576-4949 (phone)
305-576-4980 (fax)

9255 W Sunset Blvd
Suite 1100
Los Angeles, CA 90069
310-860-9914 (phone)
310-860-0073 (fax)

endemolusa.tv
imdb.com/company/co0011366
facebook.com/EndemolUS
twitter.com/endemolUS

Accepts query letters from produced or represented writers. Project types include TV. Genres include reality, comedy, and drama.

Cris Abrego
Co-Chairman and Co-CEO
imdb.com/name/nm0918141

ENDERBY ENTERTAINMENT
Production company and financing company

18034 Ventura Blvd, Suite 445, Encino, CA, United States, 91316
818-708-1602

info@enderbyentertainment.com
enderbyentertainment.com
imdb.com/company/co0209163

Does not accept any unsolicited material. Project types include feature films and short films. Genres include science fiction, action, drama, and thriller.

Rick Dugdale
President
imdb.com/name/nm1067987

ENDGAME ENTERTAINMENT
Production company

9100 Wilshire Blvd, Suite 100W
Beverly Hills, CA 90212
310-432-7300 (phone)
310-432-7301 (fax)

reception@endgameent.com
endgameent.com
imdb.com/company/co0112971
linkedin.com/company/endgame-entertainment

Does not accept any unsolicited material. Project types include TV, feature films, and theater. Genres include thriller, comedy, action, reality, science fiction, animation, drama, non-fiction, detective, crime, and romance.

Julie Goldstein
imdb.com/name/nm0326252

Adam Del Deo
imdb.com/name/nm0215534

James Stern
imdb.com/name/nm0827726

Lucas Smith
imdb.com/name/nm0809156

ENDLESS MEDIA
Production company

604 Arizona Ave
Santa Monica, CA 90401
323-373-3507

submissions@endlessmedia.com (script submissions)
info@endlessmedia.com (general)
endlessmedia.com
imdb.com/company/co0479754
facebook.com/endlessmediallc

Accepts query letters from unproduced, unrepresented writers via email. Project types include feature films. Genres include thriller, action, science fiction, detective, romance, crime, comedy, and drama. Established in 2011.

Najeeb Khuda
CEO
najeeb@endlessmedia.com

ENDLESS MOON PRODUCTIONS
Production company

1212 N Velasco
Ste 110
Angleton, TX 77515

6millionsteps@gmail.com
imdb.com/company/co0344179
facebook.com/Endless-Moon-
Productions-144411228958150

Does not accept any unsolicited material. Genres include documentary.

ENERGY ENTERTAINMENT
Production company

9107 Wilshire Blvd Suite #600
Beverly Hills, CA 90212
310-746-4872

info@energyentertainment.net
energyentertainment.net
imdb.com/company/co0120782
linkedin.com/company/energy-entertainment

Does not accept any unsolicited material. Project types include feature films. Genres include thriller, science fiction, non-fiction, drama, comedy, horror, and fantasy. Established in 2001.

Angelina Chen
Manager
imdb.com/name/nm3255914

Michelle Arenal
imdb.com/name/nm2797145

Brooklyn Weaver
imdb.com/name/nm0915819
Assistant: David Binns

ENSEMBLE PRODUCTIONS
Production company and distributor

3000 W Olympic Blvd., Suite 2405
Santa Monica, CA 90404
310-264-3930

imdb.com/company/co0384018

Does not accept any unsolicited material. Project types include TV. Genres include drama.

ENTERBRAIN
Production company and distributor

6-1
Sanbancho
Chiyoda, Tokyo 102-8431
Japan
+81-3-3265-7013 (phone)
+81-3-3265-7405 (fax)

fmd-international@ml.enterbrain.co.jp
enterbrain.co.jp
imdb.com/company/co0125532

Does not accept any unsolicited material. Project types include TV. Genres include animation and horror.

Masayuki Aoyagi
Senior managing director (Executive)
imdb.com/name/nm4396933

ENTERTAINMENT BY BONNIE AND CLYDE

1440 Colt Circle
Castle Rock, CO 80109
303-681-2955

facebook.com/pages/Bonnie-and-Clyde-
    Entertainment-Inc/134059286625283

Does not accept any unsolicited material. Project types include TV.

Duane Chapman
Producer
imdb.com/name/nm2406592

Beth Chapman
Producer
imdb.com/name/nm1726593

ENTERTAINMENT FARM (EF)
Production company

2-5-1-6F
Atago
Minato, Tokyo 105-6206
Japan
03-6888-7037

info@efarm.co.jp
imdb.com/company/co0130059

Does not accept any unsolicited material. Project types include TV. Genres include drama.

Taizo Son
Executive
imdb.com/name/nm2180943

ENTERTAINMENT INDUSTRY INCUBATOR
Production company

407 Lincoln Rd.
Ste. 6-B
Miami Beach, FL 33139
305-672-9297

info@eincubator.org
eincubator.org
imdb.com/company/co0182428

Does not accept any unsolicited material. Project types include short films. Genres include family.

ENTERTAINMENT IN MOTION
Distributor and sales agent

5455 Centinela Ave, Los Angeles , CA, United States, 90066
310-574-9996 (phone)
310-574-0690 (fax)

imdb.com/company/co0237609

Does not accept any unsolicited material. Project types include TV, short films, and feature films. Genres include thriller, family, and drama.

ENTERTAINMENT ONE
Production company, distributor, and sales agent

175 Bloor St E, North Tower
Ste 1400
Toronto, ON M4W 3R8
Canada
416-646-2400

info@entertainmentone.ca
entertainmentone.com
imdb.com/company/co0212327
linkedin.com/company/entertainment-one

Does not accept any unsolicited material. Genres include drama and action.

Xavier Marchand
Producer
imdb.com/name/nm0545421

ENTERTAINMENT ONE GROUP
Production company

9465 Wilshire Blvd, Suite 500
Los Angeles, CA 90212
310-407-0960

22 Harbor Park Dr
Port Washington
New York 11050

eonetv@entonegroup.com
entonegroup.com
imdb.com/company/co0309705
linkedin.com/company/entertainment-one

Does not accept any unsolicited material. Project types include TV, feature films, and commercials. Genres include reality, family, comedy, romance, non-fiction, thriller, animation, drama, and horror.

Jeff Hevert
imdb.com/name/nm2062114

Michael Rosenberg
imdb.com/name/nm0742283

ENTERTAINMENT STUDIOS
Production company and distributor

9903 Santa Monica Blvd., Suite 418
Beverly Hills, CA 90212
310-277-3500

es.tv
imdb.com/company/co0127629

linkedin.com/company/entertainment-studios
facebook.com/esdottv
twitter.com/ESdotTV

Does not accept any unsolicited material. Project types include TV. Genres include detective and drama.

Byron Allen
CEO/Executive Producer
imdb.com/name/nm2902750

ENTICING ENTERTAINMENT
Production company

701 Brazos St, Suite 1050
Austin, TX 78701

imdb.com/company/co0296449

Does not accept any unsolicited material. Project types include feature films. Genres include drama and thriller.

David Tice
Producer
imdb.com/name/nm3790215

ENTITLED ENTERTAINMENT
Production company

2038 Redcliff St
Los Angeles, CA 90039
323-469-9000 (phone)
323-660-5292 (fax)

entitledentertainment.com
imdb.com/company/co0076662
facebook.com/entitledent

Does not accept any unsolicited material. Project types include feature films, TV, and theater. Genres include crime, drama, family, comedy, and non-fiction.

Scott Disharoon
Partner
imdb.com/name/nm0228318

James Burke
Partner
imdb.com/name/nm0121711

ENTITLED ENTERTAINMENT
Production company

81 Cleveland Ln
Princeton, NJ 08540

entitledentertainment.com
imdb.com/company/co0076662
facebook.com/entitledent

Does not accept any unsolicited material. Genres
include crime and drama.

ENUFF PRODUCTIONS
Production company

4315 Park Ave Unit 2D
Union City, NJ 07087

dontlookmovie@gmail.com
imdb.com/company/co0483792
facebook.com/pages/Dont-Look/507346489308303
twitter.com/DONTLOOKMOVIE

Does not accept any unsolicited material. Genres
include horror.

ENVISION MEDIA ARTS
Production company

EMA, LLC
℅ The Lot
1041 N Formosa Ave
Writer's Building, Suite 11
West Hollywood, CA 90046
310-459-8080

EMA, LLC
c/o Falco Ink
475 Park Ave South
15th Floor
New York, NY 10016
212-445-7100

info@ema.la
ema.la
imdb.com/company/co0340433
facebook.com/EnvisionMediaArts
twitter.com/EnvisionMA

Accepts query letters from unproduced, unrepresented
writers via email. Project types include TV and feature
films. Genres include myth, drama, action, romance,
family, comedy, and fantasy. Established in 2002.

David Buelow
310-459-8080
db@ema.la
imdb.com/name/nm2149164

Lee Nelson
CEO
310-459-8080
ln@ema.la
imdb.com/name/nm0625540

David Tish
Director of Development
dtish@envisionma.com
imdb.com/name/nm2953843

ENVOI ENTERTAINMENT
Production company

1 Transfer Place
Toronto, ON M1S 5H8
Canada

imdb.com/company/co0531731

Does not accept any unsolicited material. Project types
include short films. Genres include horror and thriller.

EONE TELEVISION
Production company and distributor

45 Warren St
London England United Kingdom W1T 6AG
011-442-079073773

134 Peter St Suite 700
Toronto ON Canada M5V 2H2
141-664-62400

9465 Wilshire Blvd, Suite 500, Beverly Hills, CA,
United States, 90212
310-407-0960 (phone)
310-407-0961 (fax)

tvinfo@entonegroup.com
eonetv.com/home
imdb.com/company/co0332906

Does not accept any unsolicited material. Project types
include TV. Genres include drama, fantasy, thriller,
and family.

EPIC LEVEL ENTERTAINMENT, LTD.
Production company

7095 Hollywood Blvd #688
Hollywood, CA 91604
818-752-6800 (phone)
818-752-6814 (fax)

info@epiclevel.com
epiclevel.com
imdb.com/company/co0183217

Accepts query letters from unproduced, unrepresented writers via email. Project types include TV, commercials, and feature films. Genres include myth, reality, science fiction, non-fiction, animation, thriller, horror, fantasy, and action.

Paige Barnett
imdb.com/name/nm1831309

John Rosenblum
Producer
jfr@jfr.com
jfr.com

Cindi Rice
Producer
imdb.com/name/nm1394761
linkedin.com/in/cindirice
twitter.com/cindirice

EPIC PICTURES GROUP
Production company, distributor, and sales agent

6725 Sunset Blvd, Suite 330, Hollywood, CA, United States, 90028
323-207-4170 (phone)
270-477-9976 (fax)

epic-pictures.com
imdb.com/company/co0222455

Does not accept any unsolicited material. Project types include feature films and TV. Genres include drama, thriller, action, myth, and family.

EPIC TV
Studio and distributor

22224 Collington Dr.
Boca Raton, FL 33428
561-926-2723

info@epicsportstv.com
epictv.com
imdb.com/company/co0138396
facebook.com/WatchEpicTV
twitter.com/watchepictv

Does not accept any unsolicited material. Project types include TV.

EPIGRAM ENTERTAINMENT
Production company

3745 Longview Valley Rd
Sherman Oaks, CA 91423
818-461-8937 (phone)
818-461-8919 (fax)

epigrament@sbcglobal.net
imdb.com/company/co0176819

Accepts query letters from unproduced, unrepresented writers via email. Project types include feature films, TV, and commercials. Genres include romance, comedy, and drama.

Ellen Baskin
imdb.com/name/nm2302395

Val McLeroy
Partner
imdb.com/name/nm0572890

EPIPHANY PICTURES, INC.
Production company

10625 Esther Ave
Los Angeles, CA 90064
310-815-1266 (phone)
310-815-1269 (fax)

epiphanysubmissions@gmail.com.com
epiphanypictures.com
imdb.com/company/co0023944

Accepts query letters from unproduced, unrepresented writers via email. Project types include feature films, commercials, and TV. Genres include animation, action, reality, sociocultural, fantasy, comedy, non-fiction, myth, drama, romance, science fiction, thriller, and family.

Dan Halperin
310-452-0242
dan@epiphanypictures.com
imdb.com/name/nm0356917

Scott Frank
scott@epiphanypictures.com
imdb.com/name/nm0291082

Dave Schilling
Story Editor
dwsreader@gmail.com

EPITOME PICTURES
Production company

220 Bartley Dr
Toronto, ON M4A 1G1
Canada
416-752-7627 (phone)
416-752-7837 (fax)

info@epitomepictures.com
epitomepictures.com
imdb.com/company/co0066494
facebook.com/Epitome-Pictures-
     Inc-227956453907482
twitter.com/stephenstohn

Does not accept any unsolicited material. Project types include TV. Genres include drama.

Linda Schuyler
Director
imdb.com/name/nm0776946

EPOCH FILMS
Production company

9290 Civic Center
Drive Beverly Hills, CA 90210
310-275-9333 (phone)
310-275-7696 (fax)

435 Hudson St, 3rd Floor
New York, NY 10014
212-226-0661 (phone)
212-226-4893 (fax)

112-114 Great Portland St., 1st Floor
London, England W1W6PA

44207-908-6060 (phone)
44207-908-6061 (fax)

lon@epochfilms.com
epochfilms.com
imdb.com/company/co0130058

Does not accept any unsolicited material. Project types include commercials. Genres include drama and comedy.

Mindy Goldberg
Founder/Producer (NY)
imdb.com/name/nm1666061

Jerry Solomon
Managing Partner/Executive Producer (LA)
imdb.com/name/nm0813355

EQUILIBRIUM MEDIA COMPANY
Production company

1259 S. Orange Grove Ave.
Los Angeles, CA 90019
323-939-3555 (phone)
323-939-7523 (fax)

info@eq-ent.com
eq-ent.com
imdb.com/company/co0232623
facebook.com/EquilibriumEnt
twitter.com/EquilibriumEnt

Accepts query letters from unproduced, unrepresented writers. Project types include feature films. Genres include action and comedy.

Cherif Aziz
Senior Vice President Sales & Marketing
cherif@eq-ent.com

Susan Newell
Vice-President
susan@eq-ent.com

Alex Wood
Creative Executive
alex@eq-ent.com

Yoram Barzilai
Head of Production
yoram@eq-ent.com

Demian Lichtenstein
CEO
demian@eq-ent.com

Dave Hagen
Editor
dave@eq-ent.com

Miklos Wright
Head of Post Production & Senior Editor
miklos@eq-ent.com

Shajen Lichtenstein
Director of Operations
shajen@eq-ent.com

ERGO MEDIA
Distributor

PO Box 2037
Teaneck, NJ 07666
877-539-4748 (phone)
201-692-0663 (fax)

info@jewishvideo.com
jewishvideo.com
imdb.com/company/co0070357

Does not accept any unsolicited material. Project types include feature films and TV. Genres include comedy and drama.

EROS ENTERTAINMENT
Production company and distributor

Unit 23, Sovereign Park
Coronation Rd.
London NW10 7QP
UK
+ 44208-963-8700 (phone)
+ 44208-963-0154 (fax)

UK-business@erosintl.co.uk
erosentertainment.com
imdb.com/company/co0099414

Does not accept any unsolicited material. Genres include comedy, action, drama, and romance.

EROS INTERNATIONAL
Production company and sales agent

550 County Ave
Secaucus, NJ 07094
201-558-9001 (phone)
201-558-9002 (fax)

US-business@erosentertainment.com
erosentertainment.com
imdb.com/company/co0141109
facebook.com/erosnow
twitter.com/ErosNow

Does not accept any unsolicited material. Project types include TV. Genres include horror, drama, and action.

Sunil Lulla
Producer
imdb.com/name/nm2602251

ESCAPE ARTISTS
Production company

10202 W Washington Blvd
Astaire Building, 3rd Floor
Culver City, CA 90232
310-244-8833 (phone)
310-204-2151 (fax)

info@escapeartistsent.com
escapeartistsent.com
imdb.com/company/co0035535
facebook.com/EscapeArtistsEnt
twitter.com/EAfilms

Does not accept any unsolicited material. Project types include TV and feature films. Genres include comedy, action, fantasy, romance, myth, reality, science fiction, and drama.

Todd Black
Founder
todd_black@spe.sony.com
imdb.com/name/nm0085542

Jason Blumenthal
Producer
jason_blumenthal@spe.sony.com
imdb.com/name/nm0089820

Steve Tisch
Partner
steve_tisch@spe.sony.com

ESCAPE REALITY
Production company

3815 Hughes Ave
Culver City, CA 90232
310-841-4369

escapereality.tv

Accepts query letters from produced or represented writers. Project types include feature films and TV. Genres include drama, period, and thriller. Established in 2001.

Jason Blumenthal
Producer
imdb.com/name/nm0089820

Steve Tisch
Producer
imdb.com/name/nm0005494

Laura Fuest Silva
Producer
imdb.com/name/nm1557596

Frank Sutera
Executive Producer
imdb.com/name/nm1281372

David Bloomfield
Executive Producer
imdb.com/name/nm1837022

Lacy Boughn
Development Executive
imdb.com/name/nm2064419

Todd Black
Partner
imdb.com/name/nm0085542

ESPACE SAROU
Distributor

4-8-208
Nanpeidaicho
Shibuya, Tokyo 150-0036
Japan
03-3496-4871 (phone)
03-3496-2791 (fax)

info@espace-sarou.co.jp
espace-sarou.co.jp

imdb.com/company/co0064859

Does not accept any unsolicited material. Project types include feature films. Genres include comedy and drama.

Hideyuki Kai
President
imdb.com/name/nm3146786

ESPARZA / KATZ PRODUCTIONS
Production company

1201 W 5th St, Suite T210
Los Angeles , CA 90017
213-542-4420

imdb.com/company/co0061612
linkedin.com/company/esparza-katz-productions-inc

Does not accept any unsolicited material. Project types include TV and feature films. Genres include drama.

Robert Katz
Executive Producer
imdb.com/name/nm0441831

ESPERANZA FILMS
Production company

1014 Cedar St
Santa Monica, CA 90405
310-314-1164 (phone)
310-581-9967 (fax)

info@esperanza.com
esperanza.com
imdb.com/company/co0018966

Does not accept any unsolicited material. Project types include feature films and TV. Genres include drama and thriller.

Rene Simon Cruz, Jr.
Producer/Director
imdb.com/name/nm0989083

E-SQUARED
Production company

531A North Hollywood Way
Suite 237

Burbank, CA 91505
818-760-1901

info@e2-esquared.com
e2-esquared.com
imdb.com/company/co0109424

Accepts query letters from unproduced, unrepresented writers. Project types include feature films. Genres include action.

Chris Emerson
esquaredasst@sbcglobal.net
imdb.com/name/nm0256193

Matt Cavanaugh
Post Production Sound Assistant
linkedin.com/pub/matt-cavanaugh/19/283/511

ESSENTIAL ENTERTAINMENT
Production company

QUT Creative Precinct Level 3 Z1 the works 34 Parer Place via Musk Ave Kelvin Grove QLD 4059 - See more at: http://www.essential-media.com/contactus#map-4
07 31362534

PO Box 169 Annandale NSW 2038 Australia
61 2 8568 3100 (phone)
61 2 9519 2326 (fax)

9000 Sunset Blvd. Suite 600
Los Angeles, CA 90069
310-550-9100

Essential Media Canada 258 Wallace Ave - Suite 201 | Toronto ON M6P 3M9 | Canada
- See more at: http://www.essential-media.com/contactus#map-3
416-849-0058 (phone)
416-849-0058 (fax)

info@essential-ent.com
essential-media.com
imdb.com/company/co0048134
linkedin.com/company/essential-media-&-entertainment
facebook.com/essentialmediaandentertainment
twitter.com/info_essential

Does not accept any unsolicited material. Project types include feature films. Genres include comedy and drama.

ETERNE FILMS
Production company

99 Main St, Suite 100
Colleyville, TX 76034
817-337-4900

info@eternefilms.com
eterne.org
imdb.com/company/co0292041

Does not accept any unsolicited material. Project types include feature films. Genres include drama.

Steve Riach
CEO
imdb.com/name/nm3727746

EUROCINEMA
Distributor

4045 Sheridan Ave
Suite 390
Miami Beach, FL 33141

contactus@eurocinema.com
eurocinema.com
imdb.com/company/co0107775
facebook.com/eurocinema
twitter.com/Eurocinema

Does not accept any unsolicited material. Genres include action and thriller.

EUROPACORP
Production company and distributor

20 Rue Ampère, Saint-Denis Cedex, France, 93200
011-331-55995000 (phone)
011-331-53830307 (fax)

345 N Maple Dr Suite 123
Beverly Hills CA 90210
310-205-0255

contact@europacorp.com
europacorp.com
imdb.com/company/co0048273

Does not accept any unsolicited material. Project types include TV and feature films. Genres include action, comedy, thriller, and drama.

EUROPEAN FILM BONDS
Production company

European Film Bonds A/S
Knabrostræde 30
1210 Copenhagen K
453-334-9300 (phone)
453-334-9309 (fax)

filmbonds@filmbonds.com
filmbonds.com
imdb.com/company/co0311084

Project types include feature films. Genres include drama, documentary, and animation.

EVAMERE
Production company

38 W 21st St. 12th Floor
New York, NY 10010
212-337-3327

contact@evamere.com
evamere.com
imdb.com/company/co0200982

Does not accept any unsolicited material. Project types include feature films.

John Hart
Producer
imdb.com/name/nm0366359

EVENSTART FILMS
Production company

New York, NY
212-219-2020 (phone)
212-219-2323 (fax)

info@evenstarfilms.com
evenstarfilms.com
imdb.com/company/co0009776
facebook.com/evenstarfilms
twitter.com/evenstarfilms

Does not accept any unsolicited material. Project types include feature films. Genres include drama.

David Urrutia
Producer
imdb.com/name/nm0882102

Elizabeth Cuthrell
Producer
imdb.com/name/nm0193876

EVER SO CLOSE
Production company

444 Brickel Ave
Suite 51-246
Miami, FL 33131

contact@eversoclose.com
imdb.com/company/co0238825

Does not accept any unsolicited material. Genres include romance, comedy, and drama.

EVERYMAN PICTURES
Production company

Santa Monica
1512 16th St Suite 3
Santa Monica, CA 90404
310-460-7080 (phone)
310-460-7081 (fax)

imdb.com/company/co0136709

Does not accept any unsolicited material. Project types include feature films and TV. Genres include drama and comedy.

Jennifer Perini
imdb.com/name/nm0673805
Assistant: Kristopher Fogel and Lauren Downey

Jay Roach
jay.roach@fox.com
imdb.com/name/nm0005366

EVERYWHERE STUDIOS
Production company

14724 Ventura Blvd., Suite 400
Sherman Oaks, CA 91403
310-461-3060

dsuttles@everywhere-studios.com
everywhere-studios.com
imdb.com/company/co0538933
linkedin.com/company/everywhere-studios
twitter.com/EW_Studios

Does not accept any unsolicited material. Project types include feature films. Genres include family, fantasy, and drama. Established in 2014.

DAVID CALVERT-JONES
Chairman
imdb.com/name/nm1965869

DAN ANGEL
CCO
imdb.com/name/nm0029445

EVOLUTIONARY FILMS
Production company, distributor, and sales agent

3 Mills Studios
Three Mill Ln
London E3 3DU
UK
+44 (0208-215-3340

info@evolutionaryfilms.com
evolutionaryfilms.com
imdb.com/company/co0517041
facebook.com/evofilmsuk
twitter.com/EvoFilmsUK

Does not accept any unsolicited material. Project types include TV. Genres include action and drama.

John Adams
Producer
imdb.com/name/nm2095027

EVOLVING PICTURES ENTERTAINMENT
Production company

15303 Ventura Blvd., 9th Floor
Sherman Oaks, CA 91403
877-215-3646

info@evolvingpicturesentertainment.com
evolvingpicturesentertainment.com
imdb.com/company/co0047632
facebook.com/evolvingpictures

Does not accept any unsolicited material. Project types include feature films and TV. Genres include comedy, horror, and drama.

Jean-Pierre Pereat
VP
imdb.com/name/nm0673004

EXCLUSIVE FILM DISTRIBUTION
Sales agent

9100 Wilshire Blvd
Ste 401
Beverly Hills, CA 90210
310-300-9000

info@exclusivefilmdistribution.com
exclusivemedia.com
imdb.com/company/co0249132
web.facebook.com/ExclusiveMedia
twitter.com/ExclusiveEMG

Does not accept any unsolicited material. Genres include action, horror, thriller, and drama.

EXCLUSIVE MEDIA
Production company and distributor

33 St James's St,
London,
SW1A 1HD, United Kingdom
44-0203-002-9510

9100 Wilshire Blvd,
Suite 401 East,
Beverly Hills,
310-300-9000 (phone)
310-300-9001 (fax)

info@exclusivemedia.com
exclusivemedia.com
imdb.com/company/co0234935
facebook.com/ExclusiveMedia
twitter.com/ExclusiveEMG

Does not accept any unsolicited material. Project types include feature films. Genres include crime, comedy, documentary, fantasy, drama, action, thriller, horror, and romance.

Nigel Sinclair
nigelsinclair@spitfirepix.com
imdb.com/name/nm0801691
Assistant: Patricia Scott

Simon Oakes
Vice President, CEO & President of Hammer
imdb.com/name/nm0642975

Guy East
geast@exclusivemedia.com
imdb.com/name/nm0247524

Marc Schipper
CEO
imdb.com/name/nm2649227

EXECUTE ENTERTAINMENT
Production company

5731 Ibizan Court Orlando, FL 32810
954-727-5764

imdb.com/company/co0100946
twitter.com/MMJTHARSIS

Does not accept any unsolicited material. Project types include short films. Genres include drama.

EXILE ENTERTAINMENT
Production company

732 El Medio Ave.
Pacific Palisades, CA 90272
310-573-1523 (phone)
310-573-0109 (fax)

exile_ent@yahoo.com
imdb.com/company/co0063047

Accepts query letters from unproduced, unrepresented writers. Project types include feature films. Genres include horror, comedy, and drama.

Gary Ungar
imdb.com/name/nm1316083

EXODUS DISTRIBUTION
Distributor

8525 E Ruby Dr
Tucson, AZ 85730
720-800-3485

customercare@mediamakers.com
imdb.com/company/co0493066

Does not accept any unsolicited material. Genres include comedy and drama.

EXODUS FILM GROUP
Production company

1211 Electric Ave
Venice, CA 90291
310-684-3155

info@exodusfilmgroup.com
exodusfilmgroup.com
imdb.com/company/co0080906

Does not accept any unsolicited material. Project types include feature films. Genres include family, comedy, and animation.

Max Howard
Producer
max@exodusfilmgroup.com
imdb.com/name/nm0397492

EXPRESSION ENTERTAINMENT
Sales agent

Los Angeles, CA, United States

expressionent.com
imdb.com/company/co0531388

Does not accept any unsolicited material. Project types include TV. Genres include romance, drama, family, and comedy.

EYEBOOGIE
Production company

6425 Hollywood Blvd., 3rd Floor
Los Angeles, CA 90028
323-315-5750

info@eyeboogie.com
eyeboogie.com
imdb.com/company/co0146935
linkedin.com/company/eyeboogie-inc
facebook.com/Eyeboogie-103614233028042
twitter.com/eyeboogie

Does not accept any unsolicited material. Project types include TV.

Tom Herschko
Head of TV
imdb.com/name/nm1929330

Woody Thompson
Producer
imdb.com/name/nm0860853

EYE CANDY FILMS
Production company

7026 Old Katy Rd. Suite 310
Houston, TX 77024
713-802-2639

william@eyecandyinc.com
eyecandyinc.com
imdb.com/company/co0299199
facebook.com/eyecandyfilmspvtltd

Does not accept any unsolicited material. Genres include fantasy, horror, and drama.

EYE IN THE SKY PRODUCTIONS
Production company

1950 Old Cuthbert Rd
Cherry Hill, NJ 08043
323-703-3782

dboorboor@eyeintheskyentertainment.com
imdb.com/company/co0065381

Does not accept any unsolicited material. Project types include TV and feature films. Genres include thriller.

EYE ON THE BALL
Production company

PO Box 46877
Los Angeles, CA 90046
323-935-0634 (phone)
323-935-4188 (fax)

imdb.com/company/co0102936

Accepts query letters from unproduced, unrepresented writers. Project types include feature films. Genres include comedy.

Sergio Arau
Producer
keepyoureye@aol.com
imdb.com/name/nm0033190

Yareli Arizmendi
Producer
arauarizmendi@aol.com
imdb.com/name/nm0034976

FABRICATION FILMS
Production company

8701 W. Olympic Blvd.
Los Angeles, CA 90035
310-289-1232 (phone)
310-289-1292 (fax)

fabricationfilms.com
imdb.com/company/co0136539
linkedin.com/company/fabrication-films
facebook.com/Fabrication-Films-159394167453037/
    info

Does not accept any unsolicited material. Project types include feature films. Genres include drama, action, and thriller.

Kjehl Rasmussen
CEO
imdb.com/name/nm0711365

Jodie Skalla
Vice President of Acquisitions
imdb.com/name/nm2431792

FACE FILMS
Production company

Unit B
Academy Buidling
London N1 6LQ
UK

info@facefilms.com
facefilms.com
imdb.com/company/co0177771

Does not accept any unsolicited material. Project types include feature films. Genres include comedy, action, thriller, and drama.

FACE PRODUCTIONS
Production company

335 N Maple Dr, Suite 135
Beverly Hills, CA 90210
310-205-2746 (phone)
310-285-2386 (fax)

faceproductions.com.hk
imdb.com/company/co0130379
facebook.com/faceproductions
twitter.com/faceprodlv

Does not accept any unsolicited material. Project types include feature films. Genres include action, drama, and comedy.

Samantha Sprecher
imdb.com/name/nm0819616
Assistant: Kia Hellman

Billy Crystal
imdb.com/name/nm0000345
Assistant: Kia Hellman

FACETS MULTIMEDIA DISTRIBUTION
Distributor and sales agent

1517 W Fullerton Ave
Chicago, IL 60614
773-281-9075 (phone)
773-929-5437 (fax)

sales@facets.org
facets.org
imdb.com/company/co0049521
facets.org/analytics/facebook.htm

Does not accept any unsolicited material. Project types include TV. Genres include fantasy and action.

FACTORY ENTERTAINMENT GROUP
Production company

3423 N Hiatus Rd
Sunrise, FL 33351
954-638-5544 (phone)
954-903-4315 (fax)

Factoryentertainmentgroup@hotmail.com
imdb.com/company/co0383836

Does not accept any unsolicited material. Genres include horror and action.

FACTORY FILM STUDIO
Production company, distributor, and sales agent

445 Adelaide St W
Toronto, ON M5V 1T1
Canada
877-318-0535

submissions@factoryfilmstudio.com
factoryfilmstudio.com
imdb.com/company/co0314809
linkedin.com/company/factory-film-studio
facebook.com/FactoryFilmStudio
twitter.com/factory_film

Accepts query letters from unproduced, unrepresented writers via email. Project types include TV and feature films. Genres include action.

Michael Patrick Lilly
Producer
imdb.com/name/nm2583200

FADE TO BLACK PRODUCTIONS
Production company

9120 Sunset Blvd. Suite 100
Los Angeles, CA 90069
310-278-9440 (phone)
310-278-9443 (fax)

fadetoblackproductions.com
imdb.com/company/co0251339
facebook.com/Fade-to-Black-
    Productions-203803069480

Does not accept any unsolicited material. Project types include feature films. Genres include drama.

Tom Ford
Principal, Producer, Writer
imdb.com/name/nm1053530

FAKE EMPIRE
Production company

5555 Melrose Ave
Marx Brothers Building #207
Hollywood, CA 90038
323-956-8766

fakeempire.com
imdb.com/company/co0299663

facebook.com/pages/Fake-Empire/177699632283128
twitter.com/fakeempireteam

Does not accept any unsolicited material. Project types include feature films. Genres include family, thriller, romance, comedy, and drama. Established in 2010.

Jay Marcus
Creative Executive
imdb.com/name/nm1682408

Lisbeth Rowinski
President
imdb.com/name/nm2925164
Assistant: Ritu Moondra

FAKE EMPIRE TELEVISION
Production company

400 Warner Blvd
Building 138, Room 1101
Burbank, CA 91522
818-954-2420

fakeempire.com/about
facebook.com/FakeEmpire6
twitter.com/fakeempireteam

Accepts scripts from produced or represented writers. Project types include feature films and TV. Genres include family, drama, and comedy.

Josh Schwatz
imdb.com/name/nm0777300

Stephanie Savage
imdb.com/name/nm1335634

Leonard Goldstein
imdb.com/name/nm2325264
Assistant: Brittany Sever

Stephanie Savage
imdb.com/name/nm1335634
Assistant: Kendall Sand

FALCONER PICTURES
Production company

100 Wilshire Blvd. Suite 400
Santa Monica, CA 90401
310-452-3350 (phone)
310-388-5910 (fax)

falconerpictures.com
imdb.com/company/co0395531

Does not accept any unsolicited material. Project types include feature films. Genres include drama, action, thriller, comedy, and crime.

Sam Saab
Partner
imdb.com/name/nm5668114
twitter.com/samfalc

Douglas Falconer
CEO
doug@falconerpictures.com
imdb.com/name/nm0266000

FAMILY CHRISTIAN ENTERTAINMENT
Production company

5300 Patterson Ave SE
Grand Rapids, MI 49530

familychristian.com
imdb.com/company/co0516222

Does not accept any unsolicited material. Project types include feature films. Genres include drama.

Rick Jackson
Owner
imdb.com/name/nm7040528

FANDOR
Production company and distributor

522 Washington St, San Francisco, CA, United States, 94111
415-368-0330

info@fandor.com
fandor.com
imdb.com/company/co0393851

Does not accept any unsolicited material. Project types include TV, short films, and feature films. Genres include drama, action, family, documentary, thriller, comedy, and romance.

FANTASTIC FILMS INTERNATIONAL
Production company, distributor, and sales agent

3854 Clayton Ave, Los Angeles , CA, United States, 90027
323-661-7088 (phone)
323-661-7188 (fax)

info@ffimail.com
fantasticfilmsinternational.com/home
imdb.com/company/co0113360

Does not accept any unsolicited material. Project types include TV, feature films, and short films. Genres include action, family, drama, and thriller.

FARAH FILMS & MANAGEMENT
Studio

11640 Mayfield, Suite 208
Los Angeles, CA 90049
310-979-4533

submissions@farahfilms.com (script submissions)
info@farahfilms.com (general)
imdb.com/company/co0194807

Accepts query letters from unproduced, unrepresented writers via email. Project types include feature films. Genres include drama, science fiction, and action.

FARBFILM-VERLEIH
Production company

Boxhagener Str. 106
Berlin D-10245
Germany
+49 30 29 77 29 44 (phone)
+49 30 29 77 29 79 (fax)

info@farbfilm-verleih.de
farbfilm-verleih.de
imdb.com/company/co0167917
facebook.com/farbfilmverleih
twitter.com/farbfilmverleih

Does not accept any unsolicited material. Genres include comedy.

En la cama
Director
imdb.com/title/tt0474642

FAR HILLS PICTURES
Production company

552 Rose Ave, Venice, CA, United States, 90291
310-827-9100 (phone)
310-827-9101 (fax)

info@farhillspictures.com
farhillspictures.com
imdb.com/company/co0292569

Does not accept any unsolicited material. Project types include TV. Genres include family, romance, and drama.

FARMHOUSE PRODUCTIONS
Production company

235 Carlaw Ave
Suite 206
Toronto, ON M4M 2S1
Canada
647-344-4753

farmhouseproductions.ca
imdb.com/company/co0333173
facebook.com/farmhouseproductionsinc
twitter.com/farmhousegh

Does not accept any unsolicited material. Project types include TV. Genres include comedy and horror.

FARRELL/MINOFF PRODUCTIONS
Production company

14011 Ventura Blvd., Suite 401
Sherman Oaks , CA 91423
818-789-5766 (phone)
818-789-7459 (fax)

imdb.com/name/nm0268286

Does not accept any unsolicited material. Project types include TV. Genres include drama.

Mike Farrell
Producer/Director/Actor
imdb.com/name/nm0268286

Marvin Minoff
Producer
imdb.com/name/nm0591545

FARRELL PAURA PRODUCTIONS
Production company

11150 Santa Monica Blvd., Suite 450
Los Angeles, CA 90025
310-477-7776

imdb.com/company/co0134381

Does not accept any unsolicited material. Project types include TV and feature films. Genres include comedy.

Catherine Paura
Principal
imdb.com/name/nm0667474

Joseph Farrell
Principal
imdb.com/name/nm1289705

FASTBACK PICTURES
Production company and distributor

323-469-5719

info@fastbackpictures.com
fastbackpictures.com
imdb.com/company/co0151624

Does not accept any unsolicited material. Project types include short films and feature films. Genres include drama, comedy, thriller, and documentary.

Pascal Franchot
Producer
323-717-5569
pascal@fastbackpictures.com
imdb.com/name/nm0289994

FASTLANE ENTERTAINMENT
Production company

1316 Third St Promenade, Suite 109
Santa Monica, CA 90401
310-857-6868 (phone)
310-388-5830 (fax)

nfo@fastlaneent.com
fastlaneent.com
imdb.com/company/co0173838

Does not accept any unsolicited material. Project types include feature films.

Frank Miniaci
Founder/CEO
imdb.com/name/nm2131455

FASTNET FILMS
Production company

20 Herbert Place
Dublin 2, Ireland
+353 1 639 4000 (phone)
+353 1 657 6678 (fax)

enquiries@fastnetfilms.com
fastnetfilms.com
imdb.com/company/co0010293
twitter.com/FastnetFilms

Does not accept any unsolicited material. Project types include feature films. Genres include reality, drama, and documentary.

Aoife McGonigal
imdb.com/name/nm3502464

Ian Jackson
Head of Development
imdb.com/name/nm4127212

Megan Everett
Head of Development
imdb.com/name/nm3210746

FEAR FILM
Production company

2450 Hollywood Blvd.
Suite 201
Hollywood, FL 33020
954-839-0585 (phone)
954-484-5520 (fax)

contact@fearfilm.com
fearfilm.com
imdb.com/company/co0085511

Does not accept any unsolicited material.

FEARLESS FILMS
Production company

422 Adelaide St West
Toronto, ON M5V 1S7
Canada
416-504-9694

info@fearlessfilms.com
fearless.ca

imdb.com/company/co0145302

Does not accept any unsolicited material. Project types include TV. Genres include comedy and drama.

FEBRUARY FILMS
Production company

Studio 108, 72 Great Titchfield St
London W1W 7QW
UK

films@februaryfilms.com
februaryfilms.com
imdb.com/company/co0048978

Does not accept any unsolicited material. Project types include feature films and TV. Genres include drama and thriller.

Abner Pastoll
Producer
imdb.com/name/nm0665016

FEDERGREEN ENTERTAINMENT
Production company

194 Glemholme Ave
Toronto, ON Canda M6E 3C4
416-898-3456 (phone)
416-658-9913 (fax)

info@federgreenentertainment.com
federgreenentertainment.com
imdb.com/company/co0290587

Does not accept any unsolicited material. Project types include short films, TV, and feature films. Genres include thriller and science fiction.

Avi Federgreen
Producer
imdb.com/name/nm0270098

FEDORA ENTERTAINMENT
Production company

11846 Ventura Blvd
Suite 140
Studio City, CA 91604
818-508-5310

imdb.com/company/co0287780

linkedin.com/company/fedora-entertainment
facebook.com/pages/Fedora-Entertainment/
    1419843928261420

Does not accept any unsolicited material. Project types include TV. Genres include drama and comedy.

Michael Wimer
Producer
imdb.com/name/nm1057590

Marla A. White
imdb.com/name/nm0925187
linkedin.com/in/marlawhite

Peter Tolan
Producer
imdb.com/name/nm0865847

FEMMEWERKS PRODUCTIONS
Production company

3523 McKinney Ave.
#732
Dallas, TX 75204

femmewerks@yahoo.com
imdb.com/company/co0297867

Does not accept any unsolicited material. Genres include action, horror, and science fiction.

FEVERPITCH PICTURES
Production company

1810 Markley St
Norristown, PA 19401
928-563-1915 (phone)
928-484-9028 (fax)

info@feverpitchpictures.com
feverpitchpictures.com
imdb.com/company/co0206272
linkedin.com/company/feverpitch-pictures
facebook.com/feverpitch

Does not accept any unsolicited material. Project types include feature films. Genres include action, drama, comedy, and horror.

Jeffrey D. Erb
Partner
imdb.com/name/nm2075994

FG ENTERTAINMENT

Production company, distributor, and financing company

1217 N Miller Rd
Suite 2
Scottsdale, AZ 85257

imdb.com/company/co0355326

Does not accept any unsolicited material. Project types include TV and short films. Genres include comedy.

Casey Fingerhut
Director
imdb.com/name/nm3731960
facebook.com/boatangel

FIDDLER FILMS, INC.

Production company

1111 5th Ave S
Naples, FL 34102
239-435-1818

lou@fiddlerfilms.com
fiddlerproductions.com
imdb.com/company/co0067856
linkedin.com/company/fiddler-films
facebook.com/fiddlerfilms
twitter.com/FiddlerFilms

Does not accept any unsolicited material. Project types include feature films and short films. Genres include fantasy, romance, and drama. Established in 1999.

FIERCE ENTERTAINMENT

Production company

7656 Sunset Blvd.
Los Angeles, CA 90046
310-860-1174 (phone)
310-860-9446 (fax)

fierceentertainment.com
imdb.com/company/co0095383
facebook.com/FierceEntertainmentManagement

Does not accept any unsolicited material. Project types include TV and feature films.

Christopher Petzel
Founder/CEO
imdb.com/name/nm0678850

FIFTY FATHOMS PRODUCTIONS

Production company

4th Floor Shepherd's Building Central
Charecroft Way
London W14 0EE
UK
+44208-222-4601

adamlebovits@fiftyfathomsproductions.com
tigeraspect.co.uk/fifty-fathoms
imdb.com/company/co0468322

Does not accept any unsolicited material. Project types include TV. Genres include drama and horror.

FIGA FILMS

Production company, distributor, and sales agent

1249 Hyperion Ave., Los Angeles, CA, United States, 90029
323-258-5241 (phone)
323-229-9816 (fax)

contact@figafilms.com
figafilms.com
imdb.com/company/co0203302

Does not accept any unsolicited material. Project types include TV. Genres include family, romance, and drama.

FILAMENT PRODUCTIONS

Production company

1000 Dean St, Suite 303
Brooklyn, NY 11238

office@filamentprods.com
filamentprods.com
imdb.com/company/co0363211
facebook.com/profile.php
twitter.com/FilamentProds

Does not accept any unsolicited material. Project types include feature films. Genres include drama.

Adam Spielberg
Producer
imdb.com/name/nm1437616

FILM

Production company

1-19-1
Koyanagi
Fuchu, Tokyo 183-0013
Japan

recruit@film.co.jp
film.co.jp
imdb.com/company/co0246645

Does not accept any unsolicited material. Project types
include TV. Genres include drama and animation.

Shin'ya Koto
Producer
imdb.com/name/nm4631415

FILM 360
Production company

9111 Wilshire Blvd
Beverly Hills, CA 90210
310-272-7000

imdb.com/company/co0192833

Does not accept any unsolicited material. Project types
include feature films. Genres include comedy, drama,
action, period, crime, science fiction, family, fantasy,
and thriller. Established in 2009.

Daniel Rappaport
Producer
imdb.com/name/nm0710883

Eric Kranzler
Producer
imdb.com/name/nm1023394

Scott Lambert
Producer
imdb.com/name/nm0483300

FILM 44
Production company and distributor

1526 Cloverfield Blvd
Santa Monica, CA 90404
310-586-4940

info@film44.com
imdb.com/company/co0152188

Does not accept any unsolicited material. Project types
include feature films and TV. Genres include thriller,
action, drama, myth, science fiction, and fantasy.

Braden Aftergood
imdb.com/name/nm2302240

Rebecca Hobbs
imdb.com/name/nm1778008

Peter Berg
Partner
imdb.com/name/nm0000916

FILM AND MUSIC ENTERTAINMENT (F&ME)
Production company

14 Newburgh St
2nd Floor
London W1F 7RT
UK
+44 (0203-713-0028 (phone)
+44 (0207-691-9712 (fax)

office@fame.uk.com
fame.uk.com
imdb.com/company/co0024285

Does not accept any unsolicited material. Project types
include commercials. Genres include comedy and
drama.

Mike Downey
Producer
imdb.com/name/nm0236026

FILM BRIDGE INTERNATIONAL
Production company and distributor

1316 Third St Promenade, Suite 105, Santa Monica,
CA, United States, 90401
310-656-8680 (phone)
310-656-8683 (fax)

contact@filmbridgeinternational.com
filmbridgeinternational.com
imdb.com/company/co0040970

Does not accept any unsolicited material. Project types
include TV. Genres include family and drama.

FILMCOLONY

Production company

4751 Wilshire Blvd Third Floor
Los Angeles, CA 90010
323-549-4343 (phone)
323-549-9824 (fax)

info@filmcolony.com
filmcolony.com
imdb.com/company/co0159642
linkedin.com/company/filmcolony
twitter.com/filmcolony

Does not accept any unsolicited material. Project types include feature films and TV. Genres include crime, thriller, fantasy, romance, comedy, family, and drama. Established in 1995.

Anand Shah
imdb.com/name/nm4337795

Richard Gladstein
President
imdb.com/name/nm0321621
twitter.com/filmcolony

Melanie Donkers
Director of Development
imdb.com/name/nm1410650

FILMDISTRICT

Production company and distributor

1540 2nd St
Suite 200
Santa Monica, CA 90401
310-315-1722 (phone)
310-315-1723 (fax)

contact@filmdistrict.com
filmdistrict.com
imdb.com/company/co0314851
facebook.com/FDFilms
twitter.com/FilmDistrict

Does not accept any unsolicited material. Project types include feature films. Genres include fantasy, crime, drama, thriller, action, romance, and horror. Established in 2010.

Josie Liang
imdb.com/name/nm4169347

Josh Peters
imdb.com/name/nm5444016

Peter Schlessel
Founder
imdb.com/name/nm0772283
Assistant: Jessica Freenborn

Graham King
Partner
imdb.com/name/nm0454752

Tim Headington
Partner
imdb.com/name/nm2593874

Lia Buman
imdb.com/name/nm2513975
Assistant: Patrick Reese

FILMED IMAGINATION

Production company

8017 Hemet Place
Los Angeles, CA 90046
323-963-4880

info@filmedimagination.com
filmedimagination.com
imdb.com/company/co0229508
linkedin.com/company/filmed-imagination
linkedin.com/company/filmed-imagination
twitter.com/flmdimagination

Does not accept any unsolicited material. Project types include commercials, feature films, and TV. Genres include fantasy.

Daniel Dreifuss
Producer
imdb.com/name/nm1897448

Marius Haugan
Producer
imdb.com/name/nm2235104

FILMENGINE

Production company and financing company

345 Maple Dr, Suite 222, Beverly Hills, CA, United States, 90210
424-288-4448 (phone)
424-288-4588 (fax)

reception@filmenginela.com
filmenginela.com
imdb.com/company/co0063593

Does not accept any unsolicited material. Project types include TV and feature films. Genres include thriller, family, action, and drama.

FILM EXCHANGE
Production company

One O'Connor Plaza
Suite 930
Victoria, TX 77901
361-935-8843

anthony@filmexchange.org
filmexchange.org
imdb.com/company/co0491589

Does not accept any unsolicited material. Genres include drama and comedy.

FILM FINANCES, INC.
Production company and financing company

Heinrich-Pesch-Strasse 7
Koeln/Cologne Germany 50739

Floragatan 4a
Stockholm Sweden 114 31
011-460-87621759

250 The Esplanade Suite 204
Toronto ON Canada M5A 1J2
416-778-6397 (phone)
416-406-7418 (fax)

15 Conduit St
London United Kingdom W1S 2XJ
011-442-076296557 (phone)
011-442-074917530 (fax)

2-14-10 Higashi-Nakano
Nakano-Ku 13 Japan 164-0003
011-810-353325256 (phone)
011-810-353325257 (fax)

205/122 Lang Rd
Moore Park NSW Australia 2021
011-612-83532600 (phone)
011-612-83532601 (fax)

129 Mulberry Ln Leslie Ave
Magalissig GT South Africa 2191
011-270-824114088

9000 Sunset Blvd, Suite 1400, Los Angeles, CA, United States, 90069
310-275-7323 (phone)
310-275-1706 (fax)

ffi.com

Does not accept any unsolicited material. Project types include feature films and TV. Genres include family, drama, action, and thriller.

FILM FINANCIAL SERVICES
Financing company

Los Angeles, CA, United States
310-916-9569

info@filmfinancialservices.com
imdb.com/company/co0201840

Does not accept any unsolicited material.

David Sheldon
Executive
310-916-9569
imdb.com/name/nm0791007

FILM GARDEN ENTERTAINMENT
Production company and distributor

22287 Mulholland Hwy. #206
Calabasas, CA 91302
818-783-3456 (phone)
818-752-8186 (fax)

filmgarden.tv
imdb.com/company/co0011492
linkedin.com/company/film-garden-entertainment
facebook.com/pages/Film-Garden-Entertainment/
   202254163142169

Does not accept any unsolicited material. Project types include TV. Genres include period, non-fiction, and reality. Established in 1994.

FILM HARVEST
Production company

750 Lillian Way, Suite 6
LA, CA 90038
310-926-4131 (phone)
323-481-8499 (fax)

info@filmharvest.com
filmharvest.com
imdb.com/company/co0251161

Does not accept any unsolicited material. Project types include feature films. Genres include horror, action, science fiction, documentary, thriller, drama, and non-fiction. Established in 2009.

Eben Kostbar
Producer
eben@filmharvest.com
imdb.com/name/nm1670295

Joseph McKelheer
Executive Producer
joe@filmharvest.com
imdb.com/name/nm1559624

Elana Kostbar
info@filmharvest.com
imdb.com/name/nm3657939

FILM HOUSE GERMANY
Production company and financing company

Wallstraße 15a
Berlin 10179
Germany
+49 30 24 65 65 0 (phone)
+49 30 24 65 65 24 (fax)

info@filmhousegermany.com
filmhousegermany.de
imdb.com/company/co0351198

Does not accept any unsolicited material. Project types include feature films. Genres include thriller.

Marc Hansell
Producer
imdb.com/name/nm3701555

FILM IT PRODUCTIONS
Production company and distributor

2020 16th Ave
Denver, CO 80206
720-620-0536

filmitproductions7@gmail.com
film-itproductions.com
imdb.com/company/co0165162

Does not accept any unsolicited material. Project types include feature films. Genres include drama.

Darla Rae
CEO (Executive)
imdb.com/name/nm2031440

FILMMAKERS
Production company

3 2 6
Minami Aoyama
Minato, Tokyo 107 0062
Japan
03 5474 3970 (phone)
03 5474 3967 (fax)

film-makers@nifty.com
imdb.com/company/co0244671

Does not accept any unsolicited material. Project types include feature films. Genres include drama.

FILMMATES ENTERTAINMENT
Production company, distributor, and sales agent

P.O. Box 67503, Los Angeles , CA, United States, 90067
760-564-3133 (phone)
310-551-3355 (fax)

info@filmmates.net
filmmates.net
imdb.com/company/co0121235

Does not accept any unsolicited material. Project types include TV. Genres include family, drama, romance, and comedy.

FILM MOVEMENT
Distributor

109 W 27th St, Suite 9B, New York City , NY, United States, 10001

212-941-7744 (phone)
212-941-7812 (fax)

info@filmmovement.com
imdb.com/company/co0087326

Does not accept any unsolicited material. Project types include TV and feature films. Genres include romance, thriller, action, family, and drama.

FILMNATION ENTERTAINMENT

345 N Maple Dr, Suite 202
Beverly Hills, CA 90210
310-859-0088 (phone)
310-859-0089 (fax)

150 W 22nd St.
9th Floor
New York, NY 10011
917-484-8900 (phone)
917-484-8901 (fax)

wearefilmnation.com
imdb.com/company/co0251858
linkedin.com/company/filmnation-entertainment-llc
facebook.com/filmnation
twitter.com/filmnation

Accepts query letters from unproduced, unrepresented writers. Project types include feature films. Genres include fantasy, action, thriller, horror, crime, and drama. Established in 2008.

Glen Basner
gbasner@wearefilmnation.com
imdb.com/name/nm0059984

Patrick Chu
Director of Development
pchu@wearefilmnation.com
imdb.com/name/nm1776958

FILMOUT RELEASING
Distributor

2633 Mckinney Ave
#130-151
Dallas, TX 75204

barak@filmoutreleasing.com
imdb.com/company/co0163143

Does not accept any unsolicited material. Genres include comedy, horror, and action.

FILM PHARM INC.
Production company and distributor

Denver, CO 80210
818-314-0452

info@filmpharm.com
filmpharm.com
imdb.com/company/co0153978

Does not accept any unsolicited material. Project types include feature films. Genres include documentary.

FILM REPUBLIC
Sales agent

91 Great Russell St
London WC1B 3PS
UK
+44(0) 7835 999 112

info@filmrepublic.biz
filmrepublic.biz
imdb.com/company/co0199136
linkedin.com/company/film-republic-international-sales
facebook.com/filmrepublicinternationalsales
twitter.com/filmrepublic

Does not accept any unsolicited material. Project types include feature films. Genres include drama.

Xavier Rashid
Producer
imdb.com/name/nm5579306

FILMS BOUTIQUE
Sales agent

+49 30 695 378 50 (phone)
+49 30 695 378 51 (fax)

info@filmsboutique.com
filmsboutique.com
imdb.com/company/co0237531

Does not accept any unsolicited material. Project types include short films. Genres include drama.

Jean-Christophe Simon
Executive
imdb.com/name/nm0800192

FILM SCIENCE
Production company

201 Lavaca St Suite 502
Austin, TX 78701
917-501-5197

info@filmscience.com
filmscience.com
imdb.com/company/co0160719

Accepts query letters from unproduced, unrepresented writers. Project types include feature films. Genres include family, comedy, and drama.

Anish Savjani
Executive
anish@filmscience.com
imdb.com/name/nm1507013

FILMS GUERNSEY LTD
Production company and financing company

c/o American Film Services, 9126 Cordell Dr, Los Angeles , CA, United States, 90069

gjorge@financefilm.com
imdb.com/company/co0001173

Does not accept any unsolicited material. Project types include feature films. Genres include action and thriller.

FILMSIGNAL
Production company

1360 Ashland Ave.
Santa Monica, CA 90405
310-452-1152 (phone)
310-227-8241 (fax)

info@filmsignal.com
filmsignal.com
imdb.com/company/co0319945

Does not accept any unsolicited material. Project types include short films and TV. Genres include comedy and documentary.

Sharon Everitt
Director
sharonpolito@mac.com
imdb.com/name/nm1410798

FILMS MEDIA GROUP
Distributor

PO Box 2053
Princeton, NJ 08543
800-257-5126 (phone)
609-275-3767 (fax)

132 W 31st St, 17th Floor
New York, NY 10001
800-322-8755 (phone)
800-678-3633 (fax)

custserv@filmsmediagroup.com
films.com
imdb.com/company/co0173349

Does not accept any unsolicited material. Project types include TV and feature films. Genres include documentary.

FILMSMITH PRODUCTIONS
Production company

3400 Airport Dr
Bldg D
Santa Monica, CA 90405
310-260-8866 (phone)
310-397-7155 (fax)

filmsmith@mac.com
imdb.com/company/co0017423

Accepts query letters from unproduced, unrepresented writers. Project types include feature films and TV. Genres include drama, thriller, crime, and comedy.

FINE FILMS
Production company and distributor

2-5-1 5F Atago
Minatoku, Tokyo 105-6205
Japan
+81 3 6809 1855

fukuda@finefilms.co.jp
finefilms.co.jp

imdb.com/company/co0130307
facebook.com/finefilms.inc
twitter.com/finefilms_inc

Does not accept any unsolicited material. Project types include TV, short films, and feature films. Genres include action.

Yoshihisa Kato
President (Executive)
imdb.com/name/nm2497665

FIPPY & THUMP INTERNATIONAL PRODUCTIONS
Production company

215 W. 88th St, Suite 3C
New York, NY 10024
212-873-9841 (phone)
212-787-6875 (fax)

curkau@msn.com
geocities.ws/gitawei

Does not accept any unsolicited material. Project types include feature films. Genres include drama. Established in 2014.

FIRESIDE FILMS
Production company

3322 Shorecrest
Dallas, TX 75235
214-350-9323 (phone)
214-905-9069 (fax)

akillerwithin@yahoo.com
imdb.com/company/co0115013
facebook.com/FireSideFilms

Does not accept any unsolicited material. Genres include drama.

FIRESIDE RELEASING
Distributor

100 Congress Ave
Ste 210
Austin, TX 78701
512-499-8176 (phone)
512-263-5929 (fax)

info@firesidereleasing.com

firesidereleasing.com
imdb.com/company/co0203788

Does not accept any unsolicited material. Genres include drama, thriller, and documentary.

FIRST EARTH ENTERTAINMENT
Production company and sales agent

7625 Dean Martin Dr
Ste 105
Las Vegas, NV 89139
818-275-1292 (phone)
866-950-2675 (fax)

info@firstearthentertainment.com
imdb.com/company/co0261414

Does not accept any unsolicited material. Project types include TV. Genres include action and comedy.

Michela Angelini
Producer
imdb.com/name/nm3240331

FIRST GENERATION FILMS
Production company and financing company

98 Ave Rd
Ste 201
Toronto, ON M5R 2H3
Canada
416-901-4545 (phone)
416-901-6547 (fax)

fg-films.com
imdb.com/company/co0011291

Does not accept any unsolicited material. Project types include TV. Genres include thriller.

FIRST INDEPENDENT PICTURES
Production company and distributor

2999 Overland Ave, Suite 218, Los Angeles , CA, United States, 90064
310-838-6555 (phone)
310-838-9972 (fax)

firstindependentpictures.com
imdb.com/company/co0260976

Does not accept any unsolicited material. Project types include TV. Genres include drama, family, and thriller.

Angel An
Director of Development
310-860-3173
imdb.com/name/nm2998042

FIRST RUN FEATURES
Production company and distributor

The Film Center Building, 630 Ninth Ave, Suite 1213
New York City, NY 10036
212-243-0600 (phone)
212-989-7649 (fax)

info@firstrunfeatures.com
firstrunfeatures.com
imdb.com/company/co0002318
facebook.com/firstrunfeatures
twitter.com/firstrun

Does not accept any unsolicited material. Project types include short films and feature films. Genres include thriller, romance, fantasy, drama, and comedy. Established in 1979.

Marc Mauceri
imdb.com/name/nm1439609

Seymour Wishman
President
imdb.com/name/nm0936544

FIRST STREET FILMS
Production company

1514 17th St
Ste 201
Santa Monica, CA 90404
310-260-8881

imdb.com/company/co0003297
linkedin.com/company/first-street-films

Does not accept any unsolicited material. Project types include TV. Genres include comedy, thriller, family, drama, and non-fiction. Established in 1998.

FIRST TAKE MEDIA
Production company

319 Sterling Browning Rd
San Antonio, TX 78232
210-523-8824

firsttakemedia.co.uk
imdb.com/company/co0395223
facebook.com/firsttakefilms

Does not accept any unsolicited material. Genres include documentary.

FIVE BY EIGHT PRODUCTIONS
Production company

4312 Clarissa Ave
Los Angeles, CA 90027
917-658-7545

sean@fivebyeight.com
fivebyeight.com
imdb.com/company/co0173956

Does not accept any unsolicited material. Project types include feature films, TV, and short films. Genres include thriller, drama, romance, and comedy. Established in 2006.

Michael Connors
mike@fivebyeight.com
imdb.com/name/nm2155421

Sean Mullen
sean@fivebyeight.com
imdb.com/name/nm2013693

FIVE SMOOTH STONE PRODUCTIONS
Production company

106 Oakland Hills Court
Duluth, GA 30097
770-476-7171

imdb.com/company/co0332052

Does not accept any unsolicited material. Project types include feature films. Genres include non-fiction, action, and drama.

Rick Middlemas
Partner
linkedin.com/in/rickmiddlemass

FIVE STAR WORLDWIDE PRODUCTIONS

Production company

40B East 17th St
Bayonne, NJ 07002
856-625-6583

csampson568@yahoo.com
imdb.com/company/co0227150

Does not accept any unsolicited material. Project types include feature films and TV. Genres include drama, action, and crime.

FLASHBACK FILMS

Production company

303 Balch Rd.
Elgin, TX 78621
512-297-5958

jake.helgren@gmail.com
imdb.com/company/co0392787

Does not accept any unsolicited material. Genres include romance and horror.

FLASHPOINT ENTERTAINMENT

Production company

1318 San Ysidro Dr
Beverly Hills, CA 90210
310-205-6300

info@flashpointentertainment.com
imdb.com/company/co0177280

Does not accept any unsolicited material. Project types include feature films. Genres include romance and drama.

Tom Johnson
310-205-6300
imdb.com/name/nm1927361

Andrew Tennenbaum
imdb.com/name/nm0990025

Laura Roman-Rockhold
310-205-6300
info@flashpointent.com
imdb.com/name/nm4099178

FLAT BLACK FILMS

Production company and distributor

4204 Ave H
Austin, TX 78751
512-374-0951

info@flatblackfilms.com
flatblackfilms.com
imdb.com/company/co0054189

Does not accept any unsolicited material. Project types include short films and feature films. Genres include fantasy, comedy, drama, documentary, and animation. Established in 1999.

FLATIRON PICTURES

Production company

Austin Studios
1901 E 51st St, Suite 207
Austin, TX 78723
917-971-8072

FlatironPictures@aol.com
imdb.com/company/co0233773
facebook.com/Flatiron-Pictures-135652183267559

Does not accept any unsolicited material. Project types include feature films. Genres include horror, action, comedy, crime, and drama. Established in 2009.

FLAVOR UNIT ENTERTAINMENT

Production company

119 Washington Ave, Suite 400
Miami Beach, FL 33139
201-333-4883 (phone)
973-556-1770 (fax)

155 Morgan St.
Jersey City, NJ 07302

info@flavorunitentertainment.com
imdb.com/company/co0050873

Accepts query letters from unproduced, unrepresented writers via email. Project types include feature films and TV. Genres include romance, drama, family, and comedy.

Shakim Compere
CEO
201-333-4883
imdb.com/name/nm1406277
Assistant: Mark Jean

Otis Best
201-333-4883
imdb.com/name/nm1454006

Queen Latifah
CEO
201-333-4883
imdb.com/name/nm0001451

FLIPTHISTRUMPCARD PRODUCTIONS
Production company

53 Pate Dr
Middletown, NJ 07748
732-856-9014

contact@flipthistrumpcard.com
imdb.com/company/co0384848

Does not accept any unsolicited material. Project types include TV. Genres include action and drama.

FLOREN SHIEH PRODUCTIONS
Production company

20 W 22nd St
Ste 415
New York, NY 10010
212-898-0890

katherine@florenshieh.com
imdb.com/company/co0287709

Accepts query letters from unproduced, unrepresented writers. Project types include feature films. Genres include drama.

Aimee Shieh
Producer
imdb.com/name/nm1848263

Clay Floren
Producer
imdb.com/name/nm2850202

Sean Woodruff
Story Editor
linkedin.com/in/seanswoodruff

FLOWER FILMS INC.
Production company

7119 W. Sunset Blvd
#1123
West Hollywood, CA 90046
323-876-7400

imdb.com/company/co0148520
linkedin.com/company/flower-films
facebook.com/pages/Flower-Films/104073512961756

Does not accept any unsolicited material. Project types include feature films and TV. Genres include family, drama, romance, comedy, thriller, and fantasy. Established in 1995.

Drew Barrymore
Partner
imdb.com/name/nm0000106

Ember Truesdell
ember@flowerfilms.com
imdb.com/name/nm1456092

Chris Miller
imdb.com/name/nm0588091
Assistant: Steven Acosta

FLOYD COUNTY PRODUCTIONS
Production company

1123 Zonolite Rd NE
24
Atlanta, GA 30306
404-343-6434

imdb.com/company/co0284276
linkedin.com/company/floyd-county-productions

Does not accept any unsolicited material. Project types include TV. Genres include animation and comedy.

FLYING MAN PICTURES
Production company and distributor

407-521-7371 (phone)
407-295-5730 (fax)

imdb.com/company/co0118725

Does not accept any unsolicited material. Project types include short films. Genres include comedy.

F/N ENTERTAINMENT
Production company

2320 Gracy Farms Ln
123
Austin, TX 78758
512-656-6709

fnentertainment.net
imdb.com/company/co0507173
linkedin.com/company/fn-entertainment-llc

Does not accept any unsolicited material. Genres include action, comedy, and horror.

FOCUS FEATURES
Production company and distributor

100 Universal City Plaza Building 9128
Universal City, CA 91608
818-777-7373

press@filminfocus.com
focusfeatures.com
imdb.com/company/co0042399
facebook.com/FocusFeatures
twitter.com/focusfeatures

Does not accept any unsolicited material. Project types include feature films and TV. Genres include non-fiction, drama, romance, thriller, documentary, fantasy, horror, crime, action, comedy, and animation. Established in 1975.

Andrew Karpen
imdb.com/name/nm2537917

James Schamus
imdb.com/name/nm0770005

Christopher Koop
imdb.com/name/nm3096137

Josh McLaughlin
imdb.com/name/nm2249958

Jeb Brody
imdb.com/name/nm1330162
Assistant: Rebecca Arzoian

Peter Kujawski
imdb.com/name/nm1081654

FOCUS FILMS
Production company and distributor

London
UK
+44207-435-9004 (phone)
+44207-431-3562 (fax)

focus@focusfilms.co.uk
focusfilms.co.uk
imdb.com/company/co0137973

Does not accept any unsolicited material. Project types include feature films. Genres include crime and drama.

Malcolm Kohll
Producer
imdb.com/name/nm0463325

FOGGY NOTIONS UNLIMITED
Production company

713 Downing Dr
Richardson, TX 75080
972-948-4946 (phone)
972-783-1966 (fax)

info@foggynotion.biz
foggynotions.biz
imdb.com/company/co0218912

Does not accept any unsolicited material. Project types include short films. Genres include horror and drama.

FOLLOWME PRODUCTIONS
Production company

Atlanta, GA
909-764-8556 (phone)
404-935-0605 (fax)

imdb.com/company/co0314417

Does not accept any unsolicited material. Genres include science fiction, drama, action, and family.

FONTANA DISTRIBUTION
Distributor

111 Universal Hollywood Dr.
Suite 500
Universal City, CA 91608

imdb.com/company/co0186297
linkedin.com/company/fontana-distribution

Does not accept any unsolicited material. Genres include documentary.

FOOTNOTES FILMS
Production company

2866
Keele St
Toronto, ON M3M2G8
Canada

imdb.com/company/co0499478

Does not accept any unsolicited material. Project types include feature films and TV. Genres include comedy, drama, and action.

FOOTPRINT FEATURES
Production company

424-259-3002

adam@footprintfeatures.com
imdb.com/company/co0291634

Does not accept any unsolicited material.

Adam Saunders
Producer
imdb.com/name/nm0766719

FORCE OF NATURE FILMS
Production company

4628 Canyon Trail S #705
Euless, TX 76040
817-510-3741

imdb.com/company/co0483796

Does not accept any unsolicited material. Genres include horror and thriller.

FORENSIC FILMS
Production company

1 Worth St, 2nd Floor
New York, NY 10013
212-966-1110 (phone)
212-966-1125 (fax)

forensicfilms@gmail.com
imdb.com/company/co0024292
twitter.com/forensicfilms

Accepts query letters from unproduced, unrepresented writers via email. Project types include feature films. Genres include comedy, romance, drama, crime, and thriller.

Scott Macauley
Producer
imdb.com/name/nm0531337
linkedin.com/in/scottmacaulay

Robin O'Hara
Producer
imdb.com/name/nm0641327

FORESIGHT UNLIMITED
Production company and distributor

2934 1/2 Beverly Glen Circle
Suite 900
Bel Air, CA 90077
310-275-5222 (phone)
310-275-5202 (fax)

info@foresight-unltd.com
foresight-unltd.com
imdb.com/company/co0139768
facebook.com/foresightunlimited

Accepts query letters from unproduced, unrepresented writers via email. Project types include feature films. Genres include science fiction, crime, comedy, drama, action, romance, and thriller.

Tamara Birkemoe
imdb.com/name/nm1736077

Mark Damon
CEO
imdb.com/name/nm0198941

FOREST PARK PICTURES
Production company

11210 Briarcliff Ln
Studio City, CA 91604-4277
323-654-2735 (phone)
323-654-2735 (fax)

imdb.com/company/co0042178

Accepts query letters from unproduced, unrepresented writers. Project types include feature films. Genres include thriller, horror, and drama. Established in 2002.

Tove Christensen
Partner
323-848-2942 ext. 265
imdb.com/name/nm0159922

Hayden Christensen
Partner
323-848-2942 ext. 265
imdb.com/name/nm0159789

FORGET ME NOT PRODUCTIONS
Production company

New York

info@4getmenotproductions.com
4getmenotproductions.com
imdb.com/company/co0290453
linkedin.com/company/forget-me-not-productions
facebook.com/ForgetMeNotProductions

Accepts query letters from unproduced, unrepresented writers via email. Project types include feature films. Genres include drama.

Harry Azano
Producer
harryazano@gmail.com

Jennifer Gargano
jennifergargano@4getmenotproductions.com
imdb.com/name/nm2470854

FORMOSA FILMS
Production company

Communication House
26 York St
London W1U 6PZ
UK
+44 20 7993 6241

office@formosafilms.com
formosafilms.com
imdb.com/company/co0188187

Does not accept any unsolicited material. Project types include TV. Genres include thriller.

Neil Thompson
Producer
imdb.com/name/nm1578200

FORTIS FILMS
Production company

8581 Santa Monica Blvd, Suite 1
West Hollywood, CA 90069
310-659-4533 (phone)
310-659-4373 (fax)

imdb.com/company/co0015475
linkedin.com/company/fortis-films

Accepts query letters from unproduced, unrepresented writers. Project types include TV and feature films. Genres include comedy, drama, and romance.

Sandra Bullock
Partner
310-659-4533
imdb.com/name/nm0000113

Maggie Biggar
Partner
310-659-4533
imdb.com/name/nm0081772

FORTISSIMO FILMS
Production company, distributor, and sales agent

14/F, Harbour Commercial Building 122-124
Connaught Rd Central
Hong Kong China
011-852-23118081 (phone)
011-852-23118023 (fax)

525 Broadway Suite 601
New York City NY 10012
646-593-0250 (phone)
208-730-6956 (fax)

15 Thanet St
London United Kingdom WC1H 9QL
011-442-074986978

Van Diemenstraat 100, Amsterdam , Netherlands,
1013 CN
011-312-06273215 (phone)
011-312-06261155 (fax)

info@fortissimo.nl
fortissimofilms.com
imdb.com/company/co0071294

Does not accept any unsolicited material. Project types
include TV and feature films. Genres include comedy,
drama, family, thriller, and romance.

FORTITUDE INTERNATIONAL
Production company, distributor, and sales agent

8730 Wilshire Blvd, Suite 350, Beverly Hills, CA,
United States, 90211
424-284-1330

info@fortitudeint.com
fortitudeint.com
imdb.com/company/co0465798

Does not accept any unsolicited material. Project types
include TV and feature films. Genres include family,
thriller, drama, and action.

FORTRESS FEATURES
Production company

2727 Main St
Santa Monica, CA 90405
323-467-4700

fortressfeatures.com
imdb.com/company/co0194394
facebook.com/FortressMovies
twitter.com/fortressmovies

Does not accept any unsolicited material. Project types
include feature films. Genres include drama, horror,
thriller, action, crime, and comedy. Established in
2004.

Bonnie Forbes
imdb.com/name/nm1424832

Patrick Rizzotti
Partner
imdb.com/name/nm0729948

Brett Forbes
Partner
imdb.com/name/nm1771405

FORTUNE FILMS
Production company and distributor

Spectrum Studios
2 Manor Gardens
London N7 6ER
UK
+44203-714-7540

info@fortune-films.com
fortune-films.com
imdb.com/company/co0174260

Does not accept any unsolicited material. Project types
include short films. Genres include comedy, drama,
and action.

Tiernan Hanby
Producer
imdb.com/name/nm2034149

FORWARD ENTERTAINMENT
Distributor and sales agent

9255 Sunset Blvd, Suite 805
West Hollywood, CA 90069
310-278-6700 (phone)
310-278-6770 (fax)

forward-entertainment.com
imdb.com/company/co0151385

Accepts query letters from unproduced, unrepresented
writers via email. Project types include TV and feature
films. Genres include documentary and non-fiction.

Vera Mihailovich
Partner
vmihailovich@forward-ent.com
imdb.com/name/nm2250568

Connie Tavel
Partner
ctavel@forward-ent.com
imdb.com/name/nm0851679

FORWARD PASS
Production company

12233 W Olympic Blvd
Ste 340
Los Angeles, CA 90064
310-207-7378 (phone)
310-207-3426 (fax)

imdb.com/company/co0035930
linkedin.com/company/forward-pass-inc

Does not accept any unsolicited material. Project types include feature films. Genres include sociocultural, thriller, non-fiction, drama, detective, crime, and period.

Michael Mann
imdb.com/name/nm0000520

FOURBOYS FILMS
Production company

4000 Warner Blvd
Burbank, CA 91522
818-954-4378 (phone)
818-954-5359 (fax)

info@fourboysfilms.com
fourboysfilms.com
imdb.com/company/co0106524
twitter.com/FourBoysEnt

Does not accept any unsolicited material. Project types include TV and feature films. Genres include drama, comedy, and animation. Established in 2001.

David Hunt
Partner
imdb.com/name/nm0402408
linkedin.com/pub/david-hunt/24/888/742

Patricia Heaton
Partner
imdb.com/name/nm0005004

A.J. Morewitz
President
818-954-4378
imdb.com/name/nm1031450

FOURTH ROW FILMS
Production company

27 W. 20th St, Suite 1006, New York City, NY, United States, 10011

212-974-0082 (phone)
212-627-3090 (fax)

info@4throwfilms.com
imdb.com/company/co0117932

Does not accept any unsolicited material. Project types include TV and feature films. Genres include action, family, and drama.

FOUR TRIAD PRODUCTIONS
Production company

4265 San Felipe Ste 960
Houston, TX 77027

Fred@fourtriadproductions.com
fourtriadproductions.com
imdb.com/company/co0486043

Does not accept any unsolicited material. Project types include short films.

FOX 2000 PICTURES
Production company and distributor

10201 W Pico Blvd
Los Angeles, CA 90035
310-369-1000 (phone)
310-369-4258 (fax)

foxmovies.com
imdb.com/company/co0017497
linkedin.com/groups/20th-Century-Fox-3745273
facebook.com/pages/Fox-2000-Pictures/
    106316459407327
twitter.com/20thcenturyfox

Does not accept any unsolicited material. Genres include crime, horror, thriller, animation, comedy, drama, science fiction, action, family, myth, fantasy, and romance. Established in 1996.

Elizabeth Gabler
elizabeth.gabler@fox.com
imdb.com/name/nm1992894

Riley Kathryn Ellis
Executive
riley.ellis@fox.com

FOX BROADCASTING COMPANY
Production company and distributor

10201 W Pico Blvd, Los Angeles, CA, 90064, United States
310-369-1000

1211 Ave of the Americas
New York NY 10036
212-556-2400

fox.com
imdb.com/company/co0030121

Does not accept any unsolicited material. Project types include feature films, short films, and TV. Genres include crime, action, drama, and detective.

David Madden
Producer, Executive, Director, Writer
310-295-3455
imdb.com/name/nm0534574

FOX DIGITAL STUDIOS
Production company and distributor

10201 W Pico Blvd
Los Angeles, CA 90035
310-369-1000

david.brooks@fox.com
foxdigitalstudios.com
imdb.com/company/co0365818
facebook.com/FoxDigitalStudio

Accepts query letters from produced or represented writers. Project types include TV and feature films. Genres include comedy, horror, crime, drama, and thriller.

David Worthen Brooks
Creative Director
imdb.com/name/nm3652161

FOX INTERNATIONAL CHANNELS
Production company and distributor

6-25-14-6F
Jingumae
Shibuya, TOKYO 150-0001
Japan
03-5469-6733

foxad@fox.com
tv.foxjapan.com
imdb.com/company/co0376922

Does not accept any unsolicited material. Project types include feature films and TV. Genres include action and thriller.

Masato Itô
Actor
imdb.com/name/nm6153819

FOX INTERNATIONAL PRODUCTIONS (FIP)
Production company and distributor

10201 W Pico Blvd
Los Angeles, CA 90035
310-369-1000

foxinternational.com
imdb.com/company/co0237611

Does not accept any unsolicited material. Genres include action, crime, drama, romance, thriller, and family. Established in 2008.

Marco Mehlitz
imdb.com/name/nm0576438

Anna Kokourina
imdb.com/name/nm3916463

Sanford Panitch
President
310-369-1000
sanford.panitch@fox.com
imdb.com/name/nm0659529

FOX SEARCHLIGHT PICTURES
Production company and distributor

10201 W Pico Blvd
Building 38
Los Angeles, CA 90035
310-369-1000 (phone)
310-369-2359 (fax)

foxsearchlight.com
imdb.com/company/co0028932
linkedin.com/company/fox-searchlight-pictures
facebook.com/foxsearchlight
twitter.com/foxsearchlight

Does not accept any unsolicited material. Genres include fantasy, thriller, romance, crime, drama, horror, action, comedy, and family. Established in 1994.

Stephen Gilula
310-369-1000
stephen.gilula@fox.com
imdb.com/name/nm2322989

FRACTAL FEATURES
Production company

4223 S Pipkin Rs
Ste 100
Lakeland, FL 33811
863-529-5554 (phone)
863-337-4933 (fax)

kevin@fractalfeatures.com
fractalfeatures.com
imdb.com/company/co0506502

Does not accept any unsolicited material. Genres include drama and comedy.

FRAME 29 FILMS
Studio

7070 Bruns Dr
Mobile, AL 36695

horst@frame29films.com
frame29films.com
imdb.com/company/co0413096
facebook.com/frame29films

Does not accept any unsolicited material. Project types include feature films. Genres include drama, action, and thriller. Established in 2012.

Horst Sarubin
Creative Executive
horst@frame29films.com
imdb.com/name/nm0765689

Drew Hall
Creative Executive
drew@frame29films.com
imdb.com/name/nm0355527

FRAMESTORE CFC
Production company and studio

133 Spring St
New York NY 10012
212-775-0600 (phone)
212-775-0606 (fax)

9 Noel St
London United Kingdom W1F 8GH
011-442-072082600 (phone)
011-442-072082626 (fax)

5455 Av. de Gaspé Suite 900
Montreal QC Canada H2T 3B3
514-277-0004

8616 National Blvd
Culver City CA 90232
310-975-7300

19-23 Wells St, London , United Kingdom, W1T 3PQ
011-442-073448000 (phone)
011-442-073448001 (fax)

film@framestore.com
framestore.com
imdb.com/company/co0014175

Does not accept any unsolicited material. Project types include TV and feature films. Genres include science fiction, thriller, drama, and family.

Danielle Nadal
Head (Traffic)
imdb.com/name/nm1826006

FRANCISCO PRODUCTIONS
Production company

franciscoproductions.net
imdb.com/company/co0306508
facebook.com/pages/Francisco-Productions-LLC/
    231000013617995

Accepts query letters from unproduced, unrepresented writers via email. Project types include feature films. Genres include period and drama. Established in 2012.

Gabriel Francisco
Producer
imdb.com/name/nm3943533
twitter.com/therealgabef

Jeremy Profe
Director
imdb.com/name/nm3942977
twitter.com/mrprofe

Rafael Francisco
Producer
imdb.com/name/nm3315277
twitter.com/therealrafe

FREDERATOR STUDIOS

2829 N. Glenoaks Blvd., Ste. 203
Burbank CA 91504
818-848-8348

22 W 21st St, 7th Floor
New York City, NY 10010
212-779-4133 (phone)
917-591-7577 (fax)

hey@frederator.com
frederator.com
imdb.com/company/co0070267
linkedin.com/company/frederator-networks-inc-
facebook.com/frederatorstudios
twitter.com/channelfred

Accepts query letters from unproduced, unrepresented writers via email. Project types include TV, short films, and feature films. Genres include family, animation, and comedy. Established in 1998.

Fred Selbert
646-274-4601
fred@frederator.com
imdb.com/name/nm0782288
twitter.com/fredseibert
Assistant. Zoe Barton - zoe@frederator.com

Carrie Miller
carrie@frederator.com

Eric Homan
eric@frederator.com
imdb.com/name/nm2302704

Kevin Kolde
kevin@frederator.com

FREDERIC GOLCHAN PRODUCTIONS
Production company

c/o Radar Pictures
10900 Wilshire Blvd, 14th Floor
Los Angeles, CA 90024
310-208-8525 (phone)
310-208-1764 (fax)

fgfilm@aol.com
imdb.com/company/co0093754

Does not accept any unsolicited material. Genres include crime, thriller, drama, comedy, and action.

Frederic Golchan
asstgolchan@gmail.com
imdb.com/name/nm0324907
linkedin.com/pub/frederic-golchan/0/625/b16
Assistant: Gaillaume Chiasoda

FRED KUENERT PRODUCTIONS

1601 Hilts Ave. #2
Los Angeles, CA 90024
310-470-3363 (phone)
310-470-0060 (fax)

imdb.com/company/co0180697

Accepts query letters from unproduced, unrepresented writers via email. Project types include feature films. Genres include action, science fiction, fantasy, thriller, and horror.

Fred Kuenert
fkuehnert@earthlink.net
imdb.com/name/nm0473896
linkedin.com/pub/fred-kuehnert/4/352/848

FREEDOM FILMS
Production company

15300 Ventura Blvd. #508
Sherman Oaks, CA 91403
818-906-2339 (phone)
818-906-2342 (fax)

info@freedomfilmsllc.com
freedomfilms.com
imdb.com/company/co0102942

Does not accept any unsolicited material. Project types include feature films. Genres include thriller, family, horror, action, crime, and drama.

Alexandria Klipstein
Creative Executive
imdb.com/name/nm2317077

Scott Robinson
imdb.com/name/nm1558904

Brain Presley
CEO
imdb.com/name/nm0696169

FREEMAN FILM
Production company

100 Crescent Court
Ste 1450
Dallas, TX 75201
214-550-1222

info@freemanfilm.com
freemanfilm.com
imdb.com/company/co0250872

Does not accept any unsolicited material. Genres include drama.

FREE SOUL DANCE COMPANY
Production company

1451 S Miami Ave
Miami, FL 33130
305-799-9756

imdb.com/company/co0321886
facebook.com/freesouldancemiami

Does not accept any unsolicited material. Project types include short films. Genres include documentary.

FREE SPIRIT FILMS
Production company

96 Joseph Duggan Rd
Toronto, ON M4L 3Y2
Canada
416-690-8900

ali_@freespiritfilms.ca
freespiritfilms.ca
imdb.com/company/co0207356

Does not accept any unsolicited material. Genres include family.

FREE STONE PRODUCTION
Distributor

3-25-18-217
Jingumae
Shibuya, Tokyo 150-0001
Japan

info@freestone.main.jp
freestone.jp
imdb.com/company/co0345028

Does not accept any unsolicited material. Project types include TV. Genres include comedy.

Miyuki Takamatsu
International Sales (Executive)
imdb.com/name/nm5977121

FREESTYLE RELEASING
Production company, distributor, and sales agent

6310 San Vicente Blvd, Suite 500, Los Angeles, CA, United States, 90048
323-330-9920 (phone)
323-330-9939 (fax)

freestylereleasing.com
imdb.com/company/co0134711

Does not accept any unsolicited material. Project types include feature films, short films, and TV. Genres include family, comedy, thriller, drama, and action.

FRELAINE

8383 Wilshire Blvd
5th Fl
Beverly Hills, CA 90211
323-848-9729 (phone)
323-848-7219 (fax)

imdb.com/company/co0176000

Accepts query letters from unproduced, unrepresented writers. Project types include feature films. Genres include period, fantasy, thriller, and action.

James Jacks
Executive
imdb.com/name/nm0413208

FREMANTLE MEDIA

Production company and sales agent

1 Stephen St
London W1P 1PA
UK
+44 (0)20 7691 6000

contactus@fremantlemedia.com
fremantlemedia.com
imdb.com/company/co0035637
facebook.com/FremantleMediaGroup
twitter.com/FremantleMedia

Does not accept any unsolicited material. Project types include short films, feature films, and TV. Genres include action.

Cécile Frot-Coutaz
Producer
imdb.com/name/nm1227571

FREMANTLE MEDIA LATIN AMERICA

Production company and distributor

5200 Blue Lagoon Dr.
Ste 200
Miami, FL 33126
305-267-0821 (phone)
305-267-0459 (fax)

pressenquiries@fremantlemedia.com
fremantlemedia.com
imdb.com/company/co0187786

Does not accept any unsolicited material.

FRESH AND SMOKED

Production company

Studio City
10700 Ventura Blvd. Ste. 2D
Studio city, CA 91604
818-505-1311 (phone)
818-301-2135 (fax)

bdtd@freshandsmoked.com
freshandsmoked.com
imdb.com/company/co0223352
facebook.com/pages/Fresh-Smoked/
    116615628395984
twitter.com/freshandsmoked

Accepts scripts from unproduced, unrepresented writers. Project types include commercials, feature films, and TV. Genres include animation, crime, reality, science fiction, detective, fantasy, action, drama, comedy, family, thriller, myth, romance, horror, and non-fiction.

Angela McIntyre
angela@freshandsmoked.com

Jeremy Gosch
Director
jeremy@freshandsmoked.com
imdb.com/name/nm0331443

Monika Gosch
Producer
monika@freshandsmoked.com
imdb.com/name/nm2815838

FRESH PRODUCE FILMS

Production company

11684 Ventura Blvd Suite 214
Studio City, CA 91604
843-937-6337

imdb.com/company/co0044390
linkedin.com/company/fresh-produce-films-inc

Does not accept any unsolicited material. Genres include thriller and horror.

FRIED FILMS

Production company

100 N Crescent Dr, Suite 350
Beverly Hills, CA 90210
310-694-8150 (phone)
310-861-5454 (fax)

imdb.com/company/co0053780

Accepts query letters from unproduced, unrepresented writers. Project types include feature films and TV. Genres include comedy, family, action, drama, thriller, detective, crime, and romance. Established in 1990.

Robert Fried
Producer
imdb.com/name/nm0294975

Tyrrell Shaffner
Development Executive
424-210-3607
imdb.com/name/nm1656222

FRIENDLY FILMS
Production company

100 N Crescent Dr, Suite 350
Beverly Hills, CA 90210
310-432-1818 (phone)
310-432-1801 (fax)

info@friendly-films.com
friendly-films.com
imdb.com/company/co0186321

Accepts query letters from unproduced, unrepresented writers. Project types include feature films. Genres include comedy, drama, crime, science fiction, documentary, and family. Established in 2006.

David Friendly
310-432-1800
imdb.com/name/nm0295560

FRIGHTMARE VIDEO
Distributor

PO Box 384
Grapevine, TX 76099

imdb.com/company/co0386978

Does not accept any unsolicited material. Project types include feature films. Genres include horror and thriller. Established in 1985.

FRONTIER VIDEO DIST
Production company

22043 US Hwy 19 N
Clearwater, FL 33765
727-724-3373 (phone)
727-725-8214 (fax)

frontiervideo@worldnet.att.net
imdb.com/company/co0038722

Does not accept any unsolicited material. Genres include comedy.

FRONTLOT PRODUCTIONS
Production company

PO Box 463
Alpine, NJ 07620
917-327-8528

tryno@mac.com
imdb.com/company/co0033726

Does not accept any unsolicited material. Project types include short films. Genres include comedy and action.

FRONT STREET PICTURES
Production company

1950 Franklin St
Vancouver, BC V5L 1R2
Canada
604-257-4720 (phone)
604-257-4739 (fax)

info@frontstreetpictures.com
frontstreetpictures.com
imdb.com/company/co0149567
facebook.com/front.s.pictures
twitter.com/frontstreetpics

Accepts query letters from unproduced, unrepresented writers. Project types include feature films and TV. Genres include comedy, action, crime, fantasy, drama, and thriller.

Harvey Kahn
Producer
harvey@frontstreetpictures.com
imdb.com/name/nm0434838

FR PRODUCTIONS
Production company

1531 Colorado Ave.
Santa Monica, CA 90404
310-470-9212 (phone)
310-470-4905 (fax)

frprod@earthlink.net
frproductions.org
imdb.com/company/co0168898

Does not accept any unsolicited material. Project types include feature films. Genres include crime, family, comedy, romance, thriller, and drama.

Fred Roos
frprod@earthlink.net
imdb.com/name/nm0740407

FULLER FILMS
Production company

P.O. BOX 976
Venice, CA 90294
310-717-8842

imdb.com/company/co0066675

Does not accept any unsolicited material. Project types include feature films. Genres include comedy, drama, and crime.

Paul De Souza
Producer
gopics@verizon.net
imdb.com/name/nm0996278

Henry Bean
imdb.com/name/nm0063785

FULL MOON FEATURES
Production company and distributor

1626 N Wilcox Ave, Suite 474, Hollywood, CA, United States, 90028
323-822-2100

orderdesk@fullmoonfeatures.com
fullmoondirect.com
imdb.com/company/co0362667

Does not accept any unsolicited material. Project types include TV and feature films. Genres include action, thriller, family, and drama.

FULL PLATE PRODUCTIONS
Distributor

17 Leslie St.
Suite 132
Toronto, ON M4M 3H9
Canada

casey@mymilliondollarmovie.com
imdb.com/company/co0337276
linkedin.com/company/full-plate-productions

facebook.com/Full-Plate-Productions-126473114123068

Does not accept any unsolicited material. Genres include horror, science fiction, and comedy.

FULL REAL PRODUCTIONS
Production company

2510 Canyon Ridge Ct
Arlington, TX 76006

imdb.com/company/co0271980

Does not accept any unsolicited material. Project types include short films. Genres include romance and drama.

FULTON STREET FILMS
Production company

30 Gates Ave.
Ste 302
Montclair, NJ 07042
973-680-0260

tiadionnehodge@gmail.com
tiadionnehodge.com
imdb.com/company/co0196420
facebook.com/TiaDionneHodge
twitter.com/TiaDionneHodge

Does not accept any unsolicited material. Project types include short films. Genres include comedy.

FULWELL 73
Production company

7a Bayham St
Camden
London NW1 0EY
UK
+44207-419-0304

contact@fulwell73.co.uk
fulwell73.com
imdb.com/company/co0186621
facebook.com/Fulwell73Productions
twitter.com/fulwell73

Does not accept any unsolicited material. Project types include TV. Genres include comedy.

FUNIMATION ENTERTAINMENT
Production company and distributor

1200 Lakeside Parkway
Bldg 1
Flower Mound, TX 75028
972-355-7300

feedback@funimation.com
funimation.com
imdb.com/company/co0039940
linkedin.com/company/funimation-entertainment
facebook.com/Funimation-63889783480
twitter.com/funimation

Does not accept any unsolicited material. Project types include TV and feature films. Genres include drama, action, science fiction, and animation. Established in 1994.

FUN LITTLE FILMS
Production company and distributor

2227 W Olive Ave
Burbank, CA 91506
323-467-6868

FunLittleMovies2@gmail.com
funlittlemovies.com
imdb.com/company/co0161105
linkedin.com/company/fun-little-movies
facebook.com/pages/Fun-Little-Movies/
    111880782170511
twitter.com/Funlittlemovies

Does not accept any unsolicited material. Project types include short films, commercials, and TV. Genres include animation and comedy. Established in 1988.

Frank Chindamo
President
frank@funlittlemovies.com
imdb.com/name/nm0157828

FURLINED
Production company

2803 Colorado Ave
Santa Monica, CA 90404
310-496-5060

info@furlined.com
furlined.com

facebook.com/furlinedproductions
twitter.com/furlined_

Does not accept any unsolicited material. Project types include commercials. Established in 2005.

Meghan Lang
Executive Producer
meghan@furlined.com

David Thorne
Executive Producer
david@furlined.com

Diane Mcarter
President
diane@furlined.com

FURST FILMS
Production company

8954 W Pico Blvd
2nd Floor
Los Angeles, CA 90035
310-278-6468 (phone)
310-278-7401 (fax)

info@furstfilms.com
furstfilms.com
imdb.com/company/co0022433

Accepts query letters from unproduced, unrepresented writers via email. Project types include TV and feature films. Genres include thriller, detective, action, horror, drama, reality, crime, and non-fiction.

Sean Furst
Partner
imdb.com/name/nm0299120

Bryan Furst
Principal/Producer
imdb.com/name/nm1227576

FURTHUR FILMS
Production company

100 Universal City Plaza
Building 5174
Universal City, CA 91608
818-777-6700 (phone)
818-866-1278 (fax)

250 W 57th St
Suite 808
New York, NY 10107
646-606-0120 (phone)
212-247-7482 (fax)

imdb.com/company/co0002647
facebook.com/pages/Further-Films/
    1619730804974765
twitter.com/furtherfilms

Does not accept any unsolicited material. Project types include feature films. Genres include thriller, horror, science fiction, and drama. Established in 2001.

Michael Douglas
Producer
imdb.com/name/nm0000140

FUSEFRAME
Production company

2332 Cotner Ave, Suite 200
Los Angeles, CA 90064
424-208-1765

imdb.com/company/co0353810

Does not accept any unsolicited material. Project types include feature films. Genres include thriller. Established in 2011.

Eva Konstantopoulos
imdb.com/name/nm2192285

Marcus Chait
Director of Film and New Media
imdb.com/name/nm1483939

FUSION FILMS
Production company

2355 Westwood Blvd, Suite 117
Los Angeles, CA 90064
310-441-1496

info@fusionfilms.net
imdb.com/company/co0337140

Does not accept any unsolicited material. Project types include feature films. Genres include comedy and fantasy. Established in 2013.

John Baldecchi
imdb.com/name/nm0049689

FUTURE FILM GROUP
Production company

76 Dean St, London , United Kingdom, W1D 3SQ
011-442-070096600 (phone)
011-442-070096602 (fax)

1531 14th St
Santa Monica CA 90404
310-393-7124 (phone)
310-393-7251 (fax)

info@futurefilmgroup.com
futurefilmgroup.com
imdb.com/company/co0123194

Does not accept any unsolicited material. Project types include TV and feature films. Genres include family, thriller, action, and drama.

FUZZY DOOR PRODUCTIONS
Production company

c/o Fox TV Animation
5700 Wilshire Blvd, Ste 325
Los Angeles, CA 90036
323-857-8800

imdb.com/company/co0065872
facebook.com/pages/Fuzzy-Door-Productions/
    108392932522154

Does not accept any unsolicited material. Project types include feature films and TV. Genres include comedy, fantasy, and animation. Established in 1996.

Seth MacFarlane
Founder
sethmacfarlane.org
imdb.com/name/nm0532235

GAEA
Production company and distributor

1-35-11-4F
Ebisu Nishi
Shibuya, Tokyo 150-0021
Japan

03-5728-7030 (phone)
03-5728-7033 (fax)

mail@gaea-inc.com
gaea-inc.com
imdb.com/company/co0250240

Does not accept any unsolicited material. Project types include TV. Genres include documentary.

GAETA/ROSENZWEIG FILMS
Production company

150 Ocean Park Blvd
Ste 322
Santa Monica, CA 90405
310-399-7101

imdb.com/company/co0248894

Does not accept any unsolicited material. Project types include feature films. Genres include horror, comedy, crime, thriller, drama, and action. Established in 2011.

Michael J. Gaeta
Partner
imdb.com/name/nm1357812

Alison Rosenzweig
Producer
imdb.com/name/nm0742851
linkedin.com/pub/alison-rosenzweig/64/519/b03

GAGA
Production company and distributor

TY Bldg., 2-22-18
Minami Aoyama
Minato, Tokyo 107-0062
Japan
+81 3 5786 7140 (phone)
+81 3 5786 7139 (fax)

intl@gaga.co.jp
gaga.co.jp
imdb.com/company/co0004745
facebook.com/gagaeizou

Does not accept any unsolicited material. Project types include feature films, short films, video games, and TV. Genres include science fiction.

Takao Mizuno
Board-Director and Operating Officer in Charge of Programming (Executive)
imdb.com/name/nm4715408

GAIA ENTERTAINMENT/BUZZMAN PRODUCTIONS
Production company

PO Box 567971
Atlanta, GA 31156

imdb.com/company/co0102240

Does not accept any unsolicited material.

GAIAM VIVENDI ENTERTAINMENT
Production company and distributor

833 W South Boulder Rd, P.O. Box 3095, Louisville, CO, United States, 80027
303-222-3600 (phone)
303-464-3700 (fax)

350 Madison Ave Suite 1700
New York NY 10017
212-951-3000

investorrelations@gaiam.com
corporate.gaiam.com
imdb.com/company/co0383279

Does not accept any unsolicited material. Project types include TV. Genres include drama, thriller, and family.

GAINAX
Production company

1-2-29
Kajinocho
Koganei, Tokyo 184-0002
Japan
0422-70-6006 (phone)
0422-70-6012 (fax)

license@gainax.co.jp
imdb.com/company/co0071695

Does not accept any unsolicited material. Project types include TV and feature films. Genres include animation and family.

Yoshiyuki Sadamoto
Founder (Producer)
imdb.com/name/nm0755412

GALATEE FILMS
Production company and distributor

19 Ave de Messine
Paris 75008
France
+33 1 44 29 21 40 (phone)
+33 1 44 29 25 90 (fax)

mail@galateefilms.com
imdb.com/company/co0058643
linkedin.com/company/galatee-films-sas
facebook.com/Galat%C3%A9e-
    Films-1697144633841638

Does not accept any unsolicited material. Project types include feature films. Genres include non-fiction, romance, drama, comedy, and documentary. Established in 1991.

Nicolas Mauvernay
Producer
imdb.com/name/nm1241814

Jacques Perrin
President
imdb.com/name/nm0674742

Christophe Barratier
Producer
imdb.com/name/nm0056725

GAMBIT PICTURES
Production company

10100 Santa Monica Blvd., Suite 1300
Los Angeles, CA 90067

imdb.com/company/co0177587

Does not accept any unsolicited material. Project types include feature films and TV. Genres include science fiction, drama, and thriller.

George Nolfi
Partner/Producer/Writer/Director
imdb.com/name/nm1079776

Michael Hackett
Partner/Producer
imdb.com/name/nm0352489

GARDEN THIEVES PICTURES
Production company and distributor

700 12th St NW
Suite 700
Washington, DC 20005
202-253-4949 (phone)
866-297-8103 (fax)

info@gardenthieves.com
gardenthieves.com
imdb.com/company/co0239197
facebook.com/GardenThievesPictures
twitter.com/Gardenthieves

Does not accept any unsolicited material. Project types include feature films and TV. Genres include animation, reality, comedy, drama, family, and documentary. Established in 2003.

GARLIN PICTURES
Production company

11640 Woodbridge St, Suite #106
Studio City, CA 91604
310-991-7754 (phone)
818-506-7122 (fax)

info@garlinpictures.com
imdb.com/company/co0136730

Does not accept any unsolicited material. Project types include feature films.

Josh Etting
CEO/Producer
imdb.com/name/nm0262186

Brian R. Etting
CEO/Producer
imdb.com/name/nm0262188

GARRISON FILM DISTRIBUTORS INC.
Distributor

1600 Broadway
New York, NY 10019

imdb.com/company/co0023832

Does not accept any unsolicited material. Project types include feature films. Genres include drama and documentary.

GARY HOFFMAN PRODUCTIONS

Production company

3931 Puerco Canyon Rd
Malibu, CA 90265
310-456-1830 (phone)
310-456-8866 (fax)

garyhofprods@charter.net
imdb.com/company/co0014302

Does not accept any unsolicited material. Project types include TV. Genres include comedy, thriller, drama, and crime. Established in 1988.

Gary Hoffman
President
imdb.com/name/nm0388888

GARY SANCHEZ PRODUCTIONS

Production company and distributor

1041 N Formosa Ave
West Hollywood, CA 90046
323-465-4600 (phone)
323-465-0782 (fax)

gary@garysanchezprods.com
garysanchezprods.com
imdb.com/company/co0186190
linkedin.com/company/gary-sanchez-productions
facebook.com/pages/Gary-Sanchez-Productions/
    112597388757382

Does not accept any unsolicited material. Project types include feature films and TV. Genres include drama, romance, thriller, and comedy. Established in 2006.

Gary Sanchez
gary@garysanchezprods.com
facebook.com/garysanchezprods

Will Ferrell
imdb.com/name/nm0002071

GAUCHO PRODUCTIONS

Production company

12810 Westella Dr
Houston, TX 77077
713-397-7135 (phone)
713-937-9309 (fax)

martin@gauchop.com
gauchoproductions.com
imdb.com/company/co0091826
linkedin.com/company/gaucho-productions
twitter.com/GauchoProd

Does not accept any unsolicited material. Project types include feature films. Genres include drama.

Martin Delon
Producer/Director
imdb.com/name/nm1312872

Andrea Elustondo-Sanchez
Executive Producer
imdb.com/name/nm1326834

GEARSHIFT FILMS

Production company

80 Spadina Ave
Ste 304
Toronto, ON M5V 2J4
Canada
416-840-5404 (phone)
416-214-2393 (fax)

borga@gearshiftfilms.com
gearshiftfilms.com
imdb.com/company/co0356472
facebook.com/tormentmovie
twitter.com/TormentTheMovie

Does not accept any unsolicited material. Genres include drama.

GEEK PICTURES

Production company

2-27-5 Jingumae
Shibuya-Ku
Tokyo 150-0001
Japan
+81-3-5879-2360 (phone)
+81-3-5879-2361 (fax)

geekinfo_tokyo@geekpictures.co.jp
geekpictures.co.jp

imdb.com/company/co0349217

Does not accept any unsolicited material. Project types include TV. Genres include drama.

Tamotsu Kosano
Owner (Producer)
imdb.com/name/nm4561290

GENERAL ENTERTAINMENT CO. LTD.
Production company and distributor

5-1-3-9F
Roppongi
Minato, Tokyo
Japan
03-5414-2345 (phone)
03-5414-2355 (fax)

ge@genet.co.jp
genet.co.jp
imdb.com/company/co0106951

Does not accept any unsolicited material. Project types include feature films and TV. Genres include action and animation.

Kyôichi Mori
President
imdb.com/name/nm0605264

GENESIS FILM SALES
Distributor and sales agent

45-51 Whitfield St
London W1T 4HD
UK
+44 20 3372 0977

info@genesisfilmsales.com
imdb.com/company/co0371082

Does not accept any unsolicited material. Project types include feature films. Genres include thriller, crime, and drama.

GENEXT FILMS
Production company

5610 Soto St
Huntington Park, CA 90255
714-552-2731

contact@genextfilms.com
genextfilms.com
imdb.com/company/co0234963
facebook.com/pages/GenextT-FILMS-Productions/
686554521437240

Does not accept any unsolicited material. Project types include feature films. Genres include comedy. Established in 2009.

Carlos Salas
imdb.com/name/nm2972624
Assistant: Kathy Snyder

Rossana Salas
imdb.com/name/nm2970664

GENREBEND PRODUCTIONS
Production company

233 Wilshire Blvd, Suite 400
Santa Monica, CA 90401
310-917-1064 (phone)
310-917-1065 (fax)

imdb.com/company/co0094959
twitter.com/genrebend

Does not accept any unsolicited material. Project types include feature films and TV. Genres include comedy and drama.

Tom Lavagnino
imdb.com/name/nm0491706

David Nutter
imdb.com/name/nm0638354
twitter.com/genrebend

GENRE FILMS
Production company

10201 W. Pico Blvd.
Los Angeles, CA 90035

imdb.com/company/co0301801

Does not accept any unsolicited material. Project types include feature films. Genres include family, action, and fantasy.

Simon Kinberg
Writer/Producer
imdb.com/name/nm1334526

Aditya Sood
President of Production
imdb.com/name/nm1533078

GEORGE LITTO PRODUCTIONS
Production company

339 N Orange Dr
Los Angeles, CA 90401
323-936-6350

imdb.com/company/co0050602

Does not accept any unsolicited material. Project types include feature films. Genres include action, drama, and thriller.

Andria Litto
President
imdb.com/name/nm0514787

George Litto
CEO/Producer
imdb.com/name/nm0514788

GERARD BUTLER ALAN SIEGEL ENTERTAINMENT
Production company

9200 W. Sunset Blvd.
Ste. 407
West Hollywood, CA 90069
310-278-8400

imdb.com/company/co0332840

Does not accept any unsolicited material. Project types include feature films. Genres include thriller, drama, crime, and comedy. Established in 2009.

Gerard Butler
imdb.com/name/nm0124930

GERBER PICTURES
Production company

4000 Warner Blvd
Building 138, Suite 1205
Burbank, CA 91522
818-954-3046 (phone)
818-954-3706 (fax)

gerberpics.com

imdb.com/company/co0062831
linkedin.com/company/gerber-pictures
facebook.com/pages/Gerber-Pictures/
    100942556613624

Does not accept any unsolicited material. Project types include TV and feature films. Genres include action, romance, animation, comedy, family, and drama. Established in 2001.

Bill Gerber
President
imdb.com/name/nm0314088
Assistant: James Leffler

GERSH
Studio and sales agent

41 Madison Ave, 33rd Floor, New York , NY, United States, 10010
212-997-1818 (phone)
212-997-1978 (fax)

9465 Wilshire Blvd Sixth Floor
Beverly Hills CA 90212
310-274-6611 (phone)
310-274-3923 (fax)

gershagency.com
imdb.com/company/co0018749

Does not accept any unsolicited material. Project types include TV and short films. Genres include drama, family, and comedy.

GERSHMAN FILMS
Production company

216 Kings Croft
Cherry Hill, NJ 08034
215-313-5515

oleg@gershmanfilms.com
gershmanfilms.com
imdb.com/company/co0283451

Does not accept any unsolicited material. Project types include TV. Genres include drama and documentary.

GFM FILMS
Production company, distributor, and sales agent

10 Coda Centre
189 Munster Rd
London SW6 6AW
UK
44207-186-6300 (phone)
44207-186-6301 (fax)

general@gfmfilms.co.uk
gfmfilms.co.uk
imdb.com/company/co0364793
facebook.com/GFMFilmsUK
twitter.com/GFM_Films

Does not accept any unsolicited material. Project types include feature films, TV, and short films. Genres include science fiction.

Guy Collins
Producer
imdb.com/name/nm0172335

GG FILMZ
Production company

5028 Vanalden Ave
Tarzana, CA 91356

ggfilmz.com
imdb.com/company/co0195008
facebook.com/pizzafilms
twitter.com/DeborahGGFilmz

Does not accept any unsolicited material. Project types include feature films. Genres include crime, drama, and action.

Ray Giarratana
Producer/Director/Writer
imdb.com/name/nm1568265

Deborah Giarratana
Producer
imdb.com/name/nm1072937

GHOST HOUSE PICTURES
Production company and distributor

315 S Beverly Dr, Suite 216
Beverly Hills, CA 90212
310-785-3900 (phone)
310-785-9176 (fax)

info@ghosthousepictures.com

ghosthousepictures.com
imdb.com/company/co0116611

Does not accept any unsolicited material. Project types include TV and feature films. Genres include horror, thriller, comedy, and drama.

Sam Raimi
imdb.com/name/nm0000600

GHOULARDI FILM COMPANY
Production company

2301 Nottingham Ave
Los Angeles, CA 90027
818-487-7444

imdb.com/company/co0027686

Does not accept any unsolicited material. Project types include feature films. Genres include drama.

JoAnne Sellar
Producer
imdb.com/name/nm0783280

Paul Thomas Anderson
Writer/Director/Producer
imdb.com/name/nm0000759

GIANT APE MEDIA
Production company and distributor

1200 Lakeside Parkway
Building 1
Flower Mound, TX 75028

giantape.com
imdb.com/company/co0412745
facebook.com/GiantApeMedia
twitter.com/GiantApeMedia

Does not accept any unsolicited material. Genres include crime, comedy, action, horror, and thriller.

GIANT FILMS
Production company

24 Hanway St
London W1T1UH
UK
+44 20 7290 0765

info@giantfilms.com
imdb.com/company/co0125295

Does not accept any unsolicited material. Project types include feature films. Genres include comedy.

Nick O'Hagan
Producer
imdb.com/name/nm0002532

GIANT PIRATES ENTERTAINMENT
Production company

3522 Hayden Ave
Culver City, CA 90232
310-341-2500

info@giantpirates.com
giantpirates.com
imdb.com/company/co0439261

Does not accept any unsolicited material. Genres include drama and comedy.

GIANT SCREEN FILMS
Production company

990 Grove St, Suite 200
Evanston, IL 60201
847-475-9140

info@gsfilms.com
gsfilms.com
imdb.com/company/co0082191

Does not accept any unsolicited material. Project types include feature films. Genres include non-fiction.

Don Kempf
Founder/Producer
imdb.com/name/nm0447437

Andy Wood
SVP of Development and Operations
imdb.com/name/nm2012559

GIDDEN MEDIA
Production company

10202 W. Washington Blvd. David Lean Bldg. Ste 230
Culver City, CA 90232
310-244-2988

info@giddenmedia.com
giddenmedia.com
imdb.com/company/co0386252

Does not accept any unsolicited material. Project types include TV and feature films. Genres include non-fiction and drama.

Christopher Ceccotti
Head of Development
imdb.com/name/nm5153580

Amy Baer
Producer
imdb.com/name/nm1616124

GIGANOVA PRODUCTIONS
Production company

207 Warren St NE
Washington, DC 20002
202-531-9262

giganova@giganova.com
giganova.com
imdb.com/company/co0404679

Does not accept any unsolicited material. Genres include documentary.

GIGANTIC PICTURES
Production company

164 W 25th St
Suite 4M
New York, NY 10001
212-925-5075 (phone)
212-925-5061 (fax)

info@giganticpictures.com
giganticpictures.com
imdb.com/company/co0181082
facebook.com/pages/Gigantic-Pictures/
    223176104540602

Accepts query letters from produced or represented writers. Project types include TV and feature films. Genres include drama, comedy, romance, and non-fiction.

Brian Devine
Founder
imdb.com/name/nm0222601

Pamela Ryan
Producer
pamela@giganticpictures.com
imdb.com/name/nm2135347

Jason Orans
Producer
jason@giganticpictures.com
imdb.com/name/nm0649346

GIGAPIX STUDIOS
Production company and distributor

9333 Oso Ave
Chatsworth, CA 91311
818-592-0755 (phone)
800-862-7656 (fax)

info@gigapixstudios.com
imdb.com/company/co0190777

Does not accept any unsolicited material. Project types include feature films. Genres include action and comedy.

David Pritchard
President
imdb.com/name/nm0698021

GIL ADLER PRODUCTIONS
Production company

9000 W Sunset Blvd, Ste 504
West Hollywood, CA 90069
310-550-6265

imdb.com/name/nm0012155

Does not accept any unsolicited material. Project types include TV, feature films, and commercials. Genres include thriller, horror, non-fiction, reality, and action. Established in 2001.

Gil Adler
Producer
imdb.com/name/nm0012155
linkedin.com/pub/gil-adler/6/a66/63b
Assistant: Ryan Lough

GILBERT FILMS
Production company

8409 Santa Monica Blvd.
West Hollywood, CA 90069
323-650-6800 (phone)
323-650-6810 (fax)

info@gilbertfilms.com
gilbertfilms.com
imdb.com/company/co0084122
twitter.com/gilbertfilms

Does not accept any unsolicited material. Project types include feature films. Genres include family, drama, and comedy.

Gary Gilbert
President
imdb.com/name/nm1344784

Jordan Horowitz
Vice-President, Production and Development
imdb.com/name/nm0395302

GIL NETTER PRODUCTIONS
Production company

1645 Abbot Kinney Blvd, Suite 320
Venice, CA 90291
310-566-5477 (phone)
310-899-6722 (fax)

imdb.com/name/nm0626696
linkedin.com/company/gil-netter-production
facebook.com/pages/Gil-Netter-Productions/
    110136129048415

Does not accept any unsolicited material. Project types include feature films. Genres include comedy, action, family, romance, and drama.

Gil Netter
Producer
imdb.com/name/nm0626696

GINNUNGAGAP FILMWERKS
Production company and distributor

9715 W Broward Blvd
#126
Plantation, FL 33324
954-834-3220

ginfilm@gmail.com
ginnungagapfilmwerks.com

imdb.com/company/co0341075
facebook.com/ginfilms
twitter.com/ginfilm

Does not accept any unsolicited material. Project types include short films. Genres include action, science fiction, and fantasy.

GI PICTURES
Production company

545 8th Ave Suite 401
New York, NY 10018

info@nehst.com
imdb.com/company/co0273836

Accepts query letters from unproduced, unrepresented writers via email. Project types include feature films. Genres include action and drama.

Dana Offenbach
President of Nehst Studios
imdb.com/name/nm0644382

Larry Meistrich
Producer
imdb.com/name/nm0577134

GIRLS CLUB ENTERTAINMENT
Production company

30 Sir Francis Drake Blvd
PO Box 437
Ross, CA 94957
415-233-4060 (phone)
415-233-4082 (fax)

info@girlsclubentertainment.com
imdb.com/company/co0119654

Does not accept any unsolicited material. Project types include TV and feature films. Genres include comedy, romance, reality, drama, non-fiction, and crime.

Jennifer Siebel Newsom
Founder
jennifersiebelnewsom.com
imdb.com/name/nm1308076

GITLIN PRODUCTIONS
Production company

1310 Montana Ave Second Floor
Santa Monica, CA 90403
310-209-8443 (phone)
310-728-1749 (fax)

gitlinproduction@aol.com
imdb.com/company/co0203509
facebook.com/pages/Gitlin-Productions/
214188072076647

Accepts query letters from unproduced, unrepresented writers via email. Project types include TV and feature films. Genres include non-fiction, drama, comedy, reality, and action.

Mimi Polk Gitlin
Producer
imdb.com/name/nm0689316

GITTES, INC.
Production company

10202 W. Washington Blvd.
Poitier Bldg., Ste. 1200
Culver City, CA 90232-3195
310-244-4333 (phone)
310-244-1711 (fax)

imdb.com/company/co0177589

Does not accept any unsolicited material. Project types include feature films. Genres include drama and comedy.

Edward Wang
Director of Development
310-244-4334
edward_wang@spe.sony.com
imdb.com/name/nm0910882

Harry Gittes
Producer
harry_gittes@spe.sony.com
imdb.com/name/nm0321228

GIZMO FILMS
Production company

13 Queensborough Mews
London W2 3SG
UK
+44 (0) 7799 494090

c.arden@gizmofilms.com
gizmofilms.com
imdb.com/company/co0390176

Does not accept any unsolicited material. Project types
include TV. Genres include drama and documentary.

Robert Mullan
Producer
imdb.com/name/nm2759405

GK FILMS
Production company

1540 2nd St, Suite 200
Santa Monica, CA 90401
310-315-1722 (phone)
310-315-1723 (fax)

contact@gk-films.com
gk-films.com
imdb.com/company/co0209646
facebook.com/GKFilms
twitter.com/gkfilms

Does not accept any unsolicited material. Project types
include feature films and TV. Genres include romance,
crime, fantasy, science fiction, action, thriller, comedy,
drama, family, non-fiction, and animation. Established
in 2007.

Graham King
CEO
imdb.com/name/nm0454752
Assistant: Leah Williams, Michelle Reed

GKIDS
Production company and distributor

225 Broadway, #2610, New York, NY, United States,
10007
212-349-0330 (phone)
212-528-0500 (fax)

eric@gkids.com
gkids.tv
imdb.com/company/co0255038

Does not accept any unsolicited material. Project types
include TV. Genres include family, drama, animation,
and comedy.

GLASS MAN FILMS
Production company

+44 7968 418 077

info@glassmanfilms.co.uk
glassmanfilms.co.uk
imdb.com/company/co0405288

Does not accept any unsolicited material. Genres
include drama, thriller, and action.

Richard Mansell
Producer
imdb.com/name/nm1943389

GLASSY CO. LTD.
Distributor

4-1-6-306
Konan
Minato, Japan 108-0075
Japan
03-5463-8003 (phone)
03-5463-8060 (fax)

info@glassymovie.jp
imdb.com/company/co0136178

Does not accept any unsolicited material. Project types
include feature films. Genres include comedy and
drama.

GLOBAL 3 MEDIA
Distributor and sales agent

224 Tulip Trail Bend
Cedar Park, TX 78613
310-384-3391

nichollewalton-durban@global3media.com (script
submissions)
info@global3media.com (general)
global3media.com
imdb.com/company/co0494165
facebook.com/Global3Media

Accepts query letters from unproduced, unrepresented
writers via email. Genres include crime, action, and
comedy.

GLOBAL HORIZON ENTERTAINMENT
Production company

6960 E Girard Ave
Suite 103
Denver, CO 80224
303-504-4148

s_f_griffen@msn.com
ghentertainment.com
imdb.com/company/co0209648

Does not accept any unsolicited material. Genres include drama.

GLOBAL SCREEN PARTNERS
Production company

1504 Bay Rd.
Ste. 2805
Miami Beach, FL 33139
305-534-5366

info@globalscreenpartners.com
imdb.com/company/co0102142

Does not accept any unsolicited material.

GLOBAL VISION ENTERTAINMENT
Production company

909 Lake Carolyn Pkwy.
Suite 1950
Irving, TX 75039
972-506-7084 (phone)
972-506-7024 (fax)

info@globalvisionent.com
globalvisionentertainment.net
imdb.com/company/co0166049
facebook.com/GlobalVisionEntertainment

Does not accept any unsolicited material. Project types include TV.

GLOBALWATCH FILM PRODUCTIONS
Production company and distributor

1 Berkeley St
Mayfair
London W1J 8DJ
UK
+44(0203-086-9616

pandrews@globalwatch.com
globalwatchfilmproductions.com

imdb.com/company/co0464583
linkedin.com/company/4981931
facebook.com/GlobalWatch-Film-
    Productions-1431183367097570
twitter.com/GlobalWatchFilm

Does not accept any unsolicited material. Genres include drama, comedy, crime, and romance.

Paul G. Andrews
Producer
imdb.com/name/nm6214368

GLORY ROAD PRODUCTIONS
Production company

23638 Lyons Ave.
Newhall, CA 91321
424-202-2510

info@gloryroadproductions.com
gloryroadproductions.com
imdb.com/company/co0132177
facebook.com/pages/Glory-Road-Productions/
    152847784771624

Does not accept any unsolicited material. Project types include feature films. Genres include action, fantasy, drama, horror, comedy, and family.

Val Mancini
Director of Development
imdb.com/name/nm4441689

Tara Bonacci
Producer
imdb.com/name/nm1742721

Erik Elseman
Executive Vice President
imdb.com/name/nm4831920

Michael Reymann
President
imdb.com/name/nm1478831

GOES HERE ENTERTAINMENTYOUR FACE
Production company

1041 N Formosa Ave
Santa Monica Bldg W, #7

West Hollywood, CA 90046
323-850-2433

imdb.com/company/co0247237
facebook.com/pages/Your-Face-Goes-Here-
    Entertainment/109721052385712

Does not accept any unsolicited material. Project types
include TV. Genres include fantasy, thriller, drama,
science fiction, horror, and romance.

Alan Ball
323-850-2433
imdb.com/name/nm0050332

GOFF PRODUCTIONS
Production company

8491 Sunset Blvd. Suite 1000
West Hollywood, CA 90069
310-666-9082

info@goffproductions.com
goffproductions.com
imdb.com/company/co0390297
twitter.com/GoffProductions

Does not accept any unsolicited material. Project types
include TV and feature films. Genres include family
and drama. Established in 2012.

Gina G. Goff
Partner/Producer
imdb.com/name/nm0324574

Laura A. Kellam
Partner/Producer
imdb.com/name/nm044549

GO FISH PICTURES
Production company and distributor

1000 Flower St
Glendale, CA 91201
818-695-7742

imdb.com/company/co0108632

Does not accept any unsolicited material. Project types
include feature films.

GOFUN PICTURES
Production company

1-9-11-804
Tsukiji
Chuo, Tokyo 104-0045
Japan
03-3541-2223 (phone)
03-3541-2224 (fax)

info@gofun-p.net
gofun-p.net
imdb.com/company/co0375812

Does not accept any unsolicited material. Project types
include TV. Genres include comedy.

Taishi Nishimura
President (Producer)
imdb.com/name/nm4975096

GO GIRL MEDIA

3450 Cahuenga Blvd West #802
Los Angeles, CA 90068
310-472-8910

info@gogirlmedia.com
gogirlmedia.com
imdb.com/company/co0177675
facebook.com/pages/Go-Girl-Media/
    185402498145525

Accepts query letters from unproduced, unrepresented
writers via email. Project types include TV and feature
films. Genres include comedy, non-fiction, family,
reality, animation, and drama. Established in 2004.

Don Priess
Head of Production
don@gogirlmedia.com
imdb.com/name/nm1043744

Susie Singer Carter
CEO
susie@gogirlmedia.com
imdb.com/name/nm0802053

GOIN' BALLISTIC
Production company

1035 S. Semoran Blvd.
Suite 1026
Winter Park, FL 32792-5383
321-972-8663

GoinBallisticInfo@Gmail.com
imdb.com/company/co0353077
facebook.com/GoinBallistic

Does not accept any unsolicited material. Genres
include crime, action, and drama.

GOIS
Production company and distributor

3-6-11-5F
Kami Meguro
Meguro, Tokyo 153-0051
Japan
+81 3-5721-8200 (phone)
+81 3-5721-8201 (fax)

gois@gois.co.jp
gois.co.jp
imdb.com/company/co0423357

Does not accept any unsolicited material. Project types
include feature films. Genres include drama.

Yoshikazu Fukuo
President (Producer)
imdb.com/name/nm6224526

GOLD CIRCLE FILMS
Production company and distributor

233 Wilshire Blvd, Suite 650
Santa Monica, CA 90401
310-278-4800 (phone)
310-278-0885 (fax)

info@goldcirclefilms.com
goldcirclefilms.com
imdb.com/company/co0076476
linkedin.com/company/gold-circle-films
facebook.com/pages/Gold-Circle-Films/
    109649739054057

Does not accept any unsolicited material. Project types
include feature films. Genres include horror, science
fiction, drama, comedy, thriller, action, family, and
romance. Established in 2000.

Guy Danella
Producer
twitter.com/GADanella

Paul Brooks
President
imdb.com/name/nm0112189

Brad Kessell
imdb.com/name/nm1733186

GOLDCREST FILMS
Production company, distributor, sales agent, and
financing company

1 Lexington St
London W1F 9AF
United Kingdom
+44207-437-8696 (phone)
+44207-437-4448 (fax)

799 Washington St.
New York City, NY 10014
212-243-4700 (phone)
212-624-1701 (fax)

info@goldcrestfilms.com
goldcrestfilms.com
imdb.com/company/co0045569
linkedin.com/company/goldcrest-films
facebook.com/GoldcrestFilms
twitter.com/Goldcrest_Films

Does not accept any unsolicited material. Project types
include feature films and TV. Genres include science
fiction, drama, romance, documentary, horror, and
action. Established in 1977.

Laurent Treherne
Chief Technology Officer
+44 (0)20 7437 7972
ltreherne@goldcrestfilms.com

Rob Farris
Head of Production
+44 (0)20 7437 7972
rfarris@goldcrestfilms.com

Tim Spitzer
Managing Director
212-897-3882
tspitzer@goldcrestfilms.com

Jim Gardner
Director of Operations
212-897-3890
jgardner@goldcrestfilms.com

Margaret Lewis
Producer
212-897-3966
mlewis@goldcrestfilms.com

Stephen Johnston
President
imdb.com/name/nm1158125

Patrick Malone
Managing Director
+44 (0)20 7437 7972
pmalone@goldcrestfilms.com

Martin Poultney
Director
+44 (0)20 7437 7972
mpoultney@goldcrestfilms.com

GOLDCREST PICTURES
Production company

1 Lexington St
London W1F 9AF
UK
+44 20 7437 7972 (phone)
+44 20 7437 5402 (fax)

sales@goldcrestfilms.com
goldcrestfilms.com
imdb.com/company/co0245613
facebook.com/GoldcrestFilms
twitter.com/Goldcrest_Films

Does not accept any unsolicited material. Project types include feature films. Genres include action and comedy.

GOLDENLIGHT FILMS
Production company

818-904-2667 (phone)
818-994-9124 (fax)

info@goldenlightfilms.com
goldenlightfilms.com
imdb.com/company/co0072737

Does not accept any unsolicited material. Project types include feature films, short films, and commercials. Genres include drama and thriller. Established in 1998.

Kimberly Quinn
Founder
imdb.com/name/nm0703910

Theodore Melfi
Founder
imdb.com/name/nm0577647
twitter.com/theodoremelfi

Shawn Askinosie
CCO
imdb.com/name/nm2999202

GOLDENRING PRODUCTIONS
Production company

4804 Laurel Canyon Blvd
Room 570
Valley Village, CA 91607
818-508-7425

info@goldenringproductions.net
goldenringproductions.net
imdb.com/company/co0047633

Does not accept any unsolicited material. Project types include feature films and TV. Genres include drama, family, animation, non-fiction, and comedy.

Jon King
jonnyfking@gmail.com

Jane Goldenring
imdb.com/name/nm0325553
linkedin.com/pub/jane-goldenring/6/480/71

GOLDOVE ENTERTAINMENT
Production company

Los Angeles, CA
818-355-7670

info@goldove.com
goldove.com
imdb.com/company/co0398176
facebook.com/GoldoveEntertainment
twitter.com/GoldoveEnt

Accepts query letters from unproduced, unrepresented writers via email. Project types include short films and feature films. Genres include action, thriller, and drama. Established in 2012.

GOLD RUSH PICTURES
Production company and distributor

1-22-8-10F
Dogenzaka
Shibuya, Tokyo
Japan
03-5428-6194 (phone)
03-5761-8953 (fax)

shinsan@mediastar.jp
imdb.com/company/co0265442

Does not accept any unsolicited material. Project types include TV. Genres include comedy, romance, and drama.

GOLDSMITH-THOMAS PRODUCTIONS
Production company

239 Central Park West, Suite 6A
New York, NY 10024
212-243-4147 (phone)
212-799-2545 (fax)

imdb.com/company/co0186672

Accepts query letters from unproduced, unrepresented writers. Project types include TV and feature films. Genres include family, drama, non-fiction, comedy, and romance.

Elaine Goldsmith-Thomas
imdb.com/name/nm0326063
linkedin.com/pub/elaine-goldsmith-thomas/20/a85/498
Assistant: Anabel Graff

GOLD VIEW COMPANY
Sales agent

3-50-5 Entopia Ogikubo, Suite 1201
Asagaya-minami, Suginami-ku
Tokyo 166 0004
Japan
+81 35347 2501

kiyo@goldview.co.jp
goldview.co.jp
imdb.com/company/co0002048

Does not accept any unsolicited material. Project types include feature films and TV. Genres include comedy, horror, and drama.

Kiyo Joo
Producer
imdb.com/name/nm0429731

GONE OFF DEEP PRODUCTION
Production company and distributor

8906 McMeans Trail
Austin, TX 78737
512-771-3669

prod@goneoffdeep.com
goneoffdeep.com
imdb.com/company/co0138239
linkedin.com/company/gone-off-deep-llc
facebook.com/GoneOffDeep
twitter.com/goneoffdeep

Does not accept any unsolicited material. Project types include TV and feature films. Genres include family, documentary, and comedy. Established in 2011.

GOOD CLEAN FUN
Production company

3733 Motor Ave
Los Angeles, CA 90034
310-842-9300

goodcleanfunllc.com
imdb.com/name/nm2275176

Does not accept any unsolicited material. Project types include TV.

Matthew Wrablik
VP of Development
imdb.com/name/nm0136160

GOOD GAME ENTERTAINMENT
Production company

4000 Warner Blvd., Building 34
Burbank, CA 91522
818-954-3414

imdb.com/company/co0177676

Does not accept any unsolicited material. Project types include TV. Genres include comedy and drama.

Kathy Ebel
VP
imdb.com/name/nm1889799

Lauren Graham
Actor/Producer/Writer
imdb.com/name/nm0334179

GOOD HUMOR TELEVISION
Production company

9255 W Sunset Blvd #1040
West Hollywood, CA 90069
310-205-7361 (phone)
310-550-7962 (fax)

imdb.com/company/co0227256

Accepts query letters from unproduced, unrepresented writers. Project types include TV. Genres include comedy and animation.

Tom Werner
imdb.com/name/nm0921492

GOOD LUCK PICTURES
Production company

PO Box 543506
Grand Prairie, TX 75054

imdb.com/company/co0238076
facebook.com/goodluckpictures
twitter.com/goodluckpics

Does not accept any unsolicited material. Genres include documentary, comedy, and thriller.

GOOD NAMES TAKEN PRODUCTIONS
Production company

Denver, CO
303-949-9212

gntproductions@gmail.com
imdb.com/company/co0299652

Does not accept any unsolicited material. Project types include short films. Genres include comedy.

Maggie Hart
Producer
imdb.com/name/nm3660553

GOOD TO BE SEEN FILMS
Production company

2560 US Highway 22
#347
Scotch Plains, NJ 07076

info@goodtobeseenfilms.com
goodtobeseenfilms.com
imdb.com/company/co0016975

Does not accept any unsolicited material. Genres include drama, comedy, and animation.

GOOD UNIVERSE
Production company, distributor, and sales agent

9777 Wilshire Blvd, Suite 400, Beverly Hills, CA, United States, 90212
310-623-9840

info@good-universe.com
imdb.com/company/co0380492

Does not accept any unsolicited material. Project types include TV. Genres include drama, action, family, and thriller.

GOOD WORLDWIDE
Production company

6380 Wilshire Blvd., 15th Floor, Los Angeles, CA, United States, 90048
323-556-6780

601 W 26th St Suite 325
New York NY 10001

info@goodinc.com
magazine.good.is
imdb.com/company/co0242621

Does not accept any unsolicited material. Project types include TV and feature films. Genres include thriller, drama, and family.

GORDONSTREET PICTURES
Production company

2241 N.Cahuenga Blvd.
Los Angeles, CA
323-467-6267

imdb.com/company/co0137407

Does not accept any unsolicited material. Project types include feature films. Genres include thriller and drama.

Ram Bergman
Producer
imdb.com/name/nm0074851

Raymond Izaac
Development
imdb.com/name/nm0412691

GORILLA PICTURES
Production company

2000 W Olive Ave
Burbank, CA 91506
818-848-2198 (phone)
818-848-2232 (fax)

info@gorillapictures.net
gorillapictures.net
imdb.com/company/co0139947

Does not accept any unsolicited material. Project types include feature films. Genres include drama, thriller, fantasy, family, action, animation, crime, and science fiction. Established in 1999.

Don Wilson
don.wilson@gorillapictures.net
imdb.com/name/nm0933310

Bill Gottlieb
CEO
bill.gottlieb@gorillapictures.net
imdb.com/name/nm1539281

GOTHAM ENTERTAINMENT GROUP
Production company

85 John St Penthouse 1
New York City, NY 10038
814-253-5151 (phone)
801-439-6998 (fax)

Los Angeles, CA

losangeles@gothamcity.com
gothamentertainmentgroup.com
imdb.com/company/co0036910
linkedin.com/company/gotham-entertainment-group

Accepts query letters from unproduced, unrepresented writers via email. Project types include TV and feature films. Genres include action, crime, drama, non-fiction, romance, science fiction, comedy, reality, and thriller.

Joel Roodman
Partner
joel@gothamentertainmentgroup.com
imdb.com/name/nm0740211

Eric Kopeloff
Partner
imdb.com/name/nm0465740

GRACE HILL MEDIA
Production company and distributor

12211 Huston St
Valley Village, CA 91607
818-762-0000

rsvp@gracehillmedia.com
gracehillmedia.com
imdb.com/company/co0195279
linkedin.com/company/grace-hill-media
.facebook.com/GraceHillMedia
twitter.com/GraceHillTweets

Does not accept any unsolicited material. Project types include feature films. Genres include documentary and family. Established in 2000.

GRACIE FILMS
Production company and distributor

10201 W. Pico Blvd., Bldg. 41/42
Los Angeles, CA 90064
310-369-7222

graciefilms@aol.com
graciefilms.com
imdb.com/company/co0035761

Does not accept any unsolicited material. Project types include feature films and TV. Genres include non-fiction, family, romance, comedy, drama, and animation.

Richard Sakai
President
imdb.com/name/nm0757017

Julie Ansell
imdb.com/name/nm0030572

James Brooks
imdb.com/name/nm0000985

GRADE A ENTERTAINMENT
Production company

149 S Barrington Ave, Suite 719
Los Angeles, CA 90049
310-358-8600 (phone)
310-919-2998 (fax)

development@gradeaent.com
imdb.com/company/co0092463
imdb.com/company/co0092463

Accepts query letters from unproduced, unrepresented writers via email. Project types include TV and feature films. Genres include fantasy.

Andy Cohen
andy@gradeaent.com
imdb.com/name/nm2221597

GRAMMNET PRODUCTIONS
Production company

2461 Santa Monica Blvd #521
Santa Monica, CA 90404
310-317-4231 (phone)
310-317-4260 (fax)

imdb.com/company/co0067942

Does not accept any unsolicited material. Project types include feature films, TV, and theater. Genres include reality, drama, non-fiction, comedy, and family.

Kelsey Grammar
imdb.com/name/nm0001288
Assistant: Xochitl L. Olivas

GRANAT ENTERTAINMENT
Production company

2115 Colorado Ave
Santa Monica, CA 90404

imdb.com/company/co0282230

Does not accept any unsolicited material. Project types include feature films.

Cary Granat
President
imdb.com/name/nm0000026

GRAND CANAL FILM WORKS
Production company

1187 Coast Village Rd
Montecito, CA 93108
818-259-8237

11135 Magnolia, SU 160
North Hollywood, CA 91601

greych@gmail.com
imdb.com/company/co0201904

Does not accept any unsolicited material. Project types include theater, TV, and feature films. Genres include reality and non-fiction.

Rick Brookwell
Partner
rbrookwell@grandcanalfw.com
imdb.com/name/nm2162558
linkedin.com/pub/rick-brookwell/9/906/407

Craig Haffner
Partner
chaffner@grandcanalfw.com
imdb.com/name/nm0353121
linkedin.com/pub/craig-haffner/9/1a6/193

GRAND HUSTLE ENTERTAINMENT
Production company

PMB 161 541 10th St
Atlanta, GA 30318

contact@grandhustlegang.com
grandhustle.com
imdb.com/company/co0184618
facebook.com/Grand-Hustle-Entertainment-39031127556

Does not accept any unsolicited material. Genres include comedy.

T. I.
Producer, Actor
imdb.com/name/nm1939267

Jason Geter
Producer
imdb.com/name/nm2327951

GRAND PRODUCTIONS
Production company and distributor

16255 Venture Blvd, Suite 400
Encino, CA 91436
818-981-1497 (phone)
818-380-3006 (fax)

grandproductions@mac.com
grandproductions.co.uk
imdb.com/company/co0000803
twitter.com/grndproductions

Does not accept any unsolicited material. Project types include feature films and TV. Genres include comedy and drama.

Gary Randall
imdb.com/name/nm0709592

GRANDVIEW PICTURES
Production company

230 Central Park West
New York, NY 10024
212-595-2206

imdb.com/company/co0076728

Does not accept any unsolicited material. Project types include feature films. Genres include drama.

Jon Kilik
Producer
imdb.com/name/nm0453091

GRANITE ENTERTAINMENT
Production company

8539 Sunset Blvd Ste. 4-136
Los Angeles, CA 90069
310-854-6220

imdb.com/company/co0272032
facebook.com/GraniteEntertainment

Does not accept any unsolicited material. Project types include TV and feature films.

Hank McCann
Partner/Producer/Casting
imdb.com/name/nm0564869

GRAN VIA PRODUCTIONS
Production company

1888 Century Park East
14th Floor
Los Angeles, CA 90067
310-859-3060 (phone)
310-859-3066 (fax)

imdb.com/company/co0071947

Does not accept any unsolicited material. Project types include feature films and TV. Genres include science fiction, fantasy, drama, and comedy.

Mark Johnson
imdb.com/name/nm0425741
Assistant: Emily Eckert (Story Editor)

Mark Ceryak
Creative Executive
imdb.com/name/nm1641437

GRAPHIC FILM COMPANY
Production company

3450 Cahuenga Blvd. W, Bldg. 609
Los Angeles, CA 90068
323-845-0821

imdb.com/company/co0074086
facebook.com/The-Graphic-Film-
    Company-114239822096103

Does not accept any unsolicited material. Project types include feature films. Genres include drama.

GRAVITAS VENTURES
Distributor

209 Richmond St, El Segundo, CA, United States, 90245
310-388-9362

gravitasventures.com
imdb.com/company/co0220024

Does not accept any unsolicited material. Project types include feature films and TV. Genres include drama, thriller, and family.

GRAY ANGEL PRODUCTIONS
Production company

69 Windward Ave
Venice, CA 90291
310-581-0010 (phone)
310-396-0551 (fax)

reverbnation.com/grayangelproductions
imdb.com/company/co0177683
facebook.com/grayangelproductions

Accepts query letters from unproduced, unrepresented writers. Project types include feature films.

Jaclyn Bashoff
imdb.com/name/nm1902472

Anjelica Huston
imdb.com/name/nm0001378

GRAZKA TAYLOR PRODUCTIONS
Production company

409 N Camden Dr, Suite 202
Beverly Hills, CA 90210
310-246-1107

imdb.com/company/co0115289

Does not accept any unsolicited material. Project types include feature films and TV. Genres include reality, non-fiction, drama, and romance.

Grazka Taylor
Producer
grazka@grazkat.com
imdb.com/name/nm0852429

GREASY ENTERTAINMENT
Production company

6345 Balboa Blvd
Building 4, Suite 375
Encino, CA 91316
310-586-2300

info@greasy.biz
greasy.biz

imdb.com/company/co0176928

Accepts query letters from unproduced, unrepresented writers via email. Project types include TV and feature films. Genres include comedy and action.

Jon Heder
imdb.com/name/nm1417647

GREAT BRITTAN
Production company

59 Lake Dr
Highstown, NJ 08520
609-426-1777

mkmainman@aol.com
imdb.com/company/co0118661

Does not accept any unsolicited material. Project types include short films. Genres include drama, fantasy, family, and sociocultural.

GREAT MEADOW PRODUCTIONS
Production company

38 Trinity Gardens
London, England SW9 8DP
UK
+44 20 7733 7621

office@greatmeadowprods.com
greatmeadowprods.com
imdb.com/company/co0176551

Does not accept any unsolicited material. Project types include feature films and TV. Genres include drama.

Robert Cooper Cooper
Producer
imdb.com/name/nm0178340

GREAT POINT MEDIA
Production company, distributor, and financing company

22 Long Acre, London, United Kingdom, WC2E 9LY
011-440-2075505

7 W 18th St #3
New York NY 10011

info@greatpointmedia.com
greatpointmedia.com

imdb.com/company/co0504760

Does not accept any unsolicited material. Genres include drama, thriller, family, action, and comedy.

GREE

Production company and distributor

6-10-1
Roppongi
Minato, Tokyo 106-6190
Japan

pr@gree.co.jp
corp.gree.net/jp/ja
imdb.com/company/co0388462

Does not accept any unsolicited material. Project types include TV, feature films, and short films. Genres include horror.

Yuta Maeda
Vice President (Executive)
imdb.com/name/nm7097771

GREEKS PRODUCTIONS

Production company

PO Box 152848
Austin, TX 78715
512-619-6918

greeksfilms.com
imdb.com/company/co0184297
facebook.com/greekproductions

Does not accept any unsolicited material. Genres include action, comedy, horror, and thriller.

GREEN APPLE ENTERTAINMENT

Distributor and sales agent

5111 Sabal Gardens Ln
Suite 1
Boca Raton, FL 33487
561-218-4703

info@greenapple-ent.com
greenapple-ent.com
imdb.com/company/co0296083
linkedin.com/company/green-apple-entertainment-inc
facebook.com/GreenAppleEnt
twitter.com/GreenAppleEnt

Does not accept any unsolicited material. Project types include feature films and TV. Genres include thriller, comedy, action, drama, crime, and romance. Established in 2005.

GREEN COMMUNICATIONS

Production company

255 Parkside Dr
San Fernando, CA 91340
818-557-0050

info@greenfilms.com
greenfilms.com
imdb.com/company/co0049963

Does not accept any unsolicited material. Project types include TV and feature films.

D'Arcy Conrique
CEO
imdb.com/name/nm1330256

Talaat Captan
President
imdb.com/name/nm0135708

GREEN HAT FILMS

Production company

4000 Warner Blvd
Building 66
Burbank, CA 91522
818-954-3210 (phone)
818-954-3214 (fax)

imdb.com/company/co0221959

Does not accept any unsolicited material. Project types include feature films. Genres include non-fiction, thriller, comedy, and drama.

Todd Phillips
imdb.com/name/nm0680846
Assistant: Joseph Garner

GREENROOM ENTERTAINMENT

Production company

4 Margaret St
3rd Fl
London W1W 8RF

UK
+44207-580-8484

8687 Melrose Ave, 9th Floor
Los Angeles, CA 90069
+310-967-2325

info@greenroom-entertainment.com
greenroom-entertainment.com
imdb.com/company/co0244382

Does not accept any unsolicited material. Project types include TV and feature films. Genres include comedy, drama, and action.

Isabel Freer
Producer
imdb.com/name/nm2478508

GREENSTREET FILMS
Production company

430 W Broadway 2nd Floor
New York City, NY 10012
212-609-9000 (phone)
212-609-9099 (fax)

general@gstreet.com
imdb.com/company/co0025423

Accepts query letters from unproduced, unrepresented writers via email. Project types include feature films. Genres include drama, horror, romance, comedy, and thriller.

John M Penotti
President
imdb.com/name/nm0006597

Matthew Honovic
Creative Executive
http://www.imdb.com/name/
nm2416270/?ref_=fn_al_nm_1

GREENTREES FILMS
Production company, distributor, and financing company

854-A 5th St
Santa Monica, CA 90403
310-899-1522 (phone)
310-496-2082 (fax)

info@greentreesfilms.com

greentreesfilms.com
imdb.com/company/co0184723
facebook.com/greentreesfilms
twitter.com/greentreesfilms

Accepts query letters from unproduced, unrepresented writers via email. Project types include feature films, TV, and commercials. Genres include drama, non-fiction, reality, and comedy.

Jack Binder
imdb.com/name/nm0082784

GRINDSTONE ENTERTAINMENT GROUP
Production company and distributor

2700 Colorado Ave
Suite 200
Santa Monica, CA 90404
310-255-5761 (phone)
310-255-3766 (fax)

thegrindstone.net
imdb.com/company/co0209560
facebook.com/GrindstoneEnt
twitter.com/GrindstoneEnt

Accepts query letters from produced or represented writers. Project types include feature films. Genres include drama, period, action, and thriller.

Teresa Sabatine
teresa@thegrindstone.net
imdb.com/name/nm3466608

Stan Wertlieb
stanwertlieb@gmail.com
imdb.com/name/nm0921627

Ryan Black
Director of Development
ryan@thegrindstone.net
imdb.com/name/nm3337383

Barry Brooker
President
barry@thegrindstone.net
imdb.com/name/nm1633269

GRINDSTONE MEDIA
Production company and distributor

66 Seventh St
Toronto, ON M8V 3B2
Canada
416-255-3640

imdb.com/company/co0181503
linkedin.com/company/juice-productions
facebook.com/pages/Juice/197862533581759
twitter.com/JuiceTweets

Does not accept any unsolicited material. Project types include TV. Genres include comedy.

GRIZZLY ADAMS PRODUCTIONS
Production company

201 Five Cities Dr SPC 172, Pismo Beach
CA 93449
877-556-8536 (phone)
805-556-0393 (fax)

admin@grizzlyadams.tv
grizzlyadams.com
imdb.com/company/co0076591
facebook.com/grizzlyadams
twitter.com/_grizzlyadams_

Does not accept any unsolicited material. Project types include feature films and TV. Genres include reality, documentary, family, drama, and non-fiction.

David W. Balsiger
imdb.com/name/nm1901322

GROSSO JACOBSON COMMUNICATIONS CORP.
Production company

373 Front St East
Toronto, Ontario MSA 1G4
Canada

767 Third Ave
New York, NY 10017

1801 Ave of the Stars, Suite 911
Los Angeles, CA 90067
310-788-8900

grossojacobson@grossojacobson.com
imdb.com/company/co0043264
facebook.com/pages/Grosso-Jacobson-
    Communications-Corp/104996346232238

Accepts query letters from unproduced, unrepresented writers via email. Project types include feature films, theater, and TV. Genres include non-fiction, crime, drama, horror, thriller, comedy, and reality. Established in 1999.

Sonny Grosso
Executive Producer
212-644-6909
imdb.com/name/nm0343780

Keith Johnson
Sr. VP Development
310-788-8900
imdb.com/name/nm1702242
linkedin.com/pub/keith-johnson/6/A09/A74

GROSS-WESTON PRODUCTIONS
Production company

10560 Wilshire Blvd, Suite 801
Los Angeles, CA 90024
310-777-0010 (phone)
310-777-0016 (fax)

gross-weston@sbcglobal.net
imdb.com/company/co0032431
linkedin.com/company/gross-weston-productions

Accepts scripts from produced or represented writers. Project types include TV, feature films, and theater. Genres include thriller, drama, reality, comedy, action, science fiction, family, romance, and non-fiction.

Ann Weston
Executive Producer
imdb.com/name/nm0922912

Mary Gross
Executive Producer
imdb.com/name/nm0343437

GROUNDSWELL PRODUCTIONS
Production company and financing company

12424 Wilshire Blvd.
Suite 1120
Los Angeles, CA 90025
310-385-7540 (phone)
310-385-7541 (fax)

info@groundswellfilms.com

groundswellfilms.com
imdb.com/company/co0173527
linkedin.com/company/groundswell-productions

Does not accept any unsolicited material. Project types include TV, feature films, and theater. Genres include horror, action, crime, thriller, drama, comedy, non-fiction, and romance. Established in 2006.

Kelly Mullen
Vice-President
imdb.com/name/nm4133402

Janice Williams
imdb.com/name/nm1003921

GRÜNBERG FILM
Production company

Blankenburger Chaussee 84
Berlin 13125
Germany
+49(0)30 - 94 32 999

info@gruenbergfilm.de
gruenbergfilm.com
imdb.com/company/co0070475
linkedin.com/in/gruenbergfilm

Does not accept any unsolicited material. Project types include feature films, short films, and TV. Genres include action.

Andreas Grünberg
Producer
imdb.com/name/nm0345060

GRUVE DIGITAL PRODUCTIONS
Production company and distributor

450 Shrewsbury Plaza, Suite 108
Shrewsbury, NJ 07702

imdb.com/company/co0125296

Does not accept any unsolicited material. Project types include feature films and TV. Genres include drama.

GUARDIAN ENTERTAINMENT, LTD
Production company

71 5th Ave
New York, NY 10003

212-727-4729 (phone)
212-727-4713 (fax)

guardian@guardianltd.com
guardianltd.com
imdb.com/company/co0093360
linkedin.com/company/guardian-entertainment-ltd

Accepts query letters from unproduced, unrepresented writers via email. Project types include TV, feature films, and commercials. Genres include science fiction, drama, horror, reality, non-fiction, and thriller.

Anita Agair
agair@guardianltd.com

Richard Miller
rmiller@guardianltd.com

GUGGENHEIM PRODUCTIONS
Production company and distributor

3121 S St. NW
Washington, DC 20007

gpifilms@gpifilms.com
imdb.com/company/co0011170
facebook.com/GuggenheimProductions

Does not accept any unsolicited material. Project types include short films. Genres include documentary.

GULFCOAST FILM PARTNERS
Production company

2710 Del Prado Blvd
2-198
Cape Coral, FL 33904
213-260-1019 (phone)
888-521-0694 (fax)

sales@1pro.com
1pro.com
imdb.com/company/co0239766
linkedin.com/company/gulfcoast-film-partners-llc

Does not accept any unsolicited material. Genres include thriller.

GUNN FILMS
Production company

500 S Buena Vista St
Old Animation Building, Suite 3-A7
Burbank, CA 91521
818-560-6156 (phone)
818-842-8394 (fax)

andrew.gunn@disney.com
imdb.com/company/co0007784

Does not accept any unsolicited material. Project types include feature films and TV. Genres include fantasy, drama, action, romance, comedy, science fiction, thriller, and family. Established in 2001.

Andrew Gunn
Producer
andrew.gunn@disney.com
imdb.com/name/nm0348151

GUSH PRODUCTIONS
Distributor

San Francisco, CA
415-644-8741

info@gushproductions.com
imdb.com/company/co0475971
facebook.com/pages/GUSH-productions/
    183116245059192

Does not accept any unsolicited material. Genres include documentary. Established in 2009.

Samantha Grant
Founder
linkedin.com/in/gushproductions

GUY WALKS INTO A BAR
Production company

236 W 27th St #1000
New York, NY 10001
212-941-1509

info@guywalks.com
guywalks.com

Does not accept any unsolicited material. Project types include TV, feature films, and commercials. Genres include comedy, animation, romance, family, fantasy, and science fiction.

Todd Komarnicki
imdb.com/name/nm0464548

GVI
Production company

1775 K St. NW
Suite 220
Washington, DC 20006
202-293-4488

g-v-i.com
imdb.com/company/co0096772
linkedin.com/company/838606
facebook.com/pages/GVI-Washington-DC/
    180439831973170
twitter.com/GVIDC

Does not accept any unsolicited material. Project types include feature films, short films, and TV. Genres include documentary. Established in 1983.

H2O MOTION PICTURES
Production company

8549 Hedges Place
Los Angeles, CA 90069
323-654-5920 (phone)
323-654-5923 (fax)

23 Denmark St., 3rd Floor
London, WC2H 8NH, U.K
44207-240-5656

h2o@h2omotionpictures.com
h2omotionpictures.com
imdb.com/company/co0333174
facebook.com/h2omotionpictures

Does not accept any unsolicited material. Project types include feature films.

Andras Hamori
President
imdb.com/name/nm0358877

HAAS SILVER LEVENE FILM STUDIOS (HSL)
Production company

37 Warren St
London W1T 6AD
UK
+44(0)20 7383 3200 (phone)
+44 (0)20 7383 4168 (fax)

haassilevmab@films1.fsnet.co.uk
silverlevene.co.uk
imdb.com/company/co0273710

Does not accept any unsolicited material. Project types
include feature films. Genres include animation,
drama, and thriller.

Timothy W. Haas
Producer
imdb.com/name/nm3006820

HAFT ENTERTAINMENT
Production company

38 Gramercy Park North, #2C
New York, NY 10010
212-586-3881 (phone)
212-459-9798 (fax)

imdb.com/company/co0045494

Accepts query letters from produced or represented
writers. Project types include feature films and short
films.

Steven Haft
President/Producer
imdb.com/name/nm0353187

HA HA PRODUCTIONS
Production company

36 Lennox St
Suite #3
Toronto, ON M6G 1J5
Canada
416-536-2711

imdb.com/company/co0369184

Does not accept any unsolicited material. Project types
include TV. Genres include comedy and drama.

HALCYON INTERNATIONAL PICTURES
Production company and sales agent

2620 S Maryland Parkway
Ste 970
Las Vegas, NV 89109
310-388-6087

halcyonpix.com

imdb.com/company/co0190716

Does not accept any unsolicited material. Project types
include TV and feature films. Genres include horror
and comedy.

Ray Haboush
Producer
imdb.com/name/nm0352303

HALCYON VALOR PRODUCTIONS
Production company

P.O. Box 1757
Montclair, NJ 07042
908-752-9337

jamisonmlocascio@gmail.com
halcyonvalor.com
imdb.com/company/co0393069

Does not accept any unsolicited material. Genres
include drama and thriller.

HALESTORM ENTERTAINMENT
Production company

5132 N 300 West
Provo, UT
801-655-5180 (phone)
801-655-5181 (fax)

contact@hstorm.com
halestormentertainment.com
imdb.com/company/co0000345

Does not accept any unsolicited material. Project types
include feature films. Genres include comedy.

Kurt Hale
Partner/COO/Producer
imdb.com/name/nm1109378

Dave Hunter
Partner/Writer/Director
imdb.com/name/nm111268

HALF FULL ENTERTAINMENT
Production company

500 S. Buena Vista St. Old Animation Bldg., Ste. 2F3
Burbank, CA 91521
818-560-6868

halffullentertainment.com
imdb.com/company/co0308384
facebook.com/HalfFullEntertainment

Does not accept any unsolicited material. Project types include TV. Genres include comedy.

HALFIRE ENTERTAINMENT
Production company

HALFIRE ENTERTAINMENT
2021 Killarney Dr
Ottawa Ontario K2A 1P9
Canada

8730 W Sunset Blvd., Penthouse West
Los Angeles, CA 90069

halfireentertainment.com
imdb.com/company/co0432767

Does not accept any unsolicited material.

Stephanie Fontana
Director of Development
imdb.com/name/nm0284952

Noreen Halpern
President/Producer
imdb.com/name/nm0356957

HALLBROOK PRODUCTIONS
Production company

565 Dutch Valley Rd
Atlanta, GA 30324
404-892-0042

hallbrook@hallbrookproductions.com
hallbrookproductions.com
imdb.com/company/co0191386
linkedin.com/company/hallbrook-productions
facebook.com/HallBrook-Productions-
   Inc-356095461114678

Does not accept any unsolicited material. Project types include short films. Genres include comedy.

HAMMER FILMS
Production company

52 Haymarket
London, United Kingdom,

SW1Y 4RP
+44 20 3002 9510

info@hammerfilms.com
hammerfilms.com
imdb.com/company/co0103101

Does not accept any unsolicited material. Project types include TV and feature films. Genres include thriller, action, drama, comedy, horror, and documentary. Established in 1934.

Simon Oakes
imdb.com/name/nm2649227

HAMZEH MYSTIQUE FILMS
Studio

61 Blaney St
Swampscott , MA 01907-2546
781-596-1281 (phone)
781-599-2424 (fax)

info@hamzehmystiquefilms.com
hamzehmystiquefilms.com
imdb.com/company/co0057291
linkedin.com/company/hamzeh-mystique-films-inc
facebook.com/HAMZEH-MYSTIQUE-
   FILMS-52962073821

Does not accept any unsolicited material.

Ziad H. Hamzeh
President
imdb.com/name/nm0359144

Marc Sandler
VP of Development/Creative Affairs
imdb.com/name/nm0761983

HANDPICKED FILMS
Production company

8228 W Sunset Blvd
Los Angeles, CA 90046
323-654-2256

imdb.com/company/co0163220
linkedin.com/company/hand-picked-films-inc

Does not accept any unsolicited material. Project types include short films, feature films, and commercials. Genres include non-fiction, period, drama, documentary, comedy, thriller, and romance. Established in 2015.

Michel Shane
imdb.com/name/nm0788062

Darren VanCleave
Executive
imdb.com/name/nm2168166

Anthony Romano
Producer
imdb.com/name/nm0738853

HANDSOMECHARLIE FILMS
Production company

1720-1/2 Whitley Ave
Los Angeles, CA 90028
323-462-6013

imdb.com/company/co0224040
facebook.com/pages/Handsomecharlie-Films/
    210957442439474
twitter.com/handsomecharlie

Does not accept any unsolicited material. Project types include short films and feature films. Genres include drama, action, period, documentary, romance, horror, comedy, and non-fiction. Established in 2007.

Natalie Portman
President
imdb.com/name/nm0000204

HANNIBAL PICTURES
Production company

8265 Sunset Blvd, Suite 107
West Hollywood, CA 90046
323-848-2945 (phone)
323-848-2946 (fax)

contactus@hannibalpictures.com
hannibalpictures.com
imdb.com/company/co0059168
facebook.com/pages/Hannibal-Pictures/
    158994507487285

Accepts query letters from unproduced, unrepresented writers via email. Project types include feature films. Genres include science fiction, thriller, action, crime,

non-fiction, romance, drama, and comedy. Established in 1999.

Richard Rionda Del Castro
imdb.com/name/nm0215502

Kristy Eberle-Adams
imdb.com/name/nm5554723

Cam Cannon
Director of Development
imdb.com/name/nm1359191

HANNOVER HOUSE
Production company

1428 Chester St
Springdale, AR 72764
479-751-4500 (phone)
479-751-4999 (fax)

HannoverHouse@aol.com
hannoverhouse.com
imdb.com/company/co0098047
facebook.com/HHSE.hannoverhouse

Does not accept any unsolicited material. Project types include feature films. Genres include science fiction, family, and drama.

Eric Parkinson
President / CEO
imdb.com/name/nm0003826

HANWAY FILMS
Production company, distributor, and sales agent

24 Hanway St London, W1T 1UH
United Kingdom
+44 0207-290-0750

info@hanwayfilms.com
hanwayfilms.com
imdb.com/company/co0133023

Does not accept any unsolicited material. Project types include short films, TV, and feature films. Genres include romance.

Jeremy Thomas
Producer
recordedpicture.com
imdb.com/name/nm0859016

HAPPY MADISON PRODUCTIONS

Production company and distributor

10202 W Washington Blvd Judy Garland Building
Culver City, CA 90232
310-244-3100 (phone)
310-244-3353 (fax)

imdb.com/company/co0059609
twitter.com/happymadison

Does not accept any unsolicited material. Project types include TV, short films, and feature films. Genres include comedy, fantasy, drama, romance, animation, action, and thriller. Established in 1999.

Heather Parry
imdb.com/name/nm1009782
twitter.com/heatherparry

Judit Maull
Executive
imdb.com/name/nm1263796

Doug Robinson
imdb.com/name/nm2120562
Assistant: Brianna Riofrio

Adam Sandler
Partner
imdb.com/name/nm0001191
twitter.com/AdamSandler

Jack Giarraputo
Partner
imdb.com/name/nm0316406
Assistant: Rachel Simmer

HARBOR LIGHT ENTERTAINMENT

Production company

1438 N Gower St
Los Angeles, CA 90028
323-397-4928

imdb.com/company/co0213272
linkedin.com/company/harbor-light-entertainment

Does not accept any unsolicited material. Project types include feature films.

Stuart Calcote
Producer
imdb.com/name/nm3129931

Edwin Marshall
Producer
imdb.com/name/nm0550862

HARDLINE PRODUCTIONS AND ENTERTAINMENT

Production company

60 Perimeter Center Place
#442
Atlanta, GA 30346
US
678-793-8402 (phone)
678-530-1020 (fax)

jeff@hardlineproductions.com
imdb.com/company/co0308426

Does not accept any unsolicited material.

HARDY, SON AND BAKER

Production company

26 Aybrook St
London W1U 4AN
England

contact@hardybaker.com
hardybaker.com
imdb.com/company/co0432343

Does not accept any unsolicited material. Genres include drama.

Tom Hardy
Executive
imdb.com/name/nm0362766

HARMONY GOLD

Production company, distributor, and sales agent

7655 Sunset Blvd, Los Angeles , CA, United States, 90046
323-851-4900 (phone)
323-851-5599 (fax)

info@harmonygold.com
harmonygold.com
imdb.com/company/co0004023

Does not accept any unsolicited material. Project types include TV, feature films, and short films. Genres include thriller, drama, family, action, and detective.

HARMS WAY PRODUCTIONS
Production company

4158 Camellia Ave
Studio City, CA 91604
818-486-0946

imdb.com/company/co0177691

Does not accept any unsolicited material. Project types include TV and feature films.

Kristin Harms
Producer
imdb.com/name/nm0363599

HARPO FILMS, INC.
Production company

345 N Maple Dr, Suite 315
Beverly Hills, CA 90210
310-278-5559

sylvia@myagsc.com
imdb.com/company/co0004231
facebook.com/pages/Harpo-Productions/
	108466999178602

Does not accept any unsolicited material. Project types include TV and feature films. Genres include drama, romance, comedy, fantasy, horror, and non-fiction.

Oprah Winfrey
imdb.com/name/nm0001856
facebook.com/oprahwinfrey
twitter.com/Oprah

HARTBREAK FILMS
Production company

14622 Ventura Blvd. Suite 102
Sherman Oaks, CA 91403

info@hartbreak.com
hartbreak.com
imdb.com/company/co0035722

Does not accept any unsolicited material. Project types include TV. Genres include family.

Paula Hart
Producer
imdb.com/name/nm0366472

HARTSWOOD FILMS
Production company

3A Paradise Rd
Richmond
Surrey
TW9 1RX
+44 (0) 20-3668-3060 (phone)
+44 (0) 20-3668-3050 (fax)

Nations and Regions Office
17 Cathedral Rd
Cardiff
CF11 9HA
+44 (0)29-2023-3333 (phone)
+44 (0)29-2022-5878 (fax)

films.tv@hartswoodfilms.co.uk
hartswoodfilms.co.uk
imdb.com/company/co0023675
facebook.com/pages/Hartswood-Films/
	132967313406613
twitter.com/hartswoodfilms

Does not accept any unsolicited material. Project types include TV. Genres include crime, comedy, horror, thriller, detective, and drama. Established in 1980.

Beryl Vertue
Chairman
imdb.com/name/nm0895054

Elaine Cameron
Head of Development
imdb.com/name/nm0131569

Sue Vertue
Producer
imdb.com/name/nm0895056
twitter.com/suevertue

Debbie Vertue
Director of Operations
imdb.com/name/nm0895055

HASBRO, INC./HASBRO FILMS
Production company

Burbank
2950 N Hollywood Way Suite 100
Burbank, CA 91504
818-478-4320

hasbro.com/?US
imdb.com/company/co0130376

Accepts query letters from unproduced, unrepresented writers. Project types include video games and feature films. Genres include comedy, family, non-fiction, fantasy, science fiction, animation, and action.

Daniel Persitz
Creative Executive
imdb.com/name/nm1974626
linkedin.com/pub/daniel-persitz/35/224/36a

HAT TRICK PRODUCTIONS
Production company and distributor

33 Oval Rd
London NW1 7EA
UK
+44 20 7184 7777 (phone)
+44 20 7184 7778 (fax)

reception@hattrick.com
hattrick.com
imdb.com/company/co0103628
facebook.com/pages/Hattrick-Productions/
    114980688515764
twitter.com/HatTrickProd

Does not accept any unsolicited material. Project types include TV. Genres include comedy.

Jimmy Mulville
Producer
imdb.com/name/nm0612556

HAWKLI PRODUCTIONS
Production company

9500 SW 92nd St
Miami, FL 33176
305-596-5150 (phone)
305-279-4393 (fax)

imdb.com/company/co0121966

Does not accept any unsolicited material.

HAYDEN REELS
Production company

59 Crittenden St, NE
Washington, DC 20011
202-529-8946

haydenreels@aol.com
imdb.com/company/co0341935

Does not accept any unsolicited material. Project types include TV.

HAYMAKER
Production company

150 W 22nd St., 3rd Fl.
New York, NY 10011

4146 Lankershim Blvd. Suite 401
North Hollywood, CA 91602

contact@haymakertv.com
haymakertv.com
imdb.com/title/tt162099

Does not accept any unsolicited material.

Irad Eyal
Producer
imdb.com/name/nm1164455

Aaron Rothman
Producer
imdb.com/name/nm4169818

HAYZE ENTERTAINMENT GROUP
Production company and financing company

100 E Whitestone Blvd
Ste 148-306
Cedar Park, TX 78613
323-715-0217 (phone)
605-225-2833 (fax)

info@hayze-entertainment.com
hayze-entertainment.com
imdb.com/company/co0197651

Does not accept any unsolicited material. Project types include TV. Genres include documentary, animation, and horror.

Buddie Hasty
Cedar Park, TX
imdb.com/name/nm2573262

HAZY MILLS PRODUCTIONS
Production company and distributor

4024 Radford Ave
Building 7 - 2nd Floor
Studio City, CA 91604
818-840-7568

imdb.com/company/co0147414

Does not accept any unsolicited material. Project types include feature films and TV. Genres include non-fiction, comedy, family, drama, horror, and reality. Established in 2004.

Kiel Elliott
Development Executive
linkedin.com/pub/kiel-elliott/28/644/b3b
twitter.com/KielElliott

Sean Hayes
imdb.com/name/nm0005003
facebook.com/seanhayesmusic
twitter.com/theseanhayes
Assistant: Jessie Kalick

HBO FILMS
Production company, studio, and distributor

1100 Ave of the Americas
New York, NY 10036
212-512-1208

contacthbo@hbo.com
hbo.com/movies
imdb.com/company/co0005861
linkedin.com/company/hbo
facebook.com/pages/HBO-Films/104072436296883
twitter.com/HBO

Does not accept any unsolicited material. Project types include TV. Genres include comedy, drama, family, romance, non-fiction, and thriller. Established in 1983.

Len Amato
President, Films
imdb.com/name/nm0024163
facebook.com/len.amato1

Kary Antholis
President, Miniseries
imdb.com/name/nm0030794

HD FILMS, INC
Studio

4000 Warner Blvd., Bldg. 34 Suite 316
Burbank, CA 91522
818-954-4990 (phone)
818-954-4440 (fax)

hdfilms.com
linkedin.com/company/hd-films-inc
facebook.com/pages/HD-Films-Inc/
109959029029416

Does not accept any unsolicited material. Project types include TV. Genres include science fiction.

Jace Hall
Principal/Producer
imdb.com/name/nm0995727

HDNET FILMS
Production company and distributor

8269 E. 23rd Ave
Denver, CO 80238
303-542-5600

viewer@axs.tv
hdnetmovies.com
imdb.com/company/co0094788
linkedin.com/company/hdnet
facebook.com/hdnetmovies
twitter.com/HDNetMovies

Accepts query letters from unproduced, unrepresented writers. Project types include TV and feature films. Genres include comedy, crime, drama, thriller, documentary, reality, science fiction, and romance. Established in 2001.

Mark Cuban
CEO
mcuban@axs.tv

HEADLINE FEATURES
Distributor

2001 E 51st
Austin, TX 78723
214-686-0939

alex@riotstudios.com
imdb.com/company/co0493537

Does not accept any unsolicited material. Genres include comedy and drama.

HEADLINE PICTURES
Production company and distributor

Fifth Floor
22 Golden Square
London W1F 9JW
UK
+44 (0203-763-2440

info@headline-pictures.com
headline-pictures.com
imdb.com/company/co0195590

Does not accept any unsolicited material. Project types include TV. Genres include family and drama.

Stewart Mackinnon
Producer
imdb.com/name/nm1217161

HEART FIRE PRODUCTIONS
Production company and distributor

127 W Fairbanks Ave
#501
Winter Park, FL 32789
407-739-8620 (phone)
407-643-9151 (fax)

changeworld@aol.com
imdb.com/company/co0193669

Does not accept any unsolicited material. Project types include short films. Genres include drama. Established in 2005.

HEARTH CREATIVE
Production company

P.O. Box 2502
Colorado Springs, CO 80901
323-743-3180

contact@hearthcreative.org
imdb.com/company/co0277853

Does not accept any unsolicited material. Project types include feature films. Genres include drama and comedy.

HEAVY DUTY ENTERTAINMENT
Production company and distributor

6121 Sunset Blvd, Ste 103
Los Angeles, CA 90028
323-209-3545 (phone)
323-653-1720 (fax)

info@heavydutyentertainment.com
heavydutyentertainment.com
imdb.com/company/co0205983

Does not accept any unsolicited material. Project types include TV and feature films. Genres include action, drama, science fiction, comedy, and horror.

Jeff Balis
Producer
imdb.com/name/nm0050276
linkedin.com/pub/jeff-balis/3/a45/659

Rhoades Rader
Producer
imdb.com/name/nm0705476

HEEL AND TOE PRODUCTIONS
Production company

2058 Broadway
Santa Monica, CA 90404
310-288-6289

imdb.com/company/co0022072
facebook.com/pages/Heel-and-Toe-Films/
    129670757225127

Does not accept any unsolicited material. Project types include feature films and TV. Genres include action, drama, and romance. Established in 2001.

Katie Jacobs
Executive Producer
katie.jacobs@fox.com
imdb.com/name/nm0414498

Paul Attanasio
Executive Producer
paul.attanasio@fox.com
imdb.com/name/nm0001921

HEMISPHERE ENTERTAINMENT
Production company

20058 Ventura Blvd
#316
Woodland Hills, CA 91364
818-888-2263 (phone)
818-888-3651 (fax)

hemisphereentertainment.com
imdb.com/company/co0184074

Accepts query letters from unproduced, unrepresented writers. Project types include feature films. Genres include horror, romance, family, crime, thriller, action, and drama.

Jamie Elliot
COO
imdb.com/name/nm0254242

Ralph E. Portillo
CEO
imdb.com/name/nm1589685

Brad Wilson
Vice President of Development & Production
imdb.com/name/nm0933085

HENCEFORTH PICTURES
Production company

15260 Ventura Blvd Ste 1040
Sherman Oaks, CA 91403
424-832-5517 (phone)
424-832-5564 (fax)

inquiries@henceforthpictures.com
henceforthpictures.com
imdb.com/company/co0375280

Does not accept any unsolicited material. Project types include TV and feature films. Genres include action, thriller, crime, and drama. Established in 2009.

Justine Jones
VP, Development
imdb.com/name/nm3540960

William Monahan
Principal
imdb.com/name/nm1184258

HENDERSON PRODUCTIONS
Production company

4252 W Riverside Dr
Burbank, CA 91505
805-966-5832 (phone)
805-701-0918 (fax)

info@henderson-productions.com
henderson-productions.com
imdb.com/company/co0050874
twitter.com/HendersonProd

Does not accept any unsolicited material. Project types include feature films and theater. Genres include comedy, romance, family, and drama.

Garry Marshall
Producer
imdb.com/name/nm0005190

Bill Henderson
Founder
bill@henderson-productions.com

HENRY ISLAND PRODUCTIONS
Production company

610 Venice Blvd.
Venice, CA 90291
310-577-5200

info@henryislandproductions.com
imdb.com/company/co0242278

Does not accept any unsolicited material. Project types include TV and feature films.

Brian Neal
Producer
imdb.com/name/nm5563983

HENSON ALTERNATIVE
Production company

1416 N LaBrea Ave
Hollywood, CA 90028
323-802-1500 (phone)
323-802-1825 (fax)

henson.com/alternative.php
imdb.com/company/co0250340

Does not accept any unsolicited material. Project types include TV. Genres include comedy.

Lisa Henson
CEO of The Jim Henson Co.
imdb.com/name/nm0378229

HENSON ENTERTAINMENT
Production company and distributor

1776 Eye St NW
Washington, DC 20006
310-494-0344

hensonentertainment.weebly.com
imdb.com/company/co0356459

Does not accept any unsolicited material.

HERE NOW PRODUCTIONS
Production company

9107 Wilshire Blvd.
Beverly Hills, CA 90210
310-461-3530

imdb.com/company/co0220218

Does not accept any unsolicited material. Project types include feature films. Genres include drama and comedy.

Mark Webber
Actor/Producer/Director/Writer
imdb.com/name/nm0916406

HERIZON PRODUCTIONS
Production company

11700 Slater St, Overland Park,, KS, United States, 66210

sharon@herizonproductions.com

imdb.com/company/co0228408

Does not accept any unsolicited material. Project types include short films. Genres include documentary.

HERO FILMS
Production company

1581 Harbor Island Dr
Tampa, FL 31108
813-245-6773

jesschwarzkopf@yahoo.com
imdb.com/company/co0032041

Does not accept any unsolicited material. Genres include drama, crime, and action.

HEROIC TELEVISION INC
Production company

403-53 Colgate Ave
Toronto ON Canada M4M 1N6
416-462-1230

info@heroicfilmcompany.com
heroictv.ca
imdb.com/company/co0186655
facebook.com/Heroic-TV-173534516015656
twitter.com/HeroicTeeVee

Does not accept any unsolicited material. Project types include TV. Genres include action, comedy, family, and animation.

John May
Producer
imdb.com/name/nm0562007

HERO PICTURES INTERNATIONAL
Production company

12016 Wilshire Blvd., Suite 1
Los Angeles, CA 90025
310-207-4280 (phone)
310-207-4515 (fax)

info@heropictures.net
imdb.com/company/co0255875

Accepts query letters from unproduced, unrepresented writers via email. Project types include feature films.

Koldo Eguren
President
imdb.com/name/nm3222573

HERRICK ENTERTAINMENT
Production company and distributor

50 Washington St Seventh Floor
Norwalk CT 06854
203-854-5867

2295 Corporate Blvd NW Suite 222
Boca Raton FL 33431
561-241-9880 (phone)
561-241-9887 (fax)

2 Ridgedale Ave, Suite 370, Cedar Knolls, NJ, United
States, 07927
973-539-1390 (phone)
973-539-0596 (fax)

nh@herrickco.com
herrickentertainment.com
imdb.com/company/co0239021

Does not accept any unsolicited material. Project types
include feature films and TV. Genres include family,
action, drama, and thriller.

HEXTC
Production company

560-36th St.
1st Floor
Union City, NJ 07087
877-571-3797

hextc@ureach.com
hextc.org
imdb.com/company/co0487930
facebook.com/hextc

Does not accept any unsolicited material. Project types
include short films. Genres include drama.

HEYDAY FILMS
Production company

4000 Warner Blvd
Building 81, Room 207
Burbank, CA 91522

818-954-3004 (phone)
818-954-3017 (fax)

5 Denmark St.
London WC2H 8LP
UK
+44 20 78 36 63 33 (phone)
+44 20 78 36 64 44 (fax)

imdb.com/company/co0159772
facebook.com/pages/Heyday-Films/
    107919542570242
twitter.com/Heydayfilms

Does not accept any unsolicited material. Project types
include feature films and TV. Genres include action,
comedy, crime, science fiction, thriller, fantasy, family,
and drama. Established in 1997.

Jeffrey Clifford
President
imdb.com/name/nm0166641
Assistant: Kate Phillips

David Heyman
Partner
imdb.com/name/nm0382268
Assistant: Ollie Wiseman (011) 442078366333

HGTV
Production company and distributor

9721 Sherrill Blvd
Knoxville, TN 37932
865-694-2700 (phone)
865-690-6595 (fax)

hgtv.com
imdb.com/company/co0004908
web.facebook.com/hgtv
twitter.com/hgtv

Does not accept any unsolicited material. Project types
include feature films and TV. Genres include reality
and documentary.

HIGH HORSE FILMS
Production company

100 Universal City Plaza
Building 2128, Suite E
Universal City, CA 91608

323-939-8802 (phone)
323-939-8832 (fax)

highhorse.co.uk/film.html
imdb.com/company/co0024903

Accepts query letters from unproduced, unrepresented writers. Project types include feature films and TV. Genres include romance, comedy, and drama. Established in 1990.

Cynthia Chvatal
Producer
imdb.com/name/nm0161558

William Petersen
imdb.com/name/nm0676973

HIGH INTEGRITY PRODUCTIONS
Production company

11054 Ventura Blvd
Suite 324
Studio City, CA 91604 USA
714-313-9606

highintegrityproductions.com
imdb.com/company/co0188415
facebook.com/pages/High-Integrity-Productions/
166109760098778

Accepts query letters from unproduced, unrepresented writers. Project types include feature films. Genres include animation, romance, thriller, and horror.

Dale Noble
909-883-0417
dale@highintegrityproductions.com
imdb.com/name/nm2303672
linkedin.com/pub/dale-noble/11/414/a0a

HIGHLAND FILM GROUP
Production company

9200 Sunset Blvd. Suite 600
West Hollywood, CA 90069
310-271-8400 (phone)
310-278-7500 (fax)

sales@highlandfilmgroup.com
imdb.com/company/co0303030
facebook.com/Highlandfilmgroup
twitter.com/thehighlandfilm

Does not accept any unsolicited material. Project types include feature films. Genres include thriller, crime, and drama.

HIGH STAR ENTERTAINMENT
Production company, distributor, and sales agent

20 Mowat Ave
Toronto, ON M6K 3E8
Canada

info@highstarentertainment.co
highstarentertainment.com
imdb.com/company/co0466536

Does not accept any unsolicited material. Genres include drama.

Bruno Marino
Producer
imdb.com/name/nm3012041

HIGH TREASON PRODUCTIONS
Production company

8200 Wilshire Blvd, Suite 200
Beverly Hills, CA 90211
323-556-0727 (phone)
323-556-0827 (fax)

info@hightreasonproductions.com
hightreasonproductions.com
imdb.com/company/co0192071

Does not accept any unsolicited material. Project types include feature films. Genres include horror, comedy, and thriller.

James Martin
Producer
imdb.com/name/nm1006311

Eduardo Levy
Producer
imdb.com/name/nm2037687

HINTS MUSIC CO.
Production company

4-17-12-3B
Nishi Azabu
Minato, Tokyo 106-0031

Japan
03-5778-0441 (phone)
03-5778-0442 (fax)

store_manager@hintsmarket.com
hintsmarket.com
imdb.com/company/co0388189

Does not accept any unsolicited material. Project types
include TV. Genres include reality.

Masakazu Satô
Producer
imdb.com/name/nm4757605

HIRATA OFFICE
Production company

2-8-15-404
Akasaka
Minato, Tokyo
Japan
03-3587-0088 (phone)
03-3587-0502 (fax)

info@hirataoffice.co.jp
hirata-office.jp
imdb.com/company/co0191907

Does not accept any unsolicited material. Project types
include TV. Genres include comedy.

HIT ENTERTAINMENT
Production company

230 Park Ave, 12th Fl
New York City, NY 10003
212-463-9623

FisherPriceConsumerRelations@Mattel.com
hitentertainment.biz
imdb.com/company/co0029268

Does not accept any unsolicited material. Project types
include TV. Genres include comedy and family.

HIT & RUN PRODUCTIONS
Production company

222 Riverside Dr. Suite 8B
New York, NY 10025
212-864-0800

hitandrunproductions.com
imdb.com/company/co0011026

Does not accept any unsolicited material. Project types
include feature films.

Hilary Shor
President/Producer
imdb.com/name/nm0794892

HIT THE GROUND RUNNING PRODUCTIONS
Production company

52 E 17 St
Hialeah, FL 33010

imdb.com/company/co0097899

Does not accept any unsolicited material. Genres
include thriller.

HOBOKEN PICTURES
Production company

15 Church Towers
#10N
Hoboken, NJ 07030
310-593-1940

hobokenpics@aol.com
imdb.com/company/co0107371

Does not accept any unsolicited material. Project types
include feature films and TV. Genres include drama
and comedy.

HOLDING PICTURES
Production company

120 Broadway, Suite 200
Santa Monica, CA 90401
310-260-7070 (phone)
310-260-7050 (fax)

holdingpictures.com
imdb.com/company/co0230335

Does not accept any unsolicited material. Project types
include feature films. Genres include comedy, drama,
and horror.

Jamie Gregor
Story Editor
imdb.com/name/nm1439017

Charlie Lyons
CEO/Producer
imdb.com/name/nm1854001

HOLE IN THE WALL PRODUCTIONS
Production company

411 S Bayshore Blvd
Sefety Harbor, FL 34695
727-432-5862

cccomm@tampabay.rr.com
imdb.com/company/co0403405

Does not accept any unsolicited material. Genres include documentary and drama.

HOLLYWOOD CLASSICS
Distributor and sales agent

Suite 31, Beaufort Court
Admirals Way
London E14 9XL
UK
+44 (0)20 7517 7525 (phone)
+44 (0)20 7517 7535 (fax)

info@hollywoodclassics.com
hollywoodclassics.com
imdb.com/company/co0231775

Does not accept any unsolicited material. Project types include feature films.

Julia Kelly
Producer
imdb.com/name/nm6366794

HOLLYWOOD GANG PRODUCTIONS
Production company

4000 Warner Blvd
Building 139, Room 201
Burbank, CA 91522
818-954-4999 (phone)
818-954-4448 (fax)

imdb.com/company/co0129244

Does not accept any unsolicited material. Project types include feature films. Genres include action, drama, fantasy, thriller, and science fiction.

Gianni Nunnari
imdb.com/name/nm0638089

HOLLYWOOD WEEKLY MAGAZINE FILM FESTIVAL
Production company and sales agent

12301 Wilshire Blvd.
Suite 500
Los Angeles, Ca 90025
424-371-9900

hollywoodpublisher@gmail.com
hollywoodweeklymagazine.com
linkedin.com/in/prather-jackson-53054814
facebook.com/hollywoodweeklymagazine
twitter.com/hollywoodweekly

Accepts scripts from unproduced, unrepresented writers. Project types include short films and feature films. Genres include documentary, animation, comedy, fantasy, horror, drama, and action. Established in 2014.

Prather Jackson
Executive Producer
hollywoodpublisher@gmail.com

HOME BOX OFFICE (HBO)
Production company

2500 Broadway Suite 400
Santa Monica, CA 90404
310-382-3000 (phone)
310-201-9293 (fax)

1100 Ave of the Americas
Room H13-16
New York City, New York 10036
212-512-1000 (phone)
212-512-5698 (fax)

homeboxoffice.com
imdb.com/company/co0008693

Does not accept any unsolicited material. Project types include TV and feature films. Genres include sociocultural, fantasy, science fiction, crime, comedy, documentary, period, non-fiction, drama, action, family, and romance. Established in 1972.

HOMEGROWN PICTURES
Production company

1684 Ventura Blvd, Suite 800
Studio City, CA 91604

omegrownfilms@mac.com
homegrownpictures.net
imdb.com/company/co0069694
linkedin.com/company/homegrown-pictures

Does not accept any unsolicited material. Project types include TV and feature films. Genres include drama and romance.

Stephanie Allain
Producer
imdb.com/name/nm0019858

HONEST ENGINE TV
Production company

432 W 45th St, 7th Floor
New York, NY 10036
212-947-2341 (phone)
646-867-2782 (fax)

feedback@honestenginetv.com
honestenginetv.com
imdb.com/company/co0252513

Does not accept any unsolicited material. Project types include TV. Genres include comedy.

Meghan O'Hara
Founder/Producer
imdb.com/name/nm0641306

Nick McKinney
Founder/Producer
imdb.com/name/nm0571903

HOOSICK FALLS PRODUCTIONS
Production company

1633 Stanford St
Santa Monica, CA 90404
310-453-2700 (phone)
310-453-2701 (fax)

info@hfpla.com
hoosickfallsla.com
imdb.com/company/co0097609
web.facebook.com/Hoosick-Falls-
Productions-203037395320

Does not accept any unsolicited material. Project types include TV. Genres include comedy.

George Verschoor
Executive Producer
imdb.com/name/nm0004461

HOPSCOTCH PICTURES
Production company

616 N Robertson Blvd., Suite B
Beverly Hills, CA 90211
310-358-0630 (phone)
310-358-0631 (fax)

imdb.com/company/co0177700

Does not accept any unsolicited material. Project types include feature films.

Sukee Chew
Manager/Producer
imdb.com/name/nm0156819

HORIZON ALTERNATIVE TELEVISION
Production company

4000 Warner Blvd.
Burbank, CA 91522

warnerbros.com/studio/divisions/television/warner-
horizon-television

Does not accept any unsolicited material. Project types include TV.

HORIZON ENTERTAINMENT
Production company

1025 S Jefferson Parkway
New Orleans, LA 70125
504-483-1177 (phone)
504-483-1173 (fax)

jsasst@horizonent.tv
horizonent.tv
imdb.com/company/co0225725

Accepts query letters from unproduced, unrepresented writers. Project types include feature films and TV. Genres include family, reality, romance, drama, crime, comedy, thriller, and action. Established in 2000.

Jason Sciavicco
Executive Producer
imdb.com/name/nm2217296

Melissa Dembrun Sciavicco
imdb.com/name/nm2847926

HORROR, INC.
Production company

54 Jaconnet St
Newton, MA 02461

imdb.com/company/co0345614

Does not accept any unsolicited material. Project types include feature films and TV. Genres include horror.

Robert Barsamian
President/Producer
imdb.com/name/nm6452819

HOSTILE DISTRIBUTION
Distributor

1879 Difford Dr.
Niles, OH 44446
330-646-7899

hostile@doorwayproductions.net
imdb.com/company/co0176894

Does not accept any unsolicited material. Genres include thriller and horror.

HOTPLATE PRODUCTIONS
Production company

16000 Ventura Blvd, Suite 600
Encino, CA 91436
818-385-1934

imdb.com/company/co0381865

Does not accept any unsolicited material. Project types include TV. Genres include drama and crime.

Josh Gold
VP of Production & Development
imdb.com/name/nm2236268

Kathryn Morris
Actor/Producer
imdb.com/name/nm0606700

HOUNDSTOOTH
Production company

Austin, TX, United States
512-782-2232

info@houndstoothstudio.com
imdb.com/company/co0387492

Does not accept any unsolicited material.

David Crumley
Executive
512-782-2232
imdb.com/name/nm2096594

HUAYI BROTHERS FILM COMPANY
Production company and distributor

Lou Tai Duan, Wenyu River, Tianzhu, Shunyi, Beijing, China, 101312
011-861-064579338 (phone)
011-861-064570230 (fax)

huayimedia.com/entest/main1.html

Does not accept any unsolicited material. Project types include feature films and TV. Genres include family, action, drama, and thriller.

HUDSON FILM GROUP
Production company

155 Washington St
Jersey City, NJ 07302
201-721-6196 (phone)
201-721-6828 (fax)

info@hudsonfilmgroup.com
imdb.com/company/co0094566

Does not accept any unsolicited material. Project types include TV and short films. Genres include drama and documentary.

HUGHES CAPITAL ENTERTAINMENT
Production company and distributor

22817 Ventura Blvd, Suite 471
Woodland Hills, CA 91364
818-484-3205

info@trihughes.com
trihughes.com
imdb.com/company/co0186618

Accepts scripts from produced or represented writers. Project types include feature films. Genres include action, romance, family, comedy, and drama.

Patrick Hughes
imdb.com/name/nm1449018
linkedin.com/pub/patrick-hughes/19/911/141

Jacob Clymore
jc@trihughes.com

HUMANOIDS
Production company

8033 Sunset Blvd. # 628
Hollywood, CA 90046

77 Beak St, Suite 149
Soho, London W1F 9DB
United Kingdom

contact@humanoids.com
humanoids.com
imdb.com/company/co0240669
facebook.com/humanoidsinc
twitter.com/humanoidsinc

Does not accept any unsolicited material. Project types include feature films. Genres include action, horror, fantasy, drama, and science fiction.

HUMMINGBIRD JAPAN
Production company

1-16-6 Dougenzaka 10F A&B
Shibuya, Tokyo 150-0043
Japan
03-5428-5405 (phone)
03-3476-0211 (fax)

hatsuon@humbird.co.jp
humbird.co.jp
imdb.com/company/co0181692

Does not accept any unsolicited material. Project types include TV. Genres include drama.

Hajime Nihei
Dean (Legal)
imdb.com/name/nm2303231

HUNGRY BEAR PRODUCTIONS
Production company

5960 Tension Dr
Fort Worth, TX 76112

info@hungrybear.com
hungrybearproductions.com
imdb.com/company/co0189050
twitter.com/HungryBearEnt

Does not accept any unsolicited material. Project types include TV and feature films. Genres include science fiction, drama, family, horror, and comedy. Established in 2000.

HUNGRY EYES FILM AND TELEVISION
Production company

895 Davenport Rd
Toronto, ON M6G 2B4
Canada
416-654-6222 (phone)
416-654-1551 (fax)

info@hungryeyes.ca
hungryeyes.ca
imdb.com/company/co0088281
facebook.com/HungryEyesFilmandTV
twitter.com/HungryEyesFilms

Accepts query letters from unproduced, unrepresented writers. Genres include drama.

Sudz Sutherland
Producer
imdb.com/name/nm0840075

HUNTER FILMS
Production company

500 23rd St South
Birmingham, AL 35233
205-870-4996

imdb.com/company/co0056196

Does not accept any unsolicited material. Project types include feature films. Genres include drama.

Hugh Hunter
Partner/Producer
imdb.com/name/nm1227818

Alan Hunter
Partner/Producer
imdb.com/name/nm0402694

HURRICANE ENTERTAINMENT FILMS
Production company

1000 Universal Studios Plaza
Orlando, FL 32819
808-456-6544

peterparker1481@hotmail.com
imdb.com/company/co0010716

Does not accept any unsolicited material. Project types include TV.

HUTCH PARKER ENTERTAINMENT
Production company

204 Santa Monica Blvd Suite A
Santa Monica, CA 90401
310-576-4944

hutchparkerentertainment@gmail.com
imdb.com/company/co0381873

Accepts scripts from produced or represented writers. Project types include feature films. Genres include romance and thriller. Established in 2012.

Hutch Parker
Founder
imdb.com/name/nm0404446

Aaron Ensweiler
Vice-President
imdb.com/name/nm3943221

HYDE PARK ENTERTAINMENT
Production company, distributor, and sales agent

3500 W Olive Ave
Suite 300
Burbank, CA 91505

818-783-6060 (phone)
818-783-6319 (fax)

contact@hydeparkentertainment.com
hydeparkentertainment.com
imdb.com/company/co0036225

Does not accept any unsolicited material. Project types include commercials and feature films. Genres include fantasy, romance, science fiction, drama, comedy, crime, thriller, and action. Established in 1999.

Ashtok Amritraj
imdb.com/name/nm0002170

HYDRA ENTERTAINMENT
Production company

5410 Wilshire Blvd, Suite 400, Los Angeles, CA, United States, 90036
323-931-6633

info@hydra-entertainment.com
hydra-entertainment.com
imdb.com/company/co0558033

Does not accept any unsolicited material. Project types include feature films and TV. Genres include action, drama, thriller, and family.

HYPNOTIC
Production company and distributor

12233 W Olympic Blvd, Suite 255
Los Angeles, CA 90064
310-806-6930 (phone)
310-806-6931 (fax)

imdb.com/company/co0035615

Does not accept any unsolicited material. Project types include short films, feature films, and TV. Genres include horror, thriller, action, crime, comedy, and drama. Established in 2001.

Doug Liman
imdb.com/name/nm0510731

IAC GROUP
Production company

555 W 18th St
New York, NY 10011
212-314-7300

iac.com
linkedin.com/company/iac-group

Does not accept any unsolicited material. Project types include feature films. Genres include documentary.

Barry Diller
Chairman & Senior Executive
imdb.com/name/nm1660377

Victor Kaufman
Victor Kaufman
imdb.com/name/nm3215413

IA FILMS INC.
Production company

6608 Serena Cove
Austin, TX 78730

imdb.com/company/co0046263

Does not accept any unsolicited material. Project types include short films. Genres include drama, comedy, documentary, and romance.

IBID FILMWORKS
Production company

515 Fifth Ave, Suite 3A
Brooklyn, NY 11215

info@ibidfilmworks.com
ibidfilmworks.com
imdb.com/company/co0182518
linkedin.com/company/ibid-filmworks

Does not accept any unsolicited material. Project types include feature films. Genres include crime, comedy, and drama.

Jody Girgenti
Partner/Producer
imdb.com/name/nm1761255

Marc Meyers
Partner/Producer
imdb.com/name/nm1836315

ICARUS FILMS
Production company, distributor, and sales agent

32 Court St, 21st Floor, Brooklyn , NY, United States, 11201
718-488-8900 (phone)
718-488-8642 (fax)

mail@icarusfilms.com
icarusfilms.com
imdb.com/company/co0033000

Does not accept any unsolicited material. Project types include feature films and TV. Genres include action, thriller, family, and drama.

ICARUS PRODUCTIONS
Production company

1100 Madison Ave, Suite 6A
New York, NY 10028
212-581-3020

imdb.com/company/co0125551
facebook.com/Icarus-Productions-277048249094131

Does not accept any unsolicited material. Project types include feature films. Genres include comedy and drama.

Mike Nichols
Director/Producer/Writer
imdb.com/name/nm0001566

ICHIGO ICHIE FILMS
Production company, distributor, and sales agent

New York
646-652-6924

Tokyo,
Japan
+81 50-5809-3152

contact@iifilmsllc.tokyo
iifilmsllc.tokyo
imdb.com/company/co0258608

Does not accept any unsolicited material. Project types include feature films. Genres include thriller.

Hiro Masuda
President (Producer)
imdb.com/name/nm2384884

ICM PARTNERS
Production company

730 Fifth Ave
New York NY 10019
212-556-5600 (phone)
212-556-5665 (fax)

Marlborough House Third Floor 10 Earlham St
London United Kingdom WC2H 9LN
011-442-078368564

10250 Constellation Blvd, Los Angeles, CA, 90067,
United States
310-550-4000 (phone)
310-550-4100 (fax)

careersla@icmtalent.com
icmpartners.com
imdb.com/company/co0043609

Does not accept any unsolicited material. Project types
include commercials and TV. Genres include non-
fiction and sociocultural.

Steve Alexander
Agent, Producer
310-550-4000
imdb.com/name/nm5433337

ICON ENTERTAINMENT INTERNATIONAL
Production company, distributor, and sales agent

808 Wilshire Blvd
4th Fl
Santa Monica, CA 90401
310-434-7300

imdb.com/company/co0000700
linkedin.com/company/icon-entertainment-
    international
facebook.com/pages/Icon-Productions/
    108055215890057

Does not accept any unsolicited material. Project types
include TV and feature films. Genres include crime,
comedy, action, horror, drama, thriller, non-fiction,
and science fiction. Established in 1989.

Mel Gibson
Founder
imdb.com/name/nm0000154

ICON FILM DISTRIBUTION
Distributor

27a Floral St
London WC2E 9EZ
UK

info@iconfilmdistribution.co.uk
iconmovies.co.uk
imdb.com/company/co0106133

Does not accept any unsolicited material. Project types
include feature films. Genres include comedy.

ICONIC MEDIA PRODUCTIONS
Production company

5670 Wilshire Blvd. #19264
Los Angeles, CA 90036

judibell@iconicmediaprod.com
imdb.com/company/co0382482
facebook.com/IconicMediaProductions

Does not accept any unsolicited material. Project types
include feature films. Genres include drama.

Judi Bell
CEO/Producer
imdb.com/name/nm2230559

Matt Nicholas
Writer/Producer
imdb.com/name/nm3818521

IDEAL PARTNERS FILM FUND
Production company

630 Fifth Ave, Suite 1465
New York, NY 10111
212-396-9209

imdb.com/company/co0195669

Does not accept any unsolicited material. Project types
include feature films. Genres include drama and
thriller.

Jana Edelbaum
Partner/Producer
imdb.com/name/nm0248944

Rachel Cohen
Partner/Producer
imdb.com/name/nm1707602

IDENTITY FILMS

8520 Mulholland Dr
Los Angeles, CA 90046
323-654-3000 (phone)
323-654-3010 (fax)

info@identityfilm.com
identityfilm.com
facebook.com/Identity.Films.TV
twitter.com/IdentityFilms

Does not accept any unsolicited material. Project types include TV and feature films. Genres include drama.

Tara Ahamed
Director of Development
imdb.com/name/nm3925704

Anthony Mastromauro
Co-Founder/CEO/Producer
imdb.com/name/nm0557829

IDG FILMS

One Exeter Plaza, 15th Floor
Boston, MA 02116
617-534-1200

idg.com

Does not accept any unsolicited material. Project types include feature films.

David Lee
Producer
imdb.com/name/nm0497115

Steven Squillante
Producer
imdb.com/name/nm1115325

IDP DISTRIBUTION
Distributor

1133 Broadway
Ste 1120
New York, NY 10010

212-367-9435 (phone)
212-367-0853 (fax)

imdb.com/company/co0080471
linkedin.com/company/idp-distribution

Does not accept any unsolicited material. Project types include feature films. Genres include drama and thriller.

ID SOFTWARE
Production company

1500 N Greenville Ave
Richardson, TX 75080
972-613-3589

idsoftware.com
imdb.com/company/co0020170

Does not accept any unsolicited material.

IDW PUBLISHING
Production company

5080 Santa Fe
San Diego, CA 92109

idwpublishing-47542@happyfox.com
idwpublishing.com
imdb.com/company/co0188055
twitter.com/IDWPublishing

Does not accept any unsolicited material. Project types include feature films. Genres include horror.

Ted Adams
Founder/CEO/Executive Producer
imdb.com/name/nm0011389

Robbie Robbins
Founder/Executive
imdb.com/name/nm4730671

IFC
Production company and distributor

11 Penn Plaza, 15th Floor, New York City , NY, United States, 10001
646-273-7200 (phone)
646-273-7250 (fax)

2425 W Olympic Blvd Suite 670E
Santa Monica CA 90404
310-998-9300

200 Jericho Quadrangle
Jericho NY 11753
516-803-4500 (phone)
516-803-4506 (fax)

ifc.com
imdb.com/company/co0015762

Does not accept any unsolicited material. Project types include TV and feature films. Genres include drama, thriller, and family.

IFC FILMS
Production company, distributor, and sales agent

11 Penn Plaza, 18th Floor, New York, NY, United States, 10001
646-273-7200 (phone)
646-273-7250 (fax)

ifcfilms.com
imdb.com/company/co0015762

Does not accept any unsolicited material. Project types include feature films and TV. Genres include action, family, thriller, and drama.

IKM PRODUCTIONS
Production company

601 W 26th St, Suite 1255
New York, NY 10001
212-533-1951 (phone)
212-255-3382 (fax)

imdb.com/company/co0205492

Does not accept any unsolicited material. Project types include TV and feature films. Genres include thriller and comedy.

James K. Jones
Producer
imdb.com/name/nm1300158

Patrick Moses
Producer
imdb.com/name/nm2095313

ILLUMINATION ENTERTAINMENT
Production company

2230 Broadway St
Santa Monica, CA 90404
310-593-8800

info@illuminationent.com
behindthegoggles.net
imdb.com/company/co0221986
linkedin.com/company/illumination-entertainment
facebook.com/pages/Illumination-Entertainment/
    173587985995833

Does not accept any unsolicited material. Project types include feature films and short films. Genres include family, animation, drama, and comedy. Established in 2007.

Christopher Meledandri
Founder
imdb.com/name/nm0577560
Assistant: Rachel Feinberg and Katie Kirnan

ILLUSION INDUSTRIES
Production company

10000 Celtic Dr, O'Connor Building
Baton Rouge, LA 70809

2424 N Ontario St
Burbank, CA 91504
818-565-5986

admin@illusionindustries.com
illusionindustries.com
imdb.com/company/co0304148
facebook.com/IllusionIndustriesInc

Does not accept any unsolicited material. Project types include feature films. Genres include horror.

Todd Tucker
President
imdb.com/name/nm2586719

Ronald Halvas
CEO
imdb.com/name/nm359772

IMAGEEPOCH
Production company

5-7-12-3F
Ohtsuka
Bunkyo, Tokyo 112-0012
Japan

info@imageepoch.co.jp
imdb.com/company/co0205366

Does not accept any unsolicited material. Project types
include TV. Genres include comedy, action, drama,
and animation.

Ryoei Mikage
Founder (Producer)
imdb.com/name/nm2400281

IMAGEFIELD
Production company

1-2-9-4F
Shinjuku
Shinjuku, Tokyo 160-0022
Japan
03-5919-2332 (phone)
03-5919-2331 (fax)

info@im-field.com
im-field.com
imdb.com/company/co0318236

Does not accept any unsolicited material. Project types
include TV. Genres include drama.

IMAGE FORUM
Distributor

2-10-2
Shibuya
Shibuya, Tokyo 150-0002
Japan
03-5766-1119

info@imageforum.co.jp
imageforum.co.jp
imdb.com/company/co0143475
facebook.com/imageforum.japan
twitter.com/image_forum

Does not accept any unsolicited material. Project types
include feature films. Genres include documentary.

IMAGEMOVERS
Production company

100 Universal City
Bungalow 5170
Los Angeles, CA 91608

imdb.com/company/co0038131
linkedin.com/company/imagemovers
facebook.com/pages/ImageMovers/114718638545017

Does not accept any unsolicited material. Project types
include TV and feature films. Genres include romance,
fantasy, period, thriller, drama, family, action, comedy,
and animation. Established in 1997.

Robert Zemeckis
Partner
imdb.com/name/nm0000709

Steve Starkey
Partner
imdb.com/name/nm0823330

Jack Rapke
Partner
imdb.com/name/nm0710759

IMAGINE ENTERTAINMENT
Production company and distributor

9465 Wilshire Blvd
7th Floor
Beverly Hills, CA 90212
310-858-2000 (phone)
310-858-2020 (fax)

contact@imagine-entertainment.com
imdb.com/company/co0003687
linkedin.com/company/imagine-entertainment
facebook.com/pages/Imagine-Entertainment/
    103825922989076
twitter.com/ImaginEntertain

Does not accept any unsolicited material. Project types
include feature films and TV. Genres include crime,
comedy, action, horror, drama, family, fantasy, science
fiction, non-fiction, romance, animation, and thriller.
Established in 1986.

Ron Howard
Founder
r.howard@imagine-entertainment.com
imdb.com/name/nm0000165

IMAX CORPORATION

Production company and distributor

110 E 59th St Suite 2100
New York NY 10022
212-821-0100 (phone)
212-371-1174 (fax)

3003 Exposition Blvd, First Floor, Santa Monica , CA,
United States, 90404.l
310-255-5500 (phone)
310-315-1759 (fax)

info@imax.com
imax.com
imdb.com/company/co0057495

Does not accept any unsolicited material. Project types
include TV. Genres include drama and family.

Mark Welton
President (IMAX Theatres)
imdb.com/name/nm2302583

IM GLOBAL

Production company

8201 Beverly Blvd.
5th Floor
Los Angeles, CA 90048
310-777-3590 (phone)
323-657-5354 (fax)

info@imglobalfilm.com
imglobalfilm.com
imdb.com/company/co0323227
facebook.com/imglobalfilm
twitter.com/imglobalfilm

Does not accept any unsolicited material. Project types
include TV and feature films. Genres include fantasy,
thriller, action, and comedy.

Brian Kavanaugh-Jones
Head (Automatik Film Division)
office@automatikent.com
imdb.com/name/nm2271939
Assistant: Alex Saks

IMG WORLDWIDE

Distributor

McCormack House Burlington Ln, Chiswick
London United Kingdom W4 2TH
011-442-082335300

5500-34th St West
Bradenton FL 34210
800-872-6425

767 Fifth Ave 44th Floor
New York City NY 10153
212-489-8300

304 Park Ave South
New York City NY
212-774-6735 (phone)
212-246-1596 (fax)

One Burlington Ln
London United Kingdom W4 2TH
011-442-082335300

2049 Century Park East Suite 4100
Los Angeles CA 90067
424-653-1900 (phone)
424-653-1914 (fax)

1360 E 9th St, Suite 100, Cleveland , OH, United
States, 44114
216-522-1200 (phone)
216-522-1145 (fax)

speakers@imgworld.com
img.com/home.aspx
imdb.com/company/co0484205

Does not accept any unsolicited material. Project types
include TV and feature films. Genres include action,
family, drama, and thriller.

IMPACT PARTNERS

Production company and distributor

45 Main St,, Suite 506, Brooklyn, NY, United States,
11201

info@impactpartnersfilm.com
impactpartnersfilm.com
imdb.com/company/co0242489

Does not accept any unsolicited material. Project types
include feature films and TV. Genres include drama,
family, comedy, and action.

IMPACT PICTURES

Production company

9200 W Sunset Blvd, Suite 800
West Hollywood, CA 90069
310-247-1803

imdb.com/company/co0014411

Does not accept any unsolicited material. Project types include feature films. Genres include science fiction, comedy, romance, drama, crime, horror, fantasy, thriller, and action. Established in 1994.

Paul Anderson
imdb.com/name/nm0027271
Assistant: Sarah Crompton

Jeremy Bolt
Producer
imdb.com/name/nm0093337

IMPACT PRODUCTIONS

Production company

3939 S. Harvard Ave
Tulsa, OK 74135
918-87-2000

info@impactprod.org
impactproductions.com
imdb.com/company/co0089412
facebook.com/impactproductions01
twitter.com/tcnewman

Does not accept any unsolicited material. Project types include feature films. Genres include family and drama.

IMPALER FILM STUDIOS

Production company

5470 E Busch Blvd.
Suite 192
Temple Temple, FL 33617
813-399-9098

impalerfilms@yahoo.com
imdb.com/company/co0410129

Does not accept any unsolicited material. Project types include feature films. Genres include action and non-fiction. Established in 2015.

IMPERIAL DISTRIBUTING CORPORATION

Distributor

729 Seventh Ave.
New York, NY

imdb.com/company/co0031647

Does not accept any unsolicited material. Project types include feature films. Genres include thriller, action, crime, and horror.

IMPRINT ENTERTAINMENT

Production company

100 Universal City Plaza
Bungalow 7125
Universal City, CA 91608
818-733-5410

info@imprint-ent.com
imprint-ent.com
imdb.com/company/co0247764
facebook.com/pages/IMPRINT-
    ENTERTAINMENT/120818451267628
twitter.com/ImprintEnt

Does not accept any unsolicited material. Project types include TV, commercials, and feature films. Genres include action, thriller, comedy, reality, romance, drama, crime, non-fiction, fantasy, and horror. Established in 2008.

I'M READY PRODUCTIONS

Production company

515 N. Sam Houston Pkwy
Suite 215
Houston, TX 77060
281-445-2300 (phone)
281-445-2301 (fax)

info@imreadyproductions.com
imreadyproductions.com
imdb.com/company/co0199937
facebook.com/jecaryous.johnson
twitter.com/jecaryous

Does not accept any unsolicited material. Genres include comedy and romance.

IN CAHOOTS

Production company

4024 Radford Ave
Editorial Building 2, Suite 7
Studio City, CA 91604
818-655-6482 (phone)
818-655-8472 (fax)

imdb.com/company/co0166950

Does not accept any unsolicited material. Project types include TV and feature films. Genres include drama, comedy, and thriller. Established in 2010.

Ken Kwapis
imdb.com/name/nm0477129

Reynolds Anderson
Creative Executive
imdb.com/name/nm1568030

INCENDIARY FEATURES

Production company

209 E. Ben White Blvd.
Ste. 100B
Austin, TX 78704
323-377-1250

james@incendiaryfeatures.com
incendiaryfeatures.com
imdb.com/company/co0240547
twitter.com/IncendiaryFlix

Does not accept any unsolicited material. Genres include horror and thriller.

INCEPTION MEDIA GROUP

Distributor

13412 Ventura Blvd, Suite 200, Sherman Oaks, CA, United States, 91423
310-582-5948

info@inceptionmg.com
imdb.com/company/co0287555

Does not accept any unsolicited material. Project types include feature films. Genres include action.

INCOGNITO PICTURES

Production company and distributor

2711 N. Sepulveda Blvd
Ste 147
Manhattan Beach, CA 90266
424-242-5882

info@incognitopictures.com
incognitopictures.com
imdb.com/company/co0295349
facebook.com/pages/Incognito-Pictures/
    167198753371256
twitter.com/IncognitoPics

Does not accept any unsolicited material. Project types include feature films. Genres include thriller, drama, action, and comedy. Established in 2011.

Jack Selby
Chairman
imdb.com/name/nm3095212

Scott G. Stone
CEO
imdb.com/name/nm1680597
linkedin.com/pub/scott-stone/53/162/214

INDEPENDENT

Production company and sales agent

6 Hatton Place
London EC1N 8RU
UK
44 20 7257 8734 (phone)
44 20 7240 9029 (fax)

mail@independentfilmcompany.com
independentfilmcompany.com
imdb.com/company/co0212724
en-gb.facebook.com/pages/Independent/63247437072
twitter.com/IndepFilmCo

Does not accept any unsolicited material. Genres include drama.

Luc Roeg
Producer
imdb.com/name/nm0736312

INDEPENDENT FILM SALES

Production company, distributor, and sales agent

6 Hatton Place, EC1N 8RU
+44 20 7257 8734 (phone)
+44 20 7240 9029 (fax)

mail@independentfilmcompany.com
independentfilmcompany.com
imdb.com/company/co0200632
en-gb.facebook.com/IndepFilmCo
twitter.com/IndepFilmCo

Does not accept any unsolicited material. Project types include feature films. Genres include drama and thriller.

INDEPENDENT TELEVISION GROUP
Production company

8306 Wilshire Blvd., Suite 995
Beverly Hills, CA 90211
310-854-2300

indytvgroup.com
imdb.com/company/co0286591

Does not accept any unsolicited material. Project types include TV. Genres include drama.

Steven Jensen
Producer
imdb.com/name/nm0421688

INDEPENDENT TELEVISION (ITV)
Distributor

200 Grays Inn Rd
London WC1X 8HF
UK
+44 0 20 7843 8000 (phone)
+44 0 20 7843 8158 (fax)

dutyoffice@itv.com
itv.com
imdb.com/company/co0015194

Does not accept any unsolicited material. Project types include feature films. Genres include thriller and drama.

Kate Bartlett
Producer
imdb.com/name/nm1321998

INDIAN PAINTBRUSH
Production company

1660 Euclid St
Santa Monica, CA 90404
310-566-0160

imdb.com/company/co0215519

Does not accept any unsolicited material. Project types include feature films. Genres include thriller, science fiction, drama, comedy, action, romance, family, animation, and horror.

INDIA TAKE ONE PRODUCTIONS
Production company

7955 W 3rd St
Los Angeles, CA 90048
323-634-1566 (phone)
323-634-1566 (fax)

M-165, Greater Kailash, Part 2
New Delhi - 110048, India
91 11 4163 8648 (fax)

info@indiatakeone.com
indiatakeone.com
imdb.com/company/co0210547

Does not accept any unsolicited material. Project types include feature films. Genres include non-fiction and drama.

Tabrez Noorani
Producer
imdb.com/name/nm0634782

INDICAN PRODUCTIONS
Production company

9200 Sunset Blvd Penthouse 22
West Hollywood, CA 90069

imdb.com/company/co0023589

Does not accept any unsolicited material. Project types include feature films. Genres include drama, crime, and non-fiction. Established in 1995.

Julia Ormond
Founder
julia.ormond@fox.com
imdb.com/name/nm0000566

INDIE GENIUS PRODUCTIONS

Production company

225 W 14th St
Minneapolis, MN 55403
612-666-6649

westmemphisthree@gmail.com
imdb.com/company/co0097647

Accepts query letters from unproduced, unrepresented writers. Project types include feature films. Genres include documentary. Established in 2007.

Curt Johnson
curt_johnson@indiegeniusprod.com

INDIE-PICTURES

Production company

2934 Beverly Glen Circle, PMB 392, Los Angeles , CA, United States, 90077
310-289-9595

ttaylor@indie-pictures.com
imdb.com/company/co0164676

Does not accept any unsolicited material. Project types include feature films. Genres include horror.

Herb Hamsher
Producer
imdb.com/name/nm0359099

INDIEVEST PICTURES

Production company

1416 N La Brea Ave
Los Angeles, CA 90028
888-299-9961

info@indievest.com
indievest.com
imdb.com/company/co0198316
facebook.com/IndieVest

Does not accept any unsolicited material. Project types include feature films.

Mark Burton
President
imdb.com/name/nm0123666

Matt Wall
Vice President of Development
imdb.com/name/nm0908457

INDIGENOUS FILM WORKS

Production company and distributor

141 Regal Row
Dallas, TX 75247
214-498-2238

bjones@indigenousfilmworks.com
imdb.com/company/co0284679

Does not accept any unsolicited material. Genres include comedy and horror.

INDIGO FILMS

Production company

155 N Redwood Dr. Suite 250
San Rafael, CA 94903
415-444-1700 (phone)
415-444-1720 (fax)

info@indigofilms.com
indigofilms.com
imdb.com/company/co0033065
linkedin.com/company/indigo-films
facebook.com/indigofilmsentertainment
twitter.com/IndigoFilms

Does not accept any unsolicited material. Project types include TV. Genres include horror and drama.

James Cox
VP of Development
imdb.com/name/nm0185063

INDOMITABLE ENTERTAINMENT

Production company and distributor

599 Broadway
8th Floor
New York NY 10012
212-352-1071 (phone)
212-727-3860 (fax)

520 Broadway
Suite 3035
Santa Monica, CA 90401

310-664-8700 (phone)
310-664-8711 (fax)

info@indomitable.com
indomitableentertainment.com
imdb.com/company/co0274022
facebook.com/pages/Indomitable-Entertainment/
    20750471594844
twitter.com/IndomitableEnt

Accepts query letters from unproduced, unrepresented writers via email. Project types include TV and feature films. Genres include drama, thriller, comedy, and action.

Stuart Pollok
Executive Producer
imdb.com/name/nm0689415

Chris Mirosevic
Director of Film Services
imdb.com/name/nm1746156

Dominic Ianno
Founder, CEO
imdb.com/name/nm1746156

Robert Deege
Vice President of Business & Creative Affairs
imdb.com/name/nm1830098
linkedin.com/in/rdproducerdirector
twitter.com/rdeege

INDUSTRY ENTERTAINMENT
Production company

New York, NY
212-566-1066

955 S Carrillo Dr, Suite 300
Los Angeles, CA 90048
323-954-9000 (phone)
323-954-9009 (fax)

imdb.com/company/co0024345
linkedin.com/company/industry-entertainment

Does not accept any unsolicited material. Project types include TV and feature films. Genres include crime, romance, horror, family, thriller, science fiction, drama, action, comedy, and fantasy. Established in 1982.

Keith Addis
Partner
imdb.com/name/nm0011688

INEFFABLE PICTURES
Production company

9247 Alden Dr
Beverly Hills, CA 90210
424-653-1122

info@ineffablepictures.com
ineffablepictures.com
imdb.com/company/co0343339
facebook.com/pages/Ineffable-Pictures
twitter.com/IneffablePics

Does not accept any unsolicited material. Project types include feature films. Genres include science fiction, fantasy, drama, action, and comedy. Established in 2010.

Jesse Israel
Executive
imdb.com/name/nm2368220
linkedin.com/pub/dir/jesse/israel

Raphael Kryszek
President
imdb.com/name/nm1398360
linkedin.com/pub/raphael-kryszek/0/a6/a75

Ross Putman
Creative Executive
imdb.com/name/nm3819444
linkedin.com/pub/ross-putman/29/78b/68

INEVITABLE FILM GROUP
Production company

8484 Wilshire Blvd, Suite 465
Beverly Hills, CA 90211
310-220-4360

inevitablefilmgroup.com
imdb.com/company/co0206616
linkedin.com/company/inevitable-film-group-inc.

Does not accept any unsolicited material. Project types include TV and feature films. Genres include horror and drama.

Stephen Wozniak
Principal/Producer
imdb.com/name/nm0941966

Ron Farber
Principal/Producer
imdb.com/name/nm2618786

INFERNO ENTERTAINMENT
Financing company

imdb.com/company/co0205214

Does not accept any unsolicited material. Project types include feature films. Genres include comedy, family, science fiction, horror, action, crime, drama, fantasy, romance, and thriller. Established in 2010.

INFERNO FILM PRODUCTIONS
Sales agent

PO Box 696
Littleton, CO 80160-0696
303-587-9792

ifilm@infernofilm.com
infernofilm.com
imdb.com/company/co0033331

Does not accept any unsolicited material. Project types include TV and feature films. Genres include action.

Trygve Lode
Actor
imdb.com/name/nm0006999

INFINITUM NIHIL
Production company

9100 Wilshire Blvd, Ste 400W
Beverly Hills, CA 90212
323-651-2034

infinitumnihil.com
imdb.com/company/co0135149
facebook.com/pages/Infinitum-Nihil/
    108165115878775
twitter.com/infinitumnihil

Does not accept any unsolicited material. Project types include feature films. Genres include drama, action,

comedy, family, myth, romance, and fantasy. Established in 2004.

Christi Dembrowski
President
imdb.com/name/nm0218259
Assistant: Dawn Sierra & Erik Schmudde

Johnny Depp
Founder
imdb.com/name/nm0000136

Margaret French Isaac
imdb.com/name/nm0410504
Assistant: Brandon Zamel

Bobby DeLeon
imdb.com/name/nm3765677

Norman Todd
Director of Development
imdb.com/name/nm0865249

Sam Sarkar
imdb.com/name/nm0765274

INFORMANT MEDIA
Production company and financing company

9190 Olympic Blvd, Suite 440
Beverly Hills, CA 90212
310-470-9309 (phone)
310-347-4497 (fax)

michaelasimpson@informantmedia.com
informantmedia.com
imdb.com/company/co0242459
facebook.com/InformantMedia
twitter.com/InformantMedia

Accepts query letters from produced or represented writers. Project types include feature films and TV. Genres include action, thriller, comedy, fantasy, drama, romance, and science fiction. Established in 2010.

Elsa Ramo
Legal Counsel
imdb.com/name/nm1721649

Tracey Becker
Producer
tracey@informantmedia.com
imdb.com/name/nm1240204

Rick Bitzelberger
development@informantmedia.com

Melina Lizette
melina@informantmedia.com

Michael Simpson
CEO
michaelasimpson@informantmedia.com
imdb.com/name/nm0801121

Judy Cairo
Partner
judycairo@informantmedia.com
imdb.com/name/nm0003437

Jeremy Po
jeremypo@informantmedia.com

Howard Meltzer
howardmeltzer@informantmedia.com

Eric Brenner
Partner
ericbrenner@informantmedia.com
imdb.com/name/nm3665102

IN FRONT PRODUCTIONS
Production company

2000 Ave Of The Stars
Century City, CA 90067
424-288-2000

aelkin@caa.com
imdb.com/company/co0077065

Does not accept any unsolicited material. Project types include TV. Genres include romance and comedy. Established in 1992.

Danny Jacobson
Manager
imdb.com/name/nm0414816

INGENIOUS FILM PARTNERS
Production company

15 Golden Square
London W1F 9JG
UK
+44 20 73 19 40 00 (phone)
+44 20 73 19 40 01 (fax)

generalenquiries@ingeniousmedia.co.uk
ingeniousmedia.co.uk
imdb.com/company/co0136728
twitter.com/HelloIngenious

Does not accept any unsolicited material. Project types include feature films and short films. Genres include science fiction and action.

Duncan Reid
Producer
imdb.com/name/nm1442542

INGENIOUS MEDIA
Production company and distributor

15 Golden Square
London W1F 9JG
United Kingdom
+44 (0)20 7319 4000

hello@ingeniousmedia.co.uk
theingeniousgroup.co.uk
imdb.com/company/co0209925
twitter.com/HelloIngenious

Does not accept any unsolicited material. Project types include TV and feature films. Genres include fantasy.

INK FACTORY

73 Wells St
London W1T 3QG
UK
+44-20-7096-1698

2105 Colorado Ave
suite 101
Santa Monica, CA 90404
310-721-5409

info@inkfactoryfilms.com
inkfactoryfilms.com
imdb.com/company/co0312385
twitter.com/the_ink_factory

Does not accept any unsolicited material. Project types include feature films. Genres include thriller, drama, and action. Established in 2010.

Stephen Cornwell
Principal
310-721-5409
steven@inkonscreen.co.uk
imdb.com/name/nm4051169
linkedin.com/pub/stephen-cornwell/18/b5b/788

Rhodri Thomas
Executive
rhodri@inkonscreen.co.uk
imdb.com/name/nm2905579
facebook.com/rhodri.thomas.908
twitter.com/rodwan1

INNOVATIVE PRODUCTIONS
Production company

PO Box 25751
Tamarac, FL 33321
407-493-2940

innovativephotoprod.com
imdb.com/company/co0014805

Does not accept any unsolicited material. Genres include comedy.

INPHENATE
Production company

9701 Wilshire Blvd
10th Floor
Beverly Hills, CA 90212
310-601-7117 (phone)
310-601-7110 (fax)

inphenate.com
imdb.com/company/co0145670
twitter.com/Inphenate

Does not accept any unsolicited material. Project types include feature films and TV. Genres include reality, comedy, drama, and non-fiction.

Glenn Rigberg
Owner
imdb.com/name/nm0726572
linkedin.com/in/phenate

INSTIGATOR STUDIOS
Production company

14100 US HWY N.
Suite 118
Clearwater, FL 33764
727-244-2206

ray@instigatorstudios.com
imdb.com/company/co0370835
facebook.com/InstigatorStudios13

Does not accept any unsolicited material. Genres include action and drama.

INSTITUT FRANÇAIS DU JAPON
Distributor

15
Ichigaya Funagawaramachi
Shinjuku, Tokyo 162-8415
Japan
03-5206-2500 (phone)
03-5206-2501 (fax)

tokyo@institutfrancais.jp
institutfrancais.jp
imdb.com/company/co0440822

Does not accept any unsolicited material. Project types include TV. Genres include comedy.

INTANDEM FILMS
Distributor and sales agent

131-151 Great Titchfield St
London W1W 5BB
UK
+44 20 7851 3800 (phone)
+44 20 7851 3830 (fax)

info@intandemfilms.com
imdb.com/company/co0127149

Does not accept any unsolicited material. Project types include feature films. Genres include thriller and action.

Andrew Brown
Producer
imdb.com/name/nm1614472

INTEGRATED FILMSI
Production company and distributor

2912 Colorado Ave. Ste. 100
Santa Monica, CA 90404
310-998-8648 (phone)
310-998-8680 (fax)

imdb.com/company/co0085255

Does not accept any unsolicited material. Project types include feature films. Genres include horror.

Chris Winvick
Development
imdb.com/name/nm0936111

INTELLIGENT MEDIA
Sales agent

8439 W Sunset Blvd, Suite #308, West Hollywood, CA 90069
323-203-3255

Clifton Works
23 Grove Park Terrace
London W4 3QE
UK
+44208-996-6060

contact@intelligentmedia.com
intelligentmedia.com
imdb.com/company/co0317678

Does not accept any unsolicited material. Project types include feature films. Genres include horror, romance, comedy, and action.

Amanda Potts
Executive
imdb.com/name/nm2302663

INTERACTIVECORP
Production company and distributor

555 W 18th St, New York , NY, United States, 10011
212-314-7300

info@iac.com
iac.com

Does not accept any unsolicited material. Project types include TV. Genres include family and drama.

INTERCULTURAL LINK
Production company

7-17-12 #314
Roppongi
Minato-Ku, Tokyo 106-0032
Japan
81 90 9810 8249

hhaginojp@yahoo.co.jp
imdb.com/company/co0316027

Does not accept any unsolicited material. Project types include feature films. Genres include romance, comedy, and action.

INTERFILM
Production company and distributor

2-4-6-205
Fujimi
Chiyoda, Tokyo
Japan
03-3512-2346

info@interfilm.co.jp
interfilm.co.jp
imdb.com/company/co0228071

Does not accept any unsolicited material. Project types include TV. Genres include animation.

INTERLOPER FILMS
Production company

1622 Pepper Dr
Los Angeles, CA 90068
626-296-0068

coordinator@interloperfilms.com
interloperfilms.com
imdb.com/company/co0101529

Does not accept any unsolicited material. Project types include feature films. Genres include non-fiction.

David Timoner
Principal
imdb.com/name/nm0863755

Ondi Timoner
Principal
imdb.com/name/nm0863756

INTERMEDIA FILMS

Production company

9242 Beverly Blvd., Suite 201
Beverly Hills, CA 90210
310-777-0007 (phone)
310-777-0008 (fax)

info@intermediafilm.com
intermediafilm.com
imdb.com/company/co0010183

Does not accept any unsolicited material. Project types include feature films. Genres include drama, action, and comedy.

Konstantin Thoeren
Chairman
imdb.com/name/nm0858328

Linda Benjamin
President
imdb.com/name/nm0071326

INTERNATIONAL ARTS ENTERTAINMENT

Production company

8899 Beverly Blvd., Ste 800
Los Angeles, CA 90048
310-550-6760 (phone)
310-550-8839 (fax)

imdb.com/company/co0062824
facebook.com/internationalartsentertainmentgroup

Does not accept any unsolicited material.

Alan Greenspan
Producer
imdb.com/name/nm2325162

Robyn Morrison
Development
imdb.com/name/nm1308467

INTERNATIONAL DIGITAL ARTIST (IDA)

Production company and distributor

6-11-14-303
Sotokanda
Chiyoda, Tokyo 101-0021
Japan

03-6803-2035 (phone)
03-6803-2045 (fax)

info@ida-e.jp
ida-entertainment.com
imdb.com/company/co0318063

Does not accept any unsolicited material. Project types include feature films, TV, and short films. Genres include action.

Junya Okabe
President (Producer)
imdb.com/name/nm1001587

INTERNATIONAL FILM DISTRIBUTION CONSULTANTS

Distributor

1901 Ave Of The Stars
Suite 930
Los Angeles, CA 90067
310-788-2803 (phone)
310-788-2823 (fax)

general@ifdcinc.com
ifdcinc.com
imdb.com/company/co0195875

Does not accept any unsolicited material. Project types include feature films. Genres include fantasy, drama, and romance.

INTERNATIONAL FILM GROUP

Production company and distributor

7910 Ivanhoe Ave., Sutie 529, La Jolla , CA, United States, 92037

ifg@ifgfilms.com
imdb.com/company/co0077821

Does not accept any unsolicited material. Project types include feature films and TV. Genres include family, drama, action, and thriller.

INTERVISION PARTNERS

Production company

122 E 42nd St., Suite 2900
New York, NY 10168
212-949-3400 (phone)
212-949-7534 (fax)

usa@intervisionsitv.com
intervisionsitv.com
imdb.com/company/co0209777

Does not accept any unsolicited material. Project types include TV and feature films. Genres include drama.

Jerry Wolff
Partner/Producer
imdb.com/name/nm2872765

IN THE DARK ENTERTAINMENT
Production company

3005 George Mason Ave.
Suite D
Orlando, FL 32792
407-310-8996

imdb@itdentertainment.com
http/www.imdb.com/company/co0194116
linkedin.com/company/in-the-dark-entertainment-inc-

Does not accept any unsolicited material. Genres include thriller.

INTREPID PICTURES
Production company

10323 SANTA MONICA BLVD., SUITE 111
LOS ANGELES, CA 90025
310-566-5000

info@intrepidpictures.com
intrepidpictures.com
imdb.com/company/co0059753

Does not accept any unsolicited material. Project types include feature films and TV. Genres include comedy, action, thriller, and horror. Established in 2004.

Melinda Nishioka
Director of Development
melinda@intrepidpictures.com
imdb.com/name/nm2325559

Trevor Macy
Founder
imdb.com/name/nm1006167

Marc D. Evans
Founder
imdb.com/name/nm2162955

INTRINSIC VALUE FILMS
Production company

1 State St Plaza, 24th Floor
New York, NY 10004
212-989-7200 (phone)
212-202-7808 (fax)

406 Grand Blvd
Venice, CA 90291
310-857-6733

info@intrinsicvaluefilms.com
intrinsicvaluefilms.com
imdb.com/company/co0072994

Accepts query letters from unproduced, unrepresented writers via email. Project types include feature films. Genres include thriller, horror, drama, and comedy.

Joseph Lagana
Head of Development
joseph@intrinsicvaluefilms.com
intrinsicvaluefilms.com
imdb.com/name/nm1246447

Aimee Schoof
Producer
imdb.com/name/nm0774779

Isen Robbins
Producer
imdb.com/name/nm0730358

INTUITION PRODUCTIONS
Production company

1635 N Cahuenga Blvd
Los Angeles, CA 90028
323-464-1682

imdb.com/company/co0119811
linkedin.com/company/intuition-productions

Does not accept any unsolicited material. Project types include TV. Genres include drama.

Keri Selig
Producer
imdb.com/name/nm0783146

INVENTURE ENTERTAINMENT
Production company

44 E 32nd St, 9th Floor
New York, NY 10016
212-863-9656

info@inventureentertainment.com
imdb.com/company/co0180061

Does not accept any unsolicited material. Project types
include feature films.

Daniel Rosenberg
Producer
imdb.com/name/nm1360674

INVICTUS ENTERTAINMENT GROUP
Production company and financing company

1821 Randstead St
Suite 1
Philadelphia, PA 19103

IEGroup.USA@gmail.com
imdb.com/company/co0340928

Does not accept any unsolicited material. Project types
include TV and feature films. Genres include crime
and thriller.

Chelsea Bishop
Producer
imdb.com/name/nm2810519

INVINCIBLE PICTURES
Distributor

1600 N 5th St, Philadelphia, PA, United States, 19122
267-773-8971

info@invinciblepictures.com
imdb.com/company/co0234824

Does not accept any unsolicited material.

Tom Ashley
Executive
imdb.com/name/nm6526252

ION MEDIA NETWORKS
Production company and distributor

601 Clearwater Park Rd.
West Palm Beach, FL 33401
561-659-4122

ionmedia.tv
imdb.com/company/co0186092
linkedin.com/company/ion-media-networks

Does not accept any unsolicited material. Project types
include TV. Genres include fantasy, family, drama,
comedy, and crime. Established in 2006.

IONOGEN STUDIOS
Production company

Denver, CO
303-726-5210

michael@ionogenstudios.com
imdb.com/company/co0175587

Does not accept any unsolicited material. Genres
include drama.

IRISH DREAMTIME
Production company

irishdreamtime.com
imdb.com/company/co0088199

Does not accept any unsolicited material. Project types
include feature films and TV. Genres include comedy,
action, non-fiction, crime, drama, thriller, and
romance. Established in 1996.

Beau St. Clair
imdb.com/name/nm0820429

Keith Arnold
Head of Development
imdb.com/name/nm2993265

Pierce Brosnan
Founder
imdb.com/name/nm0000112

IRISH FILM BOARD
Production company and distributor

23 Dock Rd, Queensgate, Galway, Ireland
011-353-91561398 (phone)
011-353-91561405 (fax)

8285 Sunset Blvd Suite 2
West Hollywood CA 90046
323-654-3252 (phone)
323-654-3251 (fax)

14-16 Lord Edward St
Dublin Ireland
011-353-91561398 (phone)
011-353-16773394 (fax)

info@irishfilmboard.ie
irishfilmboard.ie
imdb.com/company/co0091878

Does not accept any unsolicited material. Project types include feature films and TV. Genres include action, drama, thriller, romance, comedy, and family.

IRONCLAD PICTURES
Production company

25 Broadway
12th Fl
New York, NY 10004
310-985-5459

ash@ironcladpictures.com
ironcladpictures.com
imdb.com/company/co0345344
facebook.com/IroncladPictures

Does not accept any unsolicited material. Project types include feature films. Genres include drama and crime.

Jordan Yale Levine
Founder/Producer
imdb.com/name/nm2775149

Ash Christian
Founder/Producer
imdb.com/name/nm1101381

IRON FILMS
Production company

390 NE 59th Terrace
Miami, FL 33137
786-243-0085 (phone)
305-466-5648 (fax)

imdb.com/company/co0214120

Does not accept any unsolicited material. Project types include short films. Genres include action and drama. Established in 2005.

IRON OCEAN FILMS
Production company

1317 Luanne Ave
Fullerton, CA 92831
323-957-9706

imdb.com/company/co0221536

Does not accept any unsolicited material. Project types include short films and feature films. Genres include crime, thriller, and drama.

Michelle Purple
imdb.com/name/nm0321977

Jessica Biel
imdb.com/name/nm0004754

IRONWORKS PRODUCTIONS
Production company

IRONWORKS PRODUCTIONS INC.
131 GORE DRIVE, BARRIE, ONTARIO CANADA
L4N 0A8
705-333-1679

517 W 35th St 2nd Floor
New York City, NY 10001
212-216-9780 (phone)
212-239-9180 (fax)

ironworksproductions@pobox.com
ironworksproductions.ca
imdb.com/company/co0159206

Accepts query letters from unproduced, unrepresented writers via email. Project types include feature films and TV. Genres include comedy, non-fiction, romance, drama, reality, and thriller.

Isa Freeling
imdb.com/name/nm2303742

Bruce Weiss
imdb.com/name/nm0918933

IRWIN ENTERTAINMENT
Production company

710 Seward St
Los Angeles, CA 90038
323-468-0700 (phone)
323-464-1001 (fax)

Collin Reno
William Morris Endeavor

9601 Wilshire Blvd,
Beverly Hills, CA 90210
310-859-4526

irwinentertainment.com
imdb.com/company/co0193199
linkedin.com/company/irwin-entertainment
twitter.com/irwinent

Does not accept any unsolicited material. Project types include feature films and TV. Genres include comedy and reality.

John Irwin
President
john@irwinentertainment.com
imdb.com/name/nm1685815

IS.FIELD
Production company and distributor

1-1-15-4F
Nishi Shimbashi
Minato, Tokyo 105-0003
Japan
050-5846-6969 (phone)
03-6680-8380 (fax)

is@is-field.com
is-field.com
imdb.com/company/co0280264

Does not accept any unsolicited material. Project types include TV. Genres include drama.

Kenji Seki
Producer
imdb.com/name/nm4386502

ISH ENTERTAINMENT
Production company

104 W 27th St Second Floor
New York, NY 10001
212-654-6445

info@ish.tv
ish.tv
imdb.com/name/nm4851905
twitter.com/ishteevee

Does not accept any unsolicited material. Project types include TV, short films, and feature films. Genres include documentary and reality. Established in 2008.

Chris Choun
imdb.com/name/nm1780111

Wendy Roth
Executive Vice President of Production
imdb.com/name/nm0745046

Melissa Cooper
Director of Development
imdb.com/name/nm2435108

Michael Saffran
Executive
imdb.com/name/nm5249575

Madison Merritt
imdb.com/name/nm3117402

Michael Hirschorn
President
imdb.com/name/nm1337695
linkedin.com/pub/michael-hirschorn/41/451/483

ISHIHARA PRODUCTIONS CO. LTD.
Production company and distributor

4-20-2-3F
Fuda
Chofu-City, Tokyo 182-0024
Japan

yujiro@ishihara-pro.co.jp
ishihara-pro.co.jp
imdb.com/company/co0100337

Does not accept any unsolicited material. Project types include TV. Genres include drama.

Tetsuya Watari
President (Executive)
imdb.com/name/nm0913911

ISLAND FILM GROUP
Production company, distributor, and sales agent

PO Box 3261
Honolulu, HI 96801
808-536-7955

info@islandfilmgroup.com

islandfilmgroup.com
imdb.com/company/co0242821
facebook.com/pages/Island-Film-Group/
212576402101302

Does not accept any unsolicited material. Project types include TV. Genres include drama.

Angela Laprete
Producer
imdb.com/name/nm1004581

IS OR ISN'T ENTERTAINMENT
Production company

8391 Beverly Blvd., Suite 125
Los Angeles, CA 90048
310-854-0972

info@isorisnt.com
isorisnt.com
imdb.com/company/co0116545
facebook.com/IsOrIsntEntertainment

Does not accept any unsolicited material. Project types include TV. Genres include drama.

Lisa Kudrow
Actor/Partner
imdb.com/name/nm0001435

Dan Bucatinsky
Partner/Producer/Writer
imdb.com/name/nm0117857

ITCHY PRODUCTIONS
Production company

Denver, CO 80222
720-628-6756

itchyproductions.ga@gmail.com
imdb.com/company/co0212375

Does not accept any unsolicited material. Project types include short films. Genres include horror.

Leslie Snyder-Newquist
Writer / Actor (Assistant)
imdb.com/name/nm2554723

ITHACA PICTURES
Production company

8711 Bonner Dr
West Hollywood, CA 90048
310-967-0112 (phone)
310-967-3053 (fax)

imdb.com/company/co0200829

Does not accept any unsolicited material. Project types include feature films. Genres include drama and non-fiction.

Richard Romero
Producer
imdb.com/name/nm2484143

Michael Fitzgerald
Executive
imdb.com/name/nm028033

ITN DISTRIBUTION
Distributor and sales agent

9663 Santa Monica Blvd
859
Beverly Hills, CA 90210
702-882-6926

stuart@itndistribution.com
itndistribution.info
imdb.com/company/co0005266
facebook.com/ITNDISTRIBUTION

Does not accept any unsolicited material. Genres include thriller and drama.

IVANHOE PICTURES
Production company

42 Liang Ma Qiao Rd Guangming Hotel Office
Building 707
Beijing China 100125

430 W Broadway, 2nd Floor, New York, NY, United States, 10012
212-609-9000 (phone)
212-609-9099 (fax)

1840 Century Park East
Los Angeles CA 90067

info@ivanhoepictures.com
ivanhoepictures.com/s/home.asp
imdb.com/company/co0452320

Does not accept any unsolicited material. Project types include feature films and TV. Genres include drama, thriller, and family.

IZUMI NETWORK GROUP CO.
Production company

8-5-32-5F
Akasaka
Minato, Tokyo 107-0052
Japan
03-5770-1811

info@izumitvp.co.jp
izumitvp.co.jp
imdb.com/company/co0347609

Does not accept any unsolicited material. Project types include TV. Genres include comedy.

Keisuke Matsumoto
Producer
imdb.com/name/nm4972833

JACKHOLE PRODUCTIONS
Production company

6834 Hollywood Blvd
Los Angeles, CA 90028
323-860-5900

imdb.com/company/co0071163
facebook.com/pages/Jackhole-Productions/
    112075485472368

Accepts query letters from produced or represented writers. Project types include TV. Genres include comedy and reality.

Jimmy Kimmel
Partner
imdb.com/name/nm0453994

Doug DeLuca
Producer
imdb.com/name/nm0217891

Adam Carolla
Partner
imdb.com/name/nm0004805

Daniel Kellison
Partner
imdb.com/name/nm0446058

JAEN ENTERTAINMENT
Production company

6903 Hana Rd.
Edison, NJ 08817
732-762-4277 (phone)
732-777-0227 (fax)

imdb.com/company/co0102699

Does not accept any unsolicited material. Project types include TV. Genres include comedy, drama, and thriller.

JAFFE/BRAUNSTEIN FILMS
Production company

12301 Wilshire Blvd Suite 110
Los Angeles, CA 90025
310-207-6600 (phone)
310-207-6069 (fax)

imdb.com/company/co0012412
facebook.com/pages/JaffeBraunstein-Films/
    111191708899467

Accepts scripts from produced or represented writers. Project types include TV and feature films. Genres include thriller, drama, comedy, horror, romance, and science fiction.

Howard Braunstein
imdb.com/name/nm0105946
linkedin.com/pub/howard-braunstein/0/a6/3a6

Michael Jaffe
Partner
imdb.com/name/nm0415468
Assistant: Lynn Delaney

JAKAN FILMS
Production company

220 Miracle Mile #216
Coral Gables, FL 33139
305-774-0111 (phone)
305-774-0155 (fax)

imdb.com/company/co0062708

Does not accept any unsolicited material. Genres include documentary.

JAKKS PACIFIC
Production company

21749 Baker Parkway
Walnut, CA 91789
877-875-2557

imdb.com/company/co0072553
facebook.com/jakkspacifictoys

Does not accept any unsolicited material. Project types include TV. Genres include science fiction.

Joel Bennett
CFO/EVP
imdb.com/name/nm0071547

JAMAAD PRODUCTIONS
Production company

66 Hillside Ave
Tenafly, NJ 07670
212-229-0021

garyobennett@gmail.com
imdb.com/company/co0315898
facebook.com/JamaadProductions

Does not accept any unsolicited material. Genres include drama, romance, and family.

JAMES MORGAN FILMS
Production company

26 Charlotte St,
London

james@jamesmorgan.co.uk
jamesmorgan.co.uk
facebook.com/jamesmorganfoto
twitter.com/jamesmorganfoto

Accepts scripts from unproduced, unrepresented writers via email. Project types include feature films, commercials, and short films. Established in 2009.

James Morgan
Creative Director
075-189-02552
james@jamesmorgan.co.uk
jamesmorgan.co.uk
Assistant: Emily studio@jamemsorgan.co.uk

JANE STARTZ PRODUCTIONS
Production company

244 Fift h Ave, 11th Floor
New York, NY 10001
212-545-8910 (phone)
212-545-8909 (fax)

imdb.com/company/co0048322

Accepts query letters from unproduced, unrepresented writers. Project types include TV and feature films. Genres include animation, thriller, romance, fantasy, comedy, family, and drama.

Jane Startz
President
imdb.com/name/nm0823661

Kane Lee
Vice-President
imdb.com/name/nm1634508

JANE STREET ENTERTAINMENT
Production company

100 Ave Of The Americas, 11th Floor
New York, NY 10013

janestreetentertainment.com
imdb.com/company/co0363484
facebook.com/JaneStreetEntertainment

Does not accept any unsolicited material. Project types include TV.

Donna Macletchie
Producer
imdb.com/name/nm2338190

Linda Lea
Producer
imdb.com/name/nm1103775

JANICEK ENTERTAINMENT
Production company

4100 E Dry Creek Rd
Denver, CO 80122
303-267-5221

info@janicekmedia.com
janicekmedia.com
imdb.com/company/co0029739
facebook.com/Janicek-Media-
    Creative-127428747364468
twitter.com/JanicekMedia

Does not accept any unsolicited material. Genres
include comedy.

JANSON ASSOCIATES INC.
Distributor

88 Semmens Rd.
Harrington Park, NJ 07640
201-784-8488 (phone)
201-784-3993 (fax)

steve@janson.com
janson.com
imdb.com/company/co0046042

Does not accept any unsolicited material. Project types
include TV. Genres include drama and thriller.

JANUARY FILMS
Production company

47 Ulster St.
Toronto, ON M5S 1E4
Canada
416-967-7078 (phone)
416-960-8656 (fax)

imdb.com/company/co0203337

Does not accept any unsolicited material. Project types
include feature films and TV. Genres include thriller.

Julia Rosenberg
Producer
imdb.com/name/nm0742250

JAPAN CREATIVE MANAGEMENT
Production company

3-3-10-301
Aoyama
Minato, Tokyo

Japan
03-5775-4222

official@jcm-aoyama.com
imdb.com/company/co0189777

Does not accept any unsolicited material. Project types
include feature films and TV. Genres include thriller
and horror.

Kazuhiko Akamine
C.E.O. (Executive)
imdb.com/name/nm2429807

JAPAN VIDEO DISTRIBUTION (JVD) CO. LTD.
Production company and distributor

2-3-19-5F
Shibuya
Shibuya, Tokyo 150-0002
Japan
03-3409-9920

info@jvd.ne.jp
jvd.ne.jp
imdb.com/company/co0100424

Does not accept any unsolicited material. Project types
include TV. Genres include horror.

JARET ENTERTAINMENT
Production company

6973 Birdview Ave
Malibu, CA 90265
310-589-9600

info@jaretentertainment.com
jaretentertainment.com
imdb.com/company/co000426

Does not accept any unsolicited material. Project types
include TV and feature films.

Seth Jaret
Producer/Manager
imdb.com/name/nm0418684

JAR PICTURES
Production company

4100 W Alameda Ave. 4th Floor
Burbank, CA 91505
818-955-5400

imdb.com/company/co0376813

Does not accept any unsolicited material. Project types include TV. Genres include drama and comedy.

Tom Mazza
EVP & Head of Worldwide TV
imdb.com/name/nm2301903

JAVELINA 98 PRODUCTIONS
Production company

8402 Nahas Ct
Pearland, TX 77584
832-925-9274

Javelina98@yahoo.com
imdb.com/company/co0480919

Does not accept any unsolicited material. Genres include thriller and horror.

JAY SILVERMAN PRODUCTIONS
Production company

1541 N Cahuenga Blvd
Los Angeles, CA 90028
323-466-6030 (phone)
323-466-7139 (fax)

bethany@jaysilverman.com
jaysilverman.com
imdb.com/company/co0241733
linkedin.com/profile/view
twitter.com/silvermanjay

Accepts query letters from produced or represented writers. Project types include TV and feature films. Genres include drama. Established in 1981.

Jay Silverman
Executive Producer/Director
bethany@jaysilverman.com

JEAN DOUMANIAN PRODUCTIONS
Production company

595 Madison Ave Suite 2200
New York City, NY 10022

212-486-2626 (phone)
212-688-6236 (fax)

jdpnyc.com
imdb.com/company/co0028809
facebook.com/jeandoumanianproductions
twitter.com/jdp_theater

Accepts query letters from unproduced, unrepresented writers. Project types include feature films and TV. Genres include comedy, non-fiction, romance, drama, horror, thriller, and period.

Saul Nathan-Kazis
Associate Director of Theatrical Development
imdb.com/name/nm2651163
linkedin.com/pub/saul-nathan-kazis/23/3/910

Patrick Daly
Vice-President
imdb.com/name/nm4794210
linkedin.com/pub/patrick-daly/20/449/aa

Kathryn Willingham
Development Associate
imdb.com/name/nm5187379
linkedin.com/pub/kathryn-willingham/a/a85/1a5

Jean Doumanian
Founder
imdb.com/name/nm0235389

JEFF MORTON PRODUCTIONS
Production company

10201 W Pico Blvd Building 226
Los Angeles, CA 90035
310-467-1123 (phone)
818-981-4152 (fax)

scoutspence@mindspring.com
imdb.com/company/co0184974

Does not accept any unsolicited material. Project types include feature films and TV.

Jeff Morton
Producer
scoutspence@mindspring.com
imdb.com/name/nm0608005

JERRY BRUCKHEIMER FILMS
Production company

1631 10th St
Santa Monica, CA 90404
310-664-6260 (phone)
310-664-6261 (fax)

jbfilms.com
imdb.com/company/co0217391
facebook.com/JBFilms
twitter.com/BruckheimerJB

Does not accept any unsolicited material. Project types include feature films and TV. Genres include horror, thriller, myth, reality, family, fantasy, crime, comedy, detective, science fiction, non-fiction, action, and drama.

Charlie Vignola
Director of Development
linkedin.com/pub/charlie-vogel/38/213/398

Mike Stenson
President
imdb.com/name/nm0826679

Jerry Bruckheimer
imdb.com/name/nm0000988
linkedin.com/in/jerrybruckheimer
twitter.com/BRUCKHEIMERJB

JERRY WEINTRAUB PRODUCTIONS
Production company

190 N Canon Dr, Suite 204
Beverly Hills, CA 90210
310-273-8800 (phone)
310-273-8502 (fax)

imdb.com/company/co0024560

Does not accept any unsolicited material. Project types include feature films. Genres include action, comedy, non-fiction, drama, family, thriller, science fiction, and crime.

JERSEY FILMS
Production company

PO Box 491246
Los Angeles, CA 90049
310-550-3200 (phone)
310-550-3210 (fax)

imdb.com/company/co0010434

Does not accept any unsolicited material. Project types include feature films. Genres include action, thriller, romance, non-fiction, drama, and comedy.

Nikki Grosso
310-477-7704
imdb.com/name/nm0343777

Danny DeVito
Executive
imdb.com/name/nm0000362

JET TONE PRODUCTIONS
Production company and distributor

21/F Park Commercial Centre
No. 180 Tung Lo Wan Rd
Hong Kong
China
852-2336-1102 (phone)
852-2337-9849 (fax)

jettone@netvigator.com
jettone.net
imdb.com/company/co0074316

Accepts query letters from unproduced, unrepresented writers via email. Project types include feature films. Genres include action, crime, comedy, animation, thriller, romance, drama, and science fiction.

Wong Kar-wai
imdb.com/name/nm0939182

JEWISH BROADCASTING SERVICE
Distributor

1 Bridge Plaza North
Suite #145
Fort Lee, NJ 07024
201-242-9460 (phone)
201-363-9241 (fax)

mail@jbstv.org
imdb.com/company/co0502458

Does not accept any unsolicited material. Project types include TV. Genres include drama and comedy.

JIM GUNN PRODUCTIONS INC.
Production company and distributor

2805 E. Oakland Park Blvd.
#445
Fort Lauderdale, FL 33306
954-214-4460

jimgunn@jimgunn.com
jimgunn.com
imdb.com/company/co0061121
twitter.com/JimGunnXXX

Does not accept any unsolicited material. Project types include feature films. Established in 1993.

JINGA FILMS
Sales agent

+44207-287-0050 (phone)
+44207-494-9492 (fax)

info@jingafilms.com
jingafilms.com
imdb.com/company/co0233741
twitter.com/JingaFilms

Does not accept any unsolicited material. Project types include short films and TV. Genres include action and horror.

Julian Richards
Director
imdb.com/name/nm0003332

J.K. LIVIN' PRODUCTIONS
Production company

64 Market St
Venice, CA 90291
310-857-1555

jklivinfoundation.org
imdb.com/company/co0097218

Does not accept any unsolicited material. Project types include feature films. Genres include action.

Matthew McConaughey
Partner/Producer/Actor
imdb.com/name/nm0000190

Mark Gustawes
President of Production
imdb.com/name/nm0349126

JOBRO PRODUCTIONS AND FILM FINANCE
Production company

225 Commissioners St
Suite 204
Toronto, ON M4M 0A1
Canada
647-648-3183

info@jobrofilmfinance.com
jobroproductions.com
imdb.com/company/co0496439
facebook.com/jobrofilmfinance
twitter.com/jobropff

Does not accept any unsolicited material. Genres include thriller.

Jonathan Bronfman
Producer
imdb.com/name/nm5558225

JOEL SCHUMACHER PRODUCTIONS
Production company

10960 Wilshire Bvld. Suite 1900
Los Angeles, CA 90024
310-472-7602 (phone)
310-270-4618 (fax)

imdb.com/company/co0094915

Does not accept any unsolicited material. Project types include commercials, feature films, and TV. Genres include action, fantasy, thriller, romance, comedy, crime, drama, and science fiction.

Joel Schumacher
310-472-7602
imdb.com/name/nm0001708
Assistant: Jeff Feuerstein

Aaron Cooley
Producer
818-260-6065
imdb.com/name/nm0177583
linkedin.com/pub/aaron-cooley/39/2b7/432

JOHN CALLEY PRODUCTIONS
Production company

10202 W Washington Blvd
Crawford Building
Culver City, CA 90232
310-244-7777 (phone)
310-244-4070 (fax)

imdb.com/company/co0125552

Does not accept any unsolicited material. Project types include TV and feature films. Genres include comedy, romance, drama, thriller, detective, and action.

John Calley
Producer
310-244-7777
imdb.com/name/nm1886942
linkedin.com/pub/john-calley/8/252/4a0

Lisa Medwid
310-244-7777
imdb.com/name/nm1886942

JOHN CARRABINO MANAGEMENT
Production company

5900 Wilshire Blvd., Suite 406
Los Angeles, CA 90036
323-857-4650

imdb.com/name/nm4222011
facebook.com/pages/John-Carrabino-Management/
    161867210499754

Does not accept any unsolicited material. Project types include TV.

John Carrabino
Owner/Manager
imdb.com/name/nm0139920

JOHN DOE MEDIA
Production company

8265 Sunset Blvd., Suite 105
West Hollywood, CA 90046
424-235-3688

info@johndoemedia.com
imdb.com/company/co0268174
facebook.com/JDMGtheBlog

Does not accept any unsolicited material. Project types include TV.

D. Renard Young
Producer
imdb.com/name/nm1511022

JOHN GOLDWYN PRODUCTIONS
Production company

5555 Melrose Ave, Dressing Room. 112
Los Angeles, CA 90038
323-956-5054 (phone)
323-862-0055 (fax)

imdb.com/company/co0177677

Does not accept any unsolicited material. Project types include feature films and TV. Genres include detective, non-fiction, drama, thriller, comedy, action, and crime. Established in 1991.

John Goldwyn
President
imdb.com/name/nm0326415
Assistant: Jasen Laks

Hilary Marx
Creative Executive
imdb.com/name/nm1020576
Assistant: Rebecca Crow

Erin David
Creative Executive
imdb.com/name/nm1716252
Assistant: Rebecca Crow

JOHNNY TOO PRODUCTION
Production company

1548 Brickell Ave
Miami, FL 33129
305-534-9123

imdb.com/company/co0205689

Does not accept any unsolicited material.

JOHNSON BROTHERS PRODUCTIONS
Production company and distributor

1285 Christmas Tree Rd
Dunn, NC 28334
910-891-5946 (phone)
678-716-9149 (fax)

PO Box 713
443 Bowie
Lone Star, TX 75668
512-650-5851 (phone)
678-716-9149 (fax)

duane@jbrothers.net
imdb.com/company/co0337638
linkedin.com/company/johnson-brothers-productions

Does not accept any unsolicited material. Project types include short films and TV. Genres include documentary.

JOHN WELLS PRODUCTIONS
Production company

4000 Warner Blvd
Building 1
Burbank, CA 91522-0001
818-954-1687 (phone)
818-954-3657 (fax)

jwppa@warnerbros.com
imdb.com/company/co0037310

Accepts query letters from unproduced, unrepresented writers. Project types include feature films and TV. Genres include horror, drama, action, family, comedy, science fiction, romance, and thriller.

John Wells
Principal
imdb.com/name/nm2187561
Assistant: Kristin Martini

Andrew Stearn
President
imdb.com/name/nm1048942
Assistant: Quinn Tivey quinn.tivey@jwprods.com

Claire Polstein
President
imdb.com/name/nm0689856
Assistant: Tessie Groff

JON SHESTACK PRODUCTIONS
Production company

409 N Larchmont Blvd
Los Angeles, CA 90004
323-468-1113

imdb.com/company/co0168855

Does not accept any unsolicited material. Project types include feature films. Genres include animation, fantasy, science fiction, thriller, romance, drama, comedy, crime, and family. Established in 2006.

Jonathan Shestack
imdb.com/name/nm0792871

Ginny Brewer Pennekamp
imdb.com/name/nm2555285

JORGENSEN PICTURES
Production company

500 S Buena Vista St
Animation Building 3F-6
Burbank, CA 91521
323-459-6199 (phone)
818-560-4014 (fax)

info@jorgensenpictures.com
jorgensenpictures.com
imdb.com/company/co0014340

Accepts query letters from unproduced, unrepresented writers. Project types include feature films and TV. Genres include crime, romance, drama, non-fiction, reality, and comedy.

Stacy Jorgensen
stacy@littleenginefilms.com

Gina Matthews
Partner
imdb.com/name/nm0560033

Grant Scharbo
Partner
imdb.com/name/nm0770090
linkedin.com/pub/grant-scharbo/12/734/43b

JORVA PRODUCTIONS
Production company

8383 Wilshire Blvd, #518, Beverly Hills, CA, United States, 90211
323-944-0381

contact@jorvaproductions.com
jorvaproductions.com
imdb.com/company/co0501021

Does not accept any unsolicited material. Project types include feature films and TV. Genres include romance, drama, thriller, and family.

JOSEPHSON ENTERTAINMENT
Production company

1201 W 5th St Suite M-170
Los Angeles, CA 90017
213-534-3995

imdb.com/company/co0046572

Does not accept any unsolicited material. Project types include feature films and TV. Genres include science fiction, crime, fantasy, horror, drama, romance, family, sociocultural, animation, comedy, thriller, and action.

Barry Josephson
Principal
imdb.com/name/nm0430742
Assistant: Sean Bennett

JOURNEYMAN PICTURES
Production company

225 W 13th St
New York, NY 10011
212-989-1038 (phone)
212-989-3907 (fax)

info@journeyman-pictures.com
journeyman-pictures.com
imdb.com/company/co0065292

Does not accept any unsolicited material. Project types include feature films. Genres include drama.

Paul Mezey
Producer
imdb.com/name/nm0583796

Becky Glupczynski
Producer
imdb.com/name/nm1014894

JOURNEY PRODUCTIONS INC.
Production company

2870 Peachtree Rd.
Ste. 216
Atlanta, GA 30305

404-355-1438 (phone)
801-459-9715 (fax)

info@journeyproductions.com
imdb.com/company/co0108331

Does not accept any unsolicited material. Genres include documentary.

JUNCTION FILMS
Production company

9615 Brighton Way, Suite M110
Beverly Hills, CA 90210
220 3377 (phone)
220 3550 (fax)

info@junctionfilms.com
junctionfilms.com
imdb.com/company/co0099841

Does not accept any unsolicited material. Project types include feature films. Genres include crime, comedy, reality, horror, drama, action, science fiction, and thriller. Established in 2001.

Donald Kushner
Producer
imdb.com/name/nm0476291

Alwyn Kushner
Producer
imdb.com/name/nm1672379

Brad Wyman
Producer
310-246-9799
imdb.com/name/nm0943829

JUNE BEALLOR PRODUCTIONS
Production company

100 Universal City Plaza, Bldg. 6147
Universal City, CA 91608
818-777-9000 (phone)
818-866-2222 (fax)

info@junebeallorproductions.com
junebeallorproductions.com
imdb.com/company/co0044270

Does not accept any unsolicited material. Project types include TV and feature films. Genres include documentary. Established in 1994.

June Beallor
Producer
imdb.com/name/nm0063706

JUNGLE
Production company

5-2-18-106
Mita
Minatoku, Tokyo 108-0073
Japan
03-5765-8381 (phone)
03-5765-3020 (fax)

info@jungle-tokyo.com
jungle-tokyo.com
imdb.com/company/co0007219

Does not accept any unsolicited material. Project types include TV and feature films. Genres include action and fantasy.

JUNGLE WALK, CO.
Production company and distributor

2-51-34-1F
Sangenjaya
Setagaya, Tokyo 154-0024
Japan
03-5432-6398 (phone)
03-5432-6389 (fax)

contact@junglewalk.co.jp
junglewalk.co.jp/index_e.html
imdb.com/company/co0234852

Does not accept any unsolicited material. Project types include TV. Genres include drama.

Kenji Kobayashi
Founder (Producer)
imdb.com/name/nm2730002

JUNIPER PLACE PRODUCTIONS
Production company

4024 Radford Ave, Bungalow 1
Studio City, CA 91604
818-655-5043 (phone)
818-655-8402 (fax)

imdb.com/company/co0203560

Does not accept any unsolicited material. Project types include TV. Genres include drama.

Jennifer Stempel
Director of Development
imdb.com/name/nm4009105

Jeffrey Kramer
Principal
imdb.com/name/nm0469552
linkedin.com/pub/jeffrey-kramer/6/89/850

JUST MEDIA
Production company

700 Kalamath St
Ste 201
Denver, CO 80204
303-871-9015

info@just-media.org
just-media.org
imdb.com/company/co0112075

Does not accept any unsolicited material. Project types include short films and feature films. Genres include family and documentary.

Henry Ansbacher
Executive Director (Producer)
imdb.com/name/nm1461938

JVCO PRODUCTIONS
Production company and distributor

300 Convent St
Suite 1330
San Antonio, TX 78205
210-901-5139

jvcofanfilms@gmail.com
jvcoproductions.com
imdb.com/company/co0498748

Does not accept any unsolicited material. Project types include TV. Genres include action and drama.

K5 MEDIA GROUP
Production company and distributor

1999 Ave of the Stars Suite 1100
Century City CA 90067

424-253-1122 (phone)
424-253-1123 (fax)

K5 Media Group GmbH, Konradinstrasse 5, Munich, Germany, 81543
011-498-937505590 (phone)
011-498-9375055905 (fax)

info@k5international.com
k5mediagroup.com/home
imdb.com/company/co0352546

Does not accept any unsolicited material. Project types include TV. Genres include thriller, drama, and family.

K7 GLOBAL
Production company and sales agent

Attn: George M. Kostuch
6872 Lasalle Ave.
Baton Rouge, LA 70806

george@k7pictures.com
k7pictures.com
imdb.com/company/co0483147
facebook.com/K7GLOBAL

Does not accept any unsolicited material. Project types include feature films and TV. Genres include science fiction.

George M. Kostuch
Producer
imdb.com/name/nm0467529

KABOOM! ENTERTAINMENT
Production company and distributor

20 Eglinton Ave W
Ste 603, PO Box 2041
Toronto, ON M4R 1K8
Canada
416-783-8383 (phone)
416-783-8384 (fax)

berry@kaboom-ent.com
kaboom-ent.com
imdb.com/company/co0090067
facebook.com/kaboment
twitter.com/kaboomkids

Does not accept any unsolicited material. Project types include TV. Genres include comedy, animation, and family.

KALEIDOSCOPE
Distributor and sales agent

104-108 Oxford St
London W1D 1 LP
UK
+44 (0203-397-4410

sales@kaleidoscopefilmdistribution.com
kaleidoscopefilmdistribution.com
imdb.com/company/co0198256
facebook.com/KaleidoscopeHomeEntertainment

Does not accept any unsolicited material. Project types include TV and feature films. Genres include animation.

KALEIDOSCOPE ENTERTAINMENT
Production company and distributor

25 Lesmill Rd.
Suite 5
Toronto, ON M3B 2T3
Canada
416-443-9200 (phone)
416-443-8685 (fax)

arleneh@kalent.com
imdb.com/company/co0178768

Does not accept any unsolicited material. Genres include fantasy, drama, and animation.

Paul McConvey
Producer
imdb.com/name/nm1107664

KALEIDOSCOPE FILM DISTRIBUTION
Distributor and sales agent

16 Dufours Place
6th Fl
London W1F 7SP
UK
+44 20 3397 4410

info@kaleidoscopefilmdistribution.com
kaleidoscopefilmdistribution.com

imdb.com/company/co0331256

Does not accept any unsolicited material. Project types include TV. Genres include documentary, thriller, drama, comedy, and action.

Spencer Pollard
Producer
imdb.com/name/nm2759244

KALEIDOSCOPE HOME ENTERTAINMENT
Distributor and sales agent

104-108 Oxford St
London W1D 1LP
UK
+44 (0) 20 3397 4410

info@kaleidoscopehomeentertainment.com
kaleidoscopehomeentertainment.com
imdb.com/company/co0296674
facebook.com/KaleidoscopeHomeEntertainment

Does not accept any unsolicited material. Project types include short films, TV, and feature films. Genres include action, thriller, and drama.

Spencer Pollard
Producer
imdb.com/name/nm2759244

KALYAN STUDIOS
Production company

Victoria, BC
250-508-2082

ziakalyan@gmail.com
kalyanstudios.com
imdb.com/company/co0544299
linkedin.com/company/kalyan-studios
facebook.com/kalyanstudios
twitter.com/kalyanstudios

Does not accept any unsolicited material. Project types include feature films, commercials, and short films. Genres include thriller, comedy, crime, action, drama, romance, and detective. Established in 2014.

Zia Kalyan
Director
250-508-2082
ziakalyan@gmail.com
ziakalyan.com
imdb.com/name/nm7126433
ca.linkedin.com/in/ziakalyan
facebook.com/zkalyan
twitter.com/ziakalyan

KAMALA FILMS
Production company

375 Greenwich St, 5th Floor
New York, NY 10013
212-219-4161

info@kamalafilms.com
imdb.com/company/co0172185
twitter.com/kamalafilms

Does not accept any unsolicited material. Project types include feature films. Genres include drama.

Marissa McMahon
Producer
imdb.com/name/nm0997470

KAMKOL PRODUCTIONS LLC
Production company

2227 US Hwy 1
#294
North Brunswick, NJ 08902

kamkol.productions@gmail.com
kamkol.com
imdb.com/company/co0088284
facebook.com/pages/Kamkol-Productions-LLC/
    115490423848
twitter.com/indiancowboy

Does not accept any unsolicited material. Project types include short films and TV. Genres include comedy and thriller.

KANA TOMOKO PRODUCTIONS
Production company

1-3-18 C-507, Shibuya, Shibuya-ku
Tokyo 150-0002
Japan

+81 3 33 57 51 40 (phone)
+81 3 34 98 22 60 (fax)

office@kanatomoko.jp
kanatomoko.jp
imdb.com/company/co0285163

Does not accept any unsolicited material. Project types include TV. Genres include family and documentary.

KAPITAL ENTERTAINMENT
Production company

8687 Melrose Ave
9th Floor
West Hollywood, CA 90069
310-854-3221

imdb.com/company/co0275279

Does not accept any unsolicited material. Project types include TV. Genres include comedy and drama.

Aaron Kaplan
akaplan@kapital-ent.com
imdb.com/name/nm3483168

Cailey Buck
Director of Development
linkedin.com/pub/cailey-buck/19/120/980

KAPLAN/PERRONE ENTERTAINMENT
Production company

280 S Beverly Dr, #513
Beverly Hills, CA 90212
310-285-0116

imdb.com/company/co0094257

Accepts scripts from produced or represented writers. Project types include feature films and TV. Genres include comedy, romance, drama, action, and thriller.

Aaron Kaplan
Partner
linkedin.com/pub/aaron-kaplan/3/74b/507

Alex Lerner
Manager
linkedin.com/pub/alex-lerner/1a/64b/845

KARCH BROTHERS ENTERTAINMENT
Production company and distributor

P.O. Box 631
Haslet, TX 76052
817-899-5831

jackie@karchbros.com
karchbros.com
imdb.com/company/co0454013

Does not accept any unsolicited material. Genres include horror, thriller, and drama.

KARTEMQUIN FILMS
Production company

1901 W. Wellington
Chicago, IL 60657
773-472-3348

info@kartemquin.com
kartemquin.com
imdb.com/company/co0076348

Does not accept any unsolicited material. Project types include feature films. Genres include drama and non-fiction.

KARZ ENTERTAINMENT
Production company

4000 Warner Blvd Building 138, Suite 1205
Burbank, CA 91522
818-954-1698 (phone)
818-954-1700 (fax)

karzent@aol.com
imdb.com/company/co0033868

Does not accept any unsolicited material. Project types include TV and feature films. Genres include thriller, horror, action, romance, documentary, drama, fantasy, family, crime, and comedy. Established in 1998.

Mike Karz
President
imdb.com/name/nm0440344

KASDAN PICTURES
Production company

9220 W Sunset Blvd, Suite 108
West Hollywood, CA 90069
310-281-2340

imdb.com/company/co0003216

Does not accept any unsolicited material. Project types include feature films. Genres include drama, thriller, and comedy.

Lawrence Kasdan
Writer/Producer/Director
imdb.com/name/nm0001410

KASPI CREATIVE LAB
Production company and studio

Matbuat ave 23M, Baku, AZ1073
Republic of Azerbaijan
994-502-457272

shamkhal@kaspi-global.com
kaspi-global.com

Accepts query letters from produced or represented writers. Project types include commercials, feature films, short films, and TV. Genres include horror, comedy, detective, action, and drama. Established in 2013.

shamkhal hasanli
CEO
shamkhal@kaspi-global.com

KASSEN BROTHERS PRODUCTIONS
Production company

141 W 28th St, Suite 301
New York, NY 10001
212-244-2865 (phone)
212-244-2874 (fax)

imdb.com/company/co0183529

Accepts query letters from unproduced, unrepresented writers. Project types include TV. Genres include non-fiction, action, comedy, and drama.

Mark Kassen
President
imdb.com/name/nm0440860

Patrick Petrocelli
imdb.com/name/nm2332569

Mark Olsen
Director of Development
imdb.com/name/nm1565746

Adam Kassen
212-244-2865
imdb.com/name/nm0440859

KATALYST FILMS

6806 Lexington Ave
Los Angeles, CA 90038
323-785-2700 (phone)
323-785-2715 (fax)

info@katalystfilms.com
katalystfilms.com
imdb.com/company/co0102320
facebook.com/katalyst

Accepts scripts from unproduced, unrepresented writers. Project types include feature films and TV. Genres include action, drama, crime, reality, comedy, animation, science fiction, thriller, and romance. Established in 2000.

Ashton Kutcher
Partner
imdb.com/name/nm0005110
facebook.com/Ashton

Jason Goldberg
Partner
imdb.com/name/nm0325229
linkedin.com/pub/jason-goldberg/22/120/131

KATCO
Production company

8687 Melrose Ave
West Hollywood, CA 90069
310-854-3223

imdb.com/company/co0483718

Does not accept any unsolicited material. Project types include feature films and TV. Established in 2014.

Tracy Katsky
Executive
818-789-1182
tracykb@gmail.com
Assistant: Danyelle Foord

KAUFMAN COMPANY
Production company

15030 Ventura Blvd, Suite 510
Sherman Oaks, CA 91403
818-223-9840

info@thekaufmancompany.com
thekaufmancompany.com
imdb.com/company/co0043378

Does not accept any unsolicited material.

Paul Kaufman
Producer
imdb.com/name/nm2092500

KAZUMO CO.
Production company

1-37-14-106
Tomihaya, Shibuya
Tokyo 151-0063
Japan
+81 3-5478-1081 (phone)
+81 3-5478-1090 (fax)

info@kazumo.jp
kazumo.jp
imdb.com/company/co0305526

Does not accept any unsolicited material. Project types include feature films and TV. Genres include thriller.

Hiroaki Saitô
Producer
imdb.com/name/nm1927381

KCNC
Distributor

1044 Lincoln St.
Denver, CO 80203
303-861-4444 (phone)
303-830-6380 (fax)

mailroom@kcncnews4.com
imdb.com/company/co0133741

Does not accept any unsolicited material. Genres include documentary.

KEKULE PRODUCTIONS
Production company

1598 Franklin St.
Denver, CO 80218
773-960-1984

info@kekuleproductions.com
seanjsjourdan.com
imdb.com/company/co0190614

Does not accept any unsolicited material. Project types include feature films. Genres include action, thriller, and drama.

KELLER ENTERTAINMENT GROUP
Production company

1093 Broxton Ave, Suite #246
Los Angeles, CA 90024
310-443-2226 (phone)
310-443-2194 (fax)

kellerentertainment.com
imdb.com/company/co0007667
linkedin.com/company/keller-entertainment-group-inc

Does not accept any unsolicited material. Project types include feature films and TV. Genres include family, action, and drama.

Max Keller
Chairman/CEO
imdb.com/name/nm0445720

Micheline Keller
President
imdb.com/name/nm0445732

KENNEDY/MARSHALL COMPANY
Production company

619 Arizona Ave
Santa Monica, CA 90401
310-656-8400 (phone)
310-656-8430 (fax)

kennedymarshall.com
imdb.com/company/co0013175
facebook.com/pages/The-KennedyMarshall-Company/
  274557862638636
twitter.com/KenedyMarshall

Does not accept any unsolicited material. Project types include TV and feature films. Genres include detective, thriller, family, drama, comedy, non-fiction, romance, science fiction, and action.

Grey Rembert
imdb.com/name/nm0718880

Frank Marshall
imdb.com/name/nm0550881

KENSINGTON COMMUNICATIONS
Production company and distributor

451 Adelaide St West
Toronto, ON M5V 1T1
Canada
416-504-9822 (phone)
416-504-3608 (fax)

info@kensingtontv.com
kensingtontv.com
imdb.com/company/co0101456
linkedin.com/company/kensington-communications
facebook.com/KensingtonTV
twitter.com/kensingtonTV

Does not accept any unsolicited material. Genres include documentary.

KERNER BROADCASTING
Production company

250 Worth Ave
Palm Beach, FL 33480
561-832-2000

imdb.com/company/co0279802

Does not accept any unsolicited material.

KERNER ENTERTAINMENT COMPANY
Production company

1888 Century Park East
Suite 1005
Los Angeles, CA 90067
310-815-5100 (phone)
310-815-5110 (fax)

imdb.com/company/co0127668

Does not accept any unsolicited material. Project types include feature films. Genres include action, drama, fantasy, animation, family, and comedy.

Jordan Kerner
President
imdb.com/name/nm0449549
linkedin.com/pub/jordan-kerner/29/48/a96

Ben Haber
imdb.com/name/nm1852209

KESHET MEDIA GROUP
Production company, studio, and distributor

7 Greenland St
London United Kingdom W1NW1 0ND
011-442-037710050

12 Raul Valenberg St, P.O.B. 58151, Tel Aviv, Israel, 61580
011-972-37676031 (phone)
011-972-37676007 (fax)

2900 Olympic Blvd
Santa Monica CA 90404
310-255-4686

Building 208 The Entertainment Quarter Moore Park
Sydney NSW Australia 2021
011-612-93317334

110 S. Fairfax Ave. Suite #220
Los Angeles CA 90036
323-452-0619

info@keshetinternational.com
keshetinternational.com
imdb.com/company/co0455760

Does not accept any unsolicited material. Project types include TV and feature films. Genres include drama and action.

KESTREL COMMUNICATIONS
Production company

1100 Spring St, Suite 770
Atlanta, GA 30309
404-888-0336

contact@kestrelcom.com
imdb.com/company/co0197764
linkedin.com/company/kestrel-communications-llc

Does not accept any unsolicited material. Project types include TV and feature films. Genres include comedy and drama.

Robert L. Rearden Jr.
Producer
imdb.com/name/nm4299673

KEY CREATIVES
Production company

1800 N. Highland Ave., Suite 500
Los Angeles, CA 90028
323-785-7950

imdb.com/company/co0124523
linkedin.com/company/key-creatives

Does not accept any unsolicited material. Project types include feature films and TV. Genres include science fiction.

Ken Kamins
CEO, Producer
imdb.com/name/nm1353341

KEY FILMS
Production company

5613 Versailles Ct.
Colleyville, TX 76034

imdb.com/company/co0136532

Does not accept any unsolicited material. Project types include feature films. Genres include drama and crime.

Charles Key
Producer
imdb.com/name/nm2105495

K-FACTORY
Production company

1-19-11-3F
Dogenzaka
Shibuya, Tokyo
Japan

marlon@takumibando.com
imdb.com/company/co0180984

Does not accept any unsolicited material. Project types include TV. Genres include drama.

Eiji Ohtsuka
Producer
imdb.com/name/nm1119218

KFM PRODUCTIONS
Production company

15455 Dallas Pkwy
Suite 375
Addison, TX 75001

kfmproductions.com
imdb.com/company/co0495520
web.facebook.com/KFMProductions

Does not accept any unsolicited material. Project types include short films. Genres include drama and thriller.

KGB FILMS
Production company and distributor

5555 Melrose Ave, Lucy Bungalow 101
Los Angeles, CA 90038
323-956-5000 (phone)
323-224-1876 (fax)

turbo@kgbfilms.com
imdb.com/company/co0184250
linkedin.com/company/kgb-films
facebook.com/kgbfilms

Accepts query letters from unproduced, unrepresented writers via email. Project types include feature films, TV, and short films. Genres include drama, crime, comedy, romance, and non-fiction. Established in 1994.

Justin Hogan
Producer
imdb.com/name/nm0389556
linkedin.com/pub/frank-scherma/0/332/440

Rosser Goodman
President
rossergoodman.com
imdb.com/name/nm0329223

KHARA CORPORATION
Production company and distributor

1-2-29
Kajino

Koganei, Tokyo 184-0002
Japan
080-3403-5917

joboffer@khara.co.jp
khara.co.jp
imdb.com/company/co0195433

Does not accept any unsolicited material. Project types include TV. Genres include animation.

Hideaki Anno
President (Executive)
imdb.com/name/nm0030417

KICKSTART PRODUCTIONS

Production company

594 Broadway,
Ninth Floor
New York, New York
10012

343 Railway St suite 101
Vancouver,
British Columbia
V6A 1A4
604-684-3465

1066 Tung Chau West St,
Alexandria Industrial Bldg,
Suite 306, 3/F, Block A
Lai Chi Kok, Kowloon
852-9528-0442

3212 Nebraska Ave
Santa Monica, CA 90404
310-264-1757

hiny@kickstartent.com
kickstartent.com
imdb.com/company/co0163548
facebook.com/pages/Kick-Start-Productuons-Inc/
    170721556324763
twitter.com/kickstartpro

Does not accept any unsolicited material. Project types include feature films. Genres include action, comedy, family, animation, and science fiction. Established in 1999.

Susan Norkin
imdb.com/name/nm0635379

Jason Netter
President
imdb.com/name/nm0626697

Samantha Olsson Shear
imdb.com/name/nm2427387
linkedin.com/pub/samantha-shear/6/a67/a18

Loris Kramer Lunsford
Executive Producer
imdb.com/name/nm0469603
linkedin.com/in/loriskl

KILLER FILMS

Production company and distributor

18th East 16th St, 4th Floor
New York, NY 10003
212-473-3950 (phone)
212-807-1456 (fax)

killerfilms.com
imdb.com/company/co0030755
facebook.com/killerfilms

Accepts query letters from unproduced, unrepresented writers. Project types include TV, feature films, and short films. Genres include comedy, drama, crime, romance, family, thriller, and horror. Established in 1995.

Pamela Koffler
Partner
imdb.com/name/nm0463025
Assistant: Gabrielle Nadig

Christine Vachon
Partner
imdb.com/name/nm0882927
Assistant: Gabrielle Nadig

David Hinojosa
Director of Development
imdb.com/name/nm3065267
Assistant: Gabrielle Nadig

KIM AND JIM PRODUCTIONS

Production company

787 N. Palm Canyon Dr
Palm Springs, CA 92262
760-574-1858

info@kimandjimproductions.com
kimandjimproductions.com
imdb.com/company/co0338692
facebook.com/kimandjimproductions
twitter.com/kimwaltrip

Accepts query letters from unproduced, unrepresented writers. Project types include feature films. Genres include horror, fantasy, romance, action, thriller, comedy, and drama.

Jim Casey
Vice Chairman
jim@kimandjimproductions
imdb.com/name/nm2816633

Kim Waltrip
Vice Chairman
assist@kimandjimproductions.com
imdb.com/name/nm0910601
linkedin.com/in/kimwaltrip

KINDAI EIGA KYOKAI
Production company and distributor

5-4-16-5F
Akasaka
Minato, Tokyo 107-6122
Japan
03(3582)4904 (phone)
03(3582)4959 (fax)

kindai@kindaieikyo.com
kindaieikyo.com
imdb.com/company/co0014599

Does not accept any unsolicited material. Project types include TV and feature films. Genres include horror.

Kaneto Shindô
Producer
imdb.com/name/nm0793881

KINETIC FILMWORKS
Production company

6660 Suset Blvd #l193
Hollywood, CA 90028
818-505-3347

kineticfilmworks@aol.com
kineticfilmworks.com

imdb.com/company/co0224342

Accepts query letters from unproduced, unrepresented writers via email. Project types include feature films. Genres include horror. Established in 2013.

Jeffrey Miller
Partner
imdb.com/name/nm0588577

Gary Jones
Partner
imdb.com/name/nm0428109
linkedin.com/in/garybjones

KINGDOM COUNTY PRODUCTIONS
Production company

106 Main St, Suite 2
Burlington, VT 05401
802-357-4616

info@kingdomcounty.com
kingdomcounty.com
imdb.com/company/co0154942
facebook.com/kingdomcounty

Does not accept any unsolicited material. Project types include feature films. Genres include drama.

KINGDOM POWER STUDIOS
Production company

1000 N Belt Line Rd
Suite #104
Irving, TX 75062
214-924-0094

dallas@act4jesus.com
kingdompowerministries.org
imdb.com/company/co0251386

Does not accept any unsolicited material. Project types include feature films. Genres include drama. Established in 2007.

KING MIDAS WORLD ENTERTAINMENT
Production company

3960 Howard Hughes Parkway, Suite 500
Las Vegas, NV 89169
702-990-3979 (phone)
702-562-1541 (fax)

kingmidasworldentertainment.com
imdb.com/company/co0242105
facebook.com/King-Midas-World-
   Entertainment-219953374755070

Does not accept any unsolicited material. Project types include feature films. Genres include action and drama.

KINGSBOROUGH PICTURES
Production company

446, Boul Saint-Laurent, Bureau 805
Montreal, Quebec
Canada H2W1Z5
514-985-2272

361 Beloit Ave
Los Angeles, CA 90049
310-476-1613

info@kingsboroughpictures.com
kingsboroughpictures.com
imdb.com/company/co0025097
facebook.com/KingsboroughPictures

Does not accept any unsolicited material. Project types include feature films. Genres include drama.

KINGSGATE FILMS, INC.
Production company

7024 Melrose Ave, Suite 420
Los Angeles, CA 90038
323-937-6110 (phone)
323-937-6102 (fax)

imdb.com/company/co0013909

Does not accept any unsolicited material. Project types include feature films. Genres include drama and comedy.

Greg Shapiro
Producer
imdb.com/name/nm0788513

KING'S INDIAN PRODUCTIONS
Production company

335 E 5 St, Suite 2F
New York, NY 10003

info@kingsindian.com
kingsindian.com

Does not accept any unsolicited material. Project types include feature films. Genres include thriller and drama.

John Hume
President
imdb.com/name/nm1124685

KING SIZE FILM PRODUCTIONS
Production company

32302 Camino Capistrano #203
San Juan Capistrano, CA 92675
714-928-7600

imdb.com/company/co0286028

Does not accept any unsolicited material. Project types include feature films. Genres include drama.

Michael Zanetis
President/Producer/Writer
imdb.com/name/nm4509769

KINODANCE
Distributor and sales agent

88 Winslow
#2
Somerville, MA 02144
617-571-4742

akovgan@kinodance.com
kinodance.org
imdb.com/company/co0284867

Does not accept any unsolicited material. Project types include TV. Genres include drama.

KINO FILMS
Production company and distributor

6-5-1-8F
Nishi Shinjuku
Shinjuku, Tokyo 163-1309
Japan
+81 03-5908-2262 (phone)
+81 03-5908-2232 (fax)

kinofilms-master@kinoshita-group.co.jp

kinofilms.jp
imdb.com/company/co0280680

Does not accept any unsolicited material. Project types include TV and feature films. Genres include science fiction and thriller.

Naoya Kinoshita
President (Executive)
imdb.com/name/nm3291233

KINO INTERNATIONAL
Production company and distributor

333 W 39th St, Suite 503, New York City , NY, United States, 10018
212-629-6880 (phone)
212-714-0871 (fax)

contact@kino.com
kinolorber.com
imdb.com/company/co0047947

Does not accept any unsolicited material. Project types include TV and feature films. Genres include drama, action, and thriller.

KINO LORBER
Production company and distributor

333 W 39th St, Suite 503, New York , NY, United States, 10018
212-629-6880

kinolorber.com
imdb.com/company/co0291948

Does not accept any unsolicited material. Project types include feature films and TV. Genres include drama, comedy, family, and thriller.

KINTOP PICTURES
Production company and distributor

7955 W 3rd St
Los Angeles, CA 90048
323-634-1570 (phone)
323-634-1575 (fax)

info@indiatakeone.com
indiatakeone.com
imdb.com/company/co0004925
linkedin.com/company/kintop-pictures

facebook.com/pages/Kintop-Pictures/
162544103769669

Accepts query letters from unproduced, unrepresented writers. Project types include TV and feature films. Genres include drama, horror, thriller, romance, family, comedy, and documentary.

Deepak Nayar
Founder
imdb.com/name/nm0623235

KIPPSTER ENTERTAINMENT
Production company

420 W End Ave, Suite 1G
New York, NY 10024
212-496-1200

imdb.com/company/co0310346

Does not accept any unsolicited material. Project types include TV and feature films. Genres include drama and non-fiction.

Perri Kipperman
Founder
imdb.com/name/nm1069530

David Sterns
Founder
imdb.com/name/nm3992907
linkedin.com/pub/david-stern/46/85/711

KIRIYA PICTURES
Production company

2-2-15-UCF917
Minami Aoyama
Minato, TOKYO 107-0062
Japan

kiripic@gmail.com
kiriya.com
imdb.com/company/co0214811

Does not accept any unsolicited material. Project types include TV and feature films. Genres include action and drama.

Kazuaki Kiriya
Producer
imdb.com/name/nm1589546

KIRMSER PONTURO GROUP
Production company

10 Rockefeller Plaza, Suite 910
New York, NY 10020
212-554-3430

info@kirmserponturo.com
kirmserponturo.com

Does not accept any unsolicited material. Project types include feature films. Genres include non-fiction and drama.

Tony Ponturo
Producer
imdb.com/name/nm5501182

Fran Kirmser
Producer
imdb.com/name/nm6134040

KISMET ENTERTAINMENT GROUP
Production company

8350 Wilshire Blvd., Suite 200
Beverly Hills, CA 90211
323-556-0748 (phone)
323-556-0601 (fax)

info@kismetent.com
kismetent.com
imdb.com/company/co0076370

Accepts query letters from unproduced, unrepresented writers. Project types include feature films. Genres include action and horror.

Todd Knowlton
Vice President
imdb.com/name/nm1539856

David E. Allen
Chairman/CEO/Producer
imdb.com/name/nm0020431

KISMETIC PRODUCTIONS
Production company

27 Heather Dr
Kings Park, NJ
917-848-7432

info@kismeticproductions.com

kismeticproductions.com
imdb.com/company/co0141355
linkedin.com/company/kismetic-productions-inc

Does not accept any unsolicited material. Project types include TV. Genres include documentary.

KITTY FILMS
Production company and distributor

7-3-1-4F
Minami Aoyama
Minato, Tokyo 107-0062
Japan
03-5469-1103

info@5-ace.co.jp
imdb.com/company/co0067065

Does not accept any unsolicited material. Project types include TV and feature films. Genres include drama and romance.

Shosuke Taga
Producer
imdb.com/name/nm0846464

KIWI FILM HOUSE
Production company

UK
+44 7 482 272 877

info@kiwifilmhouse.uk
kiwifilmhouse.uk
imdb.com/company/co0525672

Does not accept any unsolicited material. Project types include TV and feature films. Genres include drama.

Chelsea Grant
Director
imdb.com/name/nm6132746

KLA PRODUCTIONS
Production company

15707 Coit Rd
Suite C #146
Dallas, TX 75248
972-596-1974

info@KLAproductions.com

klaproductions.com
imdb.com/company/co0442737
linkedin.com/company/kla-productions

Does not accept any unsolicited material. Project types include short films. Genres include comedy, romance, drama, and action.

KLASKY-CSUPO
Production company

1238 N. Higland Blvd.
Hollywood , CA 90038
323-468-2600

mail@klaskycsupo.com
klaskycsupo.com
imdb.com/company/co0013196

Does not accept any unsolicited material. Project types include TV and feature films.

Gabor Csupo
Chairman
imdb.com/name/nm0190780

Arlene Klasky
Chairman
imdb.com/name/nm0458312

KLOCKWORX, THE
Production company and distributor

3-9-1-701
Meguro, Tokyo 153-0063
Japan
03.5725.3444 (phone)
03.5725.3445 (fax)

info@klockworx.com
klockworx.com
imdb.com/company/co0005849

Does not accept any unsolicited material. Project types include TV, short films, and feature films. Genres include action.

Itaru Fujimoto
President (Producer)
imdb.com/name/nm1380008

KNIGHT MEDIACOM INT'L
Production company, distributor, and sales agent

7949 Eastridge Dr
La Mesa, CA 91941
619-573-9919

rknight@knightmedia.com
knightmedia.com
imdb.com/company/co0297126

Does not accept any unsolicited material. Project types include TV. Genres include drama and fantasy.

KNIGHTSBRIDGE MEDIA
Production company and distributor

Moorgate House
5-8 Dysart St
London EC2A 2BX
UK
+44 (0)7412 988839

info@knightsbridgemedia.com
knightsbridgemedia.com
imdb.com/company/co0216612

Does not accept any unsolicited material. Project types include TV. Genres include crime, drama, and action.

Nick Rai
Manager
imdb.com/name/nm4169363

KNIGHTSBRIDGE THEATRE FILMS
Production company

1944 Riverside Dr
Los Angeles, CA 90039
323-667-0955

knightsbridgetheatre.com
imdb.com/company/co0351642
facebook.com/pages/Knightsbridge-Theatre/
  119758671421319

Does not accept any unsolicited material. Project types include feature films. Genres include thriller.

Joseph P. Stachura
Founder/Producer/Director/Writer
imdb.com/name/nm0821018

KNOW RULES MEDIA
Production company

141 Adelaide St West
Suite 1200
Toronto, ON M5H 3L5
Canada
416-902-1442

hello@knowrulesmedia.com
knowrulesmedia.com
imdb.com/company/co0406901
facebook.com/KnowRulesMedia
twitter.com/knowrulesmedia

Does not accept any unsolicited material. Genres include crime and drama.

Sanzhar Sultanov
Producer
imdb.com/name/nm3343487

KNOXSKORNER

Production company and distributor

1044 curtiss
Schertz, TX 78154
210-232-2256

istigmal@aol.com
imdb.com/company/co0172562

Does not accept any unsolicited material. Genres include action and comedy.

KOAN

Production company, distributor, and sales agent

PO Box 982557
Park City, UT 84098
435-645-7244 (phone)
435-645-8644 (fax)

dcarter@koaninc.com
koaninc.com
imdb.com/company/co0111135

Does not accept any unsolicited material. Project types include TV. Genres include drama, family, and thriller.

Gil Aglaure
Producer
imdb.com/name/nm2249135

KOKUEI COMPANY

Production company and distributor

8-3-102
Ginza
Chuo, Tokyo 104-0061
Japan
+03 3571 6378 (phone)
+03 3571 64000 (fax)

info@kokuei-tcc.co.jp
kokuei-tcc.co.jp
imdb.com/company/co0065587

Does not accept any unsolicited material. Project types include TV. Genres include drama and romance.

KOMIXX ENTERTAINMENT

Production company

9155 W Sunset Blvd
Los Angeles, CA 90069
310-385-7140

Amadeus House
27b Floral St
Covent Garden
London
WC2E 9DP
+44203-428-5396

info@komixx.com
komixx.com
imdb.com/company/co0296470
linkedin.com/company/komixx-entertainment-komixx-films
twitter.com/komixx

Does not accept any unsolicited material. Project types include short films, TV, and feature films. Genres include romance, comedy, and action.

Richard Randolph
Creative Director
+44207-861-3869
info@komixx.com
Assistant: Maddie Stewart

KOMUT ENTERTAINMENT

Production company

imdb.com/company/co0028360

Does not accept any unsolicited material. Project types include TV. Genres include drama, comedy, and thriller.

David Kohan
Partner
imdb.com/name/nm0463172
Assistant: Melissa Strauss
Melissa.Strauss@wbconsultant.com

Max Mutchnick
Partner
imdb.com/name/nm0616083
twitter.com/MaxMutchnick

KONO FILMS
Financing company

16190 N. 99th Way
Scottsdale, AZ 85260
480-621-0841 (phone)
480-621-0841 (fax)

napoleon@konomag.com
imdb.com/company/co0309196

Does not accept any unsolicited material. Project types include commercials. Genres include thriller and crime.

Napoleon Smith III
Producer
imdb.com/name/nm3418341

K/O PAPER PRODUCTS
Production company

100 Universal City Plaza
Building 5125
Universal City, CA 91608
818-733-9645 (phone)
818-733-6988 (fax)

imdb.com/company/co0315120

Does not accept any unsolicited material. Project types include feature films and TV. Genres include drama, fantasy, science fiction, action, and animation. Established in 1997.

Alex Kurtzman
Principal
imdb.com/name/nm0476064

Roberto Orci
Principal
imdb.com/name/nm0649460

KOUWA INTERNATIONAL
Production company

2-8-10-5F
Ebisu Nishi
Shibuya, Tokyo 150-0021
Japan

info@kouwa-int.com
kouwa-int.com
imdb.com/company/co0057545

Does not accept any unsolicited material. Project types include feature films. Genres include drama.

Toshiya Nomura
Producer
imdb.com/name/nm2402249

KRAININ PRODUCTIONS, INC.

25211 Summerhill Ln
Stevenson Ranch, CA 91381
661-259-9700

imdb.com/company/co0016568

Does not accept any unsolicited material. Project types include feature films and TV.

Julian Krainin
Producer/Director
imdb.com/name/nm0469313

Joel Adams
Development
imdb.com/name/nm0011073

KRANE MEDIA, LLC.

7932 Woodrow Wilson Dr
Los Angeles, CA 90046
323-650-0942 (phone)
323-650-9132 (fax)

info@thekranecompany.com
corporationwiki.com/California/Los-Angeles/krane-media-llc/47682359.aspx
imdb.com/company/co0323526

Does not accept any unsolicited material. Project types include feature films and TV. Genres include action, comedy, crime, thriller, science fiction, romance, and drama. Established in 1993.

Jonathan Krane
imdb.com/name/nm0006790

Konni Corriere
konni@thekranecompany.com
imdb.com/name/nm0180955

KRASNOFF FOSTER ENTERTAINMENT
Production company

5555 Melrose Ave Marx Brothers Building, Suite 110
Los Angeles, CA 90038
323-956-4668

community-sitcom.wikia.com/wiki/
    Krasnoff_Foster_Entertainment
imdb.com/company/co0174525

Accepts query letters from unproduced, unrepresented writers. Project types include feature films and TV. Genres include romance, drama, comedy, non-fiction, and action.

Gary Foster
Partner
imdb.com/name/nm0287811
Assistant: Haley Totten

Russ Krasnoff
Partner
310-244-3282
imdb.com/name/nm0469929
Assistant: Beth Maurer

KRASNOW PRODUCTIONS
Production company

3450 Cahuenga Blvd. West #202
Los Angeles, CA 90068
323-798-5560

imdb.com/company/co0112977

Does not accept any unsolicited material. Project types include TV.

Stuart Krasnow
Founder/President
imdb.com/name/nm0469950

KROFFT PICTURES
Production company

4024 Radford Ave
Building 5, Suite 102
Studio City, CA 91604
818-655-5314 (phone)
818-655-8235 (fax)

smkroft@aol.com
imdb.com/company/co0068404

Accepts query letters from unproduced, unrepresented writers via email. Project types include feature films and TV. Genres include comedy, animation, and family.

Sid Krofft
imdb.com/name/nm0471898

Marty Krofft
President
marty@krofft pictures.com
imdb.com/name/nm0471897

KTXA DALLAS
Distributor

5233 Bridge St
Fort Worth, TX 76103

rj.adams1@gmail.com
imdb.com/company/co0170597

Does not accept any unsolicited material. Project types include TV. Genres include comedy.

KUDOS
Production company

12-14 Amwell St
London EC1R 1UQ
UK
+44 (0) 20 7812 3270

info@kudos.co.uk
kudos.co.uk
imdb.com/company/co0502009

facebook.com/Kudostv
twitter.com/KudosTV

Does not accept any unsolicited material. Project types include TV. Genres include thriller and crime.

KUDOS FILM AND TELEVISION
Production company and distributor

12-14 Amwell St,
London, EC1R 1UQ
United Kingdom
+44 20 7812 3270 (phone)
+44 20 7812 3271 (fax)

info@kudos.co.uk
kudosproductions.co.uk
imdb.com/company/co0110977
facebook.com/Kudostv
twitter.com/KudosTV

Does not accept any unsolicited material. Project types include short films, feature films, and TV. Genres include thriller, science fiction, and drama.

KUDOS PRODUCTIONS LTD.
Production company

12 - 14 Amwell St
London EC1R 1UQ
UK
+44207-812-3270 (phone)
+44 (0) 20 7812 3271 (fax)

info@kudosfilmandtv.com
kudosfilmandtv.com
imdb.com/company/co0103807
facebook.com/Kudostv
twitter.com/KudosTV

Does not accept any unsolicited material. Project types include feature films. Genres include comedy, drama, and romance.

KULTUR INTERNATIONAL VIDEO
Production company

195 Hwy. 36
C/O Kultur Video
West Long Branch, NJ 07764

info@kultur.com

kulturvideo.com
imdb.com/company/co0029366
facebook.com/pages/Kultur-International-Films/
    76834863929
twitter.com/KulturFilms

Does not accept any unsolicited material. Project types include TV. Genres include documentary.

LACANADA DISTRIBUTION
9056 Santa Monica Blvd. Suite 203A
West Hollywood, CA 90069
310-278-9747

imdb.com

Does not accept any unsolicited material. Project types include TV. Genres include crime, thriller, and drama.

Dan Paulson
Producer
imdb.com/name/nm0667340

LADY IN THE TREE PRODUCTIONS
Production company

21700 Oxnard St, Suite 2030
Woodland Hills, CA 91367

imdb.com/company/co0338875

Does not accept any unsolicited material. Project types include feature films.

Jessalyn Gilsig
Actor/Producer
imdb.com/name/nm0319698

LAETITIA
Production company

Tokyo,
Japan

webmanager@laetitia.co.jp
laetitia.co.jp
imdb.com/company/co0249344

Does not accept any unsolicited material. Project types include TV. Genres include drama.

LAF STUDIOS
Production company, studio, and distributor

295 Princeton Hightstown Rd
Princeton Junction, NJ 08550
888-864-9838

vf_assistant@lafstudios.com
lafstudios.com
imdb.com/company/co0181188

Does not accept any unsolicited material. Project types include short films. Genres include comedy.

LAGO FILM GMBH
Production company

6399 Wilshire Blvd, Suite 1002
Los Angeles, CA 90048
310-653-7826

lago@lagofilm.com
lagofilm.com
imdb.com/company/co0183386

Does not accept any unsolicited material. Project types include feature films. Genres include comedy, drama, and horror.

Luane Gauer
imdb.com/name/nm4293864
linkedin.com/pub/luane-gauer/30/775/950

Marco Mehlitz
Producer
imdb.com/name/nm0576438

LAGUNA PRODUCTIONS
Production company, distributor, and sales agent

28385 Constellation Rd, Valencia , CA, United States, 91355
661-257-7450 (phone)
661-257-7456 (fax)

info@lagunaproductions.com
lagunaproductions.com
imdb.com/company/co0060655

Does not accept any unsolicited material. Project types include TV and feature films. Genres include comedy, family, thriller, romance, and drama.

LAGUNA RIDGE PICTURES
Production company

3452 E. Foothill Blvd., Suite 125
Pasadena, CA 91107

imdb.com/company/co0371912
facebook.com/Laguna-Ridge-
    Pictures-1565541666995774

Does not accept any unsolicited material. Project types include feature films. Genres include drama and action.

Matt Luber
Producer
imdb.com/name/nm1825319

Brandon Birtell
Producer
imdb.com/name/nm1771385

LAHA FILMS
Production company

137 W 57th St, 7th Floor
New York, NY 10019
914-834-3311 (phone)
914-833-2717 (fax)

imdb.com/company/co0117940

Does not accept any unsolicited material. Project types include feature films. Genres include drama.

Leslie Holleran
Producer
imdb.com/name/nm039097

LAINIE PRODUCTIONS
Production company

18389 E Main St
Galliano, LA 70354

imdb.com/company/co0391080

Does not accept any unsolicited material. Project types include feature films. Genres include comedy.

Cynthia Guidry
Producer
imdb.com/name/nm4789595

Lainie Guidry
Producer
imdb.com/name/nm461371

LAKE CAMP PRODUCTIONS
Production company

5555 Morningside Dr
Houston, TX 77005
713-367-1114

lakecampproductions@gmail.com
lakecampproductions.com
imdb.com/company/co0219949
linkedin.com/company/lake-camp-productions
facebook.com/lakecampproductions

Does not accept any unsolicited material. Project types include short films and feature films. Genres include family, drama, comedy, and action. Established in 1998.

LAKE PARADISE ENTERTAINMENT
Production company

13547 Ventura Blvd. Ste 186
Sherman Oaks, CA 91423

lakeparadiseentertainment.com/
    Lake_Paradise_Entertainment/Welcome.html
imdb.com/company/co0251365

Does not accept any unsolicited material. Project types include TV.

Viki Cacciatore
Principal
imdb.com/name/nm0127972

Holly M Wofford
Principal
imdb.com/name/nm1033680

LAKESHORE ENTERTAINMENT
Production company and distributor

9268 W Third St
Beverly Hills, CA 90210
310-867-8000 (phone)
310-300-3015 (fax)

info@lakeshoreentertainment.com
lakeshoreentertainment.com
imdb.com/company/co0005323
linkedin.com/company/lakeshore-entertainment

Accepts query letters from produced or represented writers. Project types include feature films. Genres

include science fiction, comedy, romance, thriller, action, fantasy, horror, crime, and drama. Established in 1994.

Tom Rosenberg
CEO
310-867-8000
imdb.com/name/nm0742347
Assistant: Tiffany Shinn

Richard Wright
Executive Vice President of Production
imdb.com/name/nm0002999

Robert McMinn
Sr. Vice-President
310-867-8000
imdb.com/name/nm0573372

LANDING PATCH PRODUCTIONS
Production company

8491 Sunset Blvd., Suite 700
West Hollywood, CA 90069
323-650-0150

imdb.com/company/co0178803
facebook.com/OfficialPaulyShore
twitter.com/PaulyShore

Does not accept any unsolicited material. Project types include feature films. Genres include comedy.

LANDSCAPE ENTERTAINMENT
Production company and distributor

9465 Wilshire Blvd Suite 500
Beverly Hills, CA 90212
310-248-6200 (phone)
310-248-6300 (fax)

imdb.com/company/co0070807

Accepts query letters from unproduced, unrepresented writers. Project types include TV and feature films. Genres include thriller, animation, science fiction, action, non-fiction, drama, crime, family, and comedy. Established in 2007.

Tyler Mitchell
Head of Development
imdb.com/name/nm1624685

Bob Cooper
Chairman
imdb.com/name/nm0178341
Assistant: Sandy Shenkman

LANE MANAGEMENT GROUP
Studio and distributor

13017 Woodbridge St, Studio City , CA, United
States, 91604
818-990-6366 (phone)
818-475-5000 (fax)

lmg@lanemanagement.com
lanemanagement.com
imdb.com/company/co0080647

Does not accept any unsolicited material. Project types
include TV and feature films. Genres include thriller,
family, and drama.

LANGLEY PARK PRODUCTIONS
Production company

4000 Warner Blvd
Building 144
Burbank, CA 91522
818-954-2930

imdb.com/company/co0297907

Does not accept any unsolicited material. Project types
include feature films. Genres include crime, romance,
comedy, drama, thriller, and action.

Kevin McCormick
Producer
818-954-2930
imdb.com/name/nm0566557
Assistant: Shamika Pryce

Rory Koslow
818-954-2930
imdb.com/name/nm1739372
Assistant: Kari Cooper

Aaron Schmidt
Creative Executive
818-954-2930
aaron.schmidt@langleyparkpix.com
imdb.com/name/nm2087164

LARCO PRODUCTIONS
Production company

2111 Coldwater Canyon Dr
Beverly Hills, CA 90210
323-350-5455

imdb.com/company/co0077868

Does not accept any unsolicited material. Project types
include feature films. Genres include thriller and
drama.

LARRIKIN ENTERTAINMENT
Production company

1801 Ave Of The Stars, Suite 921
Los Angeles, CA 90067
310-461-3030

imdb.com/company/co0369620
linkedin.com/company/larrikin-entertainment

Accepts scripts from produced or represented writers.
Project types include feature films.

Robert Lundberg
Producer
imdb.com/name/nm2302909

David Jones
Producer
imdb.com/name/nm1965869

Greg Coote
imdb.com/name/nm0178505
Assistant: Wayne Lin

LARRY LEVINSON PRODUCTIONS
Production company

500 S. Sepulveda Blvd., Suite 610
Los Angeles, CA 90049
310-440-7834

imdb.com/company/co0045255
linkedin.com/company/larry-levinson-productions

Does not accept any unsolicited material. Project types
include TV and feature films. Genres include drama.

Larry Levinson
President/Producer
imdb.com/name/nm0506062

LARRY THOMPSON ORGANIZATION
Production company

9663 Santa Monica Blvd, Suite 801
Beverly Hills, CA 90210
310-288-0700 (phone)
310-288-0711 (fax)

ltbeverlyhills@aol.com
larrythompsonorg.com
imdb.com/company/co0025504
facebook.com/larry.thompson.758737
twitter.com/LTBeverlyHills

Does not accept any unsolicited material. Project types include feature films. Genres include drama and thriller.

LASCAUX FILMS
Production company

3030 Olive St
Ste 260
Dallas, TX 75219
972-499-6590

info@lascauxfilms.com
imdb.com/company/co0348388
twitter.com/lascauxfilms

Does not accept any unsolicited material. Project types include feature films. Genres include comedy, romance, documentary, and drama. Established in 2009.

LAST ASYLUM ENTERTAINMENT
Distributor

5642 Dyer St
Dallas, TX 75206
214-363-0162 (phone)
214-363-8871 (fax)

lastasylum@aol.com
imdb.com/company/co0244365

Does not accept any unsolicited material. Genres include comedy.

LAST STRAW PRODUCTIONS
Production company

4000 Warner Blvd., Bldg. 133, Suite 209
Burbank, CA 91522
818-954-1064

imdb.com/company/co0055726
linkedin.com/company/last-straw-productions

Does not accept any unsolicited material. Project types include feature films and TV. Genres include drama.

Anthony LaPaglia
President/Actor/Producer
imdb.com/name/nm0001439

LATHAM ENTERTAINMENT
Production company

3200 Northline Ave
Greensboro, NC
336-315-1440

info@walterlatham.com
lathamentertainment.com
imdb.com/title/tt0368833

Does not accept any unsolicited material. Project types include feature films and TV.

Walter Latham
Producer/President
imdb.com/name/nm0490124

LATINO PUBLIC BROADCASTING
Production company and distributor

2550 N Hollywood Way, Suite 420, Burbank , CA, United States, 91505
818-847-9656 (phone)
818-847-9663 (fax)

info@lpbp.org
lpbp.org
imdb.com/company/co0098605

Does not accept any unsolicited material. Project types include TV. Genres include drama, family, thriller, and action.

LATIN WORLD ENTERTAINMENT
Studio and distributor

3470 NW 82nd Ave, Suite 670
Doral, FL 33122

305-572-1515 (phone)
305-572-1510 (fax)

9777 Wilshire Blvd. Suite 811
Beverly Hills, CA 90210
310-275-5757 (phone)
310-275-5759 (fax)

latinwe.com
imdb.com/company/co0106344
linkedin.com/company/latin-world-entertainment

Does not accept any unsolicited material. Project types include TV. Genres include drama.

Luis Balaguer
Partner/Producer/Manager
imdb.com/name/nm2230500

Sofia Vergara
Partner/Actor/Producer
imdb.com/name/nm0005527

LATITUDE PRODUCTIONS
Production company

833 20th St, Suite 201
Santa Monica, CA 90403
310-488-8448

curtis.burch@latitudeproductions.com
latitudeproductions.com
imdb.com/company/co0191689

Does not accept any unsolicited material. Project types include feature films. Genres include comedy.

LATIUM ENTERTAINMENT
Production company

1616 Vista Del Mar
Hollywood, CA 90028
323-836-7330

latiument.com
facebook.com/LatiumEntertainment
twitter.com/latiumartists

Does not accept any unsolicited material. Project types include TV.

Charles Chavez
Producer/Manager
imdb.com/name/nm7042525

LAUGHING COW PRODUCTIONS
Production company

794 Springdale Rd NE
Atlanta, GA 30306
404-712-9569

info@laughingcowproductions.com
laughingcowproductions.com
imdb.com/company/co0387588
linkedin.com/company/laughing-cow-productions
facebook.com/Laughing-Cow-
    Productions-257460134364768
twitter.com/laughingcowprod

Does not accept any unsolicited material. Project types include feature films. Genres include drama, comedy, and family. Established in 2012.

LAUNCHPAD PRODUCTIONS
Production company and distributor

4335 Van Nuys Blvd Suite 339
Sherman Oaks, CA 91403
818-788-4896

queries@launchpadprods.com
imdb.com/company/co0164701

Accepts query letters from unproduced, unrepresented writers via email. Project types include feature films. Genres include horror, drama, thriller, period, science fiction, crime, and comedy. Established in 2005.

Angelique Higgins
President
ahiggins@launchpadprods.com
imdb.com/name/nm1583157

David Higgins
Partner
imdb.com/name/nm0383370

LAURA ZISKIN PRODUCTIONS
Production company

10202 W Washington Blvd
Astaire Building, Suite 1310
Culver City, CA 90232
310-244-7373 (phone)
310-244-0073 (fax)

imdb.com/company/co0095403

Accepts query letters from unproduced, unrepresented writers. Project types include feature films and TV. Genres include fantasy, action, thriller, science fiction, drama, and romance. Established in 1995.

Pamela Williams
President
imdb.com/name/nm0931423
linkedin.com/pub/pam-williams/39/650/246

David Jacobson
Director of Development
imdb.com/name/nm5138376

LAURENCE MARK PRODUCTIONS
Production company

10202 W Washington Blvd
Poitier Building
Culver City, CA 90232
310-244-0055 (fax)

imdb.com/company/co0027956

Accepts query letters from unproduced, unrepresented writers. Project types include TV and feature films. Genres include drama, thriller, romance, science fiction, fantasy, family, horror, action, and comedy.

Laurence Mark
Principal
310-244-5239
imdb.com/name/nm0548257

David Blackman
310-244-5239
imdb.com/name/nm1844320
linkedin.com/pub/david-blackman/64/92a/b50
Assistant: Peter Richman

Tamara Chestna
Director of Development
310-244-5239
imdb.com/name/nm2309894

LAVA BEAR FILMS
Production company

3201-B South La Cienega Blvd
Los Angeles, CA 90016
310-815-9600

lavabear.com

imdb.com/company/co0296971
facebook.com/pages/Lava-Bear-Films/
    186604781434034
twitter.com/lavabearfilms

Does not accept any unsolicited material. Project types include feature films. Genres include drama, comedy, action, science fiction, thriller, crime, family, fantasy, and romance. Established in 2011.

Tory Metzger
President
tmetzger@lavabear.com
imdb.com/name/nm0582762
Assistant: Jon Frye

David Linde
Principal
310-815-9603
dlinde@lavabear.com
imdb.com/name/nm0511482
Assistant: Allison Warren

LAWLESS ENTERTAINMENT
Production company

11279 Dona Lisa Dr
Studio City, CA 91604
323-201-2678 (phone)
323-654-2516 (fax)

info@lawlessent.com
lawlessent.com
facebook.com/lawlessent

Does not accept any unsolicited material. Project types include feature films. Genres include fantasy and family.

Catherine Malatesta
President/Producer
imdb.com/name/nm5116055

LAW OFFICES OF ATTORNEY BELHIA MARTIN
Distributor and sales agent

1100 Poydras St
Suite 2900
New Orleans, LA 70163
504-813-0658

attybelhiamartin.com
imdb.com/company/co0409464

Does not accept any unsolicited material. Project types include feature films and TV. Genres include comedy, family, drama, and romance.

Belhia Martin
Legal Counsel
imdb.com/name/nm5482619

Belhia Martin
Legal Counsel
imdb.com/name/nm5482619

LAWRENCE BENDER PRODUCTIONS
Production company

8530 Wilshire Blvd Ste 520
Beverly Hills, CA 90211
323-951-1180

imdb.com/company/co0093776
facebook.com/pages/Lawrence-Bender-Productions/
  154135381289513

Accepts query letters from unproduced, unrepresented writers. Project types include feature films. Genres include drama, thriller, comedy, action, and crime.

Kevin Brown
imdb.com/name/nm0114019

Janet Jeffries
imdb.com/name/nm0420377
linkedin.com/pub/janet-jeffries/6/b02/760

Lawrence Bender
Partner
imdb.com/name/nm0004744
Assistant: Vincent Gatewood

LAWRENCE GORDON PRODUCTIONS
Production company

12011 San Vicente Blvd., Suite 350
Los Angeles, CA 90049
310-472-4786

imdb.com/company/co0041635

Does not accept any unsolicited material. Genres include action, drama, horror, and comedy.

Lawrence Gordon
Producer
imdb.com/name/nm0330383

Phillip Westgren
Director of Development
imdb.com/name/nm4043152

LBYL FILMS SALES AND DISTRIBUTION
Production company, distributor, and sales agent

896 Manhattan Ave
Unit 24
Brooklyn, NY 11222
347-227-8847 (phone)
347-227-8847 (fax)

contactus@lbylfilms.net
lbylfilms.net
imdb.com/company/co0444491

Does not accept any unsolicited material. Project types include theater and TV. Genres include action, drama, and comedy.

LD ENTERTAINMENT
Production company and distributor

14301 Caliber Dr, Suite 300
Oklahoma City, OK 73134
405-463-7100

9000 Sunset Blvd
Suite 600
West Hollywood, CA 90069
310-275-9600

info@ldentertainment.com
ldentertainment.com
imdb.com/company/co0192696
linkedin.com/company/ld-entertainment
facebook.com/pages/LD-Entertainment/
  268087043237145
twitter.com/tweetLD

Does not accept any unsolicited material. Project types include feature films. Genres include thriller, drama, crime, comedy, action, and horror. Established in 2007.

Mickey Liddell
CEO
imdb.com/name/nm0509176

LEE DANIELS ENTERTAINMENT
Production company

315 W 36th St
New York City, NY 10018
212-334-8110 (phone)
212-334-8290 (fax)

info@leedanielsentertainment.com
leedanielsentertainment.com
imdb.com/company/co0048235
facebook.com/lee.daniels.71868
twitter.com/leedanielsent

Accepts query letters from unproduced, unrepresented writers via email. Project types include feature films and TV. Genres include comedy, period, thriller, romance, crime, and drama. Established in 2001.

Lee Daniels
imdb.com/name/nm0200005
Assistant: Tito Crafts

Lisa Cortes
imdb.com/name/nm0181263

LEFT BANK PICTURES
Production company

7th Floor, The Place, 175 High Holborn
London, WC1V 7AA
+44 20 7759 4600 (phone)
+44 20 7759 4606 (fax)

info@leftbankpictures.co.uk
leftbankpictures.co.uk
imdb.com/company/co0208971
facebook.com/Left-Bank-Pictures-142032905824406
twitter.com/leftbankpics

Does not accept any unsolicited material. Project types include TV. Genres include drama.

Andy Harries
Producer
imdb.com/name/nm0364170

LEFT HOOK ENTERTAINMENT
Production company

2008 S Bentley Ave. #202
Los Angeles, CA 90025

imdb.com/company/co0227075
facebook.com/Lefthook-Entertainment-
    LLC-184287184918970

Does not accept any unsolicited material. Project types include feature films. Genres include horror and thriller.

Justin Hogan
Producer
imdb.com/name/nm0389556

LEGACY DISTRIBUTION
Distributor

160 Trowbridge Rd
Atlanta, GA 30350
770-394-3262

dana@legacydistribution.com
imdb.com/company/co0319207

Does not accept any unsolicited material. Project types include TV. Genres include science fiction and horror.

LEGACY ENTERTAINMENT PARTNERS
Studio

8424 Santa Monica Blvd., A140
West Hollywood, CA 90069
310-903-0356

gena@2elevenfilms.com
legacyentp.com
imdb.com/company/co0355526
facebook.com/legacyentp

Accepts query letters from unproduced, unrepresented writers via email. Project types include feature films and TV. Genres include horror, crime, and action.

Gena Vazquez
Executive
imdb.com/name/nm3220594

Lonnie Ramati
Executive of Business Affairs
imdb.com/name/nm1252942

LEGENDARY ENTERTAINMENT
Production company and distributor

535 Boylston St Suite 401
Boston MA 02116
857-250-0760

2900 W Alameda Ave, Suite 1500, Burbank, CA,
United States, 91505
818-688-7003

legendary.com
imdb.com/company/co0506361

Does not accept any unsolicited material. Project types
include feature films. Genres include action, family,
and thriller.

Jon Jashni
President (Chief Creative Officer)
323-769-4050
imdb.com/name/nm0419169

LEGENDARY PICTURES
Production company and distributor

The Pointe 2900 W. Alameda Ave
Burbank, CA, 91505
818-954-3888 (phone)
818-954-3884 (fax)

legendary.com/home
imdb.com/company/co0159111
linkedin.com/company/legendary-entertainment
facebook.com/legendary
twitter.com/Legendary

Does not accept any unsolicited material. Project types
include feature films and TV. Genres include thriller,
drama, romance, action, comedy, crime, science
fiction, family, fantasy, and non-fiction. Established in
2004.

Jillan Share
Vice President, Creative Affairs
jillian.zaks@legendarypictures.com
imdb.com/name/nm2949271
linkedin.com/pub/jillian-share/a/69/624

Jennifer Preston Bosari
Creative Executive
jpreston@legendary.com

Alex Garcia
Senior Vice President
imdb.com/name/nm1247503
linkedin.com/pub/alex-garcia/40/166/19a

Thomas Tull
818-954-3888
imdb.com/name/nm2100078

Alex Hedlund
Creative Executive
818-954-3888
imdb.com/name/nm2906163

LE GRISBI PRODUCTIONS
Production company

8733 W Sunset Blvd., Suite 101
West Hollywood, CA 90069
310-652-6120

imdb.com/company/co0307345

Does not accept any unsolicited material. Project types
include TV and feature films. Genres include drama
and comedy.

John Lesher
Producer
imdb.com/name/nm0971956

Sean Murphy
Director of Development
imdb.com/name/nm0614699

LEOMAX ENTERTAINMENT
Production company

8439 Sunset Blvd., Suite 300
Los Angeles, CA 90069
323-785-3000 (phone)
323-785-3010 (fax)

info@leomaxe.com
imdb.com/company/co0200371

Does not accept any unsolicited material. Project types
include feature films. Genres include horror.

Ingo Vollkammer
Producer
imdb.com/name/nm1703840

LEOPARD FILMS
Production company

1-3 St Peters St
Islington
London N1 8JD
UK
+44207-704-3300 (phone)
+44207-704-3301 (fax)

enquiry@leopardfilms.com
leopardfilms.com
imdb.com/company/co0129221

Does not accept any unsolicited material. Genres
include reality, documentary, and drama.

Michael Winter
Producer
imdb.com/name/nm1546986

LES FILMS SÉVILLE
Production company, distributor, and sales agent

455 Rue St. Antoine Ouest, Bureau 300, Montreal,
QC, Canada, H2Z 1J1
514-878-2282 (phone)
514-878-2419 (fax)

info@filmsseville.com
filmsseville.com/accueil
imdb.com/company/co0184496

Does not accept any unsolicited material. Project types
include feature films and TV. Genres include family,
drama, thriller, romance, and action.

LESLIE IWERKS PRODUCTIONS
Production company

1322 2nd St Suite 35
Santa Monica, 90401 CA
310-458-0490 (phone)
310-458-7212 (fax)

info@leslieiwerks.com
imdb.com/company/co0188417
linkedin.com/company/leslie-iwerks-productions-inc-
facebook.com/pages/Leslie-Iwerks-Productions/
    121694324555254
twitter.com/leslieiwerks

Does not accept any unsolicited material. Project types
include feature films, TV, and short films. Genres
include documentary. Established in 2006.

Michael Tang
imdb.com/name/nm4046664
linkedin.com/pub/michael-e-tang/21/140/11a

Jane Kelly Kosek
Producer
imdb.com/name/nm1165704

Leslie Iwerks
President
leslie@leslieiwerks.com
imdb.com/name/nm0412649
linkedin.com/pub/leslie-iwerks/9/94b/882
facebook.com/leslie.iwerks
twitter.com/leslieiwerk

LEVANTINE ENTERTAINMENT
Production company

J.P. Morgan Tower
600 Travis, Suite 6800
Houston, TX 77002
713-222-6900 (phone)
713-222-1614 (fax)

1 Rockefeller Plaza
Suite 1502
New York, NY 10020
212-218-3130

info@levnatineentertainment.com
levantineentertainment.com
imdb.com/company/co0267401

Does not accept any unsolicited material. Genres
include drama.

LEVEL 10 FILMS
Production company

6399 Wilshire Blvd. Suite 1018
Los Angeles, CA 90048
310-424-5063

level10films.com
imdb.com/company/co0278157
facebook.com/Level-10-Films-149020675166149

Does not accept any unsolicited material. Project types include TV and feature films. Genres include thriller, comedy, and horror.

Micah Goldman
Producer
imdb.com/name/nm2542772

Michael Wormser
Producer
imdb.com/name/nm2347031

LEVEL 33 ENTERTAINMENT
Distributor

10801 National Blvd, Suite 602, Los Angeles, CA, United States, 90064
424-354-8662

info@level33ent.com
level33entertainment.com
imdb.com/company/co0295653

Does not accept any unsolicited material. Project types include feature films and TV. Genres include thriller, family, and drama.

LEVELK
Distributor and sales agent

Gl. Kongevej 137 B, Third Floor, Frederiksberg , Denmark, 1850
011-454-8443072

241 Centre St
New York City NY 10013

tine.klint@levelk.dk
levelk.dk
imdb.com/company/co0464162

Does not accept any unsolicited material. Project types include TV and feature films. Genres include family, drama, and thriller.

LEVITATION STUDIO
Production company

15 Hargrove Ln
Palm Coast, FL 32137
386-693-6193

contact@levitationstudio.com

levitationstudio.com
imdb.com/company/co0467662
linkedin.com/company/levitation-studio-inc-
facebook.com/levitationstudio
twitter.com/LvtStudio

Does not accept any unsolicited material. Project types include short films. Genres include drama.

LIAISON FILMS
Production company

44 Rue Des Acacias
Paris 75017
France
+33-1-55-37-28-28 (phone)
+33-1-55-37-98-44 (fax)

contact@liasonfilms.com
imdb.com/company/co0120310

Does not accept any unsolicited material. Project types include feature films. Genres include crime, action, thriller, and drama.

Stephane Sperry
President
stephane.sperry@liasonfilms.com
imdb.com/name/nm0818373

LIBERTY STUDIOS INC.
Production company

9948 Hibert St, Suite 200
San Diego, CA 92131
858-271-0695 (phone)
858-271-0330 (fax)

info@libertystudiosinc.com
libertystudiosinc.com
imdb.com/company/co0043672
twitter.com/LibertyStudios_

Does not accept any unsolicited material. Project types include feature films. Genres include drama and period. Established in 2014.

Mark Schmidt
Founder
imdb.com/name/nm2005149

Randy Williams
Founder
imdb.com/name/nm3623229

LIBRA BABY BURLEY PRODUCTIONS
Production company

1229 15th St NW
Washington, DC 20005
917-690-6687 (phone)
703-995-4345 (fax)

imdb.com/company/co0253881
linkedin.com/company/libra-baby-burley-productions-
    llc
facebook.com/pages/Libra-Baby-Burley-Productions/
    109470189075996

Does not accept any unsolicited material. Project types
include TV. Genres include non-fiction. Established in
2007.

LICHT ENTERTAINMENT
Production company

132 S Lasky Dr, Suite 200
Beverly Hills, CA 90212
310-205-5500

imdb.com/company/co0183802

Does not accept any unsolicited material. Project types
include TV and feature films.

Aaron Wilder
Producer
imdb.com/name/nm1198288

Andy Licht
Producer
imdb.com/name/nm0508988

LIFESIZE ENTERTAINMENT
Production company and sales agent

194 Elmwood Dr
Suite 2
Parsippany, NJ 07054
973-884-4884 (phone)
973-428-9550 (fax)

info@lifesizeentertainment.com

lifesizeentertainment.com
imdb.com/company/co0065512

Does not accept any unsolicited material. Project types
include TV and feature films. Genres include thriller.

Bruce Frigeri
Producer
imdb.com/name/nm2500995

LIGHT BRIGADE FILMS
Production company

Box 172
77 Beak St
London W1F9DB
UK

megan@lightbrigadefilms.com
lightbrigadefilms.com
imdb.com/company/co0450779
facebook.com/Light-Brigade-Films-348594851819744
twitter.com/LightBdeFilms

Does not accept any unsolicited material. Project types
include feature films and TV. Genres include drama,
science fiction, fantasy, and thriller.

LIGHTHOUSE ENTERTAINMENT
Production company

409 N Camden Dr, Suite 202
Beverly Hills, CA 90210
310-246-0499 (phone)
310-246-0899 (fax)

lighthouseentertainment.com/award-winning-
    dj-2.html
imdb.com/company/co0018183

Does not accept any unsolicited material. Project types
include TV and feature films. Genres include drama
and thriller.

Steven Siebert
Manager, Producer
imdb.com/name/nm0796796

LIGHTNING BOLT FILMS
Production company

233 N Orlando Ave
Cocoa Beach, FL 32931
321-784-4881

john@lightningboltfilms.com
lightningboltfilms.com
imdb.com/company/co0413544

Does not accept any unsolicited material. Project types include short films. Genres include drama and comedy.

LIGHTNING ENTERTAINMENT
Production company

301 Arizona Ave, 4th Floor
Santa Monica, CA 90401
310-255-7999 (phone)
310-255-7998 (fax)

lightning-ent.com
imdb.com/company/co0003258

Does not accept any unsolicited material. Project types include feature films. Genres include drama.

Richard Guardian
Co-President
imdb.com/name/nm1862651

Joseph Dickstein
SVP of Acquisitions
imdb.com/name/nm0225737

LIGHTSHIP ENTERTAINMENT
Production company

6150 Metrowest Blvd
Suite 208
Orlando, FL 32835
407-447-4450 (phone)
407-447-4451 (fax)

lightshiptv.com
facebook.com/lightshipmedia
twitter.com/lightshiptv

Does not accept any unsolicited material. Project types include TV. Genres include documentary.

LIGHTSTORM ENTERTAINMENT
Production company and distributor

919 Santa Monica Blvd
Santa Monica, CA 90401
310-656-6100 (phone)
310-656-6102 (fax)

imdb.com/company/co0038663
linkedin.com/company/lightstorm-entertainment

Does not accept any unsolicited material. Project types include feature films. Genres include family, fantasy, action, crime, drama, horror, romance, science fiction, and thriller.

Rae Sanchini
Partner
imdb.com/name/nm0761093

Jon Landau
COO
imdb.com/name/nm0484457
linkedin.com/pub/jon-landau/8/35b/509

Geoff Burdick
imdb.com/name/nm0120971
linkedin.com/pub/geoff-burdick/8/592/a2a

James Cameron
CEO
imdb.com/name/nm0000116

LIKELY STORY
Production company

150 W 22nd St, 9th Floor
New York, NY 10011
917-484-8931

345 N. Maple Dr.
Suite 202
Beverly Hills, CA 90210

info@likely-story.com
likely-story.com
imdb.com/company/co0190175

Does not accept any unsolicited material. Project types include feature films.

Anthony Bregman
917-484-8931
info@likely-story.com
imdb.com/name/nm0106835

Stefanie Azpiazu
Vice President (Development & Production)
917-484-8931
info@likely-story.com
imdb.com/name/nm1282412

L'IL BIG SIS PRODUCTIONS
Production company

P.O. Box 225843
Dallas, TX 75222

imdb.com/company/co0528242

Does not accept any unsolicited material. Project types include short films. Genres include comedy.

LINCOLN SQUARE PRODUCTIONS
Production company

77 W 66th St
New York, NY 10023
212-456-2020

imdb.com/company/co0253555
facebook.com/LSProd

Does not accept any unsolicited material. Project types include TV. Genres include drama.

Phyllis McGrady
SVP, Creative Development
imdb.com/name/nm0569735

Ben Sherwood
President, ABC News
imdb.com/name/nm1639636

LINDA LISCO
Production company and sales agent

360 E Randolph
1206
Chicago, IL 60601
312-201-1000 (phone)
312-201-1000 (fax)

llisco@llisco.com
imdb.com/company/co0354157

Does not accept any unsolicited material. Project types include TV. Genres include drama.

Linda Lisco
Manager
imdb.com/name/nm4677187

LINDA PUBLISHERS
Production company

1-8-4-1503
Higashi Azabu
Minato, Tokyo 106-0044
Japan
(03) 3568 7974

oshiete@lindapublishers.com
lindapublishers.com
imdb.com/company/co0345828

Does not accept any unsolicited material. Project types include TV. Genres include drama.

Katsunori Shimbo
President (Executive)
imdb.com/name/nm4976619

LINE COMMUNICATIONS
Production company and distributor

3-22-7-2F
SHiba
Minato 105-0014
Japan
03-5444-8931 (phone)
03-5444-8930 (fax)

line@i-one-net.com
i-one-net.com
imdb.com/company/co0211434

Does not accept any unsolicited material. Project types include feature films. Genres include action and comedy.

Atsuko Kaneyoshi
President (Executive)
imdb.com/name/nm6756500

LINN SAND AGENCY
Production company

10940 Wilshire Blvd.
Ste. 1400

Los Angeles, CA 90024
310-871-7266

lsandagency@sbcglobal.net
imdb.com/company/co0094285

Does not accept any unsolicited material.

Linn Sand
Owner
lsandagency@sbcglobal.net

LIN OLIVER PRODUCTIONS
Production company

8271 Beverly Blvd.
Los Angeles , CA 90068
323-782-1495

info@linoliverproductions.com
linoliverproductions.com
imdb.com/company/co0094816
linkedin.com/company/lin-oliver-productions

Does not accept any unsolicited material. Project types include TV. Genres include animation.

LIN PICTURES
Production company

729 Seward St.
Los Angeles, CA 90038
323-785-5300

info@linpictures.com
linpictures.com
imdb.com/company/co0226345
linkedin.com/company/lin-pictures-inc-
facebook.com/LinPictures

Does not accept any unsolicited material. Project types include TV and feature films. Genres include thriller, romance, science fiction, family, fantasy, crime, action, drama, and comedy. Established in 2008.

Seanne Winslow Wehrenfennig
Head of Development
imdb.com/name/nm2253990
linkedin.com/pub/seanne-winslow-wehrenfennig/11/aba/4a2

Mark Bauch
Creative Executive
imdb.com/name/nm3113076

Dan Lin
CEO
imdb.com/name/nm1469853
linkedin.com/pub/dan-lin/11/338/893
Assistant: Ryan Halprin

Jennifer Gwartz
imdb.com/name/nm0350311
Assistant: Jeremy Katz

LIONSGATE
Production company, studio, and distributor

2700 Colorado Ave
Santa Monica, CA 90404
310-449-9200 (phone)
310-255-3870 (fax)

general-inquiries@lgf.com
lionsgate.com
imdb.com/company/co0173285
linkedin.com/company/lionsgate
facebook.com/lionsgate
twitter.com/Lionsgate

Does not accept any unsolicited material. Project types include TV and feature films. Genres include romance, science fiction, thriller, comedy, family, fantasy, action, crime, drama, horror, and non-fiction. Established in 1997.

Jon Feltheimer
CEO
jfeltheimer@lionsgate.com
imdb.com/name/nm1410838

Matthew Janzen
Vice President of Production & Development
imdb.com/name/nm0418432
linkedin.com/pub/matthew-janzen/49/950/b0a

Jina Jones
Creative Executive
imdb.com/name/nm1061205
linkedin.com/pub/jina-jones/7/311/97b

LIONS GATE FAMILY ENTERTAINMENT
Production company

2700 Colorado Blvd.
Santa Monica, CA 90404
310-449-9200

general-inquiries@lgf.com
lionsgatefilms.com
imdb.com/company/co0150906

Does not accept any unsolicited material. Project types include feature films. Genres include family.

Ken Katsumoto
Executive VP
imdb.com/name/nm0441546

LIPSYNC PRODUCTIONS
Production company

195 Wardour St
Soho
London W1F 8ZG
UK
+44207-292-3000 (phone)
+44207-292-3001 (fax)

info@lipsync.co.uk
lipsync.co.uk
imdb.com/company/co0087854

Does not accept any unsolicited material. Project types include TV. Genres include drama and comedy.

Robin Guise
Producer
imdb.com/name/nm2284822

LIQUID 9 LLC
Production company, studio, sales agent, and financing company

843 W. Randolph St
Chicago, IL 60607
312-361-1190

515 Southwest Blvd
Kansas City, MO 64108
816-960-6699 (phone)
Liquid 9 LLC (fax)

scripts@liquid9.tv (script submissions)
chris.oconnor@liquid9.tv (general)
liquid9.tv
linkedin.com/profile/view
facebook.com/liquid9
twitter.com/co2kc

Accepts scripts from unproduced, unrepresented writers via email. Project types include commercials, TV, feature films, and short films. Genres include documentary, comedy, and animation. Established in 2003.

chris oconnor
Partner
913-219-0115
chris.oconnor@liquid9.tv
Assistant: Ann Stranghoener

LIQUID CHERRY PRODCUTIONS
Production company

4250 Perimeter Park South
Ste. 105
Atlanta, GA 30341

imdb.com/company/co0085150

Does not accept any unsolicited material.

LIQUID JUNGLE ENTERTAINMENT
Production company

1630 Ringling Blvd
Sarasota, FL 34236

liquidjungle@live.com
imdb.com/company/co0272067
facebook.com/liquidjungleentertainment

Does not accept any unsolicited material. Project types include short films. Genres include horror.

LIQUID LUCK PRODUCTIONS
Production company and distributor

Denver, CO
303-518-8909

liquidluckproductions@gmail.com
imdb.com/company/co0414701

Does not accept any unsolicited material. Project types include short films. Genres include comedy and drama.

LIQUID THEORY
Production company and distributor

4425 W. Riverside Dr
Burbank, CA 91505
818-859-7903

liquid-theory.com
imdb.com/company/co0113186
linkedin.com/company/liquid-theory
facebook.com/pages/Liquid-Theory-Inc/
    173907856002737
twitter.com/TheLiquidTheory

Accepts query letters from produced or represented writers. Project types include TV and feature films. Genres include thriller, reality, animation, comedy, romance, science fiction, documentary, horror, and drama. Established in 2001.

Austin Reading
President
imdb.com/name/nm1474879
linkedin.com/pub/austin-reading/4/328/782
twitter.com/TheLiquidTheory

Mike Goldberg
mgoldberg@apa-agency.com

Julie Reading
President
imdb.com/name/nm1474880
linkedin.com/pub/julie-reading/4/329/3b

Matt Lambert
matt@liquid-theory.com
imdb.com/name/nm1479457

Marc Kamler
mkamler@apa-agency.com

Julius Saito
jsaito@liquid-theory.com

LITTLE AIRPLANE PRODUCTIONS
Production company

207 Front St
New York, NY 10038
212-965-8999 (phone)
212-965-0834 (fax)

hello@littleairplane.com
littleairplane.com
imdb.com/company/co0174821

Does not accept any unsolicited material. Project types include feature films. Genres include family.

Tom Brown
Head of Production
imdb.com/name/nm0114805

Josh Selig
Founder
imdb.com/name/nm1012154

LITTLE FAITH PICTURES
Production company

12908 Portifino St
Fort Worth, TX 76126
817-706-6279

imdb.com/company/co0442587

Does not accept any unsolicited material. Genres include drama and animation.

LITTLE ISLAND PRODUCTIONS
Production company

20 Greek St
London W1D 4DU
UK
+44 (0) 20 7851 1330 (phone)
+44 (0) 20 7851 1301 (fax)

enquiries@littleislandproductions.co.uk
littleislandproductions.co.uk
imdb.com/company/co0446669
facebook.com/Little-Island-
    Productions-368388623296177
twitter.com/littleislandpr

Does not accept any unsolicited material. Project types include TV. Genres include drama.

Helen Flint
Producer
imdb.com/name/nm0282391

LITTLE MAGIC FILMS
Production company

130 N Sycamore Ave
Los Angeles, CA 90036
323-424-4822

kiki@littlemagicfilms.com
littlemagicfilms.com
imdb.com/company/co0042025

Does not accept any unsolicited material. Project types include TV and feature films. Genres include thriller, romance, drama, and horror.

Kiki Miyake
Founder/President/Producer
imdb.com/name/nm0594380

LITTLE MORE CO.
Production company and distributor

3-56-6
Sendagaya
Shibuya, Tokyo 151-0051
Japan
03-3401-1042 (phone)
03-3401-1052 (fax)

info@littlemore.co.jp
littlemore.co.jp/en
imdb.com/company/co0007473

Does not accept any unsolicited material. Project types include TV. Genres include drama and science fiction.

Tomoko Nakano
Producer
imdb.com/name/nm2397509

LIVING DEAD GUY PRODUCTIONS
Production company

100 Universal City Plaza, Hitchcock Bungalow 5195
Universal City, CA 91608
818-777-1000

hello@livingdeadguy.com
livingdeadguy.com
imdb.com/company/co0138108

Does not accept any unsolicited material. Project types include TV. Genres include thriller, fantasy, science fiction, and drama.

Bryan Fuller
Writer/Producer
imdb.com/name/nm0298188

LIZARD TRADING COMPANY
Production company

9696 Culver Blvd. West, Suite 203
Culver City, CA 90232
310-558-8110

info@lizardtradingcompany.com
lizardtradingcompany.com
imdb.com/company/co0313428

Does not accept any unsolicited material. Project types include TV.

Elyse Seder
VP of Development
imdb.com/name/nm2100138

Matt Cabral
SVP of Production
imdb.com/name/nm0127746

LJS COMMUNICATIONS
Production company

1841 Broadway, Suite 812
New York, NY 10023
646-374-3940

lschiller@ljscommunications.com
lawrenceschiller.com

Does not accept any unsolicited material. Project types include feature films. Genres include drama.

LLEJU PRODUCTIONS
Production company and distributor

3050 Post Oak Blvd.,
Suite 460
Houston, Texas 77056
866-579-6444 (phone)
713-583-2214 (fax)

info@lleju.com
lleju.com
imdb.com/company/co0250136
facebook.com/pages/Houston-TX/Lleju-Productions-
    and-Films/111483634134
twitter.com/LLeju

Accepts query letters from unproduced, unrepresented writers. Project types include feature films. Genres include action, thriller, drama, comedy, horror, and crime. Established in 2008.

Cooper Richey
imdb.com/name/nm3295785

Keith Perkins
imdb.com/name/nm1344801

Bill Perkins
Executive
imdb.com/name/nm2645116

LLOYD ENTERTAINMENT
Production company

610 S Main St, #513
Los Angeles, CA 90014
213-489-1485

support@lloydentertainment.com
lloydentertainment.com
imdb.com/company/co0183880

Does not accept any unsolicited material. Project types include TV and feature films. Genres include drama.

Lauren Lloyd
Producer/Manager
imdb.com/name/nm0516056

LOADED FILMS
Production company

Grand Chariot Toyotama 508, Toyotama-kita 6-15-18
Nerima-ku, Tokyo 176-0012 JAPAN
+81-3-6914-9810

info@loadedfilms.jp
loadedfilms.jp
imdb.com/company/co0194446

Does not accept any unsolicited material. Project types include TV and feature films. Genres include drama, comedy, and action.

Jason Gray
Producer
imdb.com/name/nm1807406

LOCOMOTIVE DISTRIBUTION
Production company and sales agent

79 Fifth Ave, 14th Floor
New York, NY 10003
212-201-0206

info@locomotivegroup.com
locomotivegroup.com
imdb.com/company/co0352117
facebook.com/LocoDistro
twitter.com/LocoDistro

Does not accept any unsolicited material. Genres include romance, drama, and comedy.

LOGISTICS CINEMA PRODUCTIONS
Production company

3725 FM 2125
Brownwood, TX 76801
325-217-0336

joepepper7@aol.com
imdb.com/company/co0486493

Does not accept any unsolicited material.

LOGO
Production company

1540 Broadway, 31st Floor
New York, NY 10036
212-654-3005

logoonline.com
imdb.com/company/co0154766

Does not accept any unsolicited material. Project types include feature films and TV. Genres include drama.

Brian Graden
President
imdb.com/name/nm0333536

Dave Mace
VP of Original Programming
imdb.com/name/nm0532069

LOLOMOMO INC.
Sales agent and financing company

Suite 305, 1065 Canadian PL, Mississauga, ON, Canada
905-766-3094

leo@lolomomo.com

laowaigai.com

Accepts scripts from unproduced, unrepresented writers via email. Project types include TV, short films, and feature films. Genres include action, myth, thriller, horror, sociocultural, documentary, animation, romance, detective, crime, comedy, non-fiction, fantasy, family, science fiction, period, drama, and reality. Established in 2012.

Leo Xu
GM
905-766-3094
xuyfleo@gmail.com

LONDINE PRODUCTIONS
Production company

1626 N. Wilcox Ave.
Ste. 480
Hollywood, CA 90028
310-822-9025 (fax)

imdb.com/company/co0183894

Accepts query letters from unproduced, unrepresented writers via email. Project types include TV and feature films. Genres include thriller, comedy, and drama. Established in 1983.

Cassius Weathersby
President
cassiusii@aol.com
imdb.com/name/nm0915780

Joshua Weathersby
imdb.com/name/nm1500833

Nadine Weathersby
imdb.com/name/nm2325321

LONDINIUM FILMS
Production company

9025 Wilshire Blvd, Suite 400
Beverly Hills, CA 90211
310-883-5101

Ealing Studios
Ealing Green
London W5 5EP UK
44 (0) 20 8584 5282

contact@thelondinium.com
imdb.com/company/co0398495
facebook.com/MovieLondinium

Does not accept any unsolicited material. Project types include feature films. Genres include comedy.

Ben Latham-Jones
Producer
imdb.com/name/nm4695347

LONDINIUM FILMS LTD.
Production company

Ealing Studios, Ealing Green, London, United Kingdom, W5 5EP
011-442-085845282

contact@thelondinium.com
imdb.com/company/co0398495

Does not accept any unsolicited material.

Ben Latham- Jones
Producer
011-442-085845282
imdb.com/name/nm4695347

LONE STAR FILM GROUP
Production company

335 N. Maple Dr, Suite 127
Beverly Hills, CA 90210
310-285-0700

imdb.com/company/co0041075
facebook.com/Lone-Star-Film-
    Group-125557800832123

Does not accept any unsolicited material. Project types include feature films. Genres include comedy.

Erica Westheimer
Production Executive
imdb.com/name/nm0922757

Fred Westheimer
CEO
imdb.com/name/nm2120938

LONE STAR FUNDS
Financing company

2711 N Haskell Ave, Suite 1700, Dallas, TX, United States, 75204
214-754-8300

InvestorRelations@lonestarfunds.com

Does not accept any unsolicited material. Project types include TV. Genres include thriller and drama.

LONE STAR PICTURES INTERNATIONAL
Production company and distributor

5919 Greenville Ave
Ste 153
Dallas, TX 75206
214-522-2389

lonestarpictures@aol.com
imdb.com/company/co0044597

Does not accept any unsolicited material. Genres include science fiction, action, and thriller.

LONE WOLF MEDIA
Production company

10 Cottage Rd
South Portland, ME 04106
207-799-9500

info@lonewolfdg.com
lonewolfmedia.com
linkedin.com/company/lone-wolf-documentary-group
facebook.com/lonewolfdg
twitter.com/LoneWolf_Media

Does not accept any unsolicited material. Project types include TV. Genres include non-fiction.

Kirk Wolfinger
President
imdb.com/name/nm0938367

Lisa Quijano Wolfinger
Producer/Director/Writer
imdb.com/name/nm0938368

LONGRIDE
Distributor

3-11-6-4F
Ginza

Chuoku, TOKYO 104--0061
Japan
03-6264-4113? (phone)
03-6264-4114 (fax)

info@longride.jp
longride.jp
imdb.com/company/co0150828
twitter.com/longride_movie

Does not accept any unsolicited material. Project types include feature films. Genres include drama.

Norio Hatano
President (Executive)
imdb.com/name/nm2704711

LONG SHOT PICTURES
Production company and distributor

2516 Woodgate Blvd
Studio 204
Orlando, FL 32822
321-223-7929

dinojgallina.com
imdb.com/company/co0211251
linkedin.com/company/long-shot-pictures
facebook.com/LongShotPictures

Does not accept any unsolicited material. Genres include drama and crime.

LOOK AT THE MOON PRODUCTIONS
Production company

12917 Stallion Court
Potomac, MD 0854
240-672-1414

imdb.com/company/co0243594

Does not accept any unsolicited material. Project types include feature films. Genres include comedy and romance.

Sig Libowitz
Producer
imdb.com/name/nm0508904

LOOKOUT ENTERTAINMENT
Production company

54 Hermosa Ave
Hermosa Beach, CA 90254
310-798-3000

yvonne@lookoutentertainment.com
lookoutentertainment.com
imdb.com/company/co0045796
linkedin.com/company/lookout-entertainment
facebook.com/lookoutentertainment

Does not accept any unsolicited material. Project types include feature films. Genres include crime and drama.

Yvonne Bernard
Producer
imdb.com/name/nm1017627

LOOK OUT POINT
Production company

Lookout Point
3rd Floor
64 N Row
London
W1K 7DA
+44 (0)20 3761 4690

info@lookoutpoint.tv
lookoutpoint.tv
imdb.com/company/co0327262

Does not accept any unsolicited material. Project types include TV and feature films. Genres include drama, action, and crime.

Simon Vaughan
Producer
imdb.com/name/nm0891001

LOS HOOLIGANS PRODUCTIONS
Production company

4900 Old Manor Rd
Austin, TX 78723
512-334-7777

imdb.com/company/co0082018

Does not accept any unsolicited material. Genres include action, thriller, horror, and crime.

LOST MARBLES PRODUCTIONS
Production company

10866 Wilshire Blvd., Floor 10
Los Angeles, CA 90024

imdb.com/company/co0278999

Does not accept any unsolicited material. Project types include TV. Genres include comedy.

Marty Adelstein
Producer
imdb.com/name/nm137435

LOTUS ENTERTAINMENT
Production company and distributor

1875 Century Park East, Suite 2150, Los Angeles, CA, United States, 90067
310-836-2000 (phone)
310-623-4585 (fax)

info@lotusentertainment.com
lotusentertainment.com
imdb.com/company/co0428352

Does not accept any unsolicited material. Project types include feature films and TV. Genres include drama, action, thriller, and family.

LOTUS PICTURES

10760 Missouri Ave. #304
Los Angeles, CA 90025
310-435-5770

lotuspics@aol.com
imdb.com/company/co0351849

Does not accept any unsolicited material. Project types include TV and feature films.

Joseph Salemi
VP
imdb.com/name/nm3687589

Michele Berk
Producer
imdb.com/name/nm0075277

LOUISIANA OFFICE OF ENTERTAINMENT INDUSTRY DEVELOPMENT, FILM DIVISION
Production company, distributor, and sales agent

Capitol Annex Building, 1051 N. Third St., Baton Rouge, LA, United States, 70802
225-342-5403

LED-Entertainment@la.gov
louisianaentertainment.gov

Does not accept any unsolicited material. Project types include TV and feature films. Genres include family, drama, thriller, and action.

LOUVERTURE FILMS
Production company

101 W. 23rd St, #283
New York, NY 10011

info@louverturefilms.com
louverturefilms.com
imdb.com/company/co0176028

Does not accept any unsolicited material. Project types include feature films. Genres include drama.

Joslyn Barnes
Partner/Writer/Producer
imdb.com/name/nm0055656

Danny Glover
Partner/Actor/Producer
imdb.com/name/nm0000418

LUCASFILM LTD.
Production company and distributor

PO Box 29919
San Francisco, CA 94129
415-662-1800

lucasfilm.com
imdb.com/company/co0071326
linkedin.com/company/lucasfilm
facebook.com/lucasfilm

Does not accept any unsolicited material. Project types include feature films. Genres include action, fantasy, and science fiction. Established in 1971.

Kathleen Kennedy
President
imdb.com/name/nm0005086

George Lucas
imdb.com/name/nm0000184

LUCERNE MEDIA
Distributor

37 Ground Pine Rd.
Morris Plains, NJ 07950
201-538-1401 (phone)
201-538-0855 (fax)

imdb.com/company/co0056215

Does not accept any unsolicited material. Project types include TV and short films. Genres include family.

LUCID POST
Production company

139 Regal Row
Dallas, TX 75247

info@lucidpost.com
lucidipedia.com
imdb.com/company/co0168215

Does not accept any unsolicited material. Genres include thriller, drama, and action.

LUCINE DISTRIBUTION
Distributor

POBox 2987
Hollywood, CA 90078
213-926-2987

vahegm@yahoo.com
lucinedistribution.com
imdb.com/company/co0171850

Does not accept any unsolicited material. Genres include comedy and drama.

LUCKY 50 PRODUCTIONS
Production company

801 W Bay Dr Ste 800
Largo, FL 33770

imdb.com/company/co0191774

Does not accept any unsolicited material. Project types include feature films.

Martin Barab
President
imdb.com/name/nm0052774

Philippe Martinez
Chairman/CEO
imdb.com/name/nm0553662

LUCKY CROW FILMS
Production company

4335 Van Nuys Blvd.
Suite 355
Sherman Oaks, CA 91403
818-783-7529 (phone)
818-783-7594 (fax)

info@indieproducer.net
imdb.com/company/co0102838

Accepts query letters from unproduced, unrepresented writers via email. Project types include feature films and TV. Genres include drama and documentary. Established in 2004.

Kerry David
President
kerrydavid.com
imdb.com/name/nm0202968
linkedin.com/in/kerrydavid

Jon Gunn
President
imdb.com/name/nm0348197

LUCKY DAY STUDIOS
Studio

129 Hawthorne Dr
Nicholasville, KY 40356
310-737-8576

info@luckydaystudios.com
luckydaystudios.com
imdb.com/company/co0273765
facebook.com/luckydaystudio

Does not accept any unsolicited material. Project types include feature films. Genres include horror and thriller.

Jeff Day
Co-Founder/CEO
imdb.com/name/nm3026263

Tom Lockridge
Co-Founder/President
imdb.com/name/nm3330959

LUCKY DOC PRODUCTIONS
Production company

18101 Heron Walk Dr
Tampa, FL 33647
813-951-2628

jack@jlsii.com
imdb.com/company/co0485681

Does not accept any unsolicited material. Project types include TV. Genres include comedy. Established in 2014.

LUCKY HAT ENTERTAINMENT
Production company

1438 N. Gower St.
Hollywood, CA 90028
323-993-7001 (phone)
323-993-7002 (fax)

info@lucky-hat.com
lucky-hat.com
imdb.com/company/co0238733

Does not accept any unsolicited material. Project types include feature films.

LUCKY MONKEY PICTURES
Production company

125 E. 95th St
New York, NY 10128
212-860-1642 (phone)
212-860-1152 (fax)

lmpassist@luckymonkeypictures.com
luckymonkeypictures.com
imdb.com/company/co0101005
facebook.com/pages/Lucky-Monkey-Pictures/
    136269279775936
twitter.com/luckymonkeypics

Does not accept any unsolicited material. Project types include feature films. Genres include thriller.

LUDISIAN LEGION ENTERTAINMENT
Production company

2114 Farrington St.
Dallas, TX 75207
214-636-6130

jalonzo808@gmail.com
ludusstudios.com
imdb.com/company/co0353436
facebook.com/Ludisian.Legion.Entertainment

Does not accept any unsolicited material. Project types include short films. Genres include drama, fantasy, romance, and thriller. Established in 2010.

LUMANITY PRODUCTIONS
Production company

8391 Beverly Blvd. Suite 461
Los Angeles, CA 90048
323-448-6949 (phone)
416-823-6650 (fax)

info@lumanity.com
imdb.com/company/co0117925
imdb.com/company/co0117925

Does not accept any unsolicited material. Project types include feature films. Genres include comedy, drama, and thriller.

Robert Budreau
President/Producer/Director/Writer
imdb.com/name/nm1519253

Charles Roberts
Development
imdb.com/name/nm0730905

LUMEN ACTUS
Studio

4119 Burbank Blvd.
Burbank, CA 91505

tom@lumenactus.com
lumenactus.com
imdb.com/name/nm4300383
linkedin.com/company/lumen-actus-llc
facebook.com/LumenActus

Does not accept any unsolicited material. Project types include feature films. Genres include science fiction, horror, and thriller.

Thomas Konkle
Partner/Writer/Director
imdb.com/name/nm1015100

David Beeler
Partner/Writer/Producer
imdb.com/name/nm0066417

LUMENAS STUDIOS
Production company

625 S. 600 West
Salt Lake City, UT 84101
801-355-1510 (phone)
801-665-1240 (fax)

info@lumenas.com
lumenas.com
imdb.com/company/co0241441
linkedin.com/company/lumenas-studios

Does not accept any unsolicited material. Genres include family.

Darin McDaniel
Producer/Director/Writer
imdb.com/name/nm0567388

LUMIERE MEDIA
Production company

120 S Main St 2A
Doylestown PA 18901
215-230-1944 (phone)
215-230-1977 (fax)

info@lumieremedia.com
lumieremedia.com
imdb.com/company/co0153711

Does not accept any unsolicited material. Project types include TV. Genres include documentary.

Stephanie Wolf
Director
imdb.com/name/nm1683433

LYNDA OBST PRODUCTIONS
Production company

10202 W Washington Blvd
Astaire Building, Suite 1000
Culver City, CA 90232
310-244-6122 (phone)
310-244-0092 (fax)

lyndaobstproductions.com
imdb.com/company/co0071668
facebook.com/pages/Lynda-Obst-Productions/
770496236344357

Does not accept any unsolicited material. Project types include TV and feature films. Genres include thriller, drama, action, crime, comedy, romance, family, and fantasy.

Lynda Obst
Producer
lyndaobst.com
imdb.com/name/nm0643553
twitter.com/LyndaObst

Rachel Abarbanell
President
imdb.com/name/nm1561964

LYONS PARTNERSHIP L.P.

Production company and distributor

830 S. Greenville Ave
Allen, TX 75002
972-478-5300

imdb.com/company/co0106874

Does not accept any unsolicited material. Genres include family and drama.

M8 ENTERTAINMENT, INC.

Production company

15260 Ventura Blvd, Suite 710
Sherman Oaks, CA 91403
818-325-8000 (phone)
818-325-8020 (fax)

info@media8ent.com
imdb.com/company/co0309138

Does not accept any unsolicited material. Project types include TV and feature films. Genres include drama, romance, comedy, and action. Established in 1993.

Stewart Hall
President
818-826-8000
info@media8ent.com
imdb.com/name/nm1279593

MACARI/EDELSTEIN

Production company

439 N Canon, Suite 220
Los Angeles, CA 90036
310-550-9909

imdb.com/company/co0094798

Does not accept any unsolicited material. Project types include feature films.

Neal Edelstein
Producer/Partner
imdb.com/name/nm0249050

Mike Macari
Producer/Partner
imdb.com/name/nm1079551

MACGILLIVRAY FREEMAN FILMS

Production company and distributor

P.O. Box 205, Laguna Beach, CA, United States, 92652
949-494-1055 (phone)
949-494-2079 (fax)

info@macfreefilms.com
macgillivrayfreeman.com
imdb.com/company/co0053632

Does not accept any unsolicited material. Project types include TV. Genres include drama, family, and reality.

MACMILLAN ENTERTAINMENT

Production company and studio

175 Fifth Ave
New York, NY 10010
646-307-5151

us.macmillan.com
imdb.com/company/co0454269
facebook.com/macmillanentertainment

Does not accept any unsolicited material. Project types include TV and feature films. Genres include science fiction, crime, thriller, drama, and action.

John Sargent
CEO of Macmillan Publishers
imdb.com/name/nm0765120

Brendan Deneen
Producer
imdb.com/name/nm1559263

MADBROOK FILMS
Production company

15 E 62nd St
New York, NY 10065
212-981-2626

info@madbrookfilms.com
madbrookfilms.com
imdb.com/company/co0497936
facebook.com/madbrookfilms
twitter.com/MadbrookFilms

Does not accept any unsolicited material. Project types include feature films. Genres include thriller, drama, and science fiction.

Boyd Holbrook
Actor/Director
imdb.com/name/nm2933542

Madeleine Sackler
Producer/Director
imdb.com/name/nm2153450

MAD CHANCE PRODUCTIONS
Production company

4000 Warner Blvd
Building 81, Room 208
Burbank, CA 91522
818-954-3500 (phone)
818-954-3586 (fax)

imdb.com/company/co0034487
facebook.com/pages/Mad-Chance-Productions

Does not accept any unsolicited material. Project types include feature films. Genres include romance, drama, family, science fiction, action, thriller, fantasy, and comedy.

Andrew Lazar
Producer
imdb.com/name/nm0493662
Assistant: Wynn Wygal

MAD COW PRODUCTIONS
Production company

17530 Ventura Blvd, Suite 201
Encino, CA 91316

madcowproductions.co.uk
imdb.com/company/co0093766

Does not accept any unsolicited material. Project types include TV. Genres include comedy.

Madeleine Smithberg
President/Producer
imdb.com/name/nm0810431

MAD HATTER ENTERTAINMENT
Production company

9229 Sunset Blvd, Suite 225
West Hollywood, CA 90069
310-860-0441

info@madhatterentertainment.com
imdb.com/company/co0266260
facebook.com/pages/Mad-Hatter-Entertainment/
    223926789347

Does not accept any unsolicited material. Project types include feature films and TV. Genres include horror, thriller, action, drama, animation, science fiction, myth, crime, fantasy, comedy, and family. Established in 2004.

Michael Connolly
mike@madhatterentertainment.com
imdb.com/name/nm0175326
Assistant: Kyle Smeehuyzen (Development Assistant)

MAD HORSE FILMS
Production company

queries@madhorsefilms.com
madhorsefilms.com
imdb.com/company/co0382776
facebook.com/mad.horse.films

Does not accept any unsolicited material. Project types include feature films. Genres include action, thriller, horror, and science fiction.

Alexandru Celea
Vice President of Production
imdb.com/name/nm5088556
linkedin.com/pub/dir/%20/Celea

John Swetnam
Principal
imdb.com/name/nm4291727

MADHOUSE ENTERTAINMENT
Production company

10390 Santa Monica Blvd #110
Los Angeles, CA 90025
310-587-2200 (phone)
323-782-0491 (fax)

query@madhouseent.net
madhouseent.net
imdb.com/company/co0202761
twitter.com/madhouse_ent

Accepts query letters from unproduced, unrepresented writers via email. Project types include feature films and TV. Genres include comedy, thriller, crime, science fiction, action, drama, and romance. Established in 2006.

Adam Kolbrenner
imdb.com/name/nm2221807

Robyn Meisinger
President
imdb.com/name/nm1159733
linkedin.com/pub/robyn-meisinger/13/523/403

Ryan Cunningham
Manager
imdb.com/name/nm1400515
linkedin.com/pub/ryan-cunningham/23/459/649

Chris Cook
Manager
imdb.com/name/nm2303601
linkedin.com/pub/chris-cook/10/82A/7B7

MADJACK ENTERTAINMENT
Production company and studio

13400 Riverside Dr, Suite 108
Sherman Oaks, CA 91423
818-728-7660 (phone)
818-461-8818 (fax)

production@madjackentertainment.com
madjackentertainment.com
imdb.com/company/co0398109
linkedin.com/company/madjack-entertainment
facebook.com/madjackent

Does not accept any unsolicited material. Project types include TV.

Sam Mettler
Executive Producer
imdb.com/name/nm1457529

MADRIK MULTIMEDIA
Production company

1201 W 5th St
Ste F222
Los Angeles, CA 90017
213-596-5180

info@madrik.com
madrik.com
imdb.com/company/co0150567
linkedin.com/company/madrik-multimedia

Accepts query letters from unproduced, unrepresented writers. Project types include short films. Genres include comedy. Established in 2003.

Chris Adams
Partner
chris@madrik.com
imdb.com/name/nm1886228
linkedin.com/in/madrikadams

MADROSE PRODUCTIONS
Production company

14 Rons Edge Rd
Springfield, NJ 07081
347-683-8877

madroseproductions@gmail.com
imdb.com/company/co0329444
facebook.com/Madrose-
    Productions-126895157331535

Does not accept any unsolicited material. Genres include comedy.

MAGIC ELEVATOR
Studio

13636 Ventura Blvd, Suite 370
Sherman Oaks, CA 91423

contact@magicelevator.com
magicelevator.com
imdb.com/company/co0339493
facebook.com/Magic-Elevator-166227893440353

Does not accept any unsolicited material. Genres include drama, science fiction, family, and horror.

Jeff Solema
VP/Producer
imdb.com/name/nm4221414

Berenika Maciejewicz
Producer
imdb.com/name/nm3559189

MAGIC LANTERN ENTERTAINMENT
Production company

2304 Dunlavy St
Houston, TX 77006
713-626-0644

info@magiclanternent.com
magiclanternent.com

Does not accept any unsolicited material. Project types include feature films and TV. Genres include family.

Jeff Segal
President/Founder
imdb.com/name/nm0781796

Jack Crosby
Chairman
imdb.com/name/nm0188997

MAGIC STONE PRODUCTIONS
Production company

7319 Beverly Blvd.
Los Angele, CA 90036
323-549-9020

wearemagicstone.com
imdb.com/company/co0219979

Does not accept any unsolicited material. Project types include feature films. Genres include comedy.

Michael Stephenson
Producer/Director
imdb.com/name/nm0827294

MAGNEPIX DISTRIBUTION
Distributor

433 N Camden Dr
Ste 600
Beverly Hills, CA 90210
310-209-8961

magnepix.com
imdb.com/company/co0215386

Accepts query letters from unproduced, unrepresented writers via email. Genres include science fiction and action.

MAGNET RELEASING
Production company

49 W 27th St
7th Floor
New York, NY 10001
212-924-6701 (phone)
212-924-6742 (fax)

1614 W. 5th St
Austin, Texas 78703
512-474-0303 (phone)
512-474-0305 (fax)

booking@magpictures.com
magnetreleasing.com
imdb.com/company/co0219575
facebook.com/magnetreleasing

Does not accept any unsolicited material. Project types include feature films. Genres include romance, myth, thriller, horror, fantasy, action, science fiction, crime, comedy, and family.

Eamonn Bowles
President
imdb.com/name/nm2113054
linkedin.com/pub/eamonn-bowles/9/363/42

MAGNIFORGE ENTERTAINMENT
Production company

1730 Connecticut Ave NW
Suite 4C
Washington, DC 20009
202-558-6469

info2@magniforge.com
imdb.com/company/co0168260

Does not accept any unsolicited material.

MAGNOLIA ENTERTAINMENT
Production company

9595 Wilshire Blvd., Suite 601
Beverly Hills, CA 90212
310-247-0450 (phone)
310-247-0451 (fax)

imdb.com/company/co0096710

Does not accept any unsolicited material. Project types include feature films. Genres include thriller and drama.

Shelley Browning
CEO/Producer/Manager
imdb.com/name/nm0115212

MAGNOLIA MAE FILMS
Production company

285 W Broadway, Suite 300
New York, NY 10013
212-366-5044

info@magnoliamaefilms.com
magnoliamaefilms.com
imdb.com/company/co0002648
facebook.com/MagnoliaMaeFilms

Does not accept any unsolicited material. Project types include feature films. Genres include drama.

Gabrielle Tana
Producer
imdb.com/name/nm0848932

MAGNOLIA PICTURES
Production company and distributor

49 W 27th St
7th Fl
New York, NY 10001
212-924-6701 (phone)
212-924-6742 (fax)

1614 W 5th St
Austin, TX 78703
512-474-0303 (phone)
512-474-0305 (fax)

acquisitions@magpictures.com
magpictures.com
imdb.com/company/co0134717

Does not accept any unsolicited material. Project types include feature films. Genres include thriller, horror, drama, documentary, and action.

MAINLINE RELEASING
Production company

301 Arizona Ave, 4th Floor Penthouse
Santa Monica, CA 90401
310-255-7999 (phone)
310-255-7998 (fax)

info@mainlinereleasing.com
mainlinereleasing.com
imdb.com/company/co0036169
linkedin.com/company/mainline-releasing-lightning-
    entertainment

Does not accept any unsolicited material. Project types include feature films and TV. Genres include drama, horror, thriller, and family.

Marc Greenberg
Founder
imdb.com/name/nm0338554

Rich Goldberg
Founder
imdb.com/name/nm5304088

MAIN STREET FILMS
Production company

1176 Main St, Suite C
Irvine, CA 92614
949-660-9000 (phone)
949-468-2854 (fax)

825 Little Farms Ave, Suite B
Metaire, LA 70003
504-636-6555

info@mainstreetfilms.net
mainstreetfilms.net
imdb.com/company/co0423950
facebook.com/MSFilms
twitter.com/MainStreet_Film

Does not accept any unsolicited material. Project types include TV and feature films. Genres include comedy and drama.

Harrison Kordestani
President/Producer
imdb.com/name/nm1626595

Craig Chang
Chairman/Producer
imdb.com/name/nm4978624

MAJESTIC ENTERTAINMENT
Production company

2747 Paradise Rd, Suite 501
Las Vegas, NV 89109
702-369-6978 (phone)
310-470-0932 (fax)

lorenzo@majesticfilmworks.com
imdb.com/company/co0305423
facebook.com/MajesticENT

Does not accept any unsolicited material.

Lorenzo Doumani
CEO
imdb.com/name/nm0235387

MAJESTIC SERVICES
Production company and financing company

majestic.com
facebook.com/majesticsvc

Accepts scripts from unproduced, unrepresented writers. Project types include short films and feature films. Genres include detective, drama, action, romance, documentary, family, non-fiction, crime, sociocultural, and comedy. Established in 2010.

Tremain Davidson
CEO
608-774-4080
tremaina.davidson@gmail.com

MAKER STUDIOS
Production company and distributor

3562 Eastham Dr, Culver City, CA, United States, 90232
310-606-2182

info@makerstudios.com
makerstudios.com
imdb.com/company/co0308828

Does not accept any unsolicited material. Project types include TV and feature films. Genres include action, comedy, and drama.

Gabriel Lewis
Executive Vice President (Development & Strategy)
310-606-2182
imdb.com/name/nm6392883

MAKOTOYA
Production company and distributor

5-4-1-304
Nishi Oi
Shinagawa, Tokyo 140-0015
Japan
03-3771-8447 (phone)
03-3771-8447 (fax)

info@makotoyacoltd.jp
makotoyacoltd.jp
imdb.com/company/co0290820

Does not accept any unsolicited material. Project types include feature films and TV. Genres include drama and horror.

Keiko Kusakabe
President (Producer)
imdb.com/name/nm0476189

MALONE PICTURES
Production company

2528 Elm St.
Dallas, TX 75226
214-760-9911

info@malonepictures.com
malonepictures.com
imdb.com/company/co0316781
linkedin.com/company/malone-pictures
facebook.com/malonepictures

Does not accept any unsolicited material. Genres include documentary.

MALPASO PRODUCTIONS
Production company

4000 Warner Blvd
Building 81
Suite 101
Burbank, CA 91522-0811
818-954-3367 (phone)
818-954-4803 (fax)

imdb.com/company/co0010258

Does not accept any unsolicited material. Project types include feature films. Genres include thriller, romance, non-fiction, crime, fantasy, and drama. Established in 1967.

Clint Eastwood
imdb.com/name/nm0000142

Robert Lorenz
imdb.com/name/nm0520749

MALTMAN ENTERTAINMENT
Production company

29219 Canwood St, Suite 100
Agoura Hills, CA 91301
818-707-7786

info@maltmanentertainment.com
imdb.com/company/co0217986

Does not accept any unsolicited material. Project types include feature films and TV. Genres include comedy and horror.

Mark A. Altman
Producer
imdb.com/name/nm0022913

MANAGE-MENT
Production company

1103 1/2 Glendon Ave
Los Angeles, CA 90024
310-208-4411 (phone)
310-208-6736 (fax)

info@manage-ment.com
manage-ment.com
imdb.com/company/co0223070

Does not accept any unsolicited material. Project types include TV. Genres include comedy and drama.

MANAGEMENT 360
Production company and studio

9111 Wilshire Blvd, Beverly Hills , CA, United States, 90210
310-272-7000 (phone)
310-272-0084 (fax)

management360.com
imdb.com/company/co0092453

Does not accept any unsolicited material. Project types include TV. Genres include thriller, romance, drama, reality, and family.

Darin Friedman
Partner (Producer)
imdb.com/name/nm1788306

MANCAT FILMS
Production company

927 Chadwick Dr
Richardson, TX 75080

fivetonedinc@gmail.com
chariotmovie.com
imdb.com/company/co0403196

Does not accept any unsolicited material. Project types include short films. Genres include drama, thriller, and documentary.

MANCE MEDIA
Distributor

1439 N Gower St, Building 2, Suite 38, Hollywood, CA, United States, 90028

323-468-3180 (phone)
323-972-1752 (fax)

contact@mancemedia.com
mancemedia.com
imdb.com/company/co0379747

Does not accept any unsolicited material. Project types include short films and TV. Genres include thriller, family, reality, and drama.

MANDALAY PICTURES
Production company

4751 Wilshire Blvd, 3rd Floor
Los Angeles, CA 90010
323-549-4300

info@mandalay.com
mandalay.com
imdb.com/company/co0013922
linkedin.com/company/mandalay-pictures
facebook.com/pages/Mandalay-Pictures/
109759129042274

Does not accept any unsolicited material. Project types include feature films. Genres include horror, drama, action, family, thriller, comedy, and romance. Established in 1995.

Peter Guber
imdb.com/name/nm0345542

MANDALAY TELEVISION
Production company

4751 Wilshire Blvd, 3rd Floor
Los Angeles, CA 90010
323-549-4300 (phone)
323-549-9832 (fax)

info@mandalay.com
mandalay.com
imdb.com/company/co0018094
facebook.com/pages/Mandalay-Entertainment/
112716635409080

Does not accept any unsolicited material. Project types include TV. Genres include action, period, drama, romance, comedy, and thriller.

MANDEVILLE FILMS
Production company

500 S Buena Vista St
Animation Building, 2G
Burbank, CA 91521-1783
818-560-1000 (phone)
818-842-2937 (fax)

mandfilms.com
imdb.com/company/co0064942
facebook.com/MandFilms
twitter.com/mandfilms

Does not accept any unsolicited material. Project types include feature films and TV. Genres include action, drama, romance, and family. Established in 1994.

Todd Lieberman
Partner
imdb.com/name/nm0509414
Assistant: Jacqueline Lesko

David Hoberman
Partner
imdb.com/name/nm0387674
Assistant: Derek Steiner

Laura Cray
Creative Executive
imdb.com/name/nm1733050
twitter.com/lauracray
Assistant: Liz Bassin

MANDRAKE SPRINGS PRODUCTIONS
Production company

1250 NE Loop 410
Ste. 500
San Antonio, TX 78209

imdb.com/company/co0340422

Does not accept any unsolicited material. Genres include comedy.

MANDY FILMS
Production company

9201 Wilshire Blvd, Suite 206
Beverly Hills, CA 90210
310-246-0500 (phone)
310-246-0350 (fax)

mandy.com/index.php?country=BD
imdb.com/company/co0032786

Accepts query letters from unproduced, unrepresented writers. Project types include feature films and TV. Genres include action, thriller, science fiction, fantasy, drama, and comedy.

Amanda Goldberg
imdb.com/name/nm0325144

Leonard Goldberg
President
imdb.com/name/nm0325252

MANGU TV
Production company and distributor

145 6th Ave
Suite #6E
New York, NY 10013
212-463-9503

Ojai, CA
805-646-8800

info@mangustaproductions.com
mangustaproductions.com
imdb.com/company/co0203045
facebook.com/MangustaProductions
twitter.com/Mangu_tv

Does not accept any unsolicited material. Project types include feature films. Genres include romance, drama, comedy, and documentary.

Sol Tryon
Producer
imdb.com/name/nm0874501
linkedin.com/pub/sol-tryon/4/611/746

Shannon McCoy Cohn
Producer
imdb.com/name/nm3101571

Blake Ashman
imdb.com/name/nm0039137

Giancarlo Canavesio
Owner
imdb.com/name/nm2184875
linkedin.com/pub/giancarlo-canavesio/11/6a2/938

MANIFEST FILM COMPANY
Production company and distributor

5709 Franklin Ave.
Los Angeles, CA 90028
412-996-8410

info@manifestfilms.com
manifestfilm.com
imdb.com/company/co0005048
facebook.com/ManifestFilm
twitter.com/ManifestFilm

Accepts query letters from unproduced, unrepresented writers. Project types include feature films. Genres include comedy, thriller, drama, period, and crime. Established in 1998.

Janet Yang
President
janetyang2013@gmail.com
janetyang.com
imdb.com/name/nm0946003

MAN IN HAT
Production company

175 Varick St
New York, NY 10013
646-494-3837

info@maninhat.com
maninhat.com
imdb.com/company/co0351336
linkedin.com/company/man-in-hat
facebook.com/pages/ManInHat/195266753840189
twitter.com/ManInHatNY

Does not accept any unsolicited material. Project types include commercials, short films, and feature films. Genres include drama. Established in 2011.

Alessandro Penazzi
Producer
imdb.com/name/nm3958443

Bruno Mourral
Director
imdb.com/name/nm3681751

MANIS FILM
Production company

469 Lawrence Ave West
Toronto, ON M5M 1C6
Canada

info@manisfilm.com
imdb.com/company/co0413004

Does not accept any unsolicited material. Genres include thriller and drama.

Randy Manis
Producer
imdb.com/name/nm1159655

MANKIND ENTERTAINMENT
Production company

1717 W 6th St, Suite #445
Austin, TX 78703

john@mankind-ent.com
mankind-ent.com
imdb.com/company/co0297190
linkedin.com/company/mankind-entertainment-llc

Does not accept any unsolicited material. Project types include feature films. Genres include drama.

John Torres Martinez
Producer
imdb.com/name/nm2336847

MANN MADE FILMS
Production company

Altrincham
Manchester Greater Manchester
UK
+44 (0780-876-2053

staff@mannmadefilms.com
mannmadefilms.com
imdb.com/company/co0189843

Does not accept any unsolicited material. Project types include short films and feature films. Genres include horror, action, drama, and thriller.

Scott Mann
Producer
imdb.com/name/nm1470993

MAPLE SHADE FILMS
Production company

4000 Warner Blvd
Building 138, Room 1103
Burbank, CA 91522
818-954-3137

imdb.com/company/co0100155

Accepts query letters from unproduced, unrepresented writers. Project types include feature films. Genres include fantasy, thriller, action, and drama.

Ed McDonnell
President
imdb.com/name/nm0568093

MARBALEE MEDIA
Production company

PO Box 6374
Denver, CO 80206
303-733-2681

lroper@marbaleemedia.com
imdb.com/company/co0416345

Does not accept any unsolicited material. Genres include science fiction, comedy, and family.

MARBLE FILMS
Production company and distributor

2-11-23-6F
Sangenjaya
Setagaya, Tokyo 154-0024
Japan
03-5779-6039 (phone)
03-5433-2120 (fax)

info@marblefilm.jp
marblefilm.jp
imdb.com/company/co0393031

Does not accept any unsolicited material. Project types include TV. Genres include drama and science fiction.

Masanori Yamamoto
President (Executive)
imdb.com/name/nm3550913

MARBLEMEDIA DISTRIBUTION
Distributor

74 Fraser Ave
Ste 200
Toronto, ON M6K 3E1
Canada
416-646-2711 (phone)
416-646-2717 (fax)

connect@marblemedia.com
marblemedia.com
imdb.com/company/co0196029
facebook.com/marblemedia
twitter.com/marblemedia

Does not accept any unsolicited material. Genres include non-fiction, reality, animation, and comedy.

Mark J.W Bishop
Producer
imdb.com/name/nm1720649

MARC PLATT PRODUCTIONS
Production company

100 Universal City Plaza
North Hollywood, CA 91608
818-777-1122

imdb.com/company/co0093810

Accepts query letters from unproduced, unrepresented writers. Project types include TV and feature films. Genres include action, thriller, fantasy, crime, comedy, family, romance, horror, and drama.

Marc Platt
Producer
818-777-1122
platt@nbcuni.com
imdb.com/name/nm0686887
facebook.com/pages/Marc-E-Platt/112127405470433
Assistant: Joey Levy

Jared LeBoff
818-777-9961
imdb.com/name/nm1545176

Adam Siegel
President
818-777-9544
imdb.com/name/nm2132113

MARC PRODUCTION ENTERPRISES
Production company

143 Comanche Circle
Hutto, TX 78634
512-759-2244 (phone)
512-846-1703 (fax)

info@marcmovies.com
marcmovies.com
imdb.com/company/co0348455
linkedin.com/pub/ray-verduzco/1/9a3/729
facebook.com/marc.pe.3760
twitter.com/rayverduzco

Does not accept any unsolicited material. Project types include feature films. Genres include action and thriller. Established in 2011.

MARDEORO FILMS

826 Winthrop Rd
San Marino, CA 91108
626-799-1388 (phone)
626-799-2388 (fax)

mardeoro@mardeorofilms.com
imdb.com/company/co0176050

Does not accept any unsolicited material. Project types include feature films. Genres include drama.

Vivian Wu
Producer
imdb.com/name/nm0943180

Oscar Luis Costo
Producer/Director/Writer
imdb.com/name/nm0182724

MARIA
Production company

36 view street north perth
93285718

mciminata@gmail.com
facebook.com/mariaciminata

Accepts query letters from produced or represented writers. Project types include TV. Genres include comedy and animation. Established in 2015.

maria ciminata
Actor
93285718
mciminata@gmail.com
facebook.com.au/mariaciminata
Assistant: MANAGER

MARINELAND
Distributor

9600 Oceanshore Blvd
St. Augustine, FL 32080
904-471-1111 (phone)
904-460-1330 (fax)

media@georgiaaquarium.org
marineland.net
imdb.com/company/co0086100
facebook.com/MarineStudios
twitter.com/MarinelandFL

Does not accept any unsolicited material. Project types include TV, short films, and feature films. Genres include thriller, science fiction, horror, drama, family, non-fiction, and documentary. Established in 1955.

MARKERSTONE PICTURES
Production company

6124 Berkshire Rd.
McKinney, TX 75070
972-333-5840

mark.lawyer@markerstonepictures.com
markerstonepictures.com
imdb.com/company/co0388571
linkedin.com/company/markerstone-pictures
facebook.com/MarkerstonePictures

Does not accept any unsolicited material. Genres include science fiction and crime.

MARK GORDON COMPANY
Production company

12200 W Olympic Blvd, Suite 250, Los Angeles , CA, United States, 90064
310-943-6401 (phone)
310-943-6402 (fax)

imdb.com/company/co0085751

Does not accept any unsolicited material. Project types include feature films and TV. Genres include family, action, drama, and thriller.

MARKHAM STREET FILMS INC
Production company and distributor

PO Box 31073 College Square
Toronto, Ontario M6G 4A7
Canada
416-536-1390 (phone)
416-536-7986 (fax)

info@markhamstreet.com
markhamstreetfilms.com
imdb.com/company/co0128500
facebook.com/Markham-Street-Films-162792013737901
twitter.com/markhamstreet

Does not accept any unsolicited material. Genres include comedy.

Michael McNamara
Director
imdb.com/name/nm0573710

MARK VICTOR PRODUCTIONS
Production company

2932 Wilshire Blvd, Suite 201
Santa Monica, CA 90403
310-828-3339 (phone)
310-828-9588 (fax)

info@markvictorproductions.com
markvictorproductions.com
imdb.com/company/co0184007

Accepts query letters from unproduced, unrepresented writers via email. Project types include TV and feature films. Genres include non-fiction, action, thriller, animation, reality, and horror.

Sarah Johnson
Director of Development
310-828-3339
imdb.com/name/nm1154417

Mark Victor
310-828-3339
markvictorproductions@hotmail.com
imdb.com/name/nm0896131

MARK YELLEN PRODUCTION

Production company

183 S Orange Dr
Los Angeles, CA 90036
323-935-5525 (phone)
323-935-5755 (fax)

markyellen.com
imdb.com/company/co0184083

Accepts query letters from unproduced, unrepresented writers via email. Project types include commercials, feature films, and TV. Genres include action and family. Established in 2003.

Mark Yellen
Producer
323-935-5525
mark@myfilmconsult.com
imdb.com/name/nm0947390
linkedin.com/in/markyellen

MARLBORO ROAD GANG PRODUCTIONS

Production company

334 E 90th St
New York, NY 10128
212-996-7932 (phone)
310-451-4000 (fax)

imdb.com/company/co0123076
linkedin.com/company/marlboro-road-gang-
    productions

Does not accept any unsolicited material. Project types include TV and feature films. Genres include drama and crime.

Aaron Lubin
Producer
imdb.com/name/nm0523892

Ed Burns
Actor/Writer/Director/Producer
imdb.com/name/nm0122654

MARLON R. PRODUCTIONS

Production company

1932 N Druid Hills
Atlanta, GA 30318
404-692-1677

marlonrproductions.com
imdb.com/company/co0412750
facebook.com/MarlonRProductions

Does not accept any unsolicited material. Project types include TV.

MARLOWES

Production company

Victoria Embankment, Blackfriars,
London , England EC4Y 0HJ
UK
44 020 7193 7227

miles@marlowes.eu
miles@marlowes.eu
imdb.com/company/co0247110
twitter.com/MilesMarlowes

Does not accept any unsolicited material. Project types include short films, TV, and feature films. Genres include comedy and horror.

Yemi Adenle
Producer
imdb.com/name/nm2465793

MAROBRU PRODUCTIONS

Production company

515 W 57th St, 3rd Floor
New York, NY 10019
212-265-3600

marobru.net
facebook.com/Marobru-Inc-350963014939959

Does not accept any unsolicited material. Project types include TV. Genres include comedy.

Michele Armour
Producer
imdb.com/name/nm1723268

MARS CO.

Production company

2-9-15
Tomigaya
Shibuya, Tokyo 151-0063
Japan
03-5478-7000 (phone)
03-5478-7001 (fax)

mars@mars-company.jp
mars-company.jp
imdb.com/company/co0282098

Does not accept any unsolicited material. Project types include TV. Genres include drama.

Kazuhide Matsui

President (Executive)
imdb.com/name/nm4960069

MARSH ENTERTAINMENT

12444 Ventura Blvd., Suite 203
Studio City, CA 91604
818-509-1135

marshproductions.com/Home.html
imdb.com/company/co0005422
twitter.com/marshentertain

Does not accept any unsolicited material. Project types include TV. Genres include drama.

Sherry Marsh

Producer/Manager
imdb.com/name/nm1639567

MARTIN CHASE PRODUCTIONS

Production company

500 S Buena Vista St
Burbank, CA 91521
818-560-3952 (phone)
818-560-5113 (fax)

imdb.com/company/co0110950
facebook.com/martinchaseproductions

Does not accept any unsolicited material. Project types include feature films and TV. Genres include family. Established in 2000.

Debra Chase

Founder
818-526-4252
imdb.com/name/nm0153744

MARTY KATZ PRODUCTIONS

Production company

22337 Pacific Coast Highway #327
Malibu, CA 90265
310-589-1560 (phone)
310-589-1565 (fax)

martykatzproductions@earthlink.net
martykatzproductions.com
imdb.com/name/nm0441794
linkedin.com/company/marty-katz-productions-inc
facebook.com/martykatzproductions
twitter.com/martykatzprods

Accepts query letters from unproduced, unrepresented writers via email. Project types include feature films. Genres include drama, comedy, action, romance, thriller, and non-fiction. Established in 1996.

Campbell Katz

Vice President of Production & Development
imdb.com/name/nm0441645

Marty Katz

Producer
imdb.com/name/nm0441794
linkedin.com/pub/marty-katz/8/9a2/481

MARVEL ENTERTAINMENT

Production company and distributor

Marvel Animation Studios 623 Circle 7 Dr
Glendale CA 91201
818-931-8021

Marvel Studios 500 S Buena Vista St
Burbank CA 91521
818-560-9100

417 Fifth Ave, New York, NY, United States, 10016
212-576-4000

Europa House 54 Great Marlborough St
London United Kingdom W1F 7JU
011-442-078582000

marvel.com

imdb.com/company/co0047120

Does not accept any unsolicited material. Project types include feature films and short films. Genres include action, fantasy, animation, family, and science fiction.

Joe Quesada
Chief Creative Officer
212-576-4000
imdb.com/name/nm0703315

MARVISTA ENTERTAINMENT
Production company and distributor

10277 W Olympic Blvd
Los Angeles, CA 90067
424-274-3000 (phone)
424-274-3050 (fax)

info@marvista.net
marvista.net
imdb.com/company/co0118519
linkedin.com/company/mar-vista-entertainment-inc.
facebook.com/MarVistaEntertainment
twitter.com/MarVistaEnt

Accepts query letters from unproduced, unrepresented writers via email. Project types include feature films and TV.

Fernando Szew
CEO
310-737-0950
fszew@marvista.net
imdb.com/name/nm2280496
linkedin.com/pub/fernando-szew/3b/511/7a8

Robyn Snyder
Executive Vice-President Production and Development
310-737-0950
rsnyder@marvista.net
imdb.com/name/nm2237557

MAS AND MORE ENTERTAINMENT
Production company

674 Echo Park Ave
Los Angeles, CA 90026
213-250-9162

mas@masandmore.com

masandmore.com
imdb.com/company/co0137420

Does not accept any unsolicited material. Project types include feature films. Genres include drama.

Miguel Mas
CEO/Director
imdb.com/company/co0137420

Ricardo Ochoa Fernandez
VP
imdb.com/name/nm2808010

MASEKI GEINOU CO.
Production company

3-24-3-4F
Shiba
Minatoku, Tokyo 105-0014
Japan
03-5442-8255

maseki01@maseki.co.jp
maseki.co.jp
imdb.com/company/co0219884

Does not accept any unsolicited material. Project types include feature films. Genres include comedy.

MASIMEDIA
Production company

11620 Oxnard St
North Hollywood, California 91606
818-358-4803

submissions@masimedia.net
masimedia.net
imdb.com/company/co0155931

Accepts scripts from unproduced, unrepresented writers via email. Project types include feature films and TV. Genres include documentary and horror. Established in 2006.

Anthony Masi
President
818-358-4803
anthony@masimedia.net
imdb.com/name/nm1502845
twitter.com/MasiMedia

MASS HYSTERIA ENTERTAINMENT
Production company

2920 W. Olive Ave. #208
Burbank, CA 91505
818-459-8200

info@masshysteriafilms.com
masshysteriafilms.com

Accepts query letters from unproduced, unrepresented writers via email. Project types include feature films and TV.

Daniel Grodnik
President
310-285-7800
grodzilla@earthlink.net
imdb.com/name/nm0342841
linkedin.com/pub/dan-grodnik/9/176/44

MASSIVE FILM PROJECT
Production company

618 Indiana Ave #1
Venice, CA 90291
310-908-9004

info@massive.la
imdb.com/company/co0419667

Does not accept any unsolicited material. Project types include feature films. Genres include drama.

Andy Kleinman
Producer
imdb.com/name/nm2035742

MATADOR PICTURES
Production company

20 Gloucester Place
London W1U 8HA
011-442-077344544 (phone)
011-442-077347794 (fax)

admin@matadorpictures.com
imdb.com/company/co0045407
facebook.com/pages/London-United-Kingdom/
    Matador-Pictures/206766474356
twitter.com/matadorpictures

Does not accept any unsolicited material. Project types include feature films. Genres include action, drama, comedy, and romance. Established in 1999.

Orlando Cubit
Development Executive
+44 (0) 20-7009-9640
imdb.com/name/nm4919747

Nigel Thomas
Producer
+44 (0) 20-7009-9640
imdb.com/name/nm0859302

Lucia Lopez
+44 (0) 20-7009-9640
imdb.com/name/nm2389416

MATRIARCH MULTIMEDIA GROUP
Production company and distributor

1150 S. LaBrea Ave
Los Angeles, CA 90019
323-963-8717

info@matriarchmultimedia.com
matriarchmultimedia.com
imdb.com/company/co0312785
facebook.com/matriarchmultimedia
twitter.com/matriarchmginc

Does not accept any unsolicited material. Project types include TV and feature films. Genres include comedy and horror.

Cassandra Cooper
Founder/CEO/Producer
imdb.com/name/nm2111621

MATSUDA FILM PRODUCTIONS
Production company

3-18-4 Towa
Adachi-ku, Tokyo 120-0003
Japan
+81 3 3605 9981 (phone)
+81 3 3605 9982 (fax)

katuben@attglobal.net
matsudafilm.com
imdb.com/company/co0190630

Does not accept any unsolicited material. Project types include TV. Genres include drama.

MATT BATTAGLIA PRODUCTIONS

Production company

3435 E. Thousand Oaks Blvd #6876
Thousand Oaks, CA 91359
323-851-2868

info@mattbattagliaproductions.com
imdb.com/company/co0286886

Does not accept any unsolicited material. Project types include feature films and TV. Genres include reality, drama, documentary, and action. Established in 2011.

Matt Battaglia
Producer
mattbattaglia.com
imdb.com/name/nm0061307
linkedin.com/pub/matt-battaglia/23/5a8/56b
facebook.com/matt.battaglialouisville
twitter.com/mattbattaglia

MAVEN PICTURES

Production company

148 Spring St
New York, NY 10012

info@mavenfilmsllc.com
mavenfilmsllc.com
imdb.com/company/co0337243
facebook.com/MavenPictures
twitter.com/Maven_Pictures

Does not accept any unsolicited material. Project types include feature films. Genres include thriller, romance, comedy, action, and drama. Established in 2011.

Alex Francis
Producer
imdb.com/name/nm2123360

Hardy Justice
Sr. Vice-President
imdb.com/name/nm1155511
linkedin.com/pub/hardy-justice/47/16a/486

Celine Rattray
Producer
imdb.com/name/nm1488027

Trudie Styler
CEO
imdb.com/name/nm0836548
linkedin.com/pub/trudie-styler/70/653/702

Jenny Halper
Development Executive
imdb.com/name/nm3794516
linkedin.com/pub/jenny-halper/42/6a7/12

Nic Marshall
Director of Operations
imdb.com/name/nm2090942
linkedin.com/pub/nic-marshall/a/254/971

MAVERICK 523 FILMS

Distributor

P.O. BOX 591850
San Antonio, TX 78259
210-550-4554

info@maverick523films.com
imdb.com/company/co0176251

Does not accept any unsolicited material. Genres include drama.

MAVERICK ENTERTAINMENT GROUP

1191 E Newport Center Dr., Suite 210
Deerfield Beach, FL 33442
954-422-8811 (phone)
954-429-0565 (fax)

info@maverickentertainment.cc
maverickentertainment.cc
imdb.com/company/co0060687
linkedin.com/company/maverick-entertainment-group
facebook.com/maverickent

Accepts scripts from unproduced, unrepresented writers via email. Project types include feature films. Genres include action, comedy, and horror.

Pam White
Vice President
imdb.com/name/nm4983373

Doug Schwab
President
imdb.com/name/nm0776979

MAXIM MEDIA INTERNATIONAL
Distributor and sales agent

6929 N Hayden Rd
Ste C4-246
Scottsdale, AZ 85250
480-966-4070 (phone)
480-966-4570 (fax)

contact@emaximmedia.com
emaximmedia.com
imdb.com/company/co0155911

Accepts scripts from produced or represented writers. Project types include TV. Genres include horror.

MAXIMUM FILMS & MANAGEMENT
Production company, distributor, and financing company

33 W 17th St, 11th Floor
New York, NY 10011
212-414-4801 (phone)
212-414-4803 (fax)

lauren@maximumfilmsny.com
imdb.com/company/co0223939

Does not accept any unsolicited material. Project types include theater, TV, and feature films.

Marcy Drogin
212-414-4801
imdb.com/name/nm1216320

MAXIMUS GROUP
Production company and sales agent

140 Colony Center Dr
Suite 201
Woodstock, GA 30188
678-990-9032 (phone)
678-990-9037 (fax)

lwheeler@maximusmg.com
maximusmg.com
imdb.com/company/co0347713

Does not accept any unsolicited material. Project types include TV. Genres include comedy and drama.

MAYA ENTERTAINMENT GROUP
Production company and distributor

1201 W 5th St, Suite T210
Los Angeles, CA 90017
213-542-4420 (phone)
213-534-3846 (fax)

info@maya-entertainment.com
imdb.com/company/co0136764
linkedin.com/company/maya-entertainment
facebook.com/MayaEntertainment
twitter.com/MayaEnt

Does not accept any unsolicited material. Project types include feature films and TV. Genres include drama, reality, comedy, and non-fiction. Established in 2008.

Christina Hirigoyen
Development Executive
213-542-4420
imdb.com/name/nm3491113

Moctesuma Esparza
213-542-4420
imdb.com/name/nm0260800
linkedin.com/pub/moctesuma-esparza/32/938/678

MAYHEM PICTURES

725 Arizona Ave, Suite 402
Santa Monica, CA 90401
310-393-5005 (phone)
310-393-5017 (fax)

mayhempictures.tripod.com
imdb.com/company/co0093869

Does not accept any unsolicited material. Project types include feature films, short films, and TV. Genres include non-fiction, comedy, reality, and family. Established in 2003.

Brad Butler
Creative Executive
310-393-5005
brad@mayhempictures.com
imdb.com/name/nm2744089
linkedin.com/pub/brad-butler/44/159/48a

Mark Ciardi
Producer
310-393-5005
mark@mayhempictures.com
imdb.com/name/nm0161891

MAZRI
Production company

3-2-5-4F
Minami Aoyama
Minato, Tokyo 107-0062
Japan
03.5414.2112 (phone)
03.5414.2114 (fax)

info@mazri.com
mazri.com
imdb.com/company/co0357599

Does not accept any unsolicited material. Project types include TV. Genres include documentary.

Masafumi Watanabe
Producer
imdb.com/name/nm5992503

MBST ENTERTAINMENT
Production company

345 N Maple Dr, Suite 200
Beverly Hills, CA 90210
310-385-1820 (phone)
310-385-1834 (fax)

imdb.com/company/co0057791
facebook.com/pages/MBST-Entertainment/
    101026643283195

Accepts query letters from unproduced, unrepresented writers. Project types include theater, feature films, and TV. Genres include comedy, romance, action, and drama. Established in 2005.

Larry Brezner
Partner
310-385-1820
imdb.com/name/nm010836
linkedin.com/pub/larry-brezner/11/b49/844

Jonathan Brandstein
Partner
310-385-1820
imdb.com/name/nm0104844

MCCALLUM FINE ARTS ACADEMY
Production company

5600 Sunshine Dr
Austin, TX 78756
512-414-7506 (phone)
512-841-7319 (fax)

stephanie.phillips@austinisd.org
austinschools.org/campus/mccallum/fine_arts
imdb.com/company/co0341957
facebook.com/mccallumfineartsacademy
twitter.com/MACFineArts

Does not accept any unsolicited material. Project types include short films. Genres include drama.

MCLARTY MEDIA
Production company

900 Seventeenth St, NW
Suite 800
Washington, DC 20006
202-419-1420

info@maglobal.com
maglobal.com/index.php?q
imdb.com/company/co0250980

Does not accept any unsolicited material. Genres include action, thriller, and drama.

MECHANIKS
Production company

905 Electric Ave
Venice , CA 90291
310-460-7280 (phone)
310-396-7566 (fax)

works@mechaniks.com
mechaniks.com
imdb.com/company/co0119989
facebook.com/Mechaniks-161685533862261

Does not accept any unsolicited material. Project types include feature films. Genres include drama.

Andrea Kikot
Producer
imdb.com/name/nm1118602

MEDALLION RELEASING
Production company and sales agent

1428 Chester St
Springdale, AR 72764
479-751-4500

hannoverhouse@aol.com
imdb.com/company/co0517329

Does not accept any unsolicited material. Project types
include feature films and TV. Genres include romance,
thriller, and action.

MEDIA 8 ENTERTAINMENT

15260 Ventura Blvd., Suite 710
Sherman Oaks, CA 91403
818-325-8000 (phone)
818-325-8020 (fax)

info@media8ent.com
media8entertainment.com
imdb.com/company/co0051264
facebook.com/Media8eye

Does not accept any unsolicited material. Project types
include feature films. Genres include action, drama,
comedy, and thriller.

Stewart Hall
President and Board Member
imdb.com/name/nm1279593

MEDIA DISTRIBUTION PARTNERS
Distributor and sales agent

15315 Magnolia Blvd
Suite 308
Sherman Oaks, CA 91403
310-735-4792

15315 Magnolia Blvd
Suite 308
Sherman Oaks, CA 91403

info@mediadistributionpartners.com
mediadistributionpartners.com
imdb.com/company/co0336888

Does not accept any unsolicited material. Genres
include thriller and drama.

MEDIA HOUSE CAPITAL
Production company

15260 Ventura Blvd., Suite 1040
Sherman Oaks, CA 91403
310-890-4137 (phone)
818-382-7811 (fax)

5542 Short St
Burnaby, British Columbia, V5J 1L9
604-419-8178 (phone)
604-435-4384 (fax)

mediahousecapital.com
imdb.com/company/co0311137

Does not accept any unsolicited material. Project types
include feature films. Genres include drama and
romance.

David Bodanis
COO
imdb.com/name/nm2034591

Aaron L. Gilbert
Managing Director
imdb.com/name/nm0317943

MEDIAKITE
Production company and distributor

247 W 30th St
New York, NJ 10001

production@mediakite.com
mediakite.com
imdb.com/company/co0270722

Does not accept any unsolicited material. Project types
include TV. Genres include documentary.

MEDIA MATTERS BOUTIUQE
Production company

5705 Orchid Ln
Dallas, TX 75230
214-906-6878

imdb.com/company/co0390346

Does not accept any unsolicited material. Project types
include TV.

MEDIA NATION PMC
Production company

414 S Irving Blvd.
Los Angeles, CA 90020
323-931-1141

facebook.com/pages/Media-Nation-PMC/
106989022667576

Does not accept any unsolicited material. Project types include TV. Genres include drama.

David Craig
Executive Producer
imdb.com/name/nm0185829

Linda Berman
Executive Producer
imdb.com/name/nm0075802

MEDIANET
Production company

4-3-12 Toranomon
Minato-Ku
Tokyo
Japan
03-3432-1288 (phone)
03-3431-1360 (fax)

kokusai@medianet.co.jp
medianet.co.jp
imdb.com/company/co0199339

Does not accept any unsolicited material. Project types include TV, feature films, and video games. Genres include action and animation.

Ryuichirou Kanazawa
CEO (Executive)
imdb.com/name/nm1672368

MEDIA RIGHTS CAPITAL
Production company, distributor, and sales agent

9665 Wilshire Blvd
2nd Floor
Beverly Hills, CA 90212
310-786-1600 (phone)
310-786-1601 (fax)

sarons@rubenstein.com
mrcstudios.com
imdb.com/company/co0194736
linkedin.com/company/media-rights-capital

facebook.com/pages/Media-Rights-Capital/
132502213451543

Does not accept any unsolicited material. Project types include TV and feature films. Genres include comedy, romance, drama, thriller, and animation. Established in 2004.

Asif Satchu
www.imdb.com/name/nm2640007
Assistant: Maggie Settli

Charlie Goldstein
imdb.com/name/nm0326177

Modi Wiczyk
imdb.com/name/nm1582943
Assistant: Maggie Settli

Whitney Timmons
Director of Television
linkedin.com/pub/whitney-timmons/9/707/4a2

MEDIA SUITS
Production company and distributor

2-7-3-3F
Ebisunishi
Shibuya, Tokyo 150-0021
Japan
03-5428-1079 (phone)
03-5428-1089 (fax)

info@mediasuits.co.jp
imdb.com/company/co0000246

Does not accept any unsolicited material. Project types include feature films. Genres include drama.

Kumi Kobata
President (Executive)
imdb.com/name/nm1803302

MEDIA TALENT GROUP
Production company

9200 Sunset Blvd, Suite 550
West Hollywood, CA 90069
310-275-7900 (phone)
310-275-7910 (fax)

imdb.com/company/co0130439

Accepts query letters from unproduced, unrepresented writers. Project types include feature films and TV. Genres include crime, comedy, thriller, and drama. Established in 2009.

Chris Davey
310-275-7900
imdb.com/name/nm1312702
linkedin.com/pub/chris-davey/3/a24/641

Geyer Kosinski
310-275-7900
imdb.com/name/nm0467083

MEDIA WORLD TELEVISION
Production company

11426 Goodnight Ln
Dallas, TX 75229
972-241-9595

makingfilms.com/MakingFilms/home.html
imdb.com/company/co0110021
linkedin.com/company/media-world-television

Does not accept any unsolicited material. Project types include short films. Genres include documentary, horror, and comedy.

MEDUSA FILM
Production company and distributor

Via Aurelia Antica 422/424
Rome, Lazio 00165
Italy
+39-06-663-901 (phone)
+39-06-66-39-04-50 (fax)

info.mcdusa@mcdusa.it
medusa.it
imdb.com/company/co0117688
facebook.com/medusafilm
twitter.com/medusa_film

Does not accept any unsolicited material. Project types include feature films. Genres include comedy, drama, crime, horror, documentary, family, romance, and thriller. Established in 1916.

Faruk Alatan
imdb.com/name/nm0016092

Luciana Migliavacca
imdb.com/name/nm3096618

Pier Paolo Zerilli
imdb.com/name/nm1047259
linkedin.com/pub/pier-paolo-zerilli/7/95a/a05

MEGAFILMS
Production company and distributor

2601 S. Bayshore Dr
PH2
Coconut Grove, FL 33133
305-644-4810

imdb.com/company/co0244523
facebook.com/megafilmsvideo

Does not accept any unsolicited material. Genres include reality and thriller.

MEGA FILMS
Production company

1411 Broadway
New York, NY 10018
212-819-9446 (phone)
212-819-1498 (fax)

imdb.com/company/co0089752

Does not accept any unsolicited material. Genres include thriller and drama.

Morris S. Levy
Producer
imdb.com/name/nm1459257

MEGALOMEDIA
Production company and distributor

6207 Bee Cave Rd, Suite 125
Austin, TX 78746
512-347-9901

info@megalomedia.com
megalomedia.com
imdb.com/company/co0070416
facebook.com/Megalomedia-Inc-143303572373963
twitter.com/Megalomedia_Inc

Does not accept any unsolicited material. Project types include TV.

MELBAR ENTERTAINMENT GROUP
Production company and distributor

22 St. Clair Ave East
14th Floor
Toronto, ON M4T 2S3
Canada
416-569-1477 (phone)
416-861-8754 (fax)

melbargroup@live.ca
imdb.com/company/co0079795

Does not accept any unsolicited material. Genres
include comedy.

MELEE ENTERTAINMENT

144 S Beverly Dr, Suite 402
Beverly Hills, CA 90212
310-248-3931 (phone)
310-248-3921 (fax)

acquisitions@melee.com
melee.com
imdb.com/company/co0109181
facebook.com/pages/Melee-Entertainment
twitter.com/MeleeEnt

Does not accept any unsolicited material. Project types
include feature films. Established in 2003.

Brittany Williams
Creative Executive
310-248-3931
imdb.com/name/nm2950356

Bryan Turner
CEO
310-248-3931
imdb.com/name/nm0877440
linkedin.com/pub/bryan-turner/1b/3a7/952

MEMBRANE PICTURES
Production company

mothizfound@gmail.com
facebook.com/membranepictures

Accepts scripts from unproduced, unrepresented
writers. Project types include TV and feature films.
Genres include documentary, animation, thriller,

fantasy, science fiction, and action. Established in
2013.

Tim Humphries
Creative Director
mothizfound@gmail.com

MEMORY TECH
Production company

5-2-39-4F
Akasaka
Minato, Tokyo 107-0052
Japan
03-3405-8485 (phone)
03-3405-7602 (fax)

web_inq@memory-tech.co.jp
memory-tech.co.jp
imdb.com/company/co0144079

Does not accept any unsolicited material. Project types
include TV. Genres include comedy, animation, and
drama.

MENO FILM COMPANY
Production company

122 Hudson St, 5th Floor
New York, NY 10013
646-613-1260

1300 NW Northrup Ave
Portland, OR 97209

imdb.com/company/co0156951

Does not accept any unsolicited material. Project types
include feature films. Genres include science fiction
and horror.

Gus Van Sant
Director
imdb.com/name/nm0001814

MERCHANT IVORY PRODUCTIONS
Production company, studio, and distributor

250 W. 57th St.
Suite 1825
New York, NY 10019
212-582-8049 (phone)
212-706-8340 (fax)

contact@merchantivory.com
merchantivory.com
imdb.com/company/co0055367
facebook.com/pages/Merchant-Ivory-Productions/
    105682432798518
twitter.com/merchantivory

Accepts query letters from unproduced, unrepresented writers via email. Project types include feature films and TV. Genres include reality, drama, and non-fiction. Established in 1961.

James Ivory
Principal
imdb.com/name/nm0412465

Neil Jesuele
Director of Development
212-582-8049
njesuele@merchantivory.com
imdb.com/name/nm3134373
linkedin.com/pub/neil-jesuele/19/80b/a70

Paul Bradley
Producer
paul@merchantivory.co.uk
imdb.com/name/nm0103364

Simon Oxley
Producer
simon@merchantivory.co.uk
imdb.com/name/nm1774746
linkedin.com/pub/simon-oxley/35/b59/64b

MERV GRIFFIN ENTERTAINMENT
Production company and distributor

130 S El Camino Dr
Beverly Hills, CA 90212
310-385-2700 (phone)
310-385-2728 (fax)

imdb.com/company/co0093384

Does not accept any unsolicited material. Project types include TV, feature films, and short films. Genres include romance, crime, non-fiction, thriller, reality, documentary, action, comedy, drama, and period. Established in 1964.

Ron Ward
Vice Chairman
imdb.com/name/nm2302243

Tony Griffin
imdb.com/name/nm0341389

Robert Pritchard
President
imdb.com/name/nm2923017
linkedin.com/pub/rob-pritchard/5/425/a26

METAMORPHIC FILMS
Production company

9107 Wilshire Blvd.
Los Angeles, CA 90210
310-461-3530

info@metamorphicfilms.com
metamorphicfilms.com
imdb.com/company/co0215943
twitter.com/MetamorphicFilm

Does not accept any unsolicited material. Project types include feature films. Genres include science fiction and horror.

Teresa Zales
Producer
imdb.com/name/nm1536187

METATV PRODUCTIONS
Production company

1149 N. Gower St, #106E
Los Angeles, CA 90038
323-785-2233

metatv@metatvproductions.com
metatvproductions.com

Does not accept any unsolicited material. Project types include TV.

Charles Duncombe
Producer
imdb.com/name/nm5720358

Jean-Michel Michenaud
Producer
imdb.com/title/tt0243345

MET FILM
Production company

Ealing Studios
Ealing Green
London W5 5EP
UK
+44 20 8280 9112 (phone)
+44 20 8280 9111 (fax)

info@metfilm.co.uk
metfilm.co.uk
imdb.com/company/co0243632

Does not accept any unsolicited material. Project types include TV. Genres include thriller, comedy, and drama.

Anna Mohr-Pietsch
Producer
imdb.com/name/nm2429805

MET FILM PRODUCTION
Production company

Ealing Studios
Ealing Green
London W5 5EP
UK
+44 (0)20 8280 9127 (phone)
+44 (0)20 8280 9111 (fax)

mfp@metfilm.co.uk
metfilmproduction.co.uk
imdb.com/company/co0250736

Does not accept any unsolicited material. Project types include feature films. Genres include drama.

Anna Mohr-Pietsch
Producer
imdb.com/name/nm2429805

METRODOME DISTRIBUTION
Production company and distributor

Suite 31, Beaufort Court
Admirals Way
London E14 9XL
UK
+44207-517-7550

info@metrodomegroup.com
metrodomegroup.com
imdb.com/company/co0076345

Does not accept any unsolicited material. Project types include feature films. Genres include comedy.

Jezz Vernon
Producer
imdb.com/name/nm5741488

METRODOME INTERNATIONAL
Sales agent

Suite 31 Beaufort Court
Admirals Way
London E14 9XL
UK
+44 (0) 20 7517 7550

info@metrodomeinternational.com
metrodomeinternational.com
imdb.com/company/co0497531

Does not accept any unsolicited material. Project types include feature films and TV. Genres include drama and crime.

Jezz Vernon
Producer
imdb.com/name/nm5741488

METRO GOLDWYN MAYER
Production company, studio, and distributor

245 N Beverly Dr
Beverly Hills, CA 90210
310-449-3000

unitedartists.com
imdb.com/company/co0026841
linkedin.com/company/united-artists
facebook.com/mgm
twitter.com/MGM_Studios

Does not accept any unsolicited material. Project types include feature films and TV. Genres include action, drama, and crime. Established in 1919.

METRO-GOLDWYN MEYER (MGM)
Distributor

245 N Beverly Dr
Beverly Hills, CA 90210
310-449-3000

mgm.com

imdb.com/company/co0016037
facebook.com/mgm
twitter.com/MGM_Studios

Does not accept any unsolicited material. Project types include feature films. Genres include science fiction, comedy, action, thriller, family, crime, horror, myth, romance, and drama.

Dene Stratton
CFO
310-449-3000
imdb.com/name/nm4682676

Cassidy Lange
310-449-3000
imdb.com/name/nm3719738

Gary Barber
310-449-3000
imdb.com/name/nm0053388

METRO INTERNATIONAL ENTERTAINMENT
Sales agent

19 Lincoln's Inn Fields
London WC2A 3ED
+44207-396-5301

sales@metro-films.com
metro-films.com
imdb.com/company/co0441114
linkedin.com/in/metrointernationalfilms
facebook.com/MetroIntEnt
twitter.com/metrofilmsales

Does not accept any unsolicited material. Project types include feature films. Genres include thriller.

Will Machin
Producer
imdb.com/name/nm1313453

MGA ENTERTAINMENT
Production company

16300 Roscoe Blvd., Suite 150
Van Nuys, CA 91406
818-894-2525 (phone)
800-222-4685 (fax)

mgae.com

imdb.com/company/co0124725

Does not accept any unsolicited material. Project types include feature films. Genres include family.

Issac Larin
Producer
imdb.com/title/tt2034403

MGA FILMS
Distributor

9029 E Mississippi Ave. Suite K304
Denver, CO 80247
970-215-4708

MGAfilms@frii.com
imdb.com/company/co0031671

Does not accept any unsolicited material. Genres include documentary.

MGMT. ENTERTAINMENT
Production company

9220 W Sunset Blvd, Suite 106
West Hollywood, CA 90069
310-558-2540

imdb.com/name/nm2889228
facebook.com/mgmtent

Does not accept any unsolicited material.

David Schiff
Partner/Producer/Manager
imdb.com/name/nm0771467

MG STUDIOS
Production company

205 Tree Fork Ln
Suite 113
Longwood, FL 32750
407-679-9291 (phone)
407-667-9291 (fax)

info@sgstudios.com
mgstudios.com
imdb.com/company/co0182244

Does not accept any unsolicited material. Genres include comedy and family.

MICA ENTERTAINMENT
Production company

10250 Constellation Blvd, Suite 2320, Century City, CA, United States, 90067
310-569-6101

info@micaentertainment.com
imdb.com/company/co0379354

Does not accept any unsolicited material.

Dale Armin Johnson
Producer
imdb.com/name/nm5030216

MICHAEL DE LUCA PRODUCTIONS
Production company

10202 W Washington Blvd
Astaire Building, Suite 3028
Culver City, CA 90232
310-244-4990 (phone)
310-244-0449 (fax)

imdb.com/company/co0174505
twitter.com/michaelde_luca

Does not accept any unsolicited material. Project types include feature films. Genres include comedy, drama, thriller, and action.

Josh Bratman
Development Executive
310-244-4916
imdb.com/name/nm2302300
Assistant: Sandy Yep

Michael De Luca
Producer
310-244-4990
imdb.com/name/nm0006894
Assistant: Kristen Detwiler

Alissa Phillips
310-244-4918
imdb.com/name/nm1913014
Assistant: Bill Karesh

MICHAELGION
Production company

6-32-4-2F Jingumae
Shibuya, Tokyo 150-0001
Japan
+81 3 5774 0521 (phone)
+81 3 5774 0523 (fax)

harada@michaelgion.jp
momoirosora.jp
imdb.com/company/co0336324

Does not accept any unsolicited material. Project types include feature films. Genres include drama.

Hiroshi Harada
Producer (Executive)
imdb.com/company/co0336324

MICHAEL GRAIS PRODUCTIONS
Production company

321 S Beverly Dr, Suite M
Beverly Hills, CA 90210
323-857-4510 (phone)
323-319-4002 (fax)

michael.grais@gmail.com
michaelgrais.com
imdb.com/company/co0177680

Accepts query letters from unproduced, unrepresented writers via email. Project types include TV and feature films. Genres include horror and thriller.

Michael Grais
323-857-4510
michaelgrais@yahoo.com
michaelgrais.com
imdb.com/name/nm0334457

MICHAEL MAILER FILMS
Production company

81 Worth St
New York, NY 10013
212-966-9494 (phone)
212-966-9490 (fax)

michaelmailerfilms.com
imdb.com/company/co0160601

Does not accept any unsolicited material. Project types include feature films. Genres include thriller.

Allison Keir
Creative Executive
imdb.com/name/nm2608240

Michael Mailer
President, Producer
imdb.com/name/nm0537550

MICHAEL MELTZER PRODUCTIONS
Production company

12207 Riverside Dr, Suite 208
Valley Village, CA 91607
818-766-8339

imdb.com/company/co0310316

Does not accept any unsolicited material. Project types include feature films. Genres include horror, drama, and comedy.

Michael L. Meltzer
Owner/Producer
imdb.com/name/nm0578444

MICHAEL TAYLOR PRODUCTIONS
Production company

2370 Bowmont Dr
Beverly Hills, CA 90210
954-749-5141 (phone)
213-740-3395 (fax)

mt@mtjibs.com
mtjibs.com
imdb.com/company/co0183466
linkedin.com/profile/view
facebook.com/MTJibs-Michael-C-Taylor-
   Productions-282919248444498

Accepts query letters from unproduced, unrepresented writers via email. Project types include feature films and TV. Genres include reality and non-fiction.

Michael Taylor
Producer
213-821-3113
mtjibs.com
imdb.com/name/nm0852888
Assistant: Yolanda Rodriguez

MICHAEL VINE ASSOCIATES
Production company

29 Mountview Rd
London N4 4SS
UK
+44 020 8348 5899 (phone)
+44 020 8348 (fax)

mpvine@aol.com
imdb.com/company/co0095056

Does not accept any unsolicited material. Project types include feature films. Genres include horror.

MICHELE BALDWIN ENTERPRISES
Production company

191 N Ave
Dunellen, NJ 08812

imdb.com/company/co0478509

Does not accept any unsolicited material. Project types include TV. Genres include comedy and thriller.

MICHELLE KRUMM PRODUCTIONS
Production company

3826 Clayton Ave
Los Angeles, CA 90027

imdb.com/company/co0292601

Does not accept any unsolicited material. Project types include feature films. Genres include thriller and drama.

Michelle Krumm
Producer
imdb.com/name/nm2325301

MICO
Production company

5-5 Kamiyama-cho
Shibuya-ku
Tokyo 150-0047
Japan
+81 3 5453 5161

sales@micojapan.com
imdb.com/company/co0068236

Does not accept any unsolicited material. Project types include TV. Genres include drama.

MIDDKID PRODUCTIONS
Production company

10202 W Washington Blvd
Fred Astaire Building, Suite 2010
Culver City, CA 90232
310-244-2688 (phone)
310-244-2603 (fax)

imdb.com/company/co0177102

Accepts query letters from unproduced, unrepresented writers. Project types include TV. Genres include detective, drama, and crime.

Marney Hochman Nash
imdb.com/name/nm2701117
Assistant: Kent Rotherham

Shawn Ryan
imdb.com/name/nm0752841
Assistant: Kent Rotherham

MIDNIGHT SUN PICTURES
Production company

10960 Wilshire Blvd, Suite 700
Los Angeles, CA 90024
310-902-0431 (phone)
310-450-4988 (fax)

imdb.com/company/co0071900

Accepts query letters from produced or represented writers. Project types include TV and feature films. Genres include drama, comedy, romance, and horror.

Renny Harlin
310-902-0431
imdb.com/name/nm0001317

MIFUNE PRODUCTIONS CO. LTD.
Production company

9-30-7
Seijo
Setagaya, Tokyo 157-0066
Japan
03.3484.2020

mifune@mifuneproductions.co.jp
mifuneproductions.co.jp
imdb.com/company/co0096017
facebook.com/mifune.toshiro.39

Does not accept any unsolicited material. Project types include TV, short films, and feature films. Genres include action and drama.

Shirô Mifune
Executive
imdb.com/name/nm0585871

MIKE LOBELL PRODUCTIONS
Production company

9477 Lloydcrest Dr
Beverly Hills, CA 90210
323-822-2910 (phone)
310-205-2767 (fax)

imdb.com/company/co0007564

Accepts query letters from unproduced, unrepresented writers. Project types include feature films. Genres include romance, drama, action, and comedy. Established in 1973.

Mike Lobell
Producer
323-822-2910
imdb.com/name/nm0516465
Assistant: JanetChiarabaglio

MIKE'S MOVIES
Distributor

627 N. Las Palmas
Los Angeles , CA 90004
323-462-4690 (phone)
323-462-4699 (fax)

baker7@pacbell.net
imdb.com/company/co0027736
facebook.com/Mikes-Movies-
  More-149302591764275

Does not accept any unsolicited material. Project types include feature films.

Michael Peyser
Producer
imdb.com/name/nm0679017

MILESTONE FILM AND VIDEO
Production company, distributor, and sales agent

PO Box 128
Harrington Park, NJ 07640
201-767-3117

milefilms@gmail.com
milestonefilms.com
imdb.com/company/co0056222
facebook.com/pages/Milestone-Film/22348485426
twitter.com/milestonefilms

Does not accept any unsolicited material. Genres include horror.

MILK & MEDIA
Production company and studio

1975 Century Park East
Suite 700
Los Angeles, CA. 90067
323-851-4800 (phone)
323-851-4808 (fax)

milkmediastudios.com
imdb.com/company/co0268194
linkedin.com/company/milk-&-media-studios

Accepts query letters from unproduced, unrepresented writers via email. Project types include TV and feature films. Genres include thriller, drama, and horror.

Elton Brand
Producer
imdb.com/name/nm1580954

Harry Knapp
Producer
imdb.com/name/nm0460485

MILKWOOD PRODUCTIONS
Production company

27 Newman St
London, England W1T IAR
UK
+44 (0207-323-1191

info@milkwood.tv
imdb.com/company/co0245454

Does not accept any unsolicited material. Project types include TV. Genres include comedy.

Nick Parish
Director
imdb.com/name/nm3105905

MILLAR/GOUGH INK
Production company

500 S Buena Vista St
Animation Building 1E16
Burbank, CA 91521
818-560-4260 (phone)
818-560-4216 (fax)

imdb.com/company/co0188223

Accepts query letters from unproduced, unrepresented writers. Project types include TV and feature films. Genres include action, science fiction, family, and drama.

Alfred Gough
818-560-4260
imdb.com/name/nm0332184
Assistant: Mal Stares

Miles Millar
818-560-4260
imdb.com/name/nm0587692
Assistant: Mal Stares

MILLENNIUM FILMS
Production company

6423 Wilshire Blvd
Los Angeles, CA 90048
310-388-6900 (phone)
310-388-6901 (fax)

info@millenniumfilms.com
millenniumfilms.com
imdb.com/company/co0002572
facebook.com/OfficialMillenniumfilms
twitter.com/MillenniumFilms

Accepts query letters from unproduced, unrepresented writers via email. Project types include feature films. Genres include comedy, science fiction, non-fiction, thriller, action, fantasy, detective, and drama. Established in 1992.

Boaz Davidson
Head of Development & Creative Affairs
imdb.com/name/nm0203246

Trevor Short
CFO
imdb.com/name/nm0795121

Avi Lerner
Founder
imdb.com/name/nm0503592

hartly mesay
SVP
hartlymesay@gmail.com

MILNE STUDIO
Production company

335 W Josephine St
San Antonio, TX 78212
855-228-3456

info@milnestudio.com
milnestudio.com
imdb.com/company/co0422509
twitter.com/milnestudio

Does not accept any unsolicited material. Project types include short films. Genres include comedy and thriller.

MILU ENTERTAINMENT
Production company

1155 Brickell Bay Dr
3009
Miami, FL 33131
310-579-2324

info@miluent.com
miluent.com
imdb.com/company/co0466194
twitter.com/miluent

Does not accept any unsolicited material. Genres include thriller.

MIMRAN SCHUR PICTURES
Production company

1411 5th St
Suite 200
Santa Monica, CA 90401
310-526-5410 (phone)
310-526-5405 (fax)

info@mimranschurpictures.com
mimranschurpictures.com
imdb.com/company/co0272027
facebook.com/pages/Mimran-Schur-Pictures/
   210823324999
twitter.com/mimranschur

Accepts query letters from produced or represented writers. Project types include feature films. Genres include drama. Established in 2009.

David Mimran
310-526-5410
imdb.com/name/nm3450764
linkedin.com/pub/jordan-schur/78/747/6b1
Assistant: Caroline Haubold

Jordan Schur
310-526-5410
imdb.com/name/nm2028525
linkedin.com/pub/jordan-schur/78/747/6b1

Lauren Pettit
Creative Executive
310-526-5410
imdb.com/name/nm2335692
linkedin.com/pub/lauren-pettit/13/aa8/241
twitter.com/LaLaLaLooo

MIND NUGGET MEDIA
Production company

26 N Ladow Ave
Millville, NJ 08332
856-776-6004

james.ohagan@me.com
imdb.com/company/co0475814
facebook.com/MindNuggetMedia

Does not accept any unsolicited material. Project types include feature films. Genres include comedy and horror.

MINDSHARE ENTERTAINMENT
Production company and distributor

498 Seventh Ave
New York City NY 10018
212-297-7000 (phone)
212-297-7001 (fax)

Central Saint Giles, 1 St Giles High St, London,
United Kingdom, WC2H 8AR
011-442-079694040 (phone)
011-442-079694000 (fax)

mindshareworld.com
imdb.com/company/co0130535

Does not accept any unsolicited material. Project types
include feature films and TV. Genres include thriller,
comedy, action, family, and drama.

MINDSHIFT PRODUCTIONS
Production company

236 Gleave Terr
Toronto, ON L9T8N6
Canada
647-871-6377

info@mindshift-productions.com
mindshift-productions.com
imdb.com/company/co0512318

Does not accept any unsolicited material. Genres
include drama and action.

Mays Saffar
Producer
imdb.com/name/nm5036609

MIRADA
Production company

4235 Redwood Ave
Los Angeles, CA 90066
424-216-7470

mirada.com
imdb.com/title/tt0040597
facebook.com/MiradaStudios
twitter.com/miradastudios

Does not accept any unsolicited material. Project types
include feature films, theater, and TV. Genres include
myth, animation, drama, and fantasy. Established in
2010.

Guillermo del Toro
imdb.com/name/nm0868219

Javier Jimenez
imdb.com/name/nm3901643

Guillermo Navarro
imdb.com/name/nm0622897

MIRAMAX FILMS
Distributor

2450 Colorado Ave, Suite 100E, Santa Monica, CA,
United States, 90404
310-409-4321

1-4 King St
London United Kingdom SW1Y 6QY

miramax.com
imdb.com/company/co0567610

Does not accept any unsolicited material. Project types
include TV and feature films. Genres include drama,
family, and thriller.

Charles Croft
Coordinator (Production)
310-460-7406
imdb.com/name/nm6983354

MIRANDA ENTERTAINMENT
Production company

7337 Pacific View Dr
Los Angeles, CA 90068
323-874-3600 (phone)
323-851-5350 (fax)

imdb.com/company/co0067754

Does not accept any unsolicited material. Project types
include TV and feature films. Genres include horror,
comedy, and thriller.

Carsten Lorenz
Producer
323-874-3600
clorenz1@aol.com
imdb.com/name/nm0520696

MISHER FILMS
Production company

12233 Olympic Blvd, Suite 354
Los Angeles, CA 90064
310-405-7999 (phone)
310-405-7991 (fax)

misherfilms.com
imdb.com/company/co0085725

Does not accept any unsolicited material. Project types include feature films and TV. Genres include crime, drama, and action.

Kevin Misher
310-405-7999
kevin.misher@misherfilms.com
imdb.com/name/nm0592746
Assistant: Sarah Ezrin

MISSIONARY FILM PRODUCTION
Production company

324 E. Par St
Suite 202
Orlando, FL 32804
407-529-6989

scottbpoiley@gmail.com
imdb.com/company/co0359367

Does not accept any unsolicited material. Genres include drama and thriller.

MISTER SMITH ENTERTAINMENT
Sales agent

77 Dean St
London W1D 3SH
UK
44 20 7494 1724

info@mistersmithent.com
imdb.com/company/co0379163

Does not accept any unsolicited material. Project types include TV, feature films, and short films. Genres include crime, drama, and thriller.

David Garrett
Producer
imdb.com/name/nm2303675

MISTY MUNDAE MEDIA
Production company

Post Office Box 152
Butler, NJ 07405
973-838-3030 (phone)
973-492-8988 (fax)

PopCinema@aol.com
imdb.com/company/co0134281

Does not accept any unsolicited material. Project types include TV and short films. Genres include horror.

MIZUNO HARUO JIMUSHO
Production company and distributor

1-7-3
Irifune
Chuoku, Tokyo 104-0042
Japan
03-5541-9983 (phone)
03-5541-9984 (fax)

nakano@mizunoharuo.com
imdb.com/company/co0151401

Does not accept any unsolicited material. Project types include TV. Genres include drama.

MMC JOULE FILMS
Production company

5450 Bee Caves Rd
Bldg 4A
Austin, TX 78746
512-328-3310

imdb.com/company/co0258441

Does not accept any unsolicited material. Genres include drama.

MOB CINEMA PARTNERS
Distributor

3-24-5
Kami Meguro
Meguro, Tokyo 153-0051
Japan
03-5773-9230 (phone)
03-5773-9231 (fax)

info@mobcast.jp
mobcast.net
imdb.com/company/co0208597

Does not accept any unsolicited material. Project types include TV. Genres include comedy and drama.

MOCKINGBIRD PICTURES
Production company

Los Angeles, CA

info@mockingbirdpictures.com
mockingbirdpictures.com
imdb.com/company/co0124412
facebook.com/MockingbirdPictures
twitter.com/mockingbirdpics

Accepts query letters from unproduced, unrepresented writers via email. Project types include feature films. Genres include drama.

Bonnie Curtis
imdb.com/name/nm0193268

Kelly Thomas
Executive Producer
imdb.com/name/nm1684437
twitter.com/Tom_Tom_Kel

Julie Lynn
imdb.com/name/nm0528724

MODE FILMS
Production company and distributor

6-7F
Ichibancho
Chiyoda, Tokyo 102-0082
Japan
+81 3-4334-3470 (phone)
+81 3-5210-3240 (fax)

info@modcfilms.co.jp
modefilms.co.jp
imdb.com/company/co0392492

Does not accept any unsolicited material. Project types include TV. Genres include comedy.

Yasushi Miyamae
CMO (Producer)
imdb.com/name/nm5243006

MODERCINE
Production company

18 4th Place, Suite 2
Brooklyn, NY 11231

info@moderncine.com
moderncine.com
imdb.com/company/co0100731
facebook.com/moderncine
twitter.com/Moderncine

Does not accept any unsolicited material. Project types include feature films and short films. Genres include comedy, horror, crime, and thriller.

Andrew van den Houten
CEO
imdb.com/name/nm0886156
linkedin.com/pub/andrew-van-den-houten/b/530/ba1
facebook.com/andrew.vanhouten

Robert Tonino
CFO
imdb.com/name/nm1720736

MODERN DISTRIBUTORS
Distributor and sales agent

18 4th Place, Ste 2
Brooklyn, NY 11231, USA

info@moderndistrib.com
imdb.com/company/co0422477

Does not accept any unsolicited material. Genres include drama, crime, and horror.

MOJO FILMS
Production company

4024 Radford Ave.
Bungalow 1
Studio City, CA 91604
818-655-6292

imdb.com/company/co0042403

Accepts query letters from unproduced, unrepresented writers. Project types include TV and feature films. Established in 2007.

Mary-Beth Basile
Producer
imdb.com/name/nm1039389

Gary Fleder
Director
818-655-6292
garyfleder.com
imdb.com/name/nm0001219
linkedin.com/pub/gary-fleder/a/17/35

MOMENTUM PICTURES
Production company and distributor

20 Soho Square
2nd Fl
London W1D 3QW
UK
+44 20 7534 0400 (phone)
+44 20 7534 0404 (fax)

publicity@momentumpictures.co.uk
momentumpictures.co.uk
imdb.com/company/co0049085

Does not accept any unsolicited material. Project types include TV and feature films. Genres include thriller and horror.

Hamish Moseley
Producer
imdb.com/name/nm3266149

MOMENTUM WORLDWIDE
Production company

250 Hudson St
2nd Floor
New York, NY 10013
646-638-5400

momentumww.com
imdb.com/company/co0268253
linkedin.com/company/2593
facebook.com/MomentumWorldwide
twitter.com/MomentumWW

Accepts query letters from unproduced, unrepresented writers via email. Project types include commercials and TV. Genres include horror, romance, science fiction, thriller, fantasy, action, detective, comedy, crime, family, reality, myth, non-fiction, animation, sociocultural, and drama.

MONARCH FILMS
Production company and distributor

368 Danforth Ave.
Jersey City, NJ 07305
201-451-3770 (phone)
201-451-3877 (fax)

monarchfilms@aol.com
mfilms.com
imdb.com/company/co0101927

Does not accept any unsolicited material. Genres include horror.

MONGREL INTERNATIONAL
Distributor and sales agent

1028 Queen St
West Toronto, ON M6J 1H6
Canada
888-607-3456

international@mongrelmedia.com
mongrelmedia.com
imdb.com/company/co0499584
facebook.com/mongrelmedia
twitter.com/MongrelMedia

Does not accept any unsolicited material. Genres include romance.

Charlotte Mickie
Producer
imdb.com/name/nm0585334

MONIKER ENTERTAINMENT
Production company and distributor

8306 Wilshire Blvd, #2649, Beverly Hills, CA, United States, 90211
323-744-1148

monikerentertainment.com
imdb.com/company/co0246158

Does not accept any unsolicited material. Project types include TV. Genres include drama, action, family, romance, and thriller.

MONKEYBOY
Production company

Zionskirchstr. 69
Berlin-Prenzlauer Berg 10119
Germany
+49 30 2594 0944

jan.dressler@themonkeyboy.de
themonkeyboy.de
imdb.com/company/co0510516

Does not accept any unsolicited material. Genres
include drama and thriller.

Jan Dressler
Producer
imdb.com/name/nm6936276

MONKEY TOWN PRODUCTIONS
Production company and distributor

1-5-1-306
Fujimi
Chiyoda, Tokyo 102-0071
Japan
+81 3 32 64 28 23 (phone)
+81 3 32 64 28 23 (fax)

sarumachi@aol.com
imdb.com/company/co0108341

Does not accept any unsolicited material. Project types
include feature films. Genres include drama and
romance.

Masahiro Kobayashi
Producer
imdb.com/name/nm0462029

MONOGRAM
Production company

2-19-13
Takaban
Meguro, Tokyo 152-0004
Japan
03-3760-5852 (phone)
03-5941-5511 (fax)

info@mono-g.com
monogram.co.jp
imdb.com/company/co0382878

Does not accept any unsolicited material. Project types
include TV. Genres include drama.

MONSTER DISTRIBUTES
Distributor

Rear 51 Merrion Square
Dublin 2
Ireland
+353-1-6114934 (phone)
+353-1-6114935 (fax)

andrew@monsterdistributes.com
monsterentertainment.tv
imdb.com/company/co0155799
linkedin.com/company/monster-distributes-ltd.

Does not accept any unsolicited material. Project types
include short films and TV. Genres include comedy
and animation.

MONSTERFOOT PRODUCTIONS
Production company

3450 Cahuenga Blvd West
Loft 105
Los Angeles, CA 90068
323-850-6116 (phone)
323-378-5232 (fax)

imdb.com/company/co0275343
linkedin.com/company/monsterfoot-productions
facebook.com/MonsterfootProductions
twitter.com/MONSTERFOOTprod

Accepts query letters from unproduced, unrepresented
writers. Project types include feature films and TV.
Genres include non-fiction and reality. Established in
2006.

Ahmet Zappa
CEO
323-850-6116
ahmetzappa.com
imdb.com/name/nm0953257
linkedin.com/in/ahmetzappa
twitter.com/AhmetZappa

MONTAGE
Production company and distributor

4-10-18
Kami Kitazawa
Setagaya, Tokyo 156-0057
Japan

03-3303-9871 (phone)
03-3303-9824 (fax)

desk@montage.co.jp
montage.co.jp/hp
imdb.com/company/co0322014

Does not accept any unsolicited material. Project types include feature films. Genres include documentary.

Tokio Komatsubara
Executive
imdb.com/name/nm1233052

MONTAGE ENTERTAINMENT
Production company

2118 Wilshire Blvd. Suite 297
Santa Monica, CA 90403
310-966-0222

david@montageentertainment.com
montageentertainment.com
imdb.com/company/co0100820

Accepts query letters from unproduced, unrepresented writers via email. Project types include feature films and TV.

David Peters
Producer
310-966-0222
david@montageentertainment.com
imdb.com/name/nm0007070

Bill Ewart
Producer
310-966-0222
bill@montageentertainment.com
imdb.com/name/nm0263867

MONTECITO PICTURES
Production company

9465 Wilshire Blvd, Suite 920
Beverly Hills, CA 90212
310-247-9880 (phone)
310-247-9498 (fax)

1482 E. Valley Rd
Suite 477
Montecito, CA 93108

805-565-8590 (phone)
805-565-1893 (fax)

montecitopicturecompany.com
imdb.com/company/co0118469

Does not accept any unsolicited material. Project types include feature films and TV. Genres include action, thriller, non-fiction, comedy, period, family, and drama. Established in 2000.

Tom Pollock
Partner
imdb.com/name/nm0689696
Assistant: Krystee Morgan

Alex Plapinger
Executive Vice President of Production
310-247-9880
imdb.com/name/nm3292687
linkedin.com/pub/alex-plapinger/4/544/808

Ivan Reitman
Partner
imdb.com/name/nm0718645
Assistant: Eric Reich

Joe Medjuck
Partner
imdb.com/name/nm0575817

MONTONE/YORN (UNNAMED YORN PRODUCTION COMPANY)

2000 Ave of the Stars
3rd Floor North Tower
Los Angeles, CA 90067

facebook.com

Accepts query letters from unproduced, unrepresented writers. Genres include fantasy, comedy, family, and action. Established in 2008.

Rick Yorn
imdb.com/name/nm0948833

MOODY STREET PICTURES
Production company and distributor

282 Moody St, Third Floor, Waltham , MA, United States, 02453
781-647-5626

info@moodystreetpictures.com
moodystreetpictures.com
imdb.com/company/co0108421

Does not accept any unsolicited material. Project types include TV. Genres include drama, thriller, comedy, and family.

MOOK PRODUCTIONS
Production company

64 Marion Ave.
New Providnce, NJ 07974
212-229-8019 (phone)
845-357-3217 (fax)

rob_owl@hotmail.com
imdb.com/company/co0167613

Does not accept any unsolicited material. Project types include short films. Genres include comedy.

MOONLITE FILMWERKS
Production company

1307 Paige St
Houston, TX 77003

info@moonlitefilmwerks.com
moonlitefilmwerks.com
imdb.com/company/co0287283

Does not accept any unsolicited material. Genres include thriller and science fiction.

MOONSTONE ENTERTAINMENT
Sales agent

P.O. Box 1599
Studio City, CA 91614-0599
818-985-3003 (phone)
818-985-3009 (fax)

submissions@moonstonefilms.com
moonstonefilms.com
imdb.com/company/co0023327
facebook.com/MoonstoneEntertainment
twitter.com/MoonstoneEnt

Accepts query letters from unproduced, unrepresented writers via email. Project types include feature films. Genres include action and comedy.

Shahar Stroh
Director Development & Acquisitions
818-985-3003
shahar@moonstonefilms.com
imdb.com/name/nm2325576

Yael Stroh
President
yaels@moonstonefilms.com
imdb.com/name/nm0834806

MORCAMAN PRODUCTIONS
Production company

425 Maxwell
Irving, TX 75061
469-231-2360

morcaman.com
imdb.com/company/co0432865

Does not accept any unsolicited material. Project types include short films. Genres include animation.

MORENA FILMS
Production company, distributor, and sales agent

Fernando VI, 17-2, Madrid , Spain, 28004
011-349-17002780 (phone)
011-349-13194432 (fax)

morenafilms@morenafilms.com
morenafilms.com
imdb.com/company/co0080779

Does not accept any unsolicited material. Project types include feature films and TV. Genres include thriller, family, drama, and action.

MORGAN CREEK PRODUCTIONS
Production company

10351 Santa Monica Blvd
Los Angeles, CA 90025
310-432-4848 (phone)
310-432-4844 (fax)

morgancreek.com
imdb.com/company/co0033472
linkedin.com/company/morgan-creek-productions
facebook.com/morgancreekproductions
twitter.com/Morgan__Creek

Does not accept any unsolicited material. Project types include feature films. Genres include romance, crime, drama, and action.

Andrew Moncrief
Creative Executive
linkedin.com/pub/andrew-moncrief/11/262/325

MORNINGSTAR ENTERTAINMENT
Production company

350 N Glenoaks Blvd
Suite 300
Burbank, CA 91502
818-559-7255 (phone)
818-559-7551 (fax)

mstar@morningstarentertainment.com
morningstarentertainment.com
imdb.com/company/co0050956
linkedin.com/companies/morningstar-entertainment
facebook.com/pages/Morningstar-Entertainment/
    91568286971

Accepts query letters from unproduced, unrepresented writers via email. Project types include TV. Genres include non-fiction and reality. Established in 1980.

Gary Tarpinian
President
linkedin.com/pub/gary-tarpinian/33/3a/367

MORTON JANKEL ZANDER (MJZ)
Production company

2201 S Carmelina Ave
Los Angeles, CA 90064
310-826-6200 (phone)
310-826-6219 (fax)

DIRECTORS
CONTACT
SALES
LA
NY
UK
40 WOOSTER STREET
NEW YORK, NEW YORK 10013
646-613-1401 (phone)
646-613-1404 (fax)

DIRECTORS
CONTACT
SALES
LA
NY
UK
45A BREWER STREET
LONDON, ENGLAND W1F 9UE
44207-434-4000 (phone)
44207-434-4000 (fax)

mjz.com
imdb.com/company/co0102914
facebook.com/MJZ.MJZ
twitter.com/MJZitter

Does not accept any unsolicited material. Project types include commercials and short films. Established in 1990.

David Zander
President
imdb.com/name/nm1536307

MOSAIC
Production company

9200 Sunset Blvd, Tenth Floor, Los Angeles , CA, United States, 90069
310-786-4900 (phone)
310-777-2108 (fax)

imdb.com/company/co0262627

Does not accept any unsolicited material. Project types include TV, feature films, and short films. Genres include comedy, romance, thriller, drama, and family.

Jimmy Miller
Principal (Manager/Producer)
imdb.com/name/nm0588612

MOSAIC MEDIA GROUP
Production company

9200 W Sunset Blvd
10th Floor
Los Angeles, CA 90069
310-786-4900 (phone)
310-777-2185 (fax)

imdb.com/company/co0037759
linkedin.com/company/mosaic-media-group

Accepts query letters from unproduced, unrepresented writers. Project types include TV and feature films. Genres include drama, myth, comedy, action, and family.

Mike Falbo
310-786-4900
mfalbo@mosaicla.com
imdb.com/name/nm3824648
Assistant: Mark Acomb

David Householter
310-786-4900
dhouseholter@mosaicla.com
imdb.com/name/nm0396720
Assistant: Brendan Clougherty

Jimmy Miller
310-786-4900
jmiller@mosaicla.com
imdb.com/name/nm0588612
Assistant: Alyx Carr

MOSHAG PRODUCTIONS
Production company

1531 Wellesley Ave
Los Angeles, CA 90025
310-820-6760 (phone)
310-820-6960 (fax)

moshag@aol.com
imdb.com/company/co0061487

Accepts query letters from unproduced, unrepresented writers via email. Project types include feature films and TV.

Mark Mower
Producer
imdb.com/name/nm0610272

MOTT STREET PICTURES
Production company

801 N. Fairfax Ave, Suite 322
Los Angeles, CA 90046
310-279-9797

mottstreetpictures.com
imdb.com/company/co0321036

facebook.com/Mott-Street-
Pictures-100705350016814
twitter.com/mottstreetpics

Does not accept any unsolicited material. Project types include feature films. Genres include fantasy and drama.

Alex Sagalchik
Producer
imdb.com/name/nm4215812

MOVIE CENTRAL
Production company and distributor

Corus Quay
25 Dockside
Drive Toronto,
ON M5A 0B5
416-479-6784

info@moviecentral.ca
moviecentral.ca
imdb.com/company/co0263130
linkedin.com/company/movie-central
facebook.com/moviecentral
twitter.com/moviecentral

Does not accept any unsolicited material. Genres include thriller.

MOVIE-EYE ENTERTAINMENT
Distributor

6-2-1-4F
Ginza
Chuo, Tokyo 104-0061
Japan
+81 03-5537-0151 (phone)
+81 03-5537-0152 (fax)

me-tokyo@movie-eye.co.jp
imdb.com/company/co0123420

Does not accept any unsolicited material. Project types include TV. Genres include drama.

Taku Ushiyama
Chief Operating Officer (Executive)
imdb.com/name/nm2431376

MOVIE MOGUL, INC.
Production company

9100 Wilshire Blvd
Suite 520E
Beverly Hills, California
90210
424-245-4331

mogul-inc.com

Does not accept any unsolicited material. Project types include feature films.

Deborah Harpur
CEO
imdb.com/name/nm2970095

MOVIE PACKAGE COMPANY
Studio

287 S Robertson Blvd., Suite 101
Beverly Hills, CA 90211

moviepackageco.com
imdb.com/company/co0314488
twitter.com/moviepackageco

Does not accept any unsolicited material. Project types include feature films.

Shaun Redick
Producer
imdb.com/name/nm2211720

Ray Mansfield
Producer
imdb.com/name/nm1796751

MOVING PICTURES
Production company

8447 Wilshire Blvd., Suite 212
Beverly Hills, CA 90212
310-288-5464

imdb.com/name/nm3082970

Does not accept any unsolicited material. Project types include TV and feature films. Genres include romance and comedy.

Peter Jaysen
Head/Producer
imdb.com/name/nm0419779

MOXIE PICTURES
Production company

5890 W Jefferson Blvd
Los Angeles, CA 90016
310-857-1000 (phone)
310-857-1004 (fax)

18 E. 16th St.
4th Floor
New York City, NY 10003
212-807-6901 (phone)
212-807-1456 (fax)

info@moxiepictures.com
moxiepictures.com
imdb.com/company/co0119462
linkedin.com/company/moxie-pictures
facebook.com/moxiepictures
twitter.com/MoxiePictures

Does not accept any unsolicited material. Project types include TV and feature films. Genres include comedy, romance, documentary, reality, and drama. Established in 2005.

Robert Fernandez
CEO
fernandez@moxiepictures.com
imdb.com/name/nm0273045

Dan Levinson
President
danny@moxiepictures.com
imdb.com/name/nm1829495
linkedin.com/pub/dan-levinson/6/91b/1a5

Katie Connell
Head of Production
katie@moxiepictures.com

MOZARK PRODUCTIONS
Production company

4024 Radford Ave, Bldg. 5
Studio City, CA 91604
818-655-5779 (phone)
818-655-5129 (fax)

imdb.com/company/co0023587

Does not accept any unsolicited material. Project types include feature films and TV. Genres include drama and comedy.

Linda Bloodworth Thomason
Writer/Producer/Director
imdb.com/name/nm0089124

MPI MEDIA GROUP
Studio

16101 S 108th Ave
Orland Park, IL 60467
800-777-2223

info@mpimedia.com
mpimedia.com
imdb.com/company/co0028092
facebook.com/mpimediagrp
twitter.com/mpimediagroup

Does not accept any unsolicited material. Project types include TV. Genres include comedy, drama, and horror.

Malik Ali
Founder
imdb.com/name/nm5307398

Greg Newman
EVP
imdb.com/name/nm0628103

MPS DALLAS
Production company

141 Regal Row
Dallas, TX 75247
214-630-1655 (phone)
214-630-1761 (fax)

mpsfilm.com
imdb.com/company/co0088352
facebook.com/MPS.Studios
twitter.com/MPSSTUDIOS

Does not accept any unsolicited material. Genres include family, thriller, and drama.

MRB PRODUCTIONS
Production company

311 N. Robertson Blvd., #513
Beverly HIlls, CA 90211
323-965-8881

matthew@mrbproductions.com
mrbproductions.com
imdb.com/company/co0122884
linkedin.com/company/mrb-productions
facebook.com/pages/MRB-Productions-Inc/
    113037758751306
twitter.com/MRBProductions1

Does not accept any unsolicited material. Project types include feature films and TV. Genres include drama, romance, crime, documentary, comedy, and thriller. Established in 2001.

Brenda Bank
Producer
brenda@mrbproductions.com
imdb.com/name/nm1870773
Assistant: Erica Weiss

Matthew Brady
Executive Producer
matthew@mrbproductions.com
imdb.com/name/nm0103683

Luke Watson
Vice-President
luke@mrbproductions.com
imdb.com/name/nm2362830
linkedin.com/pub/luke-watson/15/60a/683

Astrid Downs
Executive Producer
astrid@mrbproductions.com

MR. MUDD
Production company and distributor

137 N Larchmont Blvd, #113
Los Angeles, CA 9004
323-932-5656 (phone)
323-932-5666 (fax)

mrmudd.com
imdb.com/company/co0040322

Does not accept any unsolicited material. Project types include feature films. Genres include romance, comedy, family, and drama. Established in 1998.

Lianne Halfon
Producer
imdb.com/name/nm0355147

John Malkovich
imdb.com/name/nm0000518

Russell Smith
Producer
imdb.com/name/nm0809833
linkedin.com/pub/russell-smith/2a/687/39

M'S WORLD CORP.
Production company and distributor

2-13-12-3F
Hamamatsucho
Minato, TOKYO 105-0013
Japan
03-6430-9290 (phone)
03-3432-6750 (fax)

info@msworld.co.jp
imdb.com/company/co0282333

Does not accept any unsolicited material. Project types include feature films. Genres include action.

MTI HOME VIDEO
Production company and distributor

14216 SW 136th St
Miami, FL 33186
305-255-8684 (phone)
305-233-6943 (fax)

mti@mtivideo.com
mtivideo.com
imdb.com/company/co0077442

Accepts scripts from produced or represented writers. Genres include drama and comedy.

MTV ANIMATION
Studio

1515 Broadway, 25th Floor
New York , NY 10128

imdb.com/company/co0054176

Does not accept any unsolicited material.

Chris Lin
SVP of Production/Series Development
imdb.com/name/nm4930153

MULLER ENTERTAINMENT
Production company

6301 Riverside Dr
Soundstage Building One
Irving, TX 75039
972-869-0700 (phone)
972-869-7791 (fax)

info@mullerentertainment.com
mullerentertainment.com
imdb.com/company/co0092222
linkedin.com/company/muller-entertainment
facebook.com/Muller-Entertainment-177962416639

Does not accept any unsolicited material. Project types include short films. Genres include science fiction.

MULTI-VALENCE PRODUCTIONS
Production company

2005 Palo Verde, Suite 200
Long Beach, CA 90815
562-208-0476

alexandergarcia06@gmail.com
imdb.com/company/co0315075

Does not accept any unsolicited material. Project types include feature films. Genres include drama and fantasy.

Alexander Garcia
Producer/Writer
imdb.com/name/nm0305094

MULTIVISIONNAIRE PICTURES
Production company

3080 W Valley Blvd., Suite B
Alhambra, CA 91803
626-737-8357 (phone)
626-727-8642 (fax)

multivisionnaire.com
facebook.com/MultiVisionnaire-Pictures-146663175347473

Does not accept any unsolicited material. Project types include feature films.

Erika Kao-Haley
Executive Producer
imdb.com/name/nm2537107

MUN2 TELEVISION
Production company

2470 W 8th Ave
Hialeah, FL 33010
305-884-8200

msnlatino.telemundo.com
imdb.com/company/co0139459
facebook.com/Telemundo
twitter.com/Telemundo

Does not accept any unsolicited material. Project types include short films and TV. Genres include comedy.

MURPHY BOYZ MANAGEMENT
Sales agent

270 Sparta Ave., Ste 104
Sparta, NJ 07871
973-702-9000 (phone)
973-702-1550 (fax)

ray@murphyboyz.com
murphyboyz.com
imdb.com/company/co0128885

Does not accept any unsolicited material. Project types include TV and commercials. Genres include drama and family.

MUSE DISTRIBUTION INTERNATIONAL
Production company and distributor

3451 St-Jacques West
Montreal, QC H4C 1H1
Canada
514-866-6873 (phone)
514-876-3911 (fax)

bpalik@muse.ca
muse.ca
imdb.com/company/co0026632
facebook.com/museent
twitter.com/MuseEntertains

Does not accept any unsolicited material. Project types include TV and feature films. Genres include action, drama, and thriller.

MUSEFILM PRODUCTIONS
Production company and distributor

15 Brooks Ave, Unit B, Venice , CA, United States, 90291
310-306-2001 (phone)
310-574-2614 (fax)

musefilm.com
imdb.com/company/co0019350

Does not accept any unsolicited material. Genres include family, thriller, crime, romance, drama, action, and comedy.

MUSE PRODUCTIONS
Production company

15-B Brooks Ave
Venice, CA 90291
310-306-2001

musefilm.com
imdb.com/company/co0019350
web.facebook.com/museproductions
twitter.com/museproductions

Does not accept any unsolicited material. Project types include feature films. Genres include thriller and drama.

MUSHI PRODUCTIONS
Production company

2-30-5
Fujimidai
Nerima, Tokyo 177-0034
Japan
03-3990-4153 (phone)
03-3990-4154 (fax)

postmaster@mushi-pro.co.jp
mushi-pro.co.jp
imdb.com/company/co0064052

Does not accept any unsolicited material. Project types include feature films, video games, short films, and TV. Genres include action and animation.

Satoshi Ito
Producer
imdb.com/name/nm0411739

MUSIC BOX FILMS
Distributor

173 N Morgan St, Chicago, IL, United States, 60607
312-241-1320

info@musicboxfilms.com
musicboxfilms.com
imdb.com/company/co0235025

Does not accept any unsolicited material. Project types include TV. Genres include reality, drama, comedy, and family.

MUTUAL FILM COMPANY
Production company

3535 Hayden Ave.
Ste 340
Culver City, CA 90232
310-558-9800 (phone)
310-558-9890 (fax)

inquiries@mutualfilm.com
imdb.com/company/co0007500

Does not accept any unsolicited material. Project types include feature films and TV. Genres include romance, thriller, and comedy.

Gary Levinsohn
Producer
imdb.com/name/nm0506013

Shelly Clippard
VP of Production & Development
imdb.com/name/nm0166953

MXN
Studio

1930 Curson Ave
Los Angeles, CA 90046
323-977-0377

imdb.com/company/co0237694

Does not accept any unsolicited material. Project types include feature films and TV. Genres include comedy.

Mason Novick
Producer/Manager
imdb.com/name/nm1259504

MY2CENTENCES
Production company

9229 Sunset Blvd., Suite 601
West Hollywood, CA 90069
310-777-0323 (phone)
310-777-0324 (fax)

info@my2c.com
imdb.com/company/co0077666

Does not accept any unsolicited material. Project types include feature films. Genres include drama.

Chris Williams
Partner
imdb.com/name/nm0930282

Craig Singer
Partner
imdb.com/name/nm0801916

MY PRODUCTIONS
Production company

3005 S Lamar Blvd
Austin, TX 78704
512-784-1060

my-productions.com
imdb.com/company/co0178889

Does not accept any unsolicited material. Project types include short films. Genres include comedy and family.

MYRIAD PICTURES
Production company, distributor, sales agent, and financing company

11900 W Olympic Blvd
Suite 400
Los Angeles, CA 90064
310-279-4000 (phone)
310-279-4001 (fax)

info@myriadpictures.com
myriadpictures.com

imdb.com/company/co0033226
linkedin.com/company/myriad-pictures
facebook.com/MyriadPictures1
twitter.com/MyriadPictures

Does not accept any unsolicited material. Project types include feature films and TV. Genres include fantasy, action, family, non-fiction, thriller, drama, romance, horror, and comedy. Established in 1993.

Kirk D'Amico
CEO
imdb.com/name/nm0195136
linkedin.com/pub/kirk-d-amico/10/bb2/180
twitter.com/kirkdamico

MYSTERE VISIONS ENTERTAINMENT
Production company

2131 N. Collins St
Suite 433-725
Arlington, TX 76011
682-999-8366

info@mysterevision.com
mysterevisions.com
imdb.com/company/co0375203
faccbook.com/MysterEVE/info

Project types include feature films. Genres include science fiction, drama, horror, and thriller.

Lien Mya Nguyen
Owner/Producer
682-999-8366
imdb.com/name/nm3168876

Eddie Brown, Jr.
Owner/Producer
682-999-8366
imdb.com/name/nm2726815

MYSTICARTS PICTURES
Studio

1918 W. Magnolia Blvd., Suite 206
Burbank, CA 91505
818-563-4121 (phone)
818-563-4318 (fax)

mysticartpictures.com
imdb.com/company/co0053465

facebook.com/MysticArtPictures
twitter.com/mysticart

Does not accept any unsolicited material. Project types include TV and feature films. Genres include drama.

Katy Wallin
CEO/President/Producer
imdb.com/name/nm0002359

MYSTIC STUDIOS PRODUCTIONS
Production company

4255 JohnsCreek Pkwy Suite B
Atlanta, GA 30024
404-663-5158

immtalent@yahoo.com
imdb.com/company/co0409328

Does not accept any unsolicited material.

MYTHIC FILMS
Production company

20501 Ventura Blvd., Ste 325
Woodland Hills, CA 91364
323-660-9441 (phone)
323-660-9450 (fax)

studio@mythicfilms.com
mythicfilms.com
imdb.com/company/co0235454

Does not accept any unsolicited material. Project types include feature films. Genres include non-fiction and drama.

Ralph Hemecker
Producer, Writer, Director
imdb.com/name/nm0375973

NABU FILMS
Production company

7125 Lennox Ave Int 156
Van Nuys, CA 91405
818-646-0354

info@nabufilms.com
imdb.com/company/co0238576

Does not accept any unsolicited material.

Jessica Villegas
Producer
imdb.com/name/nm3096521

NACH-ZACH VISION
Production company

Sofia-1582, bul Kopenhagen 23A, office 1.2A
Bulgaria
+359-2-4422206

marinov_atanas@yahoo.com
nach-zach.com
imdb.com/company/co0437270

Does not accept any unsolicited material. Project types include TV, short films, and feature films. Genres include comedy and drama. Established in 2009.

Atanas Marinov
Producer
marinov_atanas@yahoo.com

NAHB PRODUCTIONS
Production company

1201 15th St NW
Washington, DC 20005
202-266-8100 (phone)
202-266-8054 (fax)

skyetrimble123@yahoo.com
nahbproductions.com
imdb.com/company/co0142435

Does not accept any unsolicited material. Project types include TV.

NALA FILMS
Production company

2016 Broadway Pl.
Santa Monica, CA 90404
310-264-2555

info@nalafilms.com
nalafilms.com
imdb.com/company/co0154622
facebook.com/NALAFilms
twitter.com/nalafilms

Does not accept any unsolicited material. Project types include feature films and TV. Genres include drama and thriller.

Emilio Barroso
CEO
imdb.com/name/nm1950898

NAMANCO PRODUCTIONS
Production company

7 Audubon Pl
New Orleans, LA 70118
504-866-2888

300 E 51st St, Apt 11A
New York, NY 10022
212-688-6310

imdb.com/company/co0010060
linkedin.com/company/namanco-productions-inc

Does not accept any unsolicited material. Project types include feature films. Genres include drama.

Jimmy Walsh
Executive Producer
imdb.com/name/nm1255801

NAMASTE FILMS INC.
Production company

301 Pruitt Rd.
Suite 1032
Spring, TX 77380
323-395-0937 (phone)
310-601-1804 (fax)

contact@namastefilms.com
namastefilmproductions.com
imdb.com/company/co0153873

Does not accept any unsolicited material. Project types include TV. Genres include drama.

NANCY TENENBAUM FILMS
Production company

43 Lyons Plain Rd
Weston, CT 06883
203-221-6830 (phone)
203-221-6832 (fax)

ntfilms2@aol.com
imdb.com/company/co0012648
linkedin.com/company/nancy-tenenbaum-films
facebook.com/pages/Nancy-Tenenbaum-Films/
159473827409156

Does not accept any unsolicited material. Project types
include feature films. Genres include comedy.
Established in 1996.

Nancy Tenenbaum
President
imdb.com/name/nm085494
Assistant: Lyndsy Celestino

NAPOLI PICTURES
Production company

1450 Brickell Ave
Suite 1420
Miami, FL 33131
786-200-4581 (phone)
305-371-4642 (fax)

info@napolipictures.com
imdb.com/company/co0205933

Does not accept any unsolicited material. Genres
include drama.

NAT GEO WILD
Production company and distributor

1145 17th StrNW
Washington, DC 20036
800-647-5463

channel.nationalgeographic.com/wild
imdb.com/company/co0286617
twitter.com/natgeowild

Does not accept any unsolicited material. Genres
include documentary.

NATURAL EIGHT CO.
Production company

1-26-30-9F
Higashi
Shibuya, Tokyo 150-0011
Japan

info@naturaleight.co.jp

imdb.com/company/co0305810

Does not accept any unsolicited material. Project types
include TV. Genres include documentary.

Yuka Ôhashi
President (Manager)
imdb.com/name/nm2320290

NBC ENTERTAINMENT
Production company and distributor

30 Rockefeller Plaza, New York, NY, United States,
10112
212-664-4444 (phone)
212-664-5998 (fax)

100 Universal City Plaza
Universal City CA 91608
818-777-1000

imdb.com/company/co0048970

Does not accept any unsolicited material. Project types
include TV and feature films. Genres include thriller,
action, and drama.

Sean Serio
Creative Director
818-777-1000
imdb.com/name/nm6321758

NBC PRODUCTIONS
Production company

3000 W Alameda Ave
Burbank, CA 91523-0001
818-840-4444

nbcuni.com
imdb.com/company/co0065874

Does not accept any unsolicited material. Project types
include TV and feature films. Genres include horror,
crime, family, comedy, non-fiction, thriller, romance,
documentary, science fiction, action, drama, and
fantasy. Established in 1947.

NBC STUDIOS
Production company and distributor

30 Rockefeller Plaza
New York, NY - 10112
212-664-4444

nbcucareers@nbcuni.com
nbcuni.com
imdb.com/company/co0022762
facebook.com/nbcuniversal
twitter.com/NBCUniversal

Does not accept any unsolicited material. Project types include feature films and TV. Genres include detective, documentary, thriller, comedy, non-fiction, action, drama, and crime.

NBCUNIVERSAL
Studio and distributor

30 Rockefeller Plaza, New York, NY, United States, 10112
212-664-4444

2290 W. 8th Ave
Hialeah FL 33010
305-884-8200

100 Universal City Plaza Bldg 1320, Suite 4A
Universal City CA 91608
818-777-1000

nbcumv.com
imdb.com/company/co0557199

Does not accept any unsolicited material. Project types include TV. Genres include family and drama.

Mark Binke
818-777-8137
imdb.com/name/nm1337285

Mark Binke
Executive Vice President (Production)
818-777-8137
imdb.com/name/nm1337285

NBC UNIVERSAL
Production company

30 Rockefeller Plaza
New York, NY 10112
212-664-4444

nbcuniversal.com
facebook.com/nbcuniversal

twitter.com/NBCUniversal

Does not accept any unsolicited material. Project types include feature films and TV. Genres include drama, period, comedy, thriller, reality, crime, and documentary. Established in 2009.

Pearlena Igbokwe
imdb.com/name/nm2303684

Steve Burke
President
imdb.com/name/nm4446434

Marci Klein
Executive Producer
imdb.com/name/nm0458885

NBC UNIVERSAL TELEVISION DISTRIBUTION
Production company, distributor, and sales agent

3340 Peachtree Rd. NE
Suite 711
Atlanta, GA 30326
404-812-3712

30 Rockafeller Plaza
New York City, NY 10112
212-664-4444

3400 W. Olive Ave.
Burbank, CA 91505
818-840-4444 (phone)
818-866-1430 (fax)

454 N. Columbus Dr.
5th Floor
Chicago, IL 60611
312-836-5725

nbcuni.com
imdb.com/company/co0129175
linkedin.com/company/nbcuniversal-inc-
facebook.com/nbcuniversal
twitter.com/NBCUniversal

Does not accept any unsolicited material. Project types include feature films and TV. Genres include family, drama, action, fantasy, science fiction, animation, comedy, thriller, reality, horror, crime, documentary, and detective. Established in 1971.

Jerry DiCanio
imdb.com/name/nm3034292

Jennifer Nicholson-Salke
President
imdb.com/name/nm2323622
linkedin.com/pub/jennifer-vessio/6/b6b/436

NBR MEDIA
Production company and sales agent

1003 Riverside Dr
Old Hickory, TN 37138
323-828-9911

nadia@nbrmedia.com
nbrmedia.com
imdb.com/company/co0431893

Does not accept any unsolicited material. Project types include TV. Genres include science fiction and thriller.

N DESIGN
Production company

3-47-21-2F
Ogikubo
Suginami, Tokyo 167-0051
Japan
03-3392-1055 (phone)
03-3392-1377 (fax)

info@ndesign.co.jp
ndesign.co.jp
imdb.com/company/co0226013
facebook.com/ndesign.co.jp

Does not accept any unsolicited material. Project types include TV, feature films, and video games. Genres include science fiction and action.

Kôji Nozaki
President (Producer)
imdb.com/name/nm1590974

NEAL STREET PRODUCTIONS
Production company and distributor

26-28 Neal St
London WC2H 9QQ
UK

+44207-240-8890 (phone)
+44207-240-7099 (fax)

post@nealstreetproductions.com
nealstreetproductions.com
imdb.com/company/co0165439
twitter.com/nealstprods

Does not accept any unsolicited material. Project types include feature films, short films, and TV. Genres include fantasy.

Sam Mendes
Producer
imdb.com/name/nm0005222

NECROPIA ENTERTAINMENT
Production company

9171 Wilshire Blvd, Suite 300
Beverly Hills, CA 9021
323-865-0547

imdb.com/company/co0368091

Does not accept any unsolicited material. Project types include feature films. Genres include action, fantasy, horror, myth, and science fiction.

Guillermo de Toro
Director
imdb.com/name/nm0868219

NEO ART AND LOGIC
Production company

5225 Wilshire Blvd Ste. 501
Los Angeles, CA 90036
323-451-2040

aaron@neoartandlogic.com
imdb.com/company/co0038165

Accepts query letters from unproduced, unrepresented writers via email. Project types include feature films and TV. Genres include family, drama, horror, comedy, fantasy, action, documentary, thriller, science fiction, and animation. Established in 2000.

Joel Soisson
imdb.com/name/nm0812373

Aaron Ockman
imdb.com/name/nm1845744
linkedin.com/pub/aaron-ockman/7/530/94b

W. K. Border
imdb.com/name/nm0096176

Kirk Morri
Executive
imdb.com/name/nm0606294

NEOCLASSICS FILMS
Distributor and sales agent

3710 S Robertson Blvd Suite 230
Culver City CA 90232
310-559-9200 (phone)
310-559-9267 (fax)

650 W Georgia St, Suite 1925, Vancouver , BC,
Canada, V6B 4N8
604-899-0150 (phone)
604-899-0200 (fax)

info@neoclassicsfilms.com
neoclassicsfilms.com
imdb.com/company/co0229678

Does not accept any unsolicited material. Project types
include feature films. Genres include family, drama,
thriller, and action.

NERVE DAMAGE FILMS
Production company

5806 Maple St.
Houston, TX 77074

imdb.com/company/co0341242

Does not accept any unsolicited material. Project types
include short films. Genres include fantasy and
romance.

NEST CO.
Production company

1-3-12-703
Kami Meguro
Meguro, Tokyo 153-0051
Japan

03-5708-5415 (phone)
03-5708-5416 (fax)

info@nest-web.jp
nest-web.jp
imdb.com/company/co0392433

Does not accept any unsolicited material. Project types
include TV. Genres include drama.

Takashi Saitô
President (Manager)
imdb.com/name/nm5246851

NEST FAMILY ENTERTAINMENT
Production company

1421 S. Beltline Rd
Ste 300
Coppell, TX 75019
800-634-4298

PO Box 293446
Lewisville, TX 75029
800-634-4298

nestlearning.com/nestentertainment.aspx
imdb.com/company/co0004117
facebook.com/NestLearning
twitter.com/NestLearning

Does not accept any unsolicited material. Genres
include comedy, family, and animation.

NETFLIX
Production company and distributor

345 N Maple Dr Suite 300
Beverly Hills CA 90210
310-734-2900

100 Winchester Circle, Los Gatos, CA, United States,
95032
408-540-3700 (phone)
408-540-3737 (fax)

netflix.com
imdb.com/company/co0144901

Does not accept any unsolicited material. Project types
include TV and feature films. Genres include drama,
comedy, action, and family.

NETTAI

Distributor

1-5-23-303
Okusawa
Setagaya, Tokyo 158-0083
Japan
+81 337289919 (phone)
+81 337289919 (fax)

ikeponia@fs.catv.ne.jp
imdb.com/company/co0210893

Does not accept any unsolicited material. Project types include TV. Genres include comedy.

Fumiaki Ikeda
Managing Director (Executive)
imdb.com/name/nm3021410

NEVER NOMINATED PRODUCTIONS

Production company

6565 Sunset Blvd.
Los Angeles, CA
323-466-9200

imdb.com/company/co0422094

Does not accept any unsolicited material. Project types include TV.

Courtland Cox
SVP of Development
imdb.com/name/nm1202338

NEW AMSTERDAM ENTERTAINMENT

Production company

142 W 44th St, PH-2
New York, NY 10036
212-922-1930 (phone)
212-997-1936 (fax)

mail@newamsterdamnyc.com
newamsterdamnyc.com
imdb.com/company/co0010962
facebook.com/pages/New-Amsterdam-Entertainment-
    Inc
twitter.com/wix

Does not accept any unsolicited material. Project types include TV and feature films. Genres include science

fiction, thriller, documentary, action, fantasy, horror, and drama. Established in 1996.

Richard Rubinstein
CEO
imdb.com/name/nm0748283

Katherine Kolbert
imdb.com/name/nm0463946

Sara Reiner
imdb.com/name/nm2200017
linkedin.com/pub/dir/Sara/Reiner

Michael Messina
imdb.com/name/nm0582175

NEW ARTISTS ALLIANCE

Production company

16633 Ventura Blvd, #1440
Encino, CA 91436
818-784-8341

info@naafilms.com
newartistsalliance.com
imdb.com/company/co0237280
facebook.com/naafilms
twitter.com/naafilms

Accepts query letters from unproduced, unrepresented writers via email. Project types include feature films. Genres include thriller, horror, drama, and action. Established in 2003.

John Suits
john@naafilms.com
imdb.com/name/nm2986811

Gabe Cowan
gabe@naafilms.com
imdb.com/name/nm1410462
linkedin.com/pub/gabriel-cowan/79/849/863

NEWARTS ENTERTAINMENT

Production company and distributor

Suite 6C 1620 Manhattan Ave
Union City, NJ 07087

imdb.com/company/co0345226

Does not accept any unsolicited material. Project types include short films. Genres include documentary.

NEWCOAST ENTERTAINMENT

Production company and financing company

314 E. 13th St
Houston, TX 77008
832-426-4148

info@newcoastent.com
imdb.com/company/co0357048

Does not accept any unsolicited material. Project types
include TV and feature films. Genres include
documentary and comedy.

NEW CRIME PRODUCTIONS

Production company

1041 N Formosa Ave
Formosa Building, Room 219
West Hollywood, CA 90016
323-850-2525

newcrime@aol.com
imdb.com/company/co0079035
facebook.com/pages/New-Crime-Productions/
    111870248875959

Accepts query letters from unproduced, unrepresented
writers via email. Project types include feature films.
Genres include drama, thriller, comedy, and romance.

John Cusack
Executive
imdb.com/name/nm0000131
facebook.com/pages/John-Cusack/176246839075056

NEW FIERCE ENTERTAINMENT, INC.

Production company

8306 Wilshire Blvd., #904, Beverly Hills, CA, United
States, 90211
310-860-1174 (phone)
310-860-9946 (fax)

info@fierceentertainment.com
fierce-entertainment.com
imdb.com/company/co0095383

Does not accept any unsolicited material. Project types
include feature films and TV. Genres include family,
drama, comedy, action, and thriller.

NEW FILMS INTERNATIONAL

Production company and sales agent

14320 Ventura Blvd. # 619
Sherman Oaks, CA 91423
818-501-2720 (phone)
818-501-2780 (fax)

info@newfilmsint.com
newfilmsint.com
imdb.com/company/co0084783
facebook.com/NewFilmsInternational

Does not accept any unsolicited material. Project types
include feature films. Genres include thriller, romance,
and drama.

NEW HORIZONS

Production company and distributor

11600 San Vicente Blvd
Los Angeles, CA 90049
310-820-6733 (phone)
310-207-6819 (fax)

cynthiab@newhorizonspix.com
newhorizonspictures.com
imdb.com/company/co0061080

Does not accept any unsolicited material. Project types
include feature films and TV. Genres include thriller,
action, science fiction, and horror.

NEW KINGDOM PICTURES

Distributor

PO Box 140082
Orlando, FL 32814

info@newkingdompictures.com
newkingdompictures.com
facebook.com/newkingdompictures

Does not accept any unsolicited material. Genres
include family.

NEW LEAF LITERARY & MEDIA

Production company

110 W 40th St, Suite 410
New York, NY 10018
646-248-7989 (phone)
646-861-4654 (fax)

assist@newleafliterary.com
newleafliterary.com
imdb.com/company/co0415802
facebook.com/NewLeafLiterary
twitter.com/NewLeafLiterary

Does not accept any unsolicited material. Project types include feature films.

NEW LINE CINEMA
Studio

116 N Robertson Blvd
Los Angeles, CA 90048
310-854-5811 (phone)
310-854-1824 (fax)

warnerbros.com
imdb.com/company/co0046718
linkedin.com/company/2470
facebook.com/warnerbrosent
twitter.com/Warnerbrosent

Does not accept any unsolicited material. Project types include TV and feature films. Genres include action, comedy, drama, thriller, science fiction, family, documentary, period, fantasy, crime, non-fiction, and romance. Established in 1967.

Toby Emmerich
President
imdb.com/name/nm0256497
Assistant: Joshua Mack

Walter Hamada
imdb.com/name/nm1023578

Sam Brown
imdb.com/name/nm1354041
Assistant: Celia Khong

Richard Brener
imdb.com/name/nm0107196
Assistant: Kristin Schmidt

NEW MEXICO STATE FILM OFFICE
Production company and distributor

Joseph Montoya Building, 1100 St. Francis Dr, 1st Floor, Suite 1004, Santa Fe, NM, United States, 87501

505-476-5600 (phone)
505-476-5601 (fax)

info@nmfilm.com
nmfilm.com
imdb.com/company/co0328919

Does not accept any unsolicited material. Project types include TV and feature films. Genres include comedy, action, family, drama, and thriller.

Tobi E. Ives
Senior Manager (Production)
imdb.com/name/nm2628826

NEW PICTURES
Production company

5th Fl
66-68 Margaret St
London W1W 8SR
UK
+44 20 7078 8014

enquiries@newpictures.co.uk
newpictures.co.uk
imdb.com/company/co0022057

Does not accept any unsolicited material. Project types include TV. Genres include action and crime.

Charles Pattinson
Producer
imdb.com/name/nm0666495

NEW REAL FILMS
Production company and distributor

720A College St
Toronto, Ontario M6G 1C3
Canada
416-533-2530 (phone)
416-533-2617 (fax)

info@newrealfilms.com
newrealfilms.com
imdb.com/company/co0068560
facebook.com/New-Real-Films-17235363807
twitter.com/newrealfilms

Does not accept any unsolicited material. Project types include feature films. Genres include fantasy.

Leonard Farlinger
Producer
imdb.com/name/nm0267695

NEW REDEMPTION PICTURES
Production company

3000 W. Olympic Blvd, Bldg. 3
Santa Monica, CA 90404
310-315-4820

imdb.com/company/co0079347

Does not accept any unsolicited material. Project types include feature films and TV. Genres include comedy.

NEW REGENCY FILMS
Production company

10201 W Pico Blvd
Bldg 12
Los Angeles, CA 90035
310-369-8300 (phone)
310-969-0470 (fax)

270 Lafayette St.
Suite 1505
New York City, NY 10012
212-966-3166 (phone)
212-966-3443 (fax)

info@newregency.com
newregency.com
imdb.com/company/co0025101

Does not accept any unsolicited material. Project types include feature films. Genres include comedy, drama, family, science fiction, action, romance, and crime.

Mimi Tseng
CFO
imdb.com/name/nm2303729

David Manpearl
imdb.com/name/nm1818404

Justin Lam
Creative Executive
imdb.com/name/nm3528759

Arnon Milchan
Chairman
imdb.com/name/nm0586969

NEW RENAISSANCE PICTURES
Production company

15346 Saranac Dr
Whittier, CA 90604
650-722-2082

contact@newrenaissanceonline.com
newrenaissanceonline.com
imdb.com/company/co0164317
linkedin.com/company/new-renaissance-pictures
facebook.com/newrenaissancepictures

Does not accept any unsolicited material. Project types include feature films and TV. Genres include comedy, horror, and science fiction.

NEW SCHOOL MEDIA
Production company

345 N Maple Dr
Suite 315
Beverly Hills, CA 90210
310-984-5353

inquiries@newschoolmedia.com
newschoolmedia.com
imdb.com/company/co0249950

Does not accept any unsolicited material. Project types include feature films. Genres include comedy and action.

Brian Levy
imdb.com/name/nm2546392
linkedin.com/pub/brian-levy/92/3b4/816

NEW SELECT
Distributor

Ginza Aurore Bldg.
5-13-14 Ginza Chuo-Ku
Tokyo 104 0061
Japan
+81 3 5565 4568 (phone)
+81 3 3549 2705 (fax)

acquisition@new-select.com
new-select.jp
imdb.com/company/co0145657
facebook.com/%E3%82%A2%E3%83%83%AB%E3%83%83%90%E3%83%9
twitter.com/albatros_dvd

Does not accept any unsolicited material. Project types include TV. Genres include horror.

Shoko Otsuyama O'Connell
Acquistion & Marketing (Executive)
imdb.com/name/nm3110529

NEW WAVE ENTERTAINMENT
Production company and distributor

35 W. 36th St.
10th Floor
New York, NY 10018
212-594-2414 (phone)
212-239-1034 (fax)

2660 W Olive Ave
Burbank, CA 91505
818-295-5000 (phone)
818-295-5002 (fax)

nwe.com
imdb.com/company/co0024003
facebook.com/NewWaveEntertainment
twitter.com/NWESocial

Does not accept any unsolicited material. Project types include TV, feature films, and commercials. Genres include romance, myth, sociocultural, reality, crime, comedy, action, science fiction, horror, detective, fantasy, thriller, non-fiction, family, animation, and drama.

Paul Apel
CEO
818-295-5000
imdb.com/name/nm1318269
linkedin.com/pub/paul-apel/4/b10/682

Gregory Woertz
EVP Chief Financial Office
818-295-5000
gwoertz@nwe.com
imdb.com/name/nm0937343

NEW WORLD DISTRIBUTION
Production company and distributor

27068 La Paz Rd Suite 546
Aliso Viejo, CA 92656

newworlddistro.com

imdb.com/company/co0382224
linkedin.com/company/new-world-distribution
facebook.com/NewWorldDistro
twitter.com/NewWorldDistro

Does not accept any unsolicited material. Genres include documentary, drama, comedy, and family.

NEW YORK STATE GOVERNOR'S OFFICE FOR MOTION PICTURE & TV DEVELOPMENT
Production company, studio, and distributor

633 Third Ave, 33rd Floor, New York City , NY, United States, 10017
212-803-2330

nyfilm@esd.ny.gov
nylovesfilm.com

Does not accept any unsolicited material. Project types include feature films and TV. Genres include thriller, drama, action, and family.

NEXT ACTOR STUDIO
Production company

5522 Chaucer
Houston, TX 77005
713-532-2867

info@nextactor.com
nextactor.com
imdb.com/company/co0161190
facebook.com/nextactor
twitter.com/NextActorStudio

Does not accept any unsolicited material. Genres include drama and action.

NEXT EVOLUTION PRODUCTIONS
Production company

100 Manhattan Ave
Suite 704
Union City, NJ 07087
917-579-9874 (phone)
413-342-4742 (fax)

Nextevoproductions@gmail.com
nextevoproductions.com
imdb.com/company/co0298961

Does not accept any unsolicited material. Project types include TV. Genres include drama.

NEXUS ENTERTAINMENT
Production company

PO Box 740472
Houston, TX 77074
713-905-0301 (phone)
713-721-3409 (fax)

contact@nexus-films.com
imdb.com/company/co0060624
facebook.com/Nexus-
  Entertainment-133788416817952
twitter.com/NexusFilms

Does not accept any unsolicited material. Project types include short films and feature films. Genres include drama, action, comedy, crime, documentary, and family. Established in 1998.

NEXUS PRODUXIONS
Production company and distributor

5555 Morningside
Houston, TX 77005
713-367-1114

lakecampproductions@gmail.com
nexusproduxions.com
imdb.com/company/co0218882

Does not accept any unsolicited material. Project types include feature films. Genres include period, drama, and comedy. Established in 2007.

NICK WECHSLER PRODUCTIONS
Production company

Santa Monica, CA
310-309-5759 (phone)
310-309-5716 (fax)

info@nwprods.com
imdb.com/company/co0156991

Does not accept any unsolicited material. Project types include feature films and TV. Genres include animation, drama, family, action, thriller, comedy, horror, science fiction, crime, and fantasy. Established in 2005.

Elizabeth Bradford
Director of Development
lizzy@nwprods.com
imdb.com/name/nm4504768
linkedin.com/pub/elizabeth-bradford/82/857/9

Nick Wechsler
nick@nwprods.com
imdb.com/name/nm0917059

Felicity Aldridge
Creative Executive
felicity@nwprods.com
imdb.com/name/nm4504820
linkedin.com/pub/felicity-aldridge/98/615/923

NI-COLA ENTERTAINMENT
Production company

6711 Timbercove Ln
New Port Richey, FL 34653

nikomademitro@moonieandthespiderqueen.com
moonieandthespiderqueen.com
imdb.com/company/co0350626

Does not accept any unsolicited material. Genres include science fiction.

NIGEL BRITTEN MANAGEMENT
Production company

28 Woodbastwick Rd
London SE26 5LH
UK
+ 44 (0) 20 8778 7444

office@nbmanagement.com
nbmanagement.com
imdb.com/company/co0081275

Does not accept any unsolicited material. Project types include TV and feature films. Genres include thriller.

Nigel Britten
Producer
imdb.com/name/nm1528881

NIGHT AND DAY PICTURES
Production company

527 W. 7th St.
Suite 402
Los Angeles, CA 90036
323-930-2212

info@nightanddaypictures.com
nightanddaypictures.com
imdb.com/company/co0253348
twitter.com/different_duck

Accepts query letters from unproduced, unrepresented writers via email. Project types include feature films.

Rachel Berk
Creative Executive
imdb.com/company/co0157684
linkedin.com/pub/rachel-berk/29/2a9/812

Michael Roiff
President
michael@nightanddaypictures.com
imdb.com/name/nm1988698

NIGHTFILM PRODS.
Production company

817 6th St
Apt. G
Santa Monica, CA 90403
310-699-4451 (phone)
310-699-4451 (fax)

nightfilm@yahoo.com
imdb.com/company/co0285237

Does not accept any unsolicited material.

NIGHT FOX ENTERTAINMENT
Production company

8484 Wilshire Blvd, Suite 515, Beverly Hills, CA, United States, 90211
323-596-0200

info@nightfoxent.com
imdb.com/company/co0364244

Does not accept any unsolicited material.

Timothy L. Christian
Executive
imdb.com/name/nm4005199

NIKKATSU
Production company and distributor

3-28-12 Hongo
Bunkyo-ku
Tokyo 113-0033
Japan
+81 3 56 89 10 14 (phone)
+81 3 56 89 10 44 (fax)

international@nikkatsu.co.jp
nikkatsu.com
imdb.com/company/co0022792
facebook.com/nikkatsumovie
twitter.com/nikkatsu100

Does not accept any unsolicited material. Project types include feature films, short films, and TV. Genres include action.

Yûji Ishida
Producer
imdb.com/name/nm1097451

NINETY-SEVEN FILM PRODUCTION & DISTRIBUTION
Distributor

1775 Broadway
Ste 417
New York, NY 10019
212-265-8787 (phone)
212-265-8873 (fax)

contact@97filmproduction.com
97filmproduction.com
imdb.com/company/co0240071

Does not accept any unsolicited material.

NINJAS RUNNIN' WILD PRODUCTIONS
Production company

7024 Melrose Ave, Suite 420
Los Angeles, CA 90038
323-937-6100

focusfeatures.com/that_awkward_moment/
    castncrew?member=ninjas_runnin__wild
imdb.com/company/co0308755
facebook.com/FocusFeatures

facebook.com/pages/Ninjas-Running-Wild/
129825350400624
twitter.com/FocusFeatures

Accepts scripts from produced or represented writers.
Project types include feature films.

Zac Effron
imdb.com/name/nm1374980

Jason Barrett
Producer
imdb.com/name/nm2249074

NIPPON ANIMATION CO. LTD.
Production company and distributor

7-10-11 Ginza, Chuo-ku
Tokyo 104-0061
Japan

mail@nippon-animation.co.jp
imdb.com/company/co0008236

Does not accept any unsolicited material. Project types
include TV. Genres include animation, fantasy, and
drama.

NIRVANA MOTION PICTURES
Sales agent

4140 Legacy Dr
#330-205
Plano , TX 75024
505-615-0494

info@nirvanaentertainment.com
nirvanaentertainment.com
imdb.com/company/co0168074

Does not accept any unsolicited material. Project types
include TV. Genres include drama.

Sushma Morthania
Producer
imdb.com/name/nm2585785

NISHIMURA MOTION PICTURE MODEL MAKERS GROUP
Production company and distributor

2-2-11-102
Moto Asakusa

Taito, Tokyo 111-0041
Japan
03-5828-5584

info@nishi-eizo.com
nishi-eizo.com
imdb.com/company/co0211511

Does not accept any unsolicited material. Project types
include TV. Genres include action and drama.

Yoshihiro Nishimura
President
imdb.com/name/nm1883583

NITROPLUS
Production company and distributor

1-4-4-8F
Yanagibashi
Taito, Tokyo 111-0052
Japan

info@nitroplus.co.jp
nitroplus.co.jp
imdb.com/company/co0228822
facebook.com/nitroplus
twitter.com/nitroplus_staff

Does not accept any unsolicited material. Project types
include TV and feature films. Genres include science
fiction and animation.

Taoru Deji
Executive
imdb.com/name/nm3756985

NO BUDGET MOVIE COMPANY
Production company and distributor

4378 Sea Rock Ct
Apopka, FL 32712
609-709-1709

artwsmithjr@earthlink.net
nobudgetmovieco.com
imdb.com/company/co0175511

Does not accept any unsolicited material. Project types
include TV, feature films, and short films. Genres
include horror, action, fantasy, comedy, reality, drama,
science fiction, and family. Established in 2006.

NOC FILMS

Production company and distributor

817 W Howard Ln
Building B, Suite 503
Austin, TX 78753
512-497-4938

nocfilms@gmail.com
imdb.com/company/co0142470

Does not accept any unsolicited material. Project types include feature films and short films. Genres include comedy, action, drama, and crime. Established in 2004.

NO DEALS WITH THE DEVIL FILMWORKS

Production company, distributor, and sales agent

191 N Ave
Suite 163
Dunellen, NJ 08812
917-587-7756 (phone)
732-548-7956 (fax)

info@nodealswiththedevil.com
imdb.com/company/co0197086

Does not accept any unsolicited material. Project types include TV and feature films. Genres include crime, comedy, and documentary.

Adrian Washington
Producer
imdb.com/name/nm1967657

NO KILL SOCIETY

Production company

nokillsociety.com

Does not accept any unsolicited material. Project types include feature films. Genres include thriller, crime, and detective. Established in 2014.

Wes Shafer
Director
cuwes@icloud.com

NO MORE TALK PRODUCTIONS

Production company and distributor

P.O. Box 1727
Seffner, FL 33583

production@nomoretalk.com
imdb.com/company/co0249627

Does not accept any unsolicited material. Genres include comedy.

NORTH BY NORTHWEST ENTERTAINMENT

Production company and distributor

903 W Broadway
Spokane, WA 99201
509-324-2949 (phone)
509-324-2959 (fax)

100 Andover Park West
Suite 150-121
Tukwila, WA 98188
206-293-8860 (phone)
206-293-8860 (fax)

601 W. Board St
Boise, ID 83702
208-345-7870 (phone)
208-345-7999 (fax)

contact@nxnw.net
nxnw.net
imdb.com/company/co0022821

Does not accept any unsolicited material. Project types include feature films. Genres include thriller.

Dave Tanner
CEO/Partner
509-252-2570
dtanner@nxnw.net

NORTH END PICTURES

Production company and distributor

600 Union Ave
Suite 100
Elizabeth, NJ 07208
212-275-7898

northendpictures@aol.com
imdb.com/company/co0205833

Does not accept any unsolicited material. Project types include TV and feature films. Genres include comedy, thriller, and drama.

NORTHLAND PRODUCTIONS
Production company

1006 Haines Ave
Dallas, TX 75208
301-403-5288 (phone)
972-672-8942 (fax)

11272 Russwood Circle
Dallas TX 75229
972-672-8942

info@northlandproductions.com
northlandproductions.com
imdb.com/company/co0469443
facebook.com/northlandproductionsvideo

Does not accept any unsolicited material. Genres include thriller.

NOVA PICTURES
Production company

6496 Ivarene Ave.
Los Angeles, CA 90068
323-462-5502 (phone)
323-463-8903 (fax)

info@novapictures.com (script submissions)
pbarnett@novapictures.com (general)
novapictures.com
imdb.com/company/co0094813

Accepts query letters from unproduced, unrepresented writers via email. Project types include feature films.

Peter Barnett
Executive Producer
imdb.com/name/nm0055963

NOW & THEN PRODUCTIONS
Production company

1023 1/2 Abbot Kinney Blvd.
Venice, CA 90291
310-260-7073 (phone)
310-260-7060 (fax)

nowandthenproductions.com

imdb.com/company/co0202735
facebook.com/Now-and-Then-
    Productions-179584492087943

Does not accept any unsolicited material. Project types include feature films. Genres include drama.

David Duchovny
Principal, Producer, Actor
imdb.com/name/nm0000141
facebook.com/DavidDuchovnyOfficial
twitter.com/davidduchovny

Susanna Jolly
Executive Vice President
imdb.com/name/nm3104740

Tea Leoni
Principal, Producer, Actor
imdb.com/name/nm0000495
facebook.com/TeaLeoni
twitter.com/TheTeaLeoni

Eric Knight
Development
imdb.com/name/nm0460896
linkedin.com/in/theericknight

NUBIA FILMWORKS LLC
Production company

1516 K St S.E, Suite #303
Washington, DC 20003
202-547-1591

info@nubiafilmworks.com
nubiafilmworks.com
imdb.com/company/co0213763
facebook.com/NocturnalAgony
twitter.com/nubiafilmllc

Accepts query letters from unproduced, unrepresented writers. Project types include feature films and TV. Genres include drama.

Shuaib Mitchell
President
imdb.com/name/nm2712648
linkedin.com/pub/shuaib-mitchell/7/2b6/72b
facebook.com/shuaib.mitchellnubiafilmworks

Tara Hayman
Creative Executive
tarah@nubiafilmworks.com

Mary Colbert
Creative Executive
240-432-6265
maryj@nubiafilmworks.com

Calvin "C-Note" Jackson
Development Executive
calvinj@nubiafilmworks.com

NU IMAGE FILMS
Production company

6423 Wilshire Blvd
Los Angeles, CA 90048
310-388-6900 (phone)
310-388-6901 (fax)

info@millenniumfilms.com
millenniumfilms.com
imdb.com/company/co0024720
facebook.com/OfficialMillenniumfilms
twitter.com/MillenniumFilms

Does not accept any unsolicited material. Project types include feature films. Genres include comedy, science fiction, drama, and action.

Christine Crow
Director of Development
310-388-6900
imdb.com/name/nm4579268

John Thompson
Head of Development
310-388-6900
imdb.com/name/nm0860315

Mark Gill
President
310-388-6900
imdb.com/name/nm1247584

Boaz Davidson
310-388-6900
imdb.com/name/nm0203246

NUMBER 9 FILMS
Production company and distributor

Linton House
24 Wells St, 1st Fl
London W1T 3PH
UK
+44207-323-4060 (phone)
+44207-323-0456 (fax)

info@number9films.co.uk
number9films.co.uk
imdb.com/company/co0119108

Does not accept any unsolicited material. Project types include feature films, short films, and TV. Genres include thriller.

NUYORICAN PRODUCTIONS
Production company

1100 Glendon Ave, Suite 920
Los Angeles, CA 90024
310-943-6600 (phone)
310-943-6609 (fax)

imdb.com/company/co0021149

Does not accept any unsolicited material. Project types include commercials, feature films, and TV. Genres include action, reality, comedy, non-fiction, and drama.

Tiana Rios
Creative Executive
imdb.com/name/nm1018804

Jennifer Lopez
imdb.com/name/nm0000182

O2 FILMES

Rua Baumann, 930
Vila Leopoldina
São Paulo, SP 05318-000
Brazil
+55 1138 39 94 00 (phone)
+55 11 38 32 48 11 (fax)

O2 FILMES / RIO DE JANEIRO
Rua Pereira da Silva, 602
Laranjeiras
22221-140 Rio De Janeiro - RJ
Brasil
+55 21 31 72 99 00

faleconosco@o2filmes.com
o2filmes.com.br
imdb.com/company/co006939
facebook.com/o2filmes
twitter.com/o2filmes

Does not accept any unsolicited material. Project types include feature films. Genres include documentary and drama.

Paulo Morelli
imdb.com/name/nm0603758
linkedin.com/pub/paulo-o2-filmes/22/118/41a
twitter.com/paulomorelli

OAKDALE PICTURES
Production company

15450 Kivett Ln
Reno, NV 89521
775-225-4447 (phone)
775-852-6259 (fax)

info@oakdalepictures.us
imdb.com/company/co0303853
facebook.com/Oakdale-Pictures-301094076896

Does not accept any unsolicited material. Project types include feature films. Genres include drama.

OCCUPANT FILMS
Production company

5225 Wilshire Blvd., Suite 600
Los Angeles , CA 90036
323-934-9106 (phone)
323-937-0550 (fax)

joe@occupantfilms.com
occupantfilms.com

Does not accept any unsolicited material. Project types include feature films. Genres include comedy, family, and horror.

OCEAN PICTURES
Production company

9830 Wilshire Blvd.
Beverly Hills, CA 90212

imdb.com/company/co0035477

Does not accept any unsolicited material. Project types include feature films.

OCEAN PRODUCTIONS
Production company

PO Box 470729
Celebration, FL 34747
407-556-7401

info@oceanproductionsfl.com
oceanproductionsfl.com
imdb.com/company/co0365554

Does not accept any unsolicited material. Genres include horror.

OCEAN SKY ENTERTAINMENT
Production company

12021 Wilshire Blvd., Suite 117
Los Angeles, CA 90025
310-472-7096

la@oceanskyentertainment.com
oceanskyentertainment.com
imdb.com/company/co0249300
facebook.com/pages/Ocean-Sky-Entertainment/
    360929067560

Does not accept any unsolicited material. Project types include feature films. Genres include drama and romance.

ODDLOT ENTERTAINMENT

2141 N. Southport Ave.
Chicago, IL 60614

9601 Jefferson Blvd, Suite A
Culver City, CA 90232
310-652-0999 (phone)
310-652-0718 (fax)

info@oddlotent.com
oddlotent.com
imdb.com/company/co0113140
facebook.com/oddlotent

Does not accept any unsolicited material. Project types include feature films. Genres include drama.

Gigi Pritzker
CEO
imdb.com/name/nm0698133

Stacy Keppler
Director of Development
imdb.com/name/nm4139143

ODENKIRK PROVISSIERO ENTERTAINMENT
Production company

1936 N Bronson Ave
Los Angeles, CA 90068
323-785-7700 (phone)
323-785-7701 (fax)

odenkirkprovissiero@gmail.com
odenkirk-provissiero.com
imdb.com/company/co0113457

Does not accept any unsolicited material. Project types include TV. Genres include comedy.

ODESSA ENTERTAINMENT
Distributor

3-9-18-4F
Ginza
Chuo, Tokyo 104-0061
Japan
03-5148-6085 (phone)
03-5148-6086 (fax)

info@odessa-e.co.jp
odessa-e.co.jp
imdb.com/company/co0341880
facebook.com/BLACKJACK.BlurayBOX

Does not accept any unsolicited material. Project types include TV. Genres include romance, comedy, and drama.

ODNA ENTERTAINMENT
Production company

12233 W. Olympic Blvd. Ste. 260
Los Angeles, CA 90064
310-777-3555

imdb.com/company/co0248625

Does not accept any unsolicited material. Project types include feature films. Genres include drama, action, and thriller.

ODYSSEY PICTURES CORPORATION
Distributor

2321 Coit Rd, Suite E, Plano, TX, United States, 75075
972-867-0055 (phone)
972-867-0034 (fax)

info@odysseypix.com
odysseypix.com
imdb.com/company/co0028533

Does not accept any unsolicited material. Project types include TV and feature films. Genres include family and drama.

O ENTERTAINMENT
Production company

31878 Camino Capistrano, Suite 101
San Juan Capistrano, CA 92675
949-443-3222 (phone)
949-443-3223 (fax)

imdb.com/company/co0009845

Does not accept any unsolicited material. Project types include feature films and TV. Genres include comedy.

OFFICE 27
Distributor

7-5-11-509
Roppongi
Minato, Tokyo 106-0032
Japan
03-6804-5404 (phone)
03-6804-5408 (fax)

info@office27.net
imdb.com/company/co0405339

Does not accept any unsolicited material. Project types include TV and feature films. Genres include romance.

Yô Nakamura
President (Manager)
imdb.com/name/nm5429819

OFFICE HARA CO.
Production company

3-18-11-306
Kamiuma
Setagaya, Tokyo 154-0011
Japan
03-5433-3311 (phone)
03-5433-3312 (fax)

hara001@pg7.so-net.ne.jp
officehara-j.com
imdb.com/company/co0263954

Does not accept any unsolicited material. Project types include TV. Genres include horror and comedy.

Nobuko Fukuda
President (Executive)
imdb.com/name/nm4861034

OFFICE REGULUS
Production company

1-22-16-102
Wakaba
Shinjuku, Tokyo 160-0011
Japan
03-3359-0288 (phone)
03-3359-0289 (fax)

toiawase@o-regulus.co.jp
o-regulus.co.jp
imdb.com/company/co0231949

Does not accept any unsolicited material. Project types include feature films. Genres include drama.

Hiroaki Yotsumoto
President (Producer)
imdb.com/name/nm4761817

OFFICE SHIROUS
Production company and distributor

3F, 5-1-38 Akasaka
Minato-Ku
Tokyo 107-0052
Japan
81 3-3585-6807 (phone)
81 3-3585-6859 (fax)

shirous@dion.ne.jp

imdb.com/company/co0056951

Does not accept any unsolicited material. Project types include TV, feature films, and short films. Genres include action.

Shiro Sasaki
Producer
imdb.com/name/nm0765822

OFFSPRING ENTERTAINMENT
Production company

8755 Colgate Ave
Los Angeles, CA 90048
310-247-0019 (phone)
310-550-6908 (fax)

imdb.com/company/co0163665
facebook.com/pages/Offspring-Entertainment

Does not accept any unsolicited material. Project types include feature films. Genres include drama, comedy, and family.

Adam Shankman
Executive
imdb.com/name/nm0788202

Jennifer Gibgot
Producer
imdb.com/name/nm0316774
linkedin.com/pub/jennifer-gibgot/73/184/435

OFF THE KERB PRODUCTIONS
Production company

Hammer House, 3rd Fl
113-117 Wardour St
London W1F 0UN
UK
+44 020-7437 0607 (phone)
+44 020-7437 0647 (fax)

westend@offthekerb.co.uk
offthekerb.co.uk
imdb.com/company/co0237511
facebook.com/offthekerb
twitter.com/offthekerb

Does not accept any unsolicited material. Project types include short films. Genres include comedy.

Lee Evans
Actor
imdb.com/name/nm0262968

OFRENDA
Production company

3467 N. Knoll Dr
Los Angeles, CA 90068
323-851-6145

donna@ofrenda.com
ofrenda.com
imdb.com/company/co0100061

Does not accept any unsolicited material. Project types
include feature films. Genres include drama.

OGURA JIMUSYO CO.
Production company

4-19-6 Ebisu
Shibuya-Ku
Tokyo 150-0013
Japan
+81-(0)3-5424-8661 (phone)
+81-(0)3-5424-8662 (fax)

info@ogurajimusyo.jp
ogurajimusyo.jp
imdb.com/company/co0076576

Does not accept any unsolicited material. Project types
include feature films and TV. Genres include horror.

Satoru Ogura
Producer
imdb.com/name/nm0644840

OHARA BROS. CO.
Production company

2-15-14-307
Sangenjaya
Setagaya, Tokyo 154-0024
Japan
03-6661-0667 (phone)
03-6661-0667 (fax)

info@oharabros.com
oharabros.com
imdb.com/company/co0283799

Does not accept any unsolicited material. Project types
include TV and feature films. Genres include horror
and action.

Gô Ohara
President (Producer)
imdb.com/name/nm1504996

OH SEVEN PRODUCTIONS
Production company

1717 Knoll Court
Dallas, TX 75029
469-525-2511

imdb.com/company/co0348370

Does not accept any unsolicited material. Genres
include action and drama.

OHTA PRO
Production company

3-1-2F
Samoncho
Shinjuku, Tokyo 160-0017
Japan
03-3359-6266

info@ohtapro.co.jp
imdb.com/company/co0191365

Does not accept any unsolicited material. Project types
include TV. Genres include comedy.

Tsutomu Isono
Executive
imdb.com/name/nm2431610

OIZUMI STUDIOS
Production company

2-10-5
Higashi-Oizumi
Nerima, Tokyo 178-8567
Japan
03-3978-3111

info@anime-bb.com
toei-anim.co.jp
imdb.com/company/co0192019

Does not accept any unsolicited material. Project types include TV. Genres include drama.

Hiroshi Takahashi
CEO
imdb.com/name/nm2438124

OLD CHARLIE PRODUCTIONS
Production company

10100 Santa Monica Blvd. Suite 1300
Los Angeles, CA 90067

listings.findthecompany.com/l/21507101/Old-
    Charlie-Productions-Inc-in-Los-Angeles-CA

Does not accept any unsolicited material. Project types include TV. Genres include comedy.

OLD CITY ENTERTAINMENT
Production company and distributor

453 S. Spring St
Suite 439
Los Angeles, CA 90013
213-465-4822

wjsaunders@oldcityentertainment.com
williamjsaunders.com
imdb.com/company/co0271474

Does not accept any unsolicited material. Project types include short films, feature films, commercials, and TV.

William Saunders
Director
wjsaunders@oldcityentertainment.com
linkedin.com/pub/william-saunders/50/703/a32

OLIVE BRIDGE ENTERTAINMENT
Production company

10202 W Washington Blvd
Culver City, CA 90232
310-244-1269

olivebridge.com
imdb.com/company/co0219609

Does not accept any unsolicited material. Project types include TV and feature films. Genres include family,

romance, action, period, drama, and comedy. Established in 2003.

Alicia Emmrich
imdb.com/name/nm1445355

Will Gluck
imdb.com/name/nm0323239

Richard Schwartz
imdb.com/name/nm1108160
linkedin.com/pub/dir/Richard/Schwartz

Jodi Hildebrand
imdb.com/name/nm1637492

OLIVE RANCH ROAD PRODUCTIONS
Production company

1614 Montcalm St
Orlando, FL 32806
407-341-080

picturekevin@gmail.com
oliveranchroadproductions.com
imdb.com/company/co0477010
facebook.com/OLIVE-RANCH-ROAD-
    Productions-466670690125944/videos

Does not accept any unsolicited material. Project types include short films. Genres include crime and drama.

OLLIN STUDIO
Production company and studio

1041 N Formosa Ave Fairbanks Building, suite 1
West Hollywood CA 90046
323-850-3553

Porfirio Diaz 39, Col. Noche Buena, Distrito Federal, Mexico, 03720
011-555-5638686

contacto@ollinstudio.com
ollinstudio.com
imdb.com/company/co0156605

Does not accept any unsolicited material. Project types include feature films, TV, and short films. Genres include family, action, romance, thriller, and drama.

Robin D'Arcy
Executive (Producer)
imdb.com/name/nm0006866

OLMOS PRODUCTIONS INC.

Production company

500 S Buena Vista St
Old Animation Building, Suite 1G
Burbank, CA 91521
818-560-8651 (phone)
818-560-8655 (fax)

olmosonline@yahoo.com
edwardjamesolmos.com/fvcs
imdb.com/company/co0000821
facebook.com/people/Edward-James-Olmos/
    1777260806
twitter.com/edwardjolmos

Does not accept any unsolicited material. Project types
include commercials, feature films, and TV. Genres
include non-fiction, reality, drama, family, and
comedy. Established in 1980.

Edward Olmos

President
edwardjamesolmos.com
imdb.com/name/nm0001579
facebook.com/EdwardJOlmos

OLYMPUS PICTURES

Production company

12424 Whilshire Blvd.
Suite 1120
Los Angeles, CA 90025
310-452-3335 (phone)
310-452-0108 (fax)

getinfo@olympuspics.com
olympuspics.com
imdb.com/company/co0238585

Does not accept any unsolicited material. Project types
include feature films. Established in 2007.

Amanda Beckner

Creative Executive
rrdecter@olympuspics.com
linkedin.com/pub/amanda-beckner/43/a2a/924

Leslie Urdang

imdb.com/name/nm0881811

O'MALLEY PRODUCTIONS

Production company

20335 Ventura Blvd., #416
Woodland Hills, CA 91364
818-884-7012 (phone)
818-884-7031 (fax)

info@omalleyproductions.com
omalleyproductions.com
imdb.com/company/co0287576
facebook.com/pages/OMalley-Productions/
    106897616017333

Does not accept any unsolicited material. Project types
include TV.

OMANTRA FILMS

Production company and distributor

9415 Culver Blvd.
Culver City, CA 90232
310-558-0606 (fax)

raj@omantrafilms.com
omantrafilms.com
imdb.com/company/co0388642
facebook.com/omantraraj
twitter.com/omantrafilms

Does not accept any unsolicited material. Project types
include feature films. Genres include drama, romance,
and family.

OMBRA FILMS

Production company

12444 Ventura Blvd, Suite 103
Studio City, CA 91604
818-509-0552

info@ombrafilms.com
imdb.com/company/co0320014
facebook.com/ombrafilms

Accepts query letters from unproduced, unrepresented
writers via email. Project types include TV and feature
films. Genres include thriller, horror, and fantasy.
Established in 2011.

Jaume Collet-Serra

Producer
imdb.com/name/nm1429471

Pablo Larcuen
Producer
imdb.com/name/nm3631130

Juan Sola
Producer
imdb.com/name/nm4928159

OMEGA THEATRE PRODUCTIONS
Production company

3918 Alhambra Dr W
Jacksonville, FL 32207
904-398-5727

imdb.com/company/co0190392
linkedin.com/company/omega-theatre-productions-llc

Does not accept any unsolicited material. Project types include feature films. Genres include non-fiction. Established in 2006.

OMGACT ENTERTAINMENT
Distributor and sales agent

Tokyo,
Japan
81-3-6459-2333 (phone)
81-3-6459-2333 (fax)

contact@omgact.com
omgact.com
imdb.com/company/co0392373

Does not accept any unsolicited material. Project types include feature films. Genres include drama, comedy, and horror.

Shinji Nishimura
Producer
imdb.com/name/nm5337838

O.N.C. ENTERTAINMENT INC
Production company

11150 Santa Monica Blvd, Suite 450
Los Angeles, CA 90025
310-477-0670 (phone)
310-477-7710 (fax)

imdb.com/company/co0176401

Does not accept any unsolicited material. Project types include feature films. Genres include thriller, family, comedy, crime, romance, and action.

Michael Nathanson
President
michaelnathanson@oncentertainment.com
imdb.com/name/nm0622296
linkedin.com/pub/michael-nathanson/6/20/a15
Assistant: Robyn Altman

ONE EYED FILMS
Production company, distributor, and sales agent

11 Ellerslie Rd
London W12 7BN
UK
+44 20 8740 1491

info@oneeyedfilms.com
oneeyedfilms.com
imdb.com/company/co0172952

Does not accept any unsolicited material. Project types include TV. Genres include horror, drama, and comedy.

Betina Goldman
Producer
imdb.com/name/nm2757038

ONEIDA INDIAN NATION
Production company

2037 Dream Catcher Plaza
Oneida, NY 13421
315-829-8900

info@oneida-nation.org
oneidaindiannation.com

Does not accept any unsolicited material. Project types include feature films. Genres include drama.

ONE RACE FILMS
Production company

9100 Wilshire Blvd
East Tower, Suite 535
Beverly Hills, CA 90212
310-401-6880 (phone)
310-401-6890 (fax)

info@oneracefilms.com
oneracefilms.com
imdb.com/company/co0313548
facebook.com/One-Race-Films-142737939251519

Accepts query letters from unproduced, unrepresented writers via email. Project types include feature films and TV. Genres include action, crime, drama, thriller, and science fiction. Established in 1995.

Thyrale Thai

thyrale@oneracefilms.com
imdb.com/name/nm1394166
linkedin.com/pub/thyrale-thai/9/1b6/3a5

Samantha Vincent

samantha@oneracefilms.com
imdb.com/name/nm2176972
linkedin.com/pub/samantha-vincent/6/4b0/7b0

Vin Diesel

imdb.com/name/nm0004874

ONEZERO FILMS

Production company

8285 W Sunset Blvd, #2
West Hollywood, CA 90046
323-656-5852

info@onezerofilms.com
imdb.com/company/co0507032
twitter.com/onezerofilms

Does not accept any unsolicited material. Project types include feature films. Genres include drama.

ON-RIDE ENTERTAINMENT

Production company and distributor

7 Mallards Crest Court
Sicklerville, NJ 08081
856-318-9576 (phone)
856-318-9576 (fax)

onrideent.com
imdb.com/company/co0397244

Does not accept any unsolicited material. Project types include TV. Genres include thriller.

ON THE SCENE PRODUCTIONS

Production company

5900 Wilshire Blvd
14th floor
Los Angeles , CA 90036
323-930-1030 (phone)
323-930-1840 (fax)

publicists@onthescene.com
onthescene.com
imdb.com/company/co0166544

Does not accept any unsolicited material. Genres include documentary.

ON TRACK MOTION PICTURES

Production company

2618 Texas Ave
Houston, TX 77003

imdb.com/company/co0495395

Does not accept any unsolicited material. Project types include short films. Genres include thriller.

ONWARD AND SIDEWAYS PRODUCTIONS

Production company and distributor

100 Manhattan Ave
Union City, NJ 07087
347-684-1927

Davidwenzelnyc@aol.com
onwardandsidewaysmedia.yolasite.com
imdb.com/company/co0313048
twitter.com/intenttweet

Does not accept any unsolicited material. Genres include drama.

OOPS DOUGHNUTS PRODUCTIONS

Production company

6030 Wilshire Blvd.
Suite 101
Los Angeles, CA 90036
323-936-9811 (phone)
818-560-6185 (fax)

blog.s206684.gridserver.com
imdb.com/company/co0248742
facebook.com/OopsDoughnuts

Accepts query letters from unproduced, unrepresented writers. Project types include commercials, TV, and feature films.

Betsy Sullenger
Producer
imdb.com/name/nm0998095

Andy Fickman
imdb.com/name/nm0275698
Assistant: Whitney Engstrom

OOZE TALENT & LITERARY AGENCY
Production company

London, England
UK
+44 (0203-189-1893

info@oozetalent.com
oozetalent.com
imdb.com/company/co0443649
twitter.com/oozetalent

Does not accept any unsolicited material. Project types include commercials.

Shereen Boucher
Producer
imdb.com/name/nm4579159

OPEN CITY FILMS
Production company

122 Hudson St.
5th Floor
New York, NY 10013
212-255-0500 (phone)
212-255-0455 (fax)

oc@opencityfilms.com
imdb.com/company/co0091401
twitter.com/opencityfilms

Accepts query letters from unproduced, unrepresented writers via email. Project types include feature films and TV. Genres include reality and non-fiction.

Joana Vicente
linkedin.com/pub/jason-kliot/49/a39/982

Jason Kilot
imdb.com/name/nm0459852

OPENING NIGHT PRODUCTIONS
Production company

939 8th Ave, Suite #400
New York, NY 10019
212-757-8155 (phone)
212-757-8156 (fax)

info@openingnightproductions.com
openingnightproductions.com
imdb.com/company/co0238196

Does not accept any unsolicited material. Project types include feature films. Genres include drama and science fiction.

OPEN JAR FILMS
Production company

201 Brookside Ave
Lawrence Harbor, NJ 08879
732-421-5906

openjarfilms@hotmail.com
openjarfilms.com
imdb.com/company/co0462637
linkedin.com/in/djreale
facebook.com/openjarfilms
twitter.com/openjarfilms

Does not accept any unsolicited material. Project types include TV. Genres include fantasy, thriller, and action.

OPEN ROAD FILMS
Production company

12301 Wilshire Blvd.
Suite 600
Los Angeles, CA 90025
310-696-7575

openroadfilms.com
imdb.com/company/co0178575
facebook.com/OpenRoadFilms
twitter.com/OpenRoadFilms

Does not accept any unsolicited material. Project types include feature films, TV, and short films. Genres include action, documentary, drama, and crime. Established in 2002.

Keri Safran
VP Media
imdb.com/name/nm1518819

OPEN SESAME COMPANY
Distributor

1- 14 - 6 - 3 F Ginza Chuo-ku
Tokyo 104-0061
Japan
+81 3 5159 0871 (phone)
+81 3 3561 6262 (fax)

info@synergy-r.jp
imdb.com/company/co0238692

Does not accept any unsolicited material. Project types include TV. Genres include documentary.

Ritsuko Abe
Co-President (Executive)
imdb.com/name/nm3032009

OPTICAL ENTERTAINMENT COMPANY
Production company

3291 Eastman Ave
Palm Bay, FL 32905

imdb.com/company/co0389010

Does not accept any unsolicited material. Project types include short films.

ORBIT FILMS
Production company

137 N Larchmont Blvd. Suite 459
Los Angeles, CA 90004
323-837-5009 (phone)
323-464-4577 (fax)

info@orbit-films.com
orbit-films.com
imdb.com/company/co0015570

Does not accept any unsolicited material. Project types include feature films. Genres include thriller and drama.

ORBIT PICTURES
Production company

11755 Wilshire Blvd. Suite 2400
Los Angeles, CA 90025
310-914-4999 (phone)
310-914-4996 (fax)

phillip@orbitpics.com
orbitpics.com
imdb.com/company/co0102391

Does not accept any unsolicited material. Project types include feature films.

OREGON PUBLIC BROADCASTING
Production company and distributor

7140 SW Macadam Ave, Portland, OR, United States, 97219
503-244-9900

opb.org
imdb.com/company/co0074280

Does not accept any unsolicited material. Project types include TV and feature films. Genres include family, reality, thriller, and drama.

ORIAHSPHERE ENTERTAINMENT
Production company

300 Ava Rd
Toronto, ON M6C 1X4
Canada

info@oriahsphere.com
oriahsphere.com
imdb.com/company/co0349177
twitter.com/OriahEnt

Does not accept any unsolicited material. Genres include comedy, thriller, and action.

Alex Lebovici
Producer
imdb.com/name/nm3078006

ORIGINAL FILM
Production company

5930 W Jefferson Blvd
Los Angeles, CA 90016
310-445-9000 (phone)
310-575-6990 (fax)

bruce@originalfilm.com
originalfilm.com
imdb.com/company/co0011134
linkedin.com/company/original-film
facebook.com/OriginalFilm
twitter.com/originalfilmla

Does not accept any unsolicited material. Project types include TV and feature films. Genres include action, thriller, comedy, crime, and drama. Established in 1994.

Joe Piccirillo
Executive Producer
joe@originalfilm.com
imdb.com/name/nm6311600
linkedin.com/pub/joseph-piccirillo/6/2a2/7a5

Bruce Mellon
Executive Producer
bruce@originalfilm.com
imdb.com/name/nm0578089
linkedin.com/pub/bruce-mellon/1/3a2/730

ORIGINAL MEDIA

345 Hudson St
New York, NY 10014
646-780-4888 (phone)
212-683-3162 (fax)

175 Varick St, 7th Floor
New York, NY 10014
212-683-3086

originalmedia.com
imdb.com/company/co0132156
facebook.com/pages/Original-Media/
    119848194726628
twitter.com/OriginalMediaTV

Accepts scripts from unproduced, unrepresented writers. Project types include feature films and TV. Genres include family, drama, romance, thriller, and comedy.

Michael Saffran
COO
linkedin.com/pub/michael-saffran/27/242/5b9

Patrick Moses
SVP Current Series and Development
linkedin.com/pub/dir/patrick/moses

Charlie Corwin
Co Creator
imdb.com/name/nm1231965

Chelsey Trowbridge
imdb.com/name/nm2399791

Colleen Ocean Hall
SVP Unscripted Development
imdb.com/name/nm5066841
linkedin.com/pub/dir/Colleen/Hall

Jessica Matthews
VP Scripted Development
linkedin.com/pub/jessica-matthews/7b/6b8/b24

ORIGIN PICTURES
Production company

23 Denmark St
3rd Fl
London WC2H 8NH
UK
+44 20 7836 6818

info@originpictures.co.uk
originpictures.co.uk
imdb.com/company/co0237790

Does not accept any unsolicited material. Project types include TV. Genres include drama.

ORION ENTERTAINMENT
Production company

10397 W. Centennial Rd
Littleton, CO 80127
720-891-4835

orionentertainment.com
imdb.com/company/co0461823
facebook.com/pages/Orion-Entertainment/
    549250715115896
twitter.com/orionmultimedia

Does not accept any unsolicited material. Project types include TV.

ORLANDO ENTERTAINMENT
Production company

4

307 W. 6th St., Ste. 207
Royal Oak, MI 48067
310-403-2003 (phone)
313-255-1020 (fax)

orlandoent@sbcglobal.net
imdb.com/company/co0150015

Does not accept any unsolicited material. Project types include TV and feature films. Genres include horror.

ORPHANAGE ANIMATION STUDIOS
Production company

6725 Sunset Blvd., Suite 220
Los Angeles, CA 90028
323-469-6700

imdb.com/company/co0315050

Does not accept any unsolicited material. Project types include feature films. Genres include animation.

ORRICHIO FILMS
Production company, distributor, and sales agent

431 Church Rd
Milford, NJ 08848
908-246-5364

johnnyo@ptd.net
orrichio.com
imdb.com/company/co0210435
facebook.com/ParanormalCaptivityMovie
twitter.com/johnorrichio

Does not accept any unsolicited material. Project types include TV. Genres include horror and thriller.

OSCILLOSCOPE PICTURES
Production company

511 Canal St Suite 5E
New York City, NY 10013
212-219-4029 (phone)
212-219-9538 (fax)

info@oscilloscope.net
oscilloscope.net
imdb.com/company/co0230412
facebook.com/oscopelabs
twitter.com/oscopelabs

Does not accept any unsolicited material. Project types include feature films. Genres include drama and romance.

Dan Berger
imdb.com/name/nm3088964
linkedin.com/pub/dan-berger/8/83B/93A

Tom Sladek
linkedin.com/pub/tom-sladek/7/388/4a9

Amanda Lebow
imdb.com/name/nm4144904

David Laub
imdb.com/name/nm3000864

OSPREY MOVIE
Production company

10375 Richmond Ave
Suite 1515
Houston, TX 77042
713-398-3780 (phone)
713-364-4870 (fax)

syed@ospreythemovie.com
ospreythemovie.com
imdb.com/company/co0450408

Does not accept any unsolicited material. Project types include feature films. Genres include drama, thriller, and action. Established in 2016.

OSTROW AND COMPANY PRODUCER'S REPRESENTATIVES
Production company, distributor, and sales agent

468 N Camden Dr
3rd Fl
Beverly Hills, CA 90210
310-276-5007

info@ostrowandcompany.com
imdb.com/company/co0304071
facebook.com/Ostrow-and-
    Company-146594952085919

Does not accept any unsolicited material.

O'TAYE PRODUCTIONS
Production company

12001 Ventura Place
Suite 340
Studio City, CA 91604
818-232-8580 (phone)
818-232-8108 (fax)

imdb.com/company/co0201867

Accepts query letters from unproduced, unrepresented writers. Project types include TV.

Jennifer Bozell
Head of Development
linkedin.com/pub/jennifer-bozell/5/74b/876

Taye Diggs
imdb.com/name/nm0004875

OUAT MEDIA
Distributor and sales agent

2844 Dundas St West
Toronto, ON M6P 1Y7
Canada
416-979-7380 (phone)
416-492-9539 (fax)

info@ouatmedia.com
ouatmedia.com
imdb.com/company/co0195375
facebook.com/ouatmedia
twitter.com/ouatmedia

Does not accept any unsolicited material. Project types include short films. Genres include reality and comedy.

Benjamin Feuer
Director
imdb.com/name/nm1984776

OUTERBANK ENTERTAINMENT
Production company

4000 Warner Blvd.
Burbank, CA 91522
818-954-3281 (phone)
818-977-9990 (fax)

imdb.com/company/co0048032

Accepts query letters from unproduced, unrepresented writers via email. Project types include feature films and TV.

Kevin Williamson
President
310-858-8711
kevin@outerbanks-ent.com
imdb.com/name/nm0932078

OUTLAW PRODUCTIONS
Production company

11054 Cashmere St
Los Angeles, CA 90049
310-476-9891 (phone)
708-435-6670 (fax)

madison@outlawfilm.com
outlawfilm.com
imdb.com/company/co0014629
web.facebook.com/outlawfilm
twitter.com/Outlaw_Film

Does not accept any unsolicited material. Project types include TV. Genres include action, horror, drama, family, and comedy.

OUT OF THE BLUE ENTERTAINMENT
Production company

c/o Sony Pictures Entertainment
10202 W Washington Blvd
Astaire Building, Suite 1200
Culver City, CA 90232-3195
310-244-7811 (phone)
310-244-1539 (fax)

info@outoftheblueent.com
imdb.com/company/co0052395

Accepts query letters from unproduced, unrepresented writers via email. Project types include TV and feature films.

Toby Conroy
Creative Executive
imdb.com/name/nm1926762

Sidney Ganis
imdb.com/name/nm0304398
linkedin.com/pub/sidney-ganis/4/143/315

OVATION STUDIOS
Production company and distributor

2850 Ocean Park Blvd
Santa Monica, CA 90405
310-430-7575

info@ovationtv.com
ovationtv.com
imdb.com/company/co0448489
facebook.com/OvationTV
twitter.com/ovationtv

Does not accept any unsolicited material. Project types include TV. Genres include fantasy, comedy, and romance.

OVERBROOK ENTERTAINMENT
Production company

10202 W. Washington Blvd.
Poitier Building
Culver City, CA 90232
310-432-2400 (phone)
310-432-2401 (fax)

overbrookent.com
imdb.com/company/co0072775
twitter.com/officialjaden

Accepts query letters from unproduced, unrepresented writers. Project types include TV and feature films. Established in 1998.

Gary Glushon
310-432-2400
imdb.com/name/nm2237223
linkedin.com/pub/gary-glushon/a/270/455

Will Smith
310-432-2400
imdb.com/name/nm0000226

OVERNIGHT PRODUCTIONS
Production company

15 Mercer St, Suite 4
New York, NY 10013
212-625-0530

overnightprod.com/co

Does not accept any unsolicited material. Project types include feature films. Established in 2008.

Rick Schwartz
212-625-0530
imdb.com/name/nm0777408
linkedin.com/in/rickschwartzproducer

OVERTON FILMS
Production company

819 S. Rusk St
Kilgore, TX 75662
818-915-2713

chip@overtonfilms.net
overtonfilms.net
imdb.com/company/co0509458
linkedin.com/company/overton-films
twitter.com/overtonfilms

Does not accept any unsolicited material. Genres include drama and documentary.

OWN: OPRAH WINFREY NETWORK
Production company

5700 Wilshire Blvd
Ste 120
Los Angeles, CA 90036
323-602-5500

oprah.com/own
linkedin.com/company/oprah-winfrey-network
facebook.com/ownTV
twitter.com/OprahWinfreyNet

Does not accept any unsolicited material. Genres include animation, documentary, family, and reality.

Oprah Winfrey
CEO
imdb.com/name/nm0001856
twitter.com/oPRAH

OXFORD SCIENTIFIC FILMS
Production company

21-22 Warwick St
2nd Fl
London W1B 5NE
UK
+44 20 3551 4600

info@oxfordscientificfilms.tv

oxfordscientificfilms.tv
imdb.com/company/co0049775

Does not accept any unsolicited material. Project types include feature films. Genres include drama, fantasy, and science fiction.

OXYMORON ENTERTAINMENT
Production company

4712 Admiralty Way, Suite 599, Marina de Rey, CA, United States, 90292
323-956-5741

oxymoronentertainment.com
imdb.com/company/co0200184

Does not accept any unsolicited material. Project types include TV and feature films. Genres include thriller, drama, and family.

OZLA PICTURES INC.
Production company

1800 Camino Palmero St
Los Angeles, CA 90046
323-876-0180 (phone)
323-876-0189 (fax)

ozla@ozla.com
imdb.com/company/co0131306

Does not accept any unsolicited material. Project types include TV and feature films. Established in 1992.

Takashige Ichise
Producer
323-876-0180
imdb.com/name/nm0406772
Assistant: Chiaki Yanagimoto

P2 FILMS
Production company and financing company

Two Ravinia Dr.
Suite 500
Atlanta, GA 30346
408-242-9284 (phone)
404-348-4259 (fax)

info@p2-films.com
imdb.com/company/co0398352
facebook.com/P2Films

Does not accept any unsolicited material. Project types include feature films and TV. Genres include thriller and horror.

Sukhi Pabla
Producer
imdb.com/name/nm2556348

PACIFICA INTERNATIONAL FILM & TV CORPORATION
Production company

PO Box 8329
Northridge, CA 91237
818-831-0360 (phone)
818-831-0352 (fax)

bizdb.org/pacifica-international-film-and-television-
   corporation-northridge-ca-91326.biz
imdb.com/company/co0185717

Does not accept any unsolicited material. Established in 2008.

Christine Iso
Executive Producer
imdb.com/name/nm1259606

PACIFIC STANDARD
Production company

9720 Wilshire Blvd
4th Floor
Beverly Hills, CA 90212
310-777-3119 (phone)
310-777-0150 (fax)

psmag.com
imdb.com/company/co0373561

Does not accept any unsolicited material. Project types include feature films. Established in 2012.

Bruna Papandrea
imdb.com/name/nm0660295

Reese Witherspoon
imdb.com/name/nm0000702

PACK CREEK PRODUCTIONS
Production company

70 Desert Solitaire
Moab, UT 84532
435-259-0924 (phone)
435-259-3594 (fax)

info@packcreekproductions.com
packcreekproductions.com
imdb.com/company/co0433125

Does not accept any unsolicited material. Project types include feature films and TV. Genres include documentary. Established in 2001.

Sheila Canavan
Producer
imdb.com/name/nm2614103

Michael Chandler
Producer
imdb.com/name/nm0151434

PAGE PRODUCTIONS
Production company

12800 Industrial Park Blvd. Suite 135
Plymouth, MN 55441
763-383-9400 (phone)
763-383-9500 (fax)

info@pageprod.com
pageprod.com
imdb.com/company/co0233268

Accepts query letters from unproduced, unrepresented writers via email. Project types include TV. Genres include reality.

PAINLESS PRODUCTIONS
Production company

1410 S Centinela Ave
Los Angeles, CA 90025
310-839-9900 (phone)
310-943-8178 (fax)

painless.tv
imdb.com/company/co0016150
linkedin.com/company/1997838
facebook.com/pages/Painless-Productions/
    135173136533996
twitter.com/painlesstv

Does not accept any unsolicited material. Project types include TV. Genres include reality, horror, and drama.

PAKA PRODUCTIONS
Production company

PO Box 370
269 Key Largo, FL 33037
305-453-8428

info@pakaproductions.com
imdb.com/company/co0082390

Does not accept any unsolicited material. Project types include short films. Genres include drama.

PALADIN
Distributor

11 Broadway, Suite 865, New York, NY, United States, 10004

assistant@paladinfilm.com
facebook.com/PaladinFilm

Does not accept any unsolicited material.

Mark Urman
Producer
imdb.com/name/nm0882004

PALERMO PRODUCTIONS
Production company

c/o Twentieth Century Fox
10201 W Pico Blvd
Building 52, Room 103
Los Angeles, CA 90064
310-369-1900

palermoproductions.com
imdb.com/company/co031209
facebook.com/PalermoProductions

Accepts query letters from unproduced, unrepresented writers. Project types include feature films and TV.

John Palermo
Producer
310-369-1911
imdb.com/name/nm0657561
Assistant: Mike Belyea

PALISADES TARTAN

Distributor

156 W 56th St, Suite 901, New York City, NY,
United States, 10019
212-265-2323 (phone)
212-265-2766 (fax)

palisadespictures.com
imdb.com/company/co0255442

Does not accept any unsolicited material. Project types
include TV. Genres include romance, drama, and
family.

PALMSTAR ENTERTAINMENT

Production company

14622 Ventura Blvd.
Suite 755
Sherman Oaks, CA 91403
646-277-7356 (phone)
310-469-7855 (fax)

contact@palmstar.com
imdb.com/company/co0037203
linkedin.com/company/palmstar-entertainment
facebook.com/PalmStarEntertainment
twitter.com/Palmstar

Does not accept any unsolicited material. Project types
include feature films. Genres include thriller, family,
non-fiction, comedy, romance, action, and drama.
Established in 2004.

Kevin Scott Frakes
CEO
imdb.com/name/nm0289694

Michael Bassick
Co-CEO
imdb.com/name/nm2471372

Stephan Paternot
Chairman
imdb.com/name/nm0665456
linkedin.com/in/stephanpaternot
facebook.com/paternot

PALOMAR PICTURES

Production company

PO Box 491986
Los Angeles, CA 90049
310-440-3494

ad@palomarpics.com
imdb.com/company/co0009947

Does not accept any unsolicited material. Project types
include TV and feature films. Established in 1992.

Joni Sighvatsson
310-440-3494
imdb.com/name/nm0797451

Aditya Ezhuthachan
Head of Development
310-440-3494
imdb.com/name/nm2149074
linkedin.com/pub/aditya-ezhuthachan/8/769/419

PANAMAX FILMS

Production company and distributor

2000 Ponce de Leon Blvd., Suite 500,
Coral Gables, FL. 33134
305-421-6336 (phone)
305-421-6389 (fax)

info@panamaxfilms.com
panamaxfilms.com
imdb.com/company/co0177895

Accepts scripts from produced or represented writers.
Project types include feature films. Genres include
drama.

PANAY FILMS

Production company

500 S Buena Vista
Old Animation Bldg, Rm 3c-6
Burbank, CA 91521
818-560-4265

imdb.com/company/co0282368
facebook.com/pages/Panay-Films/107172795984020

Does not accept any unsolicited material. Project types
include feature films. Genres include fantasy, drama,
comedy, and action.

Andrew Panay
imdb.com/name/nm0659123
Assistant: Lukas Stuart-Fry

Adam Blum
imdb.com/name/nm3597471

PANDEMONIUM

Production company

9777 Wilshire Blvd, Suite 700
Beverly Hills, CA 90212
310-550-9900 (phone)
310-550-9910 (fax)

imdb.com/title/tt0913424

Accepts query letters from unproduced, unrepresented writers via email. Project types include feature films.

Bill Mechanic
310-550-9900
imdb.com/name/nm0575312
Assistant: David Freedman

Suzanne Warren
310-550-9900
imdb.com/name/nm0913049

PANORAMA FILMS

Production company

227 A 3rd St
Palisades Park, NJ 07650
201-562-2787

rohitgaur.info@gmail.com
rohitgaur.com
imdb.com/company/co0285021
facebook.com/gaurrohit
twitter.com/rohitgaur_

Does not accept any unsolicited material. Project types include TV. Genres include comedy and drama.

PANTELION FILMS

Production company

2700 Colorado Ave.
Suite 200
Santa Monica, CA 90404
310-449-9200 (phone)
310-255-3870 (fax)

2000 Avendia Vasco de Quiroga
Álvaro Obregón, Mexico 01210
011-525-552612000

1601 Cloverfield Blvd.
Suite 200
South Tower
Santa Monica, CA 90404
310-255-3000 (phone)
310-255-3908 (fax)

info@pantelionfilms.com
pantelionfilms.com
imdb.com/company/co0325194
facebook.com/PantelionFilms

Does not accept any unsolicited material. Project types include TV and feature films. Genres include family, science fiction, romance, drama, action, and comedy. Established in 2010.

James McNamara
Chairman
imdb.com/name/nm2241044
linkedin.com/pub/jim-mcnamara/6/316/388
facebook.com/james.mcnamara.50115

Sandra Condito
President (Acquisitions & Production)
imdb.com/name/nm1354700
linkedin.com/pub/sandra-condito/2a/bb2/3a9

Paul Presburger
CEO
imdb.com/name/nm0643967
linkedin.com/pub/paul-presburger/1/569/723

Ben Odell
Head of Production & Development
310-255-5778
imdb.com/name/nm0643967
linkedin.com/pub/benjamin-odell/6/648/784
facebook.com/ben.odell.52

PANTHERA FILM FINANCE

Production company

15675 Spaulding St
Omaha, NE 68116
+402-680-2770 (phone)
+469-621-8177 (fax)

pantherafilm@gmail.com

pantherafilmfinance.com
imdb.com/company/co0291604

Does not accept any unsolicited material. Project types include feature films. Genres include drama, romance, and horror.

PANTHERA FILM FINANCE COMPANY

Production company and financing company

PO Box 45816
Omaha, NE 68130
402-680-2770 (phone)
469-621-8177 (fax)

pantherafilm@gmail.com
pantherafilmfinance.com
imdb.com/company/co0291604

Does not accept any unsolicited material. Project types include TV. Genres include romance and drama.

PANTHER FILMS

Production company

1888 Century Park East
14th Floor
Los Angeles, CA 90067
424-202-6630 (phone)
310-887-1001 (fax)

pantherfilm.com
imdb.com/company/co0201862

Does not accept any unsolicited material. Project types include feature films.

Lindsay Culpepper

424-202-6630
imdb.com/name/nm0258431
linkedin.com/pub/lindsay-culpepper/6/580/594

Brad Epstein

Producer
424-202-6630
imdb.com/name/nm0258431
linkedin.com/pub/brad-epstein/53/a35/86a

PAPA JOE ENTERTAINMENT

Production company

14804 Greenleaf St
Sherman Oaks, CA 91403

818-788-7608 (phone)
818-788-7612 (fax)

info@papjoefilms.com
imdb.com/company/co0195371

Accepts query letters from unproduced, unrepresented writers via email. Project types include TV and feature films.

Erin Alexander

818-788-7608
imdb.com/name/nm0018408
Assistant: Amelia Garrison

Joe Simpson

CEO
818-788-7608
imdb.com/name/nm1471425
Assistant: Heath Pliler

PAPER CRANE PRODUCTIONS

Production company

240 E Cedar Ave Ste E
Burbank, CA 91502

papercranellc@gmail.com
papercraneproductions.net
imdb.com/company/co0353174
facebook.com/papercraneproductions
twitter.com/PaperCraneLA

Does not accept any unsolicited material. Project types include short films, TV, and commercials. Genres include drama, science fiction, and documentary. Established in 2012.

Hugo Perez

Producer
newzdude.tumblr.com
imdb.com/name/nm3348137
linkedin.com/in/newzdude
facebook.com/newzdude
twitter.com/newzdude

Greg Wilson

Producer
imdb.com/name/nm2745424
linkedin.com/pub/greg-wilson/4/9a4/18
facebook.com/edcotafloata

Ryan Cheevers
Producer
imdb.com/name/nm2122043
linkedin.com/pub/ryan-cheevers/b0/3b3/b12
facebook.com/ryanwilliamcheevers
twitter.com/Ryan_Cheevers

Angelo Salvatore Restaino
Partner
angelo-restaino.com
imdb.com/name/nm1913564
facebook.com/angelo.restaino.14
twitter.com/jellostack

Emily Moss Wilson
Partner
emosswilson@gmail.com
emosswilson.com
imdb.com/name/nm2672860
linkedin.com/pub/emily-moss-wilson/7/983/881
facebook.com/emosswilson
twitter.com/emosswilson

PAPER STREET FILMS
Studio

265 Canal St., Suite 212
New York, NY 10013
646-524-6954 (phone)
646-417-6460 (fax)

info@paperstreetfilms.com
paperstreetfilms.com
imdb.com/company/co0222800
web.facebook.com/Paper-Street-
    Films-218217148207588

Does not accept any unsolicited material. Project types include feature films. Genres include thriller, horror, comedy, and drama. Established in 2007.

Benji Kohn
Partner
imdb.com/name/nm2803928

Emily Buder
Creative Executive
imdb.com/name/nm1692758

Bingo Gubelmann
Partner
imdb.com/name/nm1292502

Austin Stark
Partner
imdb.com/name/nm0823133

Chris Papavasiliou
Partner
imdb.com/name/nm2830113

PAPER STREET PICTURES
Production company

4240 Johns Light Trail
Austin, TX 78727
512-721-8188

imdb.com/company/co0406281
facebook.com/paperstreetpictures

Does not accept any unsolicited material. Project types include short films. Genres include thriller.

PARABLE ROAD FILMS
Production company

800 Rodeo Dr
Colleyville, TX 76034
817-781-1977

info@filmosaic.com
imdb.com/company/co0204448

Does not accept any unsolicited material.

PARADIGM STUDIO
Production company

2701 2nd Ave North
Seattle, WA 98109
206-282-2161 (phone)
206-283-6433 (fax)

info@paradigmstudio.com
imdb.com/company/co0124646
linkedin.com/in/jcomerford

Accepts query letters from unproduced, unrepresented writers via email. Project types include feature films and TV.

John Comerford
President
206-282-2161
imdb.com/name/nm0173766
linkedin.com/pub/dir/John/Comerford

B Dahlia
Manager
206-282-2161
imdb.com/name/nm1148338
linkedin.com/pub/b-dahlia/40/258/970

PARADIGM TALENT AGENCY
Production company and sales agent

124 12th Ave South Suite 410
Nashville TN 37203
615-251-4400 (phone)
615-251-4401 (fax)

360 Park Ave South 16th Floor
New York NY 10010
212-897-6400 (phone)
212-764-8941 (fax)

404 W Franklin St
Monterey CA 93940
831-375-4889 (phone)
831-375-2623 (fax)

360 N Crescent Dr, North Building, Beverly Hills ,
CA, United States, 90210
310-288-8000 (phone)
310-288-2000 (fax)

paradigmagency.com/index_temp
imdb.com/company/co0024357

Does not accept any unsolicited material. Project types
include TV. Genres include drama, comedy, and
family.

PARADISE GROUP
Production company and distributor

1631 Maria St
Burbank, CA 91504
818-558-4830 (phone)
818-558-4835 (fax)

armen@mgnfilms.us
imdb.com/company/co0164832

Does not accept any unsolicited material. Genres
include romance and drama.

PARADISO PICTURES
Production company

8104 SW 91 Ave
Miami, FL 33173

info@paradisopictures.com
paradisopictures.com
imdb.com/company/co0196197

Does not accept any unsolicited material. Genres
include comedy.

PARADOX ENTERTAINMENT
Production company

9107 Wilshire Blvd, Suite 600
Beverly Hills, CA 90210
310-271-1355 (phone)
323-655-1720 (fax)

info@paradoxent.com
paradoxent.com/investor
imdb.com/company/co0036328

Does not accept any unsolicited material. Project types
include feature films. Genres include science fiction,
drama, romance, action, comedy, and fantasy.

Janet Sheppard
CFO
imdb.com/name/nm5128822

Fredrik Malmberg
imdb.com/name/nm1573406

PARAISO PICTURES
Production company

17001 Collins Ave.
Suite 2105
Miami, FL 33160

info@paraisopictures.com
paraisopictures.com
imdb.com/company/co0158513
twitter.com/paraisopictures

Does not accept any unsolicited material. Genres
include drama.

PARALISON
Production company

Tokyo 111-0053
Japan
+81 338632623 (fax)

info@paralison-pro.com
paralison.com
imdb.com/company/co0410426
twitter.com/TanrohIshida

Does not accept any unsolicited material.

Tanroh Ishida
Actor
imdb.com/name/nm4437969

PARALLEL ENTERTAINMENT
Production company

209 10th Ave
Nashville TN 37203
615-750-2613 (phone)
615-750-2385 (fax)

9420 Wilshire Blvd, Suite 250, Beverly Hills , CA,
United States, 90212
310-279-1123 (phone)
310-279-1147 (fax)

parallelentertainment.com
imdb.com/company/co0085172

Does not accept any unsolicited material. Project types
include short films, TV, and feature films. Genres
include action, thriller, family, and drama.

Liz Bartels
Manager (Producer)
imdb.com/name/nm5879394

PARALLEL MEDIA
Production company

301 N Canon Dr,
Suite 223
Beverly Hills, CA 90210
310-858-3003 (phone)
310-858-3034 (fax)

11054 Ventura Blvd.
Suite 371
Studio City, CA 91604

323-319-3944 (phone)
323-843-9921 (fax)

info@parallelmediallc.com
parallelmediafilms.com
imdb.com/company/co0198771

Does not accept any unsolicited material. Project types
include feature films. Established in 2006.

Armen Mahdessian
Executive
linkedin.com/pub/dir/%20/Mahdessian

PARAMEDIA INC.
Production company

2120 Colorado Ave, Suite 200
Santa Monica, CA 90404

imdb.com/company/co0027238

Does not accept any unsolicited material. Project types
include TV.

PARAMOUNT HOME MEDIA DISTRIBUTION (PHMD)
Distributor and sales agent

5555 Melrose Ave.
Los Angeles, CA

paramount.com
imdb.com/company/co0381742

Does not accept any unsolicited material. Genres
include comedy and drama.

PARAMOUNT PICTURES
Production company

5555 Melrose Ave
Los Angeles, CA 90038
323-956-5000

paramount.com
imdb.com/company/co0023400
facebook.com/Paramount
twitter.com/ParamountPics

Does not accept any unsolicited material. Project types
include feature films.

Ashley Brucks
imdb.com/name/nm2087318

Marc Evans
imdb.com/name/nm0263010

Allison Small
Creative Executive
imdb.com/name/nm1861333

PARAMYTH FILMS
Production company

264 S. La Cienega Blvd., Suite 148
Beverly Hills, CA 90211

nika@paramythfilms.com
paramythfilms.com
imdb.com/company/co0340889
facebook.com/pages/Paramyth-Films/
    172134046174864
twitter.com/GreenStoryMovie

Accepts scripts from produced or represented writers.
Project types include feature films. Genres include
action, thriller, and drama.

PARIAH
Production company

9229 Sunset Blvd
Ste 208
West Hollywood, CA 90069
310-461-3460 (phone)
310-246-9622 (fax)

imdb.com/title/tt1233334
facebook.com/uk.pariah

Does not accept any unsolicited material. Project types
include TV and feature films.

Gavin Polone
Owner
310-461-3460
imdb.com/name/nm0689780
Assistant: Stephen Iwanyk

PARKCHESTER PICTURES
Production company

8750 Wilshire Blvd., Suite 301
Los Angeles, CA 90211
310-289-5988

imdb.com/company/co0185546

Does not accept any unsolicited material. Project types
include TV. Genres include drama.

PARKER ENTERTAINMENT GROUP
Production company

8306 Wilshire Blvd
Suite #1904
Beverly Hills, CA 90211
323-400-6622 (phone)
323-400-6655 (fax)

info@parkerentgroup.com
parkerentgroup.com
imdb.com/company/co0270280
linkedin.com/company/parker-entertainment-group-
    llc-
facebook.com/parkerentgroup

Accepts scripts from produced or represented writers.
Project types include feature films. Established in
2008.

Christopher Parker
President
cparker@parkerentgroup.com
imdb.com/name/nm2034521
twitter.com/indianapapi

Gregory Parker
CEO
323-400-6622
gparker@parkerentgroup.com
imdb.com/name/nm2027023

PARKER FILM COMPANY
Production company and distributor

1101 Fifth Ave Suite 300
San Rafael, CA 94901
415-456-4465

info@parkerfilmcompany.com
parkerfilmcompany.com
imdb.com/company/co0030355
twitter.com/parkerfilmco

Does not accept any unsolicited material. Project types include feature films. Genres include drama.

PARKES/MACDONALD PRODUCTIONS

Production company

1663 Euclid St
Santa Monica, CA 90404
310-581-5990 (phone)
310-581-5999 (fax)

imdb.com/company/co0112928
facebook.com/pages/ParkesMacDonald-Productions/
    176397359214607

Accepts query letters from unproduced, unrepresented writers. Project types include feature films and TV. Established in 2007.

Laurie MacDonald
Producer
310-581-5990
imdb.com/name/nm0531827

Walter Parkes
Producer
310-581-5990
imdb.com/name/nm0662748
linkedin.com/pub/dir/walter/parkes

PARKVILLE PICTURES

Production company

Unit B304, The Biscuit Factory
100 Clements Rd
London SE16 4DG
UK
+44 (0) 20 7381 4224

info@parkvillepictures.com
parkvillepictures.com
imdb.com/company/co0239891

Does not accept any unsolicited material. Project types include feature films and short films. Genres include drama, romance, and comedy.

Olivier Kaempfer
Producer
imdb.com/name/nm2954652

PARKWAY PRODUCTIONS

Production company

7095 Hollywood Blvd, Suite 1009
Hollywood, CA 90028
323-874-6207

parkwayprods@aol.com
parkway.tv
imdb.com/company/co0063736
linkedin.com/company/parkway-productions
facebook.com/Parkwayproductions

Accepts query letters from unproduced, unrepresented writers via email. Project types include feature films and TV.

Penny Marshall
323-874-6207
imdb.com/name/nm0001508

PARTICIPANT MEDIA

Production company

331 Foothill Rd
3rd Floor
Beverly Hills, CA 90210
310-550-5100 (phone)
310-550-5106 (fax)

info@participantproductions.com
participantmedia.com
imdb.com/company/co0132772
linkedin.com/company/participant-media
facebook.com/ParticipantMedia
twitter.com/_Participant

Does not accept any unsolicited material. Project types include feature films and TV. Genres include reality and non-fiction. Established in 2004.

Jonathan King
Executive Vice President of Production
310-550-5100
imdb.com/name/nm2622896
linkedin.com/pub/jonathan-king/B/A60/1B0

Erik Andreasen
310-550-5100
imdb.com/name/nm1849675

PARTIZAN ENTERTAINMENT

Production company

285 W. Broadway
Suite 330
New York, NY 10013
212-388-0123 (phone)
212-625-2040 (fax)

1545 Wilcox Ave Suite 200
Hollywood, CA 90028
323-468-0123 (phone)
323-468-0129 (fax)

partizan.com
imdb.com/company/co0482524
linkedin.com/company/partizan
facebook.com/partizan
twitter.com/wearepartizan

Does not accept any unsolicited material. Project types include TV and feature films. Genres include thriller, crime, action, fantasy, comedy, animation, romance, drama, science fiction, and horror. Established in 1991.

Lori Stonebraker
lstonebraker@partizan.us

Li-Wei Chu
Head of Production & Development
liwei.chu@partizan.us
linkedin.com/in/liweichu

Matt Tucker
matt.tucker@partizan.com

Sheila Stepanek
Executive Producer
sstepanek@partizan.us

PARTS AND LABOR
Production company

177 N 10th St
Ste A
Brooklyn, NY 11211
718-599-5244

info@partslaborfilm.com
imdb.com/company/co0226159

Does not accept any unsolicited material. Genres include comedy and drama.

PARTS AND LABOR FILMS
Production company

177 N 10th St
Brooklyn, NY 11211
718-599-5244

imdb.com/company/co0226159
facebook.com/Parts-Labor-Films-214775915277600
twitter.com/partslaborfilms

Does not accept any unsolicited material. Project types include feature films. Genres include romance and drama.

PASSCODE ENTERTAINMENT
Production company and financing company

1450 Poydras St
Suite 504
New Orleans, LA 70112

info@pass-code.com
imdb.com/company/co0421738

Does not accept any unsolicited material. Project types include TV. Genres include drama and comedy.

PASSION RIVER FILMS
Distributor and sales agent

154 Mt. Bethel Rd
Warren, NJ 07059
732-321-0711 (phone)
732-321-4105 (fax)

Info@PassionRiver.com
passionriver.com
imdb.com/company/co0195144
facebook.com/PassionRiverFilms
twitter.com/PassionRiver

Does not accept any unsolicited material. Genres include drama and documentary.

PATHE PICTURES
Production company

6 Ramillies St
4th Floor
London W1F 7TY
United Kingdom

442-073-235151 (phone)
+44207-631-3568 (fax)

reception.desk@pathe-uk.com
imdb.com/company/co0224606

Does not accept any unsolicited material. Project types include feature films and TV. Genres include non-fiction and reality.

Bradley Quirk
Creative Executive
imdb.com/name/nm1574955
facebook.com/bradley.quirk

PATHLESS LAND PICTURES
Production company

3315 Clover Trace Dr
Spring, TX 77386
713-249-6288

craig@pathlesslandpictures.com
imdb.com/company/co0456022

Does not accept any unsolicited material. Project types include short films. Genres include drama.

PATRICIA K. MEYER PRODUCTIONS
Production company

511 Hill St #313
Santa Monica , CA 90405
310-392-0422

imdb.com/company/co0061979

Does not accept any unsolicited material. Project types include TV and feature films.

Patricia K. Meyer
Writer/Producer/Director
imdb.com/name/nm0583307

PATRIOT PICTURES
Production company

PO Box 46100
West Hollywood, CA 90046
323-874-8850 (phone)
323-874-8851 (fax)

contact@patriotpictures.com
patriotpictures.com

imdb.com/company/co0083975
linkedin.com/company/patriot-pictures-llc.

Accepts query letters from unproduced, unrepresented writers via email. Project types include feature films and TV. Genres include non-fiction and reality.

Michael Mendelsohn
323-874-8850
imdb.com/name/nm0578861
linkedin.com/pub/michael-mendelsohn/19/5/b74

PAUL ROCK PRODUCED
Production company

345 N. Maple Dr.
Suite 222
Beverly Hills, CA 90210
310-275-7625 (phone)
813-464-2804 (fax)

Submit@paulrockproduced.com
paulrockproduced.com
imdb.com/company/co0499937
facebook.com/paulrockproduced

Accepts query letters from unproduced, unrepresented writers via email. Project types include feature films. Genres include fantasy, thriller, and science fiction.

PAURA PRODUCTIONS
Production company

11150 Santa Monica Blvd, Suite 450
Los Angeles, CA 90025
310-477-7776 (phone)
310-477-7710 (fax)

info@pauraprod.com
imdb.com/company/co0134381
facebook.com/pages/Paura-Productions/
    100226523363013

Accepts query letters from unproduced, unrepresented writers via email. Project types include feature films. Genres include drama, thriller, crime, and comedy.

Catherine Paura
Executive
imdb.com/name/nm0667474

Wayne Kline
Executive
imdb.com/name/nm0459679

PBS DISTRIBUTION
Distributor

10 Guest St
2nd Fl
Boston, MA 02135
617-208-0723 (phone)
617-208-0784 (fax)

wholesale@pbs.org
pbsdwholesale.org
imdb.com/company/co0290968
linkedin.com/company/pbs-distribution

Does not accept any unsolicited material. Genres include documentary.

PCH FILM
Production company

3380 Motor Ave
Los Angeles, CA 90034
310-841-5817

info@pchfilm.com
pchfilms.com
imdb.com/company/co0127673

Accepts scripts from unproduced, unrepresented writers via email. Project types include feature films. Genres include romance and comedy.

Kayla Thorton
310-841-5817
kayla@pchfilm.com
imdb.com/name/nm4267414
linkedin.com/pub/kayla-thornton/6/911/378

PEACE ARCH ENTERTAINMENT
Production company

4640 Admiralty Way, Suite 710
Marina del Rey, CA 90292
310-776-7200 (phone)
310-823-7147 (fax)

info@peacearch.com
imdb.com/company/co0078130

linkedin.com/company/peace-arch-entertainment

Does not accept any unsolicited material. Project types include feature films and TV. Established in 1986.

Sudhanshu Saria
310-776-7200
ssaria@peacearch.com
imdb.com/name/nm2738818

PEACE BY PEACE PRODUCTIONS
Production company

14757 Royal Way;
Truckee, CA 96161
530-582-8000

peacebypeace1@mac.com
peaceproductions.org
facebook.com/Peace-Productions-247180657593

Accepts query letters from unproduced, unrepresented writers via email. Project types include TV and feature films.

Alyssa Milano
Producer
323-552-1097
imdb.com/name/nm0000192
Assistant: Kelly Kall

PEACE CREATE
Production company

3-9-10-319
Edagawa
Kotoku, Tokyo 135-0051
Japan
03-3699-4883 (phone)
03-3699-4407 (fax)

peace_create@yahoo.co.jp
peace-create.bz-office.net
imdb.com/company/co0194560

Does not accept any unsolicited material. Project types include TV. Genres include documentary.

PEACEOUT PRODUCTIONS
Production company

1299 Ocean Ave, Suite 333
Santa Monica, CA 90401

imdb.com/company/co0184814

Does not accept any unsolicited material. Project types include TV. Genres include drama, crime, and romance.

PEACE POINT ENTERTAINMENT GROUP

Production company and distributor

78 Berkeley
Toronto, ON M5A 2W7
Canada
416-365-7734 (phone)
416-365-7739 (fax)

info@peacepoint.tv
peacepoint.tv
imdb.com/company/co0111968

Does not accept any unsolicited material. Project types include TV. Genres include reality, detective, fantasy, and action.

Les Tomlin
Producer
imdb.com/name/nm1381840

PEACE POINT RIGHTS

Distributor and sales agent

79 Berkeley
Toronto, ON M5A2W5
Canada
416-365-7734 (phone)
416-365-7739 (fax)

info@peacepoint.tv
peacepointrights.tv
imdb.com/company/co0408286

Does not accept any unsolicited material. Genres include documentary.

PEACHCRAFT

Production company and distributor

371 Springfield Ave
Ste 2
Summit, NJ 07901
908-673-1485

peachcraft@gmail.com

peachcraftstudios.com
imdb.com/company/co0403427
facebook.com/pages/PeachCraft-Studios-of-Drama-
    Voice-Filmmaking/168465699684

Does not accept any unsolicited material. Project types include short films and TV. Genres include comedy.

PEACHCRAFT STUDIOS

Production company

371 Springfield Ave
Summit, NJ 07901
908-673-1485

peachcraft@gmail.com
imdb.com/company/co0238663

Does not accept any unsolicited material. Project types include short films. Genres include drama.

PEARL PICTURES

Production company

10956 Weyburn Ave, Suite 200
Los Angeles, CA 90024
310-443-7773

imdb.com/company/co0036358

Does not accept any unsolicited material. Project types include TV. Genres include drama, science fiction, and thriller.

PEGGY RAJSKI PRODUCTIONS

Production company

2 Washington Square Village
Suite 14I
New York, NY 10012
323-634-7020 (phone)
323-634-7021 (fax)

imdb.com/name/nm0707475
linkedin.com/in/peggyrajski

Does not accept any unsolicited material. Project types include TV and feature films. Genres include reality and non-fiction.

Peggy Rajski
Producer
323-634-7020
rajskip@aol.com
imdb.com/name/nm0707475

PELICAN POINT CAPITAL
Production company and financing company

850 3rd Ave
New York NY 10016

660 Newport Center Dr, Suite 710, Newport Beach,
CA, United States, 92660
949-706-7888

info@pelicanpointcapital.com
pelicanpointcapital.com
imdb.com/company/co0534980

Does not accept any unsolicited material. Project types
include TV. Genres include drama and family.

PENTHOUSE
Production company and distributor

6800 Broken Sound Parkway
Ste 100
Boca Raton, FL 33487
561-912-7000 (phone)
561-912-7038 (fax)

imdb.com/company/co0001235

Does not accept any unsolicited material. Genres
include thriller and drama.

PERCEPTION FILMS
Production company

P.O. Box 200672
Austin, TX 78720
512-803-5597

jeff@perceptionfilms.com
imdb.com/company/co0134266

Does not accept any unsolicited material. Genres
include drama.

PERCOLATE PRODUCTIONS
Production company

182 Nassau St
Suite 201
Princeton, NJ 08550
908-616-7060

contact@percolateproductions.com
percolateproductions.com
imdb.com/company/co0385933
facebook.com/ContestMovie
twitter.com/ContestMovie

Does not accept any unsolicited material. Genres
include family and drama.

PERFECT STORM ENTERTAINMENT
Production company

1850 Industrial St, Penthouse
Los Angeles, CA 90021

info@theperfectstorment.com
perfectstorment.com
imdb.com/company/co0374900

Does not accept any unsolicited material. Project types
include TV and feature films. Genres include thriller,
action, and detective.

Justin Lin
Director
imdb.com/name/nm0510912

PERISCOPE ENTERTAINMENT
Production company

2338 1/2 Teviot St
Los Angeles, CA 90039
323-205-5814 (phone)
323-663-6326 (fax)

periscopeentertainment.com
imdb.com/company/co0123772
linkedin.com/company/periscope-entertainment-llc
facebook.com/PeriscopeEntertainment
twitter.com/PeriscopeNews

Does not accept any unsolicited material. Project types
include feature films. Genres include comedy,
documentary, and horror. Established in 2004.

PERMUT PRESENTATIONS
Production company

3535 Hayden Ave
4th Floor
Culver City, CA 90232
310-838-0100 (phone)
310-838-0105 (fax)

info@permutpres.com
imdb.com/company/co0011800

Accepts query letters from unproduced, unrepresented writers. Project types include feature films and TV.

David Permut
310-248-2792
imdb.com/name/nm0674303

Chris Mangano
Development Executive
310-248-2792
imdb.com/name/nm2032016

PERSISTENT ENTERTAINMENT
Production company

1221 2nd St, Suite 200,
Santa Monica, CA 90401
310-777-0126

info@persistent-ent.com
persistent-ent.com
imdb.com/company/co0123049

Does not accept any unsolicited material. Project types include feature films. Genres include drama.

PETER ENGEL PRODUCTIONS
Production company

2660 W Olive Ave
Burbank, CA 91505
818-295-5000

imdb.com/company/co0033113

Does not accept any unsolicited material. Project types include TV. Genres include comedy and drama.

Peter Engel
Principal, Producer
imdb.com/name/nm0257137

PETERS ENTERTAINMENT
Production company

21731 Ventura Blvd.
Woodland Hills, CA 91364

info@petersentertainment.net
imdb.com/company/co0004624

Does not accept any unsolicited material. Project types include feature films.

PFEFFER FILM
Production company

500 S. Buena Vista Blvd. Animation Bldg.
Burbank, CA 91521
818-560-3177 (phone)
818-843-7485 (fax)

imdb.com/company/co0094822
facebook.com/pages/Pfeffer-Film/302868926397385

Does not accept any unsolicited material. Project types include feature films. Genres include thriller, romance, and drama.

PFM PRODUCTIONS
Production company

TOKYO,
JAPAN

info@playinformoney.com
imdb.com/company/co0136969

Does not accept any unsolicited material. Project types include TV. Genres include comedy.

Shawn Pettus Brown
Producer
imdb.com/name/nm3304633

PHANTOM FILM
Distributor

3F, Yoyogi Community Bldg.,
1-11-2 Yoyogi
Shibuya-Ku, Tokyo 151-0053
Japan
+81 3 6276 4035 (phone)
+81 3 6276 4036 (fax)

info@phantom-film.com
phantom-film.com
imdb.com/company/co0140110

Does not accept any unsolicited material. Project types include feature films and TV. Genres include crime.

Daishiro Narita
Iternational Sales and Acquisitions (Executive)
imdb.com/name/nm0621449

PHASE 4 FILMS
Production company and distributor

20 Eglinton Ave W
Ste 603, PO Box 2041
Toronto, ON M4R 1K8
Canada
416-783-8383

info@phase4films.com
phase4films.com
imdb.com/company/co0332149
facebook.com/phase4films
twitter.com/phase4films

Does not accept any unsolicited material. Genres include thriller and drama.

PHILM GROUP
Production company

600 17th St
Suite 2800 South
Denver, CO 80202
720-437-8865

phil@thephilmgroup.com
thephilmgroup.com
imdb.com/company/co0543500

Does not accept any unsolicited material. Genres include action.

PHOENIX PICTURES
Production company

10203 Santa Monica Blvd
Suite 400
Los Angeles, CA 90067
424-298-2788 (phone)
424-298-2588 (fax)

info@phoenixpictures.com
phoenixpictures.com
imdb.com/company/co0029574

Accepts query letters from unproduced, unrepresented writers via email. Project types include TV and feature films.

Edward McGurn
424-298-2788
imdb.com/name/nm0570342

Ali Toukan
Creative Executive
424-298-2788
imdb.com/name/nm4371255

Douglas McKay
424-298-2788
imdb.com/name/nm1305822

PHOTO FILM
Production company

9424 SW 1st Place
Gainesville, FL 32607
352-332-1185

Joe@theouterbands.com
imdb.com/company/co0207587

Does not accept any unsolicited material.

PIC AGENCY
Production company

6161 Santa Monica Blvd Suite 300
Hollywood, CA 90038
323-461-2900 (phone)
323-461-2909 (fax)

info@picagency.com
picagency.com
imdb.com/company/co0146821
facebook.com/pages/Pic-Agency/611546502202547
twitter.com/pic_agency

Does not accept any unsolicited material. Project types include feature films. Genres include romance, thriller, crime, and drama.

PICCADILLY PICTURE
Production company

1st Fl
101 Wardour St

London W1F 0UG
UK
+44207-432-7620 (phone)
+44207-432-7629 (fax)

info@piccadillypictures.com
piccadillypictures.com
imdb.com/company/co0127592

Does not accept any unsolicited material. Project types include TV and feature films. Genres include drama, action, and thriller.

Christopher Figg
Producer
imdb.com/name/nm0276541

PICTO FILMS
Production company and distributor

2010 S Corinth St
Ste 7108
Corinth, TX 76210
310-299-2831

shaun@pictofilms.com
pictofilms.com
imdb.com/company/co0410784
twitter.com/PictoCunningham

Does not accept any unsolicited material. Project types include TV, short films, and feature films. Genres include action, fantasy, thriller, documentary, drama, and horror. Established in 2012.

PICTURE ENTERTAINMENT

4760 S Pecos Rd
Suite 103
Las Vegas, NV 89121

lee.caplin@mail.com
imdb.com/company/co0307412

Does not accept any unsolicited material. Project types include TV and feature films. Genres include crime, horror, and drama.

PICTURE FARM
Production company

7 Denmark St, 2nd Floor, London , United Kingdom, WC2H 8LZ

011-440-2073790675 (phone)
011-440-2072407088 (fax)

338 Wythe Ave Suite 3
Brooklyn NY 11211
718-218-8001

contact@picturefarmpro.com
picturefarmproduction.com
imdb.com/company/co0073284

Does not accept any unsolicited material. Project types include TV and feature films. Genres include myth, family, drama, thriller, and action.

PICTUREMAKER PRODUCTIONS
Production company

13949 Ventura Blvd. Suite 205
Sherman Oaks, CA 91423
818-783-8400 (phone)
818-783-8401 (fax)

imdb.com/company/co0067587

Does not accept any unsolicited material. Project types include TV. Genres include crime, comedy, and drama.

PICTURE SHACK ENTERTAINMENT
Production company

115 W 30th St, 6th Floor
New York, NY 10001
646-581-9148

info@pictureshackentertainment.com
imdb.com/company/co0291750
linkedin.com/company/picture-shack-entertainment
web.facebook.com/PictureShack

Does not accept any unsolicited material. Project types include TV. Genres include comedy, horror, and thriller.

PICTURE THIS! ENTERTAINMENT
Production company and distributor

7471 Melrose Ave, Suite 7, Los Angeles , CA, United States, 90046
323-852-1398 (phone)
323-658-7265 (fax)

info@picturethisent.com
picturethisent.com
imdb.com/company/co0056697

Does not accept any unsolicited material. Project types include feature films and TV. Genres include drama, thriller, action, and family.

PICTURE TREE INTERNATIONAL
Production company, distributor, and sales agent

Zur Börse 12
Berlin 10247
Germany
+49 (0) 30 4208 248 - 14 (phone)
+49 (0) 151 5445 8921 (fax)

pti@picturetree-international.com
picturetree-international.com
imdb.com/company/co0404636

Does not accept any unsolicited material. Genres include fantasy, thriller, and action.

Alec Schulmann
Producer
imdb.com/name/nm1991187

PIER 21 FILMS
Production company

9 Price St
Toronto, ON M4W 1Z1
Canada
416-967-7091

info@pier21films.com
pier21films.com
imdb.com/company/co0324839
facebook.com/pages/Pier-21-Films/223000261052826
twitter.com/pier21films

Does not accept any unsolicited material. Genres include drama.

PIERCE WILLIAMS ENTERTAINMENT
Production company

1531 14th St
Santa Monica, CA 90404
310-656-9440 (phone)
310-656-9441 (fax)

imdb.com/company/co0009226

Does not accept any unsolicited material. Project types include feature films. Genres include thriller, horror, and drama.

Mark Williams
Executive Producer
imdb.com/name/nm0931251

PIERPOLINE FILMS
Production company

96 Morton St, 2nd Floor
New York, NY 10014
212-255-2340

info@pierpolinefilms.com
pierpolinefilms.com
imdb.com/company/co0236232

Does not accept any unsolicited material. Project types include feature films. Genres include drama and thriller.

PILLER/SEGAN/SHEPHERD
Production company

7025 Santa Monica Blvd
Hollywood, CA 90038
323-817-1100 (phone)
323-817-1131 (fax)

imdb.com/company/co0310765
facebook.com/pages/PillerSeganShepherd/
    151889934858586

Accepts query letters from unproduced, unrepresented writers. Project types include TV and feature films. Established in 2010.

Shawn Piller
323-817-1100
imdb.com/name/nm0683525

Scott Shepherd
323-817-1100
imdb.com/name/nm0791863

Lloyd Segan
323-817-1100
imdb.com/name/nm0781912
linkedin.com/pub/lloyd-segan/59/991/427

PINE STREET ENTERTAINMENT

Production company

4000 Warner Blvd. Bldg. 146 Rm. 204
Burbank, CA 91522
818-954-3279 (phone)
818-977-9713 (fax)

general.info@pinestreetent.com
pinestreetent.com

Does not accept any unsolicited material. Project types include TV. Genres include drama.

PINK SLIP PICTURES

Production company

1314 N. Coronado St.
Los Angeles, CA 90026
213-483-7100 (phone)
213-483-7200 (fax)

pinkslip@earthlink.net
imdb.com/company/co0123114

Does not accept any unsolicited material. Project types include feature films and TV.

Max Wong
Producer
213-483-7100
imdb.com/name/nm0939246

Karen Firestone
Producer
949-228-2354
karenfirestone@hotmail.com
imdb.com/name/nm0278652

PIONEER PICTURES

Production company

9229 W. Sunset Blvd. Suite 608
West Hollywood, CA 90069
310-273-8825

pioneer-pictures.com
imdb.com/company/co0084033

Does not accept any unsolicited material. Project types include feature films and TV. Genres include fantasy, drama, and family.

PIPELINE ENTERTAINMENT INC.

Production company

330 W 42nd St
Suite 1106
New York, NY 10036
212-372-7509

pipeline-talent.com
imdb.com/company/co0215262

Accepts query letters from unproduced, unrepresented writers. Project types include feature films and TV. Genres include drama, crime, thriller, comedy, and action.

Virginia Donovan
Director of Film Financing
virginia@pipeline-talent.com
imdb.com/name/nm3270342

Dan De Fillipo
Manager
dan@pipeline-talent.com
imdb.com/name/nm2496568

Dave Marken
Manager
dave@pipeline-talent.com
imdb.com/name/nm2441741

PITCH BLACK PRODUCTIONS

Production company

3621 Meadowglenn Village Ln
Ste H
Atlanta, GA 30340

imdb.com/company/co0091333

Does not accept any unsolicited material.

PIVOT

Production company and distributor

331 Foothill Rd, Third Floor, Beverly Hills, CA, United States, 90210
310-550-5100 (phone)
310-550-5106 (fax)

press@pivot.tv
pivot.tv
imdb.com/company/co0440512

Does not accept any unsolicited material. Project types include TV. Genres include family and reality.

PIXAR
Production company

1200 Park Ave
Emeryville, CA 94608
510-922-3000 (phone)
510-922-3151 (fax)

publicity@pixar.com
pixar.com
imdb.com/company/co0017902
facebook.com/DisneyPixar
twitter.com/disneypixar

Does not accept any unsolicited material. Project types include feature films. Genres include family, animation, comedy, and fantasy.

John Lasseter
imdb.com/name/nm0005124

Jim Morris
Producer
imdb.com/name/nm0606640

Ed Catmull
President
imdb.com/name/nm0146216
twitter.com/edcatmull

PLACE TO B PRODUCTIONS
Production company and distributor

6950 Sundew Creek
Converse, TX 78109
210-334-7802

qualleymoon@hotmail.com
imdb.com/company/co0310473

Does not accept any unsolicited material. Project types include short films. Genres include family, drama, and comedy. Established in 2010.

PLAN B ENTERTAINMENT
Production company

9150 Wilshire Blvd
Beverly Hills, CA 90212

310-205-5166 (phone)
310-275-5234 (fax)

imdb.com/company/co0136967
facebook.com/pages/Plan-B-Entertainment/
    104009369636628

Does not accept any unsolicited material. Project types include feature films and TV. Genres include animation, drama, fantasy, action, and myth. Established in 2004.

Brad Pitt
Producer
310-275-6135
imdb.com/name/nm0000093

Jeremy Kleiner
Producer
imdb.com/name/nm1250070

Sarah Esberg
Producer
310-275-6135
imdb.com/name/nm1209665

PLANET FILMS
Production company

7606 Dockside Dr
Rowlett, TX 75088
903-952-1211

planet.films@yahoo.com
planetfilms.info
imdb.com/company/co0072743

Does not accept any unsolicited material. Genres include comedy, documentary, and drama.

PLANET HORROR PICTURES
Production company

PO Box 543
Perry, FL 32347

info@surroundfilmworks.com
imdb.com/company/co0233012

Does not accept any unsolicited material.

PLANETWORKS ENTERPRISES
Distributor and sales agent

PO BOX 5205
Limerick, PA 19468

info@planetworksent.com
planetworksent.com
imdb.com/company/co0391539

Accepts query letters from unproduced, unrepresented writers via email. Project types include TV. Genres include comedy, horror, and drama.

PLATFORM ENTERTAINMENT
Production company

128 Sierra St
El Segundo, CA 90425
310-322-3737 (phone)
310-322-3729 (fax)

platformentertainment.com
imdb.com/company/co0085659
linkedin.com/company/platform-entertainment-group
facebook.com/PlatformEntUK

Accepts query letters from unproduced, unrepresented writers. Project types include feature films. Established in 1998.

Larry Gabriel
Producer
310-322-3737
imdb.com/name/nm0300181

Daniel Levin
Producer
310-322-3737
imdb.com/name/nm0505575

Scott Sorrentino
Producer
310-322-3737
imdb.com/name/nm1391744

PLATINUM DUNES
Production company

631 Colorado Ave
Santa Monica, CA 90401
310-319-6565 (phone)
310-319-6570 (fax)

imdb.com/company/co0071240

facebook.com/pages/Platinum-Dunes/
108426449182341
twitter.com/platinumdunes

Does not accept any unsolicited material. Project types include feature films and TV. Established in 2001.

Bradley Fuller
Producer
imdb.com/name/nm0298181

Michael Bay
Partner
imdb.com/name/nm0000881

Andrew Form
Producer
imdb.com/name/nm0286320

PLATINUM STUDIOS
Production company

11835 W. Olympic Blvd. Suite 1235E
Los Angeles, CA 90064
310-807-8100 (phone)
310-887-3943 (fax)

info@platinumstudios.com
platinumstudios.com
imdb.com/company/co0018599
facebook.com/PlatinumStudios
twitter.com/PlatinumPDOS

Does not accept any unsolicited material. Project types include feature films. Genres include science fiction, action, fantasy, and thriller.

PLATYPUS PRODUCTIONS
Production company

3401 S Congress Ave
Boynton Beach, FL 33426
561-737-8000 (phone)
561-364-4474 (fax)

imdb.com/company/co0091983

Does not accept any unsolicited material. Project types include TV. Genres include comedy, documentary, and family. Established in 1983.

PLAYTONE PRODUCTIONS
Production company

PO Box 7340
Santa Monica, CA 90406
310-394-5700 (phone)
310-394-4466 (fax)

playtone.com
imdb.com/company/co0101441
facebook.com/TomHanks
twitter.com/tomhanks

Does not accept any unsolicited material. Project types include feature films and TV. Established in 1996.

Tom Hanks
Partner
310-394-5700
imdb.com/name/nm0000158

PLUM PICTURES
Production company

Plum Pictures
33 Oval Rd
London NW1 7EA
+44 (0207-184-5700

info@plumpictures.co.uk
plumpictures.co.uk
imdb.com/company/co0284770
facebook.com/plum.pictures.7
twitter.com/plumpictures

Does not accept any unsolicited material. Project types include feature films. Genres include drama and comedy. Established in 2007.

POILEY WOOD ENTERTAINMENT
Production company

200 Grandview Pl
Longwood, FL 32779

imdb.com/company/co0319524
facebook.com/PoileyWoodEntertainment

Does not accept any unsolicited material. Genres include drama and thriller.

POILEYWOOD ENTERTAINMENT
Production company

200 Grandview Place
Longwood, FL 32712

BruceMartinWood@gmail.com
imdb.com/company/co0319524
facebook.com/PoileyWoodEntertainment

Does not accept any unsolicited material. Project types include feature films. Genres include horror, thriller, and drama.

POINT ROAD FILMS

1041 N. Formosa Ave., Writer's Bldg., Suite 9
West Hollywood, 90046

facebook.com

Does not accept any unsolicited material. Project types include feature films. Genres include action, horror, and drama.

POINTS WEST PICTURES
Production company

9100 Wilshire Blvd. Suite 1000w
Beverly Hills, CA 90212

imdb.com/company/co0268748

Does not accept any unsolicited material. Project types include TV and feature films. Genres include comedy and drama.

POKER PRODUCTIONS
Production company

3395 S Jones Blvd. Ste 318
Las Vegas, NV 89146
702-838-2594 (phone)
701-221-9252 (fax)

pokerprod.com
imdb.com/company/co0243353
linkedin.com/company/poker-productions
twitter.com/Poker_Prod

Does not accept any unsolicited material. Project types include TV. Genres include drama.

POLE POLE TIMES
Production company and distributor

7F 4 4 1 Higashinakano
Tokyo 164 0003
Japan

+81 3 3227 1405 (phone)
+81 3 3227 1406 (fax)

info@polepoletimes.jp
polepoletimes.jp/times
imdb.com/company/co0023509

Does not accept any unsolicited material. Project types
include TV. Genres include documentary.

Seiichi Motohashi
Executive
imdb.com/name/nm0782570

POLSKY FILMS
Production company

8938 Keith Ave
West Hollywood, CA 90069
310-278-1454

info@polskyfilms.com
imdb.com/company/co0202713
facebook.com/pages/Polsky-Films/139696959381434

Does not accept any unsolicited material. Project types
include feature films. Genres include crime, drama,
and documentary.

Liam Satre-Meloy
Executive
imdb.com/name/nm3176310

Gabe Polsky
Producer
imdb.com/name/nm2126907

Alan Polsky
Producer
imdb.com/name/nm2611223

POLYCROME DISTRIBUTION
Distributor

13400 Riverside Dr
Suite 301
Sherman Oaks, CA 91423
818-788-8908

imdb.com/company/co0249362

Does not accept any unsolicited material.

POLYGON PICTURES
Production company

3-20-1-1F
Minami Azabu
Minato, Tokyo 106-0047
Japan
03-5789-4170

contact@ppi.co.jp
ppi.co.jp
imdb.com/company/co0176146

Does not accept any unsolicited material. Project
types include feature films. Genres include fantasy, action,
and science fiction.

Shûzô Shiota
Executive
imdb.com/name/nm2478744

POLYMORPHIC PICTURES
Production company

4000 Warner Blvd
Building 81, Suite 212
Burbank, CA 91522
818-954-3822

imdb.com/company/co0297133
facebook.com/pages/Polymorphic-Pictures/
   118207454875569

Does not accept any unsolicited material. Project types
include feature films. Established in 2010.

Polly Johnsen
Producer
imdb.com/name/nm1480881

PONY CANYON
Sales agent

2-5-10 Toranomon
Minato-Ku
Tokyo 105-8487
Japan
+81 3 55 21 80 16 (phone)
+81 3 55 21 81 07 (fax)

intl@ponycanyon.co.jp
ponycanyon.co.jp
imdb.com/company/co0017081

Does not accept any unsolicited material. Project types include TV, feature films, and short films. Genres include action.

Shûji Danzen
Producer
imdb.com/name/nm3437401

POPART FILM FACTORY
Production company

23679 Calabasas Rd, Suite 686
Calabasas, CA 91302

popartfilms@earthlink.net
popartfilmfactory.com
imdb.com/company/co0074606

Does not accept any unsolicited material. Project types include feature films. Genres include action, crime, science fiction, and drama.

POP CINEMA
Distributor

PO Box 152
Butler, NJ 07405
973-838-3030 (phone)
973-492-8988 (fax)

PopCinema@aol.com
imdb.com/company/co0212139

Does not accept any unsolicited material. Project types include feature films and TV. Genres include thriller and horror.

POPE PIUS XII PRODUCTION
Production company

PO Box 403137
Miami Beach, FL 33140
305-600-2785

info@popepiusxiimovie.com
imdb.com/company/co0279676

Does not accept any unsolicited material.

POP-UP PICTURE SHOW
Production company

521 S. Mason Rd.
Katy, TX 77450

ATG.JohnnyD@yahoo.com
popuppictureshow.com
imdb.com/company/co0491573
facebook.com/Pop-Up-Picture-Show-335904650375

Does not accept any unsolicited material. Project types include short films. Genres include horror and comedy.

PORCHLIGHT ENTERTAINMENT
Sales agent

14724 Ventura Blvd, Suite 1105
Sherman Oaks, California 91403
310-477-8400

info@porchlight.com
porchlight.com
imdb.com/company/co0074499
linkedin.com/company/porchlight-entertainment
facebook.com/PorchLight-Entertainment-
    Inc-196348720408658
twitter.com/PorchLightEnt

Does not accept any unsolicited material. Project types include TV and feature films. Genres include drama and romance.

PORCHLIGHT FILMS
Production company

94 Oxford St
Suite 31
Darlinghurst NSW 2010
Australia
61-2-9326-9916 (phone)
61-2-9357-1479 (fax)

admin@porchlightfilms.com.au
porchlightfilms.com.au
imdb.com/company/co0141203
twitter.com/porchlightfilms

Does not accept any unsolicited material. Project types include feature films and TV. Genres include horror, drama, crime, thriller, and comedy. Established in 1996.

Liz Watts
Producer
imdb.com/name/nm0915192

Anita Sheehan
Producer
imdb.com/name/nm1618460

Vincent Sheehan
Producer
vincent@porchlightfilms.com.au
imdb.com/name/nm0790636

PORTERGELLER ENTERTAINMENT
Production company

6352 De Longpre Ave
Los Angeles, CA 90028
323-822-4400 (phone)
323-822-7270 (fax)

info@portergeller.com
imdb.com/company/co0220606

Does not accept any unsolicited material. Project types include feature films and TV.

Darryl Porter
Producer
imdb.com/name/nm0692080

Michael Tyree
Producer
imdb.com/name/nm2699784

PORTFOLIO ENTERTAINMENT
Production company and distributor

901 King St West
Suite 301
Toronto, ON
M5V 3H5
416-483-9773 (phone)
416-483-6537 (fax)

portfolio@portfolio-ent.com
portfolioentertainment.com
imdb.com/company/co0024598
linkedin.com/company/portfolio-entertainment
facebook.com/portfolioent
twitter.com/portfolioent

Does not accept any unsolicited material. Project types include TV. Genres include family.

Joy Rosen
Producer
imdb.com/name/nm1103793

PORTOBELLO PICTURES
Production company

12 Addison Ave
Holland Park
London W11 4QR
UK
+ 44 (0) 20 7605 1396 (phone)
+ 44 (0) 20 7605 1391 (fax)

mail@portobellopictures.com
portobellopictures.com
imdb.com/company/co0103646

Does not accept any unsolicited material. Project types include TV. Genres include drama and thriller.

Eric Abraham
Producer
imdb.com/name/nm0008937

PORTSMOUTH PICTURES
Production company

330 N Screenland Dr
Suite 132
Burbank, CA 91505
818-842-8998

imdb.com/company/co0335797

Does not accept any unsolicited material. Genres include animation.

POSSIBILITY PRODUCTIONS
Production company

13480 Gallant Fox Circle West
Jacksonville, FL 32218
904-982-1288

imdb.com/company/co0203620

Does not accept any unsolicited material. Genres include thriller.

POSSIBLE FILMS
Production company and distributor

302A West 12th St, Suite 334, New York City , NY,
United States, 10014

info@possiblefilms.com
halhartley.com
imdb.com/company/co0102939

Does not accept any unsolicited material. Project types
include TV. Genres include drama, comedy, and
family.

POTBOILER PRODUCTIONS
Production company

9 Greek St
London W1D 4DQ
UK
+44 20 7734 7372 (phone)
+44 20 7287 5228 (fax)

info@potboiler.co.uk
potboiler.co.uk
imdb.com/company/co0110938

Does not accept any unsolicited material. Project types
include feature films. Genres include drama.

Andrea Calderwood
Producer
imdb.com/name/nm0129573

POTION PICTURES
Production company

909 Texas
Houston, TX 77002
866-621-0331

johnetteduff@aol.com
potionpictures.co.uk
imdb.com/company/co0297496
facebook.com/PotionPictures
twitter.com/potionpictures

Does not accept any unsolicited material. Genres
include romance and comedy.

POW! ENTERTAINMENT
Production company

9440 Santa Monica Blvd, Suite 620
Beverly Hills, CA 90210
310-275-9933 (phone)
310-285-9955 (fax)

info@powentertainment.com
powentertainment.com
imdb.com/company/co0109379
linkedin.com/company/stan-lee's-pow-entertainment
facebook.com/pages/POW-Entertainment/
    114580325221034

Accepts query letters from unproduced, unrepresented
writers via email. Project types include feature films
and TV. Established in 2001.

Stan Lee
CCO
imdb.com/name/nm0498278
twitter.com/TheRealStanLee

POWERHOUSE PICTURES
Production company

13 Fern Ave
Floor 2
Collingswood, NJ 08108
917-977-0613

info@powerhousepictures.com
powerhousepictures.com
imdb.com/company/co0161027

Does not accept any unsolicited material. Project types
include short films. Genres include documentary.

POWERROC PRODUCTIONS
Production company

3525 Piedmont Rd
Atlanta, GA 30305
404-358-0448

information@powerrocproductions.com
powerrocproductions.com
imdb.com/company/co0248320

Does not accept any unsolicited material. Genres
include thriller, documentary, and drama.

POWER UP FILMS
Production company and distributor

419 N Larchmont Blvd #283
Los Angeles, CA 90004
323-463-3154

info@powerupfilms.org
powerupfilms.org
imdb.com/company/co0026662
facebook.com/pages/POWER-UP-films/99261618727
twitter.com/thrashPOWrUPfLm

Accepts query letters from unproduced, unrepresented writers via email. Project types include feature films and TV. Established in 2000.

Lisa Thrasher
President of Film Production
imdb.com/name/nm1511212

Stacy Codikow
Founder
imdb.com/name/nm0168499

PRACTICAL PICTURES

Production company and distributor

2211 Corinth Ave
Los Angeles, CA 90064
310-405-7777

practicalpictures.practicalaction.org/home.php
imdb.com/company/co0172687
facebook.com/pages/Practical-Pictures/
160830843940750

Does not accept any unsolicited material.

Jason Koffeman
Creative Executive
imdb.com/name/nm1788896

PRANA STUDIOS

Studio

1145 N McCadden Place
Los Angeles, CA 90038
323-645-6500 (phone)
323-645-6510 (fax)

info@pranastudios.com
pranastudios.com
imdb.com/company/co0206196
facebook.com/PRANASTUDIOS

Does not accept any unsolicited material. Project types include feature films. Genres include action, comedy, fantasy, family, animation, and drama.

Samir Hoon
President
tescom.rs/3/samir-hoon
imdb.com/name/nm0393696
linkedin.com/pub/dir/Samir/Hoon

Arish Fyzee
Creative Director
imdb.com/name/nm0299564
linkedin.com/pub/arish-fyzee/14/38B/9A5

Kristin Dornig
Co-Creative Director & CEO
imdb.com/name/nm0233921

Danielle Sterling
VP of Development
imdb.com/name/nm1306678

PREFERRED CONTENT

Production company and distributor

6363 Wilshire Blvd, Suite 350
Los Angeles, CA 90048
323-782-9193

info@preferredcontent.net
imdb.com/company/co0323647
linkedin.com/company/preferred-content
facebook.com/preferredcontent

Does not accept any unsolicited material. Project types include feature films. Genres include action. Established in 2010.

Kevin Iwashina
Producer
imdb.com/name/nm2250990

Ross Dinerstein
Producer
imdb.com/name/nm1895871

Trace Sheehan
Producer
imdb.com/name/nm2618717

PREFERRED FILM & TV

Production company

6363 Wilshire Blvd
Los Angeles, CA 90048
323-782-9193

imdb.com/company/co0407914

Does not accept any unsolicited material. Project types include feature films and TV. Genres include thriller and horror.

PREGER ENTERTAINMENT
Production company

6175 NW 167th St, Suite G10
Hialeah, FL 33015
305-893-0207

info@pregerentertainment.com
pregerentertainment.com
imdb.com/company/co0243710

Does not accept any unsolicited material. Project types include feature films. Genres include horror, drama, science fiction, and fantasy.

PRELUDE LIMITED
Production company

400 N Congress Ave
Suite 130
West Palm Beach, FL 33401
888-607-3555

danield@preludepictures.com
imdb.com/company/co0394399

Does not accept any unsolicited material. Genres include comedy.

PRELUDE PICTURES
Production company

1711 Worthington Rd., Suite 108
West Palm Beach, FL 33409
561-683-6614 (phone)
561-683-6615 (fax)

markk@preludepictures.com
preludepictures.com
imdb.com/company/co0065424
linkedin.com/company/prelude-pictures

Does not accept any unsolicited material. Project types include feature films. Genres include comedy and drama.

PREMISE ENTERTAINMENT
Production company and distributor

5422 Carrier Dr Suite 306
Orlando, FL 32819
407-345-9800

premiseentertainment.com
imdb.com/company/co0215397
linkedin.com/company/premise-entertainment
facebook.com/PremiseEntertainment
twitter.com/premisestudio

Does not accept any unsolicited material. Project types include feature films and short films. Genres include animation, fantasy, family, documentary, and comedy. Established in 2001.

PRENTISS-WOOD FILMS
Production company

PO Box 101420
Denver, CO 80250

info@prentisswoodfilms.com
imdb.com/company/co0457435

Does not accept any unsolicited material. Project types include short films and feature films. Genres include drama, thriller, and horror.

Amanda Prentiss
Writer (Executive)
imdb.com/name/nm4885993

PRESCIENCE FILM FUND
Production company

Debello House
14-18 Heddon St
London W1B 4DA
UK
+44 20 7745 6140 (phone)
+44 20 7439 8794 (fax)

info@presciencefilm.com
presciencefilmfinance.co.uk
imdb.com/company/co0126667

Does not accept any unsolicited material. Project types include TV and feature films. Genres include crime, action, and drama.

PRESIDIO
Distributor

2-3-3 FDC Koujimachi Bldg 11F
Chiyoda-Ku
Tokyo 102-0083
Japan
+81 3 52 15 56 32 (phone)
+81 3 52 15 56 33 (fax)

t.tanaka@presidio.co.jp
presidio.co.jp
imdb.com/company/co0026526

Does not accept any unsolicited material. Project types include TV, short films, and feature films. Genres include drama.

Yasutaka Hanada
President (Executive)
imdb.com/name/nm3110383

PRESSMAN FILM
Production company

9469 Jefferson Blvd, Suite 119
Los Angeles, CA 90232
310-450-9692 (phone)
310-450-9705 (fax)

47 Murray St
New York, NY 10007
212-489-3333 (phone)
212-489-2103 (fax)

info@pressman.com
pressman.com
imdb.com/company/co0006728
linkedin.com/company/edward-r-pressman-film-corp
facebook.com/PressmanFilm
twitter.com/PRESSMANFILM

Does not accept any unsolicited material. Project types include TV and feature films. Genres include myth, drama, thriller, comedy, fantasy, and action. Established in 1969.

Edward Pressman
CEO
imdb.com/name/nm0696299
Assistant: Kelly McKee

PRESS ON FEATURES
Production company and distributor

The South Lodge
Lammas Park Gardens
London W55HZ
UK

jeff@pressonfeatures.co.uk
imdb.com/company/co0271461

Does not accept any unsolicited material. Project types include TV and feature films. Genres include thriller, action, and crime.

Simon Phillips
Producer
imdb.com/name/nm1792652

PRETTY MATCHES PRODUCTIONS
Production company

1790 Broadway, 20th Floor
New York, New York 10019
212-512-5755

imdb.com/company/co0173730

Accepts query letters from unproduced, unrepresented writers. Project types include feature films and TV. Genres include comedy, reality, romance, and non-fiction. Established in 2005.

Sarah Parker
Principal
imdb.com/name/nm0000572

Alison Benson
Producer
imdb.com/name/nm3929030
linkedin.com/pub/alison-benson/45/930/826
Assistant: Matt Nathanson

PRETTY MONKEYS
Production company and distributor

3435 Wynkoop St
Denver, CO 80216
720-431-5000

info@prettymonkeys.com
prettymonkeys.com
imdb.com/company/co0354000

Does not accept any unsolicited material. Genres include comedy and drama.

Rodney Wilson
Principal (Executive)
imdb.com/name/nm0934057

PRETTY PICTURES
Production company and distributor

100 Universal City Plaza
Building 2352-A, 3rd Floor
Universal City, CA 91608
818-733-0926 (phone)
818-866-0847 (fax)

imdb.com/company/co0011868
facebook.com/Prettypicturesfilms

Does not accept any unsolicited material. Project types include TV and feature films. Genres include thriller, non-fiction, drama, romance, and comedy.

Tore Schmidt
Producer
imdb.com/name/nm1664013

Gail Mutrux
Producer
imdb.com/name/nm0616153

PRIMAL FILMS INC.
Production company

18 Hillhurst Crescent
Courtice, Ontario
L1E 2A5
Canda

dave@primalthemovie.com
primalfilms.com
imdb.com/company/co0150008
facebook.com/PrimalFilms
twitter.com/davidjfrancis

Does not accept any unsolicited material. Project types include feature films and short films. Genres include horror, science fiction, and comedy.

PRIMARY PRODUCTIONS
Production company

440 Lafayette St, 6th Floor
New York, NY 10003
212-674-1400 (phone)
212-674-0081 (fax)

imdb.com/company/co0177016

Does not accept any unsolicited material. Project types include feature films. Genres include comedy and family.

PRIMARY WAVE ENTERTAINMENT
Production company and studio

10850 Wilshire Blvd 6th Floor
Los Angeles CA 90024
310-247-8630 (phone)
310-247-8629 (fax)

116 E 16th St, Ninth Floor, New York, NY, United States, 10003
212-661-6990 (phone)
212-661-8890 (fax)

primarywavemusic.com
imdb.com/company/co0378422

Does not accept any unsolicited material. Project types include TV. Genres include comedy, drama, thriller, family, and reality.

PRIMARY WAVE MUSIC
Production company

10850 Wilshire Blvd.
Suite #600
Los Angeles, Ca. 90024 USA
310-247-8630 (phone)
310-247-8629 (fax)

116 E 16th St, 9th Floor
New York, NY 10003
212-661-6990 (phone)
212-661-8890 (fax)

dsimone@dswent.com

primarywavemusic.com
imdb.com/company/co0352823
linkedin.com/company/primary-wave-music
facebook.com/PrimaryWave
twitter.com/PrimaryWave

Does not accept any unsolicited material. Project types include TV.

David Simone
Producer
imdb.com/name/nm0800108

Winston Simone
Producer
imdb.com/name/nm4483051

PRIMERIDIAN ENTERTAINMENT
Production company

301 N Canon Dr, Suite 223, Beverly Hills, CA, United States, 90210
310-858-3003

info@pmellc.com
imdb.com/company/co0423129

Does not accept any unsolicited material.

Joshua Solomon
Casting
310-858-3003
imdb.com/name/nm2668394

PRIMEWAVE NEXEED
Distributor

5-13-14-4F
Ginza
Chuo, Tokyo 104-0061
Japan

nex@nexeed.com
nexeed.com/seisaku
imdb.com/company/co0315548

Does not accept any unsolicited material. Project types include feature films and TV. Genres include crime, horror, and thriller.

PRINC FILMS
Production company and sales agent

9106 Cold Stream Ln
Eden Prairie, MN 55347
763-458-1967 (phone)
952-681-2722 (fax)

info@princfilms.com
princfilms.com
imdb.com/company/co0238800
facebook.com/pages/Princ-Films/169384593173970
twitter.com/princfilms

Does not accept any unsolicited material. Project types include TV. Genres include family, thriller, and drama.

Jennifer LoMaglio Methot
Executive
imdb.com/name/nm5959467

PRINCIPAL DISTRIBUTING
Distributor

1501 Broadway
New York, NY

imdb.com/company/co0006983

Does not accept any unsolicited material. Project types include feature films. Genres include horror and action.

PRINCIPATO-YOUNG ENTERTAINMENT
Production company and studio

261 Madison Ave.
9th Floor
New York, NY 10016
212-725-0010

9465 Wilshire Blvd, Suite 900
Beverly Hills, CA 90212
310-274-4474

principatoyoung.com
imdb.com/company/co0049718
linkedin.com/company/principato-young-
    entertainment
facebook.com/pages/Principato-Young-Entertainment/
    199597900062880
twitter.com/PYE_Digital

Accepts query letters from unproduced, unrepresented writers. Project types include TV and feature films. Genres include comedy.

Peter Principato
Partner
imdb.com/name/nm1213782
Assistant: Max Suchov

Paul Young
Partner
imdb.com/name/nm1116986

David Gardner
Partner
imdb.com/name/nm2148266

Allen Fischer
Partner
imdb.com/name/nm1461672

Brian Dobbins
Partner
imdb.com/name/nm1827666

PRIVATEER ENTERTAINMENT
Production company

10441 Bloomfield St.
Toluca Lake, CA 91602
(310) 717-4777

1901 E. 51st St.
Austin, TX 78723
310-717-4777

Privateer@silversailentertainment.com
silversailentertainment.com
imdb.com/company/co0475396
facebook.com/pages/Silver-Sail-Entertainment/
    270615533001183
twitter.com/SilverSail_Ent

Does not accept any unsolicited material. Project types include TV. Genres include action.

PROCESS MEDIA
Production company

225 Broadway
New York, NY 10007
212-219-3209

info@process-media.com
process-media.com
imdb.com/company/co0210895

Does not accept any unsolicited material. Genres include comedy and drama.

PROCHILD ELDER ENTERTAINMENT
Production company

P.O. Box 16328
Plantation, FL 33318

imdb.com/company/co0241624

Does not accept any unsolicited material. Genres include drama.

PRODCO, INC.
Production company

427 S Victory Blvd
Burbank, CA 91502

imdb.com/company/co0075311

Does not accept any unsolicited material. Project types include TV. Genres include drama, comedy, and family.

PRODIGY PICTURES
Production company and distributor

124 The East Mall
Toronto, ON M8Z 5V5
Canada
416-977-3473 (phone)
416-977-5909 (fax)

info@prodigypictures.com
prodigypictures.com
imdb.com/company/co0180560
linkedin.com/company/prodigy-pictures
facebook.com/Prodigy-Pictures-331298996925827

Does not accept any unsolicited material. Genres include science fiction.

Jay Firestone
Producer
imdb.com/name/nm0278649

PRODUCE A CRIME PRODUCTIONS

Production company

1933 N. Beachwood Dr.
#201
Los Angeles, CA 90068

imdb.com/company/co0160385

Does not accept any unsolicited material. Project types include short films. Genres include drama, crime, and romance.

PRODUCER CONTENT

Production company

11012 Ventura Blvd. #138 Studio City,
CA 91604
323-381-0246

support@producercontent.com
producercontent.com
imdb.com/company/co0530090
facebook.com/producercontent
twitter.com/producercontent

Accepts query letters from unproduced, unrepresented writers via email. Genres include horror and comedy.

PRODUCERS CIRCLE

Production company

435 E 52nd St
Suite 1E
New York, NY 10022
877-268-3500

9663 Santa Monica Blvd
Suite 424
Beverly Hills, CA 90210
877-268-3500

imdb.com/company/co0043341

Does not accept any unsolicited material. Project types include feature films. Genres include crime, comedy, and horror.

PRODUCERS DAVID SHELDON AND JOAN MCCALL

Production company

1437 Rising Glen Rd.
Los Angeles, CA 90069
310-652-6263

davidsheldon@hollywoodwestentertainment.com
imdb.com/company/co0397966

Does not accept any unsolicited material.

PRODUCERS DISTRIBUTION AGENCY (PDA)

Distributor

555 W 25th St, 4th Floor
New York, NY 10001, USA
212-204-7979 (phone)
212-204-7980 (fax)

office@cineticmedia.com
cineticmedia.com
imdb.com/company/co0300083

Does not accept any unsolicited material. Project types include theater. Genres include comedy, horror, and drama.

PRODUCERS GUILD OF AMERICA

Production company

8530 Wilshire Blvd., Suite 400
Beverly Hills, CA 90211
310-358-9020 (phone)
310-358-9520 (fax)

info@producersguild.org
producersguild.org
imdb.com/company/co0095073
facebook.com/pga
twitter.com/producersguild

Does not accept any unsolicited material. Project types include short films and feature films. Genres include action and comedy.

PRODUCERS REPRESENTATIVE ORGANIZATION

Production company

100 Wilshire
Suite 950
Santa Monica, CA 90401
213-207-6871

imdb.com/company/co0024053

Does not accept any unsolicited material. Genres
include thriller, drama, and crime.

PRODUCTION POINT
Production company

1223 Wilshire Blvd. Suite #947
Santa Monica, CA 90403
310-459-8989 (phone)
310-496-2780 (fax)

productionpoint.com
facebook.com/productionpoint

Does not accept any unsolicited material. Project types
include feature films. Genres include drama.

PROFILES TELEVISION PRODUCTIONS
Production company

200 N. Continental Blvd., 3rd Floor
El Segundo, CA 90245

imdb.com/company/co0095168
facebook.com/pages/Profiles-Television-Productions-
    LLC/130341067065498

Does not accept any unsolicited material. Project types
include TV.

PROLIFIC ENTERTAINMENT
Production company

25 Broadway
New York, NY 10004
212-412-9188 (phone)
347-287-6702 (fax)

general@prolific-ent.com
prolific-ent.com
imdb.com/company/co0294485
linkedin.com/company/prolific-entertainment
facebook.com/Prolific-
    Entertainment-207804189327265

Does not accept any unsolicited material. Project types
include feature films. Genres include science fiction.

PROMETHEUS ENTERTAINMENT
Production company

6430 Sunset Blvd., Suite 1450
Los Angeles, CA 90028
323-769-4000 (phone)
323-769-4060 (fax)

prometheusentertainment.com
imdb.com/company/co0031410
linkedin.com/company/prometheus-entertainment

Does not accept any unsolicited material. Project types
include feature films and TV. Genres include drama
and science fiction.

PROSPECTOR PRODUCTIONS
Production company

1495 Hancock St
Quincy, MA
617-328-1467

info@prospectorproductions.com
prospectorproductions.com
imdb.com/company/co0380089

Does not accept any unsolicited material. Project types
include TV.

PROSPECT PARK
Production company

2049 Century Park East #2550
Century City, CA 90067
310-746-4900 (phone)
310-746-4890 (fax)

imdb.com/company/co0276484

Accepts query letters from unproduced, unrepresented
writers via email. Project types include TV and feature
films. Genres include non-fiction, drama, and reality.

Jeff Kwatinetz
Executive Producer
imdb.com/name/nm0477153

Paul Frank
imdb.com/name/nm1899773

PROSPERITY FILMS
Production company and financing company

prosperityfilms.com

Does not accept any unsolicited material. Project types include feature films and TV. Genres include thriller, family, science fiction, fantasy, detective, and action. Established in 2014.

Paul Eyres
CEO
paul@prosperityfilms.com
prosperityfilms.com

PROSPERO PICTURES
Production company

1200 Bay St
Ste 400
Toronto, ON M5R 2A5
Canada
416-926-0853 (phone)
416-920-8373 (fax)

martin.katz@prosperopictures.com
imdb.com/company/co0138248
twitter.com/ProsperoPics

Does not accept any unsolicited material. Genres include fantasy.

Martin Katz
Producer
imdb.com/name/nm0441792

PROTAGONIST PICTURES
Production company and distributor

42-48 Great Portland St, London, United Kingdom, W1W 7NB
011-442-077349000

info@protagonistpictures.com
protagonistpictures.com
imdb.com/company/co0228888

Does not accept any unsolicited material. Project types include feature films. Genres include action, family, and thriller.

PROTOCOL ENTERTAINMENT
Production company and distributor

80 Spadina Ave
Ste 405
Toronto, ON M5V2J4

Canada
416-966-2711 (phone)
416-966-2711 (fax)

randy@protocolentertainment.com
imdb.com/company/co0007719

Does not accept any unsolicited material. Project types include short films. Genres include comedy.

Steve Levitan
Producer
imdb.com/name/nm0506159

PROTOZOA PICTURES
Production company

104 N 7th St
Brooklyn, NY 11211
718-388-5280 (phone)
718-388-5425 (fax)

protozoa.com
imdb.com/company/co0062935

Does not accept any unsolicited material. Project types include feature films. Genres include action, science fiction, horror, fantasy, and thriller.

Darren Aronofsky
imdb.com/name/nm0004716

PROVIDENT FILMS
Production company, distributor, and sales agent

741 Cool Springs Blvd
Franklin, TN 37067

info@providentfilms.org
providentfilms.org
imdb.com/company/co0248927
facebook.com/providentfilms
twitter.com/providentfilms

Does not accept any unsolicited material. Project types include feature films and TV. Genres include comedy, action, and drama.

Terry Hemmings
Producer
imdb.com/name/nm1978866

PUMPJACK ENTERTAINMENT
Production company

602 Ellis St.
P.O. Box 1055
Menard, TX 76859
325-396-4530

mail@pumpjackentertainment.com
imdb.com/company/co0191687

Does not accept any unsolicited material. Genres include horror.

PUNCHED IN THE HEAD PRODUCTIONS
Production company

540 President St, Suite #1D
Brooklyn, NY 11215
718-422-0704

punchedinthehead.com
imdb.com/company/co0177229

Does not accept any unsolicited material. Project types include TV.

PUNCH PRODUCTIONS
Production company

11661 San Vincente Blvd., Suite 222
Los Angeles , CA 90049
310-442-4880 (phone)
310-442-4884 (fax)

punch@punch21.com
imdb.com/company/co0090684

Does not accept any unsolicited material. Genres include drama and comedy.

PURE GRASS FILMS
Production company

16 Manette St
London W1D 4AR UK
UK

info@puregrassfilms.com
puregrassfilms.com/contact
imdb.com/company/co0193056
facebook.com/puregrassfilms

twitter.com/puregrassfilms

Does not accept any unsolicited material. Project types include TV and feature films. Genres include fantasy, drama, and science fiction.

Christophe Charlier
Producer
imdb.com/name/nm4763831

PURE GRASS FILMS, LTD.
Production company

1st Floor, 16 Manette St
London, W1D 4AR

info@puregrassfilms.com
puregrassfilms.com
imdb.com/company/co0193056
facebook.com/puregrassfilms
twitter.com/puregrassfilms

Does not accept any unsolicited material. Project types include feature films. Genres include horror, science fiction, thriller, non-fiction, drama, and action.

Ben Grass
imdb.com/name/nm2447240

PURPLE BUNNY PRODUCTIONS
Production company

10646 Windsor Court
Orlando, FL 32821
407-222-7174 (phone)
646-219-5546 (fax)

jen@purplebunnyproductions.com
imdb.com/company/co0223249
facebook.com/PurpleBunnyProductions

Does not accept any unsolicited material. Project types include short films. Genres include horror.

PURPLE BUTTERFLY PRODUCTIONS
Production company

38-15 Pellington Dr
Fair Lawn, NJ 07410
857-445-3864

pbp@teamdesertsun.com
imdb.com/company/co0179070

linkedin.com/company/manic-butterfly-productions

Does not accept any unsolicited material.

PURPLE ROSE FILMS
Production company

137 Park St
Chelsea, MI 48118
734-433-7782

purplerosefilms@aol.com
imdb.com/company/co0056223

Does not accept any unsolicited material. Project types include feature films.

PUSH IT PRODUCTIONS
Production company

121 W. Lexington Dr, Suite 635
Glendale, CA 91203
818-480-6519

pipasst1@pushitprods.com
pushitprods.com
imdb.com/company/co0456072
facebook.com/pushitprods
twitter.com/pushitprods

Does not accept any unsolicited material. Project types include TV. Genres include comedy.

QED INTERNATIONAL
Production company

1800 N Highland Ave, 5th Floor
Los Angeles, CA 90028
323-785-7900 (phone)
323-785-7901 (fax)

info@qedintl.com
qedintl.com
imdb.com/company/co0178111
facebook.com/pages/QED-International/
    97974558257
twitter.com/QEDIntl

Accepts scripts from unproduced, unrepresented writers. Project types include feature films. Genres include drama, fantasy, crime, romance, thriller, comedy, action, myth, and horror. Established in 2005.

Bill Block
imdb.com/name/nm1088848

QUADRANT FILMS
Production company

129 Yorkville Ave
Toronto, ON M5R 1C4
Canada
416-927-0016

imdb.com/company/co0041408

Does not accept any unsolicited material. Project types include feature films and TV. Genres include horror and drama.

QUADRANT PICTURES
Production company

9229 Sunset Blvd, Suite 225
West Hollywood, CA 90069
424-244-1860

assistant@quadrantpictures.com
quadrantmotionpictures.com
imdb.com/company/co0316578

Accepts query letters from unproduced, unrepresented writers via email. Project types include feature films and TV. Genres include thriller, science fiction, horror, action, family, and drama. Established in 2011.

John Schwartz
Producer
imdb.com/name/nm1862748

Doug Davison
imdb.com/name/nm0205713

QUARTERDECK ENTERTAINMENT INC.
Production company

Studio City, CA 91604
310-625-3408

boarwild@yahoo.com
quarterdeckent.com
imdb.com/company/co0495519

Does not accept any unsolicited material. Project types include short films. Genres include period. Established in 2013.

QUARTERDECK PROD CORP
Production company

81 Catalina Court
Vero Beach, FL 32963
310-625-3408

imdb.com/company/co0493882

Does not accept any unsolicited material. Project types include short films. Genres include period. Established in 2015.

QUATTRO MEDIA
Production company and distributor

171 Pier Ave, #328
Santa Monica, CA 90405
323-828-2289

imdb.com/company/co0125407
linkedin.com/company/quattro-media

Does not accept any unsolicited material. Project types include feature films.

QUICK DRAW PRODUCTIONS
Production company

920 Congress Ave
Austin, TX 78701
512-614-6200

imdb.com/company/co0316574

Does not accept any unsolicited material. Genres include thriller, drama, and fantasy.

QUINCY PICTURES
Production company

1645 Vine St
Los Angeles, CA 90028
323-798-4681

imdb.com/company/co0382331
facebook.com/Quincy-Pictures-183228448421955

Does not accept any unsolicited material. Project types include feature films. Genres include horror.

QUIXOTE ENTERTAINMENT
Production company

301 Wilmes
Austin, TX 78752
US
512-535-6076

wade@quixoteentertainnment.com
quixoteentertainment.com
imdb.com/company/co0189568
facebook.com/QuixoteEntertainment

Does not accept any unsolicited material. Project types include short films. Genres include comedy.

QUOBO PICTURES
Production company and distributor

3-27-14-6F
Shibuya
Shibuya, Tokyo 150-0002
Japan

info@quobo-pic.com
quobo-pic.com
imdb.com/company/co0398992

Does not accept any unsolicited material. Project types include TV. Genres include comedy.

QUORUM ENTERTAINMENT
Production company

PO Box 57381
Sherman Oaks, CA 91413
310-994-3474 (phone)
310-220-6778 (fax)

info@trifoldpictures.com
trifoldpictures.com
imdb.com/company/co0134277

Does not accept any unsolicited material. Project types include feature films. Genres include drama, comedy, crime, and horror.

R2 (R SQUARED)
Production company and distributor

3113 Bramble Dr
Reno, NV 89509
623-889-5530

submissions@rsquaredfilms.com
rsquaredfilms.com

imdb.com/company/co0271163

Does not accept any unsolicited material. Project types include feature films. Genres include drama.

RABBIT BANDINI PRODUCTIONS
Production company

3500 W Olive Ave
Ste 1470
Burbank, CA 91505
818-953-7510

imdb.com/company/co0132192

Does not accept any unsolicited material. Project types include feature films. Genres include thriller.

James Franco
imdb.com/name/nm0290556

Vince Jolivette
vince@rabbitbandini.com
imdb.com/name/nm0006683

RABBIT HOLE PICTURES
Production company

9100 Wilshire Blvd, Ste 1000 W
Beverly Hills, CA 90212

imdb.com/company/co0174103

Does not accept any unsolicited material. Project types include feature films. Genres include action and science fiction. Established in 2007.

RACE MAN TELL-A-PICTURES
Production company and distributor

P.O. Box 92112
Washington, DC 20017-9112
202-494-8729

info@racemantell-a-pictures.com
racemantell-a-pictures.com/new
imdb.com/company/co0100664
facebook.com/pages/The-New-N-Word/
    117282884968622
twitter.com/sowande

Does not accept any unsolicited material. Project types include short films. Genres include comedy.

RADAR DISTRIBUTION
Distributor

Los Angeles, CA

imdb.com/company/co0216907

Does not accept any unsolicited material.

RADAR PICTURES
Production company

10900 Wilshire Blvd, Suite 1400
Los Angeles, CA 90024
310-208-8525 (phone)
310-208-1764 (fax)

info@radarpictures.com
radarpictures.com
imdb.com/company/co0023815
facebook.com/pages/Radar-Pictures/
    156573061049054

Does not accept any unsolicited material. Project types include feature films. Genres include drama and action.

Ted Field
CEO
imdb.com/name/nm0276059

RADIANT PRODUCTIONS
Production company

914 Montana Ave., 2nd Floor
Santa Monica , CA 90403
310-656-1400 (phone)
310-656-1408 (fax)

imdb.com/company/co0005233
linkedin.com/company/radiant productions
facebook.com/Radiant-Productions-
    Events-345714868798695

Does not accept any unsolicited material. Project types include TV and feature films. Genres include drama and action.

@RADICAL.MEDIA
Production company and distributor

Highstreet Loft Suite 2405 #508
Jiashan Lu 31 China 200031

011-862-154665938 (phone)
011-862-154665939 (fax)

Morelands 5-23 Old St
London United Kingdom EC1V 9HL
011-440-2074624070

Rueckerstr. 8
Berlin Germany D-10119
011-490-302332290 (phone)
011-490-3023322991 (fax)

Suite 511 19a Boundary St
Rushcutters Bay NSW Australia 2011
011-610-293808911 (phone)
011-610-293807123 (fax)

1630 12th St
Santa Monica CA 90404
310-664-4500 (phone)
310-664-4600 (fax)

435 Hudson St, Sixth Floor, New York City , NY,
United States, 10014
212-462-1500 (phone)
212-462-1600 (fax)

ckim@radicalmedia.com
radicalmedia.com/usa
imdb.com/company/co0029540

Does not accept any unsolicited material. Project types
include TV. Genres include family, drama, and reality.

@RADICAL MEDIA
Studio

435 Hudson St, 6th Floor
New York, NY 10014
212-462-1500 (phone)
212-462-1600 (fax)

1630 12th St
Santa Monica, CA 90404
310-664-4500 (phone)
310-664-4600 (fax)

ckim@radicalmedia.com
radicalmedia.com
imdb.com/company/co0029540

Accepts query letters from unproduced, unrepresented
writers.

Frank Scherma
President
scherma@radicalmedia.com
imdb.com/name/nm0771075
linkedin.com/pub/frank-scherma/0/332/440
facebook.com/frank.scherma.1
twitter.com/schermarad

Jon Kamen
Chairman
carden@radicalmedia.com
imdb.com/name/nm3885651

Sidney Beaumont
Executive Producer
beaumont@radicalmedia.com
imdb.com/name/nm1359013
linkedin.com/pub/sidney-beaumont/29/806/221
facebook.com/sydney.beaumont.3
twitter.com/sydneybeaumont

Brent Eveleth
Creative Director (Group)
eveleth@radicalmedia.com
brenteveleth.com
linkedin.com/in/brenteveleth

Bob Stein
Head (Production, Media and Entertainment)
stein@radicalmedia.com
imdb.com/name/nm6539622
linkedin.com/pub/bob-stein/12/437/4AA

Justin Wilkes
President (Media and Entertainment)
310-664-4500
wilkes@radicalmedia.com
imdb.com/name/nm1461710
linkedin.com/pub/justin-wilkes/26/2/430
facebook.com/justin.wilkes.7
twitter.com/justinwilkes

Adam Neuhaus
310-664-4500
neuhaus@radicalmedia.com
imdb.com/name/nm2732887
linkedin.com/pub/adam-neuhaus/4/9a4/91b
twitter.com/AdamNeuhaus

RADICAL SHEEP PRODUCTIONS
Production company

70 Richmond St East, Suite 315
Toronto, ON M5C 2G8 CANADA
416-539-0363 (phone)
416-539-0496 (fax)

inquiries@radsheep.com
radsheep.com
imdb.com/company/co0032794

Does not accept any unsolicited material. Project types include TV. Genres include family and animation.

RADIOACTIVEGIANT
Production company and distributor

404-890-5502

3000 Olympic Blvd, Suite 2100
Los Angeles, CA 90404
310-954-9353

thelist@radioactivegiant.com
radioactivegiant.com
imdb.com/company/co0332547
facebook.com/pages/RadioactiveGiant/
    130232493665021
twitter.com/RGTVnews

Does not accept any unsolicited material. Project types include feature films. Genres include thriller.

RADIUS ENTERTAINMENT
Production company

9229 Sunset Blvd, Suite 301
Los Angeles, CA 90069
310-858-2989 (phone)
310-858-1841 (fax)

asst@radius-ent.com
radius-ent.com
imdb.com/company/co0431309

Does not accept any unsolicited material. Project types include TV. Genres include drama, romance, and comedy.

RADIUS-TWC
Production company, distributor, and sales agent

99 Hudson St, 2nd Floor, New York, NY, United States, 10014

212-845-8600 (phone)
917-368-7017 (fax)

radius.info@weinsteinco.com
radiustwc.com
imdb.com/company/co0368345

Does not accept any unsolicited material. Project types include TV and feature films. Genres include thriller, drama, family, action, and myth.

RAFFAELLA PRODUCTIONS
Production company

14320 Ventura Blvd., Suite 617
Sherman Oaks, CA 91423
310-472-0466

imdb.com/company/co0062272
linkedin.com/company/raffaella-productions

Does not accept any unsolicited material. Project types include feature films. Genres include science fiction and action.

RAGING PICTURES
Production company

Suite 865
152 City Rd
London EC1V 2NX
UK

info@ragingpictures.com
ragingpictures.com
imdb.com/company/co0441013

Does not accept any unsolicited material. Genres include action and crime.

Ara Paiaya
Producer
imdb.com/name/nm1114894

RAINBOW FILM COMPANY/ RAINBOW RELEASING
Production company and distributor

1301 Montanta Ave, Suite A
Santa Monica, CA 90403
310-271-0202 (phone)
424-238-5682 (fax)

therainbowfilmco@aol.com
rainbowfilms.com
imdb.com/company/co0067478
facebook.com/pages/Rainbow-Film-Company/
110015385727699

Accepts query letters from unproduced, unrepresented
writers via email. Project types include feature films.
Genres include comedy, romance, drama, and non-
fiction.

Henry Jaglom
President
imdb.com/name/nm0415617

RAINBOW FILMS U.S.A.
Distributor

37a Meridian Rd
Edison, NJ 08820
732-548-0775 (phone)
908-325-0424 (fax)

info@rainbowfilmsusa.com
imdb.com/company/co0113363

Does not accept any unsolicited material. Project types
include feature films, short films, and TV. Genres
include romance.

RAINMAKER ENTERTAINMENT
Production company, studio, and distributor

200-2025 W Broadway
Vancouver, BC
Canada V6J 1Z6
604-714-2600 (phone)
604-714-2641 (fax)

info@rainmaker.com
rainmaker.com
imdb.com/company/co0298750
linkedin.com/company/rainmaker-entertainment-inc
facebook.com/RainmakerEnt
twitter.com/RainmakerEnt

Does not accept any unsolicited material. Project types
include feature films and TV. Genres include family,
action, animation, comedy, and fantasy. Established in
1996.

Craig Graham
Executive Chairman & CEO
imdb.com/name/nm0333981

Michael Hefferon
President
imdb.com/name/nm1803236
linkedin.com/in/michaelhefferon
facebook.com/hefferon

RAINMAKER FILMS
Production company and financing company

375 Greenwich St
New York, NY 10013
832-287-9372

rainmakerfilms.com
imdb.com/company/co0010735

Does not accept any unsolicited material. Project types
include feature films. Genres include crime and
comedy. Established in 2015.

Grant Gurthie
President - Executive Producer
imdb.com/name/nm0349262
linkedin.com/pub/grant-guthrie/8/149/b90

RAIN MANAGEMENT GROUP
Production company

1631 21st St
Santa Monica, CA 90404
310-954-9520 (phone)
310-496-2769 (fax)

rainmanagementgroup.com
imdb.com/company/co0215833
linkedin.com/in/rain-management-group-53355813
facebook.com/RainManagementGroup
twitter.com/rainmanagement

Does not accept any unsolicited material. Project types
include TV. Genres include drama.

RAINMARK FILMS
Production company

9A Dallington St
London EC1V 0BQ

UK
+44207-566-0710

mail@rainmarkfilms.com
imdb.com/company/co0215713

Does not accept any unsolicited material. Project types
include feature films. Genres include drama.

Frank Doelger
Producer
imdb.com/name/nm0230361

RAINSTORM ENTERTAINMENT, INC.
Production company

345 N Maple Dr, Suite 105
Beverly Hills, CA 90210
818-269-3300 (phone)
310-496-0223 (fax)

steve@rainstormentertainment.com
rainstormentertainment.com
imdb.com/company/co0010764
linkedin.com/company/rainstorm-entertainment
facebook.com/RainstormEnt

Accepts query letters from unproduced, unrepresented
writers via email. Project types include feature films
and TV. Genres include non-fiction and reality.

Alec Rossel
Development Executive
818-269-3300
imdb.com/name/nm1952377

RAKONTUR
Production company

3780 Royal Palm Ave
Miami Beach, FL 33140
786-539-4180

info@rakontur.com
rakontur.com
imdb.com/company/co0100598
facebook.com/rakonturmiami
twitter.com/rakonturmiami

Does not accept any unsolicited material. Project types
include TV. Genres include documentary and crime.

RAKUEISHA
Production company and distributor

16-3
Sakuragaoka
Shibuya, Tokyo
Japan
03-5459-4460 (phone)
03-5459-4461 (fax)

cafe@rakufilm.com
rakufilm.com
imdb.com/company/co0099702

Does not accept any unsolicited material. Project types
include TV, feature films, and short films. Genres
include horror.

Shigeji Maeda
President / Producer (Executive)
imdb.com/name/nm0535346

RAMOS AND SPARKS GROUP
Production company and distributor

122 S Calhoun St
Tallahassee, FL 32301
850-412-1060

rich@ramos-sparks.com (script submissions)
bob@ramos-sparks.com (general)
ramos-sparks.com
facebook.com/Ramos-Sparks-
   Group-208153932531604
twitter.com/RamosSparks

Does not accept any unsolicited material. Project types
include feature films. Genres include drama.

RAMPAGE ENTERTAINMENT
Production company

2412 Columbia St, 2nd Floor
Vancouver, BC V5Y 3E6
Canada
604-684-8618

info@rampage-entertainment.com
rampage-entertainment.com
imdb.com/company/co0036340
facebook.com/Rampage-
   entertainment-113566512027515

Does not accept any unsolicited material. Project types include feature films. Genres include drama, horror, and comedy.

RANCH STUDIOS

Production company and distributor

6880 Goforth Rd
Kyle, TX 78640
512-535-2194 (phone)
512-668-4062 (fax)

crew@ranchstudiosfilm.com
theranchstudios.com
imdb.com/company/co0192466

Does not accept any unsolicited material. Genres include thriller, family, drama, comedy, and action.

RANDALL DARK PRODUCTIONS

Production company and distributor

7312 Covered Bridge Dr
Austin, TX 78736
818-749-3881 (phone)
512-301-1080 (fax)

randallpdark@gmail.com
randalldarknews.blogspot.com
imdb.com/company/co0228998
facebook.com/Randall-Dark-
    Productions-631762993556156

Does not accept any unsolicited material. Project types include TV and short films. Genres include documentary and reality. Established in 2007.

RANDOM HOUSE STUDIO

Production company

1745 Broadway
New York, NY 10019
212-782-9000

imdb.com/company/co0176263

Accepts query letters from unproduced, unrepresented writers. Project types include feature films. Established in 2007.

Brady Emerson
212-782-9000
imdb.com/name/nm3031708

Valerie Cates
Executive Story Editor
212-782-9000
imdb.com/name/nm1161200

RANDOM HOUSE TELEVISION

Production company

4000 W Alameda Ave, 3rd Floor
Burbank , CA 91505
818-748-1100

imdb.com/company/co0340775

Does not accept any unsolicited material. Project types include TV. Genres include drama, thriller, and crime.

RANDOM MEDIA

Production company and distributor

1246 S Stanley Ave, Los Angeles, CA, United States, 90019

info@randommedia.com
imdb.com/company/co0456190

Does not accept any unsolicited material.

Marshall Forster
imdb.com/name/nm5818134

RANDOM ORDER ENTERTAINMENT

Production company

5005 Roundtable Ln.
Garland, TX 75044
214-543-6630 (phone)
214-233-9316 (fax)

somer@randomorder.net
randomorderproductions.com/
    randomorderproductions.com/Home.html
wwww.imdb.com/company/co0205990

Does not accept any unsolicited material. Project types include short films. Genres include horror and comedy.

RAQUEL PRODUCTIONS

Production company

51 W. 52nd St
New York, NY 10019

imdb.com/company/co0373629

Does not accept any unsolicited material. Project types include TV. Genres include reality.

RAT ENTERTAINMENT
Production company

150 S Rodeo Dr
Beverly Hills, CA 90212
818-733-4603 (phone)
818-733-4612 (fax)

imdb.com/company/co0026594

Accepts query letters from unproduced, unrepresented writers. Project types include TV and feature films. Genres include reality and non-fiction. Established in 2002.

Brett Ratner
Producer
imdb.com/name/nm0711840
Assistant: Anita S. Chang

John Cheng
Producer
imdb.com/name/nm1766738

RATIO PICTURES
Production company

23875 Ventura Blvd., Suite 202B
Calabasas, CA 91302
818-222-2403

general@ratiopictures.com
imdb.com/company/co0206528

Does not accept any unsolicited material. Project types include feature films. Genres include thriller and fantasy.

RATPAC ENTERTAINMENT
Production company

4000 Warner Blvd, Burbank, CA, United States, 91522
818-954-1099

imdb.com/company/co0430860

Does not accept any unsolicited material. Project types include TV. Genres include drama, comedy, and family.

Tiffany Prasifka
Creative Executive
imdb.com/name/nm7347554

RAVEN BANNER ENTERTAINMENT
Production company

33 VILLIERS ST. SUITE 201
TORONTO, ON
M5A 1A9
CANADA
416-778-9090

mpaszt@ravenbanner.ca
ravenbannerentertainment.com
imdb.com/company/co0305404
facebook.com/RavenBannerEntertainment
twitter.com/RavenBanner

Does not accept any unsolicited material. Project types include feature films. Genres include horror and thriller.

RAVENS NEST ENTERTAINMENT
Production company

Greater London House
Hampstead Rd
London, England NW1 7QY
UK
+44 20 3384 7690

info@rooksnestent.com
rooksnestent.com
imdb.com/company/co0468177

Does not accept any unsolicited material. Project types include feature films. Genres include thriller, science fiction, and action.

Michael Sackler
Producer
imdb.com/name/nm4712091

RAW TELEVISION
Production company

3rd Floor
13-21 Curtain Rd
London, England EC2A 3LT
UK
+44207-456-0800 (phone)
+44207-456-0801 (fax)

info@raw.co.uk
raw.co.uk
imdb.com/company/co0178419

Does not accept any unsolicited material. Project types include TV. Genres include documentary.

Bart Layton
Producer
imdb.com/name/nm1717925

RCIS CREATIVE
Production company

postproduction.ronaldcopley.com

Does not accept any unsolicited material. Project types include short films and commercials. Established in 2008.

Ronald Copley
Owner
ronald@ronaldcopley.com

RCR DISTRIBUTION
Distributor

421 S Beverly Dr
8th Floor
Beverly Hills, CA 90212
310-728-1355

info@rcrmg.com
rcrmediagroup.com
imdb.com/company/co0386845

Does not accept any unsolicited material. Project types include theater. Genres include thriller.

RCR MEDIA GROUP
Production company, distributor, and financing company

421 S Beverly Dr.
Beverly Hills, CA 90212

310-728-1355 (phone)
310-579-8414 (fax)

info@rcrmg.com
rcrmediagroup.com
imdb.com/company/co0320980
linkedin.com/company/rcr-media-group
facebook.com/rcrmediagroup
twitter.com/RCRMediaGroup

Does not accept any unsolicited material. Project types include feature films. Genres include crime, horror, romance, comedy, action, drama, science fiction, and thriller. Established in 2009.

Ricardo Costa Reis
Producer/Creative Executive
imdb.com/name/nm4579160
facebook.com/notes/rcr-media-group/ricardo-costa

Eliad Josephson
CEO
imdb.com/name/nm4035615
linkedin.com/in/eliadjosephson
facebook.com/eliad.josephson

Rui Costa Reis
Chairman
imdb.com/name/nm3926066

RCR PICTURES
Production company

8840 Wilshire Blvd
Beverly Hills, CA 90211
310-358-3234 (phone)
310-358-3109 (fax)

imdb.com/company/co0301318
facebook.com/pages/RCR-Pictures/105050442868201

Accepts query letters from unproduced, unrepresented writers. Project types include feature films. Genres include science fiction, crime, romance, and drama.

Robin Schorr
Producer
imdb.com/name/nm0774908

REAL COFFEE ENTERTAINMENT
Production company and distributor

3-11-1-606
Jimbocho
Chiyoda, Tokyo
Japan
03-6380-9490 (phone)
03-6380-9491 (fax)

info@realcoffee.jp
realcoffee.jp
imdb.com/company/co0306379

Does not accept any unsolicited material. Project types include feature films. Genres include drama.

Shinya Shinozaki
President (Producer)
imdb.com/name/nm3177772

REALITY'S EDGE FILMS

Production company, distributor, and sales agent

1401 Madison St
Ste 3
Hollywood, FL 33020
954-817-5450

imdb.com/company/co0343763

Does not accept any unsolicited material. Project types include TV. Genres include horror and thriller.

REALM ENTERTAINMENT

Production company and distributor

8748 Forest Lake Dr
Port Richey, FL 34668
727-328-4634 (phone)
815-346-3485 (fax)

realmentertainment@live.com
realmentertainment.biz
imdb.com/company/co0184381
facebook.com/RealmEntertainment
twitter.com/RealmEntertain

Does not accept any unsolicited material. Project types include feature films and TV. Genres include non-fiction, animation, thriller, action, myth, detective, crime, science fiction, drama, documentary, fantasy, family, and horror. Established in 1995.

Matt Graziaplene
President
727-834-0000
driveracing@hotmail.com
imdb.com/name/nm5624895
facebook.com/RealmEntertainment
twitter.com/realmentertain

REALM STUDIOS

Production company

139 Regal Row
Dallas, TX 75247
214-905-9908

dskinner@realm.tv
realmstudios.com
imdb.com/company/co0167519

Does not accept any unsolicited material. Genres include action, thriller, and drama.

REBELLION FILMS

Production company

Ville St.Laurent QC
Canada
514-571-3930

Anthony@rblfilms.com
rblfilms.com

Does not accept any unsolicited material. Project types include TV and feature films. Genres include thriller, horror, drama, comedy, family, science fiction, and action.

REBELLION PICTURES

Production company

12100 N.E. 16th Ave, Suite 208
North Miami, FL 33161
305-895-3737 (phone)
305-895-3701 (fax)

rp@rebellionpictures.com
rebellionpictures.com
imdb.com/company/co0132400

Does not accept any unsolicited material. Project types include TV and short films. Genres include comedy and drama.

RECORDED PICTURE COMPANY

Production company

24 Hanway St
London W1T 1UH
United Kingdom
+44 20-7636-2251 (phone)
+44 20-7636-2261 (fax)

rpc@recordedpicture.com
recordedpicture.com
imdb.com/company/co0029168
twitter.com/recordedpicture

Accepts scripts from produced or represented writers.
Project types include feature films.

Jeremy Thomas
+44 20 7636 2251
imdb.com/name/nm0859016
Assistant: Karin Padgham

Peter Watson
+44 20 7636 2251
imdb.com/name/nm0914838

Alainee Kent
+44 20 7636 2251
imdb.com/name/nm1599134

RECORDED PICTURE COMPANY (RPC)

Production company

24 Hanway St.
London W1T 1UH
UK
+44 20 7636 2251 (phone)
+44 20 7636 2261 (fax)

rpc@recordedpicture.com
recordedpicture.com
imdb.com/company/co0029168

Does not accept any unsolicited material. Project types
include TV. Genres include drama.

RED BARN PICTURES

Production company

481 Walker St
Fairview, NJ 07022
917-716-4913

imdb.com/company/co0214002

Does not accept any unsolicited material. Project types
include TV and short films. Genres include
documentary.

RED BOARD PRODUCTIONS

Production company

3000 W. Olympic Blvd., Bldg. 4 Suite 1200
Santa Monica, CA 90404
310-264-4285 (phone)
310-264-4286 (fax)

imdb.com/company/co0043385

Does not accept any unsolicited material. Project types
include TV. Genres include crime and drama.

RED BOX FILMS

Production company

10 Amwell St, London EC1R 1UQ, UK
+44 (0207-323-9933 (phone)
+44 (0) 20 7323 9030 (fax)

info@redboxfilms.co.uk
redboxfilms.co.uk
imdb.com/company/co0232017

Does not accept any unsolicited material. Genres
include documentary.

Simon Chinn
Producer
imdb.com/name/nm1187711

RED C ENTERTAINMENT

Production company

301 Depot
Waco, TX 76712
602-281-0959

info@redctelevision.com
redctv.com
imdb.com/company/co0228776
facebook.com/russell.clay.58
twitter.com/redctv

Does not accept any unsolicited material. Genres
include crime, comedy, and drama.

RED CROWN PRODUCTIONS
Production company

630 5th Ave, Suite 2505
New York, NY 10111
212-355-9200 (phone)
212-719-7029 (fax)

info@redcrownproductions.com
redcrownproductions.com
imdb.com/company/co0308277
linkedin.com/company/red-crown-productions
facebook.com/redcrownproductions
twitter.com/RedCrownProd

Does not accept any unsolicited material. Project types include feature films. Genres include comedy and drama. Established in 2010.

Daniel Crown
212-355-9200
dcrown@crownnyc.com
imdb.com/name/nm3259054

Alish Erman
Creative Executive
alish@redcrownproductions.com
imdb.com/name/nm2289542

Riva Marker
Head of Production & Development
riva@redcrownproductions.com
imdb.com/name/nm1889450

RED DISTRIBUTION
Production company and distributor

345 Hudson St 6th Floor
New York, NY 10014
917-421-7601

info@redmusic.com
redmusic.com
imdb.com/company/co0016675

Does not accept any unsolicited material. Genres include comedy.

REDEEMING FEATURES
Production company and distributor

72 Great Titchfield St London UK
Soho
London, W1W 7QW
UK
0203-740-3338

72 Great Titchfield St London UK
Soho
London, W1W 7QW
UK
0203-740-3338

artists@redeemingfeatures.co.uk
redeemingfeatures.co.uk
imdb.com/company/co0126611

Does not accept any unsolicited material. Project types include feature films and TV. Genres include drama, comedy, and documentary.

Nathanael Wiseman
Producer
imdb.com/name/nm2247148

RED GIANT MEDIA
Production company

535 5th Ave, 5th Floor
New York, NY 10017
212-989-7200 (phone)
212-937-3505 (fax)

info@redgiantmedia.com
redgiantentertainment.com
imdb.com/company/co0228962

Does not accept any unsolicited material. Project types include feature films. Genres include science fiction. Established in 2008.

Isen Robbins
Producer
imdb.com/name/nm0730358
twitter.com/isen1

Aimee Schoof
Producer
imdb.com/name/nm0774779
facebook.com/aimee.schoof
twitter.com/linkedin.compubaimee-schoof475853a

Kevin Fox
imdb.com/name/nm0289100
linkedin.com/in/person
twitter.com/kfury

RED GRANITE PICTURES
Production company

9255 Sunset Blvd, Suite 710
Los Angeles, CA 90069
310-703-5800 (phone)
310-246-3849 (fax)

redgranitepictures.com
imdb.com/company/co0325207
facebook.com/RedGranitePictures

Does not accept any unsolicited material. Project types include feature films. Genres include drama.

Riza Aziz
CEO
imdb.com/name/nm4265383

Joe Gatta
imdb.com/name/nm2211910

RED HEN PRODUCTIONS
Production company

3607 W Magnolia
Ste. L
Burbank, CA 91505
818-563-3600 (phone)
818-787-6637 (fax)

imdb.com/company/co0021072
facebook.com/redhenproductions

Accepts query letters from unproduced, unrepresented writers. Genres include thriller and drama.

Stuart Gordon
818-563-3600
imdb.com/name/nm0002340

RED HOUR FILMS
Production company

629 N La Brea Ave
Los Angeles, CA 90036
323-602-5000 (phone)
323-602-5001 (fax)

redhourfilms.com
imdb.com/company/co0039303
facebook.com/RedHourFilms
twitter.com/RedHourFilms

Does not accept any unsolicited material. Project types include feature films and TV. Genres include science fiction, comedy, family, fantasy, and action.

Ben Stiller
imdb.com/name/nm0001774

Robin Mabrito
robin@redhourfilms.com
imdb.com/name/nm3142663

REDLABDIGITAL
Production company

26 Soho St
Toronto, ON M5T 1A8
Canada
416-306-6400

vinit@redabto.com
redlabdigital.com
imdb.com/company/co0343466
facebook.com/pages/Redlab-Digital/
    491080294259512
twitter.com/REDLABdigital

Does not accept any unsolicited material. Genres include drama, crime, and thriller.

RED LINE FILMS
Production company

304 Hudson St
New York, NY 10013
212-257-6230

info@redlinefilms.net
imdb.com/company/co0135556
linkedin.com/company/red-line-films
facebook.com/Red-Line-Films-114564018594411

Does not accept any unsolicited material. Project types include TV. Genres include documentary.

RED OM FILMS, INC.
Production company

3000 Olympic Blvd
Building 3, Suite 2330
Santa Monica, CA 90404
310-594-3467

imdb.com/company/co0087432

Does not accept any unsolicited material. Project types include TV and feature films. Genres include action, family, drama, and comedy.

Philip Rose
Producer
imdb.com/name/nm0741615

Lisa Gillian
Producer
imdb.com/name/nm0731359

Julia Roberts
imdb.com/name/nm0000210

RED PLANET PICTURES

Production company

2nd Floor, Axtell House, 23-24 Warwick St
London
W1B 5NQ
+44-0-20-3551-9080 (phone)
+44-0-20-3701-4780 (fax)

info@redplanetpictures.co.uk
redplanetpictures.co.uk
imdb.com/company/co0213314
twitter.com/RedPlanetTV

Does not accept any unsolicited material. Project types include TV. Genres include drama and crime.

Simon Winstone
Director of Development
simonwinstone@redplanetpictures.co.uk
imdb.com/name/nm0935654

RED ROVER FILMS

Production company

4450 W. Lakeside Dr, Suite 320
Burbank, CA 91505 USA
415-440-9300 (phone)
415-440-9303 (fax)

todd@redroverfilms.com
redroverfilms.com
imdb.com/company/co0151795

Does not accept any unsolicited material. Project types include feature films. Genres include drama, thriller, and comedy.

RED SKY PRODUCTIONS

Production company

133 Luckie St NW
Atlanta, GA 30303
404-875-8102

redskyproductions.com
imdb.com/company/co0141516

Does not accept any unsolicited material. Project types include TV. Genres include documentary.

RED STROKES ENTERTAINMENT

Production company and distributor

9465 Wilshire Blvd. Suite 319
Beverly Hills, CA 90212
310-786-7887 (phone)
310-786-7827 (fax)

imdb.com/company/co0079213
linkedin.com/company/red-strokes-entertainment

Does not accept any unsolicited material. Project types include feature films and TV. Genres include drama, family, and comedy.

RED WAGON ENTERTAINMENT

Production company

8931 Ellis Ave.
Los Angeles, CA 90034
310-853-4600

redwagonentertainment.com
imdb.com/company/co0093794

Does not accept any unsolicited material. Project types include TV and feature films. Genres include drama, fantasy, animation, and horror.

Lucy Fisher
Producer
310-244-4466
imdb.com/name/nm0279651

Douglas Wick
Producer
310-244-4466
imdb.com/name/nm0926824

REEDS FIELD
Production company and distributor

1-4-8-5F
Toranomon
Minato, Tokyo 105-0001
Japan
03-3504-8555

hkanno-j@gyosei.or.jp
hkanno-j.gyosei.or.jp
imdb.com/company/co0399829

Does not accept any unsolicited material. Project types include feature films. Genres include family and drama.

Hiroshi Kanno
CEO (Producer)
imdb.com/name/nm1733310

REELDREAMS PRODUCTIONS
Production company

139 W Park St
Lake Helen, FL 32744
407-920-1780

MWGruver@aol.com
reeldreamsproductions.com/contact.html
imdb.com/company/co0242066
facebook.com/ReelDreamsProductionsCo

Does not accept any unsolicited material. Genres include horror, thriller, and drama.

REEL FX
Production company

2115 Colorado Ave
Santa Monica, CA 90404
310-264-6440 (phone)
310-264-6441 (fax)

chuck.peil@reelfx.com
reelfx.com
imdb.com/company/co0051162
linkedin.com/company/reel-fx
facebook.com/wearereelfx
twitter.com/wearereelfx

Does not accept any unsolicited material. Project types include feature films. Genres include action, science fiction, comedy, horror, and drama.

REEL FX CREATIVE STUDIO
Production company

2115 Colorado Ave
Santa Monica, CA 90404
310-264-6440 (phone)
310-264-6441 (fax)

301 N. Crowdus St.
Dallas, TX 75226
214-979-0961 (phone)
214-979-0963 (fax)

chuck.peil@reelfx.com
reelfx.com
imdb.com/company/co0051162
linkedin.com/company/reel-fx
facebook.com/wearereelfx
twitter.com/wearereelfx

Does not accept any unsolicited material. Genres include science fiction and animation.

REEL LIFE VIDEO
Production company and distributor

1714 Fortview Rd., #106
Austin, TX 78704

reelifepictures.com
imdb.com/company/co0121191

Does not accept any unsolicited material.

REEL MEDIA INTERNATIONAL
Distributor

7000 Independence Pkwy
Ste 160-7
Plano, TX 75025
214-521-3301 (phone)
214-522-3448 (fax)

reelmedia@aol.com
reelmediaintl.com
imdb.com/company/co0113964

Does not accept any unsolicited material. Genres include comedy, science fiction, and drama.

REEL ONE ENTERTAINMENT
Production company and distributor

9107 Wilshire Blvd
Ste 625
Beverly Hills, CA 90210
310-888-2245

sales@reeloneent.com
reeloneent.com
imdb.com/company/co0036136

Does not accept any unsolicited material. Project types include feature films. Genres include drama.

REFUGEE PRODUCTIONS
Production company

8631 Hayden Pl
Culver City, CA 90232
310-244-8244

imdb.com/company/co0332207

Does not accept any unsolicited material. Project types include TV. Genres include drama and comedy.

REGENCY ENTERPRISES
Production company and distributor

10201 W. Pico Blvd., Bldg. 12
Los Angeles, CA 90035
310-369-8300 (phone)
310-969-0470 (fax)

info@newregency.com
newregency.com
imdb.com/company/co0021592
facebook.com/NewRegency
twitter.com/NewRegency

Does not accept any unsolicited material. Project types include feature films. Genres include drama, comedy, and action.

REGENT ENTERTAINMENT
Production company

10940 Wilshire Blvd, Suite 1600
Los Angeles, CA 90024
310-806-4290 (phone)
310-443-4296 (fax)

info@regententertainment.com
regententertainment.com
imdb.com/company/co0045895
linkedin.com/company/regent-entertainment

Accepts query letters from unproduced, unrepresented writers via email. Project types include feature films and TV. Genres include science fiction, horror, drama, and action.

David Millbern
Director of Development
310-806-4290
imdb.com/name/nm0587778

Roxana Vatan
imdb.com/name/nm2985872

REGENT RELEASING
Distributor

10990 Wilshire Blvd, Penthouse, Los Angeles, CA, United States, 90024
310-806-4288

info@regentreleasing.com
regentreleasing.com
imdb.com/company/co0118524

Does not accept any unsolicited material. Project types include short films, TV, and feature films. Genres include action, comedy, thriller, drama, and crime.

REHAB ENTERTAINMENT
Production company

1416 N La Brea Ave
Hollywood, CA 90028
323-645-6444 (phone)
323-645-6445 (fax)

info@rehabent.com
rehabent.com
imdb.com/company/co0235838
twitter.com/rehabent907

Accepts query letters from unproduced, unrepresented writers via email. Project types include feature films.

Brett Coker
imdb.com/name/nm1832709

REHME PRODUCTIONS
Production company

1145 Gayley Ave. Ste. 301
Los Angeles, CA 90024 USA
310-824-3371 (phone)
310-824-5459 (fax)

rehmeprod@earthlink.net
imdb.com/company/co0094895

Does not accept any unsolicited material. Project types
include TV and feature films. Genres include drama.

REINER/GREISMAN
Production company

9169 W. Sunset Blvd.
West Hollywood, CA 90069
310-285-2300 (phone)
310-285-2345 (fax)

imdb.com/company/co0185376

Accepts query letters from unproduced, unrepresented
writers. Project types include feature films. Genres
include comedy and drama.

Alan Greisman
Producer
310-205-2766
imdb.com/name/nm0340112

Rob Reiner
310-285-2328
imdb.com/name/nm0001661
Assistant: Pam Jones

REIZ INTERNATIONAL
Production company and distributor

2-1-8-311
Shimo Ochiai
Shinjuku, Tokyo 161-0033
Japan
+81 3-3565-6469 (phone)
+81 3-3565-6483 (fax)

info@r-z.co.jp
r-z.co.jp
imdb.com/company/co0291263

Does not accept any unsolicited material. Project types
include TV. Genres include drama.

Kôji Yokokawa
Founder (Executive)
imdb.com/name/nm1703027

RELATIVITY MEDIA, LLC
Studio

9242 Beverly Blvd, Suite 300
Beverly Hills, CA 90210
310-724-7700 (phone)
310-724-7701 (fax)

relativitymedia.com
imdb.com/company/co0125319
facebook.com/relativity
twitter.com/relativity

Accepts query letters from produced or represented
writers. Project types include feature films,
commercials, and TV. Genres include reality and non-
fiction.

Julie Link
facebook.com/julie.link5

Jonathan Karsh
imdb.com/name/nm1285615

RELATIVITY SPORTS
Production company and distributor

Los Angeles, CA, United States
310-724-7700

info@relativitysports.com
relativitysports.com
imdb.com/company/co0481723

Does not accept any unsolicited material. Project types
include feature films and TV. Genres include thriller,
family, and drama.

RELENTLESSGENERATOR
Production company

400 Lafayette St.
2nd FL
New York, NY 10003
646-653-8001 (phone)
same (fax)

4499 Glencoe Ave
Marina del Rey, CA 90292

1 Primrose St
London, EC2A 2EX

LA@rgenerator.com
rgenerator.com
linkedin.com/company/rgenerator
facebook.com/generator
twitter.com/generator

Accepts scripts from produced or represented writers. Project types include feature films, short films, and TV. Established in 2012.

Ryan Rodriguez
Client Manager
ryan@rgenerator.com

RELEVE ENTERTAINMENT
Production company and distributor

8200 Wilshire Blvd. Ste 300,
Beverly Hills, CA 90211
323-468-9470 (phone)
310-861-0804 (fax)

releve-ent.com
imdb.com/company/co0136337
facebook.com/ReleveEnt
twitter.com/ReleveEnt

Does not accept any unsolicited material. Project types include feature films. Genres include crime, comedy, and drama.

RELIC PICTURES
Production company

34 Beekman Place, New York, NY, United States, 10022

info@relicpictures.com
relicpictures.com
imdb.com/company/co0457773

Does not accept any unsolicited material. Project types include TV. Genres include family and drama.

REMEMBER DREAMING, LLC
Production company

8252 1/2 Santa Monica Blvd, Suite B
West Hollywood, CA 90046
323-654-3333

imdb.com/company/co0228588

Accepts query letters from unproduced, unrepresented writers. Project types include feature films and TV. Genres include non-fiction and reality.

Stan Spry
President
imdb.com/name/nm1413593
twitter.com/stanspry

Courtney Brin
courtney@freefall-films.com
imdb.com/name/nm2831504
linkedin.com/pub/courtney-brin/14/31a/27a

RENAISSANCE PICTURES
Production company

315 S Beverly Dr, Suite 216
Beverly Hills, CA 90210
310-785-3900 (phone)
310-785-9176 (fax)

imdb.com/company/co0047594

Accepts query letters from unproduced, unrepresented writers. Project types include feature films and TV. Genres include action, fantasy, drama, and horror.

Robert Tapert
Partner
imdb.com/name/nm0849964

Sam Raimi
imdb.com/name/nm0000600

RENART FILMS
Production company

135 Grand St.
3rd Floor
New York, NY 10013
212-274-8224 (phone)
212-274-8229 (fax)

info@renartfilms.com
imdb.com/company/co0199700
facebook.com/pages/Renart-Films/105553939480886

Accepts query letters from produced or represented writers. Project types include feature films. Genres include romance, drama, and comedy.

Julie Christeas
julie@renartfilms.com
imdb.com/name/nm2184127

Dan Schechter
dan@renartfilms.com
imdb.com/name/nm1633080

TJ Federico
tj@renartfilms.com
imdb.com/name/nm2077416
linkedin.com/pub/tj-federico/70/a38/64b

Timothy Duff
President
tim@renartfilms.com
imdb.com/name/nm2178779
linkedin.com/pub/timothy-duff/5/7a5/5b4

Caroline Dillon
Creative Director
caroline@renartfilms.com
imdb.com/name/nm0226974

RENEE MISSEL MANAGEMENT
Production company

2376 Adrian St, Suite A
Newbury Park, CA 91320
310-463-0638 (phone)
805-669-4511 (fax)

imdb.com/name/nm0592911
twitter.com/reneemissel

Accepts query letters from unproduced, unrepresented writers via email. Project types include feature films. Established in 1983.

Renee Missel
Producer
imdb.com/name/nm0592911
twitter.com/reneemissel

RENEE VALENTE PRODUCTIONS
Production company and distributor

9000 Sunset Blvd
Los Angeles, CA 90069
310-472-5342

valenteprod@aol.com
imdb.com/company/co0112475

Accepts query letters from unproduced, unrepresented writers via email. Project types include TV and feature films. Genres include family, reality, drama, and sociocultural. Established in 1980.

Renee Valente
Executive Producer
imdb.com/name/nm0884095

RENEGADE 83
Production company

12925 Riverside Dr, Bldg 413
Sherman Oaks, CA 91423 USA
818-480-3112 (phone)
818-480-3192 (fax)

tech@renegdae83.com
renegade83.com
imdb.com/company/co0147963
facebook.com/pages/Renegade83-Inc/
   379476538822561
twitter.com/Renegade83Inc

Does not accept any unsolicited material. Project types include TV. Genres include science fiction.

RENEGADE ANIMATION, INC.
Production company

111 E Broadway, Suite 208
Glendale, CA 91205
818-551-2351 (phone)
818-551-2350 (fax)

contactus@renegadeanimation.com
renegadeanimation.com
imdb.com/company/co0050247
linkedin.com/company/renegade-animation

Accepts query letters from unproduced, unrepresented writers via email. Project types include TV.

Ashley Postlewaite
imdb.com/name/nm1041234
linkedin.com/pub/ashley-postlewaite/0/66a/950
facebook.com/ashley.postlewaite

Alec Megibben
Storyboard Artist
linkedin.com/in/alecanimates

Darrell Van Citters
imdb.com/name/nm0885864

RENFIELD PRODUCTIONS
Production company

c/o The Lot
1041 N Formosa Ave
Writers Building, Suite 321
West Hollywood, CA 90046
323-850-3907 (fax)

development@renfieldproductions.com
renfieldproductions.com
imdb.com/company/co0034557
facebook.com/RenfieldProductions
twitter.com/renfieldprods

Accepts query letters from unproduced, unrepresented writers via email. Project types include TV. Genres include drama, non-fiction, animation, reality, action, comedy, family, and horror.

Joe Dante
Director
imdb.com/name/nm0001102
facebook.com/directorjoedante
twitter.com/joe_dante

Mike Finnell
Producer
imdb.com/name/nm0278228

RENO PRODUCTIONS
Production company

156 W 44rd St, 6th Fl
New York, NY 10036, USA
212-582-4040 (phone)
212-582-4030 (fax)

info@renoproductionsinc.com
renoproductionsinc.com

imdb.com/company/co0036576

Does not accept any unsolicited material. Project types include feature films. Genres include crime, drama, thriller, and documentary.

REPRISAL FILMS
Production company

London, England
UK

hello@reprisalfilms.com
reprisalfilms.com
imdb.com/company/co0137061

Does not accept any unsolicited material. Project types include feature films. Genres include comedy, thriller, and drama.

John Michael McDonagh
Producer
imdb.com/name/nm0567620

REPUBLIC OF EPIC
Production company

4007 McCullough Ave. #195
San Antonio, TX 78212

info@republicofepic.com
imdb.com/company/co0319225

Does not accept any unsolicited material. Genres include drama and action.

RESERVE ENTERTAINMENT GROUP
Distributor

269 S Beverly Dr, Suite 1122
Beverly Hills, CA 90210
310-360-4397 (phone)
310-388-5853 (fax)

info@thereserveent.com
thereserveent.com
imdb.com/company/co0169888

Does not accept any unsolicited material. Project types include TV. Genres include comedy and drama.

RESURGENT ENTERTAINMENT
Production company and financing company

4005 Nicholson Dr
Suite 3210
Baton Rouge, LA 70808
225-906-3575

imdb.com/company/co0209370

Does not accept any unsolicited material. Project types include TV. Genres include drama.

REVEILLE, LLC/ SHINE INTERNATIONAL
Production company

1741 Ivar Ave
Los Angeles, CA 90028
323-790-8000 (phone)
323-790-8399 (fax)

shineinternational.com

Does not accept any unsolicited material. Project types include TV. Genres include reality and non-fiction.

Carolyn Bernstein
Executive Vice-President, Scripted TV
imdb.com/name/nm3009190

Rob Cohen
imdb.com/name/nm0003418

Todd Cohen
imdb.com/name/nm1537619
linkedin.com/in/trcohen

REVEK ENTERTAINMENT
Production company

12100 Wilshire Blvd, Suite 819
Los Angeles, CA 90025
310-845-6356

asst@revekentertainment.com
revekentertainment.com
imdb.com/company/co0431506
facebook.com/pages/Revek-Entertainment/
    351904838248753
twitter.com/RevekEntertain

Does not accept any unsolicited material. Project types include feature films. Genres include thriller, drama, and horror.

REVELATIONS ENTERTAINMENT
Production company

1221 Second St
4th Floor
Santa Monica, CA 90401
310-394-3131 (phone)
310-394-3133 (fax)

info@revelationsent.com
revelationsent.com
imdb.com/company/co0075256
linkedin.com/company/revelations-entertainment
facebook.com/pages/Revelations-Entertainment/
    110579179025356

Does not accept any unsolicited material. Project types include TV and feature films. Genres include family, detective, drama, and action. Established in 1996.

Morgan Freeman
President
imdb.com/name/nm0000151

Lori McCreary
CEO
imdb.com/name/nm0566975
twitter.com/LoriMcCreary

Tracy Mercer
VP of Development
imdb.com/name/nm0580312

REVERE STUDIOS
Production company

1008 Dishman Loop
Oviedo, FL 32765
407-721-8803

ghill@reverestudios.con
reverestudios.com
imdb.com/company/co0242511
linkedin.com/company/revere-studios

Does not accept any unsolicited material. Genres include action and drama.

REVOLUTION FILMS
Production company

9-A Dallington St
London EC1Z 0BQ

UK
+44-20-7566-0700

email@revolution-films.com
revolution-films.com
imdb.com/company/co0103733
facebook.com/revolutionfilms

Does not accept any unsolicited material. Project types include feature films. Genres include period, thriller, drama, comedy, non-fiction, and action. Established in 1994.

Michael Winterbottom
Producer
imdb.com/name/nm0935863

Andrew Eaton
Producer
imdb.com/name/nm0247787

REVOLUTION MEDIA
Production company

8383 Wilshire Blvd., Suite 310
Beverly Hills, CA 90211
323-883-0056

imdb.com/company/co0442320

Does not accept any unsolicited material. Project types include TV. Genres include crime and drama.

REVOLUTION STUDIOS
Production company and distributor

2900 W Olympic Blvd, Santa Monica, CA, United States, 90404
310-255-7000 (phone)
310-255-7001 (fax)

revolutionstudios.com
imdb.com/company/co0003580

Does not accept any unsolicited material. Project types include TV. Genres include romance, comedy, drama, thriller, and family.

REVOLVER ENTERTAINMENT
Production company and distributor

86-90 Paul St | London | EC2A 4NE

86-90 Paul St | London | EC2A 4NE
+44207-243-4300 (phone)
+44207-243-4302 (fax)

hello@revolvergroup.com
revolvergroup.com
imdb.com/company/co0106208

Does not accept any unsolicited material. Project types include feature films. Genres include comedy, drama, action, and romance.

Justin Marciano
Producer
imdb.com/name/nm2459727

REVOLVER PICTURE COMPANY
Production company

955 S Carrillo Dr, Ste 100
Los Angeles, CA 90048 USA
323-964-9299

imdb.com/company/co0398773

Does not accept any unsolicited material. Project types include feature films. Genres include horror.

REVSCOPE PICTURES
Production company

7C Vernon Ln
Chatham, NJ 07928
201-400-9898

m_pleckaitis@revscopepictures.com
www/www.imdb.com/company/co0190641

Does not accept any unsolicited material. Project types include TV and feature films. Genres include comedy and horror.

RG ENTERTAINMENT LTD.
Production company

9595 Wilshire Blvd., Ste 900
Beverly Hills, CA 90212
310-246-1442 (phone)
310-246-1474 (fax)

imdb.com/company/co0313624

Does not accept any unsolicited material. Project types include feature films. Genres include fantasy and animation.

RHINO FILMS
Production company and distributor

Los Angeles, CA
310-441-6557

contact@rhinofilms.com
imdb.com/company/co0032380
linkedin.com/company/rhino-films-inc-

Does not accept any unsolicited material. Project types include feature films and TV. Genres include science fiction, non-fiction, drama, documentary, and comedy. Established in 1996.

RHOMBUS MEDIA
Production company and distributor

99 Spadina Ave
Ste 600
Toronto, ON M5V 3P8
Canada
416-971-7856 (phone)
416-971-9647 (fax)

info@rhombusmedia.com
rhombusmedia.com
imdb.com/company/co0010810
facebook.com/rhombusmedia
twitter.com/rhombusmedia

Does not accept any unsolicited material. Genres include comedy.

Kevin Krikst
Producer
imdb.com/name/nm2844322

RHOMBUS MEDIA, INC.
Production company and distributor

99 Spadina Ave. Unit#600
Toronto, Ontario
M5V 3P8
Canada
416-971-7856 (phone)
416-971-9647 (fax)

info@rhombusmedia.com
rhombusmedia.com
imdb.com/company/co0010810
linkedin.com/company/rhombus-media-inc.
facebook.com/rhombusmedia
twitter.com/rhombusmedia

Does not accept any unsolicited material. Project types include feature films. Genres include thriller, horror, crime, comedy, science fiction, and action. Established in 1979.

Niv Fichman
Producer
imdb.com/name/nm0275651

Larry Weistein
Producer
imdb.com/name/nm0918452

RHYTHM & HUES STUDIOS
Studio

The V, Vega Block, 11th Floor, Left Wing, Plot No -
17
Software Units Layout, HITEC City
Madhapur, Hyderabad - 500 081
India
+91 40 40334567

Prism Tower, A-Wing, 3rd Floor
Goregaon-Malad Link Rd
Goregaon (West), Mumbai 400062
India
+91 22 40388888

2100 E Grand Ave
El Segundo, CA 90245
310-448-7500 (phone)
310-448-7600 (fax)

401 W Georgia St, Suites No. 500 & 600
Vancouver, BC V6B 5A1, Canada
604-288-8745

info-la@rhythm.com
rhythm.com
imdb.com/company/co0075252
linkedin.com/company/rhythm-&-hues
facebook.com/RhythmAndHues
twitter.com/RhythmAndHues

Does not accept any unsolicited material. Project types include feature films. Genres include action, crime, family, drama, romance, fantasy, comedy, and science fiction. Established in 1987.

Pauline Ts'o
Lighting Supervisor
imdb.com/name/nm1173396

Heather Jennings
imdb.com/name/nm0997142

RIALTO PICTURES
Distributor

45 E 72nd St, Suite 16A, New York City , NY, United States, 10021
212-717-6773

rialtonyc@aol.com
rialtopictures.com
imdb.com/company/co0049592

Does not accept any unsolicited material. Project types include TV. Genres include drama and family.

RICE & BEANS PRODUCTIONS
Production company

30 N Raymond Ave, Suite 605
Pasadena, CA 91103
626-792-9171

vin88@pacbell.net
imdb.com/company/co0094899

Accepts query letters from unproduced, unrepresented writers via email. Project types include TV and feature films. Genres include drama and comedy.

Ben Montanio
Producer
imdb.com/name/nm0598996

Vince Cheung
Producer
imdb.com/name/nm0156588

RICHE PRODUCTIONS
Production company

9336 W Washington Blvd
Stage 4, Room 201

Culver City, CA 90232
310-202-4850

imdb.com/company/co0176392
facebook.com/pages/Riche-Productions/
126336494047525

Accepts query letters from unproduced, unrepresented writers. Project types include feature films and TV. Genres include family and action.

Peter Riche
Partner
imdb.com/name/nm0724855
linkedin.com/pub/peter-riche/70/414/ab4

Alan Riche
Partner
imdb.com/name/nm0724843
Assistant: Adrienne Novelly

RICH HIPPIE PRODUCTIONS
Production company

332 S. Beverly Dr, Suite 101
Beverly Hills, CA 90212
424-204-9033

nfo@richhippieproductions.com
richhippieproductions.com
imdb.com/company/co0459181

Does not accept any unsolicited material. Genres include thriller and drama.

RICHWATER FILMS
Production company

22 S Audley St
Mayfair
London W1K2NY
UK

info@richwaterfilms.com
imdb.com/company/co0406675

Does not accept any unsolicited material. Project types include feature films. Genres include action and horror.

Jonathan Sothcott
Producer
imdb.com/name/nm1151096

RIDGEROCK ENTERTAINMENT GROUP

1900 Church St, Ste 300,
Nashville, TN 37203 USA
615-489-6350 (phone)
888-735-1901 (fax)

gary@ridgerockentertainment.com
ridgerockentertainment.com
imdb.com/company/co0189148
facebook.com/pages/Ridgerock-Entertainment-Group/
    1429510457347803
twitter.com/ridgerockent

Does not accept any unsolicited material. Project types include feature films. Genres include drama and comedy.

RIGEL USA
Distributor

149 S. Barrington Ave, Suite 362, Los Angeles , CA, United States, 90049

info@rigel.tv
rigel.tv
imdb.com/company/co0091094

Does not accept any unsolicited material. Project types include TV. Genres include family and drama.

RIGHT COAST PRODUCTIONS
Production company and distributor

289 Springs Fireplace Rd
East Hampton, NY 11937
631-329-1200 (phone)
631-329-1947 (fax)

imdb.com/company/co0225585

Does not accept any unsolicited material. Project types include feature films. Genres include romance, family, drama, and comedy.

RINGLEADER STUDIOS
Production company

8840 Wilshire Blvd., Third Floor
Beverly Hills, CA 90211

info@ringleaderstudios.net
ringleaderstudios.net

imdb.com/company/co0156389

Does not accept any unsolicited material. Project types include TV. Genres include horror, thriller, and science fiction.

RIP CORD PRODUCTIONS

5555 Melrose Ave., Dressing Rm 115
Hollywood, CA 90038
323-956-3800 (phone)
323-862-2294 (fax)

imdb.com/company/co0193472

Does not accept any unsolicited material. Project types include feature films and TV. Genres include comedy.

RISE FILMS
Production company, distributor, and sales agent

46 Berwick St
London W1F 8SG
UK
+44203-214-6072

info@risefilms.com
risefilms.com
imdb.com/company/co0196042
facebook.com/RiseFilms
twitter.com/risefilms

Does not accept any unsolicited material. Project types include TV and feature films. Genres include documentary.

Sam Leifer
Producer
imdb.com/name/nm1746026

RITCHIE/WIGRAM PRODUCTIONS

4000 Warner Blvd, Bldg 81, Rm 215,
Burbank, CA 91522, USA
818-954-2412 (phone)
818-954-6538 (fax)

imdb.com/company/co0204562

Does not accept any unsolicited material. Genres include fantasy and science fiction.

RITZEL ENTERTAINMENT

Production company and distributor

413 New Rd
Somers Point, NJ 08244

imdb.com/company/co0214218

Does not accept any unsolicited material. Project types include TV. Genres include drama and comedy.

RIVAL PICTURES

Production company

2121 Cloverfield Blvd., Suite 116
Santa Monica, CA 90404
310-664-1954 (phone)
310-388-0536 (fax)

edparks@rivalpictures.net
rivalpictures.net
imdb.com/company/co0108383

Does not accept any unsolicited material. Project types include feature films. Genres include drama and thriller.

RIVE GAUCHE TELEVISION

Production company and distributor

15442 Ventura Blvd.
Ste. 507
Sherman Oaks, CA 91403
818-784-9912 (phone)
818-784-9916 (fax)

rgtvsales@rgitv.com
rgitv.com
imdb.com/company/co0010886
linkedin.com/company/rive-gauche-television
facebook.com/pages/Rive-Gauche-Television/
    174496655908588
twitter.com/RiveGaucheTV

Does not accept any unsolicited material. Project types include feature films. Genres include documentary. Established in 1994.

Tomas Silva
Vice President, International Sales
305-803-3090
tomas@rgitv.com

Devin Sunseri
Director of Development
818-784-9912
devin@rgitv.com

Ashley Lewelling
Director of Development
818-530-7913
ashley@rgitv.com

David Auerbach
President
818-530-7917
david@rgitv.com

Laurie Carreira
Manager, Distribution Services
818-784-9917
laurie@rgitv.com

Marine Ksadzhikyan
Senior Vice President, International Distribution
818-784-2237
marine@rgitv.com

Jonathan Kramer
CEO
818-386-1035
jon@rgitv.com
imdb.com/name/nm2883855

Bryan Gabourie
Vice President, International Distribution
818-784-9912
bryan@rgitv.com

Jay Behling
CFO
818-530-7908
jay@rgitv.com

Antonia Lianos
Director of Contract Administration
818-784-2094
antonia@rgitv.com

Sylvia Wadzinski
Assistant, International Sales & Production
818-784-9912
sylvia@rgitv.com

RIVER ROAD ENTERTAINMENT

Production company

2000 Ave of the Stars, Suite 620-N
Los Angeles, CA 90067
213-253-4610 (phone)
310-843-9551 (fax)

riverroadentertainment.net
imdb.com/company/co0120121
linkedin.com/company/river-road-entertainment

Does not accept any unsolicited material. Project types include feature films and TV. Genres include drama, non-fiction, comedy, and reality.

Tom Skapars
Creative Executive
imdb.com/name/nm2799570
linkedin.com/pub/tom-skapars/0/139/52

RIVERSTONE PICTURES
Production company

72 Wells St
London W1T 3QF
UK
+44 20 7268 9820

7955 W 3rd St,
Los Angeles CA 90048.
+323-634-1570

info@riverstonepictures.com
riverstonepictures.com
imdb.com/company/co0540798

Does not accept any unsolicited material. Project types include short films, feature films, and TV. Genres include action, reality, family, horror, and thriller.

RJ MAMRAK PRODUCTIONS
Production company and distributor

60 S Broadway
Pitman, NJ 08071
856-889-9956

rmamrak@mac.com
imdb.com/company/co0272932

Does not accept any unsolicited material. Genres include action.

RKO PICTURES, INC.
Production company and distributor

11301 W Olympic Blvd, Suite 510,
Los Angeles, CA 90064
310-277-0707 (phone)
310-566-8940 (fax)

info@rko.com
rko.com
imdb.com/company/co0050028

Does not accept any unsolicited material. Project types include feature films and TV. Genres include drama, thriller, action, and animation.

RLJ ENTERTAINMENT, INC.
Production company and distributor

232 N Main St
Stillwater, MN 55082
651-351-3990

55 Drury Ln Covent Garden
London United Kingdom WC2B 5SQ
011-440-2037348706

6320 Canoga Ave 8th Floor
Woodland Hills CA 91367
818-407-9100

8515 Georgia Ave, Suite 650, Silver Spring, MD,
United States, 20910
301-608-2115

inquires@rljentertainment.com
rljentertainment.com
imdb.com/company/co0385511

Does not accept any unsolicited material. Project types include TV. Genres include family, drama, and action.

ROADSIDE ATTRACTIONS
Studio

7920 Sunset Blvd
Suite 402
Los Angeles, CA 90046
323-882-8490

info@roadsideattractions.com
roadsideattractions.com
imdb.com/company/co0017716
linkedin.com/company/roadside-attractions
facebook.com/RoadsideAttractionsFilms
twitter.com/roadsidetweets

Accepts query letters from produced or represented writers. Project types include feature films. Genres include comedy, drama, horror, and thriller.

Gail Blumenthal
Distributor
imdb.com/name/nm0089812

Eric d'Arbeloff
Founder
imdb.com/name/nm0195396

Howard Cohen
Founder
imdb.com/name/nm1383518

ROAR

9701 Wilshire Blvd. 8th Floor
Beverly Hills , CA 90212
310-424-7800 (phone)
310-424-7824 (fax)

info@roar.la
roar.la
imdb.com/company/co0080643

Does not accept any unsolicited material. Project types include TV and feature films. Genres include thriller, action, comedy, and drama.

ROBBINSWOOD PRODUCTIONS
Production company

34-36 Scott St # 1
Newark, NJ 07102

imdb.com/company/co0215734

Does not accept any unsolicited material. Project types include TV. Genres include drama and action.

ROB CHILD AND ASSOCIATES
Production company, distributor, and sales agent

P O Box 514
Washington Crossing, PA 18977
215-369-1453

robchildassoc@gmail.com
robchild.net
imdb.com/company/co0134249

Does not accept any unsolicited material. Project types include TV. Genres include action and comedy.

ROBERT CORT PRODUCTIONS
Production company

1041 N Formosa Ave
West Hollywood, CA 90046
323-850-2644 (phone)
323-850-2634 (fax)

imdb.com/company/co0094924

Accepts query letters from unproduced, unrepresented writers. Project types include feature films and TV. Genres include drama and comedy.

Eric Hetzel
Producer
imdb.com/name/nm0381796

Robert Cort
Producer
imdb.com/name/nm0181202
Assistant: Maritza Berta

ROBERT GREENWALD PRODUCTIONS
Production company

10510 Culver Blvd
Culver City, CA 90232-3400
310-204-0404 (phone)
310-204-0174 (fax)

info@rgpinc.com
imdb.com/company/co0056700
linkedin.com/company/robert-greenwald-productions

Does not accept any unsolicited material. Project types include feature films and TV. Genres include comedy, drama, and non-fiction.

Robert Greenwald
imdb.com/name/nm0339254

Philip Kleinbart
imdb.com/name/nm0459036

ROBERT KOSBERG PRODUCTIONS
Production company

1438 N. Gower St, Bldg. 35, Box 10
Hollywood, CA 90028
323-468-4513

bobkosberg@yahoo.com (script submissions)
bobkosberg@nashentertainment.com (general)
imdb.com/company/co0094875
linkedin.com/in/robertkosberg
twitter.com/robertkosberg

Accepts query letters from unproduced, unrepresented writers via email. Project types include TV and feature films.

Jane Moore
Development
imdb.com/name/nm0601327

Robert Kosberg
Producer
imdb.com/name/nm0466946

ROBERT LAWRENCE PRODUCTIONS

Production company

1810 14th St
Suite 102
Santa Monica, CA 90404
310-399-2762

imdb.com/company/co0021936
linkedin.com/company/robert-lawrence-productions

Accepts query letters from unproduced, unrepresented writers. Project types include feature films. Genres include action, drama, and comedy.

Robert Lawrence
President
imdb.com/name/nm0492994

ROBERTS/DAVID FILMS INC.

Production company

100 Universal City Plaza
Bldg. 1320
Universal City, CA 91608
323-574-1700 (phone)
818-733-1551 (fax)

robertsdavid.com
imdb.com/company/co0109061
linkedin.com/company/roberts-david-films-inc.

Does not accept any unsolicited material. Project types include feature films and TV. Genres include reality, non-fiction, and comedy.

Lorena David
Partner
lorena@robertsdavid.com

Mark Roberts
Partner
mark@robertsdavid.com

ROBERT SIMONDS COMPANY

Production company

10202 Washington Blvd
Robert Young Building
Suite 3510
Culver City, CA 90232
310-244-5222 (phone)
310-244-0348 (fax)

imdb.com/company/co0033486
linkedin.com/company/robert-simonds-co

Does not accept any unsolicited material. Project types include feature films. Genres include thriller, comedy, action, and family. Established in 2012.

Robert Simonds
CEO
rasst@rscfilms.com
imdb.com/name/nm0800465
Assistant: Jennifer Jiang

ROBIN HOOD FILMS

Production company, distributor, and sales agent

702-450-7950

chris@robinhoodfilms.com
robinhoodfilms.com
imdb.com/company/co0031414
linkedin.com/company/robin-hood-films-movies
facebook.com/robinhoodfilms
twitter.com/robinhood_films

Does not accept any unsolicited material. Project types include TV. Genres include horror and crime.

Christopher Robin Hood
Producer
imdb.com/name/nm0393450

ROBOT COMMUNICATIONS

Production company

3-9-7 Ebisu-Minami
Tokyo 150-0022
Japan
+81 3 3760 1171

faab@robot.co.jp
imdb.com/company/co0113654

Does not accept any unsolicited material. Project types include TV. Genres include comedy.

Shuji Abe
President (Producer)
imdb.com/name/nm0008375

ROCKET SCIENCE PRODUCTIONS

Production company

5084 Coleridge Dr,
Fairfax, VA 22032, United States
703-764-8000

bepublished@rocketscienceproductions.com
rocketscienceproductions.com
imdb.com/company/co0490893
facebook.com/RocketScienceProductionsLLC
twitter.com/RSP_llc

Does not accept any unsolicited material. Project types include TV. Genres include drama.

ROCKLIN/ FAUST

Production company

10390 Santa Monica Blvd, Suite 200
Los Angeles, CA 90025
310-800-5140 (phone)
310-789-3060 (fax)

imdb.com/company/co0299281
linkedin.com/pub/nicole-rocklin/1b/a90/462

Does not accept any unsolicited material. Project types include feature films and TV. Genres include non-fiction, reality, drama, comedy, and animation.

Blye Pagon Faust
Producer
imdb.com/name/nm1421308

ROCK LYARD CO.

Production company and distributor

1-6-4-4F
Shibuya
Shibuya, Tokyo 150-0002
Japan
03-5766-1375

info@rocklyard.com
imdb.com/company/co0166223

Does not accept any unsolicited material. Project types include TV. Genres include documentary.

Takashi Teishô
President (Producer)
imdb.com/name/nm2944332

ROCK'N ROBIN PRODUCTIONS

Production company

450 W 56th St
New York, NY 10019
212-246-4367

info@rocknrobin.tv
rocknrobin.tv
imdb.com/company/co0508676
facebook.com/rocknrobintv
twitter.com/rocknrobintv

Does not accept any unsolicited material. Project types include TV. Genres include documentary.

RODDENBERRY ENTERTAINMENT

Production company

4400 Coldwater Canyon Blvd, Suite #100
Studio City, CA 91604
818-487-9431 (phone)
818-487-9440 (fax)

info@roddenberry.com
roddenberry.com
imdb.com/company/co0368541
facebook.com/roddenberry
twitter.com/roddenberry

Does not accept any unsolicited material. Project types include feature films and TV. Genres include science fiction and drama.

RODEO QUEEN PRODUCTIONS

Production company and sales agent

1104 Spruce
Pryor, OK 74361
918-645-0072

zachary@rodeoqueenproductions.com
rodeoqueenproductions.com
imdb.com/company/co0385847
facebook.com/zhadden

Does not accept any unsolicited material. Project types include TV. Genres include horror and comedy.

ROGUE STATE PRODUCTIONS

Production company

2000 Ave of the Stars, 3rd Floor
Los Angeles, CA 90067

imdb.com/company/co0381690

Does not accept any unsolicited material. Project types include TV. Genres include reality and documentary.

ROLLERCOASTER ENTERTAINMENT

Production company

21 St. Clair Ave East, Suite 1000
Toronto, ON M4T 1L9
Canada
647-290-2004 (phone)
416-696-7800 (fax)

ghowsam@gmail.com
imdb.com/company/co0277538
facebook.com/7383rollercoasters

Does not accept any unsolicited material. Genres include comedy and crime.

Gary Howsam
Producer
imdb.com/name/nm0398258

ROLLMAN ENTERTAINMENT

Production company and distributor

6767 Forest Lawn Dr
Los Angeles, CA 90068
323-850-7655

press@rollmanent.com

rollmanentertainment.com
imdb.com/company/co0352074
linkedin.com/company/rollman-entertainment
facebook.com/RollmanEntertainment
twitter.com/RollmanEnt

Does not accept any unsolicited material. Project types include TV and feature films. Genres include animation, comedy, and family. Established in 2010.

RONA EDWARDS PRODUCTIONS

Production company

8549 Wilshire Blvd.
Suite 1052
Beverly Hills, CA 90211

info@esentertainment.net
esentertainment.net
imdb.com/company/co0094948

Does not accept any unsolicited material. Project types include feature films and TV. Genres include comedy, thriller, and romance. Established in 1999.

ROOKS NEST ENTERTAINMENT

Production company

Greater London House
Hampstead Rd
London NW1 7QY
UK
+44 20 3384 7690

info@rooksnestent.com
rooksnestent.com
imdb.com/company/co0356803
twitter.com/RooksNestEnt

Does not accept any unsolicited material. Project types include feature films. Genres include comedy and drama.

Sophie Vickers
Producer
imdb.com/name/nm4153748

ROOM 101, INC.

Production company

9677 Charleville Blvd.
Beverly Hills 90212
310-271-1130

imdb.com/company/co0203017
linkedin.com/company/room-101-inc.
facebook.com/media/set

Accepts query letters from unproduced, unrepresented writers. Project types include TV and feature films. Genres include drama, crime, and horror.

Steven Schneider
Producer
imdb.com/name/nm2124081

ROOM 19 MEDIA
Production company

86 Smith St
Irvington, NJ 07111
973-202-7190

room19@room19media.com
imdb.com/company/co0123978

Does not accept any unsolicited material. Project types include short films. Genres include comedy.

ROOM 5 FILMS
Production company

373 Broadway, E22
New York, NY 10013
212-343-2800

contact@room5films.com
room5films.com
imdb.com/company/co0267662
facebook.com/pages/Room-5-Films/
    266636396750533

Does not accept any unsolicited material. Genres include documentary and drama. Established in 2011.

Heather Smith
Producer
imdb.com/name/nm3150253

ROOM 9 ENTERTAINMENT, LLC
Production company

9229 Sunset Blvd, Suite 505
West Hollywood, CA 90069
310-651-2001 (phone)
310-651-2010 (fax)

info@room9entertainment.com
imdb.com/company/co0122495

Does not accept any unsolicited material. Project types include feature films and TV. Genres include drama and non-fiction.

Michael R. Newman
imdb.com/name/nm1616293

David O. Sacks
CEO
imdb.com/name/nm1616294

Daniel Brunt
imdb.com/name/nm1616292

ROOS MEDIA GROUP

1818 7th Ave. S
Fargo, ND 58103

roosmediagroup.com

Does not accept any unsolicited material. Project types include feature films. Genres include comedy.

ROOSTER TEETH PRODUCTIONS
Production company and distributor

636 Ralph Ablanedo Dr
Austin, TX 78748
512-480-0336

rtinfo@roosterteeth.com
roosterteeth.com
imdb.com/company/co0119714
facebook.com/roosterteeth
twitter.com/roosterteeth

Does not accept any unsolicited material. Genres include horror, science fiction, and fantasy.

ROPE THE MOON PRODUCIONS
Production company

1438 N Gower St
Box 36

Hollywood, CA 90028
323-330-1856

info@thefortfilms.com
thefortfilms.com
imdb.com/company/co0134175

Does not accept any unsolicited material. Genres include family and comedy.

ROSA ENTERTAINMENT
Production company

7288 Sunset Blvd, Suite 208
Los Angeles, CA 90046
310-470-3506 (phone)
310-470-3509 (fax)

info@rosaentertainment.com
rosaentertainment.com
imdb.com/company/co0182149
facebook.com/pages/Rosa-Entertainment/
    180064202005686

Does not accept any unsolicited material. Project types include feature films and TV. Genres include drama and comedy.

Sidney Sherman
Producer
sidney@rosaentertainment.com
imdb.com/name/nm0792587

ROSEBLOOD MOVIE CO.
Production company

1875 Century Park East, Suite 2140
Los Angeles, CA 90067

info@rko.com
rko.com/roseblood.asp
imdb.com/company/co0274380

Does not accept any unsolicited material. Project types include feature films. Genres include crime, horror, thriller, and drama.

ROSEROCK FILMS
Production company

4000 Warner Blvd
Building 81
Suite 216

Burbank, CA 91522
818-954-7528 (phone)
818-954-6658 (fax)

imdb.com/company/co0182148
facebook.com/roserockfilms
twitter.com/roserock_films

Does not accept any unsolicited material. Project types include feature films.

Patricia Reed
Director of Development
818-954-7673
imdb.com/name/nm0715623

Hunt Lowry
Producer
imdb.com/name/nm0523324
linkedin.com/pub/hunt-lowry/a/841/2b8

ROTH FILMS
Production company

2900 W Olympic Blvd
Santa Monica, CA 90404
310-255-7000

imdb.com/company/co0268489

Does not accept any unsolicited material. Project types include feature films.

Palak Patel
imdb.com/name/nm2026983

Joe Roth
Producer
imdb.com/name/nm0005387

ROUGH DIAMOND PRODUCTIONS
Production company

1424 N. Kings Rd
Los Angeles, CA 90069
323-848-2900 (phone)
323-848-8142 (fax)

info@roughdiamondproductions.net
roughdiamondproductions.net
imdb.com/company/co0172893
linkedin.com/in/juliaverdin
facebook.com/roughdiamondproductions

twitter.com/juliaverdin

Does not accept any unsolicited material. Project types include feature films. Genres include thriller, horror, drama, and action. Established in 1993.

ROUGHHOUSE
Production company

1722 Whitley Ave
Hollywood, CA 90028
323-469-3161

roughhouse.com
imdb.com/company/co0291982

Accepts scripts from produced or represented writers. Project types include feature films. Genres include romance and drama.

David Green
imdb.com/name/nm0337773

ROUGHWORKS ENTERTAINMENT
Production company

5555 Collins Ave. Suite 3d
Miami Beach, FL 33140
305-926-6282

info@roughworksentertainment.com
imdb.com/company/co0187690

Does not accept any unsolicited material. Genres include drama.

ROUNDTABLE ENTERTAINMENT
Production company

5300 Melrose Ave, Suite E331
Hollywood, CA 90038
323-769-2567

imdb.com/company/co0099774

Does not accept any unsolicited material. Project types include feature films and TV. Genres include drama and comedy.

ROUTE 7 PRODUCTIONS
Production company

690 Lincoln Rd
Suite 302
Miami Beach, FL 33139
305-531-2160 (phone)
305-531-2575 (fax)

imdb.com/company/co0271786

Does not accept any unsolicited material. Genres include drama.

ROUTE ONE FILMS
Production company and studio

1041 N Formosa Ave
Santa Monica East #200
West Hollywood, CA 90046
323-850-3855 (phone)
323-850-3866 (fax)

1620 Montgomery St. #250
San Francisco, CA 94111
415-449-9122

routeonefilms.com
imdb.com/company/co0316867

Does not accept any unsolicited material. Project types include feature films.

Jay Stern
imdb.com/name/nm0827731

Chip Diggins
imdb.com/name/nm0226505

Russell Levine
imdb.com/name/nm4149902

ROVIO
Production company

Keilaranta 17, Espoo, AL, Finland, FI-02150
011-358-503008250

contact@rovio.com
imdb.com/company/co0358927

Does not accept any unsolicited material.

Mikael Hed
Executive
imdb.com/name/nm4678928

ROXWELL FILMS
Production company

650 Rose Ave, Suite 2
Venice, CA 90291
310-399-7895

info@roxwell.net
imdb.com/company/co0320829
facebook.com/RoxwellFilms
twitter.com/RoxwellFilms

Does not accept any unsolicited material. Project types include feature films. Genres include thriller and drama. Established in 2008.

ROYAL TIES PRODUCTIONS
Production company

5700 Canoga Ave, Suite 300
Woodland Hills, CA 91367

imdb.com/company/co0232279

Does not accept any unsolicited material. Project types include feature films and short films. Genres include documentary. Established in 2006.

R-SQUARED FILMS
Production company, distributor, and sales agent

3113 Bramble Dr
Reno, NV 89509
623-889-5530

submissions@rsquaredfilms.com
imdb.com/company/co0271163

Accepts query letters from unproduced, unrepresented writers via email. Project types include feature films and TV. Genres include action, drama, and family.

Buzz Remde
Producer
imdb.com/name/nm1364362

RTL PRODUCTIONS
Production company and financing company

P.O. Box 640
Woodbury, NJ 08096

pacopapo@rtlproductions.com
rtlproductions.com

imdb.com/company/co0226719
linkedin.com/in/robertolombardi

Does not accept any unsolicited material. Project types include TV. Genres include drama, fantasy, and action.

RUBICON ENTERTAINMENT
Production company

3406 Tareco Dr.
Los Angeles, CA 90068
323-850-9200 (phone)
323-378-5584 (fax)

submissions@rubiconentertainment.com
rubiconentertainment.com
imdb.com/company/co0476567
linkedin.com/company/rubicon-entertainment-llc

Accepts query letters from unproduced, unrepresented writers via email. Project types include feature films. Genres include drama and comedy.

RUBY FILMS
Production company and distributor

6 Lloyd Baker St
London WC1X 9AW
UK
+44 20 7833 9990 (phone)
+44 20 7837 5862 (fax)

info@rubyfilms.co.uk
rubyfilms.co.uk
imdb.com/company/co0104115
twitter.com/rubyfilmandtv

Does not accept any unsolicited material. Project types include TV. Genres include drama.

Alison Owen
Producer
imdb.com/name/nm0654077

RUBY-SPEARS PRODUCTIONS
Production company

3500 W. Olive Ave., Suite 300
Burbank , CA 91505
818-840-1234

rubyspearsproductions@gmail.com (script submissions)
info@rubyspears.com (general)
rubyspears.com
imdb.com/company/co0001592

Does not accept any unsolicited material. Project types include feature films and TV. Genres include animation.

RUCKUSFILM
Production company

4610 Charlotte Ave.
Nashville, TN 37209
615-298-5818 (phone)
615-292-0204 (fax)

angie@ruckusfilm.com
ruckusfilm.com
imdb.com/company/co0135857
linkedin.com/company/ruckus-film
facebook.com/Ruckus-Film-322050394512454
twitter.com/RuckusFilm

Does not accept any unsolicited material. Project types include TV and feature films. Genres include family, comedy, and fantasy.

RUFFHOUSE STUDIOS
Production company

2823 Lariat Trail
Austin, TX 78734
512-965-2957

charlie@ruffhousin.com
ruffhousin.com
imdb.com/company/co0125287
linkedin.com/in/charleswiedman
facebook.com/ruffhousin
twitter.com/ruffhousinatx

Does not accept any unsolicited material. Genres include action and drama.

RUMPUS ENTERTAINMENT
Production company

8630 Pine Tree Place
Los Angeles, CA 90069
323-774-5245

imdb.com/company/co0213473

Does not accept any unsolicited material. Project types include feature films. Genres include romance and comedy.

RUM RIVER PRODUCTIONS
Production company

5915 S. Sycamore St. Littleton, CO 80120
303-883-6421

Matt@RumRiverProductions.com
rumriverproductions.com
imdb.com/company/co0258898

Does not accept any unsolicited material. Project types include short films. Genres include horror.

RUNAWAY PRODUCTIONS
Production company

7336 Santa Monica Blvd.
Ste 751
West Hollywood, CA 90046
310-801-0885

runawaylp@gmail.com (script submissions)
lindapalmer@runawayproductions.tv (general)
runawayproductions.tv
imdb.com/company/co0097894
facebook.com/runawayproduct

Accepts query letters from unproduced, unrepresented writers via email. Project types include TV and feature films. Genres include comedy.

Linda Palmer
imdb.com/name/nm1881313

Todd Wade
imdb.com/name/nm0905520

R W PRODUCTIONS
Production company and distributor

6011 Westline Dr
Houston, TX 77036
713-522-4701 (phone)
713-522-0426 (fax)

info@rwvideo.com
rwvideo.com

imdb.com/company/co0194897
twitter.com/filmsbychampion

Does not accept any unsolicited material. Project types include TV. Genres include thriller. Established in 1987.

R.W. PRODUCTIONS

Production company

6011 Westline Dr
Houston, TX 77036
713-522-4701 (phone)
713-522-0426 (fax)

info@rwvideo.com
rwvideo.com
imdb.com/company/co0107179
linkedin.com/company/rw-productions

Does not accept any unsolicited material. Genres include comedy, horror, and thriller.

RW PRODUCTIONS

Production company

championenter@gmail.com
rwproductionsinc.com
imdb.com/company/co0253400
linkedin.com/company/rw-productions

Does not accept any unsolicited material. Project types include TV. Genres include drama and documentary.

RYAN MURPHY PRODUCTIONS

Production company

5555 Melrose Ave Modular Building, First Floor
Los Angeles, CA 90038
323-956-2408 (phone)
323-862-2235 (fax)

imdb.com/company/co0156994
facebook.com/pages/Ryan-Murphy-Productions/
    139660549406713

Does not accept any unsolicited material. Project types include feature films and TV. Genres include drama, horror, thriller, documentary, comedy, science fiction, and non-fiction. Established in 2008.

Ryan Murphy
imdb.com/name/nm0614682

Dante Di Loreto
President
imdb.com/name/nm0223994

RYDING BYKES ENTERTAINMENT

Production company

2124 NE 15th Terrace
Cape Coral, FL 33909
248-622-6926 (phone)
239-673-9499 (fax)

RydingBykes@comcast.net
imdb.com/company/co0279685

Does not accept any unsolicited material.

S3 ENTERTAINMENT GROUP

Production company and financing company

1100 Woodward Heights
Ferndale, MI 48220
248-444-7000 (phone)
248-630-2617 (fax)

info@s3eg.com
imdb.com/company/co0249736
linkedin.com/company/s3-entertainment-group
facebook.com/S3EGroup
twitter.com/S3EG

Does not accept any unsolicited material. Project types include feature films. Genres include thriller.

SABAN FILMS

Production company, distributor, and sales agent

10100 Santa Monica Blvd, Suite 110, Los Angeles, CA, United States, 90067
310-203-5850

info@sabanfilms.com
sabanfilms.com
imdb.com/company/co0481625

Does not accept any unsolicited material. Project types include TV, short films, and feature films. Genres include science fiction, drama, family, fantasy, comedy, thriller, animation, and action.

SABBATICAL PICTURES

Production company

1601 Elm St
Ste 300
Dallas, TX 75201
972-394-7334

info@sabbaticalpictures.com
sabbaticalpictures.com
imdb.com/company/co0210355

Does not accept any unsolicited material. Genres include horror and thriller.

SACRED DOGS ENTERTAINMENT LLC
Production company

311 N Robertson Blvd.
Ste. 249
Beverly Hills, CA 90211
323-656-6900

studio@sacreddogs.com
sacreddogs.com
imdb.com/company/co0121976
facebook.com/Victory.Tischler.Blue
twitter.com/vtb1

Does not accept any unsolicited material. Project types include feature films. Genres include documentary.

Arden Brotman
323-656-6900
imdb.com/name/nm2231224

Victory Tischler-Blue
Owner
323-656-6900
imdb.com/name/nm0089548

SACRED PRODUCTIONS
Production company

478 E Altamonte Dr
Suite 108 #156
Altamonte Springs, FL 32701
407-218-0880

sharon@sacredmovie.com
imdb.com/company/co0247417

Does not accept any unsolicited material. Genres include horror.

SAFADY ENTERTAINMENT
Production company and financing company

9663 Santa Monica Blvd, Suite 406
Beverly Hills, CA 90210
310-207-8600 (phone)
310-207-2288 (fax)

cchapman@safadyentertainment.com
safadyentertainment.com
imdb.com/company/co0263900
facebook.com/pages/SafadyEntertainment
twitter.com/SafadyEnt

Does not accept any unsolicited material. Project types include feature films. Genres include horror, drama, thriller, and action.

SAINTSINNER ENTERTAINMENT
Production company

397 Magnolia St
Salem, NJ 08079
856-935-5619 (phone)
856-935-8870 (fax)

casting@saintsinnerent.com (script submissions)
info@bravaent.com (general)
saintsinnerent.com
imdb.com/company/co0124581
facebook.com/saintsinnerent
twitter.com/SSETWEETS

Accepts query letters from unproduced, unrepresented writers via email. Genres include action.

SAKONNET CAPITAL PARTNERS
Financing company

155 Chestnut St
Providence, RI 02903
401-454-0800 (phone)
401-537-9154 (fax)

mcorso@sakcap.com
imdb.com/company/co0310712

Does not accept any unsolicited material. Project types include commercials. Genres include thriller and drama.

Michael Corso
Producer
imdb.com/name/nm3937322

SALIENT MEDIA, LLC
Production company and distributor

8383 Wilshire Blvd, Suite 1050, Beverly Hills , CA,
United States, 90211
323-370-1503

info@salientmedia.com
salientmedia.com
imdb.com/company/co0204251

Does not accept any unsolicited material. Project types
include TV. Genres include family, drama, thriller,
and romance.

SALT COMPANY INTERNATIONAL, THE
Sales agent

2nd Fl, Unit 19, Tileyard Studios
Tileyard Rd
London N7 9AH
UK
+44207-535-6714

info@salt-co.com
salt-co.com
imdb.com/company/co0235242

Does not accept any unsolicited material. Project types
include TV, feature films, and short films. Genres
include horror.

Samantha Horley
Producer
imdb.com/name/nm2548355

SALTIRE ENTERTAINMENT
Production company

6352 De Longpre Ave
Los Angeles, CA 90028

imdb.com/company/co0104114
facebook.com/pages/saltire-entertainment/
    107057289327193

Does not accept any unsolicited material. Project types
include feature films. Genres include myth, science
fiction, and drama.

Stuart Pollok
Producer
imdb.com/name/nm0689415

SALTIRE PRODUCTIONS
Production company

321 W Bell St
Houston, TX 77019
713-261-2951

mark@MJdocherty.com
imdb.com/company/co0525704

Does not accept any unsolicited material. Project types
include short films. Genres include action, science
fiction, and drama.

SALT PICTURES
Production company, distributor, and sales agent

1A Adpar St
3rd Fl
London W2 1DE
UK
+44 (0)20 7535 6714 (phone)
+44 (0)20 7563 7283 (fax)

info@salt-co.com
salt-co.com
imdb.com/company/co0145945

Does not accept any unsolicited material. Project types
include TV. Genres include drama and crime.

SALTY FEATURES
Production company

135 W 20th St. – 5th fl.
New York, NY 10011
212.604.9700
212-924-1601 (phone)
212-924-2306 (fax)

info@saltyfeatures.com
saltyfeatures.com
imdb.com/company/co0120227
linkedin.com/company/salty-features
facebook.com/SaltyFeatures
twitter.com/saltyfeatures

Does not accept any unsolicited material. Project types include TV and feature films. Genres include non-fiction and reality.

Yael Melamede
Producer
imdb.com/name/nm0577336

Eva Kolodner
imdb.com/name/nm0464286

SALVATORE/ORNSTON PRODUCTIONS
Production company

5650 Camellia Ave
North Hollywood, CA 91601
310-466-8980 (phone)
818-752-9321 (fax)

imdb.com/company/co0223789

Accepts query letters from produced or represented writers. Project types include feature films. Genres include action, animation, comedy, thriller, drama, romance, and crime.

David E. Ornston
Executive
imdb.com/name/nm0650361

Richard Salvatore
Executive
imdb.com/name/nm0759363

SAMACO FILMS
Production company

12041 Wilshire Blvd, Ste 20
Brentwood, CA 90025
310-979-9971 (phone)
310-979-9973 (fax)

franco@samacoproductions.com
samacofilms.com
imdb.com/company/co0435063
linkedin.com/in/samacofilms
facebook.com/SamacoFilms
twitter.com/francosama

Does not accept any unsolicited material. Project types include feature films. Genres include drama, action, and thriller.

SAMUEL GOLDWYN FILMS
Production company and distributor

30 W 26th St, Third Floor, New York, NY, United States, 10010
212-367-9435 (phone)
212-590-0124 (fax)

9570 W Pico Blvd Suite 400
Los Angeles CA 90035
310-860-3100 (phone)
310-860-3195 (fax)

info@samuelgoldwyn.com
samuelgoldwynfilms.com
imdb.com/company/co0058013

Does not accept any unsolicited material. Project types include TV and feature films. Genres include thriller, action, and drama.

SAMUELS MEDIA
Production company

345 N Canon Dr, Suite 202
Beverly Hills, CA 90210
310-395-1280

imdb.com/company/co0184827

Does not accept any unsolicited material. Project types include feature films. Genres include drama and thriller.

SAMUELSON PRODUCTIONS LIMITED
Production company

10401 Wyton Dr
Los Angeles, CA 90024-2527
310-208-1000 (phone)
323-315-5188 (fax)

info@samuelson.la
samuelson.la
imdb.com/company/co0182558
linkedin.com/company/samuelson-productions-limited

Does not accept any unsolicited material. Project types include TV and feature films. Genres include drama, action, and comedy.

Renato Celani
imdb.com/name/nm1954607

Josie Law
imdb.com/name/nm1656468

Peter Samuelson
Owner
imdb.com/name/nm0006873
Assistant: Brian Casey

Marc Samuelson
imdb.com/name/nm0760555

Saryl Hirsch
imdb.com/name/nm1950244

SANBORN STUDIOS
Production company

8100 15th St. E
Sarasota, FL 34243

imdb.com/company/co0326279

Does not accept any unsolicited material. Project types include short films. Genres include action and documentary.

SANDBAR PICTURES
Production company

4111 W. Alameda Ave Ste 505
Burbank, CA 91505
415-398-0780 (phone)
415-398-1598 (fax)

1145 N. McCadden Place
Hollywood, CA 90038
323-337-1183 (phone)
323-337-1434 (fax)

info@sandbarpictures.net
imdb.com/company/co0171098

Does not accept any unsolicited material. Project types include feature films. Genres include drama, thriller, and horror. Established in 2005.

Greg Little
Founder
imdb.com/name/nm0514571

Elizabeth Zox Friedman
Founder
imdb.com/name/nm0295288
linkedin.com/pub/lizzie-friedman/72/7b6/536
twitter.com/Frizzie93

SANDER/MOSES PRODUCTIONS
Production company

The Lot 1041 N. Formosa Ave
Formosa Building
Suite 7
West Hollywood, CA 90046
818-560-4500 (phone)
818-860-6284 (fax)

info@sandermoses.com
sandermoses.com
imdb.com/company/co0028175
facebook.com/SanderMosesProductions

Accepts query letters from unproduced, unrepresented writers via email. Project types include TV, feature films, and commercials. Genres include drama, non-fiction, and reality.

Kim Moses
imdb.com/name/nm0608593

Ian Sander
imdb.com/name/nm0761401
twitter.com/IanSander

SANDERS ARMSTRONG CASERTA MANAGEMENT

2120 Colorado Blvd, Ste 120
Santa Monica, CA 90404
310-315-2100 (phone)
310-315-2115 (fax)

imdb.com/company/co0070591

Does not accept any unsolicited material. Project types include TV. Genres include drama.

SANDIA MEDIA
Production company

6100 4th St. NW, Suite A109
Los Ranchos, NM 87107

505-345-2135 (phone)
505-814-5703 (fax)

info@sandiamedia.com
sandiamedia.com
imdb.com/company/co0248855

Does not accept any unsolicited material. Project types include feature films. Genres include comedy, romance, and drama. Established in 2008.

SAN FRANCISCO FILM SOCIETY
Production company

39 Mesa St, Suite 110, The Presidio, San Francisco , CA, United States, 94129
415-561-5000 (phone)
415-561-5099 (fax)

info@sffs.org
sffs.org
imdb.com/company/co0270763

Does not accept any unsolicited material. Project types include feature films, TV, and short films. Genres include drama, romance, and family.

Athena Kalkopoulou
Coordinator (Project Development)
415-561-5045
imdb.com/name/nm6692739

SANITSKY COMPANY
Production company

9200 Sunset Blvd.
Los Angeles, CA 90069
310-274-0120 (phone)
310 274 1455 (fax)

imdb.com/company/co0059772

Does not accept any unsolicited material. Project types include TV. Genres include drama.

Larry Sanitsky
President
imdb.com/name/nm0762792

SAPPHIRE BLUE FILMS
Production company

300 S. Lenola Rd.
Suite 3 281
Maple Shade, NJ 08052
215-900-9595 (phone)
856-206-9754 (fax)

antonne@equalverdicts.com
imdb.com/company/co0343215

Does not accept any unsolicited material. Project types include TV and feature films. Genres include drama.

SARABANDE PRODUCTIONS
Production company

715 Broadway, Suite 210
Santa Monica, CA 90401
310-395-4842 (phone)
310-395-7079 (fax)

imdb.com/company/co0064364
linkedin.com/company/sarabande-productions
twitter.com/produsarab

Does not accept any unsolicited material. Project types include TV. Genres include drama, crime, thriller, and science fiction.

SARGENT HALL PRODUCTIONS
Production company

9229 Sunset Blvd.
West Hollywood, CA 90069

imdb.com/company/co0316570

Does not accept any unsolicited material. Project types include feature films and TV. Genres include comedy and drama.

SATURN FILMS
Production company and distributor

9000 Sunset Blvd., #911
West Hollywood, CA 90069
310-887-0900 (phone)
310-248-2965 (fax)

imdb.com/company/co0010750

Does not accept any unsolicited material. Project types include feature films. Genres include action and drama. Established in 1999.

SAWBONE FILMS

Production company and distributor

10 Cottage Rd
South Portland, ME 04106
207-799-9500

lonewolfmedia.com
facebook.com/lonewolfdg
twitter.com/LoneWolf_Media

Does not accept any unsolicited material. Project types include TV. Genres include drama.

SAY TRUE FILMS

Production company

P. O. Box 1899
Winter Park, FL 32790
310-739-1406

sheri@saytruefilms.com
saytruefilms.com
imdb.com/company/co0370002
facebook.com/ATrueStoryProduction
twitter.com/SayTrueFilms

Does not accept any unsolicited material. Genres include drama and documentary.

SBK PICTURES

Production company

324 Highland Ln
Bryn Mawr, PA 19010
610-525-8785 (phone)
610-658-0809 (fax)

jeffrey_berry@sbkpictures.com
sbkpictures.com
imdb.com/company/co0171637

Does not accept any unsolicited material. Project types include TV and feature films. Genres include drama.

SB PRODUCTIONS

Production company

338 Park Dr
San Antonio, TX 78212
210-865-3074 (phone)
210-826-2889 (fax)

masbruni@mac.com
imdb.com/company/co0219980
facebook.com/serrasolsesbrothers

Does not accept any unsolicited material. Project types include TV. Genres include documentary.

SCARLET FIRE ENTERTAINMENT

Production company

561 28th Ave
Venice, CA 90291
310-302-1001 (phone)
310-302-1002 (fax)

imdb.com/company/co0052256

Does not accept any unsolicited material. Project types include TV and feature films. Genres include comedy.

Steven Pearl
Producer
310-302-1001
imdb.com/name/nm0669093

Allen Loeb
Producer
310-302-1001
imdb.com/name/nm1615610

SCARPE DIEM PRODUCTIONS

Production company

414 Washington St
New York, NY 10013
212-226-6828

info@scarpediemproductions.com
scarpediemproductions.com
imdb.com/company/co0356951

Does not accept any unsolicited material. Project types include feature films. Genres include romance, drama, fantasy, and family.

SCARY MADISON

Production company and distributor

10202 W Washington Blvd., Judy Garland Bldg.
Culver City, CA 90232
+310-244-3100 (phone)
+310-244-3353 (fax)

imdb.com/company/co0059609

Does not accept any unsolicited material. Project types include feature films. Genres include thriller.

SCENE SEVENTEEN PICTURES
Production company

P.O. Box 14084
Gainseville, FL 32604
352-378-0500

imdb.com/company/co0093905

Does not accept any unsolicited material.

SC FILMS INTERNATIONAL
Production company and distributor

1st Floor, 56 Brewer St
Soho
London W1F 9TJ
UK
44207-287-1900

info@scfilmsinternational.com
scfilmsinternational.com
imdb.com/company/co0265456
facebook.com/SCFilmsInternational
twitter.com/SC_Films

Does not accept any unsolicited material. Project types include TV. Genres include animation and comedy.

Simon Crowe
Producer
imdb.com/name/nm2995520

SCHNEIDER FILMS LLC
Production company

140 Monroe Ave.
Keansburg, NJ 07734
732-895-6262 (phone)
732-787-2181 (fax)

imdb.com/company/co0097288

Does not accept any unsolicited material. Project types include TV. Genres include comedy and action.

SCIENTIFIC GAMES CORPORATION
750 Lexington Ave
New York, NY 10022
212-754-2233

scientificgames.com
twitter.com/ScientificGames

Does not accept any unsolicited material. Project types include TV.

SCION FILMS
Production company

3rd Floor
21 Ganton St
London W1F 9BN
England
+44 20 7851 5740 (phone)
+44 20 7851 5741 (fax)

info@scionig.com
scionig.com
imdb.com/company/co0133024

Does not accept any unsolicited material. Project types include feature films. Genres include drama.

Jeff Abberley
Producer
imdb.com/name/nm1329997

SCOOTY WOOP ELITE
Production company and sales agent

1131 Alta Loma Rd. #414 West
Hollywood, CA 90069
310-749-4712

info@scootywoopelite.com
scootywoopelite.com
imdb.com/company/co0285791
twitter.com/ScootyWoopElite

Does not accept any unsolicited material. Project types include feature films. Genres include drama and thriller.

SCORE PRODUCTIONS, INC.
Production company

2401 Main St.
Santa Monica, CA 90405
604-868-7377

score@scoreproductions.com
scoreproductions.com
imdb.com/company/co0128322

Accepts query letters from produced or represented writers. Project types include TV and feature films. Genres include drama, detective, science fiction, and fantasy.

SCOTT FREE PRODUCTIONS
Production company

614 N. La Peer Dr.
Los Angeles, CA 90069
310-360-2250 (phone)
310-360-2251 (fax)

rsafilms.com
imdb.com/company/co0074212

Does not accept any unsolicited material. Project types include feature films and TV. Genres include animation, reality, drama, detective, action, non-fiction, thriller, and crime.

David Zucker
imdb.com/name/nm0001878
Assistant: Mark Pfeffer

Ridley Scott
imdb.com/name/nm0000631
Assistant: Nancy Ryan

SCOTT RUDIN PRODUCTIONS
Production company

120 W 45th St
10th Floor
New York, NY 10036
212-704-4600

imdb.com/company/co0093765
linkedin.com/company/scott-rudin-productions

Accepts query letters from unproduced, unrepresented writers. Project types include feature films. Established in 1993.

Eli Bush
Executive
212-704-4600
eli@scottrudinprod.com
imdb.com/name/nm4791912

Scott Rudin
Producer
212-704-4600
imdb.com/name/nm0748784

SCOTT SANDERS PRODUCTIONS
Production company

322 8th Ave
14th Fl
New York, NY 10001
212-792-6390

scottsandersproductions.com
imdb.com/company/co0326530

Does not accept any unsolicited material. Project types include feature films and TV. Genres include comedy and romance.

Scott Sanders
imdb.com/name/nm0761712
Assistant: Jaime Quiroz

Bryan Kalfus
imdb.com/name/nm0435729

SCOTT STUBER CO.
Production company

100 Universal City Plaza
Bungalow 4171
Universal City, CA 91608
818-777-3200 (phone)
818-777-0020 (fax)

imdb.com/company/co0376117

Does not accept any unsolicited material. Project types include feature films and TV. Genres include action, fantasy, romance, science fiction, crime, thriller, and drama.

Michael Clear
Vice President
imdb.com/name/nm2752795
linkedin.com/pub/mike-clear/4/90/42b

Nicholas David Nesbitt
Vice President
imdb.com/name/nm1704779

Scott Stuber
Principal
imdb.com/name/nm0835959

SCREEN DOOR
Production company

412 Roncesvalles Ave
Suite 207
Toronto, ON M6R2N2
Canada
416-479-4162 (phone)
416-516-0184 (fax)

development@screendoor.org
screendoor.org
imdb.com/company/co0171541

Does not accept any unsolicited material. Genres include drama.

Mary Young Leckie
Producer
imdb.com/name/nm0949229

SCREEN DOOR ENTERTAINMENT
Production company

15223 Burbank Blvd.
Sherman Oaks, CA 91411
818-781-5600 (phone)
818-781-5601 (fax)

info@sdetv.com
sdctv.com
imdb.com/company/co0099778

Accepts query letters from unproduced, unrepresented writers. Project types include TV. Genres include reality. Established in 2001.

Joel Rizor
President
imdb.com/name/nm1381432

Dave Shikiar
imdb.com/name/nm0793434

M. Alessandra Ascoli
generalinfo@sdetv.com
imdb.com/name/nm0038529

SCREEN GEMS
Production company

10202 W Washington Blvd
Culver City, CA 90232
310-244-4000 (phone)
310-244-2037 (fax)

imdb.com/company/co0010568

Does not accept any unsolicited material. Project types include TV, feature films, and short films. Genres include romance, reality, thriller, fantasy, science fiction, drama, comedy, horror, documentary, and action. Established in 1926.

Scott Strauss
Executive Vice President of Production
imdb.com/name/nm0833873

Loren Schwartz
imdb.com/name/nm2817219

Clint Culpepper
President
imdb.com/name/nm0191695

Glenn Gainor
imdb.com/name/nm0004636

Eric Paquette
imdb.com/name/nm1789841

Pamela Kunath
imdb.com/name/nm2242666

Carol Smithson
imdb.com/name/nm2972574
linkedin.com/pub/carol-smithson/10/762/7b2

James Lopez
imdb.com/name/nm5144603

SCREEN MEDIA FILMS
Production company, distributor, and sales agent

757 Third Ave
3rd Fl
New York, NY 10017

212-308-1790 (phone)
212-308-1791 (fax)

info@screenmedia.net
screenmedia.net
imdb.com/company/co0092769

Does not accept any unsolicited material. Project types include TV. Genres include action and thriller.

Suzanne Blech
Executive
imdb.com/name/nm2518335

SCREEN MEDIA VENTURES
Production company and distributor

757 Third Ave, Third Floor, New York City , NY, United States, 10017
212-308-1790 (phone)
212-308-1791 (fax)

info@screenmedia.net
screenmedia.net
imdb.com/company/co0081784

Does not accept any unsolicited material. Project types include TV and feature films. Genres include action, drama, thriller, and family.

SCYTHIA FILMS
Production company

431A Queen St W
Toronto, ON M5V 2A5
Canada
416-897-05211

info@scythiafilms.com
scythiafilms.com
imdb.com/company/co0293963
facebook.com/scythiafilmsinc
twitter.com/intentfollow

Does not accept any unsolicited material. Genres include drama.

Daniel Bekerman
Producer
imdb.com/name/nm1764941

SE8 GROUP
Production company

PO Box 691763
West Hollywood, CA 90069
310-285-6090 (phone)
310-285-6097 (fax)

imdb.com/company/co0103782

Accepts query letters from unproduced, unrepresented writers. Project types include feature films. Genres include drama and thriller.

Gary Oldman
imdb.com/name/nm0000198

Douglas Urbanski
Producer
imdb.com/name/nm0881703

SEAN CONNORS FILMS
Production company and financing company

17011 Lincoln Ave
#461
Parker, CO 80134

imdb.com/company/co0214126

Does not accept any unsolicited material. Project types include TV. Genres include action and thriller.

Sean Connors
Producer
imdb.com/name/nm2583861

SEA STAR FILMS
Production company

7124 Abbott Ave
Miami Beach, FL 33141
305-868-3843

seastarfilms.com
imdb.com/company/co0441098
facebook.com/Sea-Star-Films-25479342810

Does not accept any unsolicited material. Genres include documentary.

SECOND AND 10TH INC.
Production company

51 MacDougal St, Suite 383
New York, NY 10012
347-882-4493

imdb.com/company/co0317939

Does not accept any unsolicited material. Project types include feature films. Genres include drama.

Anne Carey
Producer
imdb.com/name/nm0136904
linkedin.com/pub/anne-carey/28/237/661

SECRET HANDSHAKE ENTERTAINMENT, LLC
Production company

7709 Melrose Ave, Suite 201, Los Angeles, CA, United States, 90046
323-822-4000

info@secrethandshakeent.com
imdb.com/company/co0252079

Does not accept any unsolicited material. Project types include short films. Genres include family.

SECTION 23 FILMS
Distributor

9396 Richmond Ave
Houston, TX 77063
713-335-0452

imdb.com/company/co0286265
facebook.com/pages/Section23-Films/
    103114626395115

Does not accept any unsolicited material. Project types include short films, feature films, and TV. Genres include science fiction, drama, animation, and action. Established in 2009.

SEDIC INTERNATIONAL
Production company and distributor

203
7-13-28 Minami-Aoyama
Minato-Ku, Tokyo 107-0062
Japan
+81 3-5766-8929 (phone)
+81 3-5766-8939 (fax)

sedic@inter.office.ne.jp
sedic.co.jp
imdb.com/company/co0240064

Does not accept any unsolicited material. Project types include short films, TV, and feature films. Genres include action.

SEE-SAW FILMS
Production company

2 Paddington St
Paddington
NSW 2021
61 (0)2 9357 0700

74 Rivington St
London, England EC2A 3AY
UK
44203-301-6268 (phone)
44844-994-5035 (fax)

info@see-saw-films.com
see-saw-films.com
imdb.com/company/co0230132

Does not accept any unsolicited material. Project types include TV. Genres include drama, crime, and thriller.

Iain Canning
Producer
imdb.com/name/nm2096617

SEISMIC PICTURES
Production company

Raleigh Studios
5358 Melrose Ave.
Suite 218W
Hollywood, CA 90028
323-960-3449

info@seismicpictures.com
seismicpictures.com
imdb.com/company/co0203691

Does not accept any unsolicited material. Project types include feature films and TV. Genres include comedy, reality, non-fiction, and drama.

Robert Schwartz
imdb.com/name/nm0777412

Alejandro Laguette
Director of Development
imdb.com/name/nm1657781

SELF-RELIANT FILM
Production company

info@selfreliantfilm.com
selfreliantfilm.com
imdb.com/company/co0422279
facebook.com/selfreliantfilm
twitter.com/selfreliantfilm

Does not accept any unsolicited material. Project types include feature films and short films. Genres include documentary and drama. Established in 2010.

Ashley Maynor
Founder
imdb.com/name/nm3579482

Paul Harrill
Founder
imdb.com/name/nm0364204

SENART FILMS
Production company

555 W 25th St, 4th Floor
New York, NY 10001
212-406-9610 (phone)
212-406-9581 (fax)

info@senartfilms.com
senartfilms.com
imdb.com/company/co0081078
linkedin.com/company/senart-films-llc
facebook.com/senartfilms

Does not accept any unsolicited material. Project types include TV and feature films. Genres include reality, non-fiction, and drama.

Robert May
Producer
imdb.com/name/nm1254338

SENATOR DISTRIBUTION
Distributor

161 Ave Of The Americas
11th Floor
New York, NY 10013
212-627-1662

9000 W Sunset Blvd
16th Floor
Los Angeles, CA 90069
310-248-4700 (phone)
310-248-4720 (fax)

general@senatorent.com
imdb.com/company/co0236626

Does not accept any unsolicited material. Genres include thriller, drama, and crime.

SENTIENT ENTERTAINMENT
Production company

2500 Broadway
Building F, Suite F-125
Santa Monica, CA 90404
310-315-3500 (phone)
424-238-4301 (fax)

info@sentientent.com
imdb.com/company/co0321306
facebook.com/Sentient-111469505597745

Does not accept any unsolicited material. Project types include TV and feature films.

Chris Tuffin
Producer
310-315-3500
imdb.com/name/nm0876195

Renee Tab
President
310-315-3500
imdb.com/name/nm2229960

S.E.P PRODUCTIONS
Production company

2630 Lacy St Studios
1st Flr Main Factory
Los Angeles, CA 90031
310-295-0875 (phone)
323-227-7919 (fax)

sep@peelhead.com
imdb.com/company/co0124590

Does not accept any unsolicited material.

SERAPHIM FILMS
Production company

310-888-4200 or 310-246-0050

assistant@seraphimfilms.com
imdb.com/company/co0045933

Does not accept any unsolicited material. Project types include feature films. Genres include fantasy, drama, horror, and animation.

Clive Barker
President
imdb.com/name/nm0000850
facebook.com/officialclivebarker

SERENDIPITY POINT FILMS
Production company

9 Price St
Toronto, ON M4W 1Z1
Canada
416-960-0300 (phone)
416-960-8656 (fax)

serendipitypoint.com
imdb.com/company/co0016814
facebook.com/SerendipityPointFilms
twitter.com/SerendipityPnt

Does not accept any unsolicited material. Project types include feature films and TV. Genres include drama, comedy, thriller, and action.

Wendy Saffer
imdb.com/name/nm2194201

Robert Lantos
Producer
imdb.com/name/nm0487190
Assistant: Cherri Campbell

SERENDIPITY PRODUCTIONS, INC.
Production company

15260 Ventura Blvd, Suite 1040
Sherman Oaks, CA 91403
818-789-3035 (phone)
818-235-0150 (fax)

imdb.com/company/co0119340

Does not accept any unsolicited material. Project types include TV and feature films. Genres include horror, drama, and non-fiction.

Daniel Heffner
danheffner@earthlink.net
imdb.com/name/nm0004527

Ketura Kestin
keturak@gmail.com
imdb.com/name/nm3109585

SEVEN ARTS PICTURES
Production company

1801 Century Park East
Suite 1830
Lost Angeles, CA 90067
323-372-3080 (phone)
323-372-3088 (fax)

8721 Sunset Blvd
Suite 209
Los Angeles, CA 90069

136-144 New Kings Rd
London, United Kingdom, SW6 4LZ
011-442-030068222 (phone)
011-442-030068220 (fax)

info@7artspictures.com
imdb.com/company/co0045848

Does not accept any unsolicited material. Project types include feature films. Genres include science fiction, comedy, thriller, and drama.

Peter Hoffman
CEO
imdb.com/name/nm0389056

SEVENTH ART RELEASING
Production company, distributor, and sales agent

6579 Pickwick St, Los Angeles, CA, United States, 90042
323-259-8259 (phone)
323-474-6371 (fax)

info@7thart.com
7thart.com
imdb.com/company/co0048319

Does not accept any unsolicited material. Project types include TV. Genres include comedy, romance, family, and drama.

S FILMS
Production company

3rd Floor, Tyler's Court
111a Wardour St
London W1F 0UJ
UK
+44 (0207-494-4049

info@sfilms.com
sfilms.com
imdb.com/company/co0104822

Does not accept any unsolicited material. Project types include TV. Genres include romance, comedy, and drama.

SHADOWCATCHER ENTERTAINMENT
Production company

4701 SW Admiral Way
Box 32
Seattle, WA 98116
206-328-6266 (phone)
206-447-1462 (fax)

kate@shadowcatcherent.com
shadowcatcherent.com
imdb.com/company/co0021127
facebook.com/ShadowCatcherEntertainment

Does not accept any unsolicited material. Project types include TV, feature films, and theater. Genres include non-fiction, comedy, animation, drama, and reality.

Norman Stephens
Producer
imdb.com/name/nm1017457

David Skinner
Executive Producer
imdb.com/name/nm1623496

Tom Gorai
Producer
imdb.com/name/nm0329753
linkedin.com/pub/tom-gorai/9/553/b86

SHAFTESBURY
Production company and distributor

163 Queen St East, Suite 100
Toronto, ON M5A 1S1
Canada
416-363-1411 (phone)
416-363-1428 (fax)

pcassavetti@shaftesbury.ca
shaftesbury.ca
imdb.com/company/co0068478
facebook.com/ShaftesburyTV
twitter.com/shaftesburytv

Does not accept any unsolicited material. Genres include documentary.

SHAFTESBURY FILMS
Production company

163 Queen St East Suite 100
Toronto, ON, Canada, M5A 1S1
416-363-1411 (phone)
416-363-1428 (fax)

4370 Tujunga Ave Suite 300
Studio City, CA 91604
818-505-3361 (phone)
818-505-3511 (fax)

info@shaftesbury.ca
shaftesbury.ca
imdb.com/company/co0014501
linkedin.com/company/shaftesbury-films-inc.
facebook.com/ShaftesburyTV
twitter.com/shaftesburytv

Does not accept any unsolicited material. Project types include TV and feature films. Genres include action, comedy, thriller, romance, family, drama, and animation. Established in 1987.

Adam Haight
Senior Vice President, Scripted Content
ahaight@shaftesbury.ca

Julie Lacey
Vice President, Creative Affairs
jlacey@shaftesbury.ca
imdb.com/name/nm0479936

Christina Jennings
Chairman & CEO
cjennings@shaftesbury.ca
imdb.com/name/nm0421126
twitter.com/CJShaftesbury

SHALLOW BEACH ENTERTAINMENT
Production company

1521 Alton Rd #434
Miami Beach, FL 33139
305-535-6522 (phone)
305-604-0593 (fax)

renee@shallowbeach.tv
shallowbeach.tv
imdb.com/company/co0189146

Does not accept any unsolicited material. Project types include short films. Genres include documentary.

SHAOLIN FILM PRODUCTIONS
Production company and distributor

231 Claremont Ave.
8
Montclair, NJ 07042
862-220-1382

shaolinfilm1@yahoo.com
imdb.com/company/co0211629

Does not accept any unsolicited material. Project types include TV. Genres include action and drama.

SHARKKBAIT ENTERTAINMENT GROUP
Production company

6278 N. Federal Highway #462
Fort Lauderdale, FL 33308
954-547-3567

info@sbentgroup.com
sbentgroup.com
imdb.com/company/co0165338
facebook.com/sbentgroup

Does not accept any unsolicited material. Project types include short films and feature films. Genres include romance, comedy, and action. Established in 2005.

SHAUN CASSIDY PRODUCTIONS
Production company

Los Angeles, CA
818-733-5976

imdb.com/company/co0000380

Accepts query letters from unproduced, unrepresented writers. Project types include TV. Genres include comedy and drama.

Shaun Cassidy
imdb.com/name/nm0001027

SHAW MEDIA
Production company and distributor

121 Bloor St East
15th Fl
Toronto, ON M4W 3M5
Canada
416-967-1174

corporate.inquiries@shawmedia.ca
shawmedia.ca
imdb.com/company/co0330730

Does not accept any unsolicited material. Genres include drama and crime.

Paul Robertson
Producer
imdb.com/name/nm1453748

SHEEP NOIR FILMS
Production company

438 W 17th Ave
Vancouver, BC V5Y 2A2
604-762-8933 (fax)

info@sheepnoir.com
sheepnoir.com
imdb.com/company/co0047875

Does not accept any unsolicited material. Project types include feature films and TV. Genres include drama.

Nathaniel Geary
imdb.com/name/nm0311303

Marc Stephenson
Producer
604-762-8933
marc@sheepnoir.com
imdb.com/name/nm0827287
facebook.com/marc.stephenson.353

Wendy Hyman
Producer
imdb.com/name/nm0405207

SHEPHARD/ROBIN COMPANY
Production company

c/o Raleigh Studios
5300 Melrose Ave, Suite 225E
Los Angeles, CA 90038
323-871-4412 (phone)
323-871-4418 (fax)

imdb.com/company/co0035643

Does not accept any unsolicited material. Project types
include TV. Genres include drama.

Greer Shephard
Principal
imdb.com/name/nm0791709

Michael Robin
Principal
imdb.com/name/nm0732218

SHIGOTO FILM PRODUCTION
Production company

Haiyuu-Za Building
4-9-2roppongi
Minato-Ku, Tokyo 106-0032
Japan
81-3-3470-2881 (phone)
81-3-3470-2880 (fax)

kobayashi@shigoto-kk.co.jp
shigoto-kk.com
imdb.com/company/co0025876

Does not accept any unsolicited material. Project types
include TV. Genres include drama and romance.

Shinichi Ono
Manager
imdb.com/name/nm6411440

SHINE ON ENTERTAINMENT
Production company

4440 PGA Blvd Ste 308
Palm Beach Gardens, FL 33410
US
844-333-0844

info@shineonentertainment.com
imdb.com/company/co0479733
facebook.com/Shine-On-
    Entertainment-125790750836844

Does not accept any unsolicited material. Genres
include drama.

SHÔCHIKU BROADCASTING CO.
Production company and distributor

4-1-1-5F
Tsukiji
Chuo, Tokyo 104-0045
Japan
03-5250-2321

post@shochiku.co.jp
broadcasting.co.jp
imdb.com/company/co0484644

Does not accept any unsolicited material. Project types
include TV. Genres include drama.

SHOCHIKU COMPANY
Production company and distributor

4-1-1, Togeki Bldg
Tsukiji
Chuo-Ku, Tokyo 104-8422
Japan
+81 3 5550 1623 (phone)
+81 3 5550 1654 (fax)

ibd@shochiku.co.jp
shochiku.co.jp
imdb.com/company/co0030891

Does not accept any unsolicited material. Project types
include TV. Genres include drama.

Yoshitaka Ishizuka
Producer
imdb.com/name/nm3554553

SHOCK-O-RAMA CINEMA

Production company and distributor

PO Box 152
Butler, NJ 07405
973-838-3030

PopCinema@aol.com
imdb.com/company/co0091082

Does not accept any unsolicited material. Project types include TV. Genres include horror and drama.

SHOEBOX FILMS

Production company

48 Russel Square, London,
WC1B 4JP, United Kingdom.
+44 0207-287-2953

info@shoeboxfilms.co.uk
shoeboxfilms.co.uk
imdb.com/company/co0352835

Does not accept any unsolicited material. Project types include TV. Genres include fantasy.

SHOE MONEY PRODUCTIONS

Production company

10202 W Washington Blvd
Poitier Building, Suite 3100
Culver City, CA 90232
310-244-6188

shoemoneyproductions@mac.com
imdb.com/company/co0126698
facebook.com/pages/ShoeMoney-Productions/
    6624704006

Accepts query letters from unproduced, unrepresented writers via email. Project types include TV and feature films. Genres include drama.

Julie DeJoie
Head of Production & Development
imdb.com/name/nm1264807

Thomas Schlamme
imdb.com/name/nm0772095

SHONDALAND

Production company

323-671-4650

imdb.com/company/co0170849
facebook.com/ShondaLand

Does not accept any unsolicited material. Project types include feature films and TV. Genres include drama and comedy.

Betsy Beers
Producer
imdb.com/name/nm0066530
twitter.com/BeersBetsy

Shonda Rhimes
imdb.com/name/nm0722274
twitter.com/shondarhimes

Alison Eakle
Executive
imdb.com/name/nm2300208

SHORELINE ENTERTAINMENT

Production company

1875 Century Park East, Suite 600
Los Angeles, CA 90067
310-551-2060 (phone)
310-201-0729 (fax)

info@shorelineentertainment.com
shorelineentertainment.com
imdb.com/company/co0074988
facebook.com/ShorelineEntertainment

Does not accept any unsolicited material. Project types include TV and feature films. Genres include reality, drama, thriller, non-fiction, horror, and science fiction.

Sam Eigen
imdb.com/name/nm2073662
linkedin.com/pub/sam-eigen/1/777/256

Morris Ruskin
CEO
imdb.com/name/nm0750830

SHOUT! FACTORY

Production company and distributor

2034 Armacost Ave, First Floor, Los Angeles, CA,
United States, 90025
310-979-5880

info@shoutfactory.com
shoutfactory.com
imdb.com/company/co0110208

Does not accept any unsolicited material. Project types include TV and commercials. Genres include family and drama.

SHOWGATE
Distributor

Marumiya Bldg, 4th Fl.
1-19-13, Ginza
Chuo-ku, Tokyo 104 0061
Japan
+81 3 5524 1869 (phone)
+81 3 5524 1871 (fax)

info@showgate.jp
showgate.jp
imdb.com/company/co0219983

Does not accept any unsolicited material. Project types include TV, short films, and feature films. Genres include action.

Yuki Noguchi
Manager, Acquisition & Production Division (Executive)
imdb.com/name/nm3025614

SHOWTIME NETWORKS
Production company

1633 Broadway
New York, NY 10019
212-708-1600

10880 Wilshire Blvd
Ste 1600
Los Angeles, CA 90024
310-234-5200

sho.com
imdb.com/company/co0075105
linkedin.com/company/showtime-networks
facebook.com/showtime

Does not accept any unsolicited material. Project types include TV and feature films. Genres include science fiction, family, crime, detective, romance, thriller, drama, animation, horror, fantasy, comedy, non-fiction, action, and myth.

Christina Spade
CFO
imdb.com/name/nm5268270
linkedin.com/pub/chris-spade/11/b35/a00

Tim Delaney
imdb.com/name/nm2303906

Joan Boorstein
imdb.com/name/nm1140886

Matthew Blank
CEO
imdb.com/name/nm2303194

SIDNEY KIMMEL ENTERTAINMENT
Production company

9460 Wilshire Blvd., Suite 500
Beverly Hills, CA 90212
310-777-8818 (phone)
310-777-8892 (fax)

reception@skefilms.com
skefilms.com
imdb.com/company/co0015447
linkedin.com/company/sidney-kimmel-entertainment

Does not accept any unsolicited material. Project types include feature films. Genres include crime, comedy, drama, and romance. Established in 2004.

Matt Berenson
President
imdb.com/name/nm0073554

Jim Tauber
CCO
imdb.com/name/nm0851433

Sidney Kimmel
Chairman
imdb.com/name/nm0454004

Mark Mikutowicz
Vice-President
imdb.com/name/nm2963870

SIENNA FILMS
Production company

183 Harbord St
Toronto, ON M5S 1H5

Canada
416-703-1126

siennainfo@siennafilms.com
siennafilms.com
imdb.com/company/co0029873
facebook.com/siennafilms
twitter.com/sienna_films

Does not accept any unsolicited material. Project types include feature films and TV. Genres include romance and drama.

Jennifer Kawaja
Producer
imdb.com/name/nm0442786

SIERRA/AFFINITY
Production company and distributor

9378 Wilshire Blvd, Suite 210, Beverly Hills, CA, United States, 90212
424-253-1060 (phone)
424-653-1977 (fax)

info@sierra-affinity.com
sierra-affinity.com
imdb.com/company/co0276464

Does not accept any unsolicited material. Project types include TV. Genres include family and drama.

Kelly McCormick
Principal
imdb.com/name/nm0566555

SIERRA/ AFFINITY
Production company

9378 Wilshire Blvd.
Suite 210
Beverly Hills, CA 90212
424-253-1060 (phone)
424-653-1977 (fax)

info@sierra-affinity.com
sierra-affinity.com
imdb.com/company/co0276464
linkedin.com/company/sierra-affinity

Does not accept any unsolicited material. Project types include feature films. Genres include action, fantasy, comedy, detective, crime, thriller, romance, drama, horror, and science fiction.

Kelly McCormick
Sr. Vice-President
imdb.com/name/nm0566555

Jen Gorton
Creative Executive
imdb.com/name/nm4224815
facebook.com/jen.gorton.9

Nicholas Meyer
CEO
imdb.com/name/nm0583293

SIGLO
Production company and distributor

5-24-16-210
Nakano
Nakano, Tokyo 164-0001
Japan
+81 3 53 43 31 01 (phone)
+81 3 53 43 31 02 (fax)

cine.co.jp
imdb.com/company/co0049142

Does not accept any unsolicited material. Project types include TV. Genres include comedy and drama.

Tetsujirô Yamagami
President (Producer)
imdb.com/name/nm0945294

SIGNAL STATION PRODUCTIONS
Production company

5031 Coral Gables
Houston, TX 77069
713-503-6104

imdb.com/company/co0465023

Does not accept any unsolicited material. Project types include short films. Genres include comedy, thriller, and fantasy. Established in 2012.

SIGNATURE ENTERTAINMENT
Distributor

Charlotte St Studios
76-78 Charlotte Street
London W1T 4QS
UK
+44 (0203-657-7050

info@signature-entertainment.co.uk
signature-entertainment.co.uk
imdb.com/company/co0351891
linkedin.com/company/signature-entertainment-uk
facebook.com/SignatureEntertainmentUK
twitter.com/SignatureEntUK

Does not accept any unsolicited material. Project types include feature films. Genres include drama, action, and crime.

Marc Goldberg
imdb.com/name/nm4709773

SIGNATURE PICTURES
Production company

8285 W Sunset Blvd, Suite 7
West Hollywood, CA 90046
323-848-9005 (phone)
323-848-9305 (fax)

james@signaturepictures.com
imdb.com/company/co0119730
linkedin.com/company/signature-pictures
facebook.com/SigPix
twitter.com/sigpix

Does not accept any unsolicited material. Project types include feature films. Genres include thriller, drama, action, non-fiction, and romance.

Illana Diamant
Partner
imdb.com/name/nm0224532

Moshe Diamant
Partner
imdb.com/name/nm0224537

SIKELIA PRODUCTIONS
Production company

110 W 57th St
5th Floor
New York, NY 10019

212-906-8800 (phone)
212-906-8891 (fax)

imdb.com/company/co0141038
facebook.com/pages/Sikelia-Productions/
    1378719192355489

Does not accept any unsolicited material. Project types include feature films. Genres include action, thriller, romance, crime, and drama.

Emma Koskoff
President
imdb.com/name/nm0863374

Martin Scorsese
Principal
imdb.com/name/nm0000217
facebook.com/scorsese

Margaret Bodde
Executive Producer
imdb.com/name/nm0090784

SILLY ROBIN PRODUCTIONS
Production company

30 Slope Dr
Short Hills, NJ 07078

ribz99@aol.com
alanzweibel.com
imdb.com/company/co0033277

Does not accept any unsolicited material. Genres include comedy.

SILVER DREAM PRODUCTIONS
Production company

3452 E Foothill Blvd, Suite 620
Pasadena, CA 91107
626-799-3880 (phone)
626-799-5363 (fax)

luoyan@silverdreamprods.com
imdb.com/company/co0182728
facebook.com/silverdreamproductions

Accepts query letters from unproduced, unrepresented writers via email. Project types include feature films. Genres include drama and myth.

Luo Yan
imdb.com/name/nm0526839
Assistant: Diana Chin

SILVER/KOSTER PRODUCTIONS
Production company

353 S Reeves Dr, Penthouse
Beverly Hills, CA 90212
310-551-5245

silvers-koster.com

Accepts query letters from unproduced, unrepresented
writers via email. Project types include TV, feature
films, and commercials. Genres include reality and
non-fiction.

Karen Corcoran
Vice-President
facebook.com/karen.corcoran.505

Iren Koster
President
imdb.com/name/nm0467397
linkedin.com/pub/iren-koster/44/ba8/824

Tracey Silvers
Chairman
imdb.com/name/nm0799016
facebook.com/tracey.silvers.3

SILVERLINING MEDIA GROUP
Production company

3919 Baronne St, New Orleans, LA, United States,
70115

info@silverliningmg.com
imdb.com/company/co036355/

Does not accept any unsolicited material.

Colin Bates
Producer
imdb.com/name/nm0060885

SILVER NITRATE ENTERTAINMENT
Production company

12268 Ventura Blvd
Studio City, CA 91604

818-762-9559 (phone)
818-762-9177 (fax)

imdb.com/company/co0093834
linkedin.com/company/silver-nitrate
facebook.com/pages/Silver-Nitrate-Entertainment/
    664069326951092

Does not accept any unsolicited material. Project types
include feature films. Genres include science fiction,
drama, comedy, and animation.

Ash Shah
Principal
ash@silvernitrate.net
imdb.com/name/nm0787420

SILVER PICTURES
Production company

2434 Main St.
Santa Monica, CA 90405
310-566-6100 (phone)
310-566-6188 (fax)

imdb.com/company/co0019968
imdb.com/company/co0019968

Accepts query letters from unproduced, unrepresented
writers. Project types include TV and feature films.
Genres include thriller, family, science fiction,
animation, reality, action, non-fiction, and drama.

Alex Heineman
imdb.com/name/nm2670366

Joel Silver
Chairman
imdb.com/name/nm0005428

Sarah Meyer
Director of Development
imdb.com/name/nm1060895
twitter.com/sarahjeanious

SILVER SPEAR PICTURES
Production company

49 NE 22nd St
Miami, FL 33137

silverspearpictures.com
imdb.com/company/co0477402

facebook.com/Silver-Spear-
Pictures-717613664998426

Does not accept any unsolicited material. Genres
include crime.

SIMONSAYS ENTERTAINMENT
Production company

12 Desbrosses St
New York, NY 10013
917-797-9704

info@simonsaysentertainment.net
simonsaysentertainment.net
imdb.com/company/co0278962
facebook.com/simonsaysentertainment
twitter.com/simonsaysent

Accepts scripts from unproduced, unrepresented
writers. Project types include feature films. Genres
include romance, drama, and crime.

Ron Simons
Principal
imdb.com/name/nm1839399

April Yvette Thompson
imdb.com/name/nm1690743
facebook.com/aprilyvettethompson

SIMON WEST PRODUCTIONS
Production company

3450 Cahuenga Blvd West
Building 510
Los Angeles, CA 90068
323-845-0821 (phone)
323-845-4582 (fax)

submissions@simonwestproductions.com
imdb.com/company/co0093861

Accepts query letters from unproduced, unrepresented
writers. Project types include feature films and TV.
Genres include drama, science fiction, and action.

Simon West
Principal
imdb.com/name/nm0922346

Jib Polhemus
President
imdb.com/name/nm1015441
linkedin.com/pub/jib-polhemus/87/189/167

SIMS COMPANY
Production company

Shibuya Ku
Tokyo 150-0031
Japan
+81 03-5459-3693 (phone)
+81 03-5459-3696 (fax)

info@sims.co.jp
sims.co.jp
imdb.com/company/co0181022

Does not accept any unsolicited material. Project types
include TV. Genres include fantasy and action.

Hideki Katagiri
Director (Executive)
imdb.com/name/nm2222204

SIMSIE FILMS/ MEDIA SAVANT PICTURES

2934 1/2 Beverly Glen Circle
Suite 264
Los Angeles, CA 90077

simsiefilms@mac.com
imdb.com/company/co0182824

Accepts query letters from unproduced, unrepresented
writers. Project types include feature films. Genres
include comedy and drama.

Gwen Field
Partner
imdb.com/name/nm0275947
linkedin.com/in/gwenfield

SINGE CELL PICTURES
Production company

PO Box 69691
West Hollywood, CA 90069
310-360-7600 (phone)
310-360-7011 (fax)

imdb.com/company/co0079704

Accepts query letters from unproduced, unrepresented writers. Project types include TV and feature films. Genres include drama and comedy.

Michael Stipe
Principal
imdb.com/name/nm0005468

Sandy Stern
Principal
imdb.com/name/nm0827840

SINGLE ARROW PRODUCTIONS
Production company

700 Coquina Way
Boca Raton, FL 33432
561-416-2952

info@SingleArrow.com
imdb.com/company/co0337236

Does not accept any unsolicited material. Project types include short films. Genres include family and documentary.

SINOVOI ENTERTAINMENT
Production company

1317 N San Fernando Blvd, Suite 395
Burbank, CA 91504
818-562-6404 (phone)
818-567-0104 (fax)

maxwell@sinovoientertainment.com
imdb.com/company/co0020398

Accepts query letters from unproduced, unrepresented writers via email. Project types include feature films. Genres include drama, horror, and comedy.

Kimberly Estrada
imdb.com/name/nm1538997
facebook.com/KimberlyEstradaFanPage
twitter.com/kimberlyestrada

Maxwell Sinovoi
Principal
imdb.com/name/nm0802511

SIRENA FILMS
Production company

P.O. Box 491383, Los Angeles, CA, United States, 90049
310-826-8112

info@sirenafilms.com
sirenafilms.com
imdb.com/company/co0046509

Does not accept any unsolicited material. Project types include feature films and TV. Genres include action, family, romance, and drama.

SIREN PRODUCTIONS MEDIA
Production company

PO Box 734912
Ormond Beach, FL 32173

imdb.com/company/co0318331
facebook.com/Siren-Productions-63400566554

Does not accept any unsolicited material. Genres include horror and romance.

SIX ISLAND PRODUCTIONS
Production company and distributor

192 Spadina Ave
Suite 307
Toronto, ON M5T2C2
Canada
416-538-3455

info@sixisland.com
sixisland.com
imdb.com/company/co0075917

Does not accept any unsolicited material. Project types include TV. Genres include drama and comedy.

SIXTH SENSE PRODUCTIONS, INC.
Production company and distributor

269 S Beverly Dr, Suite 1297
Beverly Hills, CA 90212
310-247-2790 (phone)
310-247-2791 (fax)

scripts@sixthsenseproductions.com (script submissions)
info@sixthsenseproductions.com (general)
sixthsenseproductions.com
imdb.com/company/co0172317

Accepts scripts from unproduced, unrepresented writers via email. Project types include feature films. Genres include sociocultural, action, and drama.

Richard Harding
CEO
imdb.com/name/nm1502749
linkedin.com/pub/richard-harding/8/406/7B0
twitter.com/rhssp

SKETCH FILMS
Production company

B54
Ugli Campus
56 Wood Ln
London, W12 7SB
+44203-096-1225

hello@sketchfilms.co.uk
sketchfilms.co.uk
imdb.com/company/co0262357
linkedin.com/company/sketch-films
facebook.com/SketchLondon
twitter.com/sketchfilm

Does not accept any unsolicited material. Project types include feature films. Genres include action, horror, science fiction, myth, and fantasy. Established in 2009.

Len Wiseman
Writer
imdb.com/name/nm0936482

Jeremy Riggall
Owner
jeremy@sketchfilms.co.uk

SKY 21 PRODUCTIONS
Production company

2356 Sandspring Dr., SW
Atlanta, GA 30331

admin@sky21productions.com
imdb.com/company/co0230906

Does not accept any unsolicited material.

SKYDANCE PRODUCTIONS
Studio

5555 Melrose Ave
Dean Martin Building
2nd Floor
Hollywood, CA 90038
310-314-9900

hello@skydance.com
skydance.com
imdb.com/company/co0152219
linkedin.com/company/skydance-productions
facebook.com/SkydanceProductions
twitter.com/Skydance

Accepts scripts from produced or represented writers. Project types include TV and feature films. Genres include fantasy, action, science fiction, thriller, myth, family, comedy, and drama.

Dana Goldberg
CCO
imdb.com/name/nm1602154
Assistant: Matt Grimm

David Ellison
CEO
imdb.com/name/nm1911103
Assistant: Bill Bost

SKYFARM ENTERTAINMENT
Production company

25 Atlantic Ave
Toronto, ON M6K 3E7
Canada

info@skyfarment.com
skyfarment.com
imdb.com/company/co0400513
twitter.com/skyfarment

Does not accept any unsolicited material. Genres include crime and comedy.

SKYLARK ENTERTAINMENT, INC.
Production company

12405 Venice Blvd, Suite 237
Los Angeles, CA 90066
310-390-2659

imdb.com/company/co0021365
linkedin.com/company/skylark-entertainment

Does not accept any unsolicited material. Project types include feature films and TV. Genres include non-fiction, drama, and comedy.

SKYLIGHT MEDIA ENTERTAINMENT
Production company

30 Percy St
London W1T 2DB
UK
+44(0203-384-6265

info@skylightm.com
skylightm.com
imdb.com/company/co0473902

Does not accept any unsolicited material. Project types include TV and feature films. Genres include action and comedy.

Tamer Hassan
Producer
imdb.com/name/nm1268748

SKY ONE
Production company

9220 Sunset Blvd, Suite 230
West Hollywood, CA 90069
310-860-2740 (phone)
310-860-2471 (fax)

sky.com

Accepts query letters from unproduced, unrepresented writers. Project types include TV. Genres include science fiction and action.

SKY PHOENIX INC
Distributor

690029 Daniels Pkwy
#289
Ft Myers, FL 33912-7522
239-277-7597

me@skyphoenix.com
skyphoenix.com
imdb.com/company/co0232574

Does not accept any unsolicited material. Project types include short films. Genres include non-fiction. Established in 2007.

SLATE FILMS
Production company

9 Greek St
London W1D 4DQ
UK
+44207-734-7372 (phone)
+44207-287-5228 (fax)

info@slatefilms.com
slatefilms.com
imdb.com/company/co0075464

Does not accept any unsolicited material. Project types include TV. Genres include drama.

Andrea Calderwood
Producer
imdb.com/name/nm0129573

SLINGSHOT PRODUCTIONS
Production company

1A Adpar St
3rd Fl
London, England W2 1DE
UK
+44 20 7535 6720 (phone)
+44 20 7563 7283 (fax)

info@slingshot-studios.com
slingshot-studios.com
imdb.com/company/co0009090

Does not accept any unsolicited material. Project types include TV. Genres include comedy, thriller, and drama.

Arvind Ethan David
Producer
imdb.com/name/nm2366922

SLOW LEARNER
Production company and distributor

12-3-503
Udagawacho
Shibuya, Tokyo 150-0042
Japan
+81 03 3770 3717 (phone)
+81 03 3770 3718 (fax)

kosikawa@kg7.so-net.ne.jp
imdb.com/company/co0057895

Does not accept any unsolicited material. Project types include TV. Genres include documentary.

Michio Koshikawa
President (Executive)
imdb.com/name/nm1904467

SLUM GODDESS
Production company and distributor

2927 Lakeshore Blvd. W.
Suite #306
Toronto, ON M8V-1J3
Canada

Vivita@VivitaOnline.com
vivitaonline.com
imdb.com/company/co0371359

Does not accept any unsolicited material. Genres include action.

SMALL PLANET NEWS SERVICE
Production company

803 ELLENDALE DR.
Winter Park, FL 32792
407-678-1400 (phone)
407-677-9019 (fax)

becca@smallplanetnew.com
imdb.com/company/co0171831

Does not accept any unsolicited material. Project types include TV. Genres include family.

SMART ENTERTAINMENT
Production company

9595 Wilshire Blvd, Suite 900
Beverly Hills, CA 90212
310-205-6090 (phone)
310-205-6093 (fax)

assistant@smartentertainment.com
smartentertainment.com
imdb.com/company/co0158519
linkedin.com/company/smart-entertainment

Accepts query letters from unproduced, unrepresented writers via email. Project types include feature films and TV. Genres include thriller, reality, comedy, horror, and non-fiction.

Zac Unterman
zac@smartentertainment.com
imdb.com/name/nm2303352

John Jacobs
President
john@smartentertainment.com
imdb.com/name/nm0414481

SMARTY PANTS ENTERTAINMENT
Production company

1225 Bennett Dr
Unit 111
Longwood, FL 32750-7621
407-767-0199

smartypantsworld.com
imdb.com/company/co0214345
facebook.com/ilovesmartypants

Does not accept any unsolicited material. Genres include crime and action.

SMASH MEDIA FILMS
Production company

1208 Georgina Ave
Santa Monica, CA 90402
310-395-0058 (phone)
310-395-8850 (fax)

info@smashmediafilms.com
smashmediaproductions.com/films.html

Accepts query letters from unproduced, unrepresented writers via email. Project types include feature films and TV. Genres include comedy, science fiction, and drama.

Shelley Hack
Vice-President
shelley.hack@smashmediafi lms.com

Harry Winer
President
harry.winer@smashmediafilms.com
linkedin.com/pub/harry-winer/11/3ab/900

SMITHSONIAN CHANNEL

Production company, distributor, and financing company

1225 19th St NW
Ste 250
Washington, DC 20036
202-261-1700

contact@smithsoniannetworks.com
smithsonianchannel.com
imdb.com/company/co0275579
linkedin.com/company/smithsonian-networks
facebook.com/SmithsonianChannel
twitter.com/SmithsonianChan

Does not accept any unsolicited material. Project types include feature films and TV. Genres include period, reality, drama, sociocultural, documentary, and non-fiction. Established in 2006.

SMITHSONIAN INSTITUTION

Production company and distributor

1000 Jefferson Dr, Washington , DC, United States, 20560
202-633-1000

si.edu
imdb.com/company/co0102272

Does not accept any unsolicited material. Project types include short films, TV, and feature films. Genres include drama, thriller, comedy, family, action, and romance.

SMODCAST PICTURES

Production company and distributor

P.O. Box 93339
Los Angeles CA 90093
323-969-9423 (phone)
323-969-9008 (fax)

P.O. Box 400, Red Bank, NJ, United States, 07701
732-842-6933 (phone)
732-842-3772 (fax)

smodcast.com
imdb.com/company/co0326257

Does not accept any unsolicited material. Project types include TV and feature films. Genres include drama, action, family, and thriller.

SMOKEBOMB ENTERTAINMENT

Production company

163 Queen St East
Ste 100
Toronto, ON M5A 1S1
Canada
416-588-8855 (phone)
416-363-1428 (fax)

info@smokebomb.ca
smokebomb.ca
imdb.com/company/co0312868
facebook.com/SmokebombEntertainment
twitter.com/Smokebomb_Ent

Does not accept any unsolicited material. Genres include action.

Jay Bennett
Executive
imdb.com/name/nm4065787

SMOKEHOUSE PICTURES

Production company

12001 Ventura Pl., Suite 200
Studio City, CA 91604
818-432-0330 (phone)
818-432-0337 (fax)

imdb.com/company/co0184096

Does not accept any unsolicited material. Project types include feature films. Genres include thriller, comedy, and drama.

George Clooney
Partner
imdb.com/name/nm0000123

Katie Murphy
Creative Executive
imdb.com/name/nm3682023
linkedin.com/pub/katie-murphy/3/a40/659

Grant Heslov
Partner
imdb.com/name/nm0381416
Assistant: Tara Oslin

SMOKESHOW FILMS
Production company

4114 Duvawn St
Alexandria, VA 22310
703-329-0192

imdb.com/company/co0207588

Does not accept any unsolicited material. Genres include documentary.

SMOKIN' HOT PRODUCTIONS
Production company

32 Hickory Dr
Garden Level
Maplewood, NJ 07040

ezie@eziecotler.com
imdb.com/company/co0520170

Does not accept any unsolicited material. Project types include TV. Genres include comedy.

SMOKIN YOGI VISIONS
Production company, distributor, and sales agent

8530 W 35th St
Minneapolis, MN 55426
612-867-3877

info@smokinyogi.com
smokinyogi.com
imdb.com/company/co0310780

Does not accept any unsolicited material. Project types include TV. Genres include comedy and drama.

SMUGGLER FILMS
Production company

38 W 21st St, 12th Floor, New York, NY, United States, 10010
212-337-3327 (phone)
212-337-9686 (fax)

6 -10 Great Portland St 1st Flr
London United Kingdom W1W 8QL
011-440-2076367665 (phone)
011-440-2076374667 (fax)

823 Seward St Phone
Los Angeles CA 90038
323-817-3300 (phone)
323-817-3333 (fax)

waage@smugglersite.com
smugglersite.com
imdb.com/company/co0268515

Does not accept any unsolicited material. Project types include feature films and TV. Genres include action, drama, family, and thriller.

Catherine Waage
Creative Executive
imdb.com/name/nm3515444

SNEAK PREVIEW ENTERTAINMENT
Production company

6705 Sunset Blvd
2nd Floor
Hollywood, CA 90028
323-962-0295 (phone)
323-962-0372 (fax)

indiefilm@sneakpreviewentertain.com
sneakpreviewentertain.com
imdb.com/company/co0061839
linkedin.com/company/sneak-preview-entertainment

Accepts query letters from unproduced, unrepresented writers via email. Project types include feature films. Established in 1991.

Chris Hazzard
Director of Development
323-962-0295
ch@sneakpe.com
imdb.com/name/nm3302502
linkedin.com/pub/chris-hazzard/5/543/6b3
twitter.com/ChrisHazzardSF

Steven Wolfe
CEO
323-962-0295
sjwolfe@sneakpreviewentertain.com
imdb.com/name/nm0938145

SOARING FLIGHT PRODUCTIONS

Production company

1700 Pacific Ave
Ste 4100
Dallas, TX 75201

imdb.com/company/co0390458

Does not accept any unsolicited material. Project types include feature films. Genres include drama, horror, and thriller. Established in 2007.

SOBE BROOKE STUDIOS

Production company

10900 Wilshire Blvd.
Suite # 1400
Los Angeles, CA 90024
305-602-0312

1230 Peachtree St North East, 19th Floor
Atlanta, GA 30309
305-602-0312

255 Alhambra Circle
Suite # 1160
Coral Gables, FL 33134
305-602-0312

sobebrooke.com
imdb.com/company/co0459542
linkedin.com/company/sobe-brooke-studios
facebook.com/SobeBrookeStudios
twitter.com/sobebrooke

Does not accept any unsolicited material. Project types include feature films. Genres include documentary, thriller, and drama. Established in 2013.

Justin Shaner
CEO
imdb.com/name/nm5232783
linkedin.com/in/justinshaner
facebook.com/jshaner1

Jose Yacaman
Executive Vice President of Production
imdb.com/name/nm2499513
linkedin.com/pub/jose-yacaman/8/b1a/55a
facebook.com/jose.d.yacaman
twitter.com/JDYacaman

Carla Pimentel
imdb.com/name/nm4520475
linkedin.com/pub/carla-carolina-pimentel/35/438/4b8
facebook.com/carla.c.pimentel

Fernando Rojas
COO
linkedin.com/pub/fernando-rojas/49/873/4a8
facebook.com/frojash

SOBINI FILMS

Production company

10203 Santa Monica Blvd
Suite 300B
Los Angeles, CA 90067
310-432-6900 (phone)
310-432-6939 (fax)

sobini.com
imdb.com/company/co0086773
linkedin.com/in/markaminsobini
twitter.com/sobinifilms

Does not accept any unsolicited material. Project types include feature films. Genres include thriller, drama, family, and comedy.

Mark Amin
CEO
imdb.com/name/nm0024909
linkedin.com/in/markaminsobini

Cami Winikoff
COO
imdb.com/name/nm0935121

David Higgin
President
imdb.com/name/nm0383371

SOCIAL CAPITAL FILMS

Production company

1001 Bridgeway PMB 170
Sausalito, CA 94965
415-332-8877 (phone)
415-332-8467 (fax)

1010 Wilshire Blvd.
Suite 507

Los Angeles, CA 90017
866-609-7098

info@socialcapitalfilms.com
imdb.com/company/co0319624

Does not accept any unsolicited material. Project types include TV and feature films. Genres include thriller, horror, reality, science fiction, comedy, drama, family, and non-fiction.

Martin Shore
CEO
imdb.com/name/nm2005915

SOCIAL CONSTRUCT

Production company and sales agent

Charlotte St
Asheville, NC 28801

contact@socialconstructfilms.com
socialconstructfilms.com
imdb.com/company/co0300393
facebook.com/SocialConstructFilms
twitter.com/socialconstuct

Does not accept any unsolicited material. Project types include TV. Genres include drama and documentary.

Zak Kilberg
Producer
imdb.com/name/nm1815953

SODA PICTURES

Distributor

17 Blossom St
London E1 6PL
UK
+44207-377-1407 (phone)
+44207-377-1406 (fax)

info@sodapictures.com
sodapictures.com
imdb.com/company/co0110168
facebook.com/SodaPictures
twitter.com/SodaPictures

Does not accept any unsolicited material. Project types include TV, short films, and feature films. Genres include thriller.

SOGEI PRO

Production company

4-28-8-612
Yoyogi
Shibuya, Tokyo 151-0053
Japan
03-3320-1107 (phone)
03-3320-3255 (fax)

info@geipro.co.jp
geipro.co.jp
imdb.com/company/co0143185

Does not accept any unsolicited material. Project types include TV. Genres include drama.

SOGNO PRODUCTIONS

Production company

PO Box 55476
Portland, OR 97238
561-676-4696

imdb.com/company/co0197581

Accepts scripts from unproduced, unrepresented writers. Project types include feature films and TV. Genres include drama, romance, comedy, documentary, action, fantasy, and thriller.

SOLACE & SANDWISCO PRODUCTIONS

Distributor

3111 SW 10th St
Pompano Beach, FL 33069
954-975-7777

katiealloway@bookofhope.net
imdb.com/company/co0178222

Does not accept any unsolicited material. Project types include short films. Genres include drama.

SOLID JAM

Production company

2-1-405
Udagawacho
Shibuya, Tokyo 150-0042
Japan

+81 3-6416-4310 (phone)
+81 3-6416-4311 (fax)

info@solidjam.com
solidjam.com
imdb.com/company/co0433965

Does not accept any unsolicited material. Project types include TV. Genres include drama.

Hirokazu Koreeda
Executive
imdb.com/name/nm0466153

SOLIPSIST FILMS
Production company

465 N Crescent Heights Blvd
Los Angeles, CA 90048
323-272-3122 (phone)
323-375-1649 (fax)

info@solipsistfilms.com
solipsistfilms.com
imdb.com/company/co0157838

Accepts query letters from unproduced, unrepresented writers via email. Project types include TV and feature films. Genres include drama, fantasy, reality, non-fiction, detective, and thriller.

Stephen L'Heureux
Principal
imdb.com/name/nm1655017
twitter.com/SLHeureux8

David Purcell
Creative Executive
twitter.com/davepurcell

SOLSTICE FILMS
Production company

Denver, CO
504-357-7099

redwolflevina@yahoo.com
wolvenlycana.com
imdb.com/company/co0342074
facebook.com/WolvenLycana

Does not accept any unsolicited material. Genres include horror.

Stefanie Levina
CEO/Executive (Executive)
imdb.com/name/nm5348216

SOMEDAY MELISSA
Production company

P.O. Box 146
Totowa, NJ 07512
973-464-0437

judy@somedaymelissa.com
somedaymelissa.com
imdb.com/company/co0355864
facebook.com/share.php
twitter.com/intenttweet

Does not accept any unsolicited material. Project types include theater and short films. Genres include documentary.

SOMNIATE INTERNATIONAL
Production company

12 Horsham Ave
North Finchley
London N12 9BE
UK
+44084-482-48142 (phone)
+44084-482-48144 (fax)

enquiry@somniate.com
somniate.com
imdb.com/company/co0499678

Does not accept any unsolicited material. Project types include feature films. Genres include comedy and drama.

Sunny Surani
Manager
imdb.com/name/nm4452719

SONAR ENTERTAINMENT
Production company and distributor

2121 Ave of the Stars, Suite 2150, Los Angeles, CA, United States, 90067
424-230-7140

Fox Studios Australia, 38 Drr Ave Building 61, Level 1 Moore Park Australia NSW 2021

011-612-83533644 (phone)
011-612-83533645 (fax)

272 Kings Rd College House, First Floor
London United Kingdom SW3 5AW
011-442-078089170 (phone)
011-442-078089171 (fax)

contact@sonarent.com
sonarent.com
imdb.com/company/co0192886

Does not accept any unsolicited material. Project types include feature films and TV. Genres include drama and thriller.

SONOPIX PRODUCTIONS
Production company

Plot No 15, Rd No 3,
Aurora Colony-2,
Banjara Hills, Hyderabad – 500034
040-402-10979 (phone)
040-237-40979 (fax)

sonopixproductions@rediffmail.com
sonopixproductions.com
imdb.com/company/co0173363

Does not accept any unsolicited material. Project types include short films. Genres include drama.

SONY PICTURES RELEASING INTERNATIONAL
Distributor

10202 W Washington Blvd, Culver City , CA, United States, 90232
310-244-4000 (phone)
310-244-2626 (fax)

Level 26, 1 Market St
Sydney NSW Australia 2000

imdb.com/company/co0305812

Does not accept any unsolicited material. Project types include short films, feature films, and TV. Genres include drama, family, romance, science fiction, action, documentary, crime, and thriller.

Ignacio Darnaude
Executive Vice President (Creative Advertising/ International)
imdb.com/name/nm1435075

SOPHIA ENTERTAINMENT
Production company

3286 M St NW
Washington, DC 20007
814-535-1528 (phone)
202-337-1839 (fax)

chris@capitoloutdoor.com
imdb.com/company/co0502326
twitter.com/sophiaentertmnt

Does not accept any unsolicited material. Genres include documentary.

SOURCE PRODUCTIONS
Production company and distributor

2-42-13
#103 Goto Building
Toshmia-ku, Tokyo 170-0012
Japan
+81 080 1175 3029

dave@sourceproductions.ca
imdb.com/company/co0074462

Does not accept any unsolicited material. Genres include crime, thriller, action, drama, and comedy.

SOUTH AUSTIN PICTURES LLC
Production company

9420 Research Blvd
Suite 120
Austin, TX 78759
512-458-1300

info@southaustinpictures.com
imdb.com/company/co0138265

Does not accept any unsolicited material. Genres include romance, comedy, and drama.

SOUTH BEACH PRODUCTIONS
Production company

1521 Alton Rd
#617
Miami Beach, FL 33139
773-457-1175

alejandro@sobeprod.com
singleinsouthbeach.com
imdb.com/company/co0316888

Does not accept any unsolicited material. Project types include TV. Genres include romance, crime, drama, and comedy.

SPAD FILMS
Production company

444 Brickell Ave
Ste 51
Miami, FL 33131
305-401-1498 (phone)
267-373-6379 (fax)

spadfilms@mac.com
imdb.com/company/co0259096
twitter.com/spadfilms

Does not accept any unsolicited material. Genres include drama.

SPAD PRODUCTIONS
Production company

444 Brickell Ave
Miami, FL 33131
305-401-1498

spadfilms@mac.com
imdb.com/company/co0013594

Does not accept any unsolicited material. Genres include drama.

SPARK MEDIA
Production company and distributor

1823 Jefferson Place NW
Washington, DC 20036

sparkmediasolutions.com
imdb.com/company/co0021533

Does not accept any unsolicited material. Genres include documentary.

SPECTRAL ALCHEMY
Production company and distributor

1512-1/2 S Congress
Ste 9
Austin, TX 78704
646-942-7474

info@spectralalchemy.com
spectralalchemy.com
mdb.com/company/co0192439
facebook.com/Mythaphi

Does not accept any unsolicited material. Genres include documentary.

SPEED KILLS PRODUCTION
Production company

1225 Alton Rd
Miami Beach, FL 33139
305-534-9123 (phone)
305-534-9125 (fax)

info@silviosardi.com
imdb.com/company/co0204813

Does not accept any unsolicited material.

SPELLMAN/CORBEN PRODUCTIONS
Production company

11111 Biscayne Blvd.
Ste. 222
Miami, FL 33181
305-891-0903 (phone)
253-660-3594 (fax)

spellmancorben@bellsouth.net
imdb.com/company/co0041094

Does not accept any unsolicited material.

S PICTURES, INC.
Production company

4420 Hayvenhurst Ave
Encino, CA 91436
818-995-1585 (phone)
818-995-1677 (fax)

info@spictures.tv
spictures.tv

Does not accept any unsolicited material. Project types include feature films and TV. Genres include science fiction, reality, comedy, and non-fiction.

Chuck Simon
818-995-1585
chuck@spictures.tv
imdb.com/name/nm1247168
facebook.com/cksimon1

SPIDERWOOD PRODUCTIONS
Production company and distributor

PO Box 19075
Austin, TX 78760
512-332-0060

info@spiderwoodstudios.com
spiderwoodproductions.com
imdb.com/company/co0138100
facebook.com/pages/Austin-TX/Spiderwood-Studios/
    344508940385
twitter.com/Spiderwood

Does not accept any unsolicited material. Genres include action and thriller.

SPIKED HEEL PRODUCTIONS
Production company

2124 NE 15th Terrace
Cape Coral, FL 33909
239-673-9499

SpikedHeel@comcast.net
spikedheelproductions.com
imdb.com/company/co0353430
faccbook.com/pages/Coleman/318888474867887

Does not accept any unsolicited material. Genres include action.

SPIN CYCLE FILMS
Production company and distributor

P.O. Box 29618
San Antonio, TX 78229-0618
512-940-1139 (phone)
512-233-2590 (fax)

jamie@spincyclefilms.com
spincyclefilms.com

imdb.com/company/co0138409
facebook.com/spincyclefilms
twitter.com/SpinCycleFilms

Does not accept any unsolicited material. Project types include short films. Genres include comedy. Established in 2004.

SPIN MASTER
Production company and distributor

450 Front St W
Toronto, ON M5V 1B6
Canada
800-622-8339 (phone)
416-364-8005 (fax)

spinmaster.com
imdb.com/company/co0158515

Does not accept any unsolicited material. Project types include feature films and TV. Genres include action.

Ronnen Harary
Producer
imdb.com/name/nm3243829

SPIRAL ENTERTAINMENT
Production company

2240 Gerrard St East
Toronto, ON M4E 2E1
Canada

info@spiralentertainment-ltd.com
spiralentertainment-ltd.com
imdb.com/company/co0321601
facebook.com/spiralentertainmentfilmandtelevision

Does not accept any unsolicited material. Project types include short films. Genres include comedy.

Darren Portelli
Producer
imdb.com/name/nm1077693

SPIRAL FILMS
Production company

902 E 5th St
Ste 204
Austin, TX 78702

imdb.com/company/co0110548

Does not accept any unsolicited material. Project types include feature films. Genres include documentary and drama. Established in 2011.

SPITFIRE PICTURES
Production company

710 Tenth St NW
Atlanta, GA 30318
404-872-7006

9100 Wilshire Blvd
#401e
Beverly Hills, CA 90212
310-300-9000 (phone)
310-300-9001 (fax)

spitfirepictures.com
imdb.com/company/co0091468

Does not accept any unsolicited material. Project types include feature films. Genres include drama, documentary, thriller, and romance. Established in 2003.

Nicholas Ferrall
Director
imdb.com/name/nm5909330
linkedin.com/pub/nick-ferrall/39/58b/356

Nigel Sinclair
CEO
imdb.com/name/nm0801691

SPO
Production company and distributor

3-8-15 Roppongi
Minato-ku,
Tokyo
Japan
+81-3-6812-5410 (phone)
+81-3-3796-3317 (fax)

info@spoinc.jp
spoinc.jp
imdb.com/company/co0010521

Does not accept any unsolicited material. Genres include drama, romance, and comedy.

Yoshiharu Kôzuki
Producer
imdb.com/name/nm3105742

SPRINGTREE STUDIOS
Production company

1426 NW 25th Terrace
Gainesville, FL 32605
US
352-338-7867

rubyproductions@springtreestudios.com
imdb.com/company/co0319305

Does not accept any unsolicited material.

SPY FILMS
Production company

49C Spadina Ave
Toronto, ON M5V 2J1
Canada

carlo@spyfilms.com
spyfilms.com
imdb.com/company/co0116111

Does not accept any unsolicited material. Project types include short films and feature films. Genres include science fiction.

Carlo Trulli
Producer
imdb.com/name/nm2359152

SPYGLASS ENTERTAINMENT
Production company

245 N Beverly Dr
Second Floor
Beverly Hills, CA 90024
310-443-5800 (phone)
310-443-5912 (fax)

spyglassentertainment.com
imdb.com/company/co0031181
linkedin.com/company/spyglass-entertainment

Does not accept any unsolicited material. Project types include feature films. Genres include action, thriller, horror, non-fiction, comedy, family, and drama.

Roger Birnbaum
Chairman
imdb.com/name/nm0083696

Gary Barber
Chairman
imdb.com/name/nm0053388

SQUAREONE ENTERTAINMENT
Production company and distributor

1680 Michigan Ave.
Suite 700
Miami Beach, FL 33139
305-777-2248

vinceoffer@squareoneent.com
imdb.com/company/co0088062
facebook.com/SquareOneEntertainmentGmbH

Does not accept any unsolicited material. Genres include comedy.

S&S PROD'S
Production company

10512 Burbank Blvd
North Hollywood, CA 91601
818-505-9981 (phone)
818-505-0469 (fax)

imdb.com/company/co0530257

Does not accept any unsolicited material. Genres include crime, thriller, and drama.

SSS ENTERTAINMENT
Production company

320 S Willaman Dr, Penthouse 2, Los Angeles, CA, United States, 90048
310-804-7850

info@sssentertainment.com
imdb.com/company/co0274103

Does not accept any unsolicited material. Project types include feature films.

Shaun S. Sanghani
President
imdb.com/name/nm2228167

STAFF-LINE
Production company

1-5-13-4F
Jinnan
Shibuya, Tokyo 150-0041
Japan
03-3770-5201 (phone)
03-3770-9666 (fax)

staff-up@staff-up.net
staff-up.net
imdb.com/company/co0161278

Does not accept any unsolicited material. Project types include TV. Genres include drama.

Kumiko Hoshi
Producer
imdb.com/name/nm2008780

STAGE 6 FILMS
Production company

10202 W Washington Blvd
Culver City, CA 90232
310-244-4000 (phone)
310-244-2626 (fax)

sonypicturesworldwideacquisitions.com
imdb.com/company/co0222021

Does not accept any unsolicited material. Project types include feature films. Genres include family, romance, comedy, thriller, animation, horror, crime, action, period, documentary, science fiction, and drama. Established in 2007.

STAIRWAY
Production company

1-12-4F
Shinanomachi
Shinjuku, Tokyo 160-0016
Japan
03-5368-5748

info@stairway.jp
stairway.jp
imdb.com/company/co0305092

Does not accept any unsolicited material. Project types include feature films and TV. Genres include crime, drama, and horror.

ST. AMOS PRODUCTIONS
Production company

3480 Barham Blvd
Los Angeles, CA 90068
323-850-9872

st.amosproductions@earthlink.net
imdb.com/company/co0009925

Accepts query letters from unproduced, unrepresented writers via email. Project types include feature films and TV. Genres include comedy, non-fiction, reality, and drama.

John Stamos
Principal
imdb.com/name/nm0001764
facebook.com/johnstamos
twitter.com/JohnStamos

STARCHILD PICTURES
Production company

2nd floor, 35 Soho Square, London W1D 3QX
44 (0203-174-0895

info@starchildpics.com
starchildpics.com
imdb.com/company/co0304886

Does not accept any unsolicited material. Project types include feature films. Genres include comedy, horror, crime, and science fiction.

Ed King
Producer
imdb.com/name/nm1132576

STARDUST PROMOTION INC.
Production company

2-3-3-2F
Ebisu Nishi
Shibuya, Tokyo 150-0021
Japan
03-3464-5593

info@stardust.co.jp

stardust.co.jp
imdb.com/company/co0166187

Does not accept any unsolicited material. Project types include feature films. Genres include drama and thriller.

Hiroko Takagi
Manager
imdb.com/name/nm3858245

STAR PARTNERS
Production company

8929 Charleston Park
Orlando, FL. 32819
407-217-5800

allen@allenschwalb.com
allenschwalb.com
imdb.com/company/co0141156

Does not accept any unsolicited material. Genres include drama, comedy, and romance.

STARR MANAGEMENT
Production company

Po Box 268
Willis, TX 77378
281-882-9480

casting@starrmgmt.com
starrmgmt.com
imdb.com/company/co0532293
linkedin.com/in/VeronicaStarr
facebook.com/starrmgmt

Does not accept any unsolicited material. Genres include drama and comedy.

STARRUNNER
Production company and distributor

Two North St
Waldwick, NJ 07463
917-414-6332

imdb.com/company/co0283400

Does not accept any unsolicited material. Project types include TV. Genres include thriller.

STARRY NIGHT ENTERTAINMENT
Production company

Los Angeles, CA
818-895-4916

975 Park AVe.
Suite 10C
New York, NY 10028
212-717-2750 (phone)
212-794-6150 (fax)

mailbox@starrymightent.com
starrynightentertainment.com
imdb.com/company/co0183209
facebook.com/pages/Starry-Night-Entertainment
twitter.com/StarryNightEnt

Accepts query letters from unproduced, unrepresented writers via email. Project types include feature films, TV, commercials, and theater. Genres include drama, comedy, non-fiction, and reality.

Michael Shulman
Partner (NY)
ms@starrynightentertainment.com

Craig Saavedra
Partner (LA)
cs@starrynightentertainment.com
facebook.com/craig.saavedra
twitter.com/CraigSAAVEDRA

STARS NORTH
Production company

P.O. Box 470181
Celebration, FL 34747-0181
321-278-6708

production@starsnorth.com
starsnorth.com
imdb.com/company/co0006777
facebook.com/StarsNorthFilms

Does not accept any unsolicited material. Genres include drama.

STARS ROAD ENTERTAINMENT
Production company

10202 W Washington Blvd
David Lean Bldg, Suite 100

Culver City, CA 90232
310-244-4646

imdb.com/company/co0242736

Does not accept any unsolicited material. Project types include feature films. Genres include horror, thriller, detective, fantasy, and crime.

Sam Raimi
Partner
imdb.com/name/nm0000600

Joshua Donen
Partner
imdb.com/name/nm0232433

Ryan Carroll
Executive
imdb.com/name/nm1498070

STARSTREAM ENTERTAINMENT
Production company

100 Skypark Dr, Monterey, CA, United States, 93940
203-661-8080

starstreamentertainment.com
imdb.com/company/co0406729

Does not accept any unsolicited material. Project types include feature films, short films, and TV. Genres include drama, romance, comedy, and family.

STAR THROWER ENTERTAINMENT
Production company

720 Huntley Dr, Suite 107, Los Angeles, CA, United States, 90069
310-855-9009

info@sthrower.com
imdb.com/company/co0306981

Does not accept any unsolicited material.

Tim White
Producer
imdb.com/name/nm0925524

START MEDIA
Production company

375 Hudson St, Fl 12, New York City, NY, United
States, 10014
212-620-5700

info@start-media.com
start-media.com
imdb.com/company/co0423025

Does not accept any unsolicited material. Project types
include feature films and TV. Genres include family,
drama, comedy, and action.

STARZ
Production company, studio, and distributor

9242 Beverly Blvd Suite 200
Beverly Hills CA 90210
424-204-4000 (phone)
424-204-4010 (fax)

521 Fifth Ave Suite 1900
New York NY 10175

8900 Liberty Circle, Englewood , CO, United States,
80112
720-852-7700 (phone)
720-852-4098 (fax)

2950 N Hollywood Way
Burbank CA 91505
818-748-4000 (phone)
818-798-4626 (fax)

info@starz.com
starzglobal.com
imdb.com/company/co0198894

Does not accept any unsolicited material. Project types
include TV. Genres include family, action, comedy,
and drama.

STATE OF THE ART INC.
Production company

2201 Wisconsin Ave. NW
Suite 350
Washington, DC 20007
202-537-0818 (phone)
202-537-0828 (fax)

office@stateart.com
stateart.com
imdb.com/company/co0142543

facebook.com/StateOfTheArtInc

Does not accept any unsolicited material. Project types
include TV. Genres include documentary.

STATE STREET PICTURES
Production company

9255 W. Sunset Blvd.
Suite 528
Los Angeles, CA 90069
323-556-2240 (phone)
323-556-2242 (fax)

State St Pictures
8075 W. 3rd St.
Suite 306
Los Angeles, CA
90048

statestreetpictures.com
imdb.com/company/co0068765
facebook.com/StateStreetPictures

Does not accept any unsolicited material. Project types
include feature films and TV. Genres include drama
and comedy.

Robert Teitel
Partner
imdb.com/name/nm0854052
facebook.com/robert.teitel

George Tillman, Jr.
Partner
imdb.com/name/nm0863387
facebook.com/gtillmanjr
twitter.com/George_Tillman

STEALTH MEDIA GROUP
Production company, distributor, and sales agent

143 S Hayworth Ave
Los Angeles CA 90048
323-920-0310 (phone)
323-920-0301 (fax)

14 Regent Hill, Brighton, United Kingdom, BN1
3ED
011-441-273739182 (phone)
011-441-273749122 (fax)

info@stealthmediagroup.com

stealthmediagroup.com
imdb.com/company/co0271065

Does not accept any unsolicited material. Project types include TV and feature films. Genres include documentary, action, family, romance, comedy, thriller, and drama.

STEAMROLLER PRODUCTIONS, INC.
Production company

100 Universal City Plaza #7151
Universal City, CA 91608
818-733-4622 (phone)
818-733-4608 (fax)

steamrollerprod@aol.com
imdb.com/company/co0003653

Accepts query letters from unproduced, unrepresented writers via email. Project types include feature films and TV. Genres include non-fiction, thriller, action, detective, reality, and crime.

Steven Seagal
imdb.com/name/nm0000219
facebook.com/sseagalofficial
Assistant: Tracy Irvine

Binh Dang
imdb.com/name/nm0199462

STEFANIE EPSTEIN PRODUCTIONS
Production company

427 N Canon Dr, Suite 214
Beverly Hills, CA 90210
310-385-0300 (phone)
310-385-0302 (fax)

billseprods@aol.com
imdb.com/company/co0171458
linkedin.com/company/stefanie-epstein-productions
twitter.com/StefanieEpstein

Accepts query letters from unproduced, unrepresented writers via email. Project types include feature films and TV. Genres include drama and comedy.

Bill Gienapp
Creative Executive
twitter.com/Type_O_Purple

Stefanie Epstein
Producer
twitter.com/StefanieEpstein

STERLING PICTURES LTD.
Production company

7 Denmark St
London, England WC2H 8LZ
UK
+44 (0) 7956 529489

admin@sterlingpictures.com
sterlingpictures.com
imdb.com/company/co0103958
facebook.com/Sterling-Pictures-154027691335690/
    info
twitter.com/SterlingPix

Does not accept any unsolicited material. Project types include TV. Genres include horror and drama.

STERLING WORLDWIDE DISTRIBUTION COMPANY
Distributor

211 W 56th St
Ste 20C
New York, NY 10019
212-227-7977

imdb.com/company/co0244839

Does not accept any unsolicited material.

STEVEN BOCHCO PRODUCTIONS
Production company

3000 Olympic Blvd, Suite 1310
Santa Monica, CA 90404
310-566-6900

yr@bochcomedia.com
imdb.com/company/co0085628
linkedin.com/company/steven-bochco-productions

Accepts query letters from unproduced, unrepresented writers. Project types include TV. Genres include drama, detective, and crime.

Dayna Kalins
President
imdb.com/name/nm0435861

Steven Bochco
Chairman
imdb.com/name/nm0004766

STICKY FILM
Production company

Portland, OR

stickyfilm@gmail.com
paulharrod.com
imdb.com/company/co0146050
twitter.com/stickyfm

Does not accept any unsolicited material. Project types include short films. Genres include comedy. Established in 2002.

Adam Pollock
Co-founder
adam.pollock@sticky.fm
linkedin.com/pub/adam-pollock/34/428/2b0

STINK FILMS
Production company

1 Alfred Mews
London W1T 7AA
UK
+44 20 7462 4000 (phone)
+44 20 7462 4001 (fax)

reception@stink.tv
imdb.com/company/co0295895

Does not accept any unsolicited material. Project types include short films. Genres include documentary.

John Hillcoat
Director
imdb.com/name/nm0384825

STOKELY CHAFFIN PRODUCTIONS
Production company

1456 Sunset Plaza Dr
Los Angeles, CA 90069
310-657-4559

imdb.com/name/nm0149563
linkedin.com/pub/stokely-chaffin/b/a98/634
facebook.com/pages/Stokely-Chaffin-Productions/
183949531616797

Accepts query letters from unproduced, unrepresented writers via email. Project types include feature films and TV. Genres include comedy, horror, non-fiction, thriller, and action.

Stokely Chaffin
Principal
imdb.com/name/nm0149563
linkedin.com/pub/stokely-chaffin/b/a98/634

STOKEY VIDEO
Production company and distributor

PO Box 6109
Monroe Twp., NJ 08831

imdb.com/company/co0002534

Does not accept any unsolicited material. Project types include TV. Genres include comedy and drama.

STONE BRIDGE FILMS
Production company

PO BOX 4474
Hallandale, FL 33008

engertpeter@msn.com
imdb.com/company/co0163296
linkedin.com/company/stone-bridge-films

Does not accept any unsolicited material. Genres include drama.

STONEBRIDGE PRODUCTIONS
Production company

PO Box 16226
Fernandina Beach, FL 32035
904-673-0083

info@americanstock.us
imdb.com/company/co0224350
linkedin.com/company/stonebridge-productions

Does not accept any unsolicited material. Genres include documentary.

STONEBROOK ENTERTAINMENT

Production company

10061 Riverside Dr, Suite 813
Toluca Lake, CA 91602
818-766-8797

imdb.com/company/co0291056
linkedin.com/company/stonebrook-entertainment

Accepts query letters from unproduced, unrepresented writers via email. Project types include TV and feature films.

Kris Wheeler
Producer
imdb.com/name/nm2699108
facebook.com/pages/Kris-Wheeler/203421416346308
twitter.com/Wheelerkris

STONE & COMPANY ENTERTAINMENT

Production company

c/o Hollywood Center Studios
1040 N Las Palmas Ave, Building 1
Los Angeles, CA 90038
323-960-2599 (phone)
323-960-2437 (fax)

info@stonetv.com
stonetv.com/home.html
imdb.com/company/co0173288
linkedin.com/company/stone-&-company-
     entertainment

Accepts query letters from unproduced, unrepresented writers via email. Project types include TV. Genres include reality and non-fiction.

David Weintraub
Producer
imdb.com/name/nm1479111
twitter.com/dwetalent

Scott Stone
Principal
imdb.com/name/nm0832164

René Brar
Development Executive
imdb.com/name/nm0105324
twitter.com/renebrar

STONELOCK PICTURES

Production company and distributor

5050 Serrania Ave, Woodland Hills , CA, United States, 91364

info@stonelockpictures.com
imdb.com/company/co0000881

Does not accept any unsolicited material. Project types include TV and feature films. Genres include drama, family, and thriller.

STONE VILLAGE PICTURES

Production company

9200 W Sunset Blvd
Suite 520
West Hollywood, CA 90069
310-402-5171 (phone)
310-402-5172 (fax)

imdb.com/company/co0003987
linkedin.com/company/stone-village-entertainment

Does not accept any unsolicited material. Project types include feature films. Genres include thriller, romance, and drama.

Dylan Russell
Partner
imdb.com/name/nm1928375

Scott Steindorff
Executive Producer
imdb.com/name/nm1127589
linkedin.com/pub/scott-steindorff/21/282/454
twitter.com/Scottsteindorff

STOREFRONT PICTURES

Production company

1112 Montana Ave
Santa Monica, CA 90403
310-459-4235

betty@storefrontpics.com
storefrontpics.com
imdb.com/company/co0096868

Does not accept any unsolicited material. Project types include feature films. Genres include fantasy, comedy, family, romance, and drama.

Susan Cartsonis
President
imdb.com/name/nm0142134
linkedin.com/pub/susan-cartsonis/5/8/359
facebook.com/susan.cartsonis
twitter.com/SusanCartsonis

STORIES
Production company

5-3-1
Akasaka
Minato, Tokyo 107-6301
Japan
03-6441-9032 (phone)
03-6441-9039 (fax)

contact@stories-llc.com
stories-llc.com
imdb.com/company/co0358181

Does not accept any unsolicited material. Project types include TV. Genres include animation.

Tomo Koizumi
Producer/ Partner (Producer)
imdb.com/name/nm4433949

STORY AND FILM
Production company and studio

2934 1/2 Beverly Glen Circle,
Suite 195
Los Angeles, CA 90077
310-480-8833

imdb.com/company/co0120778

Accepts query letters from unproduced, unrepresented writers via email.

Clark Peterson
Development Executive
imdb.com/name/nm0677075
linkedin.com/pub/clark-peterson/13/971/204

STORYHOUSE PRODUCTIONS
Production company

2233 Wisconsin Ave
Washington, DC 20007

202-342-1373 (phone)
202-342-3883 (fax)

mail@storyhousepro.com
storyhousepro.com
imdb.com/company/co0150626
linkedin.com/company/story-house-productions

Does not accept any unsolicited material. Genres include drama.

STORY HOUSE PRODUCTIONS
Production company

2233 Wisconsin Ave NW
Ste 420
Washington, DC 20007
202-342-1373 (phone)
202-342-3883 (fax)

mail@storyhousepro.com
storyhousepro.com
imdb.com/company/co0124731
facebook.com/Casting-Story-House-
    Productions-198663526812635

Does not accept any unsolicited material. Project types include TV. Genres include documentary.

STORYLINE ENTERTAINMENT
Production company

8335 Sunset Blvd, Suite 207
West Hollywood, CA 90069
323-337-9045 (phone)
323-210-7263 (fax)

info@storyline-entertainment.com
storyline-entertainment.com
imdb.com/company/co0091980
facebook.com/storylineent

Does not accept any unsolicited material. Project types include TV, feature films, and theater. Genres include non-fiction, reality, romance, comedy, and drama.

Craig Zadan
Partner
323-337-9045
craig@storyline-entertainment.com

Mark Nicholson
Vice President (Development)
323-337-9047
mark@storyline-entertainment.com

Neil Meron
Partner
323-337-9046
neil@storyline-entertainment.com

STORYWRITER CO.
Production company

2-32-2-1F
Ikejiri
Setagaya, Tokyo 154-0001
Japan
03-5433-1137 (phone)
03-5433-1130 (fax)

info@storywriterinc.com
storywriterinc.com
imdb.com/company/co0471106
facebook.com/we.are.storywriterinc

Does not accept any unsolicited material. Project types include feature films. Genres include horror.

Yasuhito Nakae
Executive
imdb.com/name/nm5870685

STRAIGHT UP FILMS
Production company

3215 La Cienega Ave
Los Angeles, CA 90034
424-238-8470

hello@straightupfilms.com
straightupfilms.com
imdb.com/company/co0167695
facebook.com/pages/Straight-Up-Films/
    243716051911
twitter.com/straightupfilms

Does not accept any unsolicited material. Project types include feature films and TV. Genres include drama, comedy, and crime.

Kate Cohen
Co-CEO/Producer
imdb.com/name/nm3154628

Marisa Polvino
Co-CEO/Producer
imdb.com/name/nm0689909
linkedin.com/pub/marisa-polvino/5/413/923

Casey A. Carroll
Director of Development
imdb.com/name/nm3554230
linkedin.com/pub/casey-a-carroll/45/6b0/802

STRAND RELEASING
Production company and distributor

6140 W Washington Blvd, Culver City , CA, United States, 90232
310-836-7500 (phone)
310-836-7510 (fax)

strand@strandreleasing.com
strandreleasing.com
imdb.com/company/co0035339

Does not accept any unsolicited material. Project types include TV and feature films. Genres include thriller, drama, and family.

STRANGE HAT FILMS
Studio

Salou, Tarragona
Spain
638173165

strangehatfilms@gmail.com
strangehatfilms.wordpress.com
facebook.com/strangehatfilms

Accepts scripts from unproduced, unrepresented writers via email. Project types include short films and feature films. Genres include sociocultural, detective, science fiction, reality, non-fiction, and documentary. Established in 2014.

Joan Vilajosana
Director of Film and New Media
joanvi.quesada@gmail.com

STRAYDOG PROMOTION CO.
Production company

3-7-26-409
Nishi Shinjuku
Shinjuku, Tokyo 160-0023
Japan
03-6698-6084 (phone)
03-6673-1302 (fax)

s-staff@straydog.info
straydog.info
imdb.com/company/co0428692

Does not accept any unsolicited material. Project types include feature films. Genres include comedy.

STRIKE ENTERTAINMENT
Production company

3000 W Olympic Blvd
Building 5, Suite 1250
Santa Monica, CA 90404
310-315-0550 (phone)
310-315-0560 (fax)

strikenz.co.nz
imdb.com/company/co0086710
linkedin.com/company/strike-entertainment_2

Accepts query letters from unproduced, unrepresented writers via email. Project types include feature films. Genres include drama, thriller, action, comedy, horror, and science fiction. Established in 2002.

STRONGHOLD PRODUCTIONS
Production company

PO Box 310781
Miami, FL 33231
310-420-2014

strongholdprods@aol.com
strongholdproductions.org/nav.html
imdb.com/company/co0087474
linkedin.com/company/stronghold-productions-
   limited

Does not accept any unsolicited material. Genres include drama and romance.

STUDIO 4°C
Production company

Tokyo,
Japan

info@studio4c.co.jp
studio4c.co.jp/top.html
imdb.com/company/co0041113
facebook.com/studio4c
twitter.com/STUDIO4C

Does not accept any unsolicited material. Project types include short films and feature films. Genres include animation and action.

Kôji Morimoto
Founder (Executive)
imdb.com/name/nm0605479

STUDIOCANAL
Production company

301 N. Canon Dr.
Suite 207
Beverly Hills, CA 90210
310-247-0994 (phone)
310-247-0995 (fax)

studiocanal.com/en
imdb.com/company/co0047476
facebook.com/STUDIOCANAL.UK
twitter.com/StudioCanalUK

Does not accept any unsolicited material. Project types include TV and feature films. Genres include romance, drama, thriller, comedy, reality, horror, non-fiction, fantasy, and crime.

Ron Halpern
Executive Vice President of Production
facebook.com/ron.halpern1

STUDIO CANAL
Production company and distributor

50 Marshall St
London, England W1F 9BQ
UK
+44 (0)20 7534 2700 (phone)
+44 (0)20 7534 2701 (fax)

info@studiocanal.co.uk
studiocanal.co.uk
imdb.com/company/co0176671
facebook.com/STUDIOCANAL

Does not accept any unsolicited material. Project types include TV. Genres include drama.

STUDIOCANAL
Production company and distributor

50 Marshall St
London
W1F 9BQ
United Kingdom
+44207-534-2700 (phone)
+44207-354-2701 (fax)

info@studiocanal.co.uk
studiocanal.co.uk
imdb.com/company/co0136720
facebook.com/STUDIOCANAL

Does not accept any unsolicited material. Project types include short films, feature films, and TV. Genres include science fiction and thriller.

STUDIO-E2
Production company and studio

5308 Great Divide Dr
Austin, TX 78738

info@studio-e2.com
studio-e2.com
imdb.com/company/co0357540
facebook.com/pages/Studio-e2/148082561874590
twitter.com/Studio_e2

Does not accept any unsolicited material. Project types include short films. Genres include drama and fantasy.

STUDIO EIGHT PRODUCTIONS
Production company

10b Salisbury Mews
London, England SW6 7DS
UK
+44203-006-2897 (phone)
+44207-610-9880 (fax)

mail@studioeight.co.uk
imdb.com/company/co0104580

Does not accept any unsolicited material. Project types include TV. Genres include family, drama, comedy, and science fiction.

Jamie Brown
Producer
imdb.com/name/nm0007077

STUDIO GHIBLI
Production company and distributor

1-4-25 Kajino-cho
Koganei-shi, Tokyo 184-0002
Japan
+81 422 50 2511 (phone)
+81 422 50 2489 (fax)

post@ghibli.co.jp
ghibli.jp
imdb.com/company/co0048420

Does not accept any unsolicited material. Project types include TV. Genres include animation.

Kôji Hoshino
chief executive officer
imdb.com/name/nm1916093

STX ENTERTAINMENT
Production company, distributor, and financing company

10202 W Washington Blvd Robert Young Building
Culver City CA 90232

3900 W Alameda Ave, 32nd Floor, Burbank, CA, United States, 91505
310-362-8721 (phone)
310-742-2300 (fax)

imdb.com/company/co0249694

Does not accept any unsolicited material. Project types include TV. Genres include drama, action, thriller, comedy, romance, and family.

Jason Babiszewski
Creative Executive
imdb.com/name/nm2380955

SUBMARINE ENTERTAINMENT
Production company

525 Broadway
Ste 601
New York, NY 10012

212-625-1410 (phone)
212-625-9931 (fax)

info@submarine.com
imdb.com/company/co0131815

Accepts query letters from produced or represented writers. Project types include feature films. Genres include drama and documentary.

Dan Braun
President
dan@submarine.com
imdb.com/name/nm2250854

Josh Braun
President
josh@submarine.com
imdb.com/name/nm2248562

SUCH MUCH FILMS
Production company

Santa Monica, CA 90405

info@suchmuchfilms.com
suchmuchfilms.com
imdb.com/company/co0112289
facebook.com/suchmuchfilms
twitter.com/SuchMuchFilms

Accepts query letters from produced or represented writers. Project types include feature films. Genres include drama and documentary.

Judi Levine
Principal
imdb.com/name/nm0505861
facebook.com/judi.levine.94

Ben Lewin
Principal
imdb.com/name/nm0506802

SUDDEN STORM PRODUCTIONS
Production company

10 Hamilton St
Toronto, ON M4M 2C5
Canada
647-476-2668

information@suddenstorm.ca

suddenstorm.ca
imdb.com/company/co0010592

Does not accept any unsolicited material. Project types include TV and feature films. Genres include crime and thriller.

Jeff Glickman
Producer
imdb.com/name/nm1093042

SULLIVAN ENTERTAINMENT
Production company, distributor, and sales agent

110 Davenport Rd
Toronto, ON M5R 3R3
Canada
416-921-7177

inquire@sullivan-ent.com
sullivan-ent.com
imdb.com/company/co0045201
linkedin.com/company/1577123
facebook.com/sullivanent
twitter.com/sullivanent

Does not accept any unsolicited material. Genres include drama, crime, and thriller.

Kevin Sullivan
Producer
imdb.com/name/nm0838195

SUMMER HILL FILMS
Production company, distributor, and sales agent

10645 N. Tatum Blvd.
Suite 200-130
Phoenix, AZ 85028
480-535-8711

info@summerhillfilms.com
summerhillfilms.com
imdb.com/company/co0276008
facebook.com/summerhillfilms
twitter.com/summerhillfilms

Does not accept any unsolicited material. Project types include TV and feature films. Genres include thriller.

Jon Bonnell
Producer
imdb.com/name/nm2284710

SUMMIT DISTRIBUTION
Distributor

1630 Stewart St
Santa Monica, CA 90404
310-309-8400

usasummitorder.com
imdb.com/company/co0225299
linkedin.com/company/summit-distribution
facebook.com/SummitDistribution

Does not accept any unsolicited material. Genres include romance, drama, and fantasy.

SUMMIT ENTERTAINMENT
Production company

1630 Stewart St
Ste 120
Santa Monica, CA 90404
310-309-8400 (phone)
310-828-4132 (fax)

imdb.com/company/co0046206
twitter.com/summitent

Does not accept any unsolicited material. Project types include feature films. Genres include drama, fantasy, thriller, science fiction, crime, comedy, action, and romance.

Patrick Wachsberger
President
310-309-8400
imdb.com/name/nm0905163

Rob Friedman
CEO
310-309-8400
imdb.com/name/nm2263981

Merideth Milton
Sr. Vice-President
310-309-8400
imdb.com/name/nm0590693

Gillian Bohrer
Vice-President
310-309-8400
imdb.com/name/nm2023551

SUMS FILM AND MEDIA
Production company

1 Duchess St
London W1W 6AN
UK
+44 (0)20 3475 4875

info@sumslondon.com
sumslondon.com
imdb.com/company/co0350441
uk.linkedin.com/in/andy-brunskill-31355812
facebook.com/Sums-Film-Media-147617295327167
twitter.com/SUMS_IT_UP

Does not accept any unsolicited material. Genres include thriller.

Andy Brunskill
Producer
imdb.com/name/nm2086436

SUN BRILLIANT
Production company

1-7-10-703
Shinjuku
Tokyo 106-0022
Japan
+81 03-5367-2796 (phone)
+81 03-5367-2797 (fax)

info@sunbrilliant.com
sunbrilliant.com
imdb.com/company/co0431907

Does not accept any unsolicited material. Project types include TV. Genres include drama and thriller.

Misa Ohkatsu
C.E.O. (Producer)
imdb.com/name/nm4688757

SUNDANCE INSTITUTE DOCUMENTARY FUND
Production company and financing company

1825 Three Kings Dr
Park City, UT 84060
435-658-3456 (phone)
435-658-3457 (fax)

dfp@sundance.org

sundance.org/programs/documentary-fund
imdb.com/company/co0120252
facebook.com/sundance
twitter.com/sundancefest

Does not accept any unsolicited material. Project types include TV. Genres include documentary.

SUNDANCETV
Production company and distributor

2425 W Olympic Blvd Suite 5050W
Santa Monica CA 90404
310-998-9300

11 Penn Plaza, New York, NY, United States, 10001
212-324-8500

sundance.tv
imdb.com/company/co0490233

Does not accept any unsolicited material. Project types include TV. Genres include comedy, drama, and family.

SUNDAY RISING FILMS
Production company

4110 19th Ave West
Bradenton, FL 34205
941-751-2600

ryan@studio26productions.com
imdb.com/company/co0278178

Does not accept any unsolicited material. Project types include TV. Genres include family. Established in 2008.

SUNDIAL PICTURES
Production company

511 Sixth Ave., Suite 375
New York, NY 10011

info@sundialpicturesllc.com
sundial-pictures.com
imdb.com/company/co0259997

Does not accept any unsolicited material. Project types include TV and feature films. Genres include comedy, documentary, drama, and thriller.

Joey Carey
Partner
imdb.com/name/nm2909903
linkedin.com/pub/joey-carey/64/932/685
twitter.com/JoeyCareyFilms

Benjamin Weber
imdb.com/name/nm3373548
linkedin.com/in/benweber1
facebook.com/benjamin.weber.3557

Stefan Norwicki
President
imdb.com/name/nm3378356
twitter.com/StefanNowicki

SUNLIGHT PRODUCTIONS
Production company

854-A Fifth St
Santa Monica, CA 90403
310-899-1522 (phone)
310-899-1262 (fax)

info@sunlightproductions.com
filmbudget.com/sunlightproductions
imdb.com/company/co0028319

Does not accept any unsolicited material. Project types include TV and feature films. Genres include non-fiction, comedy, and drama.

Mike Binder
Executive
imdb.com/name/nm0082802

SUNNYMARCH
Production company

16 Manette St
London W1D 4AR
UK

info@sunnymarch.com
facebook.com/SUNNYMARCHLtd
imdb.com/company/co0445206

Does not accept any unsolicited material. Project types include short films. Genres include action and thriller.

Benedict Cumberbatch
Producer
imdb.com/name/nm1212722

SUNSET STUDIOS

Production company, distributor, sales agent, and financing company

321 Montgomery Rd, Suite 160143
Altamonte Springs, FL 32716
407-412-7226

info@sunsetstudios.co
sunsetstudios.co
imdb.com/company/co0438683
linkedin.com/company/sunsetstudiosfl
twitter.com/SunsetStudiosFL

Does not accept any unsolicited material. Project types include feature films. Genres include family, animation, thriller, horror, and science fiction. Established in 2014.

SUNSET UNDISCOVERED

Production company

321 Montgomery Rd, Suite 160143
Altamonte Springs, FL 32716
407-412-7226

sunsetstudios.co
imdb.com/company/co0501640
facebook.com/1424592750
twitter.com/SunsetStudiosFL

Does not accept any unsolicited material. Project types include short films. Genres include thriller, horror, and documentary.

SUNSTAR PRODUCTIONS

Production company

34 Brophy Dr
Ewing, NJ 08648
609-658-3917 (phone)
609-219-0216 (fax)

nobletalent@comcast.net
imdb.com/company/co0171545

Does not accept any unsolicited material. Project types include TV. Genres include drama.

SUNSWEPT ENTERTAINMENT

Production company

Sunswept Entertainment - TV
10201 W. Pico Blvd.
Building 3/Room 204
Los Angeles, CA 90035

10201 W Pico Blvd
Building 45
Los Angeles, CA 90064
310-369-0878 (phone)
310-969-0726 (fax)

imdb.com/company/co0226011

Does not accept any unsolicited material. Project types include feature films. Genres include romance, family, fantasy, comedy, and animation. Established in 2004.

Karen Rosenfelt
Principal
imdb.com/name/nm1651942

SUNTAUR ENTERTAINMENT

Production company

1581 N Crescent Heights Blvd.
Los Angeles, CA 90046
323-656-3800

info@suntaurent.com
suntaurent.com
imdb.com/company/co0183461

Does not accept any unsolicited material. Project types include TV and feature films. Genres include drama and comedy.

Paul Aaron
Executive
imdb.com/name/nm0007477
facebook.com/aaronpaul
twitter.com/aaronpaul_8

SUNWOOD ENTERTAINMENT CORPORATION

Production company

P.O. Box 568795
Orlando, FL 32856-8795

secproductions2@yahoo.com
imdb.com/company/co0171367
facebook.com/Sunwood-Entertainment-
    Corporation-109526142448450

Does not accept any unsolicited material.

SUPER CRISPY ENTERTAINMENT
Production company

2812 Santa Monica Blvd
Ste 205
Santa Monica, CA 90404
310-453-4545

crispyfilms@gmail.com
imdb.com/company/co0326644
facebook.com/pages/Super-Crispy-Entertainment/
    220900244666693

Does not accept any unsolicited material. Project types
include feature films. Genres include comedy, drama,
and romance.

Andrea Sperling
Producer
310-453-4545
imdb.com/name/nm0818304

Jonathan Schwartz
Producer
310-453-4545
imdb.com/name/nm2009933

SUPERFINGER ENTERTAINMENT
Production company

c/o Chris Hart/UTA
9560 Wilshire Blvd
Beverly Hills, CA 90212
310-385-6715

imdb.com/company/co0181284

Accepts query letters from unproduced, unrepresented
writers via email. Project types include TV and feature
films. Genres include animation, non-fiction, comedy,
and reality.

Dane Cook
imdb.com/name/nm0176981
twitter.com/DaneCook

SUPERSAURUS
Production company

1-6-6
Irifune
Chuo, Tokyo 104-0042
Japan
+81-3-3551-5530 (phone)
+81-3-3551-4769 (fax)

info@supersaurus.jp
supersaurus.jp
imdb.com/company/co0212243

Does not accept any unsolicited material. Project types
include TV. Genres include drama.

SUURKIITOS
Production company and distributor

1-20-1-4F
Uehara
Shibuya, Tokyo
Japan
03-5738-3738

info@suurkiitos.com
suurkiitos.com
imdb.com/company/co0283325
facebook.com/suurkiitos.official
twitter.com/suurkiitos_inc

Does not accept any unsolicited material. Project types
include short films, TV, and feature films. Genres
include romance and drama.

SUZANNE DELAURENTIIS
PRODUCTIONS
Production company

10061 Riverside Dr, Suite 101
Toluca Lake, California, 91602

5555 Melrose Ave, Drier Building #217
Hollywood, CA 90036
323-956-7899

delaurentiisllc@gmail.com
suzannedelaurentiisproductions.com
imdb.com/company/co0014118

Does not accept any unsolicited material. Project types
include TV and feature films. Genres include crime
and drama.

Suzanne DeLaurentiis
Producer
imdb.com/name/nm0216560

SWEET 180
Production company

141 W 28th St #300
NYC, NY 10001
212-541-4443 (phone)
212-563-9655 (fax)

sweet180.com
twitter.com/Sweet180grados

Does not accept any unsolicited material. Project types include feature films and TV. Genres include comedy, non-fiction, drama, reality, and romance.

Nina Schreiber
Manager
nina@sweet180.com

Lillian LaSalle
Principal
lillian@sweet180.com
facebook.com/lillian.lasalle

Rachel Maran
assistant@sweet180.com

SWEET BASIL
Production company

Tokyo,
Japan
03.5418.8151

sweetbasil@sweetbasil.co.jp
imdb.com/company/co0198596

Does not accept any unsolicited material. Project types include TV. Genres include drama.

Yûji Yoshida
Producer
imdb.com/name/nm0948954

SWEN DO BRASIL
Production company and distributor

6332 Alton Rd, Miami Beach, FL, United States, 33141
305-904-6144

449 S Beverly Dr
Beverly Hills CA 90212
310-904-6144

Alameda Franca 267 Conj. 101
Sao Paulo SP Brazil 01422-000
011-551-18182442

Praia de Botafogo, 501 Torre A (Pao de Acucar) 1o. Andar
Rio de Janeiro RJ Brazil 222250-40
011-552-125866259

info@swengroup.us
swengroup.us
imdb.com/company/co0125529

Does not accept any unsolicited material. Project types include feature films and TV. Genres include drama, thriller, romance, action, and family.

SWEN ENTERTAINMENT
Distributor

1111 Lincoln Rd
Ste 400
Miami Beach, FL 33139
305-588-2825

imdb.com/company/co0304778
facebook.com/SwenGroup

Does not accept any unsolicited material. Genres include drama, crime, and action.

SWING BUD FILMS
Production company

2320 Blue Bonnet Blvd.
Houston, TX 77030

corporationwiki.com/Texas/Houston/swing-bud-films-llc/39171216.aspx
imdb.com/company/co0337341

Does not accept any unsolicited material. Genres include documentary.

SYCAMORE ENTERTAINMENT GROUP
Distributor

5555 Melrose Ave, Dreier Building, Suite 219, Los
Angeles, CA, United States, 90038
888-530-2999

info@sycamoreentertainment.com
imdb.com/company/co0367975

Does not accept any unsolicited material.

SYCAMORE PICTURES
Production company

1680 N. Vine St, Suite 905, Los Angeles, CA, United
States, 90028
323-938-1785

info@sycamorepictures.com
sycamorepictures.com
imdb.com/company/co0326604

Does not accept any unsolicited material. Project types
include TV and feature films. Genres include romance,
family, thriller, and drama.

SYNCA CREATIONS
Distributor

6-25-8-1301
Jungumae
Shibuya, Tokyo 151-0001
Japan
+81 3-6434-1524 (phone)
+81 3-6434-1209 (fax)

info@synca.jp
synca.jp
imdb.com/company/co0455400

Does not accept any unsolicited material. Project types
include TV. Genres include drama.

SYNDICADO
Production company, distributor, and sales agent

121 Beaconsfield Av.
Toronto, ON M6J 3J5
Canada
416-533-1743

info@syndicado.com
syndicado.com
imdb.com/company/co0295867
facebook.com/Syndicado

twitter.com/Syndicado

Does not accept any unsolicited material. Project types
include TV, short films, and feature films. Genres
include documentary.

Greg Rubidge
Casting Department
imdb.com/name/nm0747984

SYNERGETIC DISTRIBUTION
Distributor

9301 Wilshire Blvd Ste 507
Beverly Hills, CA 90210
310-268-1210

sales@synergeticdistribution.com
synergeticdistribution.com
imdb.com/company/co0278658

Does not accept any unsolicited material. Genres
include romance, comedy, thriller, drama, and action.

SYNKRONIZED
Production company

19201 Collins Ave
Unit 133 A
Miami, FL 33160
305-479-2643

acohen@skddvd.com
skddvd.com
imdb.com/company/co0208907
facebook.com/pages/Synkronized-Films/
    159669597422729
twitter.com/Synkronizedfilm

Does not accept any unsolicited material. Genres
include comedy and romance.

TAGGART PRODUCTIONS

9000 W Sunset Blvd
Suite 1020
West Hollywood, CA 90069
424-249-3350 (phone)
424-249-3972 (fax)

taggart-productions.com
imdb.com/company/co0316676
linkedin.com/company/taggart-productions

facebook.com/taggartproductions
twitter.com/TaggartTweet

Does not accept any unsolicited material. Project types include feature films. Genres include comedy, action, crime, thriller, and drama. Established in 2010.

Tim Nardelli
linkedin.com/pub/tim-nardelli/22/323/550
facebook.com/tim.nardelli

Michael Nardelli
President & CEO
imdb.com/name/nm1660148
linkedin.com/pub/dir/Mike/Nardell

TAGHIT
Production company

468 N Camden Dr, Suite 200
Beverly Hills, 90210

imdb.com/company/co0359898

Does not accept any unsolicited material. Project types include feature films. Genres include drama and thriller.

TAGLINE PICTURES
Production company

9250 Wilshire Blvd
Ground Floor
Beverly Hills, CA 90212
310-595-1515 (phone)
310-595-1505 (fax)

info@taglinela.com
taglinela.com
imdb.com/company/co0183460

Does not accept any unsolicited material. Project types include TV. Genres include drama and comedy.

J.B. Roberts
Partner
facebook.com/jb.roberts.9

Chris Henze
Partner
imdb.com/name/nm1771421
linkedin.com/pub/chris-henze/70/a23/78b

Kelly Kulchak
President
imdb.com/name/nm2103544

TAILLIGHT TV
Production company

30 Middleton St
Nashville, TN 37210
615-385-1034 (phone)
615-385-1024 (fax)

info@taillight.tv
taillight.tv
imdb.com/company/co0047193
linkedin.com/company/taillight-tv
facebook.com/Taillight-436861895253
twitter.com/taillighttv

Does not accept any unsolicited material. Project types include TV. Genres include reality.

TAITO
Production company and distributor

Shinjuku East Side Square 2F 6-27-30 Shinjuku, Shinjuku-Ku, Tokyo
Tokyo 160-8447
Japan

overseas_inquiries@taito.co.jp
taito.co.jp
imdb.com/company/co0118221

Does not accept any unsolicited material. Project types include video games, TV, and feature films. Genres include animation and action.

TAKE 5 PRODUCTIONS
Production company

1 Atlantic Ave
Ste 215
Toronto, ON M6K 3E7
Canada
416-583-2186 (phone)
416-532-2750 (fax)

info@take5productions.ca
take5productions.ca
imdb.com/company/co0304458
facebook.com/Take5ProductionsInc

twitter.com/take5prod

Does not accept any unsolicited material. Genres include drama and action.

John Weber
Producer
imdb.com/name/nm1222780

TAKI CORPORATION

Production company and distributor

1-10-5F
Nanpeidai
Shibuya, Tokyo
Japan
03-3496-5775 (phone)
03-3496-5776 (fax)

promotion@taki-c.co.jp
imdb.com/company/co0072435

Does not accept any unsolicited material. Project types include feature films. Genres include comedy, fantasy, and family.

TALLGRASS PICTURES

Production company

710 13th St #300
San Diego, CA 92101
916-717-4483

jennifer@tallgrasspictures.com
tallgrasspictures.com
imdb.com/company/co0405706
facebook.com/tallgrasspicturesllc

Accepts query letters from unproduced, unrepresented writers via email. Project types include feature films. Genres include science fiction, romance, action, drama, reality, fantasy, crime, and comedy.

TALLTREE PICTURES

Production company

151
Great Titchfield St
London W1W 5BB
UK
+44 20 71479948 (phone)
+44 20 71479948 (fax)

info@talltreepictures.co.uk
talltreepictures.co.uk
imdb.com/company/co0312786
facebook.com/talltreepictures
twitter.com/talltreepicture

Does not accept any unsolicited material. Project types include feature films. Genres include crime, drama, and action.

Vince Woods
Producer
imdb.com/name/nm3807209

TAMA PRODUCTION

Production company

1-4-4-1F
Saiwaicho
Higashi Kurume, Tokyo
Japan
0424-71-6976

mailbox@tamapro.co.jp
imdb.com/company/co0206399

Does not accept any unsolicited material. Project types include TV. Genres include comedy, drama, and animation.

TAMARA ASSEYEV PRODUCTION

Production company

1187 Coast Village Rd.
Suite 134
Santa Barbara, CA 93108
323-656-4731 (phone)
323-656-2211 (fax)

tamaraprod@aol.com
imdb.com/company/co0043622

Accepts query letters from unproduced, unrepresented writers. Project types include TV. Genres include drama.

Tamara Asseyev
Producer
imdb.com/name/nm0039834
linkedin.com/pub/tamara-asseyev/66/35/9b4
Assistant: Constance Mead

TAMBOURINE ARTISTS
Production company

2-25-13
Daizawa
Setagaya, Tokyo 155-0032
Japan
03-6277-8301 (phone)
03-6277-8302 (fax)

hs@tambourine.co.jp
tambourineartists.com
imdb.com/company/co0262290

Does not accept any unsolicited material. Project types include TV. Genres include drama.

TANNENBAUM COMPANY
Production company, studio, and distributor

c/o CBS Studios
4024 Radford Ave, Bungalow 16
Studio City, CA 91604
818-655-7181 (phone)
818-655-7193 (fax)

imdb.com/company/co0099776
twitter.com/tbaumco

Does not accept any unsolicited material. Project types include TV and feature films. Genres include reality, drama, comedy, and non-fiction.

Jason Wang
Creative Affairs
imdb.com/name/nm4867712
linkedin.com/pub/jason-wang/4/9A5/905

Eric Tannenbaum
Partner
imdb.com/name/nm1383548

TAPESTRY FILMS, INC.
Production company

9328 Civic Center Dr, 2nd Floor
Beverly Hills, CA 90210
310-275-1191 (phone)
310-275-1266 (fax)

imdb.com/company/co0018522
linkedin.com/company/tapestry-films

Does not accept any unsolicited material. Project types include feature films. Genres include action, comedy, romance, thriller, and family.

Robert L. Levy
imdb.com/name/nm0506597

Kat Blasband Page
imdb.com/name/nm2321097

Peter Abrams
imdb.com/name/nm0009222

Michael Schreiber
President
imdb.com/name/nm2325100

TAPESTRY INTERNATIONAL
Production company and distributor

3 Church St
Sea Bright, NJ 07760
732-559-1300 (phone)
732-559-1309 (fax)

info@tapestry.tv
imdb.com/company/co0047968

Does not accept any unsolicited material. Project types include TV. Genres include comedy and documentary.

TARA CONTENTS
Production company

4-5
Ohdenmacho
Chuo, Tokyo 103-0011
Japan
(03) 5640 5612

iseki@taracontents.com
imdb.com/company/co0195110

Does not accept any unsolicited material. Project types include TV. Genres include action, crime, and drama.

Satoru Iseki
President (Producer)
imdb.com/name/nm0410785

TAR ART
Production company

304 Hudson St, 6th Floor
New York, NY 10013
212-989-7900 (phone)
212-989-7911 (fax)

inquire@tar-art.com
tar-art.com
imdb.com/company/co0215731

Does not accept any unsolicited material. Project types include feature films. Genres include drama.

TASHMOO PRODUCTIONS
Production company

1841 Broadway, Suite 711A
New York, NY 10023
212-799-7855

1075 Duval St, Suite C21 #236
Key West, FL 33040
305-294-9382

info@tashmoo.com
tashmoo.com
imdb.com/company/co0089657

Does not accept any unsolicited material. Project types include feature films. Genres include drama and comedy.

TASKOVSKI FILMS
Production company, distributor, and sales agent

7 Granard Business Centre
Bunns Ln
London NW7 2DQ
UK
+ 44 387 65 652 046

info@taskovskifilms.com
taskovskifilms.com
imdb.com/company/co0264624
facebook.com/TaskovskiFilms
twitter.com/TaskovskiFilms

Does not accept any unsolicited material. Project types include feature films. Genres include documentary and drama.

Irena Taskovski
Producer
imdb.com/name/nm2412325

TATTVADARSANA FILMS
Production company and studio

vik.rajat@yahoo.com
facebook.com/vik.rajat

Does not accept any unsolicited material. Project types include short films and commercials. Genres include science fiction, fantasy, reality, drama, detective, crime, thriller, family, and non-fiction. Established in 2015.

Rajat Vikram
Director
vik.rajat@yahoo.com

TAURUS ENTERTAINMENT COMPANY
Distributor

5555 Melrose Ave
Marx Brothers Building, Suite 103/104
Hollywood, CA 90038
818-935-5157 (phone)
323-686-5379 (fax)

taurusentco@yahoo.com
taurusec.com
imdb.com/company/co0080449
facebook.com/TaurusEntertainmentsInc

Accepts query letters from unproduced, unrepresented writers via email. Project types include feature films and TV. Genres include action, family, animation, and drama. Established in 1991.

Robert Dudelson
rfdudelson@mac.com
imdb.com/name/nm0240055
linkedin.com/pub/robert-dudelson/5/418/a53
facebook.com/rfdudelson

James Dudelson
jgdudelson@yahoo.com
imdb.com/name/nm0240054
facebook.com/james.dudelson

TAYLOR LANE PRODUCTIONS
Production company

2446 1/2 N Gower St
Los Angeles, CA 90068
310-770-2594

info@deontaylorenterprises.com

imdb.com/company/co0203749
facebook.com/Taylor-Lane-
  Productions-200436060067111

Does not accept any unsolicited material. Project types include feature films. Genres include drama.

TAYLORMADE FILMS
Production company and distributor

Los Angeles, CA, United States
310-880-1956

taylormccluskeyllc@yahoo.com
taylormccluskey.com
imdb.com/company/co0394779

Does not accept any unsolicited material. Project types include feature films, TV, and short films. Genres include comedy, thriller, action, family, and drama.

TAYLOR-MADE PRODUCTIONS
Production company

PO Box 309
Caldwell, NJ 07006
973-226-1461 (phone)
973-226-1462 (fax)

taylormix@aol.com
taylormadeprod.com
imdb.com/company/co0019819

Does not accept any unsolicited material. Project types include short films. Genres include crime.

T&C PICTURES
Production company and sales agent

17412 Ventura Blvd
Encino, CA 91316
310-828-1340

imdb.com/company/co0207457

Does not accept any unsolicited material. Project types include feature films and TV. Genres include horror, comedy, non-fiction, documentary, crime, thriller, drama, action, and romance. Established in 2007.

Barry Rosenbush
Executive
imdb.com/name/nm0742492

Bill Borden
Producer
christine@tandcpictures.com
imdb.com/name/nm0096115

Arata Matsushima
310-828-7801
imdb.com/name/nm2606503

TDJ ENTERPRISES
Production company

3703 Patience Blvd
Dallas, TX 75236
888-201-2535

info@tdjakes.com
tdjakes.com
imdb.com/company/co0267610
facebook.com/TDJenterprises
twitter.com/bishopjakes

Does not accept any unsolicited material. Project types include TV and feature films. Genres include drama. Established in 1993.

TEAKWOOD LANE PRODUCTIONS
Production company

11845 W Olympic Blvd., Suite 1125W
Los Angeles, CA 90064

imdb.com/company/co0039827

Does not accept any unsolicited material. Project types include TV. Genres include drama, action, and thriller. Established in 1989.

TEAM DESERTSUN STUDIOS
Production company

38-15 Pellington Dr
Fair Lawn, NJ 07410
857-445-3864

info@desertsunstudios.com
imdb.com/company/co0191904

Does not accept any unsolicited material.

TEAM DOWNEY
Production company

1311 Abbot Kinney
Venice, CA 90291
310-450-5100

teamdowney.com
imdb.com/company/co0306946

Does not accept any unsolicited material. Project types include feature films. Genres include drama, comedy, and action. Established in 2010.

David Gambino
President
imdb.com/name/nm1312724
linkedin.com/pub/david-gambino/9/756/879

Robert Downey
Producer
imdb.com/name/nm0000375
facebook.com/robertdowneyjr
twitter.com/RobertDowneyJr

Susan Downey
Producer
imdb.com/name/nm1206265

TEAM G
Production company

1839 Blake Ave #5
Los Angeles, CA 90039
213-915-8106 (phone)
323-843-9210 (fax)

info@teamgproductions.com
teamgproductions.com
imdb.com/company/co0200164

Does not accept any unsolicited material. Project types include feature films. Genres include science fiction, comedy, and drama.

Trey Hock
Partner
imdb.com/name/nm2465366
twitter.com/treyhock

Jett Steiger
Partner
imdb.com/name/nm2532520

TEAM TEPES PRODUCTIONS
Production company

5470 E Busch Blvd.
Suite 192
Temple Terrace, FL 33617
813-399-9098

rdtsproductions@yahoo.com
imdb.com/company/co0414911

Does not accept any unsolicited material. Genres include action.

TEAM TODD
Production company

2900 W Olympic Blvd
Santa Monica, CA 91404
310-255-7265 (phone)
310-255-7222 (fax)

imdb.com/company/co0050544
linkedin.com/company/team-todd
facebook.com/pages/Team-Todd/25240836851

Accepts scripts from produced or represented writers. Project types include feature films. Genres include myth, drama, animation, family, and romance.

Julianna Hays
Creative Executive
imdb.com/name/nm3057670
linkedin.com/in/juliannahays

Suzanne Todd
Principal
imdb.com/name/nm0865297
linkedin.com/in/mssuzannetodd
twitter.com/teamsuz

TEA SHOP & FILM COMPANY
Production company

Third Floor
Tyler's Court
111a Wardour St
London
W1F 0UJ

info@teashopfilm.com
teashopfilm.com
imdb.com/company/co0332878
linkedin.com/company/the-tea-shop-&-film-company

Does not accept any unsolicited material. Project types include feature films. Genres include horror.

James Harris
Producer
imdb.com/name/nm2448068

TEEVEE GRAPHICS
Production company

2F Tanaka Bldg.1-1-22?Takatori Sawara-ku Fukuoka-shi, Fukuoka 814-0011 Japan
092-852-7264 (phone)
092-852-7265 (fax)

tvg-info@teeveeg.com
teeveeg.com
imdb.com/company/co0201385
facebook.com/teevee-graphicsInc-347185295320169

Does not accept any unsolicited material. Project types include TV and feature films. Genres include comedy.

TELEMUNDO STUDIOS
Production company and distributor

7355 NW 41st St
Miami, FL 33166
305-640-7700

info@telemundostudios.com
telemundostudios.com
imdb.com/company/co0210756
linkedin.com/company/telemundo-studios-miami-llc
facebook.com/TelemundoStudios
twitter.com/tlmdstudios

Does not accept any unsolicited material. Project types include TV. Genres include romance and drama. Established in 2003.

TELEPRODUCTIONS INTERNATIONAL
Production company, distributor, and sales agent

14020 Thunderbolt Place
Suite 200
Chantilly, VA 20151
703-222-2408 (phone)
703-222-3964 (fax)

info@tpiltd.com
imdb.com/company/co0195982

Does not accept any unsolicited material. Project types include TV and feature films. Genres include documentary.

Larry Y. Higgs
Producer
imdb.com/name/nm2551143

TELEVISA USA
Production company and distributor

1601 Cloverfield Blvd., South Tower, Suite 200
Santa Monica, CA 90404
310-255-5083

soniagambaro@televisa.com.mx
televisa.com/us
imdb.com/company/co0468558
linkedin.com/company/televisa
facebook.com/TelevisaUSA
twitter.com/Televisa_USA

Does not accept any unsolicited material. Project types include TV. Genres include drama and romance.

TELEVISION 360
Production company

9111 Wilshire Blvd.
Beverly Hills, CA 90210
310-272-7000

imdb.com/company/co0335036

Does not accept any unsolicited material. Project types include TV. Genres include reality, comedy, fantasy, and drama.

TEMPEST PRODUCTIONS
Production company

1211 N Windomere
Dallas, TX 75208
214-942-8830

Tempest@Tempestproductions.com
tempestproductions.org
imdb.com/company/co0068884
facebook.com/tempestaustralia

Does not accept any unsolicited material. Project types include short films. Genres include comedy and horror.

TEMPLE HILL ENTERTAINMENT
Production company

9255 W Sunset Blvd
West Hollywood, CA 90069
310-270-4383 (phone)
310-270-4395 (fax)

templehillent.com
imdb.com/company/co0069651
facebook.com/pages/Temple-Hill-Entertainment/
   336532409773139
twitter.com/TempleHillEnt

Does not accept any unsolicited material. Project types
include feature films and TV. Genres include drama,
thriller, family, comedy, and fantasy. Established in
2006.

Isaac Klausner
Creative Executive
imdb.com/name/nm2327099
linkedin.com/pub/isaac-klausner/16/25b/151
facebook.com/isaac.klausner

Wyck Godfrey
Partner
imdb.com/name/nm0324041
twitter.com/wyckgodfrey
Assistant: Jaclyn Huntling

Marty Bowen
Partner
imdb.com/name/nm2125212
Assistant: Charlie Morrison

Tracy Nyberg
Sr. Vice-President
imdb.com/name/nm2427937

TEMPLE STREET PRODUCTIONS
Production company and distributor

595 Adelaide St. E
Toronto, ON M5A 1N8
Canada
416-591-0065 (phone)
416-591-0075 (fax)

info@templestreetproductions.com
templestreetproductions.com
imdb.com/company/co0069372

facebook.com/pages/Temple-Street-Productions/
   101253038932
twitter.com/TempleStreet

Does not accept any unsolicited material. Genres
include science fiction.

Emma Green
Actress
imdb.com/name/nm2543084

TEN ACRE FILMS
Production company

PO Box 303516
Austin, TX 78703

imdb.com/company/co0516591

Does not accept any unsolicited material. Project types
include feature films. Genres include comedy, drama,
documentary, and thriller. Established in 2014.

TENAFLY FILM COMPANY
Production company

5670 Wilshire Blvd. #2540
Los Angeles, CA 90036
310-933-3190

1965 Broadway Suite 29E
New York, NY 10023

info@tenaflyfilm.com
tenaflyfilm.com
imdb.com/company/co0012094
linkedin.com/company/tenafly-film-co
twitter.com/TenaflyFilmCo

Does not accept any unsolicited material. Project types
include commercials, TV, and feature films. Genres
include comedy and drama. Established in 1996.

TENDER PRODUCTION CO.
Production company

4-12-25-2F
Minami Azabu
Minato, Tokyo 106-0047
Japan
03-5798-7775 (phone)
03-5798-7776 (fax)

info@tenderpro.net
tenderpro.net
imdb.com/company/co0376851

Does not accept any unsolicited material. Project types include TV. Genres include drama.

TEN/FOUR PICTURES
Production company

1011 N Fuller Ave, Suite C
Los Angeles, CA 90046
323-851-5400 (phone)
323-851-5401 (fax)

info@tenfourpictures.com
imdb.com/company/co0259260
facebook.com/tenfourpictures
twitter.com/tenfourpictures

Does not accept any unsolicited material. Project types include feature films. Genres include documentary, thriller, and comedy.

TEN THIRTEEN PRODUCTIONS
Production company

PO Box 3210
Santa Monica, CA 90408

imdb.com/company/co0078377

Does not accept any unsolicited material. Project types include TV and feature films. Genres include action and science fiction. Established in 1993.

TEN THIRTY-ONE PICTURES ENTERTAINMENT
Production company and distributor

888-896-1031

P.O. Box 604
Burbank, CA 91503
818-570-1031

tenthirtyonepictures.com
imdb.com/company/co0233499
linkedin.com/company/ten-thirty-one-pictures-
    entertainment-inc

Does not accept any unsolicited material. Project types include feature films. Genres include drama, thriller, and romance. Established in 2002.

TEN X TEN ENTERTAINMENT
Production company

1640 S Sepulveda Blvd
Ste 450
Los Angeles, CA 90025
310-575-1235

imdb.com/company/co0112253

Does not accept any unsolicited material. Project types include TV. Genres include reality, comedy, and documentary. Established in 2004.

Brad Austin
Director of Development
310-575-1235
imdb.com/name/nm4114614

Ken Mok
Principal
310-575-1235
imdb.com/name/nm0596298

TERNION PICTURES
Production company

1010 W Martin Luther King Jr Blvd
Austin, TX 78701
512-322-0896 (phone)
512-708-9393 (fax)

info@ternionpictures.com
ternionpictures.com
imdb.com/company/co0274496
facebook.com/TernionPictures
twitter.com/TernionPictures

Does not accept any unsolicited material. Project types include feature films and TV. Genres include crime, comedy, science fiction, animation, and romance. Established in 1992.

TERNION PRODUCTIONS
Production company

2850 Ocean Park Blvd., Suite 300
Santa Monica, CA 90405

imdb.com/company/co0236875

Does not accept any unsolicited material. Project types include TV and feature films. Genres include drama, action, and comedy.

TERRA FIRMA FILMS
Production company

3601 Wilshire Blvd
Beverly Hills, CA 90210
310-480-5676 (phone)
310-862-4717 (fax)

info@terrafirmafilms.com
terrafirmafilms.com
imdb.com/company/co0163783

Accepts query letters from unproduced, unrepresented writers via email. Project types include feature films. Genres include comedy, action, family, romance, and drama. Established in 2003.

Josh Shader
Producer
imdb.com/name/nm1003558
linkedin.com/pub/josh-shader/9/1b8/547
twitter.com/JoshShader

Adam Herz
President
imdb.com/name/nm0381221

TERRA PRODUCTIONS
Production company

9900 SW 60 CT
Miami, FL 33156
305-409-0890

towerkrauss@terramiami.com
terraproductions.com/pages/1
imdb.com/company/co0168230

Does not accept any unsolicited material. Genres include documentary.

TERRIMEL ENTERTAINMENT
Production company

5555 Melrose Ave, Dreier Bldg. Suite 210
Los Angeles, CA 90038
323-997-7735

terri@terrimelentertainment.com
terrimelentertainment.com
imdb.com/company/co0396931
facebook.com/terrimelentertainment
twitter.com/TERRIMELent

Does not accept any unsolicited material. Project types include feature films. Genres include comedy and romance.

TEXAS AVENUE FILMS
Production company

701 Texas Ave
Austin, TX 78705
512-477-8049

imdb.com/company/co0367383

Does not accept any unsolicited material. Project types include feature films. Genres include drama. Established in 2008.

TEXAS DREAM IMAGING
Production company and distributor

5105 China Berry Dr
McKinney, TX 75070
214-448-0871

tdijoey@yahoo.com
imdb.com/company/co0152087

Does not accept any unsolicited material. Project types include short films. Genres include horror.

THANKS LAB
Production company and distributor

2-14-5-203
Shibuya
Shibuya, Tokyo 150-0002
Japan
03-6805-0310 (phone)
03-5464-2529 (fax)

info@thankslab.com
imdb.com/company/co0295232

Does not accept any unsolicited material. Project types include TV. Genres include drama.

Motoo Kawabata
C.E.O. (Producer)
imdb.com/name/nm1583173

THARSIS FILMS ENTERTAINMENT
Production company

7950 NW 53rd St Suite 337
Miami, FL FL 33166

tharsisfilms@tharsisfilms.com
tharsisfilms.com
imdb.com/company/co0495675

Does not accept any unsolicited material. Genres include thriller and documentary.

THE 3D FILM FACTORY
Distributor

7974 Mission Bonita Dr. San Diego, CA 92120
619-384-4014

info@3dfilmfactory.com
3dfilmfactory.com
imdb.com/company/co0236432
facebook.com/3D-Film-Factory-153911355749

Does not accept any unsolicited material. Genres include documentary, family, animation, action, and horror.

THE 777 GROUP
Production company

12021 Wilshire Blvd. Ste. 110
Los Angeles, CA 90025
424-209-7770

info@the777group.com
the777group.com
imdb.com/company/co0133127
twitter.com/777group

Accepts query letters from unproduced, unrepresented writers via email. Project types include TV. Genres include animation, comedy, drama, and non-fiction.

Marcello Robinson
CEO
312-834-7770
info@the777group.com
imdb.com/name/nm0732883
linkedin.com/pub/marcello-robinson/6/56/912

THE AMERICAN FILM COMPANY
Production company

c/o Business Affairs, Inc.
2415 Main St, 2nd Floor
Santa Monica, CA 90405
310-392-0777

info@americanfilmco.com
theamericanfilmcompany.com
imdb.com/company/co0176864
facebook.com/theamericanfilmcompany
twitter.com/AmericanFilmCo

Accepts query letters from unproduced, unrepresented writers via email. Project types include feature films. Genres include thriller, drama, period, and non-fiction. Established in 2008.

Brian Falk
President
imdb.com/name/nm1803137
twitter.com/brifalk

THE ASYLUM
Production company, studio, and distributor

72 E Palm Ave
Burbank, CA 91502
323-850-1214 (phone)
818-260-9811 (fax)

comments@theasylum.cc
theasylum.cc
imdb.com/company/co0042909
linkedin.com/company/the-asylum
facebook.com/AsylumFilms
twitter.com/theasylumcc

Does not accept any unsolicited material. Project types include feature films. Genres include fantasy, action, horror, thriller, and science fiction. Established in 1997.

Mark Quod
Post Production Supervisor
quod@theasylum.cc
imdb.com/name/nm0704517

Micho Rutare
Director of Development
micho@theasylum.cc
imdb.com/name/nm3026436
twitter.com/MichoRutare

David Rimawi
Partner
rimawi@theasylum.cc
imdb.com/name/nm0727235

David Michael Latt
Partner
imdb.com/name/nm0490375

Joseph Lawson
Visual Effects Supervisor
lawson@theasylum.cc
imdb.com/name/nm1037472

Lisa Ries
Post Production Sound Assistant
ries@theasylum.cc
imdb.com/name/nm2917991

Paul Bales
Partner
bales@theasylum.cc
imdb.com/name/nm0050097

THE AV CLUB
Production company

2629 Main St #211
Santa Monica, CA 90405
310-396-1165

avclub.com
facebook.com/theavclub
twitter.com/theavclub

Does not accept any unsolicited material. Project types include feature films. Genres include thriller, drama, documentary, comedy, science fiction, non-fiction, and romance.

Amy Robertson
Producer
imdb.com/name/nm1516144

THE BADHAM COMPANY
Production company and distributor

c/o Paradigm Agency
360 N Beverly Dr
Beverly Hills CA 90210
310-288-8000

c/o Rain Management
1800 Stanford St
Santa Monica, CA 90404
310-481-9800

ah@badhamcompany.com
johnbadham.com
imdb.com/company/co0054883

Accepts scripts from produced or represented writers. Project types include feature films and TV. Genres include non-fiction, family, and drama.

John Badham
Producer
imdb.com/name/nm0000824

THE BEAR MEDIA
Production company

1901 E. 51st St, Box 19
Austin, TX 78723
512-660-5540

cave@thebearmedia.com
thebearmedia.com
imdb.com/company/co0271535

Does not accept any unsolicited material. Genres include documentary and comedy.

THE BORSCHT CORP.
Production company and distributor

5859 Biscayne Blvd
Miami, FL 33137

contact@borschtcorp.com
borschtcorp.com
imdb.com/company/co0362467
linkedin.com/company/borscht-corporation

facebook.com/BorschtCorp
twitter.com/borschtcorp

Does not accept any unsolicited material. Project types include short films. Genres include drama, comedy, horror, fantasy, animation, and thriller. Established in 2011.

THE BOSKO GROUP

Production company, distributor, and sales agent

1367 Mockingbird Dr
Kent, OH 44241

imdb.com/company/co0194928

Does not accept any unsolicited material. Project types include TV and feature films. Genres include thriller, science fiction, and horror.

THE BRAKEFIELD COMPANY

Production company

3727 W Magnolia Blvd., #718
Burbank, CA 91505

info@thebrakefieldcompany.com
thebrakefieldcompany.com
imdb.com/company/co0344861
facebook.com/TheBrakefieldCompany
twitter.com/TheBrakefieldCo

Does not accept any unsolicited material. Project types include feature films. Genres include drama.

Jennifer Grace Cook

Creative Executive
imdb.com/name/nm1614490

Shawna Brakefield

CEO/President
imdb.com/name/nm1113538

THE BUENA VISTA MOTION PICTURES GROUP

Production company

500 S. Buena Vista St
Burbank, CA 91521
818-560-1000

facebook.com

Does not accept any unsolicited material. Project types include feature films.

THE BUREAU

Production company

18 Phipp St
2nd Floor
London - EC2A 4NU
United-Kingdom
+44-0207-033-0555

mail@thebureau.co.uk
thebureau.co.uk

Does not accept any unsolicited material. Project types include feature films. Genres include documentary, romance, drama, thriller, and comedy. Established in 2000.

Valentina Brazzini

linkedin.com/pub/valentina-brazzini/3/896/926

Soledad Gatti-Pascual

imdb.com/name/nm0309806
linkedin.com/pub/soledad-gatti-pascual/15/99/400

Bertrand Faivre

Producer
imdb.com/name/nm0265724
linkedin.com/pub/bertrand-faivre/11/2a1/b03

THE CALLING PRODUCTION, LLC

Production company

2901 1st Ave North
St. Petersburg, FL 33713
813-505-3622 (phone)
888-569-4668 (fax)

jamestmguyer@yahoo.com
arigothemovie.com
imdb.com/company/co0234450

Does not accept any unsolicited material. Project types include feature films. Genres include drama. Established in 2015.

THE CARBERG STUDIO

Production company

3732 Idlebrook Circle
214
Casselberry, FL 32707
954-646-2965 (phone)
425-642-2969 (fax)

ccarberg@gmail.com
imdb.com/company/co0196902

Does not accept any unsolicited material. Genres include crime and action.

THE COHEN MEDIA GROUP
Production company and distributor

750 Lexington Ave, 5th Floor, New York, NY, United States, 10022
646-380-7929

750 N. San Vicente Blvd Suite 1600
West Hollywood CA 90069
310-360-6409

cohenmedia.net
imdb.com/company/co0243890

Does not accept any unsolicited material. Project types include feature films and TV. Genres include family and drama.

THE COLLECTIVE
Production company and distributor

8383 Wilshire Blvd, Suite 1050, Beverly Hills , CA, United States, 90211
323-370-1500 (phone)
323-370-1555 (fax)

767 Fifth Ave 46th Floor
New York NY 10153
212-433-1229

office@thecollective-la.com
thecollective-la.com
imdb.com/company/co0416903

Does not accept any unsolicited material. Project types include feature films and TV. Genres include family, action, and drama.

THE CUTTING EDGE GROUP
Production company

18 Rodmarton St, London, United Kingdom, W1U 8BJ
011-442-074674488

8687 Melrose Ave Ninth Floor
Los Angeles CA 90069
310-967-2380

cuttingedgegroup.com
imdb.com/company/co0212862

Does not accept any unsolicited material. Project types include feature films. Genres include crime, family, drama, action, and thriller.

THE EDELSTEIN COMPANY
Production company

10351 Santa Monica Blvd.
Los Angeles, CA 90035
323-933-4051

imdb.com/company/co0155498

Does not accept any unsolicited material. Project types include TV.

Michael Edelstein
Producer
imdb.com/name/nm024904

THE EXCHANGE
Production company, distributor, and sales agent

5670 Wilshire Blvd, Suite 2540, Los Angeles, CA, United States, 90036
310-935-3760 (phone)
424-228-3760 (fax)

info@theexchange.ws
theexchange.ws
imdb.com/company/co0360871

Does not accept any unsolicited material. Project types include feature films and TV. Genres include family, thriller, action, and drama.

THE FIGHTING ARTS OF BORNEO
Production company

3613 Bayview Rd
Miami, FL 33133

joel.fendelman@gmail.com

imdb.com/company/co0456902

Does not accept any unsolicited material. Genres include documentary.

THE FILM SALES COMPANY
Production company, distributor, and sales agent

165 Madison Ave, Suite 601, New York City, NY, United States, 10016
212-481-5020 (phone)
212-481-5021 (fax)

contact@filmsalescorp.com
filmsalescorp.com
imdb.com/company/co0178293

Does not accept any unsolicited material. Project types include TV and feature films. Genres include action, thriller, family, comedy, and drama.

THE FRED ROGERS COMPANY
Production company

2100 Wharton St, Ste 700
Pittsburgh, PA 15203
877-677-6437

info@fci.org
fci.org
imdb.com/company/co0350264
facebook.com/pages/The-Fred-Rogers-Company/
    134212499968848
twitter.com/FredRogersCo

Does not accept any unsolicited material. Project types include TV. Genres include family and animation. Established in 1971.

THE FYZZ FACILITY
Production company, distributor, and financing company

94 Cleveland St, London, United Kingdom, W1T 6NW
011-440-2073887868

The Fyzz Facility LP 9460 Wilshire Blvd. 5th Floor Beverly Hills CA 90212
310-777-4544

info@thefyzz.com
thefyzz.com

imdb.com/company/co0498672

Does not accept any unsolicited material. Project types include TV. Genres include family and drama.

THE GALLANT ENTERTAINMENT GROUP
Production company and distributor

16161 Ventura Blvd, Suite 664
Encino, CA 91436
818-905-9848 (phone)
818-906-9965 (fax)

mog@gallantentertainment.com
gallantentertainment.com
imdb.com/company/co0018692
linkedin.com/company/the-gallant-entertainment-
    group
twitter.com/GallantEntGroup

Does not accept any unsolicited material. Project types include feature films, TV, and short films. Genres include documentary, thriller, romance, action, science fiction, and drama. Established in 1992.

K.R. Gallant
Operations
krg@gallantentertainment.com

Michael Gallant
Producer
imdb.com/name/nm0302572
linkedin.com/pub/michael-o-gallant/45/733/506

THE GLOBAL FILM INITIATIVE
Production company and distributor

3701 Sacramento St, #401, San Francisco, CA, United States, 94118
415-934-9500 (phone)
415-934-9501 (fax)

gfi-info@globalfilm.org
globalfilm.org

Does not accept any unsolicited material. Project types include TV. Genres include family and drama.

THE GOATSINGERS
Production company

177 W. Broadway, 2nd Floor
New York, NY 10013
212-966-3045 (phone)
212-966-4362 (fax)

imdb.com/company/co0000042

Does not accept any unsolicited material. Project types include feature films and TV.

Harvey Keitel
President/Actor/Producer
imdb.com/name/nm0000172

THE GOLD COMPANY
Production company

499 N Canon Dr, Suite 306
Beverly Hills, CA 90210
310-270-4653

imdb.com/company/co0224609

Accepts query letters from unproduced, unrepresented writers. Project types include feature films. Genres include comedy.

Jessica Green
Executive Vice President of Production
imdb.com/name/nm2783652

Eric L. Gold
Principal
imdb.com/name/nm0324970
linkedin.com/pub/eric-l-townley/2/a14/63

THE GOLDSTEIN COMPANY
Production company

1644 Courtney Ave
Los Angeles, CA 90046
310-659-9511

garywgoldstein.com
linkedin.com/company/the-goldstein-company
facebook.com/garywgoldstein
twitter.com/garywgoldstein

Accepts query letters from unproduced, unrepresented writers via email. Project types include TV, commercials, and feature films. Genres include thriller, reality, non-fiction, comedy, action, and romance.

Gary Goldstein
Producer
gary@garywgoldstein.com
imdb.com/name/nm0326214
linkedin.com/in/garywgoldstein
twitter.com/garywgoldstein

Sandra Tomita
imdb.com/name/nm0866739

THE GOODMAN COMPANY
Production company

8491 Sunset Blvd, Suite 329
Los Angeles, CA 90069
323-655-0719

ilyssagoodman@sbcglobal.net
thegoodmancompany.com

Accepts query letters from unproduced, unrepresented writers. Project types include TV and feature films. Genres include drama, comedy, non-fiction, family, and reality.

Ilyssa Goodman
Executive
imdb.com/name/nm1058415
linkedin.com/in/ilyssagoodman

THE GOTHAM GROUP
Production company

9255 Sunset Blvd, Suite 515
Los Angeles, CA 90069
310-285-0001 (phone)
310-285-0077 (fax)

gotham-group.com
imdb.com/company/co0080580
linkedin.com/company/the-gotham-group

Does not accept any unsolicited material. Project types include TV, feature films, and commercials. Genres include science fiction, family, action, comedy, reality, non-fiction, fantasy, drama, and animation.

Julie Kane-Ritsch
jkr@gotham-group.com
imdb.com/name/nm1415970
linkedin.com/pub/julie-kane-ritsch/a/6a9/322

Peter McHugh
peter@gotham-group.com

Ellen Goldsmith-Vein
egv@gotham-group.com
imdb.com/name/nm1650412

THE GREENBERG GROUP
Sales agent

2029 S Westgate Ave
Los Angeles, CA 90025

lgreenberg@thegreenberggroup.com
thegreenberggroup.com
imdb.com/company/co0237762
linkedin.com/company/the-greenberg-group
facebook.com/pages/The-Greenberg-Group/
    741724785853691

Accepts query letters from unproduced, unrepresented writers via email. Project types include commercials, feature films, and TV. Genres include action, reality, thriller, and non-fiction.

Randy Greenberg
randy@greenberggroup.com
imdb.com/name/nm2985843
twitter.com/RandyGreenberg

THE GROUP ENTERTAINMENT
Production company

The Anchor Building
2509 Portland Ave,
Louisville KY, 40212
502-561-1162

115 W 29th St #1102
New York, NY 10001
212-868-5233 (phone)
212-504-3082 (fax)

info@thegroupentertainment.com
thegroupentertainment.com
imdb.com/company/co0181699

Does not accept any unsolicited material. Project types include feature films and TV. Genres include drama, romance, reality, comedy, action, and non-fiction.

Kyle Luker
Partner
kyle@thegroupentertainment.com
imdb.com/name/nm1739392

Jill McGrath
Partner
jill@thegroupentertainment.com

Gil Holland
Partner
imdb.com/name/nm0390693

Rebecca Atwood
Creative Executive
rebecca@thegroupentertainment.com

THE HALCYON COMPANY
Production company

8455 Beverly Blvd
Penthouse
Los Angeles, CA 90048
323-650-0222

info@thehalcyoncompany.com
thehalcyoncompany.com
imdb.com/company/co0175646
facebook.com/pages/The-Halcyon-Company/
    109874619030902
twitter.com/TheHalcyonCo

Does not accept any unsolicited material. Project types include feature films. Genres include science fiction, action, and thriller. Established in 2006.

Victor Kubicek
CEO
imdb.com/name/nm2127497

Derek Anderson
CEO
imdb.com/name/nm2203770

THE HAL LIEBERMAN COMPANY
Production company and studio

8522 National Blvd, Suite 108
Culver City, CA 90232
310-202-1929 (phone)
323-850-5132 (fax)

imdb.com/company/co0152063

facebook.com/pages/The-Hal-Lieberman-Company/
107021165998090

Accepts query letters from unproduced, unrepresented writers via email. Project types include feature films. Genres include drama, family, fantasy, horror, and thriller.

Dan Scheinkman
Vice-President
linkedin.com/pub/dan-scheinkman/7/49/a59

Hal Lieberman
Principal
imdb.com/name/nm0509386
linkedin.com/pub/hal-lieberman/13/a7b/5b8

THE HATCHERY
Production company and distributor

4751 Wilshire Blvd.
Third Floor
Los Angeles, CA 90010
323-549-4360 (phone)
818-748-4615/Attn: Dan Angel (fax)

dangel@thehatcheryllc.com
thehatchery.co.za
imdb.com/company/co0131267

Does not accept any unsolicited material. Project types include TV and feature films. Genres include family, horror, comedy, and science fiction.

Dan Angel
Founder
dangel@thehatcheryllc.com
imdb.com/name/nm0029445
linkedin.com/pub/dan-angel/5/74a/19a

THE HECHT COMPANY
Production company and distributor

5455 8th St #34
Carpinteria, CA 93013
805-745-1007

hechtco@aol.com
imdb.com/company/co0080878

Accepts query letters from unproduced, unrepresented writers via email. Project types include TV and feature films. Genres include drama, non-fiction, reality, and thriller.

Duffy Hecht
Producer
imdb.com/name/nm0372953

THE HELPERN COMPANY

10323 Santa Monica Blvd., Suite 101
Los Angeles, CA 90025

imdb.com/name/nm0375809

Does not accept any unsolicited material. Project types include feature films.

David Helpern
Producer
imdb.com/name/nm0375809

THE IMAGINARIUM STUDIOS
Production company

Ealing Studios
Ealing Green
London W5 5EP
UK
+44 20 3597 7304 (phone)
+44 20 7836 6947 (fax)

enquiries@theimaginariumstudios.com
theimaginariumstudios.com
imdb.com/company/co0373005
facebook.com/imaginariumstudiosuk
twitter.com/imaginariumuk

Does not accept any unsolicited material. Project types include short films and feature films. Genres include drama and fantasy.

Andy Serkis
Producer
imdb.com/name/nm0785227

THE INDIE ADMIN
Production company and sales agent

1003 Riverside Dr
Old Hickory, TN 37138
323-828-9911

nadia@theindieadmin.com

imdb.com/company/co0423386

Does not accept any unsolicited material. Project types include TV and feature films. Genres include crime, thriller, and action.

THE JAVELINA FILM COMPANY
Production company

200 E Grayson St
#104
San Antonio, TX 78215
210-822-8513

imdb.com/company/co0029146

Does not accept any unsolicited material. Genres include drama.

THE JIM HENSON COMPANY
Production company

1416 N La Brea Ave
Hollywood, CA 90028
323-802-1500 (phone)
323-802-1825 (fax)

37-18 Northern Blvd, Suite 400
Long Island City, NY 11101
212-794-2400 (phone)
212-439-7452 (fax)

info@henson.com
henson.com
imdb.com/company/co0095015
linkedin.com/company/the-jim-henson-company
facebook.com/hensoncompany

Does not accept any unsolicited material. Project types include feature films, commercials, TV, and theater. Genres include non-fiction, animation, comedy, fantasy, family, science fiction, and reality. Established in 1958.

Brian Henson
Chairman
imdb.com/name/nm0005008

Halle Stanford
Executive Vice President of Children's Entertainment
imdb.com/name/nm1277553
linkedin.com/pub/halle-stanford/1a/22a/647

THE KONIGSBERG COMPANY
Production company

7919 W Sunset Blvd., 2nd Floor
Los Angeles, CA 90046
323-845-1000

imdb.com/company/co006938

Does not accept any unsolicited material. Project types include feature films and TV. Genres include drama.

Frank Konigsberg
Producer
imdb.com/name/nm0465119

THE LADD COMPANY
Production company

9255 Sunset Blvd., Suite 620
West Hollywood, CA 90069
310-777-2060 (phone)
310-777-2061 (fax)

imdb.com/company/co0042559
facebook.com/The-Ladd-Company-212831953834

Does not accept any unsolicited material. Project types include feature films.

Alan Ladd Jr.
President
imdb.com/name/nm0480440

THE LEVINSON/FONTANA COMPANY
Production company

185 Broome St
New York, NY 10002
212-206-3585

tom@tomfontana.com
tomfontana.com
imdb.com/company/co0068745

Does not accept any unsolicited material. Project types include TV.

Tom Fontana
Writer/Executive Producer
imdb.com/name/nm0284956

Barry Levinson
Director/Writer/Executive Producer
imdb.com/name/nm0001469

THE LITTLEFIELD COMPANY
Production company and distributor

500 S Buena Vista St Animation Building, Suite 3D-2
Burbank, CA 91521
818-560-2280 (phone)
818-560-3775 (fax)

imdb.com/company/co0080851

Does not accept any unsolicited material. Project types
include TV. Genres include drama.

Warren Littlefield
Principal
818-560-2280
imdb.com/name/nm0514716
Assistant: Patricia Mann

THE LITTLE FILM COMPANY
Production company

The Little Film Company UK
5 Rama Court, Harrow on the Hill
Middlesex, HA1 3NG

12930 Ventura Blvd, Suite #822
Studio City, CA 91604
818-762-6999

info@thelittlefilmcompany.com
thelittlefilmcompany.com
facebook.com/The-Little-Film-
    Company-77023658332

Does not accept any unsolicited material. Project types
include feature films. Genres include comedy,
romance, action, documentary, and fantasy.

Robbie Little
Co-President
imdb.com/name/nm0514655

THE MANHATTAN PROJECT LTD.
Production company

1775 Broadway, Suite 410
New York , NY 10019
212-258-2541

imdb.com/title/tt0091472
linkedin.com/company/manhattan-project-ltd

Does not accept any unsolicited material. Project types
include feature films and TV.

Kit Golden
President
imdb.com/name/nm0325455

David Brown
Producer
imdb.com/name/nm0113360

THE MARK GOKDON COMPANY
Production company

12235 W Olympic Blvd, Suite 230
Los Angeles, CA 93064
310-843-6301 (phone)
310-923-103 (fax)

imdb.com/company/co0085751
linkedin.com/company/the-mark-gordon-company

Does not accept any unsolicited material. Project types
include feature films and TV. Genres include drama
and action.

Mark Gordon
imdb.com/name/nm0330428

THE MAZUR/KAPLAN COMPANY
Production company and distributor

3204 Pearl St
Santa Monica, CA 90405
310-450-5838

info@mazurkaplan.com
mazurkaplan.com
imdb.com/company/co0247200

Does not accept any unsolicited material. Project types
include TV and feature films. Genres include non-
fiction, thriller, fantasy, reality, family, romance, and
comedy. Established in 2009.

Paula Mazur
Producer
310-450-5838
imdb.com/name/nm0563394

Kimi Armstrong Stein
Vice-President
kimi@mazurkaplan.com
imdb.com/name/nm2148964

Mitchell Kaplan
Producer
imdb.com/name/nm3125086

THE MOVIE STUDIO
Production company

530 N Federal Highway
Ft. Lauderdale, FL 33301
954-332-6600

GSV@TheMovieStudio.org
themoviestudio.co
imdb.com/company/co0439485
facebook.com/themoviestudioorg

Does not accept any unsolicited material. Genres include horror and comedy.

THE OCTOBER PEOPLE, LLC
Production company

San Diego, CA

Seattle, WA
619-500-2854

info@theoctoberpeople.net
theoctoberpeople.net
imdb.com/company/co0397558
facebook.com/TheOctoberPeople
twitter.com/October_People

Does not accept any unsolicited material. Project types include feature films and short films. Genres include thriller and horror. Established in 2013.

THEO FILMS
Production company

124 Major St
Toronto, ON M5S 2L2
Canada

imdb.com/company/co0314380

Does not accept any unsolicited material. Project types include short films and TV. Genres include drama and fantasy.

THE ORCHARD
Production company and distributor

23 E 4th St., 3rd Floor, New York, NY, United States, 10003

theorchard.com
imdb.com/company/co0468371

Does not accept any unsolicited material. Project types include TV. Genres include comedy, family, drama, and thriller.

THE ORPHANAGE
Production company

39 Mesa St, Suite 201
San Francisco, CA 94129
415-561-2570

6725 Sunset Blvd., Suite 220
Los Angeles, CA 90028
323-469-6700 (phone)
415-561-2570 (fax)

imdb.com/company/co0089909

Does not accept any unsolicited material. Project types include feature films. Genres include thriller, family, fantasy, and science fiction.

THE PITT GROUP
Production company

8750 Wilshire Blvd.
Suite 301
Beverly Hills, CA 90211
310-246-4800 (phone)
310-275-9258 (fax)

imdb.com/company/co0034610

Accepts query letters from unproduced, unrepresented writers. Project types include feature films and TV.

Genres include crime, animation, comedy, romance, drama, and detective. Established in 2000.

Jeremy Conrady
Creative Executive
jconrady@pittgroup.com
imdb.com/name/nm262042
linkedin.com/pub/jeremy-conrady/a/b29/787

Lou Pitt
Principal
lpitt@pittgroup.com
imdb.com/name/nm2229316
linkedin.com/pub/lou-pitt/6/a28/2b5

THE PRODUCERS FILMS
Production company

111 Priory Rd
London NW6 3NN
UK
+44207-636-4226 (phone)
+44207-636-4099 (fax)

info@theproducersfilms.co.uk
theproducersfilms.co.uk
imdb.com/company/co0111274

Does not accept any unsolicited material. Project types include feature films. Genres include drama and comedy.

Jeanna Polley
Producer
imdb.com/name/nm0689571

THE RADMIN COMPANY
Production company and distributor

9201 Wilshire Blvd, Suite 102
Beverly Hills, CA 90210
310-274-9515 (phone)
310-274-0739 (fax)

queries@radmincompany.com
radmincompany.com
imdb.com/company/co0040878

Does not accept any unsolicited material. Project types include feature films. Genres include romance, comedy, and drama. Established in 1993.

Linne Radmin
CEO
imdb.com/name/nm0705709
linkedin.com/pub/linne-radmin/15/b75/951

THERE'S ENTERPRISE
Production company and distributor

4-14-19-4F
Ginza
Chuo, Tokyo 104-8138
Japan
+81.3.3542.1951 (phone)
+81.3.3542.1913 (fax)

info@theres.co.jp
imdb.com/company/co0064637

Does not accept any unsolicited material. Genres include science fiction, horror, action, and drama.

THE SAFRAN COMPANY
Production company

9663 Santa Monica Blvd.
Suite 840
Beverly Hills, CA 90210
310-278-1450

imdb.com/company/co0179825
linkedin.com/company/the-safran-company

Does not accept any unsolicited material. Project types include feature films and TV. Genres include family and comedy. Established in 2006.

Joan Mao
Director of Development
imdb.com/name/nm1619641

Peter Safran
imdb.com/name/nm0755911

THE SCORE GROUP
Production company and distributor

4931 SW 75th Ave.
Miami, FL 33155

imdb.com/company/co0067366

Does not accept any unsolicited material.

THE SEAN DANIEL COMPANY

Production company

12429 Ventura Court, 2nd Floor
Studio City, CA 91604
818-508-8165

imdb.com/name/nm0199733

Does not accept any unsolicited material. Project types include feature films. Genres include thriller, comedy, horror, and action.

Sean Daniel
Producer
imdb.com/name/nm0199733

Jason Brown
Development
imdb.com/name/nm0113798

THE SOCIETY FOR ARTS

Production company and sales agent

1112 N. Milwaukee Ave
Chicago, IL 60642
773-486-9612

christopherkamyszew@msn.com
imdb.com/company/co0272024

Does not accept any unsolicited material. Project types include TV. Genres include comedy and drama.

THE SOLUTION ENTERTAINMENT GROUP

Production company, distributor, and sales agent

6525 Sunset Blvd., Bungalow 4, Hollywood, CA, United States, 90028
323-723-3217

info@thesolutionent.com
thesolutionent.com
imdb.com/company/co0332559

Does not accept any unsolicited material. Project types include TV and feature films. Genres include family, drama, romance, thriller, and comedy.

THE STEVE TISCH COMPANY

Production company

10202 W Washington Blvd
Culver City, CA 90232
310-841-4330

imdb.com/company/co0024369

Accepts query letters from unproduced, unrepresented writers. Project types include feature films. Genres include thriller, comedy, drama, and action. Established in 1984.

Steve Tisch
Chairman
imdb.com/name/nm0005494

Lacy Boughn
Director of Development
imdb.com/name/nm2064419

THESTREAM.TV

Production company and distributor

6161 Santa Monica Blvd #401
Los Angeles, CA 90038
310-424-5197

thestreamtv@thestream.tv
thestream.tv
imdb.com/company/co0213809
facebook.com/pages/theStreamtv/316864921689297
twitter.com/thestreamtv

Does not accept any unsolicited material. Project types include TV. Genres include reality.

THE SWEET SHOP

1011 N. Fuller Ave, Suite G
West Hollywood, CA 90046
424-258-1000

pgarrett@thesweetshop.tv
thesweetshop.tv
linkedin.com/company/the-sweet-shop
facebook.com/thesweetshopfilms
twitter.com/_thesweetshop

Does not accept any unsolicited material. Project types include TV, commercials, and short films.

Laura Thoel
Executive Producer
laura@thesweetshop.tv

Preston Garrett
Head of Production
pgarrett@thesweetshop.tv

Dina Morales
Producer
dmorales@thesweetshop.tv

THE TANABE AGENCY
Production company

2-21-4
Aobadai
Meguro, Tokyo 153-0042
Japan
03-3791-2211 (phone)
03-3791-2215 (fax)

tanabe-agency.co.jp
imdb.com/company/co0165557

Does not accept any unsolicited material. Project types include TV. Genres include drama and fantasy.

Shôchi Tanabe
President (Executive)
imdb.com/name/nm4299405

THE TELEVISION SYNDICATION COMPANY (TVS)
Production company and distributor

520 Sabal Lake Dr., Suite 108
Longwood, FL 32779
407-788-6407 (phone)
407-788-4397 (fax)

mary@tvsco.com (script submissions)
cassie@tvsco.com (general)
tvsco.com
imdb.com/company/co0095845
linkedin.com/company/the-television-syndication-company
facebook.com/TelevisionSyndicationCo

Accepts query letters from unproduced, unrepresented writers via email. Project types include feature films, short films, and TV. Genres include family, drama, documentary, non-fiction, reality, and period. Established in 1989.

THE TRAVELING PICTURE SHOW COMPANY
Production company and financing company

1531 N Cahuenga Blvd, Los Angeles, CA, United States, 90028
323-769-1115

info@travelingpictureshow.tv
tpscfilms.com
imdb.com/company/co0115922

Does not accept any unsolicited material. Project types include feature films and TV. Genres include drama, fantasy, family, and thriller.

THE WALT DISNEY COMPANY
Production company, studio, and distributor

500 S Buena Vista St
Burbank, CA 91521
818-560-1000 (phone)
818-560-2500 (fax)

thewaltdisneycompany.com
imdb.com/company/co0044374
linkedin.com/company/the-walt-disney-compan
twitter.com/DisneyPost

Does not accept any unsolicited material. Project types include TV. Genres include animation, drama, non-fiction, fantasy, family, myth, action, and comedy. Established in 1923.

Rita Ferro
imdb.com/name/nm3474908
linkedin.com/pub/rita-ferro/8/31a/9aa
facebook.com/rita.ferro.980

Robert Iger
President
bob.iger@disney.com
imdb.com/name/nm2250609

Mary Ann Hughes
Vice-President
imdb.com/name/nm3134377

THE WEINSTEIN COMPANY
Production company and distributor

345 Hudson St
New York, NY 10014
646-862-3400

99 Hudson St.
New York, NY 10013
212-845-8600

Canaletto House
39 Beak St.
London, United Kingdom, W1F 9SA
011-442-074946180

9100 Wilshire Blvd, Suite 700W
Beverly Hills, CA 90212
424-204-4800

375 Greenwich St, Lobby A
New York, NY 10013-2376
212-941-3800 (phone)
212-941-3949 (fax)

info@weinsteinco.com
weinsteinco.com
imdb.com/company/co0150452
linkedin.com/company/the-weinstein-company
facebook.com/weinsteinco
twitter.com/WeinsteinFilms

Does not accept any unsolicited material. Project types include TV and feature films. Genres include romance, myth, family, thriller, drama, comedy, animation, action, and non-fiction. Established in 2005.

Collin Creighton
Vice President (Production & Development)
imdb.com/name/nm3083758

Barbara Schneeweiss
Vice President (Development & Production for TV & Film)
imdb.com/name/nm0773679
linkedin.com/pub/barbara-schneeweiss/4/360/a46

Harvey Weinstein
Co-Chairman
imdb.com/name/nm0005544
linkedin.com/pub/harvey-weinstein/91/965/aa4
Assistant: Brendon Boyea

THE WOLPER ORGANIZATION
Production company and studio

4000 Warner Blvd.
Bldg. 14, Ste. 200
Burbank, CA 91504
818-123-1421 (phone)
818-123-1593 (fax)

wolperorg.com
imdb.com/company/co0089381

Does not accept any unsolicited material. Project types include TV and feature films. Genres include drama, detective, and crime. Established in 1987.

David L. Wolper
Actor
imdb.com/name/nm0938678

Sam Alexander
Director of Development
sam.alexander@wbtvprod.com
imdb.com/name/nm3303012
linkedin.com/pub/sam-alexander/4/904/117

Kevin Nickldus
Creative Director
imdb.com/name/nm2102454
linkedin.com/pub/kevin-nicklaus/15/668/48B

Mnrkf Whlperf
Executive Producer
imdb.com/name/nm0938679

THE ZANUCK COMPANY
Production company

16 Beverly Park
Beverly Hills, CA 90210
310-248-0281 (phone)
310-203-9117 (fax)

info@zanuckco.com
zanuckco.com
imdb.com/company/co0093750

Does not accept any unsolicited material. Project types include TV and feature films. Genres include romance, family, crime, drama, thriller, period, fantasy, comedy, and action. Established in 1988.

Dean Zanuck
Producer
310-204-3989
imdb.com/name/nm0953124

Richard D Zanuck
imdb.com/name/nm0005573

THINK FAMOUS
Production company

8100 Oak Ln
Suite 401
Miami Lakes, FL 33016
305-984-5256

contact@thinkfamous.com
imdb.com/company/co0462215
facebook.com/thinkfamous
twitter.com/thinkfamous

Does not accept any unsolicited material. Project types include TV. Genres include comedy.

THIRD WINDOW FILMS
Distributor and sales agent

18B the vale
London, England nw118sg
UK
+44784-945-5537

info@thirdwindowfilms.com
thirdwindowfilms.com
imdb.com/company/co0195174
facebook.com/thirdwindowfilms
twitter.com/thirdwindow

Does not accept any unsolicited material. Project types include TV and feature films. Genres include thriller and horror.

Adam Torel
Producer
imdb.com/name/nm2880008

THIRTEEN/WNET
Production company and distributor

825 Eighth Ave
New York, NY 10019
212-560-1313 (phone)
212-560-1314 (fax)

programming@thirteen.org
thirteen.org
imdb.com/company/co0369777

facebook.com/wnet-thirteen
twitter.com/thirteenny

Does not accept any unsolicited material. Project types include TV. Genres include family and drama.

THIS AMERICAN LIFE
Production company

153 W 27th St, Suite 1104
New York, NY 10001

web@thislife.org
thislife.org
imdb.com/company/co0328661

Does not accept any unsolicited material. Project types include feature films.

THOMAS PRODUCTIONS, ROB
Production company

1438 N Gower St, Bldg. 62
Los Angeles, CA 90028
323-468-5320

slaverats.com
imdb.com/company/co0175100

Does not accept any unsolicited material. Project types include TV. Genres include comedy and drama.

THOUGHT MOMENT MEDIA
Production company

5419 Hollywood Blvd, Suite C-142
Los Angeles, CA 90027
323-380-8662

info@thoughtmoment.com
thoughtmoment.com
imdb.com/company/co0397382
facebook.com/pages/Thought-Moment-Media/
    270162619826746
twitter.com/ThoughtMoment

Accepts scripts from produced or represented writers. Project types include feature films, short films, and TV.

THOUSAND WORDS
Distributor and sales agent

110 S Fairfax Ave, Suite 370
Los Angeles, CA 90036
323-936-4700 (phone)
323-936-4701 (fax)

info@thousand-words.com
thousand-words.com
imdb.com/title/tt0763831

Accepts query letters from unproduced, unrepresented writers via email. Project types include feature films. Genres include animation, thriller, and drama. Established in 2000.

Jonah Smith
Chairman
323-936-4700
info@thousand-words.com
imdb.com/name/nm0808819

Palmer West
Chairman
323-936-4700
info@thousand-words.com
imdb.com/name/nm0922279

Michael Van Vliet
Creative Executive
323-936-4700
info@thousand-words.com
imdb.com/name/nm2702900

THREE BLIND ARTISTS ENTERTAINMENT GROUP
Production company

145 S Glenoaks Blvd, Suite 462, Burbank , CA, United States, 91502
818-392-8150

info@threeblindartists.com
imdb.com/company/co0175003

Does not accept any unsolicited material. Project types include short films. Genres include drama.

THREE POINT CAPITAL, LLC.
Financing company

West Coast Office:, 2041 Rosecrans Ave, Suite 322, Manhattan Beach, CA, United States, 90245
310-546-8111

info@tpc.us
imdb.com/company/co0298611

Does not accept any unsolicited material.

Britt Fletcher
Executive
imdb.com/name/nm4035592

THREE STRANGE ANGELS
Production company

9050 W Washington Blvd
Culver City, CA 90232
310-840-8213

imdb.com/company/co0123752

Does not accept any unsolicited material. Project types include feature films. Genres include comedy and fantasy.

THREE STRONGE ANGELS, INC.
Production company

9350 W Washington Blvd
Culver City, CA 90232
310-540-8213

imdb.com/company/co0183490

Does not accept any unsolicited material. Project types include feature films. Genres include fantasy, action, and comedy.

Lindsay Doran
310-240-8213
imdb.com/name/nm0233386
Assistant: Natasha Khrolenko

THRESHOLD ENTERTAINMENT GROUP
Production company and distributor

1649 11th St
Santa Monica, CA 90404
310-452-8899 (phone)
310-452-0736 (fax)

info@thresholdentertainment.com
thethreshold.com
imdb.com/company/co0070928
linkedin.com/company/threshold-entertainment

facebook.com/pages/Threshold-Entertainment/
104003999636737

Does not accept any unsolicited material. Project types
include TV and feature films. Genres include fantasy
and science fiction.

THRESHOLD PICTURES
Production company

1280 S. W. Ivanhoe Blvd.
Orlando, FL 32804
Usa
407-489-5595

imdb.com/company/co0206031

Does not accept any unsolicited material. Project types
include short films. Genres include comedy.

THROTTLE FILMS
Production company

3900 Willow St
Ste 200
Dallas, TX 75226
214-276-7659

info@throttlepost.com
throttle-films.com
facebook.com/pages/Throttle-Films/
195526203823261

Does not accept any unsolicited material. Genres
include crime, action, and drama.

THROUGH FILMS
Production company

137 Larmont Blvd., Suite 150
Los Angeles, CA 90004
310-993-2124

marcus@throughfilms.com
throughfilms.com
imdb.com/company/co0282631
facebook.com/pages/Through-Films-LLC/
158983616009
twitter.com/throughfilmsllc

Does not accept any unsolicited material. Project types
include feature films. Genres include drama.

THUMP
Production company

188 Davenport Rd
Ste 202
Toronto, ON M5R 1J2
Canada
416-961-6278 (phone)
416-961-5608 (fax)

norstarfilms.com
imdb.com/company/co0274348

Does not accept any unsolicited material. Project types
include TV and short films. Genres include drama and
comedy.

Ilana Frank
Producer
imdb.com/name/nm0290957

THUNDERBIRD FILMS
Production company

165 Ave Rd
Suite 301
Toronto, Ontario
M5R 3S4

533 Smithe St.
Suite 401
Vancouver, British Columbia
V6B 6H1
604-683-3555 (phone)
604-707-0378 (fax)

10675 Santa Monica Blvd
Suite B
Los Angeles, California 90025

info@hunderbirdfilms.net
thunderbird.tv
imdb.com/company/co0163158
linkedin.com/company/thunderbird-films-inc-
facebook.com/pages/Thunderbird-Films
twitter.com/TbirdFilms

Does not accept any unsolicited material. Project types
include TV. Genres include comedy and drama.

Timothy Gamble
CEO
imdb.com/name/nm0303817
linkedin.com/pub/tim-gamble/66/b4b/895
facebook.com/tim.gamble.33

Alex Raffe
Head of Production & Development
alex@thunderbirdfilms.com
imdb.com/name/nm0706244
linkedin.com/pub/alex-raffe/2/65b/509
twitter.com/thunderbird.tvteam

Danielle Kreinik
Head of Development
imdb.com/name/nm2315742
linkedin.com/in/daniellekreinik

THUNDER ROAD PICTURES
Production company

1411 5th St Suite 400
Santa Monica, CA 90401
310-573-8885

imdb.com/company/co0172670

Does not accept any unsolicited material. Project types include feature films and TV. Genres include drama, detective, crime, action, non-fiction, and thriller. Established in 2003.

Basil Iwanyk
Owner
imdb.com/name/nm0412588

Kent Kubena
Sr. VP, Film & TV Development & Production
imdb.com/name/nm0473423
linkedin.com/in/kentkubena
Assistant: Noah Winter

Peter Lawson
President of Production
imdb.com/name/nm4498662
linkedin.com/pub/peter-j-lawson/6b/b11/282

Erica Lee
Vice-President
imdb.com/name/nm3102707

TICTOCK STUDIOS
Production company

479 Columbia Art District, Holland , MI, United States, 49423
616-393-6800

Info@TicTockStudios.com
tictockstudios.com
imdb.com/company/co0235945

Does not accept any unsolicited material. Project types include TV and feature films. Genres include drama, thriller, and family.

TIGER ASPECT PRODUCTIONS
Production company

4th Fl, Shepherd's Building Central
Charecroft Way
London, England W14 0EE
UK
+44 20 7434 6700 (phone)
+44 20 8222 4700 (fax)

general@tigeraspect.co.uk
tigeraspect.co.uk
imdb.com/company/co0103644

Does not accept any unsolicited material. Project types include TV. Genres include comedy.

TIGERLILY FILMS
Production company, distributor, and sales agent

23 Blandford Court
St Peters Way
London N1 4SA
UK
+44 20 7729 9845 (phone)
+44 20 7923 1001 (fax)

joe@tigerlilyfilms.com
tigerlilyfilms.com
imdb.com/company/co0104400
facebook.com/Tigerlily-
    productions-236756949709894
twitter.com/tigerlilyfilms

Does not accept any unsolicited material. Project types include TV. Genres include comedy, documentary, thriller, and drama.

Natasha Dack
Producer
imdb.com/name/nm0196513

TIGERLILY MEDIA
Production company

567 Bishop Gate Ln
Jacksonville, FL 32204
904-858-9880 (phone)
904-858-9887 (fax)

info@tigerlilymedia.com
tigerlilymedia.com
imdb.com/company/co0184260
facebook.com/tigerlilymedia
twitter.com/wearetigerlily

Does not accept any unsolicited material. Genres include comedy and drama.

TIG PRODUCTIONS
Production company

4450 Lakeside Dr, Suite 225
Burbank, CA 91505
818-260-8707

imdb.com/company/co0012524
facebook.com/pages/Tig-Productions/
    148567138520919

Does not accept any unsolicited material. Project types include feature films and TV. Genres include drama and thriller.

TIMBER CREATIVE GROUP
Production company

649 N. Mills Ave.
Orlando, FL 32803
407-895-7001 (phone)
407-895-7002 (fax)

info@timbercreativegroup.com
imdb.com/company/co0299129

Does not accept any unsolicited material. Genres include documentary.

TIMBERGROVE ENTERTAINMENT
Production company

4349 Elmer Ave
Studio City, CA 91602

imdb.com/company/co0155840

Does not accept any unsolicited material. Project types include feature films. Genres include comedy. Established in 2001.

TIM BURTON PRODUCTIONS
Production company and distributor

8033 Sunset Blvd, Suite 7500
West Hollywood, CA 90046
310-300-1670 (phone)
310-300-1671 (fax)

timburton.com
imdb.com/company/co0081851

Does not accept any unsolicited material. Project types include feature films. Genres include action, family, and fantasy. Established in 1989.

Tim Burton
Principal
310-300-1670
kory.edwrds@timburton.com
imdb.com/name/nm0000318

Derek Frey
Executive
derek@lazerfilm.com
imdb.com/name/nm0294553
linkedin.com/in/derekfreyfilms
facebook.com/DerekFreyFilms

TIMEGATE STUDIOS
Production company and distributor

14140 Southwest Freeway
Suite 400
Sugar Land, TX 77478
281-295-4263 (phone)
281-295-4095 (fax)

timegatestudios.com
imdb.com/company/co0030115
web.facebook.com/timegatestudios

Does not accept any unsolicited material.

TIME INC. STUDIOS
Production company

225 Liberty St
New York, NY 10281
212-522-1212

timeinc.com
imdb.com/company/co0259985
linkedin.com/company/time-inc.
facebook.com/TimeInc
twitter.com/TimeInc

Does not accept any unsolicited material. Project types
include TV and feature films. Genres include drama.

TITAN BROADCAST MANAGEMENT
Distributor

888 3rd St NW
Ste A
Atlanta, GA 30318
678-904-0555 (phone)
678-904-0556 (fax)

info@titanbroadcast.com
titanbroadcast.com
imdb.com/company/co0420978

Does not accept any unsolicited material. Project types
include TV. Genres include comedy and family.

TITMOUSE, INC.
Production company

6616 Lexington Ave
Los Angeles, CA 90038
323-466-7800

sales@titmouse.net
titmouse.net
imdb.com/company/co0186051
facebook.com/titmouse.cartoons

Does not accept any unsolicited material. Project types
include TV. Genres include animation and comedy.

TIWARY ENTERTAINMENT GROUP
Production company and financing company

1 Irving Place, Suite P8C
New York, NY 10003

212-477-6698 (phone)
212-477-5259 (fax)

info@tiwaryent.com
tiwaryent.com
imdb.com/company/co0187550
linkedin.com/company/tiwary-entertainment-group-
    ltd-
facebook.com/TiwaryEnt
twitter.com/TiwaryEnt

Does not accept any unsolicited material. Project types
include feature films. Genres include drama.

TLA RELEASING
Production company, distributor, and sales agent

234 Market St
5th Fl
Philadelphia, PA 19106
215-733-0608 (phone)
215-733-0668 (fax)

contact@tlareleasing.com
tlareleasing.com
imdb.com/company/co0057093

Does not accept any unsolicited material. Project types
include TV. Genres include comedy, drama, and
thriller.

Elliot Dal Pra London
Producer
imdb.com/name/nm2467243

TMC ENTERTAINMENT
Production company and distributor

11400 W Olympic Blvd # 200
Los Angeles, CA 90064
310-806-4400

contact@tmcent.tv
imdb.com/company/co0126495

Does not accept any unsolicited material. Project types
include TV and feature films. Genres include comedy,
drama, and family. Established in 2004.

TO AND FRO PRODUCTIONS
Production company and distributor

4541 Broadway
2L
Union City, NJ 07087
201-381-0326

info.toandfro@gmail.com
toandfrofilms.com
imdb.com/company/co0221755
facebook.com/pages/To-and-Fro-Productions-LLC/
    450710795579
twitter.com/toandfrofilms

Does not accept any unsolicited material. Project types
include TV. Genres include documentary.

TOEI ANIMATION COMPANY
Production company, studio, and distributor

Toei Animation Enterprises Limited (TAE) Unit
1604-05, Island Place Tower 510 King's Rd, North
Point
Hong Kong China
011-852-25641191 (phone)
011-852-25643567 (fax)

2-10-5 Higashi Ohizumi, Nerima-ku, Tokyo, Japan,
178-8567
011-813-39783111

Toei Animation Music Publishing 58 Yokodera-machi
Shinjuku-ku
Tokyo Japan 162-0831
011-813-52613288 (phone)
011-813-52613954 (fax)

Toei Animation Incorporated (TAI) 11150 W
Olympic Blvd Suite 1150
Los Angeles CA 90064

Toei Animation Phils., Inc. (TAP) Ninth Floor, Cyber
One Building Eastwoodcity Cyberpark, E. Rodriguez
Jr. Ave, Bagumbayan, Quezon City
Metro Manila Philippines
011-632-6871720 (phone)
011-632-6877362 (fax)

Tavac Co., Ltd. Sato Building, 1-5-2 Kita-Shinjuku
Shinjuku-ku
Tokyo Japan 169-0074
011-813-33711135 (phone)
011-813-3369680 (fax)

Toei Animation Shanghai Rep. (TAS) Unit 807,
Feidiao International Plaza No.1065, Zhaojiabang Rd,
Xuhui District
Shanghai China
011-862-133680306 (phone)
011-862-133680307 (fax)

sales@toei-anim.net
corp.toei-anim.co.jp
imdb.com/company/co0062107

Does not accept any unsolicited material. Project types
include video games, TV, and short films. Genres
include animation, action, and comedy.

TOEI COMPANY
Sales agent

2-17, 3-Chome
Ginza
Chuo-ku, Tokyo 104-8108
Japan
+81 3 3535 7621 (phone)
+81 3 3535 7622 (fax)

international@toei.co.jp
toei.co.jp
imdb.com/company/co0054276
facebook.com/TOEI.co.jp
twitter.com/TOEI_PR

Does not accept any unsolicited material. Project types
include TV. Genres include animation.

Mika Enomoto
Television (Producer)
imdb.com/name/nm4418345

TOFOO FILMS
Distributor

5-4-1-306
Shinjuku
Shinjuku, Tokyo 160-0022
Japan
+81 03-5919-1542 (phone)
+81 03-5919-1543 (fax)

info@tongpoo-films.jp
tongpoo-films.jp
imdb.com/company/co0355335
facebook.com/tofoofilms

Does not accept any unsolicited material. Project types include TV. Genres include animation, drama, and science fiction.

Shigetaka Kinoshita
President (Executive)
imdb.com/name/nm5126748

TOHO-TOWA
Production company and distributor

18 Ichiban-cho
Chiyoda-ku
Tokyo 102-8537
Japan
+81-3-3556-0335 (phone)
+81-3-3556-0317 (fax)

intl-dept@tohotowa.co.jp
toho.co.jp
imdb.com/company/co0064457

Does not accept any unsolicited material. Project types include feature films and TV. Genres include thriller, animation, and drama.

Hiroyasu Matsuoka
CEO
imdb.com/name/nm2487010

TOKYO BROADCASTING SYSTEM (TBS)
Production company and distributor

5-3-6 Akasaka
Minato-ku
Tokyo 107-8006
Japan
+81 3 5571 3085 (phone)
+81 3 3505 1584 (fax)

prosales@tbs.co.jp
tbs.co.jp
imdb.com/company/co0072133

Does not accept any unsolicited material. Project types include TV, feature films, and short films. Genres include thriller.

Fumihiko Sori
Director
imdb.com/name/nm1216495

TOKYO STORY
Production company

Tokyo,
Japan

info@tokyo-story.com
imdb.com/company/co0320224

Does not accept any unsolicited material. Project types include TV. Genres include drama.

TOKYO UNIVERSITY OF THE ARTS
Production company and distributor

12-8 Ueno Park
Taito-Ku,, Tokyo 110-8714
Japan
+81 3 5685 7763 (fax)

toiawase@ml.geidai.ac.jp
geidai.ac.jp
imdb.com/company/co0285395

Does not accept any unsolicited material. Project types include TV and feature films. Genres include drama.

TOLEDO PRODUCTIONS
Production company

Ste 44
10 Richmond Mews
London, UK W1D 3DD
UK

info@toledoproductions.com
imdb.com/company/co0209419

Does not accept any unsolicited material. Project types include feature films. Genres include romance and drama.

Duncan Kenworthy
Producer
imdb.com/name/nm0448953

TOLLYWOOD
Production company and distributor

5-32-5-2F
Daizawa
Setagaya, Tokyo 155-0032
Japan

03-3414-0433 (phone)
03-3414-0463 (fax)

tollywood@nifty.com
imdb.com/company/co0249373

Does not accept any unsolicited material. Genres include animation and drama.

Takahiro Ohtsuki
President (Producer)
imdb.com/name/nm3154427

TOMBSTONE DISTRIBUTION
Distributor

1201 W 5th St
Ste T-420, 4th Fl
Los Angeles, CA 90017
310-622-8773 (phone)
310-492-5861 (fax)

info@archstonedistribution.com
tombstonedistribution.com
imdb.com/company/co0339428
facebook.com/pages/Archstone-Distribution/
    144349352276960
twitter.com/ArchstoneDistb

Does not accept any unsolicited material. Genres include comedy, horror, and fantasy.

TOMCAT FILMS
Production company, distributor, and sales agent

10645 N. Tatum Blvd.
Ste 200-130
Phoenix, AZ 85028
480-535-8711 (phone)
480-535-8712 (fax)

info@tomcatfilmsllc.com
tomcatfilmsllc.com
imdb.com/company/co0275813
facebook.com
twitter.com/tomcatfilmsllc

Does not accept any unsolicited material. Project types include TV. Genres include action and crime.

Ted Chalmers
Producer
imdb.com/name/nm0150043

TOM LYNCH COMPANY
Production company and distributor

315 S Beverly Dr, Penthouse, Beverly Hills, CA, United States, 90212
310-724-6900 (phone)
310-282-9176 (fax)

info@tomlynchco.com
tomlynchco.com
imdb.com/company/co0067602

Does not accept any unsolicited material. Project types include TV. Genres include drama, comedy, romance, and family.

TOMMY K. PICTURES
Production company

9757 Hummerbird Ln
Houston, TX 77060
310-873-7326

1697 Broadway # 622
New York, NY 10006
212-453-9954

11556 Burbank Blvd
North Hollywood, CA 90068
310-873-7326

124 Preston St
Hartford, CT 06114
310-873-7326

Tommykijas@gmail.com
imdb.com/company/co0262360
linkedin.com/company/tommy-k-pictures-inc.-

Does not accept any unsolicited material. Project types include short films, feature films, and TV. Genres include thriller, drama, comedy, horror, crime, and action. Established in 2007.

TOM WELLING PRODUCTIONS
Production company

16000 Ventura Blvd
Encino, CA 91436
818-954-4012

imdb.com/company/co0314090
linkedin.com/company/tom-welling-productions

Does not accept any unsolicited material. Project types include TV. Genres include drama. Established in 2010.

Tom Welling
Founder
imdb.com/name/nm0919991

TONIK PRODUCTIONS
Production company

27 W 24th St. Suite 1108
New York, NY 10010
212-532-6565 (phone)
212-532-6650 (fax)

info@tonikproductions.com
tonikproductions.com/home
imdb.com/company/co0078138
twitter.com/Tonik_Films

Accepts query letters from unproduced, unrepresented writers via email. Project types include feature films. Genres include drama, comedy, family, fantasy, and science fiction.

Nikki SIlver
Principal
imdb.com/name/nm1012185
linkedin.com/pub/nikki-silver/6/919/310
facebook.com/nikki.silver.75

Tonya Lewis Lee
Principal
imdb.com/name/nm1416174
linkedin.com/pub/tonya-lewis-lee/10/361/620
facebook.com/TonyaLewisLee
twitter.com/TLewisLee

TOOL OF NORTH AMERICA
Production company and distributor

2210 Broadway
Santa Monica, CA 90404
310-453-9244 (phone)
310-453-4185 (fax)

50 W 17th St, 4th Floor
New York, NY 10011
212-924-1100 (phone)
212-924-1156 (fax)

info@toolofna.com
toolofna.com
imdb.com/company/co0336975
linkedin.com/company/tool-of-north-america
facebook.com/toolofna
twitter.com/ToolofNA

Does not accept any unsolicited material. Project types include TV, feature films, and commercials. Genres include non-fiction, drama, reality, thriller, and horror. Established in 1995.

Lori Stonebraker
Executive Producer
310-453-9244
lori.stonebraker@toolofna.com
linkedin.com/pub/lori-stonebraker/91/abb/2a8

Chris Neff
Executive Producer
310-453-9244
chris.neff@toolofna.com
linkedin.com/in/cneff08

Robert Helphand
Executive Producer
310-453-9244
robert.helphand@toolofna.com
linkedin.com/pub/robert-helphand/7/19/b76

Dustin Callif
Executive Producer
310-453-9244
dustin@toolofna.com
imdb.com/name/nm2956668
linkedin.com/company/tool-of-north-america

Oliver Fuselier
Executive Producer
310-453-9244
oliver@toolofna.com
imdb.com/name/nm0299336
linkedin.com/pub/dir/oliver/fuselier

Josh Gold
Executive Producer
310-453-9244
josh@toolofna.com

TOONBOX ENTERTAINMENT
Production company, distributor, and sales agent

26 Richardson St
Toronto, ON M5A 4J9
Canada
416-362-8783 (phone)
416-362-7914 (fax)

info@toonboxent.com
toonboxent.com
imdb.com/company/co0294917
linkedin.com/company/toon-box-entertainment
facebook.com/toonboxent
twitter.com/toonboxent

Does not accept any unsolicited material. Project types include TV and feature films. Genres include comedy and animation.

Hongjoo Ahn
Producer
imdb.com/name/nm3760679

TOONZ ANIMATION INDIA
Production company, studio, and distributor

Toonz Entertainment Pte Ltd. 312A, Tanglin Rd
#01-01
Singapore Singapore 247982
011-656-2205056 (phone)
011-656-2355690 (fax)

1280, Bernard Avem Suite 400
Quatremon QC Canada H2V 1V9

731-739 Nila, Technopark Campus Trivandrum,
Kerala
India 695 581
011-914-712700929 (phone)
011-914-712700954 (fax)

4301 Hacienda Dr, Suite 200, Pleasanton, CA, United States, 94588
925-463-8833

toonz@toonzanimationindia.com
toonz.co
imdb.com/company/co0183292

Does not accept any unsolicited material. Project types include video games, TV, and feature films. Genres include drama, family, and animation.

TOTAL FRAT MOVE
Production company and distributor

2499 S Capital of Texas Hwy
Ste B203
Austin, TX 78746
951-878-5419

support@totalfratmove.com
totalfratmove.com
imdb.com/company/co0410116
facebook.com/totalfratmove
twitter.com/totalfratmove

Does not accept any unsolicited material. Project types include short films. Genres include comedy.

TOUCHDOWN PRODUCTIONS
Production company

1806 Bella Lago Ln
Tampa, FL 33618
813-505-2250 (phone)
813-265-1375 (fax)

toni@touchdownproductions.net
imdb.com/company/co0329284

Does not accept any unsolicited material.

TOUGH GUY FILMS
Production company

1914 N. 39th Ave.
Hollywood, FL 33021
954-483-5726

toughguyfilms@comcast.net
toughguyfilms.com
imdb.com/company/co0382326

Does not accept any unsolicited material. Project types include short films. Genres include thriller and action.

TOWER OF BABBLE ENTERTAINMENT
Production company

854 N Spaulding Ave
Los Angeles, CA 90046
323-230-6128 (phone)
323-822-0312 (fax)

imdb.com/company/co0179064

Accepts query letters from unproduced, unrepresented writers via email. Project types include TV and feature films. Genres include comedy and romance.

Beau Bauman
323-230-6128
info@towerofb .com
imdb.com/name/nm0062149

Jeff Wadlow
323-230-6128
info@towerofb .com
imdb.com/name/nm0905592

TOWER PRODUCTIONSTP
Production company

P.O. Box 2177
Harker Heights, TX 76548
254-690-1776 (phone)
254-690-1776 (fax)

info@towerproductions.com
towerproductionsllc.com
imdb.com/company/co0370949

Does not accept any unsolicited material. Genres include action.

TPG CAPITAL
Production company

401 Congress Ave
Suite 2750
Austin, TX 78701
512-533-6600 (phone)
512-533-6601 (fax)

1301 McKinney
9th Floor
Houston, TX 77002
713-457-5510

301 Commerce St
Suite 3300
Fort Worth, TX 76102
817-871-4000 (phone)
817-871-4001 (fax)

2100 McKinney Ave
Suite 1030
Dallas, TX 75201

469-621-3001 (phone)
469-621-3002 (fax)

owen@blicksilverpr.com
tpg.com
imdb.com/company/co0347345
linkedin.com/company/tpg-capital

Does not accept any unsolicited material. Genres include family, comedy, and drama.

TRADEMARK FILMS
Production company

14a Goodwin's Court
London WC2N 4LL
UK
+44 (0) 20 3322 8900

mail@trademarkfilms.co.uk
trademarkfilms.co.uk
imdb.com/company/co0230546

Does not accept any unsolicited material. Project types include TV. Genres include comedy, crime, and drama.

David Parfitt
Producer
imdb.com/name/nm0661406

TRANCAS INTERNATIONAL FILMS, INC.
Production company and distributor

2021 Pontius Ave
2nd Floor
Los Angeles, CA 90025
310-477-6569 (phone)
310-477-7126 (fax)

info@trancasfilms.com
imdb.com/company/co0005891
facebook.com/TrancasInternationalFilms
twitter.com/TrancasFilms

Does not accept any unsolicited material. Project types include TV and feature films. Genres include action, horror, thriller, drama, and comedy.

Malek S. Akkad

President
imdb.com/name/nm0015443
linkedin.com/pub/malek-akkad/6a/a7a/376

Louis Nader

imdb.com/name/nm0618868

TRANSCENDENT ENTERTAINMENT

Production company

Los Angeles, CA

transcendentent.com
imdb.com/company/co0269457

Does not accept any unsolicited material. Project types include TV and feature films.

Danny Rodriguez

CEO
danny@transcendentent.com
linkedin.com/pub/danny-rodriguez/5/a96/817
twitter.com/officialDannyR

TRANSIENT

Production company

1331 Brickell Ave
Ste 300
Miami, FL 33130

imdb.com/company/co0419091

Does not accept any unsolicited material. Genres include action and science fiction.

TRANSIT MEDIA COMMUNICATIONS

Distributor

22-D Hollywood Ave.
Hohokus, NJ 07423
800-343-5540 (phone)
845-774-2845 (fax)

newday.com/tmc
imdb.com/company/co0021569

Does not accept any unsolicited material. Project types include TV. Genres include crime, documentary, and comedy.

TRANS LUX DISTRIBUTING CORPORATION

Distributor

625 Madison Ave
New York, NY 10022
212-751-3110

imdb.com/company/co0107995

Does not accept any unsolicited material.

TREEHOUSE FILMS

Production company

4450 Lakeside Dr
Suite 225
Burbank, CA 91505
818-260-8707 (phone)
818-260-0440 (fax)

imdb.com/company/co0077634

Does not accept any unsolicited material. Project types include feature films. Genres include romance and drama.

Kevin Costner

Founder
imdb.com/name/nm0000126

TREEHOUSE PICTURES

Production company

400 W 14th St, New York, NY, United States, 10014
424-278-1001

9200 Sunset Blvd Suite 1232
West Hollywood CA 90069
424-278-1001 (phone)
424-278-1002 (fax)

assistant@treehousepictures.com
treehousepictures.com
imdb.com/company/co0284629

Does not accept any unsolicited material. Project types include feature films and TV. Genres include drama, action, family, and thriller.

Juliet Berman

Creative Executive
imdb.com/name/nm0075789

TRIBECA FILMS

345 N. Maple Dr.
Suite 202
Beverly Hills, CA 90210
310-651-8342

375 Greenwich St, 8th Floor
New York, NY 10013
212-941-2400 (phone)
212-941-3939 (fax)

54 Varick St,
New York, NY 10013
212-941-2001 (phone)
212-941-3997 (fax)

entries@tribecafilmfestival.org (script submissions)
info@tribecafilm.com (general)
tribecafilm.com
imdb.com/company/co0186498
linkedin.com/company/tribeca-film-festiva
facebook.com/Tribeca
twitter.com/Tribeca

Does not accept any unsolicited material. Project types include TV and feature films. Genres include comedy, drama, period, fantasy, action, crime, romance, thriller, and non-fiction. Established in 1989.

Robert De Niro

Partner
212-941-2400
imdb.com/name/nm0000134
linkedin.com/pub/robert-deniro/26/9b9/646
facebook.com/RobertDeNiroSr

Jane Rosenthal

Partner
imdb.com/name/nm0742772
linkedin.com/pub/jane-rosenthal/15/186/3B4
facebook.com/pages/Jane-Rosenthal
twitter.com/janetribeca

Berry Welsh

Director of Development
212-941-2400
imdb.com/name/nm2654730
linkedin.com/pub/berry-welsh/4/B85/742
facebook.com/berry.welsh
twitter.com/BarryPWels

TRICOAST STUDIOS

Production company and distributor

11124 Washington Blvd
Culver City, CA 90232
310-458-7707

tricoast@tricoast.com
tricoastworldwide.com
imdb.com/company/co0127287
linkedin.com/company/tricoast-studios
facebook.com/pages/Tricoast-Worldwide-Studios/
    140312726147049
twitter.com/TriCoastStudios

Does not accept any unsolicited material. Project types include feature films and TV. Genres include drama. Established in 1987.

Marcy Hamilton

CEO
marcy@tricoast.com
imdb.com/name/nm0358036

Strathford Hamilton

Founder
strath@tricoast.com
imdb.com/name/nm0358175

Andrew Williams

Sound Supervisor
andrew@tricoast.com

Daisy Hamilton

Director of Business Development
daisyhamilton@tricoast.com

Martin Wiley

Executive Producer
info@tricoastworldwide.com

TRICON DISTRIBUTION

Production company and distributor

786 King St W
Toronto, ON M5V 1N6
Canada
416-341-9926 (phone)
416-341-0173 (fax)

info@triconfilms.com
triconfilms.com
imdb.com/company/co0435145

facebook.com/TriconFilms
twitter.com/triconfilms

Does not accept any unsolicited material. Genres include documentary.

Andrea Gorfolova
Producer
imdb.com/name/nm1951166

TRICON FILMS & TELEVISION
Production company and distributor

372 Richmond St West, Suite 200, Toronto , ON, Canada, M5V 1X6
416-341-9926 (phone)
416-341-0173 (fax)

info@triconfilms.com
triconfilms.com
imdb.com/company/co0519424

Does not accept any unsolicited material. Project types include TV. Genres include family, drama, and comedy.

TRICOR ENTERTAINMENT
Production company

1149 N. McCadden Place ~ Hollywood, CA 90038
323-464-0055 (phone)
323-464-0099 (fax)

Darian@OccidentalEntertainment.com
tricorentertainment.com
imdb.com/company/co0070488

Does not accept any unsolicited material. Project types include feature films. Genres include action. Established in 1988.

Craig Darian
CEO
323-464-0055
darian@occidentalentertainment.com
craigdarian.com
imdb.com/name/nm1545768

Ron Mencer
Director of Development
imdb.com/name/nm1348889

TRILOGY ENTERTAINMENT GROUP
Production company, studio, and distributor

1207 4th St
Suite 400
Santa Monica, CA 90401
310-656-9733

trilogyent.com
imdb.com/company/co0078090
linkedin.com/company/trilogy-entertainment-group
facebook.com/pages/Riding-the-Alligator/104540316270450
twitter.com/PenDensham

Does not accept any unsolicited material. Project types include feature films and TV. Genres include comedy, action, fantasy, romance, and thriller.

Nevin Densham
Producer
imdb.com/name/nm0219719

Pen Densham
Founder
imdb.com/name/nm0219720
linkedin.com/pub/pen-densham/9/9bb/393
twitter.com/Pendensham

John Watson
Founder
imdb.com/name/nm2302370

TRILOGY FILMS
Production company and distributor

74 Church St
Montclair, NJ 07042
973-744-0856 (phone)
973-744-0858 (fax)

dawn@trilogy-films.com
trilogy-films.com
imdb.com/company/co0366755

Does not accept any unsolicited material. Project types include TV. Genres include documentary.

TRINITY MEDIA PICTURES
Production company

800 Hammond Blvd
Jacksonville, FL 32221
904-596-2400

doschaffer@tbc.org
imdb.com/company/co0333544

Does not accept any unsolicited material. Project types include short films. Genres include family.

TRIPLE CROSS PRODUCTIONS
Production company

1519 W Main St
Houston, TX 77006
713-397-1788

imdb.com/company/co0443545

Does not accept any unsolicited material. Project types include TV. Genres include thriller. Established in 2013.

TRI-STATE PICTURES
Production company

1406 Camp Craft Rd.
Suite 200
Austin, TX 78746

kristin@bracecove.net
imdb.com/company/co0498467

Does not accept any unsolicited material. Genres include science fiction and drama.

TRISTONE ENTERTAINMENT INC.
Production company

2-11-23 Sun Towers
B #8
Setagaya, TOKYO 154-0024
Japan

actor@tristone.co.jp
tristone.co.jp
imdb.com/company/co0010462

Does not accept any unsolicited material. Project types include TV. Genres include action, thriller, and crime.

Mataichirô Yamamoto
Producer
imdb.com/name/nm0945451

TRIUMPHANT ENTERTAINMENT
Production company and distributor

8350 Wilshire Blvd, Suite 200, Beverly Hills, CA, United States, 90211

Admin@triumphantpictures.com
imdb.com/company/co0207464

Does not accept any unsolicited material.

Cecil Chambers
Writer
imdb.com/name/nm1729494

TROIKA PICTURES
Production company

2019 S Westgate Ave
2nd Floor
Los Angeles, CA 90025
310-696-2859 (phone)
310-820-7310 (fax)

troikapics@gmail.com
troikapictures.com
imdb.com/company/co0246102
twitter.com/troikapictures

Does not accept any unsolicited material. Project types include feature films. Genres include fantasy, romance, thriller, action, and crime.

Robert Stein
CEO
310-696-2859
imdb.com/name/nm3355501
linkedin.com/pub/robert-stein/41/665/405

Bradley Gallo
Head of Production & Development
310-696-2859
imdb.com/name/nm0303010
linkedin.com/in/bradleygallo

Michael Helfant
COO
310-696-2859
imdb.com/name/nm0375033
linkedin.com/pub/michael-helfant/4/57/10a

TROMA ENTERTAINMENT
Production company and distributor

36-40 11th St
Long Island City, NY 11106
718-391-0110 (phone)
718-391-0255 (fax)

troma1@gmail.com
troma.com
imdb.com/company/co0019150
linkedin.com/company/troma-entertainment
facebook.com/troma.entertainment
twitter.com/tromateamvideo

Accepts scripts from unproduced, unrepresented
writers. Project types include feature films. Genres
include sociocultural, drama, action, thriller, science
fiction, fantasy, and horror. Established in 1974.

Lloyd Kaufman
President
lloyd@troma.com
lloydkaufman.com
imdb.com/name/nm0442207
linkedin.com/pub/lloyd-kaufman/0/661/541
facebook.com/pages/Lloyd-Kaufman
twitter.com/witter.comlloydkaufman

Michael Herz
Vice-President
imdb.com/name/nm0381230
linkedin.com/pub/michael-herz/10/a95/a90

TROUBADOUR FILMS
Production company, distributor, and sales agent

4566 Creekview Dr
Salt Lake City, UT 84107
801-243-9330

media@troubadourfilms.com
troubadourfilms.com
imdb.com/company/co0187995

Does not accept any unsolicited material. Project types
include TV. Genres include drama and comedy.

Jarrod Phillips
Producer
imdb.com/name/nm2326393

TROUBLEMAKER STUDIOS
Production company and distributor

4900 Old Manor Rd
Austin, TX 78723
512-334-7777 (phone)
512-391-1549 (fax)

imdb.com/company/co0035848

Does not accept any unsolicited material. Genres
include thriller and action.

TRUE VISION PRODUCTIONS
Production company and distributor

49a Oxford Rd
South Chiswick
London W4 3DD
UK
020-874-27852 (phone)
020-874-27853 (fax)

website@truevisiontv.com
truevisiontv.com
imdb.com/company/co0209004
facebook.com/True-Vision-
    Productions-176491479112374
twitter.com/truevisiontv

Does not accept any unsolicited material. Project types
include TV. Genres include documentary.

TRULY INDIE
Distributor

1614 W. 5th St
Austin, TX 78703
512-474-2909

ksanders@trulyindie.com
trulyindie.com
imdb.com/company/co0179468
linkedin.com/company/magnolia-pictures-hdnet-films-
    landmark-theatres-truly-indie
twitter.com/TrulyIndieFilm

Does not accept any unsolicited material. Project types
include feature films. Genres include documentary,
action, thriller, romance, drama, and comedy.
Established in 2005.

TRUMPETT PRODUCTIONS
Production company and financing company

P.O. Box 21
Cranfills Gap, TX 76637
817-526-1702

kimhughes10@yahoo.com
imdb.com/company/co0330747

Does not accept any unsolicited material. Project types include TV. Genres include comedy and drama.

Kim Hughes
Producer
imdb.com/name/nm4347441

TRUTH ENTERTAINMENT
Production company

2170 Buckthorne Pl
#400
Spring, TX 77380
281-292-6900

biz@truthent.com
truthentertainment.us
imdb.com/company/co0398657

Does not accept any unsolicited material. Project types include feature films. Genres include romance, drama, and thriller.

TRYGON PICTURES
Production company, distributor, and sales agent

14 Rembrandt Way
Mays Landing, NJ 08330
609-569-0270

agata@trygonfilm.com
trygonfilm.com
imdb.com/company/co0381275
facebook.com/trygonfilm
twitter.com/trygonfilm

Does not accept any unsolicited material. Project types include TV. Genres include documentary and comedy.

TSUNAMI PRODUCTIONS
Production company, distributor, and sales agent

722 Dulaney Valley Rd #364
Towson, MD 21204
410-472-2123

melissa@tsunamiproductions.com
tsunamiproductions.com
imdb.com/company/co0196219

Accepts query letters from unproduced, unrepresented writers via email. Project types include TV. Genres include comedy and drama.

Melissa McComas
Producer
imdb.com/name/nm2550923

TUGG
Distributor

4210 Spicewood Springs Rd.
Ste 200
Austin, TX 78759-8653
855-321-8844

support@tugginc.com
tugg.com
imdb.com/company/co0374670
facebook.com/TuggInc
twitter.com/tugginc

Does not accept any unsolicited material. Genres include comedy, documentary, action, and science fiction.

TURNER BROADCASTING SYSTEM (TBS)
Production company and distributor

14 N Tower
Atlanta, GA 30303
404-827-1500 (phone)
404-827-2381 (fax)

tbsinfo@turner.com
tbs.com
imdb.com/company/co0005051

Does not accept any unsolicited material. Project types include TV. Genres include horror, comedy, thriller, and drama.

TURNPIKE PICTURES
Production company

3228 Collinsworth
Fort Worth, TX 76107
817-846-2810

pfarrell@turnpikepictures.com
turnpikepictures.com
imdb.com/company/co0408834

Does not accept any unsolicited material. Genres
include drama and family.

TURTLEBACK PRODUCTIONS, INC.
Production company

11736 Gwynne Ln
Los Angeles, CA, CA 90077
310-440-8587 (phone)
310-440-8903 (fax)

turtleback-productions-inc.hub.biz
imdb.com/company/co0045039

Accepts query letters from unproduced, unrepresented
writers. Project types include TV and feature films.
Genres include drama, thriller, fantasy, and crime.
Established in 1988.

Howard Meltzer
President
310-440-8587
imdb.com/name/nm0578430
linkedin.com/pub/howard-meltzer/36/824/660

TV LAND
Production company and distributor

1515 Broadway 45th Floor
New York, NY 10036
212-846-3723 (phone)
201-422-6630 (fax)

info@tvland.com
tvland.com
imdb.com/company/co0094233
linkedin.com/company/tv-land
facebook.com/tvland
twitter.com/tvland

Accepts query letters from unproduced, unrepresented
writers via email. Project types include TV. Genres
include comedy and drama. Established in 1996.

Scott Gregory
Vice-President
linkedin.com/pub/scott-gregory/3/824/b94
facebook.com/scott.gregory.9619

Larry W. Jones
President
212-846-6000
larry.jones@tvland.com
imdb.com/name/nm1511130
linkedin.com/pub/larry-jones/6/122/1a0
facebook.com/pages/Larry-W-Jones/
579462038841440

Bradley Gardner
Producer
imdb.com/name/nm3952119

Rose Catherine Pinkney
Vice-President
imdb.com/name/nm0684384
linkedin.com/pub/rose-catherine-pinkney/38/8a2/486

TV ONE LLC
Production company and distributor

1010 Wayne Ave
Silver Spring, MD 20910
301-755-0400

tvoneonline.com
imdb.com/company/co0118331
linkedin.com/company/tv-one
facebook.com/tvonetv
twitter.com/tvonetv

Accepts query letters from produced or represented
writers. Project types include TV. Genres include
drama and comedy. Established in 2004.

Jubba Seyyid
Senior Director
linkedin.com/pub/jubba-seyyid/91/933/958
twitter.com/Jubbaman

Alfred Liggins
Chairman
301-755-0400
aliggins@tv-one.tv
imdb.com/name/nm3447190

T.V. REPAIR
Sales agent

davidjlatt@earthlink.net
imdb.com/company/co0183810

Accepts query letters from unproduced, unrepresented writers via email. Project types include TV. Genres include sociocultural and family.

David Latt
310-459-3671
davidjlatt@earthlink.net
imdb.com/name/nm0490374

TWELFTH NIGHT ENTERTAINMENT
Production company and sales agent

2534 Idlewood Dr.
Garland, TX 75040
972-202-4013

aruizesparza@msn.com
imdb.com/company/co0131405

Does not accept any unsolicited material. Genres include fantasy and family.

TWENTIETH CENTURY FOX FILM CORPORATION
Production company and studio

10201 W Pico Blvd
Los Angeles, CA 90035
310-369-1000 (phone)
310-203-1558 (fax)

foxmovies@fox.com
foxstudios.com
imdb.com/company/co0000756
facebook.com/20thCFoxStudios
twitter.com/foxbacklot

Does not accept any unsolicited material. Project types include TV and feature films. Genres include drama, non-fiction, comedy, fantasy, horror, family, myth, detective, crime, romance, thriller, and action. Established in 1935.

Steve Freedman
linkedin.com/pub/steve-timinskas/3/90a/381

David A Starke
linkedin.com/company/fox-filmed-entertainment

Ted Dodd
linkedin.com/pub/ted-dodd/5/789/801

TWENTIETH CENTURY FOX TELEVISION
Production company, studio, distributor, and financing company

10201 W Pico Blvd
Los Angeles, CA 90064
310-369-6000

info@fox.com
foxmovies.com
imdb.com/company/co0056447
linkedin.com/company/fox-filmed-entertainment
facebook.com/foxmovies
twitter.com/20thcenturyfox

Does not accept any unsolicited material. Project types include TV. Genres include drama and comedy. Established in 1949.

Jonathan Harris
Sr. Vice President Legal Affairs
linkedin.com/pub/jonathan-harris/9/A50/2B6

Gary Newman
Chairman
gary.newman@fox.com
imdb.com/name/nm3050096
linkedin.com/pub/gary-newman/8/a67/421

Dana Walden
Executive
imdb.com/name/nm0992861

TWENTIETH TELEVISION
Production company, studio, and distributor

2121 Ave of the Stars
17th Floor
Los Angeles, CA 90067
310-369-1000 (phone)
310-369-3899 (fax)

info@fox.com
fox.com
imdb.com/company/co0161074

linkedin.com/company/twentieth-television
facebook.com/pages/20th-Television/
   112762725404025
twitter.com/FOXTV

Does not accept any unsolicited material. Project types include TV. Genres include drama, comedy, and documentary. Established in 1995.

Roger Ailes
Producer
imdb.com/name/nm0014614

TWIN PYRE PRODUCTIONS
Production company

913 10th St
Huntsville, TX 77320
713-376-2218 (phone)
832-422-3798 (fax)

babaracus13@hotmail.com
imdb.com/company/co0282417

Does not accept any unsolicited material. Genres include drama.

TWINSTAR ENTERTAINMENT
Production company and studio

556 S. Fair Oaks Ave, Suite 376
Pasadena, CA 91105
949-929-1200

info@twinstarentertainment.com
twinstarentertainment.com
imdb.com/company/co0144114

Accepts scripts from unproduced, unrepresented writers. Project types include TV. Genres include family, drama, animation, and comedy. Established in 2003.

Russ Werdin
CEO
linkedin.com/pub/russ-werdin/18/600/5a6

RUSS WERDIN
CEO
rwerdin@werdin.com

TWISTED PICTURES
Production company and distributor

c/o Evolution Entertainment
901 N Highland Ave
Los Angeles, CA
323-850-3232

imdb.com/company/co0137447
facebook.com/pages/Twisted-Pictures/
   108186339203451

Accepts query letters from unproduced, unrepresented writers. Project types include TV and feature films. Genres include horror, crime, and thriller. Established in 2004.

Mark Burg
Founder
imdb.com/name/nm0121117

TWITCHING MONKEY PRODUCTIONS
Production company and distributor

P.O. Box 684966
Austin, TX 78768

twitchingmonkey.com
imdb.com/company/co0101488
facebook.com/twitchingmonkeyproductions

Does not accept any unsolicited material. Project types include short films. Genres include comedy and drama.

TWO BIRDS ENTERTAINMENT
Production company and studio

1762 N Tamarind Ave #307
Hollywood, CA 90028

jordan@twobirdsentertainment.net
twobirdsentertainment.net
imdb.com/company/co0505861
facebook.com/twobirdsentertainment

Does not accept any unsolicited material. Genres include drama and romance.

TWO SIX PRODUCTIONS
Production company and distributor

953 Hope Dr SW
Atlanta, GA 30310
404-309-4345 (phone)
404-753-5583 (fax)

twosixproductions@mac.com
imdb.com/company/co0177973

Does not accept any unsolicited material. Project types include short films. Genres include comedy.

TWO TON FILMS
Production company and studio

info@twotonfilms.com
twotonfilms.com
imdb.com/company/co0188112
facebook.com/pages/Two-Ton-Films/324667725316
twitter.com/TwoTonFilms

Accepts query letters from unproduced, unrepresented writers via email. Project types include feature films and TV. Genres include family, comedy, drama, and action.

Justin Zackham
Partner
imdb.com/name/nm0951698

Clay Pecorin
Partner
imdb.com/name/nm2668976
linkedin.com/pub/clay-pecorin/4/98a/839

TYCOON ENTERTAINMENT
Production company

30 S 15th St, Suite 1000, Philadelphia , PA, United States, 19102
267-417-0000

info@tycoonent.com
tycoonent.com
imdb.com/company/co0015206

Does not accept any unsolicited material. Project types include feature films. Genres include thriller, family, drama, and action.

TYCOR INTERNATIONAL FILM PRODUCTIONS
Production company and distributor

600 W Peachtree St Northwest,Suite 1560
Atlanta, GA

hello@tycorfilms.com

tycorinternationalfilmcompany.com
imdb.com/company/co0195525

Does not accept any unsolicited material. Project types include short films. Genres include drama.

UBERFILMS
Production company

P.O. BOX 202257
Denver, CO 80220
303-355-5211 (phone)
303-416-4282 (fax)

info@uber-films.com
imdb.com/company/co0229405

Does not accept any unsolicited material. Project types include feature films. Genres include drama.

Nicholas Chavez
Producer (Executive)
imdb.com/name/nm2796331

UCZKOWSKI PRODUCTIONS
Production company and distributor

#339 270 Sparta Ave. Ste. 104
Sparta, NJ 07871

uczkowski@mac.com
imdb.com/company/co0135108

Does not accept any unsolicited material. Project types include feature films and TV. Genres include horror.

U-FIELD CO.
Production company

1-26-8-3F
Higashi Azabu
Minato, Tokyo 106-0044
Japan
03-5545-4105 (phone)
03-5545-5900 (fax)

info@u-field.jp
u-field.jp
imdb.com/company/co0340594

Does not accept any unsolicited material. Project types include TV. Genres include comedy.

Yoshiro Maekawa
Producer
imdb.com/name/nm7322008

UFLAND PRODUCTIONS
Production company and studio

963 Moraga Dr
Los Angeles, CA 90049
310-476-4520 (phone)
310-476-4891 (fax)

ufland.productions@verizon.net
imdb.com/company/co0000904

Does not accept any unsolicited material. Project types include TV and feature films. Genres include drama, romance, and comedy. Established in 1972.

Harry Ufland
Producer
imdb.com/name/nm0880036
linkedin.com/pub/harry-ufland/3b/103/843

Mary Jane Ufland
Producer
imdb.com/name/nm0880040

UFOTABLE
Production company

1-38-11
Nogata
Nakano, Tokyo 165-0027
Japan
03-5318-1539 (phone)
03-3388-8202 (fax)

info@ufotable.com
ufotable.com
imdb.com/company/co0191504

Does not accept any unsolicited material. Project types include feature films, TV, and video games. Genres include fantasy and animation.

Hikaru Kondo
President
imdb.com/name/nm2137662

UK FILM COUNCIL
Production company and distributor

21 Stephen St
London, England W1T 1LN
UK
+44 20 7255 1444

info@ukfilmcouncil.org.uk
imdb.com/company/co0104811

Does not accept any unsolicited material. Project types include feature films. Genres include fantasy and drama.

Tuks Tad Lungu
Actor
imdb.com/name/nm5842339

UMEDIA
Production company, studio, and distributor

28 Rue Marius Aufan
Levallois-Perret France 92300

235 Ave Louise, Brussels, Belgium, 1050
011-322-5440000

83-84 Long Acre 2nd Floor
London United Kingdom WC2E 9NG
011-442-034753232 (phone)
011-322-3729138 (fax)

1331 N Sycamore Ave Unit 1
Hollywood CA 90028

info@umedia.eu
umedia.eu/en
imdb.com/company/co0305542

Does not accept any unsolicited material. Project types include TV and feature films. Genres include drama, thriller, science fiction, animation, action, family, and romance.

Lauraine Heftler
Executive (Producer)
imdb.com/name/nm1981482

UNBROKEN PICTURES
Production company

Los Angeles , CA, United States

imdb.com/company/co0289755

Does not accept any unsolicited material. Project types include feature films and TV. Genres include comedy, romance, drama, family, and action.

UNCONVENTIONAL NON-FICTION
Production company

500 Eudora St
Denver, CO 80220
303-994-1227

britta.denverfilm@gmail.com
imdb.com/company/co0271869

Does not accept any unsolicited material. Genres include documentary.

Britta Erickson
President (Producer)
imdb.com/name/nm3117919

UNDERGROUND FILMS
Production company and studio

447 S Highland Ave
Los Angeles, CA 90036
323-930-2588 (phone)
323-930-2334 (fax)

submissions@undergroundfilms.net
undergroundfilms.net
imdb.com/company/co0118811
facebook.com/UndergroundFilmsManagement

Accepts scripts from unproduced, unrepresented writers via email. Project types include TV. Genres include comedy, animation, thriller, myth, non-fiction, family, drama, romance, fantasy, action, and horror. Established in 2003.

Josh McGuire Turner
Producer
323-930-2435
josh@undergroundfilms.net
facebook.com/josh.t.mcguire

Trevor Engelson
Owner
trevor@undergroundfilms.net
imdb.com/name/nm0257333
linkedin.com/pub/trevor-engelson/3/a80/b75

Evan Silverberg
Producer
323-930-2588
evan@undergroundfilms.net

Austin Bedell
Development Assistant
austin@undergroundfilms.net
imdb.com/name/nm6551298
linkedin.com/in/austinchristopherbedell

Chris Dennis
Manager
chris@undergroundfilms.net
imdb.com/name/nm4221802

Noah Rothman
Producer
noah@undergroundfilms.net

UNDERGROUND PRODUCTIONS
Distributor

5645 Glen Errol Rd.
Atlanta, GA 30327
404-587-6776 (phone)
404-303-1598 (fax)

dow.brain@underground-productions.com (script submissions)
Undergroundprod1@aol.com (general)
underground-productions.com
imdb.com/company/co0089796

Does not accept any unsolicited material. Project types include short films. Genres include comedy.

UNDER Z GROUP
Production company and distributor

1-1-1-2F
Hitotsubashi
Chiyoda, Tokyo 100-0003
Japan
03-3213-3288 (phone)
03-3213-3281 (fax)

info@ranves.com
uzg.co.jp
imdb.com/company/co0358626

Does not accept any unsolicited material. Project types include TV. Genres include drama.

UNEARTHED FILMS
Production company

3155 Phoenix Ave.
Unit B
Oldsmar, FL 34677
813-818-7463

HeNeverDies@aol.com
unearthedfilms.com
imdb.com/company/co0015217
facebook.com/Unearthed-FIlms-152402618109784
twitter.com/unearthedfilms

Does not accept any unsolicited material. Project types include short films. Genres include horror.

UNIFIED PICTURES
Production company

19773 Bahama St
Northridge, CA 91324
818-576-1006 (phone)
818-534-3347 (fax)

info@unifiedpictures.com
unifiedpictures.com
imdb.com/company/co0136920
facebook.com/unifiedpictures
twitter.com/unifiedpictures

Accepts query letters from unproduced, unrepresented writers. Project types include feature films. Genres include comedy, detective, horror, action, crime, thriller, and drama. Established in 2004.

Paul Michael Ruffman
Senior VP Business Development
linkedin.com/pub/dir/Paul/Ruffman

Steve Goldstein
President/Business Development
imdb.com/name/nm2179640

Keith Kjarval
Founder/Producer
imdb.com/name/nm1761309

UNIFRANCE FILM INTERNATIONAL
Production company and distributor

French Cultural Center Gongti Xilu, 18 - Chaoyang District
Beijing China 100020
011-861-065535468 (phone)
011-861-065535470 (fax)

13 Rue Henner, Paris, France, 75009
011-331-47539580 (phone)
011-331-47059655 (fax)

352 W 117th St Suite 2F
New York NY 10026
212-832-8860 (phone)
212-755-0629 (fax)

contact@unifrance.org
unifrance.org
imdb.com/company/co0198790

Does not accept any unsolicited material. Project types include TV, short films, and feature films. Genres include reality, drama, family, thriller, comedy, and action.

UNIJAPAN
Production company

1-28-44-4F
Shinkawa
Chuo, Tokyo 104-0033
Japan
03-3553-4780 (phone)
03-3553-4785 (fax)

office@unijapan.org
unijapan.org
imdb.com/company/co0375963
facebook.com/unijapan

Does not accept any unsolicited material. Project types include TV. Genres include drama.

Jun'ichi Sakomoto
President (Executive)
imdb.com/name/nm2707157

UNI J OFFICE
Production company

Tokyo,
Japan

ad@j-inagawa.com
j-inagawa.com
imdb.com/company/co0266319

Does not accept any unsolicited material. Project types include feature films. Genres include horror.

Junji Inagawa
Actor
imdb.com/name/nm0408362

UNION ENTERTAINMENT
Production company

9255 Sunset Blvd, Suite 528
West Hollywood, CA 90069
310-274-7040 (phone)
310-274-1065 (fax)

info@unionent.com
ueginc.com
imdb.com/company/co0183888

Does not accept any unsolicited material. Project types include video games. Genres include animation. Established in 2006.

Richard Leibowitz
President
310-274-7040
rich@unionent.com
imdb.com/name/nm2325318
Assistant: Sarah Logie

Howard Bliss
howard@unionent.com
imdb.com/name/nm2973051
linkedin.com/pub/howard-bliss/39/b27/1b9

UNION PICTURES
Production company and distributor

34 Park Rd
Toronto, ON M4W 2N2
Canada
416-961-4400 (phone)
416-961-8600 (fax)

unionpictures.ca
imdb.com/company/co0293241

Does not accept any unsolicited material. Project types include TV. Genres include drama and comedy.

Sandra Cunningham
Producer
imdb.com/name/nm0192441

UNIQUE BRAINS
Production company

25-3F
Saneicho
Shinjuku, Tokyo 160-0008
Japan
090-4056-1895

heroshow@lgd.co.jp
imdb.com/company/co0308546

Does not accept any unsolicited material. Project types include TV. Genres include animation.

UNIQUE FEATURES
Production company

9200 W. Sunset Blvd.
Suite 404
West Hollywood, CA 90069
310-492-8009 (phone)
310-492-8022 (fax)

888 7th Ave, 16th Floor
New York, NY 10106
212-649-4980 (phone)
212-649-4999 (fax)

imdb.com/company/co0242085

Does not accept any unsolicited material. Project types include feature films and TV. Established in 2008.

Michael Lynne
Principal
310-492-8009
imdb.com/name/nm1088153

UNISON FILMS
Production company

790 Madison Ave
Suite 306
New York, NY 10065

212-226-1200 (phone)
646-349-1738 (fax)

info@unisonfilms.com
unisonfilms.com
imdb.com/company/co0143046

Does not accept any unsolicited material. Project types include feature films. Genres include comedy, drama, and romance. Established in 2004.

Cassandra Kulukundis
Producer
imdb.com/name/nm0474697

Emanuel Michael
CEO
imdb.com/name/nm1639578
linkedin.com/pub/emanuel-michael/83/863/272

UNITED BLADE ENTERTAINMENT
Production company and distributor

P.O. BOX 5075
Deltona, FL 32725
386-837-0782

initedbladeentertainment@gmail.com
imdb.com/company/co0431385
facebook.com/unitedblade

Does not accept any unsolicited material. Genres include comedy and action.

UNITED ENTERTAINMENT
Production company and distributor

1-9-2-8F Shinjuku
Tokyo 160-0022
Japan
+81 0 3-5361-3633 (phone)
+81 0 3-5361-3635 (fax)

mail@united-ent.com
united-ent.com
imdb.com/company/co0204498
facebook.com/UnitedEnt.movie
twitter.com/united_enta

Does not accept any unsolicited material. Project types include TV. Genres include comedy, romance, and drama.

Yasumasa Osada
President (Executive)
imdb.com/name/nm4071504

UNITED EQUITY GROUP
Production company

10700 Richmond Ave
Ste 252
Houston, TX 77042
956-494-4242 (phone)
713-587-0609 (fax)

corporate@uegonline.net
imdb.com/company/co0275803
facebook.com/United-Equity-
    Group-127123517298150

Does not accept any unsolicited material. Genres include comedy.

UNITED INTERNATIONAL PICTURES (UIP)
Distributor and sales agent

566 Chiswick High Rd
Bldg 5
London, England W4 5YF
UK
+44 0 20 3184 2500 (phone)
+44 0 20 3184 2501 (fax)

enquiries@uip.com
imdb.com/company/co0074139

Does not accept any unsolicited material. Project types include feature films. Genres include comedy, thriller, and action.

John Horgan
Executive
imdb.com/name/nm2065275

UNITED REVOLUTION PICTURES
Production company

504 477 Richmond W.
Toronto, ON M8Z 2T7
Canada
647-994-7845

imdb.com/company/co0010308

Does not accept any unsolicited material. Project types include TV. Genres include horror and thriller.

Manuel H. Da Silva
Producer
imdb.com/name/nm3048048

UNITED TALENT AGENCY
Distributor

9336 Civic Center Dr, Beverly Hills, CA, United States, 90210
310-273-6700 (phone)
310-247-1111 (fax)

888 Seventh Ave 9th Floor
New York NY 10106
212-659-2600

info@unitedtalent.com
unitedtalent.com
imdb.com/company/co0033208

Does not accept any unsolicited material. Project types include commercials, TV, and short films. Genres include drama and thriller.

UNIVERSAL CABLE PRODUCTIONS
Production company

100 Universal City Plaza
Building 1440, 14th Floor
Universal City, CA 91608
818-840-4444

30 Rockefeller Plaza
New York, NY 10112
212-664-4444

nbcuni.com/cable/universal-cable-productions
imdb.com/company/co0242101
facebook.com/nbcuniversal
twitter.com/NBCUniversal

Accepts query letters from unproduced, unrepresented writers. Project types include TV. Genres include drama and comedy. Established in 1997.

UNIVERSAL PICTURES
Production company and distributor

1 Central Saint Giles
St Giles High St

London WC2H 8NU
UK
+44 (0203-618-8000

enquiriesuk@nbcuni.com
universalpictures.co.uk
imdb.com/company/co0105063

Does not accept any unsolicited material. Project types include TV. Genres include drama, fantasy, and comedy.

Roma Khana
Actress
imdb.com/name/nm1866227

UNIVERSAL PICTURES INTERNATIONAL (UPI)
Production company and distributor

1 Central Saint Giles
St Giles High St
London WC2H 8N
UK
+44 20 7079 6000

enquiriesuk@nbcuni.com
universalpictures.co.uk
imdb.com/company/co0219608
facebook.com/universalpicturesuk
twitter.com/universaluk

Does not accept any unsolicited material. Project types include TV and feature films. Genres include comedy.

Clare Wise
Producer
imdb.com/name/nm0936328

UNIVERSAL STUDIOS
Production company and studio

100 Universal City Plaza
Universal City, CA 91608
818-840-4444

universalstudios.com
imdb.com/company/co0000534

Does not accept any unsolicited material. Project types include TV and feature films. Genres include thriller, comedy, crime, family, fantasy, animation, detective, drama, myth, horror, non-fiction, action, romance, and science fiction. Established in 1912.

Ron Meyer
818-840-4444
imdb.com/name/nm0005228

UNIVERSAL TELEVISION
Production company

100 Universal City Plaza
Building 1360, 3rd Floor
Universal City, CA 91608
818-777-1000

universalstudios.com
imdb.com/company/co0096447

Does not accept any unsolicited material. Project types include TV. Genres include family, thriller, romance, science fiction, myth, non-fiction, detective, crime, comedy, fantasy, action, drama, and animation.

UNIZARRE INTERNATIONAL FILM & TV PRODUCTIONS
Production company

UK
+44 (0)7740 405666

enquiries@unizarre.com
unizarre.com
imdb.com/company/co0153555

Does not accept any unsolicited material. Project types include TV. Genres include science fiction.

David Bowles
Producer
imdb.com/name/nm0101228

UNRAVAL PICTURES
Production company

PO Box 684643
Austin, TX 78768
512-507-8158

pj@unraval.com
unraval.com
imdb.com/company/co0418505
facebook.com/unravelsg

Does not accept any unsolicited material. Genres include documentary and drama.

UNSTOPPABLE ENTERTAINMENT
Production company

c/o Independent Talent Agency
76 Oxford St
London W1D 1BS
United Kingdom

info@unstoppableentertainmentuk.com
unstoppableentertainmentuk.com
imdb.com/company/co0282998
facebook.com/UnstoppableEntertainmentUK
twitter.com/UnstoppableLtd

Accepts scripts from unproduced, unrepresented writers. Project types include feature films. Genres include thriller, crime, drama, comedy, action, romance, and science fiction. Established in 2007.

Noel Clarke
Principal
noel@unstoppableentertainmentuk.com

UNTITLED ENTERTAINMENT
Production company and distributor

350 S Beverly Dr, Suite 200
Beverly Hills, CA 90212
310-601-2100

imdb.com/company/co0034249
linkedin.com/company/untitled-entertainment

Accepts query letters from unproduced, unrepresented writers. Project types include TV. Genres include drama, comedy, non-fiction, fantasy, myth, and romance.

Jason Weinberg
Partner
linkedin.com/pub/jason-weinberg/10/643/80b

UPLINK
Production company and distributor

37-18
Udagawacho
Shibuya, Tokyo 150-0042

Japan
03-6825-5501

tabela@uplink.co.jp
uplink.co.jp
imdb.com/company/co0029349

Does not accept any unsolicited material. Project types include TV. Genres include drama, comedy, and crime.

Takashi Asai
President (Producer)
imdb.com/name/nm0038306

UPLOAD FILMS

9522 Brookline Ave.
Baton Rouge, LA 70809
225-610-1639

8522 National Blvd., #106
Culver City, CA 90232
310-841-5805 (phone)
310-841-5804 (fax)

uploadfilms.com
imdb.com/company/co0195173
linkedin.com/company/upload-films

Does not accept any unsolicited material. Project types include feature films. Genres include drama, detective, action, horror, and thriller. Established in 2006.

John Portnoy
Partner
jportnoy@uploadfilms.com
imdb.com/name/nm0692471
linkedin.com/in/johnportnoy
facebook.com/kandyd

Andrew Mann
Partner
7films.dendelionblu.me/andrew-mann
imdb.com/name/nm2635886
linkedin.com/in/andrewmanntci
facebook.com/andrew.mann.9

Nick Thurlow
Producer
imdb.com/name/nm2250917
linkedin.com/pub/dir/nick/thurlow
facebook.com/nick.thurlow

UPPITV
Production company

c/o CBS Studios
4024 Radford Ave, Bungalow 9
Studio City, CA 91604
818-655-5000

imdb.com/company/co0286875

Does not accept any unsolicited material. Project types include TV. Genres include drama and comedy.

Samuel Jackson
818-655-5000
imdb.com/name/nm0000168
twitter.com/SamuelLJackson

Rebecca Windsor
Manager of Development
linkedin.com/pub/rebecca-windsor/11/603/998

UPTOWN 6 PRODUCTIONS
Production company and distributor

2904 Zuni St
Denver, CO 80211
323-823-6973

info@uptown6.com
uptown6.com
imdb.com/company/co0305597

Does not accept any unsolicited material. Project types include TV. Genres include comedy, thriller, and horror.

Adam Lipsius
Director
imdb.com/name/nm0513771

URBAN HOME ENTERTAINMENT
Production company, distributor, and sales agent

457 Hill St St.
Atlanta, GA 30312
888-254-3822

urbanhomeent@aol.com
urbanhomeent.com
imdb.com/company/co0196583

Does not accept any unsolicited material. Project types include TV. Genres include comedy and drama.

Trae Dungy
Producer
imdb.com/name/nm2561440

URBAN WOLF PRODUCTIONS
Production company

carl@urbanwolfproductions.com
imdb.com/company/co0065430

Does not accept any unsolicited material.

USA NETWORK
Production company

30 Rockefeller Plaza
21st Floor
New York, NY 10112
212-664-4444 (phone)
212-703-8582 (fax)

usanetwork.com
imdb.com/company/co0014957
facebook.com/USANetwork
twitter.com/USA_Network

Does not accept any unsolicited material. Project types include TV. Genres include drama and comedy. Established in 1971.

UT CINEMA PRODUCTION
Production company

73 Boatworkd Dr
Bayonne, NJ 07002
718-219-1418

utcinema@tut.by
utcinema.com
imdb.com/company/co0485413

Does not accept any unsolicited material. Project types include TV. Genres include drama and comedy.

UTTERLY MAD ENTERTAINMENT
Production company

PO Box 696
Maple Shade, NJ 08052
888-375-9623

wb2zeu@msn.com

imdb.com/company/co0084064

Does not accept any unsolicited material. Project types include TV. Genres include thriller and drama.

VALHALLA MOTION PICTURES
Production company

3201 Cahuenga Blvd W
Los Angeles, CA 90068-1301
323-850-3030 (phone)
323-850-3038 (fax)

vmp@valhallaent.com
valhallamotionpictures.com
imdb.com/company/co0092570
facebook.com/pages/Valhalla-Motion-Pictures/
126114487446982
twitter.com/valhallapics

Does not accept any unsolicited material. Project types include feature films and TV. Genres include thriller, drama, action, fantasy, and horror.

Gale Hurd
CEO
323-850-3030
gah@valhallapix.com
imdb.com/name/nm0005036
twitter.com/GunnerGale

VALIANT ENTERTAINMENT
Production company

424 W. 33rd St., New York City, NY, United States, 10001
323-462-3710 (phone)
323-657-5358 (fax)

inquiries@valiantentertainment.com
valiantentertainment.com
imdb.com/company/co0328290

Does not accept any unsolicited material. Project types include feature films, short films, and TV. Genres include action, romance, drama, thriller, and family.

VANDERKLOOT FILM & TELEVISION
Studio

750 Ralph McGill Blvd, NE
Atlanta, Georgia 30312
404-221-0236

bv@vanderkloot.com
vanderkloot.com
imdb.com/company/co0184000
linkedin.com/company/vanderkloot-film-&-television-
    inc.

Does not accept any unsolicited material. Project types
include short films, feature films, TV, and
commercials. Genres include drama, non-fiction,
action, family, and comedy.

William VanDerKloot
404-221-0236
william@vanderkloot.com
imdb.com/name/nm0886281
linkedin.com/in/vanderkloot

Lisa Ferrell
Executive Producer
lisa@magicklantern.com

VAN GOGH PRODUCTIONS
Production company

704 26th St S
703-299-0147

alexanderbarnett2@gmail.com
vangoghmusic.nl
imdb.com/company/co0154384

Accepts query letters from unproduced, unrepresented
writers. Project types include theater and feature films.
Genres include period and drama. Established in 2004.

Alexander Barnett
Executive Producer
703-299-0147
alexanderbarnett2@gmail.com
alexanderbarnett.com
imdb.com/name/nm1918760
linkedin.com/profile/view
facebook.com/alexander.barnett.31
twitter.com/barnettdirector
Assistant: Ashley March

VANGUARD FILMS AND ANIMATION
Production company

8703 W Olympic Blvd
Los Angeles, CA 90035
310-360-8039 (phone)
310-362-8685 (fax)

contact@vanguardanimation.com
vanguardanimation.com
imdb.com/company/co0096434
linkedin.com/company/vanguard-films-&-animation
facebook.com/pages/Vanguard-Animation/
    109408872411752

Does not accept any unsolicited material. Project types
include feature films. Genres include animation,
comedy, science fiction, and family. Established in
2002.

Robert Moreland
President Production & Development
310-888-8020
imdb.com/name/nm0603668
linkedin.com/pub/rob-moreland/7/903/aa0

John Williams
Chairman & CEO
310-888-8020
imdb.com/name/nm0930964

VANGUARD PRODUCTIONS
Production company

12111 Beatrice St
Culver City, CA 90230
310-306-4910 (phone)
310-306-1978 (fax)

info@vanguardproductions.biz
vanguardproductions.biz
imdb.com/company/co0089850
facebook.com/VanguardPublishing

Accepts query letters from unproduced, unrepresented
writers via email. Project types include feature films
and TV. Genres include non-fiction, action, drama,
family, and comedy. Established in 1986.

Terence O'Keefe
310-306-4910
terry@vanguardproductions.biz
imdb.com/name/nm0641496

VANQUISH MOTION PICTURES
Production company

10 Universal City Plaza
NBC/Universal Building, 20th Floor
Universal City, CA 91608
818-753-2319

submissions@vanquishmotionpictures.com
imdb.com/company/co0273425
facebook.com/pages/Vanquish-Motion-Pictures/
    109664999062401

Accepts query letters from unproduced, unrepresented
writers via email. Project types include TV and feature
films. Established in 2009.

Neetu Sharma
Creative Executive
818-753-2319
ns@vanquishmotionpictures.com
imdb.com/name/nm3434485

Ryan Williams
Creative Executive
818-753-2319
rs@vanquishmotionpictures.com
imdb.com/name/nm4426713

VARIENT
Production company

6007 Washington Blvd.
Los Angeles, CA 90232
310-839-1000

info@varient.com
varient.com
imdb.com/company/co0292161

Does not accept any unsolicited material. Project types
include TV. Genres include drama.

Gina Resnick
Producer
imdb.com/name/nm0720314

VARSITY PICTURES
Production company

11821 Mississippi Ave
Los Angeles, CA 90025

310-601-1960 (phone)
310-601-1961 (fax)

imdb.com/company/co0215791
facebook.com/VarsityPictures
twitter.com/varsitypictures

Accepts query letters from unproduced, unrepresented
writers. Project types include TV and feature films.
Established in 2007.

Shauna Phelan
310-601-1960
imdb.com/name/nm1016912
linkedin.com/pub/shauna-phelan/5/8b5/697
facebook.com/shauna.phelan.7

Carter Hansen
Creative Executive
310-601-1960
imdb.com/name/nm3255715
facebook.com/thecarterhansen
twitter.com/Carter_Hansen

VAUGHN STUDIOS
Production company and distributor

PO Box 340
Allenwood, NJ 08720
732-567-6870

office@vaughnstudios.com
jerseyboyhero.com
imdb.com/company/co0331034

Does not accept any unsolicited material. Project types
include short films and TV. Genres include
documentary.

VCX
Production company, distributor, and sales agent

3430 Precision Dr
North Las Vegas, NV 89032
702-638-4321

sales@vcx.com
vcx.com
imdb.com/company/co0039932

Does not accept any unsolicited material. Project types
include TV. Genres include documentary and comedy.

Norman Arno
President
imdb.com/company/co0039932

VELVET RIBBON PRODUCTIONS
Production company

4909 Mill Run Rd
Dallas, TX 75244
972-503-2581 (phone)
972-503-2783 (fax)

sgarrison@swbell.net
sharongarrison.com
imdb.com/company/co0349359
facebook.com/SharonGarrison4VRProductions

Does not accept any unsolicited material. Project types include short films. Genres include drama.

VELVET STEAMROLLER ENTERTAINMENT
Production company

10900 Wilshire Blvd Suite 1400
Los Angeles CA 90024
310-443-5335 (phone)
773-409-5662 (fax)

1829 N Orleans St, Chicago , IL, United States, 60614
312-924-0530

vs@velvetsteamroller.com
velvetsteamroller.com
imdb.com/company/co0108388

Does not accept any unsolicited material. Project types include TV, short films, and feature films. Genres include family and drama.

VENEVISION INTERNATIONAL
Production company and distributor

Final Av. La Salle, Edf. Antaraju, Caracas , Venezuela, DF 1050
011-582-127089164 (phone)
011-582-127823464 (fax)

C/ Montalban 5-3 Izq.
Madrid Spain 28014

011-349-15214103 (phone)
011-349-15311417 (fax)

121 Alhambra Plaza Suite 1400
Coral Gables FL 33134
305-442-3411 (phone)
305-448-4762 (fax)

info@venevisioninternational.com
venevisioninternational.com
imdb.com/company/co0081793

Does not accept any unsolicited material. Project types include TV and feature films. Genres include drama, action, family, thriller, and romance.

VENTURE 4TH AG LLC
Production company

Austin, TX, United States

info@venture4.com
venture4.com
imdb.com/company/co0402483

Does not accept any unsolicited material. Project types include TV. Genres include comedy, drama, romance, and family.

VENTURE FORTH PRODUCTIONS
Production company and distributor

United States

info@venture4.com
venture4.com
imdb.com/company/co0441062

Does not accept any unsolicited material. Project types include TV. Genres include romance and drama.

VERISIMILITUDE
Production company

225 W 13th St
New York, NY 10011
212-989-1038 (phone)
212-989-1943 (fax)

info@verisimilitude.com
verisimilitude.com
imdb.com/company/co0212525

Does not accept any unsolicited material. Project types include feature films. Genres include romance, drama, comedy, and thriller.

Alex Orlovsky
Partner
imdb.com/name/nm0650164

Phaedon Papadopoulos
Creative Executive
imdb.com/name/nm3011396

Hunter Gray
Partner
imdb.com/name/nm0336683

Tyler Brodie
Partner
imdb.com/name/nm0110921

VÉRITÉ FILMS
Production company

15 Beaufort Rd
Toronto, ON M4E 1M6
Canada
416-693-8245

verite@veritefilms.ca
veritefilms.ca
imdb.com/company/co0121068
facebook.com/pages/V%C3%A9rit%C3%A9-Films-
    Inc/174261756027334
twitter.com/veritecanada

Accepts query letters from unproduced, unrepresented writers. Project types include TV. Genres include drama, comedy, and family. Established in 2004.

Virginia Thompson
306-585-1737
virginia@veritefilms.ca
imdb.com/name/nm1395111

VERIZON
Production company and distributor

140 W St, New York, NY, United States, 10007
212-395-1000 (phone)
212-571-1897 (fax)

verizon.com
imdb.com/company/co0208464

Does not accept any unsolicited material. Project types include TV. Genres include reality, comedy, drama, family, thriller, and romance.

VERNON-MCKEE
Production company

7520 Lawndale Ave
Houston, Texas 77012
713-894-3158

molly@vernonmckee.com
vernonmckee.com
imdb.com/company/co0364077
facebook.com/Vernon-McKee-170438206387248

Does not accept any unsolicited material. Project types include short films. Genres include thriller. Established in 2011.

VERTEBRA FILMS
Production company

250 E 33rd St.
10016
323-461-0021 (phone)
323-461-0031 (fax)

hello@vertebrafilms.com
vertebrafilms.com
imdb.com/company/co0319489
twitter.com/VertebraFilms

Does not accept any unsolicited material. Project types include feature films. Genres include thriller and horror. Established in 2010.

Mac Cappucino
imdb.com/name/nm2225247

VERTICAL ENTERTAINMENT
Production company and distributor

2500 Broadway, Suite F-125, Santa Monica, CA, United States, 90404
424-238-4455

info@vert-ent.com
vert-ent.com
imdb.com/company/co0427244

Does not accept any unsolicited material. Project types include feature films and TV. Genres include drama, thriller, and family.

VERTIGO FILMS
Production company and studio

The Big Room Studios 77 Fortess Rd
London, United Kingdom,
NW5 1AG
+44-0-20-7428-7555 (phone)
+44-0-20-7485-9713 (fax)

mail@vertigofilms.com
vertigofilms.com
imdb.com/company/co0113509
facebook.com/VertigoFilmsUK
twitter.com/vertigofilms

Does not accept any unsolicited material. Project types include feature films. Genres include science fiction, romance, thriller, drama, action, comedy, crime, fantasy, and horror. Established in 2002.

Rupert Preston
Producer
imdb.com/name/nm0696486

Allan Niblo
Producer
imdb.com/name/nm0629242

James Richardson
Producer
imdb.com/name/nm0724597

Jim Spencer
Producer
imdb.com/name/nm2005794

NIck Love
imdb.com/name/nm0522393

VESTALIA PRODUCTIONS
Production company

210 W Glen Ave
Ridgewood, NJ 07450
201-835-7778 (phone)
201-670-4931 (fax)

vestaliaproductions@yahoo.com
imdb.com/company/co0169260

Does not accept any unsolicited material. Project types include short films. Genres include drama.

VH1
Production company

2600 Colorado Ave
Santa Monica, CA 90404
310-752-8000

info@vh1.com
vh1.com
imdb.com/company/co0045189
facebook.com/VH1
twitter.com/VH1

Accepts query letters from unproduced, unrepresented writers. Project types include TV. Genres include drama, romance, comedy, and non-fiction. Established in 1986.

Van Toffler
212-846-8000
van.toffler@vh1.com
imdb.com/name/nm0865508

VHX
Distributor

231 Front St, Suite 214, Brooklyn, NY, United States, 11201
347-689-1458

contact@vhx.tv
imdb.com/company/co0450816

Does not accept any unsolicited material.

Jamie Wilkinson
Executive
347-689-1458
imdb.com/name/nm6920411

VIACOM INC.
Production company

1515 Broadway
New York, NY 10036
212-258-6000

viacom.com
imdb.com/company/co0077647
facebook.com/viacom

twitter.com/viacom

Does not accept any unsolicited material. Project types include TV. Genres include comedy, non-fiction, and drama. Established in 1971.

Philippe Dauman
212-258-6000
philippe.dauman@viacom.com
imdb.com/name/nm2449184

VICTORIA BAY PRODUCTIONS
Production company

Hopesdm@yahoo.com
victoriabayproductions.com

Does not accept any unsolicited material. Project types include TV and feature films. Genres include fantasy. Established in 1992.

Hope Schenk
Executive Vice President of Production
hopesdm@yahoo.com

VICTORY FILM GROUP
Production company

033 Main St, Suite 400, Sarasota, FL, United States, 34237

info@victoryfilmgroup.com
imdb.com/company/co0342499

Does not accept any unsolicited material.

Stephen K. Bannon
Director
imdb.com/name/nm0052442

VIDEOARTS JAPAN
Production company and distributor

2F Akasaka Hill-Side Bld.2-18-1
Akasaka, Minato-Ku
Tokyo 107-0052
Japan
+81-3-6229-0751 (phone)
+81-3-6229-0754 (fax)

info@videoartsmusic.com
videoartsmusic.com
imdb.com/company/co0126378

Does not accept any unsolicited material. Project types include TV. Genres include documentary.

VIDEO FOCUS
Production company

2-7
Wakaba
Shinjuku, Tokyo 160-0011
Japan
03-3353-3371 (phone)
03-3353-3630 (fax)

info@videofocus.co.jp
videofocus.co.jp
imdb.com/company/co0283815

Does not accept any unsolicited material. Project types include TV and feature films. Genres include comedy, romance, and drama.

Toshiya Tsubonouchi
Producer
imdb.com/name/nm5187733

VIDEOSONIC
Production company and distributor

1, Evridamantos & Lagoumitzi St., Athens , United States, 11745

j.sarras@videosonic.gr
imdb.com/company/co0061607

Does not accept any unsolicited material. Project types include TV. Genres include drama and thriller.

VILLAGE ROADSHOW PICTURES
Production company

100 N Crescent Dr, Suite 323
Beverly Hills, CA 90210
310-385-4300 (phone)
310-385-4301 (fax)

flo@gracepr.net
vreg.com
imdb.com/company/co0108864

Does not accept any unsolicited material. Project types include feature films. Established in 1998.

Matt Skiena
310-385-4300
mskiena@vrpe.com
imdb.com/name/nm3466832

Bruce Berman
310-385-4300
imdb.com/name/nm0075732
Assistant: Suzy Figueroa

VILLANOVISION FILMS
Production company

6 Jupiter St
Colonia, NJ 07067
732-388-5551

info@villanovisions.com
imdb.com/company/co0382701

Does not accept any unsolicited material. Project types include TV. Genres include comedy, drama, and science fiction.

VINCENT CIRRINCIONE ASSOCIATES
Production company

1516 N. Fairfax Ave
Los Angeles, CA 90046
323-850-8080

reception@vcassoc.com
imdb.com/company/co0090082
linkedin.com/company/vincent-cirrincione-associates
facebook.com/vcatalent

Does not accept any unsolicited material. Project types include feature films and TV. Genres include drama and thriller.

Vincent Cirrincione
Owner/Producer
imdb.com/name/nm0162801

VINCENT NEWMAN ENTERTAINMENT
Production company

8840 Wilshire Blvd
3rd Floor
Los Angeles, CA 90211
310-358-3050 (phone)
310-358-3289 (fax)

general@liveheart-vne.com
imdb.com/company/co0163095

Accepts query letters from unproduced, unrepresented writers via email. Project types include TV. Genres include drama, thriller, myth, comedy, fantasy, and action. Established in 2011.

Vincent Newman
310-358-3050
vincent@liveheart-vne.com
imdb.com/name/nm0628304
Assistant: John Funk

John Funk
Director/Writer
linkedin.com/pub/john-funk/a/4a3/924

VINCENZO PRODUCTIONS
Production company

48 Mountainside Rd
Mendham, NJ 07945
201-776-7868

germs3@verizon.net
imdb.com/company/co0370795

Does not accept any unsolicited material. Project types include TV and feature films. Genres include thriller.

VIN DI BONA PRODUCTIONS
Production company

12233 W Olympic Blvd, Suite 170
Los Angeles, CA 90064
310-442-5600

afv.com
imdb.com/company/co0017060
linkedin.com/company/vin-di-bona-productions
facebook.com/AFVOfficial

Accepts query letters from unproduced, unrepresented writers. Project types include TV. Genres include comedy. Established in 1987.

Vin DiBona
Chairman
imdb.com/name/nm0223688

Joanne Moore
President
imdb.com/name/nm0601370

Cara Di Bona
imdb.com/name/nm0223685

VINTON ENTERTAINMENT
Production company

1100 Glendon Ave
Los Angeles, CA 90024-3503

info@vintonentertainment.com
vintonentertainment.com
imdb.com/company/co0467460
linkedin.com/company/vinton-studios
facebook.com/pages/Laika-company/
    104039669631769

Does not accept any unsolicited material. Project types
include feature films. Genres include animation.
Established in 2004.

VIPER COMICS
Production company

9400 N MacArthur Blv
Suite 124-215
Irving, TX 75063

info@vipercomics.com
vipercomics.com
imdb.com/company/co0264356
facebook.com/vipercomics
twitter.com/vipercomics

Does not accept any unsolicited material. Genres
include horror.

VIRGIN EARTH
Production company

Honey Building B2F
3-35-8 Jingumae, Shibuya-Ku
Tokyo 150-0001
Japan
+81-3-5414-7660 (phone)
+81-3-5414-7661 (fax)

info@virginearthinc.com
virginearthinc.com

imdb.com/company/co0025119

Does not accept any unsolicited material. Project types
include feature films and TV. Genres include
documentary.

Rinse Koornstra
Producer
imdb.com/name/nm5445881

VIRGIN PRODUCED
Production company

315 S Beverly Dr, Suite 506
Beverly Hills, CA 90212
310-941-7300

901,9th Floor, Notan Classic Bldg
F/891-B, Turner Rd, Bandra (West)
Mumbai 400 050 India

903 Colorado Ave
Santa Monica CA 90401
310-941-7300

media@virginproduced.com
virginproduced.com
imdb.com/company/co0310456
facebook.com/VIRGINproduced
twitter.com/VIRGINproduced

Does not accept any unsolicited material. Project types
include TV. Genres include comedy, action, drama,
fantasy, animation, and thriller. Established in 2010.

Jason Felts
CEO
310-941-7300
jfelts@virginproduced.com
imdb.com/name/nm1479777

Rebecca Farrell
imdb.com/name/nm2761874

VISCERAL PSYCHE FILMS
Production company and distributor

1-11-6-6F
Oh-I
Shinagawa, Tokyo 140-0014
Japan
03-3775-7441 (phone)
03-3775-7442 (fax)

mindmeld@visceralpsyche.com
visceralpsyche.com
imdb.com/company/co0180725
facebook.com/visceralpsyche
twitter.com/visceralpsyche

Does not accept any unsolicited material. Project types include TV. Genres include drama.

Paul Leeming
Producer
imdb.com/name/nm2283467

VISILEX PRODUCTIONS
Production company

C/O Naskret/Selzer & Associates
3 Becker Farm Rd.
Roseland, NJ 07068

charles@charleskipps.com
charleskipps.com
imdb.com/company/co0239824
twitter.com/times2ck

Does not accept any unsolicited material. Project types include TV. Genres include drama and comedy.

VISION BEQUEST FILMWORKS
Production company

P.O. Box 590843
Houston, TX 77259

leftturnyield@yahoo.com
imdb.com/company/co0230942

Does not accept any unsolicited material. Genres include drama and comedy.

VISION FILMS
Production company, distributor, and sales agent

14945 Ventura Blvd, Suite 306, Sherman Oaks, CA, United States, 91403
818-784-1702 (phone)
818-788-3715 (fax)

visionfilms@earthlink.net
visionfilms.net
imdb.com/company/co0070863

Does not accept any unsolicited material. Project types include TV and feature films. Genres include drama, action, family, and thriller.

VISION FILMS, INC.
Studio

14945 Ventura Blvd
Sherman Oaks, CA 91403
818-784-1702 (phone)
818-788-3715 (fax)

visionfilms.net
imdb.com/company/co0070863
linkedin.com/pub/vision-films/66/a61/8b1
facebook.com/VisionFilmsInc

Does not accept any unsolicited material. Project types include commercials, short films, and feature films. Genres include documentary and family. Established in 1997.

Samantha Coolbeth
Sales & Marketing Coordinator
samantha@visionfilms.net

Nathan Ross
Director of Digital Operations & Servicing
nathan@visionfilms.net

Jasmine Abrams
Contract Manager
contracts@visionfilms.net

Alex Saveliev
Director of Domestic Distribution
marketing@visionfilms.net

Adam Wright
Executive Vice-President
adam@visionfilms.net

Lise Romanoff
CEO
lise@visionfilms.net
imdb.com/name/nm0738983

Monique Green
Director of Finance
accounting@visionfilms.net

VISION-X PRODUCTIONS
Production company

3481 Lakeside Dr, NE
Suite #1904
Atlanta, GA 30326
678-732-3810

info@visionXproductions.com
visionxproductions.com
imdb.com/company/co0379681
facebook.com/ken.farrington
twitter.com/Ken_Farrington

Does not accept any unsolicited material. Project types include TV. Genres include thriller and horror.

VISIT FILMS
Production company, distributor, and sales agent

173 Richardson St, Brooklyn, NY, United States, 11222
718-312-8210 (phone)
718-362-4865 (fax)

info@visitfilms.com
visitfilms.com
imdb.com/company/co0173924

Does not accept any unsolicited material. Project types include TV. Genres include comedy, romance, family, and drama.

VISUALWORKS
Production company

1-33-8-13F
Higashi Ikebukuro
Toshima, Tokyo 170-0013
Japan
03 5911 7316 (phone)
03-5911-7317 (fax)

press@visualworks.co.jp
visualworks.co.jp
imdb.com/company/co0219083

Does not accept any unsolicited material. Project types include feature films. Genres include comedy.

Yasuzo Toyoda
Chief Executive Officer
imdb.com/name/nm2798730

VOLTAGE PICTURES
Production company, distributor, and sales agent

116 N Robertson Blvd, Suite 200, Los Angeles, CA, United States, 90048
323-606-7630 (phone)
323-315-7115 (fax)

sales@voltagepictures.com
voltagepictures.com
imdb.com/company/co0179337

Does not accept any unsolicited material. Project types include TV and feature films. Genres include family, thriller, drama, and action.

Zev Foreman
President (Production)
imdb.com/name/nm2303301

VOLTAGE PRODUCTIONS
Production company

116 N. Robertson Blvd., Suite 200
Los Angeles, CA 90048 USA
323-606-7630 (phone)
323-315-7115 (fax)

office@voltagepictures.com
voltagepictures.com
imdb.com/company/co0179337

Accepts scripts from produced or represented writers. Project types include feature films. Genres include animation, non-fiction, romance, drama, science fiction, action, and fantasy. Established in 2011.

Craig Flores
imdb.com/name/nm1997836
Assistant: Edmond Guidry

Zev Foreman
Head of Development
imdb.com/name/nm2303301

Nicolas Chartier
nicolas@voltagepictures.com
imdb.com/name/nm1291566

VON ZERNECK SERTNER FILMS
Production company

c/o HCVT
11444 W Olympic Blvd
11th Floor

Los Angeles, CA 90064
310-652-3020

vzs@vzsfilms.com
vzsfilms.com
imdb.com/company/co0094479

Does not accept any unsolicited material. Genres include thriller, non-fiction, detective, drama, and crime. Established in 1987.

Frank Von Zerneck
Partner
310-652-3020
vonzerneck@gmail.com
imdb.com/name/nm0903273

Robert M. Srtner
Partner
imdb.com/name/nm0785750

VOX3 FILMS
Production company and distributor

315 Bleecker St #111
New York, NY 10014
212-741-0406 (phone)
212-741-0424 (fax)

contact@vox3films.com
imdb.com/company/co0146502
facebook.com/pages/Vox3-Films/110031625098

Does not accept any unsolicited material. Project types include TV and feature films. Genres include drama, comedy, romance, and thriller. Established in 2004.

Christina Lurie
Partner
imdb.com/name/nm1417371

Steven Shainberg
Partner
imdb.com/name/nm078760

Andrew Fierberg
212-741-0406
imdb.com/name/nm0276404

VULCAN PRODUCTIONS
Production company

505 Fifth Ave. S., Suite 900
Seattle WA 98104
206-342-2000

info@vulcanproductions.com
vulcanproductions.com
imdb.com/company/co0042766
facebook.com/VulcanInc
twitter.com/VulcanInc

Does not accept any unsolicited material. Genres include thriller, non-fiction, and action. Established in 1983.

Jody Allen
President
206-342-2277
jody@vulcan.com
imdb.com/name/nm0666580

VURV
Production company and distributor

7660 Centurion Parkway
Suite 100
Jacksonville, FL 32256
877-394-5644 (phone)
904-493-9146 (fax)

oraclesales_us@oracle.com
imdb.com/company/co0183674

Does not accept any unsolicited material. Genres include drama.

W2 MEDIA
Distributor

310-392-0088

info@w2media.com
imdb.com/company/co0332305

Does not accept any unsolicited material.

Warren Nimchuk
Producer
imdb.com/name/nm3410149

WALDEN MEDIA
Production company

1888 Century Park East
14th Floor
Los Angeles, CA 90067
310-887-1000 (phone)
310-887-1001 (fax)

17 New England Executive Park
Suite 305
Burlington, MA 01803

info@walden.com
walden.com
imdb.com/company/co0073388
facebook.com/waldenmedia
twitter.com/waldenmedia

Accepts query letters from unproduced, unrepresented writers via email. Project types include feature films. Established in 2001.

Amanda Palmer
310-887-1000
imdb.com/name/nm2198853

Eric Tovell
Creative Executive
etovell@walden.com
Assistant: Carol Tang ctang@walden.com

Evan Turner
310-887-1000
imdb.com/name/nm1602263

WALKER CABLE PRODUCTIONS
Production company

304 N Main St
Unit 5
Conroe, Texas 77301
936-760-3279

Charlie@walkercableinc.com
walkercableinc.com
imdb.com/company/co0184185
linkedin.com/pub/walkercable-productions/44/92/759
facebook.com/WalkerCableProductions
twitter.com/WalkerCableProd

Does not accept any unsolicited material. Project types include TV and feature films. Genres include action, comedy, and family.

WALKER/FITZGIBBON TV & FILM PRODUCTION
Production company

2399 Mt. Olympus
Los Angeles, CA 90046
323-878-0500

mo@walkerfitzgibbon.com
walkerfitzgibbon.com
imdb.com/company/co0171571
linkedin.com/company/walker-fitzgibbon-tv-&-film
web.facebook.com/WFTVF
twitter.com/WalkerFitzFilm

Does not accept any unsolicited material. Project types include commercials and TV. Genres include drama, animation, comedy, and non-fiction.

Mo Fitzgibbon
323-469-6800
mo@walkerfitzgibbon.com
imdb.com/name/nm0280422

Robert W. Walker
imdb.com/name/nm0908166

WALT BECKER COMPANY
Production company

8530 Wilshire Blvd., Suite 550
Beverly Hills, CA 90211
323-871-8400

imdb.com/company/co0405377

Does not accept any unsolicited material. Project types include TV and feature films. Genres include comedy Established in 2007.

Kelly Hayes
Director of Development & Production
imdb.com/name/nm0971886
linkedin.com/pub/kelly-hayes/2a/845/717

Walt Becker
Writer/Producer
imdb.com/name/nm0065608

Ross Putman
Development
imdb.com/name/nm3819444

WALT BECKER PRODUCTIONS
Production company

8530 Wilshire Blvd.
Suite 550
Beverly Hills, CA 90212
323-871-8400 (phone)
323-871-2540 (fax)

imdb.com/company/co0236068

Does not accept any unsolicited material. Project types include TV.

Walt Becker
imdb.com/name/nm0065608

Kelly Hayes
Director of Development
imdb.com/name/nm0971886

WALT DISNEY STUDIO HOME ENTERTAINMENT
Production company

500 S. Buena Vista St.
Burbank, CA 91521-6369
818-560-1000

waltdisneystudios.com
imdb.com/company/co0049546

Does not accept any unsolicited material. Project types include feature films, TV, and short films. Genres include non-fiction, drama, comedy, horror, crime, thriller, documentary, action, animation, family, fantasy, romance, and science fiction. Established in 1952.

WANGO FILMS
Production company

281 Mutual St
Ste 2206
Toronto, ON M4Y 3C4
Canada
416-829-4049

info@wangofilms.com
wangofilms.com
imdb.com/company/co0349875
facebook.com/Wango-Films-112676668810114
twitter.com/wangofilms

Does not accept any unsolicited material. Genres include thriller.

April Mullen
Producer
imdb.com/name/nm0611983

WAREHOUZE
Production company

Fort Mason Green
Pier 1
San Francisco, CA 94123
888-874-9275 (phone)
888-874-9275 (fax)

sf-info@warehouze.tv
imdb.com/company/co0337396
linkedin.com/company/warehouze
facebook.com/warehouze
twitter.com/warehouze

Does not accept any unsolicited material. Project types include feature films and TV. Genres include drama, crime, science fiction, animation, non-fiction, and action. Established in 2007.

WARNER BROS. PICTURES
Production company and distributor

1325 Ave of the Americas 32nd Floor
New York NY 10019
212-636-5000

Warner Suite, Leavesden Studios South Way, Watford,
United Kingdom WD25 7LT
011-441-923685222 (phone)
011-441-923685221 (fax)

98 Theobalds Rd
London United Kingdom WC1X 8WB
011-442-079845200 (phone)
011-442-079845551 (fax)

4000 Warner Blvd, Burbank , CA, United States, 91522
818-954-6000

warnerbros.com
imdb.com/company/co0215074

Does not accept any unsolicited material. Project types include feature films and TV. Genres include action, thriller, drama, and family.

Greg Silverman

President (Creative Development and Worldwide Production)
818-954-1848
imdb.com/name/nm0798909

WARNER BROS. TELEVISION GROUP

Production company and distributor

4000 Warner Blvd
Burbank, CA 91522-0001
818-954-6000

info@warnerbros.com
warnerbros.com
imdb.com/company/co0253255
linkedin.com/company/2470
facebook.com/warnerbrosent
twitter.com/Warnerbrosent

Does not accept any unsolicited material. Project types include TV. Genres include comedy, action, animation, drama, family, thriller, romance, myth, non-fiction, and fantasy. Established in 2005.

Bruce Rosenblum

President
bruce.rosenblum@warnerbros.com
imdb.com/name/nm2686463

WARNER BROTHERS ANIMATION

Production company

411 N Hollywood Way
Burbank, CA 91505
818-977-8700

info@warnerbros.com
warnerbros.com
imdb.com/company/co0072876
linkedin.com/company/2470
facebook.com/warnerbrosent
twitter.com/Warnerbrosent

Does not accept any unsolicited material. Project types include TV. Genres include animation. Established in 1930.

Sam Register

Executive Vice-President, Creative
sam.register@warnerbros.com
imdb.com/name/nm1882146

WARNER BROTHERS ENTERTAINMENT INC.

Production company

4000 Warner Blvd
Burbank, CA 91522-0001
818-954-6000

warnerbros.com
imdb.com/company/co0080422
linkedin.com/company/2470
facebook.com/warnerbrosent
twitter.com/Warnerbrosent

Does not accept any unsolicited material. Project types include TV. Genres include animation, drama, family, detective, romance, thriller, science fiction, fantasy, myth, non-fiction, comedy, crime, and action. Established in 1923.

Barry Meyer

barry.meyer@warnerbros.com
imdb.com/name/nm0583028

WARNER BROTHERS HOME ENTERTAINMENT

Production company and studio

4000 Warner Blvd
Burbank, CA 91522-0001
818-954-6000

info@warnerbros.com
warnerbros.com
imdb.com/company/co0200179
linkedin.com/company/2470
facebook.com/warnerbrosent
twitter.com/Warnerbrosent

Does not accept any unsolicited material. Project types include short films, feature films, and TV. Genres include myth, romance, action, drama, science fiction, comedy, animation, family, thriller, non-fiction, horror, crime, and fantasy. Established in 2005.

Kevin Tsujihara
President
kevin.tsujihara@warnerbros.com
imdb.com/name/nm2493597

WARNER BROTHERS PICTURES
Production company

4000 Warner Blvd
Burbank, CA 91522-0001
818-954-6000

info@warnerbros.com
warnerbros.com
imdb.com/company/co0026840
linkedin.com/company/2470
facebook.com/warnerbrosent
twitter.com/Warnerbrosent

Does not accept any unsolicited material. Project types include feature films. Genres include animation, thriller, drama, detective, family, comedy, myth, romance, action, non-fiction, fantasy, and crime. Established in 1923.

Greg Silverman
imdb.com/name/nm0798909
Assistant: Cate Adams

Racheline Benveniste
Creative Executive
imdb.com/name/nm3367909
Assistant: Matthew Crespy

Lynn Harris
Executive Vice President of Production
imdb.com/name/nm0365036
Assistant: Alexandra Amin

Jeff Robinov
President
jeff.robinov@warnerbros.com
imdb.com/name/nm0732268
Assistant: Carrie Frymer

WARNER HORIZON TELEVISION
Production company

4000 Warner Blvd
Burbank, CA 91522-0001
818-954-6000

info@warnerbros.com
warnerbros.com
imdb.com/company/co0183230
linkedin.com/company/2470
facebook.com/warnerbrosent
twitter.com/Warnerbrosent

Does not accept any unsolicited material. Project types include TV. Genres include animation, non-fiction, comedy, drama, fantasy, romance, myth, family, and action. Established in 1999.

inc val
Head of Creative and Interactive
val1ant@live.com

Peter Roth
President
818-954-6000
peter.roth@warnerbros.com
imdb.com/name/nm2325137

WARNER SISTERS PRODUCTIONS
Production company

PO Box 50104
Santa Barbara, CA 93150
818-766-6952

info@warnersisters.com
warnersisters.com
imdb.com/company/co0121034
facebook.com/cass.warner
twitter.com/cassieowarner

Does not accept any unsolicited material. Genres include non-fiction and documentary. Established in 2003.

Cass Warner
imdb.com/name/nm2064300

WARP FILMS
Production company

Spectrum House 32-34 Gordon House Rd
London, United Kingdom, NW5 1LP
011-442-072848350 (phone)
011-442-072848360 (fax)

info@warpfilms.co.uk
warp.net/films

imdb.com/company/co0251927
facebook.com/warpfilms
twitter.com/WarpFilms

Accepts query letters from unproduced, unrepresented writers via email. Project types include feature films. Genres include documentary, romance, drama, horror, comedy, non-fiction, and action. Established in 2004.

Mark Herbert
imdb.com/name/nm0378591

Peter Carlton
imdb.com/name/nm1275058

WARP X

Electric Works
Digital Campus
Sheffield S1 2BJ
UK
+44114-286-6280 (phone)
+44114-286-6283 (fax)

info@warpx.co.uk
warpfilms.com
imdb.com/company/co0202028

Does not accept any unsolicited material. Project types include feature films. Genres include comedy, thriller, drama, crime, documentary, and horror. Established in 2008.

Mark Herbert
Producer
imdb.com/name/nm0378591

Barry Ryan
imdb.com/name/nm1419213

Robin Gutch
imdb.com/name/nm0349168

Mary Burke
Producer
imdb.com/name/nm1537339

WARREN MILLER ENTERTAINMENT
Production company

5720 Flatiron Parkway
Boulder CO 80301

303-253-6300 (phone)
303-253-6380 (fax)

info@warrenmillertv.com
aimstudios.tv
imdb.com/company/co0040142
facebook.com/WarrenMillerEntertainment

Accepts query letters from unproduced, unrepresented writers. Project types include feature films and TV. Genres include action, non-fiction, and reality. Established in 1952.

Jeffrey Moore
Senior Executive Producer
jmoore@aimmedia.com
imdb.com/name/nm2545455

Ginger Sheehy
imdb.com/name/nm1200078
linkedin.com/pub/ginger-sheehy/3/849/5b4
twitter.com/gst916

WARRIOR POETS
Production company

407 Broome St
New York, NY 10013
212-219-7617 (phone)
212-219-2920 (fax)

info@warrior-poets.com
warrior-poets.com
imdb.com/company/co0169151
facebook.com/WarriorPoetsProductions

Does not accept any unsolicited material. Project types include feature films and TV. Genres include drama and non-fiction. Established in 2005.

Ethan Goldman
imdb.com/name/nm1134121

Jeremy Chilnick
imdb.com/name/nm2505733
Assistant: Marjon Javadi

Morgan Spurlock
imdb.com/name/nm1041597
Assistant: Emmanuel Moran

WARRIOR PRODUCTIONS
Production company

16266 SW 14th St
Pembroke Pines, FL 33027
954-639-3419 (phone)
954-653-3778 (fax)

warriorproductions@gmail.com
imdb.com/company/co0260276
linkedin.com/company/warrior-productions
facebook.com/WarriorProductions

Does not accept any unsolicited material. Genres
include documentary.

WATER BEARER FILMS

Production company, distributor, and sales agent

3239 Gateway Circle
Charlottesville, VA 22911
434-923-8686 (phone)
434-923-8989 (fax)

Sales@Waterbearerfilms.com
imdb.com/company/co0029508

Does not accept any unsolicited material. Project types
include feature films and TV. Genres include thriller
and drama.

Michael Stimler
Producer
imdb.com/name/nm1192876

WATER'S END PRODUCTIONS

Production company

9903 Santa Monica Blvd.
No. 822
Beverly Hills, CA 90212
424-293-0714

watersendprod.com
imdb.com/company/co0472007

Does not accept any unsolicited material. Project types
include feature films. Genres include drama.
Established in 2012.

WATERSHED 5 STUDIOS

Production company

720 S Lamar Blvd.
Austin, TX 78704
512-851-2507

watershed5.com
imdb.com/company/co0231502
facebook.com/Watershed-5-67024809531
twitter.com/Watershed5

Does not accept any unsolicited material. Project types
include short films and TV. Genres include reality.

WAYANS BROTHERS ENTERTAINMENT

Production company

8730 W Sunset Blvd, Suite 290
Los Angeles, CA 90069-2247
323-930-6720 (phone)
424-202-3520 (fax)

thawkins@wayansbros.com
imdb.com/company/co0001823

Does not accept any unsolicited material. Project types
include TV. Genres include comedy, family, horror,
and crime. Established in 1980.

Rick Alvarez
imdb.com/name/nm0023315

Keenan Wayans
imdb.com/name/nm0005540

Mike Tiddes
Creative Executive
imdb.com/name/nm1639277

Shawn Wayans
imdb.com/name/nm0915465

Marlon Wayans
imdb.com/name/nm0005541
Assistant: Shane Miller

WAYFARE ENTERTAINMENT VENTURES LLC

Production company

435 W 19th St
4th Floor
New York, NY 10011
212-989-2200

info@start-media.com
wayfareentertainment.com
imdb.com/company/co0239158

linkedin.com/company/wayfare-entertainment-ventures-llc

Does not accept any unsolicited material. Project types include feature films. Genres include fantasy, myth, thriller, non-fiction, drama, action, comedy, science fiction, romance, and family. Established in 2008.

Sarah Shepard
imdb.com/name/nm2416896
linkedin.com/pub/sarah-shepard/24/145/38b

Michael Maher
start-media.com/start-motion-pictures/team/michael-j-maher
imdb.com/name/nm3052130

Jeremy Kipp Walker
imdb.com/name/nm0907844

Ben Browning
info@wayfareentertainment.com
imdb.com/name/nm1878845

WAYPOINT ENTERTAINMENT
Production company

400 S Beverly Dr, Suite 300, Beverly Hills, CA, United States, 90212
323-510-3330

info@waypointfound.com
waypointfound.com
imdb.com/company/co0353060

Does not accept any unsolicited material. Project types include feature films, short films, and TV. Genres include drama, romance, and family.

WAYWARD STUDIOS
Production company

649 SW Whitmore Dr
Port Saint Luci
Port Saint Lucie, FL 34984
772-475-4340 (phone)
772-879-0028 (fax)

waywardstudios@hotmail.com
imdb.com/company/co0221664

Does not accept any unsolicited material. Genres include horror.

WEED ROAD PRODUCTIONS
Production company

4000 Warner Blvd
Building 81, Suite 115
Burbank, CA 91522
818-954-3771 (phone)
818-954-3061 (fax)

imdb.com/company/co0093488

Does not accept any unsolicited material. Project types include feature films and TV. Genres include animation, drama, family, thriller, horror, fantasy, science fiction, non-fiction, and action. Established in 2004.

Nicki Cortese
imdb.com/name/nm2492480
Assistant: Mike Pence

Akiva Goldsman
imdb.com/name/nm0326040
Assistant: Bonnie Balmos

WEINSTOCK PRODUCTIONS
Production company

316 N Rossmore Ave
Los Angeles, CA 90004
323-791-1500

imdb.com/company/co0032259

Accepts query letters from unproduced, unrepresented writers. Project types include feature films. Genres include drama, comedy, crime, family, and thriller.

Charles Weinstock
President
imdb.com/name/nm091848
linkedin.com/pub/chuck-weinstock/19/35a/aa0

WEINTRAUB/KUHN PRODUCTIONS
Production company

1821 Wilshire Blvd, Ste 645
Santa Monica, CA 90403
310-458-3300 (phone)
310-458-3302 (fax)

dubeywein@aol.com
imdb.com/company/co0031680

Does not accept any unsolicited material. Project types include TV and feature films. Genres include thriller, myth, non-fiction, drama, science fiction, romance, family, fantasy, action, and comedy. Established in 1976.

Maxwell Meltzer
imdb.com/name/nm0578443

Fred Weintraub
President
fred@fredweintraub.com
fredweintraub.com
imdb.com/name/nm0918518

Tom Kuhn
President
imdb.com/name/nm0474166
linkedin.com/pub/tom-kuhn/18/534/292

Jackie Weintraub
imdb.com/name/nm0918520

WELLER/GROSSMAN PRODUCTIONS

Production company and distributor

5200 Lankershim Blvd, Fl5
North Hollywood, CA 91601
818-755-4800

contact@wellergrossman.com
imdb.com/company/co0102774

Accepts scripts from produced or represented writers. Project types include TV. Genres include comedy, animation, drama, and reality. Established in 1993.

Robb Weller
contact@wellergrossman.com
imdb.com/name/nm0919888

WELL GO USA ENTERTAINMENT

Production company and distributor

1601 E Plano Pkwy
Ste 110
Plano, TX 75070
972-265-4317 (phone)
972-265-4321 (fax)

wellgousa.com
imdb.com/company/co0227523
facebook.com/WellGoUSA

twitter.com/wellgousa

Does not accept any unsolicited material. Genres include drama, action, and crime.

WENDY FINERMAN PRODUCTIONS

Production company

144 S Beverly Dr, #304
Beverly Hills, CA 90212
310-694-8088 (phone)
310-694-8088 (fax)

info@wendyfinermanproductions.com
imdb.com/company/co0004317

Accepts query letters from unproduced, unrepresented writers via email. Project types include TV and feature films. Genres include drama, romance, fantasy, comedy, family, and period.

Wendy Finerman
Producer
wfinerman@wendyfinermanproductions.com
imdb.com/name/nm0277704

Lisa Zupan
Vice-President
lzupan@wendyfinermanproductions.com
imdb.com/name/nm0958702

WERC WERK WORKS

Production company

251 First Ave North, Suite 401, Minneapolis, MN, United States, 55401
612-238-0300 (phone)
612-238-0320 (fax)

info@werkmail.com
imdb.com/company/co0246269

Does not accept any unsolicited material. Project types include short films and feature films. Genres include animation and action.

Elizabeth Redleaf
Producer
612-238-0300
imdb.com/name/nm3119353

WESSLER ENTERTAINMENT

Production company

11661 San Vicente Blvd., Suite 609
Los Angeles, CA 90049

imdb.com/company/co0037906

Accepts query letters from unproduced, unrepresented writers. Project types include feature films. Genres include comedy and family.

Charles B. Wessler
President
imdb.com/name/nm0921853

WESTEND FILMS
Production company, distributor, and sales agent

5-7 Hillgate St
1st Floor
London W8 7SP
UK
+44207-494-8300 (phone)
+44207-494-8301 (fax)

info@westendfilms.com
westendfilms.com
imdb.com/company/co0237788
facebook.com/westendfilms

Does not accept any unsolicited material. Project types include TV, short films, and feature films. Genres include romance.

Sharon Harel
Producer
imdb.com/name/nm0362856

WESTERN INTERACTIVE PRODUCTIONS
Production company

3000 Custer Rd
Suite 270-180
Plano, TX 75075
214-608-5008

erick@skinnerboxthemovie.com
imdb.com/company/co0181608

Does not accept any unsolicited material.

WESTERN TRAILS VIDEO
Distributor

608 Perth St.
Victoria, TX 77904-2857
361-572-0930

imdb.com/company/co0094738

Does not accept any unsolicited material. Genres include action and science fiction.

WESTWOOD PRODUCTIONS
Production company

40
Langham St
London W1W 7AS
England
44 20 7255 2494 (phone)
44 7580 7670 (fax)

andrew@westwoodproductions.co.uk
imdb.com/company/co0221930

Project types include feature films. Genres include drama.

WE TV NETWORK
Distributor

11 Penn Plaza
19th Floor
New York, NY 10001
212-324-8500 (phone)
212-324-8595 (fax)

contactwe@wetv.com
wetv.com
imdb.com/company/co0340786
linkedin.com/company/we-tv-network-rainbow
    media-
facebook.com/WeTV
twitter.com/WEtv

Does not accept any unsolicited material. Project types include TV. Genres include reality, family, and comedy. Established in 1997.

Laurence Gellert
imdb.com/name/nm1557598

WGBH BOSTON
Distributor and sales agent

One Guest St, Boston, MA, United States, 02135
617-300-2000

wgbh.org
imdb.com/company/co0183007

Does not accept any unsolicited material. Project types include TV. Genres include thriller, drama, and family.

WGBH INTERNATIONAL
Distributor and sales agent

10 Guest St
Boston, MA 02135

pbsinternational.org
imdb.com/company/co0183007

Does not accept any unsolicited material. Project types include TV. Genres include documentary.

Tom Koch
Director
imdb.com/name/nm1045824

WHALEROCK INDUSTRIES
Production company

2900 W Olympic Blvd
3rd Floor
Sanata Monica, CA, 90404
310-255-7272 (phone)
310-255-7058 (fax)

info@bermanbraun.com
whalerockindustries.com
imdb.com/company/co0199425
linkedin.com/company/whalerock-industries

Does not accept any unsolicited material.

Chris Cowan
Executive, Head of Unscripted Television
imdb.com/name/nm0184544

Andrew Mittman
President
imdb.com/name/nm3879410

WHAT IF IT BARKS FILMS
Production company

Festival House
Tranquil Passage
Blackheath, London SE3 0BJ
UK
44 (0208-297-9999 (phone)
44 (0208-297-1155 (fax)

info@wiibfilms.co.uk
imdb.com/company/co0380799

Does not accept any unsolicited material. Project types include feature films. Genres include comedy.

Andrew O'Connor
Producer
imdb.com/name/nm0640193

WHEN ANGELS SING
Production company

1901 E 51st St
Austin, TX 78723
512-656-6553

imdb.com/company/co0342359

Does not accept any unsolicited material. Genres include family, comedy, and drama.

WHERE THERE'S A WILL PRODUCTIONS
Production company

Los Angeles, CA

development@wtawproductions.com
wtawproductions.com

Does not accept any unsolicited material. Project types include TV and feature films. Genres include horror, drama, thriller, comedy, and romance. Established in 2007.

Philip Wyler
Development Executive
development@wtawproductions.com

WHITE HORSE PICTURES
Production company

9100 Wilshire Blvd, Suite 423E
Beverly Hills, CA 90212
424-228-8000

info@whitehorsepics.com
whitehorsepics.com
imdb.com/company/co0331987
facebook.com/whitehorsepics
twitter.com/whitehorsepic

Does not accept any unsolicited material. Project types
include feature films. Genres include documentary.
Established in 2014.

WHITE LOTUS PRODUCTIONS
Production company and distributor

PO Box 162439
Miami, FL 33116
855-889-4483

info@whitelotusmovies.com
whitelotusmovies.com
imdb.com/company/co0377445
facebook.com/White-Lotus-
    Productions-173778506251

Does not accept any unsolicited material. Genres
include horror, drama, and thriller.

WHITE PINE PICTURES
Production company and distributor

822 Richmond St W
Ste 301
Toronto, ON M6J 1C9
Canada
416-703-5580 (phone)
416-703-1691 (fax)

info@whitepinepictures.com
imdb.com/company/co0068482
facebook.com/WhitePinePictures
twitter.com/WhitePine_TO

Does not accept any unsolicited material. Genres
include documentary.

Peter Raymont
Producer
imdb.com/name/nm0713394

WHITEWATER FILMS
Production company and distributor

11264 La Grange Ave
Los Angeles, CA 90025
310-575-5800 (phone)
310-575-5802 (fax)

info@whitewaterfilms.com
whitewaterfilms.com
imdb.com/company/co0109361
linkedin.com/company/whitewater-films
facebook.com/WhitewaterFilms
twitter.com/WhitewaterFilms

Does not accept any unsolicited material. Project types
include feature films. Genres include thriller, comedy,
romance, non-fiction, crime, and drama. Established
in 2008.

Nick Morton
Producer
imdb.com/name/nm1134288

Rick Rosenthal
Producer
imdb.com/name/nm0742819
linkedin.com/pub/rick-rosenthal/6/491/a63

Trent Brion
Producer
imdb.com/name/nm116357

Bert Kern
Associate Producer
imdb.com/name/nm2817387

WHIZBANG FILMS
Production company

24 Ryerson Ave
Ste 400
Toronto, ON M5T 2P3
Canada
416-516-5899 (phone)
416-516-9550 (fax)

info@whizbangfilms.com
whizbangfilms.com
imdb.com/company/co0076583
facebook.com/WhizbangFilms
twitter.com/Whizbangfilms

Does not accept any unsolicited material. Genres
include drama.

Frank Siracusa
Producer
imdb.com/name/nm0802731

WHYADUCK PRODUCTIONS INC.
Production company

4804 Laurel Canyon Blvd
PMB 502
North Hollywood, CA 91607-3765
818-980-5355

rbw@duckprods.com
duckprods.com
imdb.com/company/co0034143

Does not accept any unsolicited material. Project types include TV and feature films. Genres include drama, documentary, comedy, non-fiction, romance, and science fiction. Established in 1981.

Robert Weide
rbw@duckprods.com
imdb.com/name/nm0004332

WIDEAWAKE, INC.
Production company

8752 Rangely Ave
Los Angeles, CA 90048
310-652-9200

wideawakeinc.com
imdb.com/company/co0145942

Does not accept any unsolicited material. Project types include TV and feature films. Genres include action, family, comedy, and romance. Established in 2004.

Luke Greenfield
imdb.com/name/nm0339004

Jake Detharidge
Creative Executive
imdb.com/name/nm4681516

WIDESPREAD CREATIVE
Production company

902 E. 5th St., Ste 107
Austin, TX 78702

512-481-2182 (phone)
817-704-4379 (fax)

info@widespreadcreative.com
widespreadcreative.com
imdb.com/company/co0450404
facebook.com/WidespreadCreative

Does not accept any unsolicited material. Project types include TV. Genres include action and comedy.

WIDES PUBLISHING (WAIZU SHUPPAN)
Production company and distributor

7-7-23-7F
Nishi Shinjuku
Shinjuku, Tokyo 160-0023
Japan
+81 3 3369 9218 (phone)
+81 3 3369 1436 (fax)

wides@max.hi-ho.ne.jp
wides-web.com
imdb.com/company/co0099848

Does not accept any unsolicited material. Project types include TV. Genres include drama.

Hiroshi Okada
President (Producer)
imdb.com/name/nm2318244

WIGRAM PRODUCTIONS
Production company

4000 Warner Blvd
Building 81, Room 215
Burbank, CA 91522
818-954-2412 (phone)
818-954-6538 (fax)

imdb.com/company/co0204562

Accepts query letters from unproduced, unrepresented writers. Project types include feature films. Genres include crime, science fiction, fantasy, action, comedy, and thriller. Established in 2006.

Lionel Wigram
jeff.ludwig@wbconsultant.com
imdb.com/name/nm0927880
Assistant: Jeff Ludwig

Peter Eskelsen
Vice-President
peter.eskelsen@wbconsultant.com
imdb.com/name/nm2367411
linkedin.com/pub/peter-eskelsen/18/73a/755

WILCO CO.
Production company and distributor

3-2-1-1F
Uehara
Shibuya, Tokyo
Japan
03-5478-6551 (phone)
03-5478-6553 (fax)

info@wilco-jp.com
wilco-jp.com
imdb.com/company/co0131250

Does not accept any unsolicited material. Project types include TV. Genres include drama.

Naoki Hashimoto
President (Producer)
imdb.com/name/nm1889705

WILD AT HEART FILMS
Production company

868 W Knoll Dr, Suite 9
West Hollywood, CA 90069
310-855-1538 (phone)
310-855-0177 (fax)

info@wildatheartfilms.us
wildatheartfilms.us
imdb.com/company/co0096528
twitter.com/WildatHeartFilm

Does not accept any unsolicited material. Genres include myth, drama, animation, romance, non-fiction, family, and comedy. Established in 2000.

Jewell Sparks
Head of Development
jewell@wildatheartfilms.us
imdb.com/name/nm3876152

James Egan
CEO
jamesegan@wildatheartfilms.us
imdb.com/name/nm0250680
linkedin.com/pub/james-egan/5/7a/b31

Tammy Hirata
Creative Executive
tammy@wildatheartfilms.us

Jess Kreusler
Creative Executive
jess@wildatheartfilms.us

WILD BUNCH AG
Production company, distributor, and financing company

25 Powis Terrace
London United Kingdom W11 1JJ
011-442-077929791 (phone)
011-442-077929871 (fax)

99 Rue De La Verrerie, Paris, France, 75004
011-331-53015020 (phone)
011-331-53015049 (fax)

Schönhauser Allee 53
Berlin Germany D10437
011-493-088091700 (phone)
011-493-088091774 (fax)

wildbunch.biz
imdb.com/company/co0544845

Does not accept any unsolicited material. Project types include feature films and TV. Genres include drama, family, thriller, and action.

WILDCARD PICTURES
Production company

1475 King St West
Suite C4
Toronto, ON M6K 1J4
Canada
647-479-7447

imdb.com/company/co0190463

Does not accept any unsolicited material. Project types include short films and TV. Genres include drama.

Jen Frankel
Producer
imdb.com/name/nm2412314

WILDGAZE FILMS
Production company

53 Greek St
London W1D 3DR
UK
+44 20 7734 7065 (phone)
+44 20 7734 4250 (fax)

info@wildgaze.co.uk
imdb.com/company/co0005838

Does not accept any unsolicited material. Project types include feature films. Genres include comedy.

WILDWOOD ENTERPRISES, INC.
Production company

725 Arizona Ave, Suite 306
Santa Monica, CA 90401
310-451-8050

imdb.com/company/co0034515

Does not accept any unsolicited material. Project types include short films, TV, and feature films. Genres include romance, thriller, drama, comedy, crime, non-fiction, and fantasy.

Robert Redford
Owner
imdb.com/name/nm0000602

Bill Holderman
Development Executive
imdb.com/name/nm2250139

WILLOWOOD FILMS
Production company

225 Winona Dr
First Floor
Toronto, ON M6C 3S4
Canada

info@willowoodfilms.com
willowoodfilms.com
imdb.com/company/co0323166

Does not accept any unsolicited material. Genres include horror.

Chris Luckhardt
Producer
imdb.com/name/nm2308971

WILLOW STUDIOS
Production company, distributor, and sales agent

66 Willow Rd
East Kingston, NH 03827
603-642-3138

chris.murphy@willowstudios.com
willowstudios.com
imdb.com/company/co0325429

Does not accept any unsolicited material. Project types include TV. Genres include drama.

WIND DANCER FILMS
Production company

38 Commerce St
New York, NY 10014
212-765-4772 (phone)
212-765-4785 (fax)

6255 W. Sunset Blvd. Suite 1100
Hollywood, CA 90028
310-601-2720 (phone)
310-601-2725 (fax)

winddancer.com
imdb.com/company/co0028602

Does not accept any unsolicited material. Project types include feature films and TV. Genres include crime, drama, fantasy, romance, and comedy. Established in 1989.

Catherine Redfearn
Creative Executive
catherine_redfearn@winddancer.com
imdb.com/name/nm1976144
linkedin.com/pub/catherine-redfearn/15/19/148

Judd Payne
Head of Production
imdb.com/name/nm1450928
linkedin.com/pub/judd-payne/5/61b/52b
twitter.com/juddpayne

Dete Meserve
President
twitter.com/DeteMeserve

Matt Williams
Principal
imdb.com/name/nm0931285
Assistant: Jake Perron

David McFadzean
Principal
imdb.com/name/nm05687
Assistant: David Caruso

WINDOWSEAT, INC.
Production company

200 Pier Ave, Suite 135
Hermosa Beach, CA 90254
310-372-3650

info@windowseatpictures.com
windowseat.com
imdb.com/company/co0470347
linkedin.com/company/windowseatpictures
facebook.com/windowseatpictures
twitter.com/wearewindowseat

Does not accept any unsolicited material. Project types include feature films, TV, commercials, and short films. Genres include thriller, comedy, action, and drama. Established in 2003.

Jim Reach
Principal
310-372-3650
info@windowseat.com

Emiliano Haldeman
Sr. Vice-President
imdb.com/name/nm2541464
linkedin.com/pub/emiliano-haldeman/63/550/5b3

Bill Kiely
Director
imdb.com/name/nm2316469

Joseph McKelheer
Sr. Vice-President
joe@windowseat.com
imdb.com/name/nm1559624
linkedin.com/pub/joseph-mckelheer/6/2b1/35

Ryan Dorff
CFO
imdb.com/name/nm6459728

WINDWARD PICTURES, INC.
Production company

1401 N 450 E Bountiful, Utah 84010-3453 United States
+801-295-7514

info@windwardpictures.com
windwardpictures.com
imdb.com/company/co0307657
linkedin.com/company/windward-pictures-inc

Does not accept any unsolicited material. Project types include commercials, TV, and feature films. Genres include fantasy, romance, period, comedy, family, science fiction, myth, thriller, drama, action, and detective. Established in 1997.

Ann Sparks
President
asparks@windwardpictures.com

WINGNUT FILMS LTD.
Production company

PO Box 15 208
Miramar
Wellington 6003
New Zealand
+64-4-388-9939 (phone)
+64-4-388-9449 (fax)

reception@wingnutfilms.co.nz
imdb.com/company/co0046203
linkedin.com/pub/wingnut-films/6b/b04/516

Does not accept any unsolicited material. Project types include feature films and TV. Genres include romance, family, fantasy, thriller, crime, non-fiction, animation, horror, science fiction, and comedy.

Carolynne Cunningham
Producer
imdb.com/name/nm0192254

Peter Jackson
imdb.com/name/nm0001392

WINKLER FILMS
Production company

190 N Canon Dr Suite 500 Penthouse
Beverly Hills, CA 90210
310-858-5780 (phone)
310-858-5799 (fax)

winklerfilms@sbcglobal.net
winklerfilms.com
imdb.com/company/co0049390

Accepts query letters from unproduced, unrepresented writers. Project types include TV and feature films. Genres include drama, crime, romance, and action.

Jill Cutler
President
imdb.com/name/nm1384594

David Winkler
Producer
310-858-5780
imdb.com/name/nm0935210

Charles Winkler
310-858-5780
imdb.com/name/nm0935203
Assistant: Jose Ruisanchez

Irwin Winkler
CEO
310-858-5780
imdb.com/name/nm0005563
Assistant: Selina Gomeau

WINSOME PRODUCTIONS
Production company

PO Box 2071
Santa Monica, CA 90406
310-656-3300

info@winsomeprods.com
winsomeprods.com
imdb.com/company/co0129854

facebook.com/pages/Winsome-Productions/
    19789808323

Does not accept any unsolicited material. Project types include TV and feature films. Genres include non-fiction, drama, comedy, and action. Established in 1989.

A.D. Oppenheim
info@winsomeprods.com
imdb.com/name/nm0649148

Daniel Oppenheim
imdb.com/name/nm0649151

WISHBONE ENTERTAINMENT INC.
Production company

25 The Esplanade
3204
Toronto M5E 1W5
Canada
416-815-1999 (phone)
416-815-8111 (fax)

imdb.com/company/co0050930

Does not accept any unsolicited material. Project types include TV. Genres include crime and horror.

WITT-THOMAS PRODUCTIONS
Production company

11901 Santa Monica Blvd, Suite 596
Los Angeles, CA 90025
310-472-6004 (phone)
310-476-5015 (fax)

pwittproductions@aol.com
imdb.com/company/co0083928

Does not accept any unsolicited material. Project types include feature films. Genres include comedy, crime, drama, action, period, and romance. Established in 2010.

Tony Thomas
Partner
imdb.com/name/nm0859597
Assistant: Marlene Fuentes

Paul Witt
Partner
pwittproductions@aol.com
imdb.com/name/nm0432625
Assistant: Ellen Benjamin

WKMG
Production company

4466 John Young Pkwy.
Orland Park, FL 32804
407-521-1200 (phone)
407-521-1204 (fax)

imdb.com/company/co0112156

Does not accept any unsolicited material. Project types include TV and short films. Genres include documentary.

W!LDBRAIN ENTERTAINMENT, INC.
Production company and distributor

15000 Ventura Blvd
3rd Floor
Sherman Oaks, CA 91403
818-290-7080

info@wildbrain.com
wildbrain.com
imdb.com/company/co0077172
linkedin.com/company/wild-brain

Accepts query letters from produced or represented writers. Project types include short films, TV, and feature films. Genres include animation, fantasy, comedy, and family. Established in 1994.

Lisa Ullmann
imdb.com/name/nm0880520

Michael Polis
President
mpolis@wildbrain.com
imdb.com/name/nm1277040

Bob Higgins
imdb.com/name/nm0383338

WME ENTERTAINMENT
Distributor

Roundabout Plaza 1600 Division St Suite 300
Nashville TN 37203
615-963-3000 (phone)
615-963-3090 (fax)

100 New Oxford St
London England United Kingdom W1CA 1HB
011-442-089298400 (phone)
011-442-089298500 (fax)

1500 S Douglas Rd, Suite 230
Coral Gables FL 33134
305-938-2000 (phone)
305-938-2002 (fax)

1325 Ave of the Americas
New York NY 10019
212-586-5100 (phone)
212-246-3583 (fax)

9601 Wilshire Blvd, Third Floor, Beverly Hills, CA, United States, 90210
310-285-9000 (phone)
310-285-9010 (fax)

info@wmeentertainment.com
wmeentertainment.com
imdb.com/company/co0268644

Does not accept any unsolicited material. Project types include TV. Genres include drama and reality.

WOLFE RELEASING
Distributor

21570 Almaden Rd, San Jose, CA, United States, 95120
408-268-6782

acquisitions@wolfevideo.com
wolfereleasing.com
imdb.com/company/co0142224

Does not accept any unsolicited material. Project types include TV. Genres include drama and family.

WOLF FILMS, INC.
Production company and distributor

100 Universal City Plaza #2252
Universal City, CA 91608-1085
818-777-6969 (phone)
818-866-1446 (fax)

imdb.com/company/co0019598
twitter.com/wolffilms

Does not accept any unsolicited material. Project types include TV, feature films, and short films. Genres include drama and non-fiction.

Danielle Gelber
Executive Producer
imdb.com/name/nm1891764

Dick Wolf
CEO
imdb.com/name/nm0937725

Tony Ganz
imdb.com/name/nm0304673

WOLFMILL ENTERTAINMENT
Production company

9027 Larke Ellen Circle
Los Angeles, CA 90035
310-559-1622 (phone)
310-559-1623 (fax)

info@wolfmill.com
wolfmill.com
imdb.com/company/co0184078

Accepts query letters from unproduced, unrepresented writers via email. Project types include feature films and TV. Genres include animation. Established in 1997.

Marv Wolfman
Partner
marv@wolfmill.com
imdb.com/name/nm0938379

Craig Miller
Partner
craig@wolfmill.com
imdb.com/name/nm0003653

WOLVES CREATIVE
Production company

spencerturley.com

Does not accept any unsolicited material. Project types include feature films. Genres include animation. Established in 1995.

Spencer Turley
Owner
spencerturley@gmail.com

WOMEN IN FILM
Production company

6100 Wilshire Blvd, Suite 710, Beverly Hills , CA, United States, 90048
323-935-2211 (phone)
323-935-2212 (fax)

info@wif.org
wif.org
imdb.com/title/tt0247823
facebook.com/WIFLA
twitter.com/WIF_LosAngeles

Does not accept any unsolicited material. Project types include TV. Genres include drama and comedy.

WOMEN IN FILM
Production company and distributor

6100 Wilshire Blvd, Suite 710, Beverly Hills , CA, United States, 90048
323-935-2211 (phone)
323-935-2212 (fax)

info@wif.org
wif.org
imdb.com/company/co0052946

Does not accept any unsolicited material. Project types include feature films and TV. Genres include drama, romance, and family.

WOMEN MAKE MOVIES
Production company and distributor

115 W 29th St, Suite 1200, New York , NY, United States, 10001
212-925-0606

imdb.com/company/co0075700

Does not accept any unsolicited material. Project types include short films. Genres include documentary.

WONDERLAND SOUND AND VISION
Production company

8739 Sunset Blvd
West Hollywood, CA 90069
310-659-4451 (phone)
310-659-4451 (fax)

hello@wonderlandsoundandvision.com
wonderlandsoundandvision.com
imdb.com/company/co0080859
twitter.com/mcgswonderland
twitter.com/mcgswonderland

Does not accept any unsolicited material. Project types include TV and feature films. Genres include drama, comedy, horror, romance, science fiction, non-fiction, crime, and action. Established in 2000.

Steven Bello
Creative Executive
imdb.com/name/nm2086605

Mary Viola
imdb.com/name/nm0899193

WONDERPHIL PRODUCTIONS, LLC
Production company and distributor

1032 Irving St., #130
San Francisco, CA. 94122
310-482-1324

phil@wonderphil.biz
wonderphil.biz
imdb.com/company/co0115133

Accepts scripts from unproduced, unrepresented writers. Project types include feature films. Genres include thriller, fantasy, horror, science fiction, drama, and action.

Phil Gorn
CEO
phil@wonderphil.biz
imdb.com/name/nm1486721

Sanders Robinson
President
925-525-7583
sandman@wonderphil.biz
facebook.com/sanders.robinson.50

WON TON BABY PRODUCTIONS
Production company

65 Milltown Rd
East Brunswick, NJ 08816
732-257-4215

imdb.com/company/co0276020

Does not accept any unsolicited material. Project types include feature films, short films, theater, and TV. Genres include comedy and horror.

WORKING TITLE FILMS
Production company

9720 Wilshire Blvd
4th Floor
Beverly Hills, CA 90212
310-777-3100 (phone)
310-777-5243 (fax)

workingtitlefilms.com
imdb.com/company/co0057311
facebook.com/WorkingTitleFilms
twitter.com/Working_Title

Does not accept any unsolicited material. Project types include TV, feature films, and short films. Genres include family, drama, comedy, fantasy, action, thriller, non-fiction, crime, science fiction, and romance. Established in 1983.

Tim Bevan
Co-Chairman
imdb.com/name/nm0079677

Liza Chasin
liza.chasin@workingtitlefilms.com
imdb.com/name/nm0153877
Assistant: Johanna Byer

Amelia Granger
+44 20 7307 3000
imdb.com/name/nm0335028

Michelle Wright
imdb.com/name/nm0942657

Eric Fellner
Co-Chairman
imdb.com/name/nm0271479

WORLD FILM SERVICES, INC.
Production company

150 E 58th St
29th Floor
New York, NY 10155
212-632-3456 (phone)
212-632-3457 (fax)

imdb.com/company/co0184077

Accepts query letters from unproduced, unrepresented writers. Project types include TV and feature films. Genres include thriller, crime, comedy, action, family, drama, science fiction, non-fiction, fantasy, horror, and romance.

Dahlia Heyman
Creative Executive
imdb.com/name/nm3101094

John Heyman
CEO
imdb.com/name/nm0382274

Pamela Osowski
Creative Executive
imdb.com/name/nm1948494

WORLD INTERNATIONAL NETWORK
Production company and distributor

1306 S Spaulding Ave, Los Angeles , CA, United States, 90019
323-549-9797 (phone)
323-549-9711 (fax)

imdb.com/company/co0063285

Does not accept any unsolicited material.

WORLD OF WONDER PRODUCTIONS
Production company

6650 Hollywood Blvd, Suite 400
Hollywood, CA 90028
323-603-6300 (phone)
323-603-6301 (fax)

support@worldofwonder.net
worldofwonder.net
imdb.com/company/co0093416
facebook.com/pages/World-of-Wonder-Productions/
    187007651324618
twitter.com/worldofwonder

Does not accept any unsolicited material. Project types include feature films and TV. Genres include reality, comedy, non-fiction, crime, action, period, drama, and family. Established in 1990.

Tom Campbell
imdb.com/name/nm1737859

Chris Skura
imdb.com/name/nm1048940

Fenton Bailey
imdb.com/name/nm0047259

WORLD PRODUCTIONS
Production company and distributor

101 Finsbury Pavement
London EC2A 1RS
UK
+44020-300-23113

freddie@world-productions.com
world-productions.com
imdb.com/company/co0072097
facebook.com/worldproductionsltd
twitter.com/worldprods

Does not accept any unsolicited material. Project types include TV and feature films. Genres include drama and thriller.

Priscilla Parish
Producer
imdb.com/name/nm2566076

WORLD'S FAIR PICTURES
Production company

4096 Youngfield St
Denver, CO 80033
303-431-9536

info@worldsfairpictures.com
imdb.com/company/co0320695

Does not accept any unsolicited material. Project types include feature films. Genres include crime and thriller.

Lee Roy Kunz
Executive
imdb.com/name/nm2753333

WORLDVIEW ENTERTAINMENT, INC.

Production company

1384 Broadway
25th Floor
New York, NY 10018
212-431-3090 (phone)
212-431-0390 (fax)

info@worldviewent.com
worldviewent.com
imdb.com/company/co0001099
facebook.com/worldviewent
twitter.com/worldviewent

Does not accept any unsolicited material. Project types include feature films. Genres include drama, documentary, romance, action, and comedy. Established in 2007.

Sarah Johnson Redlich
Partner
imdb.com/name/nm3164071

Maria Cestone
imdb.com/name/nm2906036

Christopher Woodrow
imdb.com/name/nm2002108

Amanda Bowers
imdb.com/name/nm4112873

WORLDWIDE BIGGIES

Production company

545 W 45th St
5th Floor
New York, NY 10036
646-442-1700 (phone)
646-557-0019 (fax)

kari@wwbiggies.com
wwbiggies.com
imdb.com/company/co0173152
linkedin.com/company/worldwide-biggies
twitter.com/wwbiggies

Does not accept any unsolicited material. Project types include TV and feature films. Genres include non-fiction, animation, comedy, action, family, drama, fantasy, reality, and documentary. Established in 2007.

Scott Webb
imdb.com/name/nm1274591

Albie Hecht
CEO
imdb.com/name/nm0372935

Kari Kim
kari@wwbiggies.com
imdb.com/name/nm2004613

WORLDWIDE PANTS INC.

Production company and distributor

1697 Broadway
New York, NY 10019
212-975-5300 (phone)
212-975-4780 (fax)

lswdl@aol.com
imdb.com/company/co0066959
linkedin.com/company/worldwide-pants
facebook.com/pages/Worldwide-Pants/
    110473355647932

Does not accept any unsolicited material. Project types include TV and feature films. Genres include comedy, action, animation, non-fiction, drama, and romance. Established in 1991.

Rob Burnett
imdb.com/name/nm0122427

David Letterman
imdb.com/name/nm0001468

Tom Keaney
Executive
imdb.com/name/nm3174758

WORLDWIDE PRODUCTION SERVICES

Production company

2140 S Dixie Hwy
Suite 207
Coconut Grove, FL 33133
305-858-5060

wwps@me.com
worldwideproductionservices.tv
imdb.com/company/co0183146
facebook.com/Worldwide-Production-
    Services-185146051529210

Does not accept any unsolicited material. Genres include drama and crime.

WOR-TV
Production company and distributor

9 Broadcast Plaza
43 Meadowlands Parkway
Secaucus, NJ 07096
201-348-0009

viewer.services@foxtv.com
my9nj.com
imdb.com/company/co0075005
facebook.com
twitter.com/My9NJ

Does not accept any unsolicited material. Project types include TV. Genres include comedy.

WPBT2
Production company and distributor

PO Box 2
Miami, FL 33261
305-949-8321 (phone)
305-944-4211 (fax)

channel2@channel2.org
channel2.org
imdb.com/company/co0049062
facebook.com/WPBT2
twitter.com/wpbt2

Does not accept any unsolicited material. Genres include drama.

WREKIN HILL ENTERTAINMENT
Distributor

10685 Santa Monica Blvd, Los Angeles, CA, United States, 90025
310-470-3131 (phone)
310-470-3132 (fax)

info@wrekinhill.com
wrekinhillentertainment.com
imdb.com/company/co0317821

Does not accept any unsolicited material. Project types include TV, short films, and feature films. Genres

include family, animation, comedy, drama, and fantasy.

W-UP ENTERTAINMENT
Production company

5-5-12-2F
Akasaka
Minato, Tokyo 107-0052
Japan
03-3560-3134 (phone)
03-6234-4322 (fax)

info@wup-e.com
wup-e.com
imdb.com/company/co0298045

Does not accept any unsolicited material. Project types include TV and feature films. Genres include fantasy and action.

WWE STUDIOS
Production company and distributor

WWE Corporate Headquarters
Attention: (please include Department)
1241 E Main St
Stamford, CT 06902
203-352-8600

12424 Wilshire Blvd, Suite 1400
Los Angeles, CA 90025
310-481-9370 (phone)
310-481-9369 (fax)

wwe.com/inside/overtheropes/wwestudios
imdb.com/company/co0242604
facebook.com/OfficialWWEStudios
twitter.com/WWEStudios

Does not accept any unsolicited material. Project types include feature films and TV. Genres include thriller, comedy, action, drama, detective, crime, family, non-fiction, science fiction, and horror. Established in 2008.

Richard Lowell
imdb.com/name/nm1144067
Assistant: Cherie Harris Cherie.harris@wwecorp.com

Michael Luisi
President
imdb.com/name/nm0525405

X4 PRODUCTIONS
Production company

1829 Kingswood Rd.
Jacksonville, FL 32207
904-651-5913

x4productions@hotmail.com
imdb.com/company/co0524951
facebook.com/pages/X4-Productions/327248548006

Does not accept any unsolicited material. Project types include short films. Genres include drama.

XCES FILM
Production company and distributor

2-29-1-3F
Hongo
Bunkyo, Tokyo 113-0033
Japan
03-5689-8621

info@shinnihoneizo.co.jp
shinnihoneizo.co.jp
imdb.com/company/co0204329

Does not accept any unsolicited material. Genres include drama.

XENON PICTURES
Distributor

1440 9th St, Santa Monica , CA, United States, 90401
310-451-5510 (phone)
310-395-4058 (fax)

info@xenonpictures.com
xenonpictures.com/wp
imdb.com/company/co0109042

Does not accept any unsolicited material. Project types include feature films. Genres include crime, drama, and action.

X FILME CREATIVE POOL
Production company and distributor

Niederlassung München
Tölzer Straße 5
82031 Grünwald
Deutschland

49-89-6494-6324 (phone)
49-89-6494-5820 (fax)

Kurfuerstenstrasse 57
10785 Berlin
Germany
49-30-230-833-11 (phone)
49-30-230-833-22 (fax)

info@x-filme.de
x-filme.de/en
imdb.com/company/co0055954
linkedin.com/company/x-filme-creative-pool
facebook.com/XFilmeCreativePool

Does not accept any unsolicited material. Project types include TV and feature films. Genres include drama, family, comedy, romance, and action. Established in 1994.

Wolfgang Becker
imdb.com/name/nm0065615

Dani Levy
imdb.com/name/nm0506374

Stefan Arndt
stefan.arndt@x-filme.de
imdb.com/name/nm0036155

X-FILME CREATIVE POOL
Production company and distributor

+49 30 2308 3311

info@x-filme.de
imdb.com/company/co0055954

Project types include feature films. Genres include drama.

XINE PRODUCTIONS
Production company

19 DePalma Court
Somerset, NJ 08873

imdb.com/company/co0201204

Does not accept any unsolicited material. Project types include TV. Genres include comedy and drama.

XINGU FILMS LTD.
Production company

12 Cleveland Row
St. James
London SW1A 1DH
United Kingdom
44-20-7451-0600 (phone)
44-20-7451-0601 (fax)

mail@xingufilms.com
imdb.com/company/co0068740

Does not accept any unsolicited material. Project types include TV. Genres include action, non-fiction, comedy, crime, fantasy, detective, horror, romance, myth, science fiction, drama, family, thriller, and animation. Established in 1993.

Anita Sumner
imdb.com/name/nm0838856

Alex Francis
Producer
imdb.com/name/nm2123360

Trudie Styler
trudie@xingufilms.com
imdb.com/name/nm0836548

XIX ENTERTAINMENT
Production company

9000 W Sunset Blvd, Penthouse
West Hollywood, CA 90069
310-746-1919 (phone)
310-746-1920 (fax)

33 Ransomes Dock
35-37 Parkgate Rd
London SW11 4NP
44-20-7801-1919 (phone)
44-20-7801-1920 (fax)

info@xixentertainment.com
xixentertainment.com
imdb.com/company/co0286583
twitter.com/xix_news

Does not accept any unsolicited material. Project types include feature films, TV, and commercials. Genres include drama, romance, non-fiction, thriller, period, and reality. Established in 2010.

Robert Dodds
CEO
robert.dodds@xixentertainment.com
imdb.com/name/nm2142323

XLRATOR MEDIA
Production company and distributor

Los Angeles, CA, United States

info@xlratormedia.com
xlratormedia.com
imdb.com/company/co0328673

Does not accept any unsolicited material. Project types include TV. Genres include family and drama.

XPAND

1017 Cole Ave, Los Angeles , CA, United States, 90038
310-309-6705 (phone)
323-785-0037 (fax)

xpandcinema.com

Does not accept any unsolicited material.

XTEAMARTISTS
Production company, distributor, and sales agent

5060 Addison Circle #2841
Addison, TX 75001
817-271-5401

videotape@xteamartists.com
xteamartists.com
imdb.com/company/co0306177
linkedin.com/company/xteamartists-llc
facebook.com/xteamartists
twitter.com/xteamartists

Does not accept any unsolicited material. Genres include thriller and drama.

XYZ FILMS
Production company and distributor

4223 Glencoe Ave, Suite B119
Marina del Rey, CA 90292
310-956-1550 (phone)
310-827-7690 (fax)

info@xyzfilms.com
xyzfilms.com
imdb.com/company/co0244345
facebook.com/xyzfilms
twitter.com/xyzfilms

Does not accept any unsolicited material. Project types include feature films. Genres include crime, comedy, non-fiction, horror, action, drama, thriller, and science fiction.

Kyle Franke
Head of Development
310-359-9099
kyle@xyzfilms.com
imdb.com/name/nm3733941

Nate Bolotin
Partner
nate@xyzfilms.com
imdb.com/name/nm1924867

Todd Brown
Partner
info@xyzfilms.com
imdb.com/name/nm1458075

YAHOO!
Production company and distributor

2400 Broadway
1st Floor
Santa Monica, CA 90404
310-907-2700 (phone)
310-907-2701 (fax)

yahoo.com
imdb.com/company/co0054481

Accepts query letters from unproduced, unrepresented writers. Project types include commercials, TV, and short films. Genres include reality, comedy, non-fiction, and family. Established in 1995.

YAHOO! INC.
Production company and distributor

701 First Ave, Sunnyvale , CA, United States, 94089
408-349-3300

1065 Ave of The Americas 9th Floor
New York NY 10018
212-381-6800

yahoo.com
imdb.com/company/co0054481

Does not accept any unsolicited material. Project types include commercials. Genres include reality, family, non-fiction, and documentary.

YARI FILM GROUP
Production company and distributor

10850 Wilshire Blvd
6th Floor
Los Angeles, CA 90024
310-689-1450 (phone)
310-234-8975 (fax)

reception@yarifilmgroup.com
imdb.com/company/co0136740

Does not accept any unsolicited material. Project types include feature films and TV. Genres include crime, drama, family, action, animation, thriller, romance, and comedy.

Bob Yari
byari@yarifilmgroup.com
imdb.com/name/nm0946441
Assistant: Julie Milstead

David Clark
imdb.com/name/nm1354046

Ethen Adams
imdb.com/name/nm2319337

YASH RAJ FILMS (YRF)
Production company and distributor

Yash Raj Films USA Inc. 2417 Jericho Turnpike, Suite 284
Garden City NY 11040
516-280-5662

Yash Raj Films International Ltd. (UK) Vista Centre, 50 Salisbury Rd
Hounslow, Middlesex England United Kingdom TW4 6JQ
011-448-707397345 (phone)
011-448-707397346 (fax)

Yash Raj Films Private Limited. (Mumbai), 5 Shah Industrial Estate, Veera Desai Rd, Andheri (West), Mumbai, India, 400 053
011-912-230613500 (phone)
011-912-230613599 (fax)

Yash Raj Films (UAE) L.L.C. P.O. Box – 50270, 3106, The Citadel, Business Bay
Dubai United Arab Emirates
011-971-44472140 (phone)
011-971-44472139 (fax)

helpdesk@yashrajfilms.com
yashrajfilms.com
imdb.com/company/co0077190

Does not accept any unsolicited material. Project types include feature films and TV. Genres include thriller, drama, action, and family.

YELLOW RICK ROAD PRODUCTIONS
Production company

209 Doverwood Rd
Fern Park, FL 32730
212-330-0425

info@yellowrickroad.com
imdb.com/company/co0303215

Does not accept any unsolicited material. Genres include documentary.

YORK PRODUCTIONS
Production company

433 Plaza Real
Suite #275
Boca Raton, FL 33432
561-962-4175

imdb.com/company/co0257341

Does not accept any unsolicited material. Project types include short films. Genres include drama.

YORK SQUARE PRODUCTIONS
Production company

17328 Ventura Blvd, Suite 370
Encino, CA 91316
818-789-7372

assistant@yorksquareproductions.com
yorksquareproductions.com
imdb.com/company/co0378544

Accepts query letters from unproduced, unrepresented writers via email. Project types include TV, feature films, and commercials. Genres include comedy and drama.

Jonathan Mostow
Executive
imdb.com/name/nm0609236
Assistant: Emily Somers

YORKTOWN PRODUCTIONS
Production company

18 Gloucester Ln
4th Floor
Toronto ON M4Y 1L5
Canada
416-923-2787 (phone)
416-923-8580 (fax)

listings.fta-companies-ca.com/l/110671632/Yorktown-Productions-Ltd-in-Toronto-ON
imdb.com/company/co0184088

Does not accept any unsolicited material. Project types include feature films, TV, and short films. Genres include science fiction, drama, fantasy, family, comedy, romance, and action. Established in 1986.

Norman Jewison
Founder
416-923-2787
imdb.com/name/nm0422484

Michael Jewison
Producer
imdb.com/name/nm0422483

YORK ZIMMERMAN
Production company

2233 Wisconsin Ave N.W.
Suite 502
Washington DC 20007
202-337-3291 (phone)
202-337-0614 (fax)

syork@yorkzim.com

imdb.com/company/co0178450
linkedin.com/company/york-zimmerman-inc

Does not accept any unsolicited material. Genres include documentary.

YOUNGTREE PRESS
Production company

Tokyo,
Japan
053-488-4160

info@youngtreepress.net
youngtreepress.net
imdb.com/company/co0287148

Does not accept any unsolicited material. Project types include feature films. Genres include drama.

Shingo Wakagi
Founder (Producer)
imdb.com/name/nm1115569

YOUTUBE
Production company and distributor

YouTube Space 12422 W Bluff Creek Dr
Los Angeles CA 90094

1 St Giles High St
London England United Kingdom WC2H 8AG
011-442-070313000

901 Cherry Ave, San Bruno, CA, United States, 94066
650-253-0000

press@youtube.com
youtube.com
imdb.com/company/co0202446

Does not accept any unsolicited material. Project types include short films, feature films, TV, and commercials. Genres include fantasy, non-fiction, sociocultural, and reality.

YOU WANNA DO THIS OR NOT PRODS.
Production company

Burbank, CA 91505
818-292-3828

joey@youwannadothisornotprods.com
imdb.com/company/co0355962

facebook.com/joseph.napoli.39
twitter.com/joeythenap

Does not accept any unsolicited material. Genres include drama.

YRF ENTERTAINMENT
Production company and distributor

260 S Beverly Dr, Suite 201, Beverly Hills, CA, United States, 90212
310-550-8355 (phone)
310-432-0598 (fax)

info@yrfentertainment.com
yrfentertainment.com
imdb.com/company/co0362130

Does not accept any unsolicited material. Project types include TV and feature films. Genres include romance, documentary, thriller, family, drama, and reality.

ZACHARY FEUER FILMS
Production company

9348 Civic Center Dr, 3rd Floor
Beverly Hills, CA 90210
310-729-2110 (phone)
310-820-7535 (fax)

imdb.com/name/nm0275400

Accepts query letters from unproduced, unrepresented writers. Project types include TV. Genres include action, comedy, thriller, and drama.

Zachary Feuer
Producer
imdb.com/name/nm0275400

ZAK CORP.
Production company

2-25-4
Jingumae
Shibuya, Tokyo 150-0001
Japan
03-5474-8681 (phone)
03-5474-8688 (fax)

ykst@jb3.so-net.ne.jp
imdb.com/company/co0173419

Does not accept any unsolicited material. Project types include feature films. Genres include comedy.

ZAK PENN'S COMPANY

Production company

6240 W. Third St., Ste. 421
Los Angeles, CA 90036
323-939-1700

imdb.com/company/co0185423
linkedin.com/company/zak-penn's-company

Does not accept any unsolicited material. Project types include TV and feature films. Genres include fantasy, non-fiction, science fiction, thriller, family, and comedy.

Zak Penn
Producer
zak.penn@fox.com
zakpenn.blogspot.com
imdb.com/name/nm0672015
twitter.com/zakpenn
Assistant: Hannah Rosner

ZANUCK INDEPENDENT

Production company

1951 N Beverly Dr
Beverly Hills, CA 90210
310-274-5735 (phone)
310-273-9217 (fax)

imdb.com/company/co0279611

Accepts query letters from unproduced, unrepresented writers. Project types include feature films. Genres include comedy, action, drama, and thriller.

Dean Zanuck
Founder
imdb.com/name/nm0953124

ZAZIE FILMS

Production company and distributor

Dai-ni Atmosphere Aoyama 7f
2-10-8, Meguro
Tokyo 153-0063
Japan

+81 3 3494 7394 (phone)
+81 3 3494 7492 (fax)

shimura@zaziefilms.com
zaziefilms.com
imdb.com/company/co0081764

Does not accept any unsolicited material. Project types include TV and feature films. Genres include drama.

Daisuke Shimura
Managing Director (Executive)
imdb.com/name/nm2538411

ZEITGEIST FILMS

Distributor

247 Center St, Second Floor, New York, NY, United States, 10013
212-274-1989 (phone)
212-274-1644 (fax)

mail@zeitgeistfilms.com
zeitgeistfilms.com
imdb.com/company/co0078470

Does not accept any unsolicited material. Project types include feature films and TV. Genres include family, drama, and thriller.

ZELLNER BROS.

Production company

P.O. Box 49554
Austin, TX 78765
512-296-1045

info@zellnerbros.com
zellnerbros.com
imdb.com/company/co0365774
facebook.com/pages/Zellner-Bros/224603629912
twitter.com/zellnerbros

Does not accept any unsolicited material. Genres include drama.

ZEMECKIS/NEMEROFF FILMS

Production company

264 S La Cienega Blvd, Suite 238
Beverly Hills, CA 90211
310-736-6586

imdb.com/company/co0141237

Does not accept any unsolicited material. Project types include feature films. Genres include drama and comedy.

Terry Nemeroff
Producer
imdb.com/name/nm0625892

Leslie Zemeckis
Producer
imdb.com/name/nm0366667

ZENITH
Production company

1-19-13-402
Jungumae
Shibuya, Tokyo 150-0001
Japan
03-5411-7747 (phone)
03-5411-2527 (fax)

info@zenithinc.jp
zenithinc.jp
imdb.com/company/co0301116
facebook.com/pages/Zenith-inc/283583685033059
twitter.com/Zenith_Model

Does not accept any unsolicited material. Project types include TV. Genres include drama.

ZENTROPA ENTERTAINMENT
Production company

+45-36-86-87-88

receptionen@filmbyen.dk
zentropa.dk
imdb.com/company/co0136662
linkedin.com/company/zentropa
facebook.com/Zentropaproductions
twitter.com/ZentropaNews

Accepts scripts from unproduced, unrepresented writers. Project types include feature films. Genres include family, crime, science fiction, non-fiction, romance, comedy, horror, fantasy, thriller, drama, and action. Established in 1992.

Peter Aalbaek Jensen
CEO
peter.aalbaek.jensen@filmbyen.dk
imdb.com/name/nm0421639

Frederik Nemeth
CFO
frederik.nemeth@filmbyen.dk

ZEPHYR FILMS
Production company

48a Goodge St
London
W1T 4LX
UK
+440207-794-0011

info@zephyrfilms.co.uk
zephyrfilms.co.uk
imdb.com/company/co0130369

Does not accept any unsolicited material. Project types include feature films and TV. Genres include comedy, animation, thriller, crime, family, horror, romance, fantasy, drama, and action.

Chris Curling
Producer
imdb.com/name/nm0192770
linkedin.com/pub/chris-curling/15/53/BB7

Phil Robertson
Producer
imdb.com/name/nm0731990

ZEPPOTRON
Production company and distributor

Shepherd's Building Central
Charecroft Way, Shepherds Bush
London W14 0EH
UK
+44870-333-1700 (phone)
+44870-333-1800 (fax)

contact@zeppotron.com
zeppotron.com
imdb.com/company/co0104481

Does not accept any unsolicited material. Genres include comedy, drama, and action.

Charlie Brooker
Producer
imdb.com/name/nm0111765

ZEROFUNCTION PRODUCTIONS
Production company

15 Shallmar Blvd. #101
Toronto, ON M5N 1J7
Canada
647-214-1944

zero@zerofunction.com
zerofunction.com
imdb.com/company/co0247845

Does not accept any unsolicited material. Project types
include feature films. Genres include fantasy, science
fiction, and drama.

ZERO GRAVITY MANAGEMENT
Production company

4130 Cahuenga Blvd
Suite 113
Universal City, CA 91602
424-204-9970

1531 14th St
Santa Monica, CA 90404
310-656-9440

15900 Riverside Dr West
Suite 4A
New York, NY 10032
917-285-6102

info@zerogravitymanagement.com
zerogravitymanagement.com
imdb.com/company/co0086332
linkedin.com/company/zero-gravity-management
facebook.com/zerogravitymanagement
twitter.com/zerogravitymgmt

Accepts query letters from unproduced, unrepresented
writers via email. Project types include feature films.
Genres include thriller and action.

ZERO TRANS FAT PRODUCTIONS
Production company

231 W Jefferson Blvd
Dallas, TX 75208
832-315-7700

adamdonaghey@gmail.com
imdb.com/company/co0238931
facebook.com/adamdonaghey
twitter.com/adamdonaghey

Does not accept any unsolicited material. Genres
include science fiction and drama.

ZETA ENTERTAINMENT
Production company

3422 Rowena Ave
Los Angeles, CA 90027
310-595-0494

INFO@ZETAENTERTAINMENT.COM
zetaentertainment.com
imdb.com/company/co0037026

Does not accept any unsolicited material. Project types
include TV and feature films. Genres include comedy,
action, crime, horror, drama, thriller, fantasy, and
family.

Zane Levitt
President
zanewlevitt@gmail.com
imdb.com/name/nm0506254
linkedin.com/pub/zane-levitt/30/3b1/552

ZEV GUBER PRODUCTIONS
Production company

60 Melrose Place
Montclair, NJ 07042
973-509-1728 (phone)
973-509-1728 (fax)

zev@jazfilms.com
imdb.com/company/co0275909

Does not accept any unsolicited material. Project types
include TV. Genres include documentary.

ZEYLIV
Distributor

5-1-3-501
Sendagaya

Shibuya, Tokyo 151-0051
Japan
03-6273-1873 (phone)
03-6273-1872 (fax)

info@zeyliv.co.jp
zeyliv.co.jp
imdb.com/company/co0268148

Does not accept any unsolicited material. Genres
include comedy, romance, and drama.

ZIA FILMS LLC
Production company

22617 Dolorosa St.
Woodland Hills, CA 91367
818-438-2701

ziafilms@earthlink.net
ziafilms.com
imdb.com/company/co0118531

Does not accept any unsolicited material. Project types
include TV and feature films. Genres include fantasy,
science fiction, drama, action, horror, and
documentary. Established in 2012.

Darryl Anka
Writer-Director-Producer
818-438-2701
imdb.com/name/nm0030138

ZIEGER PRODUCTIONS

310-476-1679 (phone)
310-476-7928 (fax)

imdb.com/company/co0114742

Accepts query letters from unproduced, unrepresented
writers.

Michele Colucci-Zieger
Producer
imdb.com/name/nm1024135

ZING PRODUCTIONS, INC.
Production company

Bauman Management
947 S Windsor Blvd.

Los Angeles, CA 90019
310-210-4728

220 S Van Ness Ave
Hollywood, CA 90004
323-466-9464

jbauman@baumanmgt.com
zinghollywood.com

Does not accept any unsolicited material. Project types
include TV, short films, and feature films. Genres
include romance, drama, fantasy, family, comedy,
reality, and animation.

Rob Loos
President
rob@zinghollywood.com
imdb.com/name/nm0519763
linkedin.com/pub/rob-loos/5/426

ZIPPORAH FILMS
Production company, distributor, and sales agent

1 Richdale Ave
Ste 4
Cambridge, MA 02140
617-576-3603 (phone)
617-864-8006 (fax)

info@zipporah.com
zipporah.com
imdb.com/company/co0013680
facebook.com/pages/Zipporah-Films-Inc/
    173826772661674

Does not accept any unsolicited material. Project types
include TV. Genres include documentary.

Frederick Wiseman
Producer
imdb.com/name/nm0936464

ZODIAK MEDIA
Production company and distributor

Immeuble Le France
115-123
Avenue Charles de Gaulle
92200 Neuilly Sur Seine
France
33 (0) 1 53 10 91 00

Immeuble Le France
115-123
Avenue Charles de Gaulle
92200 Neuilly Sur Seine
France
+33 (0) 1 53 10 91 00

Gloucester Bldg, Kensington Village
Avonmore Rd
London W14 8RF
UK
+44 (0)20 7013 400

contactus@zodiakmedia.com
zodiakmedia.com
imdb.com/company/co0390878
facebook.com/zodiakmedia
twitter.com/ZodiakMedia

Does not accept any unsolicited material. Project types include TV and feature films. Genres include animation.

Andy Lennon
Executive
imdb.com/name/nm2858174

ZODIAK RIGHTS
Production company, distributor, and sales agent

Avon House
Avonmore Rd
London W14 8TS
UK
+44 20 7013 4400 (phone)
+44 20 7013 4401 (fax)

contactus@zodiakrights.com
zodiakrights.com
imdb.com/company/co0322128

Does not accept any unsolicited material. Project types include TV and feature films. Genres include crime, drama, and thriller.

Steve Macallister
Executive
imdb.com/name/nm3280843

ZODIAK USA
Production company

520 Broadway Suite 500
Santa Monica, CA 90401
310-460-4490 (phone)
310-460-4494 (fax)

contact@zodiakusa.com
zodiakusa.com
imdb.com/company/co0314564
linkedin.com/company/zodiak-usa
facebook.com/zodiaknyc
twitter.com/ZodiakNYC

Accepts query letters from unproduced, unrepresented writers via email. Project types include TV. Genres include animation, comedy, non-fiction, romance, and reality.

Timothy Sullivan
212-488-1699
imdb.com/name/nm2432438

Natalka Znak
CEO
imdb.com/name/nm1273500

ZUCKER PRODUCTIONS

Los Angeles, CA
310-656-9202 (phone)
310-656-9220 (fax)

imdb.com/company/co0110404
facebook.com/pages/Zucker-Productions/
    253063648039987

Accepts query letters from unproduced, unrepresented writers. Project types include TV. Genres include fantasy, drama, comedy, romance, and thriller. Established in 1972.

Jerry Zucker
Partner
imdb.com/name/nm0958387

Farrell Ingle
Creative Executive
imdb.com/name/nm3377346
linkedin.com/pub/farrell-ingle/12/3a0/2b9

Janet Zucker
Partner
imdb.com/name/nm0958384

ZUKUN LABORATORIES

Production company

2-34-5
Higashi Oizumi
Nerima, Tokyo 178-8666
Japan
03-3867-5029 (phone)
03-3867-5041 (fax)

zukun@toei.co.jp
zukun-lab.com
imdb.com/company/co0379893

Does not accept any unsolicited material. Project types include feature films. Genres include drama, action, and crime.

Index by Company Name

Find software, books, courses and more on WritersStore.com

Find software, books, courses and more on WritersStore.com

Find software, books, courses and more on WritersStore.com

Find software, books, courses and more on WritersStore.com

Find software, books, courses and more on WritersStore.com

Find software, books, courses and more on WritersStore.com

Find software, books, courses and more on WritersStore.com

Find software, books, courses and more on WritersStore.com

Index by Contact Name

Find software, books, courses and more on WritersStore.com

Find software, books, courses and more on WritersStore.com

Find software, books, courses and more on WritersStore.com

Find software, books, courses and more on WritersStore.com

Find software, books, courses and more on WritersStore.com

Find software, books, courses and more on WritersStore.com

Index by Submission Policy

Accepts query letters from produced or represented writers

3311 Productions, 60
Anderson Productions, Craig, 98
Anova Pictures, 103
Bayonne Entertainment, 137
Beth Grossbard Productions, 145
Bigel Entertainment, LLC, 147
Clifford Werber Productions Inc., 204
Constantin Film, 212
Darius Films Incorporated, 229
Dark Castle Entertainment, 230
Delve Films, 237
Endemol Entertainment, 276
Escape Reality, 284
Fox Digital Studios, 311
Gigantic Pictures, 326
Grindstone Entertainment Group, 341
Haft Entertainment, 345
Informant Media, 374
Jackhole Productions, 384
Jay Silverman Productions, 387
Kaspi Creative Lab, 397
Lakeshore Entertainment, 412
Liquid Theory, 426
Maria , 446
Midnight Sun Pictures, 464
Mimran Schur Pictures, 466
Relativity Media, LLC, 566
Renart Films, 567
Roadside Attractions, 576
Salvatore/Ornston Productions, 589
Score Productions, Inc., 593
Submarine Entertainment, 632
Such Much Films, 633
TV One LLC, 683
W!ldbrain Entertainment, Inc., 723

Accepts query letters from unproduced, unrepresented writers

25/7 Productions, 58
2929 Productions, 59

3 Arts Entertainment, 61
72 Productions, 65
Aberration Films, 70
Act III Productions, 73
Adam Fields productions, 75
Ahimsa Films, 80
Airmont Pictures, 81
Alex Rose Productions, 85
Alianza Films International, 85
American Work Inc., 95
Andrea Simon Entertainment, 98
Animus Films, 101
Article 19 Films, 116
Artists Public Domain, 118
Barnstorm Films, 134
Bauer Martinez Studios, 136
Bee Holder Productions, 141
Berlanti Television, 145
Bix Pix Entertainment, 152
Blumhouse Productions, 159
Bobker/Krugar Films, 161
Bona Fide Productions, 163
Boz Productions, 165
Broken Silence, 171
Brooklyn Films, 172
Burleigh Filmworks, 176
Burnside Entertainment, Inc., 176
Caliber Media Company, 178
Cartoon Network, 185
Chaiken Films, 190
Cheerland film Group., 192
CineMagic Entertainment, 197
Cinema Libre Studio, 198
Colleen Camp Productions, 207
Color Force, 208
Colossal Entertainment, 208
Comedy Arts Studios, 209
Completion Films, 211
Concept Entertainment, 211
Content Media Corporation PLC, 212
Contrafilm, 213
Cooper's Town Productions, 214
Crescendo Productions, 220
Crossroads Films, 222

Accepts query letters from unproduced, unrepresented writers via email

Accepts scripts from produced or represented writers

Accepts scripts from unproduced, unrepresented writers

Accepts scripts from unproduced, unrepresented writers via email

Does not accept any unsolicited material

Find software, books, courses and more on WritersStore.com

Find software, books, courses and more on WritersStore.com

Find software, books, courses and more on WritersStore.com

Find software, books, courses and more on WritersStore.com

Find software, books, courses and more on WritersStore.com

Find software, books, courses and more on WritersStore.com

Find software, books, courses and more on WritersStore.com